THE BEST BIBLE?

Ad Fontes
P R E S S

HOW TO NAVIGATE ENGLISH BIBLE TRANSLATIONS

THE BEST BIBLE?

WITH INSIGHTS INTO **12** CONTEMPORARY VERSIONS

MATTHEW J. BARRON

Published by Ad Fontes Press
Portland, Oregon 97239
adfontespress.com

Library of Congress Control Number: 2021906347
ISBN: 978-1-946138-02-6 (trade paper)

Publisher's Cataloging-in-Publication Data

NAMES: Barron, Matthew J.
TITLE: *The Best Bible? How to Navigate English Bible Translations with Insights into Twelve Contemporary Versions* / by Matthew J. Barron.
DESCRIPTION: 1st edition. | Portland, OR : Ad Fontes Press, 2021 | Summary: An overview of the process of English Bible translation and its results, including a brief history of early English Bibles and reviews with assessments of twelve contemporary English Bible versions. | Includes glossary, scripture index, and subject index.
IDENTIFIERS: LCCN 2021906347 (print) | ISBN 9781946138026 (trade paper)
SUBJECTS: LCSH: The English Bible. | BISAC: RELIGION / Biblical Reference / General. | RELIGION / Biblical Studies / General. | REFERENCE / Bibliographies & Indexes.
CLASSIFICATION: LCC BS 455 .B367 (print) | DDC 220.52—dc23
LC record available at https://lccn.loc.gov/2021906347

Table of Contents

continued on next page

The Best Bible?

Expanded Table of Contents

Expanded Table of Contents

The Best Bible?

Abbreviations & Acronyms

AD	*anno Domini*	in the year of [our] Lord (a.k.a. CE—in the common era*)
a.k.a.		also known as
BC		before Christ (a.k.a. BCE—before the common era)
c.		century
c., circa		approximately, around
cf.	*confer*	compare with
e.g.	*exempli gratia*	for the sake of example
et al.	*et alia*	and others
i.e.	*id est*	that is

MS, MSS	manuscript(s)	NT	New Testament
OT	Old Testament	SO	so also with, and so it is with

BIBLE VERSIONS

Alter	*The Hebrew Bible* by Robert Alter (2018)
AMP	*The Amplified Bible* (1965, '87, 2015)
ASV	American Standard Version (1901)
Ballantine	*The Riverside New Testament* by William G. Ballantine (1923, '34)
Bishops'	the Bishops' Bible (1568, '72)
CEB	*Common English Bible* (2011)
CEV	*Contemporary English Version* (1995, '99)
Coverdale	Miles Coverdale's Bible (1537)
CSB	*Christian Standard Bible* (2017, '20)
Douay	the Douay Old Testament (1609–10)
Douay-Rheims-Challoner	the Douay-Rheims Bible edited by Bishop Richard Challoner (1749, '72)
EasyEnglish	*EasyEnglish Bible,* online (2018)
EHV	*Evangelical Heritage Version* (2019)
ESV	*English Standard Version* (2001, '16)
Geneva	the Geneva Bible (1560, 1599)

---

* This book retains the traditional abbreviation since the approximate reckoning from Christ's birth is common only to those influenced by the spread of Christianity.

GNB, TEV	*Good News Bible	Today's English Version* (1976, '92)
Great	the Great Bible (1539)
GW	*God's Word* (1995)
HCSB	*Holman Christian Standard Bible* (2004, '09)
ICB	*International Children's Bible* (1986)
ISV	*International Standard Version* (1996, 2010)
JB	*The Jerusalem Bible* (1966)
KJV	King James Version (1611)
LEB	*The Lexham English Bible* (2010, '12)
Living, TLB	*The Living Bible* (1971)
LSB	the *Legacy Standard Bible* (2021)
LXX	the Greek Septuagint (*circa* 280 – 130 BC)
Matthew	the "Thomas Matthew" Bible (1537)
MEV	*Modern English Version* (2014)
Message, MSG	*The Message* by Eugene H. Peterson (2002, '18)
Moffatt	*The Bible. A New Translation* by James Moffatt (1922, '54)
Montgomery	*The New Testament in Modern English* by H. B. Montgomery (1924)
NAB	*The New American Bible* (1970, '86, '91)
NABRE	*The New American Bible, Revised Edition* (2010)
NASB	*New American Standard Bible* (1971, '77, '95, '20)
NCV	*New Century Version* (1990)
NEB	*The New English Bible* (1970)
NET Bible, NET	*NET Bible: New English Translation* (2006, '17, '19)
NETS	*A New English Translation of the Septuagint* (2007)
NIV	*New International Version* (1984, 2011)
NIrV	*New International Reader's Version* (1996, '98)
NJB	*The New Jerusalem Bible* (1985)
NJPS	*New Jewish Publication Society* Tanakh (1985, '99)
NKJV, RAV	*New King James Version* (a.k.a. *Revised Authorised Version*, 1982)
NLT	*New Living Translation* (1996, 2015)
NRSV	*New Revised Standard Version* (1990, 2021?)
NWT	*New World Translation of the Holy Scriptures* (1960, '84, 2013)
Phillips	*The New Testament in Modern English* by J. B. Phillips (1958, '72)
REB	*The Revised English Bible* (1989)

The Best Bible?

Rheims	the Rheims New Testament (1582)		
RSV	*Revised Standard Version* (1952, '71)		
RV	the English Revised Version (1881, '85, '95)		
TNIV	*Today's New International Version* (2005)		
TPT	*The Passion Translation* by Brian Simmons (2018, '20)		
Tyndale	William Tyndale's versions (1525–36)		
Vulg.	the Latin Vulgate of St. Jerome (*c.* late 4th c. AD)		
Weymouth	*The New Testament in Modern Speech* by R. F. Weymouth (1903, '29)		

BIBLICAL BOOKS

Old Testament (or *Tanakh*)

Gn	Genesis	**Pr**	Proverb(s)
Ex	Exodus	**Ecc**	Ecclesiastes
Lv	Leviticus	**Sg**	Song of Solomon (or Song of
Nm	Numbers		Songs, Canticles)
Dt	Deuteronomy	**Is**	Isaiah
Jos	Joshua	**Jer**	Jeremiah
Jg	Judges	**Lm**	Lamentations
Ru	Ruth	**Ezk**	Ezekiel
1Sa	I Samuel	**Dn**	Daniel
2Sa	II Samuel	**Ho**	Hosea
1Kg	I Kings	**Jl**	Joel
2Kg	II Kings	**Am**	Amos
1Ch	I Chronicles	**Ob**	Obadiah
2Ch	II Chronicles	**Jon**	Jonah
Ezr	Ezra (or 1 Esdras [Douay];	**Mi**	Micah
	2 Esdras 1–10 [LXX])	**Na**	Nahum
Ne	Nehemiah (or 2 Esdras [Douay];	**Hab**	Habbakuk
	2 Esdras 11–23 [LXX])	**Zp**	Zephaniah
Est	Esther	**Hg**	Haggai
Jb	Job	**Zc**	Zechariah
Ps, Pss	Psalm, Psalms	**Ml**	Malachi

New Testament

Mt	Matthew		1Ti	I Timothy
Mk	Mark		2Ti	II Timothy
Lk	Luke		Tt	Titus
Jn	John		Phm	Philemon
Ac	Acts of the Apostles		Heb	Hebrews
Ro	Romans		Jas	James
1Co	I Corinthians		1Pt	I Peter
2Co	II Corinthians		2Pt	II Peter
Gal	Galatians		1Jn	I John
Eph	Ephesians		2Jn	II John
Php	Philippians		3Jn	III John
Col	Colossians		Jd	Jude
1Th	I Thessalonians		Rv	Revelation (or Apocalypse)
2Th	II Thessalonians			

Apocrypha (or Deuterocanon)

1Esd	I Esdras (or Greek Esdras; 2 Esdras [Eastern Orthodox]; 3 Esdras [Douay])
2Esd	II Esdras (or Latin Esdras; 3 Esdras [Eastern Orthodox]; 4 Esdras [Douay])
Tb	Tobit
Jdt	Judith
Est+	Additions to Esther
Ws	Wisdom of Solomon
Sir	Wisdom of Sirach, Ecclesiasticus
Bar	Epistle of Baruch
Dan+	Additions to Daniel
Song of 3	Song of the Three Children
Sus	Susanna
Bel & Drag	Bel and the Dragon
Prayer Man	Prayer of Manasseh
1Mc	I Maccabees
2Mc	II Maccabees

The Best Bible?

Preface

For God's Word to have any say in God's Church, it must be understood. "For indeed, if the trumpet produces an indistinct sound, who will prepare for battle? And so you through the tongue, unless you produce a clear message, how will it be known what is spoken? For you will be speaking into the air." (**1Co 14.8–9** LEB)

The Bible is the Church's charter. It's her heritage, her founding document, and her written authority, even when it is locked behind ancient languages. But it has no force until it is displayed with a language that people can understand. If the English-speaking church is to hear God's Word with authority and clarity, she must insist on a clear English translation.

Today, millions of English-speaking Christians world-wide rely on several English translations of the Bible to understand their relationships and obligations to God and each other. With over forty translations in print, and each asserting its own merits, some find it intimidating to decide which Bible they ought to read, study, and devote themselves to. Adding to the confusion are various groups who publicly reject one translation, denounce another, and promote their preferred version as the one and only worthy of attention.

Who is to say one Bible is better than another? More importantly, what are the criteria for judging the qualities and accuracy of each?

I wrote this book to put those doubts to rest and to frame the whole endeavor of Bible translation so that you, the reader, will be equipped to decide for yourself. Not only will you gain an appreciation for the processes involved in producing translations, you will also gain insight into the production and merits of several popular versions currently in print.

Use this reference to grow your knowledge about the Bible and translation, to guide your next Bible purchase, or to inform what counsel you give someone when they ask you, "What is the best Bible?"

WHAT THIS BOOK DOES

Though ultimately intended to answer "Which Bible is best or most accurate?" this book frames the entire process of Bible translation—its goals, methods, audiences, *etc.*—to help readers arrive at a more rounded and informed decision. It offers the tools and standards for measuring what "the best" or "most accurate" ought to be. It tells the stories of our most popular versions and the circumstances from which they arose, helping answer the question "Where do our Bibles come from?" It describes the processes and methods employed in the production of these translations. And it suggests solutions to practical questions, like "Which Bible is best—for reliable Bible study? For early language learners? For reading the Bible in a year? *Et cetera.*"

This book does not, however, give attention to the ever growing number of editions available for each translation. There are far too many than can be covered in a volume this size. Rather, this book focuses on the text of the translations themselves.

HOW THIS BOOK IS STRUCTURED

This book is organized into three parts. The first reveals the kinds of decisions that translators have to make before, during, and after their translation work. It explains the intentions, philosophies, methods, and difficulties of rendering Scripture from its original languages into something that makes sense for readers and listeners today.

The second part surveys the history of our earliest English Bibles, especially those which lay the foundations upon which the popular King James version was built.

The third and final part reviews and assesses twelve of the most popular and accessible English versions commonly used today.

HOW TO USE THIS BOOK

Words followed by asterisks (*) are strewn throughout these pages. These terms are defined in the Glossary near the back of the book.

Common abbreviations and acronyms for biblical books and Bible translations are listed and expanded following the Table of Contents near the front of this book.

Each chapter concludes with a section of Endnotes. These notes either add interesting details or cite the sources of each chapter's facts.

Footnotes (indicated by superscripted, lowercase letters), instead of Endnotes (indicated by superscripted numbers), are added to Part Two, "History of English Bibles," to reveal insights and sources for the histories written therein.

Twelve contemporary Bible translations are reviewed in Part Three, "Modern English Bibles." Each review shares the same divisions:

(1) An overview (called "At a Glance") with three timelines—

   [a] one for events contemporary with the version's publication,

   [b] another placing the version's publish date alongside those of other versions, and

   [c] one more indicating significant milestones during the version's publication;

(2) the version's history;

(3) the translators' stated goals;

(4) the underlying text bases;

(5) the translation's process and method;

(6) representative samples and notable or contested passages;

(7) significant revisions;

(8) a summary estimation; and

(9) an explanation of the copyright permissions, which govern how the version may be cited in other works.

Specifics regarding the selection and method of evaluating these translations is detailed in the "Introduction" on page 195.

Finally, there are two Indices in the back of the book. The first, a Scripture Index, locates every place in the text where passages of Scripture are cited or referenced; the other is a Subject Index to help readers link relevant topics scattered throughout these pages.

THE AUTHOR'S PERSPECTIVE

Numbered scripture references in this book follow the traditional English order as found in the Geneva and King James Bibles. Therefore, references to certain passages, particularly in the major prophets and the Psalms, may differ from those printed in editions of the Jewish *Tanakh*, the Greek Septuagint, or the Latin Vulgate.

This book identifies those portions of the Septuagint not found in the Hebrew Scripture as Apocryphal, not Deuterocanonical. It frequently refers to the Hebrew-Aramaic *Tanakh* as the "Old Testament." (See page 4 and following regarding biblical canons.) Selections of Scripture presented herein should prove relevant to those who adhere to Christian beliefs, yet they should still interest critics of Bible translation in general.

My own strengths are in the Greek New Testament, for which I find occasion to translate portions into English when the need arises to study it in depth. My competence in Hebrew is elementary and limited. This is why I have given many more examples from the New Testament than from the Old.

This work is a labor of love for my Christian friends rooted in fundamentalist, Pentecostal, and evangelical Charismatic persuasions. I pray this work will equip and unite you around God's revealed Word—both living and written.

ACKNOWLEDGMENTS

The translation review chapters have benefited from the observations of those who have gone before me. Where I include their insights, I cite their works in that chapter's Endnotes.

I also relied on the knowledge and experience of those who were actually in the trenches of Bible production. I thank the editors, translators, scholars, and professors, who have participated on the teams and committees which have produced the translations described in this book. Some of these individuals have shared their insights with me over telephone and email. In particular, I thank the following for the time and attention that they have given in reviewing initial draft portions of this work. You have helped me to keep the record straight:

Dr. Barry J. Beitzel, *Professor emeritus of Old Testament and Semitic Languages, Trinity Evangelical Divinity School* (NLT); Dr. James A. Borland, *Professor emeritus of New Testament, Liberty University* (NKJV); Dr. C. John "Jack" Collins, *Professor of Old Testament, Covenant Theological Seminary* (ESV); Dr. Dorian Coover-Cox, *Acting Director of Ph.D. Studies and Professor of Old Testament Studies, Dallas Theological Seminary* (CSB); Dr. A. Andrew Das, *Professor of Religious Studies and Assistant Dean of the Faculty for Assessment and Accreditation, Elmhurst College* (CSB); Dr. Paul R. Gilchrist, *former President of Biblical Studies, Covenant College, and former Stated Clerk of the General Assembly of the Presbyterian Church in America* (NKJV); Dr. Wayne Grudem, *Research Professor of Theology and Biblical Studies, Phoenix Seminary* (ESV); Rev. Dr. David Instone-Brewer, *Senior Research Fellow in Rabbinics and the New Testament, Tyndale House, Cambridge* (NIV); Dr. Karen H. Jobes, *Gerald F. Hawthorne Professor emerita of New Testament Greek and Exegesis, Wheaton College and Graduate School* (NIV); Dr. Gordon H. Johnston, *Professor of Old Testament Studies, Dallas Theological Seminary*

(NET); Dr. John F. Kutsko, *Executive Director of the Society of Biblical Literature and Affiliate Professor of Biblical Studies, The Candler School of Theology* (NRSV); Mr. Pike Lambeth, *Executive Vice President, The Lockman Foundation* (NASB); Dr. Tremper Longman III, *Distinguished Scholar of Biblical Studies, Westmont College* (NLT); Prof. Alan R. Millard F.S.A., *Rankin Professor emeritus of Hebrew and Ancient Semitic languages, and Honorary Senior Fellow (Ancient Near East), at the School of Archaeology, Classics and Egyptology, University of Liverpool* (NIV); Dr. James D. Price, *retired Professor of Hebrew and Old Testament, Temple Baptist Seminary* (NKJV, CSB); Dr. Brian Simmons, *Lead Translator for* The Passion Translation *and Core Residential Faculty, Wagner University* (TPT); Dr. Andrew E. Steinmann, *Distinguished Professor of Theology and Hebrew, Concordia University* (CSB); Dr. Mark L. Strauss, *University Professor of New Testament, Bethel University* (NIV); Mr. Mark D. Taylor, *President and C.E.O. of Tyndale House Publishers* (NLT); Dr. Eugene C. Ulrich, *John A. O'Brien Professor emeritus of Hebrew Scripture and Theology, Department of Theology, University of Notre Dame* (NRSV); Dr. Rick Wadholm, Jr., *Adjunct Professor of Old Testament, Horizon College & Seminary, of Biblical and Theological Studies, SUM Bible College and Theological Seminary, and of Theology, North Central University* (TPT); and Dr. W. Don Wilkins, *Scholar in Residence, The Lockman Foundation* (NASB).

Please note that none of those listed here have corresponded with me as representatives of the boards or committees on which they sit. Each has consented to relate their expertise in an individual capacity only.

For their insight and suggestions, I also thank Dr. Donald L. Brake, Sr., *Dean emeritus, Multnomah Biblical Seminary, Multnomah University* and author of *A Visual History of the King James Bible* (Grand Rapids, MI: Baker Books, 2011); Dr. Loren L. Johns, *Professor of New Testament, Anabaptist Mennonite Biblical Semi-*

nary (regarding the RSV); James Snapp, Jr. author of *A Fresh Analysis of John 7:53–8:11 with a Tour of the External Evidence* (2016); Dr. Mark L. Ward, Jr., author of *Authorized: The Use & Misuse of the King James Bible* (Bellingham, WA: Lexham Press, 2018). Thanks also goes to Jeffrey Pelton (inscribeministries.com) for his edits to the bulk of this material. Any remaining deficiencies herein are clearly my own.

My many friends and family have encouraged me during the production of this book. I wish to mention two in particular: James M. V. Sligar, who first suggested this work and saw its value to critical Bible readers, and Andrew R. Pomeroy, who showed deep interest in my talks and encouraged this book's publication. Of course, I mustn't fail to mention mine own, Molly Maria, my beloved wife, who patiently endured and labored while I wrote and edited this work. To you all, I am deeply grateful!

In memoriam, Ryan J. Harter (1985 – 2019). Thank you for encouraging me to go for it.

Soli Deo gloria,
Matthew J. Barron
July 6, 2021

Part One

The Decisions
Translators Make

Textual Decisions

Laying Foundations

A fundamental decision that translators and editors make before doing their work is choosing which manuscript sources they should use in their translation. Selecting a base text* can be as simple as pulling the nearest printed edition from a bookshelf (or retrieving one with a computer). Any capable translator can grab the latest edition of the Greek New Testament and start translating. But, in order to avert scrutiny and answer criticism, they must be able to justify their choice of text.

To build on a solid foundation, translators must answer challenges to the validity and authority of their selection. These challenges are posed with questions regarding (1) canon,* (2) language primacy,* (3) tradition, (4) original composition, and (5) authoritative editions. They all deal with the texts' origin or authority.

The choice of text is complicated by the Bible's own history— by its unique development and transmission* from one generation to the next. The Bible is not a single book. Rather, it is a library collection of laws and letters, poems and prophecies, histories and apocalyptic visions. Its composition and final form took over a millennium and half to complete.[1] Though divinely inspired,* it is written by more than forty human authors whose occupations ranged from shepherds and kings, prophets and priests, to rabbis and martyrs. It records events on three continents,[2] in three different languages,[3] and under a number of political climates. Each of these works develop a single theme in concert—God's revelation (his self-disclosure) and involvement in his creation.

As the Bible developed, audiences and readers recognized the authority of these written works and collected them into a single canonical corpus*—that is, a body of authoritative texts. They preserved and copied these texts for their children and grand-children as a perpetual memorial. Or, they copied them to propagate their faith and values in the market of competing

For a list of who wrote what, visit *booklink.id/ biblical-authors*

ideas. When these families and communities migrated to live with other nations, they translated those texts into the native speech of their adopted homes. These texts were then copied and their transmission passed from one generation to the next, but not without variation. These variations are the focus of differing challenges and opinions, as we shall see.

CANON

One of the more evident challenges is that not all Bibles contain the same content. That is, some faith communities view certain books within their Bibles as authoritative (and inspired) while others do not.

A biblical canon* is the range of writings that a community deems authentic or considers authoritative. Different communities define the scope of their canon with different sets of criteria. This results in different canons. To answer the challenge of canonicity,* editors and translators must qualify their scope of biblical writings, because their choice of canon determines which books they include or omit in their translation of the Bible.

Biblical canons do not begin fully formed. An authoritative list of canonical books doesn't drop from the clouds one day and receive immediate and universal acclaim. Rather, biblical canons develop over time and are often tied to the events described in their texts.

The *Torah* (or the first five books of Moses—**Genesis, Exodus, Leviticus, Numbers, Deuteronomy**) is the earliest and first recognized section of the Hebrew canon. It records the origin of all things through God's creation, the beginnings of the human race, and the rise of nations. It recounts God's choice of the Israelite nation as a people selected specially for himself. It lists the words that God inscribed in stone through his direct agency (*i.e.*, the Ten Commandments, or *Decalogue*). It encodes God's voice through his designated prophet, Moses. Ultimately, the *Torah* bears witness to the historic covenants that God cut for himself and the people he chose to participate in those ancient agreements.

For more about the biblical canon, visit *booklink.id/canon*

The Best Bible?

The Israelites recognized the Law's authority as soon as the national covenant was ratified (Dt 31.9–13). They agreed to obey the Law (Ex 24.3–8) and exalted it among the nation's greatest treasures and stored the *Torah* for safe-keeping within their most revered and sacred space—next to the Ark of the Covenant in the most holy place of the Tabernacle (Dt 3.25–26; *cf.* Ex 25.16; Heb 9.4; 1Kg 8.9; 2Ch 5.10).

Moses's successors encouraged the covenantal community to uphold the conditions of the *Torah* (*e.g.* Jos 1.7). These prophets and inspired chroniclers recorded evidence of Israel's (and later, Judah's) progress or failure in keeping their end of the ancient agreements. They bore witness to the blessings or curses which resulted when the covenants' conditions were maintained or violated.

Sometimes, prophets spoke divine decrees that were recognized and obeyed (Mi 3.9–12 to King Hezekiah, see Jer 26.17–19). Their words were validated by the events they predicted (Is 44.28; Ezk 26.1–14; Dn 9–12) or witnessed (*e.g.*, the Temple's destruction and the Babylonian exile, 2Kg 25). Their words were then appended to the *Torah* (*e.g.* Jos 24:26) and, later, collected into a group called the "Prophets" (Hebrew *Nevi'im*). Their section starts with the "Former Prophets" (beginning with Joshua, Moses' aide, *circa* 13th c. BC) and concludes with the "Latter Prophets" (ending with the post-exilic prophet, Malachi, *post* 515 BC). This collection of prophetic and historical books validated the *Torah*'s authority and confirmed the earlier section's influence and standing within the community. Through the Prophets, the Hebrew communities of Israel and Judah witnessed the *Torah*'s authority and recognized it as canonical.

Another collection of scriptures accompanied the Prophets, called the "Writings" (Heb. *Khetuvim* or Greek *Hagiographa*). This section includes works written in various genres,* including poetry (e.g., the Psalms), wisdom literature (Proverbs, Job), and history (Chronicles). Some of these works record events that occurred after the Jews returned home from exile under Persian rule (Daniel, Ezra, Nehemiah, Esther).[4]

These three sections of Hebrew (and some Aramaic) Scriptures* were later organized into a single collection, which Jews call the *Tanakh*.[5] Jewish traditions uphold the *Tanakh* as canonical. Though arranged differently, it comprises the same material as the Protestant Old Testament (OT).

In the fourth century BC, Alexander the Great (†323 BC) spread the Greek language and Hellenistic culture as he conquered the Persian empire along his army's thirteen-year march to India. Since then, a sizable Jewish community settled in Alexandria, Egypt, where they learned to speak Greek better than they did their ancestral Hebrew. The Jewish diaspora there felt a need to translate the *Torah* into the language they spoke. So translation began on the *Torah* (*i.e.*, Pentateuch) under the reign of the Egyptian king, Ptolemy II (*ca.* 250 BC). The completed work became known as the Septuagint (abbreviated with the Roman numerals LXX in honor of the legendary seventy[-two] Israelite elders who translated it). The LXX eventually came to refer to Greek translations of the whole collection of Hebrew Scriptures, plus a few later works that the Jewish communities valued. This process was completed sometime around the mid- to late-2nd century BC.

Among the later works included in the LXX are Greek supplements to **Daniel** (namely **Susanna, Bel & the Dragon, Song of the Three Children**), and to **Esther**, and to **Jeremiah** (**Baruch** and the **Letter of Jeremiah**). Besides these are books titled **Tobit, Judith, Ecclesiasticus** (*i.e.*, **Sirach**), and the **Maccabees**. These works cover pivotal events and beliefs in Jewish history between the time of the Jews' return from Babylon until the birth of Jesus Christ. For example, **1–2 Maccabees** record how the nation of Judah cleansed the Temple after their war with King Antiochus IV (†164 BC) and won their independence from the Greek Seleucids.[6]

These Greek additions are what we call the *Apocrypha* (Gk. "hidden" books). They stage the background for Jesus Christ's ministry. Though they were never considered part of the Hebrew canon, early Christian communities, who adopted their Scriptures from Greek-speaking Jews, saw value in them. (As a result,

The Best Bible?

their status as biblical books remained in dispute until the Protestant Reformation in the 16th century.)

Initially, the early Christian movement was considered a sect of Judaism, so it was natural for the early Church to adopt whatever Scriptures were considered authoritative by the Jews. Jesus Christ even affirmed his personal authority by appealing to these Scriptures for the benefit of his Jewish audiences (**Lk 24.27, 44;** *cf.* **Jn 5.39–47**). Thus Jesus and the apostles confirmed the Jewish Scriptures as the Church's written authority by the way they used and cited them.

The body of Christian writings, *i.e.*, the New Testament (NT), was composed in Greek before the closing of the 1st century AD.[7] It includes the Gospels, the Letters (*i.e.*, Epistles), **Acts**, and **Revelation**. The early Church accepted four Gospels only (**Matthew, Mark, Luke, John**) as early eyewitness testimonies of Christ's ministry.[8] They also included the **Acts of the Apostles**, which traces the Church's beginning through the ministries of the apostles Peter and Paul. They accepted the authority of the Letters on the basis of their apostolic authorship. Paul wrote thirteen letters to churches and individuals in Asia Minor and Europe.[9] Of the rest, which we call the General (or Catholic) Epistles, John wrote three, Peter two, and James (Jesus' brother) and Jude one each.[10] John's **Revelation** (*i.e.*, the **Apocalypse** from Gk. *apokálypsis* "unveiling") was the last NT work composed while John was exiled to the island of Patmos, probably during the reign of the Roman Emperor Domitian (81–96 AD).

As the Church's influence spread into largely Greek-speaking, non-Jewish communities, the LXX became the form of Scripture that the Church used for defending her beliefs.[11] Today, the Greek Orthodox Church holds the Greek Scriptures as authoritative.[12] They share the same NT with the other Christian traditions, but they accept the Greek Apocrypha (*i.e.* Deuterocanon) as part of their OT.

The Western churches debated the Apocrypha's value before the Protestant Reformation, but it wasn't until AD 1546 at the

Council of Trent that the Roman Catholic Church formally decreed the Bible with the Apocrypha as "sacred and canonical".[13] (This Council was a response to the Protestant Reformation that was spreading throughout Europe at that time.) Today, the official Roman Catholic stance maintains that the Hebrew-Aramaic OT, most of the Greek OT additions (which Catholics call the Deuterocanon*), and the Greek NT are authentic Scriptures.[14]

The designation, Deuterocanon, is a Greco-Latin word for a "second-canon", whereas the Protocanon* ("first-canon") refers to the rest of Scripture corresponding to just the Hebrew OT canon and the Greek NT. For Eastern Orthodoxy (i.e., Greek and Slavic Orthodox churches), the Deuterocanon signifies works of lesser rank than the Protocanon.[15] For Roman Catholics, on the other hand, Deuterocanon does not imply inferior authority but merely denotes a secondary or later stage of canonical development.

The Roman Catholic Deuterocanon comprises most of the same books as the Greek Apocrypha, but it excludes **1–2 Esdras**, the **Prayer of Manasseh, Psalm 151**, and **3 Maccabees**, all of which are treated as canonical in Eastern Orthodoxy.[16]

The Tewahedo (Ethiopian Orthodox) Church holds the most extensive canon in Christendom with a total of eighty-one books. It includes most of the books of the Greek Apocrypha[17] plus the book of Enoch and eight additional writings dealing with church history and policy.

The Protestant canon consists of the Hebrew-Aramaic OT and Greek NT. Most of the Christian communities who split with Rome during the Reformation do not view the Apocrypha as authoritative. The early Reformers recognized Jewish tradition, which rejected the apocryphal books.[18] They took note of Saint Jerome, who translated the Latin Vulgate* Bible from Hebrew sources and enumerated only the Hebrew books as constituting the OT.[19] They argued to reject the Apocrypha for other reasons, too, including: The earliest lists of biblical books excluded the Apocrypha;[20] the authorship for most of the Apocrypha is unknown;[21] the books have apparent historical or doctrinal errors;[22]

The Best Bible?

they are not quoted by other authors of Scripture;[23] they are of human derivation[24] and, thus, lack divine inspiration.[25] The Reformed movement has taught that the Holy Spirit, who resides in all believers, vouches for those works that he himself inspired, which necessarily excludes the apocryphal works since they were not authored by divine prophets or apostles of Jesus Christ (**Eph 2.20**).[26] Protestants, therefore, rejected the use of the Apocrypha for establishing doctrine.[27]

Martin Luther, in his 1534 German translation, was the first in modern times to set the Apocrypha apart from the OT in its own section. The section's title page reads, "Apocrypha . . . though not the same as Holy Scripture, yet useful and good to read."[28] Later Protestant Bibles followed Luther's precedent by grouping the Apocrypha as a separate section between the two Testaments.

In the 1820s, the British and Foreign Bible Society[29] and the American Bible Society faced pressure to remove the Apocrypha entirely. Their excision has set the norm for Protestant Bibles to this day.

For more on the Apocrypha, visit *booklink.id/ apocrypha*

☐ Hebrew Canon

■ Greek Apocrypha

Hebrew *Tanakh* (Old Testament)	Composed *circa* 1400 – 400 BC
Greek *Septuagint* (LXX)	Translated *c.* 250 – 130 BC
Protestant OT Canon and Apocrypha	AD 1534
Rom. Catholic Protocanon and Deuterocanon	AD 1564

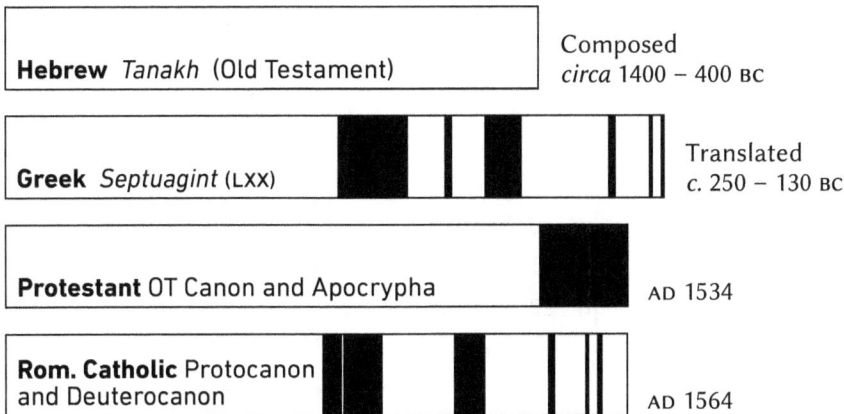

Different faith traditions put the **Apocrypha/Deuterocanon** in different places within or outside the OT in their editions of the Bible.

DIFFERING OLD TESTAMENT CANONS

Hebrew *Tanakh*	Protestant Old Test. [a]	Roman Cath. Old Test. [b]
***Torah* (Instruction)**	**Law**	**Pentateuch**
1. Genesis	1. Genesis	1. Genesis
2. Exodus	2. Exodus	2. Exodus
3. Leviticus	3. Leviticus	3. Leviticus
4. Numbers	4. Numbers	4. Numbers
5. Deuteronomy	5. Deuteronomy	5. Deuteronomy
***Nevi'im* (Prophets)**	**History**	**History**
Former Prophets	6. Joshua	6. Joshua (Iosue)
6. Joshua	7. Judges	7. Judges
7. Judges [c]	8. Ruth	8. Ruth
8. Samuel & Kings	9. 1 Samuel	9. 1 Samuel
Latter Prophets	10. 2 Samuel	10. 2 Samuel
Major Prophets	11. 1 Kings	11. 1 Kings
9. Isaiah	12. 2 Kings	12. 2 Kings
10. Jeremiah	13. 1 Chronicles	13. 1 Chronicles
11. Ezekiel	14. 2 Chronicles	14. 2 Chronicles
Minor Prophets	15. Ezra	15. Ezra (1 Esdras)
12. *(The Twelve)*	16. Nehemiah	16. Nehemiah (2 Esdras)
Hosea	17. Esther	17. Tobit (Tobias) [d]
Joel		18. Judith [d]
Amos		19. Esther
Obadiah	**Poetry**	*Additions to Esther* [d]
Jonah	18. Job	20. 1 Maccabees [d]
Micah	19. Psalms	21. 2 Maccabees [d]
Nahum	20. Proverbs	
Habakkuk	21. Ecclesiastes	**Wisdom (Sapiential Books)**
Zephaniah	22. Song of	22. Job
Haggai	Solomon	23. Psalms
Zechariah		24. The Proverbs
Malachi		25. Ecclesiastes
		26. Canticle of Canticles
		27. Wisdom [d]
(cont'd)	*(cont'd)*	28. Sirach (Ecclesiasticus) [d]

Hebrew *Tanakh*	Protestant Old Test. [a]	Roman Cath. Old Test. [b]
Kethuvim (Writings)	**Prophets**	**Prophets**
13. Psalms	*Major Prophets*	*Major Prophets*
14. Proverbs	23. Isaiah	29. Isaiah (Isaias)
15. Job	24. Jeremiah	30. Jeremiah (Jeremias)
The Scrolls (Megilloth)	25. Lamentations	31. Lamentations
16. The Song of	26. Ezekiel	32. Baruch [d]
Songs	27. Daniel	*Epistle of Jeremiah* [d]
17. Ruth [c]	*Minor Prophets*	33. Ezekiel (Ezechiel)
18. Lamentations	28. Hosea	34. Daniel
19. Ecclesiastes	29. Joel	*Add. to Daniel* [d]
20. Esther	30. Amos	
21. Daniel	31. Obadiah	*Minor Prophets*
22. Ezra [e]	32. Jonah	35. Hosea (Osee)
23. Nehemiah [e]	33. Micah	36. Joel
24. Chronicles	34. Nahum	37. Amos
	35. Habakkuk	38. Obadiah (Abdias)
	36. Zephaniah	39. Jonah (Jonas)
	37. Haggai	40. Micah (Micheas)
	38. Zechariah	41. Nahum
	39. Malachi	42. Habakkuk (Habacuc)
		43. Zephaniah
		(Sophonias)
		44. Haggai (Aggeus)
		45. Zechariah
		(Zacharias)
		46. Malachi (Malachias)

Different faith traditions name and sort the Old Testament books in different ways.

a Early Protestant Bibles included the Apocrypha (*Judith, The Book of Wisdom, Tobit, [Jesus] Sirach, Baruch, Maccabees, Additions to Esther,* and *Additions to Daniel*), but this collection was distinguished from canonical Scripture and placed together in a separate section.[107]

b Roman Catholics reject *1 Esdras* (or *3rd* or *Greek Esdras*), *2 Esdras* (or *4th* or *Latin Esdras*), and the *Prayer of Manasseh* from their canon. These books form a part of the Catholic Apocrypha and are printed as an appendix in Catholic Bibles.

c Ruth is sometimes grouped with Judges.

d Deuterocanonical books.

e Ezra and Nehemiah are frequently considered one book.

Protestant Old Testament (OT)	Eastern (Greek & Slavonic) Orthodox OT	Ethiopian Orthodox (*i.e.*, Tewahedo) OT
Law	**Pentateuch**	**Pentateuch**
1. Genesis	1. Genesis	1. Genesis
2. Exodus	2. Exodus	2. Exodus
3. Leviticus	3. Leviticus	3. Leviticus
4. Numbers	4. Numbers	4. Numbers
5. Deuteronomy	5. Deuteronomy	5. Deuteronomy
History	**History**	**History**
6. Joshua	6. Joshua (Iesous)	6. Joshua
7. Judges	7. Judges	7. Judges
8. Ruth	8. Ruth	8. Ruth
9. 1 Samuel	9. 1 Kingdoms (1 Samuel)	9. 1 and 2 Samuel
10. 2 Samuel	10. 2 Kingdoms (2 Samuel)	10. 1 and 2 Kings
11. 1 Kings	11. 3 Kingdoms (1 Kings)	11. 1 Chronicles
12. 2 Kings	12. 4 Kingdoms (2 Kings)	12. 2 Chronicles
13. 1 Chronicles	13. 1 Paraleipomenon (1 Chronicles)	13. Jubilee
14. 2 Chronicles	14. 2 Paraleipomenon (2 Chronicles)	14. Enoch
15. Ezra	*Prayer of Manasseh*	15. Ezra & Nehemiah
16. Nehemiah	15. 1 Esdras (3 Esdras, Greek Esdras)	16. Ezra (2nd) & Ezra Sutuel
17. Esther	16. 2 Esdras (*or* Ezra-Nehemiah) [108]	17. Tobit
	17. Nehemiah	18. Judith
	18. Tobit	19. Esther
	19. Judith	20. 1 Maccabees
	20. Esther	21. 2 & 3 Maccabees
	Additions to Esther	
	21. 1 Maccabees	
	22. 2 Maccabees	
	23. 3 Maccabees [109]	
(cont'd)	*(cont'd)*	*(cont'd)*

Protestant Old Testament (OT)	Eastern (Greek & Slavonic) Orthodox OT	Ethiopian Orthodox (*i.e., Tewahedo*) OT
Poetry	**Wisdom (Poetry)**	**Wisdom**
18. Job	24. Psalms [110]	22. Job
19. Psalms	25. Job	23. Psalms
20. Proverbs	26. Proverbs	24. Proverbs
21. Ecclesiastes	27. Ecclesiastics	25. Tegsats (Reproof)
22. The Song of Songs	28. Song of Solomon	26. Metsihafe Tibeb
	29. Wisdom of Solomon	(Books of Wisdom)
	30. Wisdom of Sirach	27. Ecclesiastes
		28. The Song of Songs
Prophets	**Prophets**	**Prophets**
Major Prophets	*Minor Prophets*	*Major Prophets*
23. Isaiah	31. Hosea	28. Isaiah
24. Jeremiah	32. Amos	30. Jeremiah
25. Lamentations	33. Micah	31. Ezekiel
26. Ezekiel	34. Joel	32. Daniel
27. Daniel	35. Obadiah	*Minor Prophets*
Minor Prophets	36. Jonah	33. Hosea
28. Hosea	37. Nahum	34. Amos
29. Joel	38. Habakkuk	35. Micah
30. Amos	39. Zephaniah	36. Joel
31. Obadiah	40. Haggai	37. Obadiah
32. Jonah	41. Zachariah	38. Jonah
33. Micah	42. Malachi	39. Nahum
34. Nahum	*Major Prophets*	40. Habakkuk
35. Habakkuk	43. Isaiah	41. Zephaniah
36. Zephaniah	44. Jeremiah	42. Haggai
37. Haggai	45. Baruch	43. Zechariah
38. Zechariah	46. Lamentations of Jeremiah	44. Malachi
39. Malachi	47. Epistle of Jeremiah	45. Book of Joshua the son of Sirach
	48. Ezekiel	46. Book of Josephus ben Gurion
	49. Daniel	
	Additions to Daniel	

COMPLICATED CANONS. Even when certain traditions share the same books, it's not always easy to keep them straight. Each faith community refers to the biblical books in their own way. Nowhere is this better demonstrated than how different traditions refer to the books of *Ezra*, *Nehemiah*, and the *Greek* and *Latin Esdras*.

The Hebrew canon treats *Ezra* and *Nehemiah* as a single book, as does the early translator, Jerome, who followed the Hebrew order in his Latin Vulgate.

The Greek Septuagint (LXX) also combines *Ezra-Nehemiah* into one book, but it gives that book a confusing designation—*2nd Esdras*. In the LXX, *1st Esdras* is the name for the apocryphal book of Greek *Esdras*, which is not found in the Hebrew canon.

Eastern Orthodox traditions tend to follow the LXX, but they split *Ezra* and *Nehemiah* into two books; *Ezra* they label *1 Esdras*.[30] What the LXX calls *1st Esdras*, Eastern Orthodoxy calls *2 Esdras*.

Confused yet? Just wait!

There are actually *two* apocryphal books of *Esdras*. The one in the LXX is called the *Greek Esdras*. The other is called the *Latin Esdras*. *Latin Esdras* is excluded from Protestant, Roman Catholic, and Orthodox canons, but it is still considered a part of the Apocrypha. It is printed as an appendix in Catholic Bibles and included among the Apocrypha section in some Protestant editions (*e.g.*, the Geneva Bible and the KJV).

When the KJV was first published in 1611, *Ezra* and *Nehemiah* were two separate books in the Old Testament canon, as they are in all Protestant Bibles and most Catholic ones today. The two books of *Esdras* were simply designated, *1* and *2 Esdras*. But the Catholic Douay Bible (1610), in accordance with the revised Latin Vulgate, calls them all the books of *Esdras*—*1 Esdras* (*Ezra*), *2 Esdras* (*Nehemiah*), *3 Esdras* (*Greek Esdras*), *4 Esdras* (*Latin Esdras*). (See table on page 15.)

Thanks to modern ecumenical versions, like the RSV's and NRSV's expanded Apocrypha (1977, 1989), we may finally have the designations we need to put this conundrum to rest.

We can hope anyway. ◄

Different Traditions:	Different Designations for the Same Books:			
	Ezra	Nehemiah	Greek Esdras	Latin Esdras
Hebrew Tanakh	**Ezra** (Ezra-Nehemiah)			
Greek Septuagint (LXX)	**2 Esdras** (Ezra-Nehemiah)		1 Esdras	
Jerome's Latin Vulgate	**Ezras** (Ezra-Nehemiah)			
Protestant (KJV/RSV)	**Ezra**	**Nehemiah**	1 Esdras	2 Esdras
Clementine Vulgate (Douay-Rheims)	**1 Esdras**	**2 Esdras**	3 Esdras	4 Esdras
Eastern Orthodox (Slavonic)	**1 Esdras**	**Nehemiah**	2 Esdras	3 Esdras (*omits chapters 1–2 and 15–16 of Latin Esdras*)
Ethiopian Orthodox (Tewahedo)	**1 Ezra** (Ezra-Nehemiah)		2 Ezra	Ezra Sutu'el (*omits chs. 1–2 and 15–16 of Latin Esdras*)

Different canonical traditions give different names to the same books. *Ezra*, *Nehemiah*, and the apocryphal books of *Esdras* are among the trickiest to track. (Grayed areas indicate traditions that omit one or more of these books.)

LANGUAGE PRIMACY

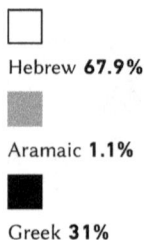

Language primacy* is a challenge to the choice of an original or authentic text. It asks, "In which language(s) were the originals composed?" If translators wish to choose a text as close as possible to the original, they will choose (in all likelihood) a text in the language in which it was originally written. In other words, they will not opt to translate a translation.

The two major divisions of the Bible were composed in two primary languages—The OT in Classical Hebrew (with a few later portions in Imperial Aramaic) and the NT in a dialect of Greek called *Koinē** (Gk. "Common"). So, the answer seems simple enough: The Bible's original composition (*i.e.*, its *autographa**) advocates for Hebrew primacy for the OT and Greek primacy for the NT.

Nonetheless some people may advocate translating from a translation. Some promote the Greek LXX for the OT, or early Syriac versions for the NT, or early Latin versions for the whole Bible. They promote these versions, because (as they argue) these versions were based on earlier Greek and Hebrew MSS than those we now possess. The original MSS copies on which those versions relied are now lost to us or have yet to be recovered (see diagram "General Transmission of the Bible" on page 22). Advocates for the use of these early versions argue for their value as lenses into the Bible's original Hebrew and Greek composition. Yet, as they promote these versions as sources for English Bible translation, their arguments for such versions still assume Hebrew and Greek primacy. (See "Conjectural Emendations" on page 38.)

Others insist that the NT—in part or in whole—was originally composed in the Aramaic language.[31] One early church historian suggested that the Gospel of **Matthew** was originally written in the Galilean Aramaic spoken by Jesus and his disciples,[32] but we lack early enough written samples to prove this one way or the other. Nonetheless, advocates of Aramaic primacy suggest that early translations of the NT into the later Syriac* language preserve the language and thought of those supposed Aramaic originals.[33]

Hebrew **67.9%**

Aramaic **1.1%**

Greek **31%**

Hebrew *Tanakh*
Old Testament

Greek
New Testament

The languages in which the Bible was composed, with the percentages of each language's contribution to the biblical composition.

The Best Bible?

TRADITION

It may surprise some to learn that we no longer have the Bible's original written documents. We cannot be sure where the physical tablets are on which God wrote the *Decalogue* (*i.e.*, the Ten Commandments, **Ex 20.2–17**). Baruch's original transcriptions of Jeremiah's prophecies are nowhere to be found (*cf.* **Jer 36.4, 32**). Even if we possessed the very first scroll of Luke's Gospel or the apostle Paul's own *autographa*,* we could not absolutely certify them as original or as some other early copy. The rest of the originals are lost to us through wars, persecutions, natural disasters, overuse, and decay. We only have access to the Bible's words through its copies. The text of those copies have passed through millennia of translation and transmission* from one generation to the next. During this development, some faith communities began giving greater weight to an early version or a translation of the originals than to the originals themselves.

For example, the Samaritan community held their version of the *Torah* (the first five books of the Hebrew OT) as authoritative. Despite its being written in a different script,[34] there are few consequential differences between the standard Hebrew *Torah* and the Samaritan one. But the exceptions are glaring: Every place in the text where "Jerusalem" is the main focus of worship, the Samaritans allude to or write "Mt. Gerizim" instead![35]

The Greek Orthodox Church esteems the Septuagint* (the Greek OT), because of its historic significance and traditional use within the early Christian church. Orthodox communities assume that any significant differences between the Hebrew and the Greek are changes made under divine inspiration.[36]

For centuries, the Roman Catholic Church placed priority on Latin translations.[37] In 1546, the Council of Trent decreed that the Latin Bible was approved for use in worship and doctrine, that it was to be "held as authentic," and that it "must not be rejected."[38] These strong words directed Catholic translators' use of the Latin editions until the middle of the twentieth century. In 1943, Pope

Pius XII clarified that the decree applied only to the Latin Rite and did not "in any way diminish the authority and value of the original texts."[39] Since then, Pope Paul VI positively encouraged the production of modern Bibles based on more original sources and "in cooperation with the separated brethren."[40] (For transmission priority in the English tradition, see page 40.)

THE MANUSCRIPT PROCESS

Once translators and editors have settled on the canon and language of their source (*i.e.*, the base texts that they are translating from), they can then proceed to establish the best possible text to work from. Arriving at a reliable text, though, has its own challenges.

Some suspect that the Bible was copied and passed down from one generation to the next, like the game of "telephone": One person starts by passing a message to another in secret. The next person secretly passes it on to yet another, and they, on to another, and so on, and so on, until it reaches the last person. The game ends when the last person openly shares the message as they've received it, and the first one reveals the original message for comparison. We laugh at the differences between the first and last iterations wondering who made which changes to the message as it passed down the line.

This illustration fails to demonstrate the actual way in which the Bible came down to us. One important difference is that we no longer have the initial record to compare later copies with. Yet, we do have many early copies from earlier sources and early versions to compare with one another. And unlike the game, the copies are not isolated in secrecy but compared openly. Here's how it actually happened:

Ancient writings were copied by hand. Scribes would carefully copy lines of text with pen and ink from hand-written documents to new or reused surfaces.[41] This process occurred several thousands of times for many centuries up until and after the introduction of the printing press in the fifteenth century AD.

Scribes were generally conservators, not innovators. It was their task to preserve the message for later readers.[42] Copying the text was not an exercise in creative expression except where opportunity allowed scribes to illustrate the margins, innovate with more efficient hand-writing, introduce reference systems, or abbreviate commonly used or theologically significant words. Any scribes who deliberately altered the words of their copies could be held accountable by their exemplars* (*i.e.,* the manuscripts that they copied from) and by copies already in circulation. For Hebrew scribes, preserving Scripture is a mission to guard and protect Jewish cultural heritage. They instituted strict scribal practices to ensure fidelity when copying the Hebrew Bible. (See "The Hebrew-Aramaic Old Testament" on page 37.)

A scribe copying the Psalms, circa 12th century. From the *Eadwine Psalter* at Trinity College, Cambridge (*MS R.17.1*).

The Christians' goal is to propagate the gospel message of Jesus Christ and to instruct believers in the faith. The practical need was to make the NT available and accessible for use in the church and for Christian missions. This is evidenced by the 5,400 partial and complete Greek manuscripts* of the NT—quite a large sum when compared to other significant, ancient literary works (see table on page 20). Today, thanks to their efforts, we have access to a number of quality Hebrew manuscripts, very many Greek ones, and an even larger number of early translations into Latin, Coptic, Syriac, Georgian, Armenian, Arabic, and other languages.

Throughout this period of hand-writing Scripture, man-made errors crept into copies of the Bible which were then perpetuated

by successive generations of copyists. These errors arose from fatigue, inattention, tricks on the eyes, ears, or memory, and on occasion, intentional change. When we compare and contrast these manuscripts with one another, we can observe the scribes' writing habits and discern how those errors occurred. This science of recognizing, diagnosing, and correcting these errors is called textual criticism.* The practice of textual criticism helps us understand how we got the Bible in the form that we have it now. More significantly, it offers clues to what the underlying original text would have been. This is invaluable for biblical exegesis,* which demands as much precision as possible to accurately discern the meaning of Scripture.

Author	Title of work	Work composed	Total MSS [111]
Tacitus [112]	*Annals*	AD 100 – 114	33
Josephus [113]	*Jewish Wars*	AD 77/8	62
	Jewish Antiquities	AD 93/4	77
Thucydides	*History*	460 – 400 BC	96
Herodotus	*Histories*	480 – 425 BC	109
Livy [114]	*History of Rome*	59 BC – AD 17	150
Sophocles	*Plays*	496 – 406 BC	193
Pliny, the Elder	*Natural History*	AD 49 – 79	200
Plato	*Tetralogies*	*ca.* 400 BC	210
Julius Cæsar	*Gallic Wars*	100 – 44 BC	251
Demosthenes	*Speeches*	*ca.* 300 BC	340
Homer [115]	*Iliad*	*ca.* 800 BC	1,900 +
Greek New Testament [116]		AD 50 – 100	*circa* 5,400
Manuscript copies of early New Testament translations			*ca.* 18,500
Old Testament Manuscripts (including all translations) [117]			*ca.* 42,000

Number of extant manuscript witnesses* for ancient literary works. *Nota bene*: These figures will necessarily be obsolete with each new published discovery of previously unknown extant MSS, yet they still serve to illustrate the relative numerical strength of biblical textual witnesses when compared to other ancient texts.

NEW DISCOVERIES OF
OLD SOURCES

It has been well over six-hundred years since pioneering translators first "Englished" the Bible. Since then, they have gained better
access and sharper insight into the Scripture's original texts, languages, and culture. Thanks to the combined studies of linguists,
archæologists, theologians, and literary stylists, a good number of
the Bibles available today are more accurate and accessible than
any previous time in history.

In the late fourteenth century AD, John Wycliffe and his fellow
Oxford scholars were limited to late copies of a Latin translation.
By the early sixteenth century, William Tyndale obtained access
to the earlier Greek and Hebrew texts, which were made available
through the alliance of Byzantine and Jewish scholars and their European printers. Tyndale and his compatriots gave readers in their
day a translation of the Bible closer to the original sources than
was Wycliffe's a century earlier. (For more, see "Wycliffe, Lollardy,
& Suppression" starting on page 171.)

Tyndale's efforts were cut short after his arrest and execution.
He had translated the NT and much of the OT. The rest of the He-
brew prophets and writings would have to wait for translation until
after the death of Mary I, Queen of England. After Mary's reign, the
Protestant exiles in Geneva published the first English Bible with an
OT translated entirely from the Hebrew. (For more, see "Tyndale &
Black-Market Bibles" starting on page 175.)

Centuries later, the British Empire (and other European imperial powers) advanced onto a number of exotic locales, including Egypt, Palestine, and the Levant, where explorers made significant discoveries relevant to biblical history and interpretation.
The Palestine Exploration Fund (founded in 1865) financed sur-
veyors and archæologists who drew detailed maps and recorded
descriptions of the city of Jerusalem and her surrounding areas.
This gave translators a rich knowledge of the geography and place
names in the Bible. *(continued on page 24)*

GENERAL TRANSMISSION OF THE BIBLE

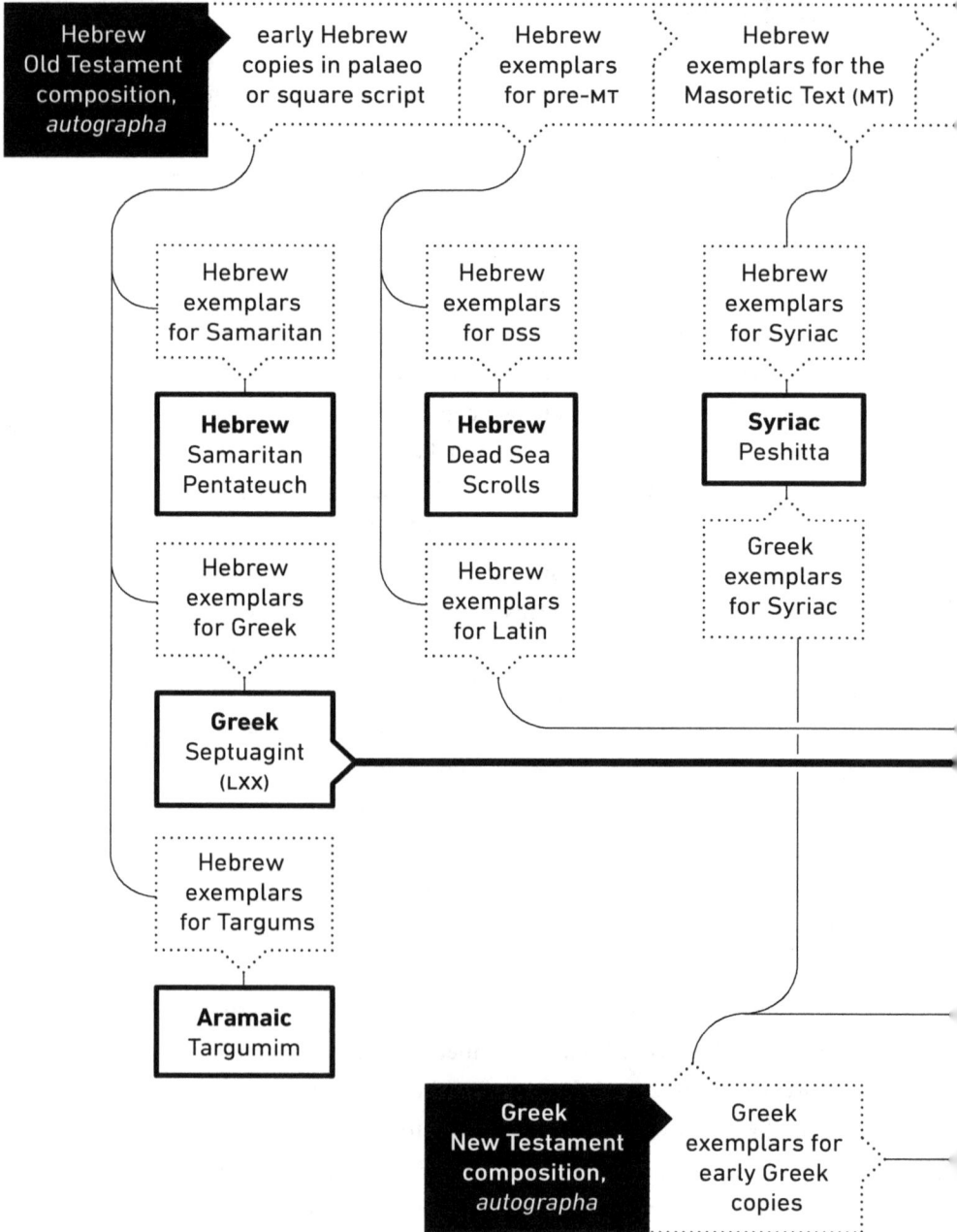

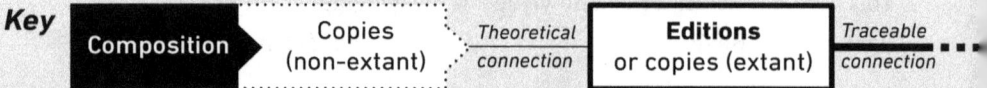

| Hebrew Old Testament composition, *autographa* | early Hebrew copies in palaeo or square script | Hebrew exemplars for pre-MT | Hebrew exemplars for the Masoretic Text (MT) |

Hebrew exemplars for Samaritan

Hebrew exemplars for DSS

Hebrew exemplars for Syriac

Hebrew Samaritan Pentateuch

Hebrew Dead Sea Scrolls

Syriac Peshitta

Hebrew exemplars for Greek

Hebrew exemplars for Latin

Greek exemplars for Syriac

Greek Septuagint (LXX)

Hebrew exemplars for Targums

Aramaic Targumim

Greek New Testament composition, *autographa*

Greek exemplars for early Greek copies

Key

| Composition | Copies (non-extant) | *Theoretical connection* | **Editions** or copies (extant) | *Traceable connection* |

```
Hebrew                Hebrew                        Hebrew
Masoretic             Aleppo &                  Biblia Hebraica
Text (MT)             Leningrad                 (BHK, BHS, BHQ)
                      Codices (MT)


                              many late
                              Hebrew
                              copies

                                          Hebrew
                                          Ben Chayyim
                                          Rabbinic
                                          Bible (MT)

                                                              English
                                                              Modern Bibles
                                                              have the benefit
      Latin          English        English                  of all extant
      Vulgate        Wycliffe       Tyndale-KJV              ancient versions
                     Bible          Tradition                and previous
                                                              translations
      Greek                                                   for reference.
      exemplars
      for Latin
                                          Greek
                     many late           Textus Receptus (TR),
                     Greek               Majority Greek Text
                     copies

      early                               Greek
      Greek                               critical editions
      copies                              (Nestle-Aland, UBS)
```

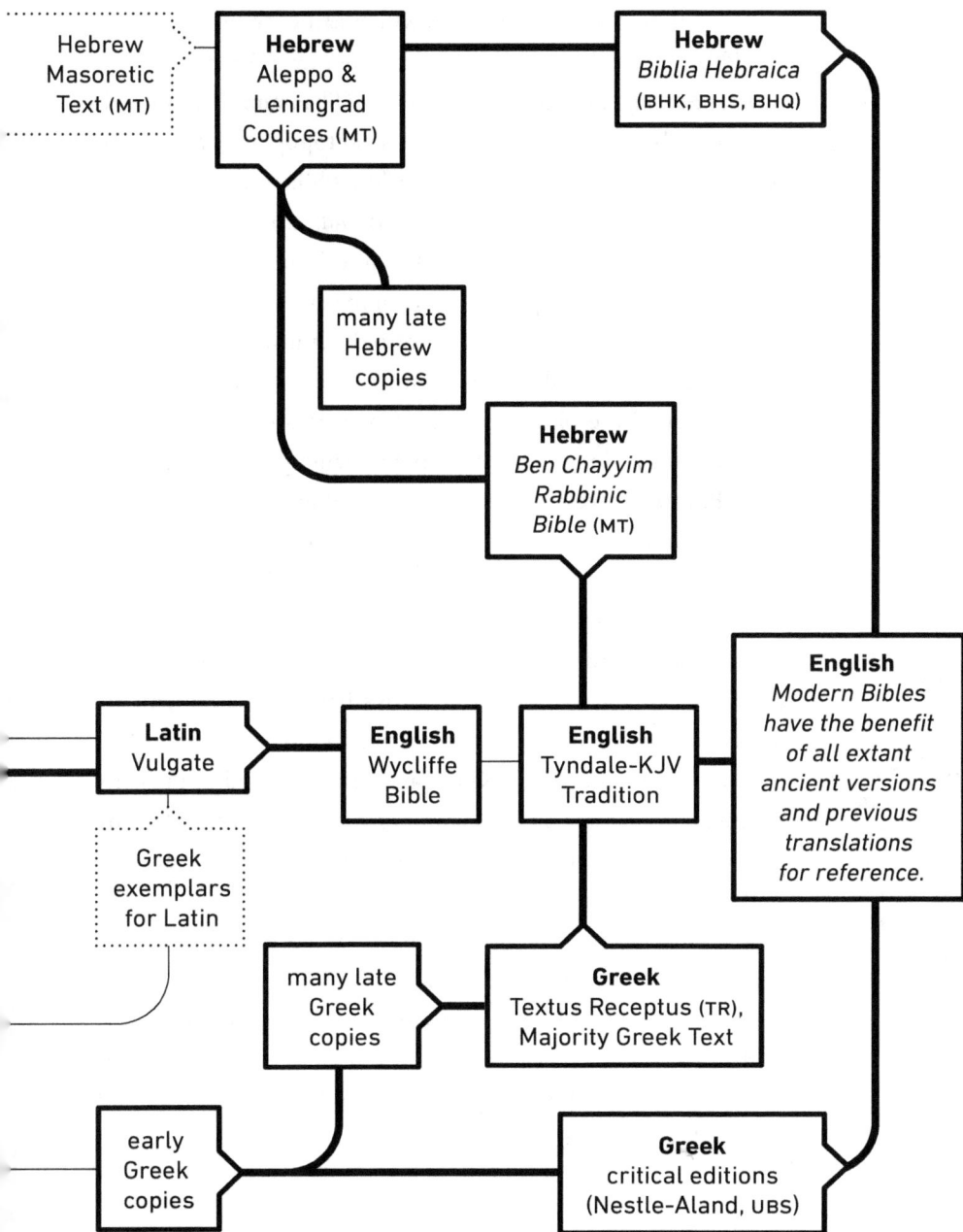

Exemplars are the MSS from which other copies are made. Their texts are reflected in copies and translations so that it's theoretically possible to reconstruct them, even if they are not extant (*i.e.,* even if they are no longer available for study).   **23**

(continued from page 21) Such discoveries affect how we interpret passages like **1Sa 17.52**, which earlier translations read, "the Philistines fell down wounded by the *way of Shaaráim.*" (Geneva 1560, *emphasis added*). The "*way of* Shaaráim" leaves the direction "to" or "from" ambiguous, but later topographical research revealed which direction was meant: "the Philistines fell down by the *way to Shaaraim.*" (RV 1881, *emphasis added*).

While American and British treasure hunters dug through the sands of Egypt in search for the tombs of the Pharaohs, some explorers sifted through archives of old manuscripts (MSS) preserved by the dry, arid climate. Some of these freshly uncovered texts included the oldest available Greek MSS of the NT. These papyrus* MSS, along with other parchments previously hidden from European eyes, challenged the standing of that Greek edition which lay behind the NT of the KJV. (For more on the NT text-bases and the *Textus Receptus,** see "The Greek New Testament" on page 26.)

Translators and text critics,* who studied the ancient MSS, in the late 19th and early 20th centuries began working with NT texts that were hundreds, if not more than a thousand, years older than the ones from which King James' men worked in the early seventeenth century. In fact, some of the more recently discovered MSS were copied within only a couple centuries after Jesus walked the shores of Galilee.

Considering the passage of time between events described in other ancient texts and the dates for existing copies of those works, a couple hundred years is a relatively short period of time. In the case of our NT's earliest MSS, less than a century slipped by since the death of the last eye-witness to the events it records.[43] (See table on page 25.)

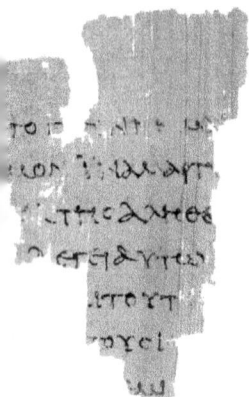

A fragment of **papyrus 52** containing portions of **Jn 18.31, 32, 33, 37, 38** is dated to *c.* AD 125–170, less than a century after the death of John, the author of **Revelation**.

The Best Bible?

Author	Work	Earliest extant* MS	Time gap (approx.)[118]
Homer	*Iliad*	*circa* 400 BC	400 years
Herodotus	*The Histories*	1st century AD	1,350 years
Sophocles	Plays	3rd cent. BC	100 – 200 years
Thucydides	*History*	3rd cent. BC	200 years
Plato	Tetralogies	AD 895	1,300 years
Demosthenes	Speeches	Some fragments, *c.* 1st c. BC (AD 1100)	1,100 + (1,400) years
Julius Cæsar	*Gallic Wars*	AD 9th cent.	950 years
Livy	*History of Rome*	AD early 5th cent.	400 years
Pliny the Elder	*Natural History*	a single 5th cent. AD fragment	400 years
Tacitus	*Annals*	1st half: AD 850; 2nd half: AD 1050; (AD 1100)	750 – 950 years
Josephus	*Jewish Wars*	AD late 3rd cent.	200 years
	Jewish Antiquities	AD 6th – 7th cent.	450 – 550 years
Old Testament			
Papyrus Fouad 266 (Greek)		1st cent. BC	1,300 years
Papyrus Rylands 458 (Greek)		2nd cent. BC	1,200 years
Dead Sea Scrolls (Hebrew)		AD 1st cent.	650 years
Greek New Testament			
$\mathfrak{P}^{46}$ (Chester Beatty Papyrus II)		*c.* AD 200	150 years
$\mathfrak{P}^{66}$ (Papyrus Bodmer II)		*c.* AD 200	130 years
$\mathfrak{P}^{67}$ (Papyrus Barcelona 1)		*c.* AD 200	140 years
$\mathfrak{P}^{4}$ (Suppl. Gr. 1120)		*c.* AD 200	140 years
$\mathfrak{P}^{52}$ (Papyrus Rylands 457)		*c.* AD 125	30 years

Approximate duration between the earliest extant* (*i.e.*, surviving) manuscripts and the events they record.

An example
of numbering
variants between
manuscripts at
1Co 15.51:

Collating (comparing) a single manuscript (MS):

Base	We shall not all sleep, but we shall all be changed
ms 1	We shall ᴧ all sleep, but we shall <u>not</u> all be changed

MS 1 varies in
two places from
the Base Text,
so we count two
variants.

Collating two MSS:

Base	We shall not all sleep, but we shall all be changed
ms 1	We shall ᴧ all sleep, but we shall <u>not</u> all be changed
ms 2	We shall not all sleep, but we shall <u>not</u> all be changed

MS 2 varies in
one place from
the Base and
in one from
MS 1. Since the
variant is the
same as one
already counted
in MS 1, we still
have only two
variants.

THE GREEK NEW TESTAMENT

The Number of Manuscripts and Variants.

Many manuscripts of the Greek NT have survived, but they do not agree with each other in every detail. These differences between MSS are called textual variants.*

We identify such variants by comparing MSS against a base text—a single important manuscript (MS) or printed edition. Once we've established our base text, we compare it against a MS and note the differences between the two texts and record each difference as a textual variant. (Such differences include additions, omissions, transpositions, or substitutions.)

Then we bring a second MS alongside for additional comparison. If a difference found in this MS is the same as that found in the first, then both differences count as only one variation from the base text—a single textual variant. Where the second MS differs from *both* the base text *and* the first MS in the same place, we record the differences as two separate variants. (See the sidebars on pages 26 and 27.)

An example of one significant variant is found at **1Ti 4.10**, where the apostle Paul explains his motives for his ministry. The traditional base text reads

> "For this we labor and *endure insult* (Gk. *oneidizometha*), because we hope in the living God."[44]

The variant reads

> "For this we labor and *strive* (Gk. *agōnizometha*), because we hope in the living God."

Critical editors tend to prefer "strive" over "endure insult" because the reading is a bit better attested* (*i.e.,* evidenced) by the earliest complete MSS (external evidence), and it seems to fit the context better (internal evidence).[45]

The Best Bible?

Another significant variant at **1Co 15.51** regards Christian resurrection (as demonstrated in the sidebars). There are more variants in this verse among many more MSS than the ones collated* here, but the reading of the base text is most probable, because it has better support from the MSS (external evidence),[46] and it better explains the rise of the other variants (internal evidence). For example, later scribes may have adjusted the base text's phrasing to avoid the embarrassment that Paul and the early disciples did, in fact, die, since Paul wrote "sleep" as a metaphor for death. They may have also edited the passage to contradict those who denied there being a future resurrection. Textual criticism allows us to weigh the evidence and select the most probable variant.

If we could compare all 5,400 or so Greek NT MSS against a single base text, the number of total variants would be quite large—approximately half a million according to conservative estimates.[47] (See table on page 27.) But the total *number* of textual variants is not as important as is the *nature* of those variants. The vast majority of differences do not even translate into English.[48] Scholars estimate that only one percent of the total number of textual variants (an estimated 5,000 out of a half-million) are both meaningful *and* sup-

Collating three MSS:

Base	We shall not all sleep, but we shall all be changed
ms 1	We shall ʌ all sleep, but we shall not all be changed
ms 2	We shall not all sleep, but we shall not all be changed
ms 3	We shall ʌ all sleep, but we shall not all be changed

MS 3 varies in two places from the Base. Since the varients are identical to MS 1, we still count just two variants.[136]

Year	Number of MSS (*estimated numbers of papyri, uncials, minuscules, and lectionaries*)		Estimated number of variants (vars.)	
AD 1516	7 – 8 manuscripts (MSS)		—	119
1550	17 MSS		—	120
1707	100 + MSS	121	*circa* 30,000 variants	122
1752	*circa* 200 MSS		—	123
before 1872	*c.* 1,000 MSS		*c.* 120,000 vars.	124
1892	3,060 MSS	125	*c.* 180,000 – 200,000 vars.	126
1908	4,026 MSS		—	127
1923	4,266 MSS	128	*c.* 250,000 vars.	129
1952	5,487 MSS	130	*c.* 300,000 vars.	131
2007	5,494 MSS	132	*c.* 400,000 vars.	133
2020	*c.* 5,400 MSS	134	*c.* 500,000 vars.	135

Number of estimated variants per number of known or utilized, extant Greek MSS.

ported by external* or internal evidences.* [49] In other words, of all those variants, the ones that make any real difference in English Bible translation affect less than four percent of the NT text.[50]

Which Greek Edition to Translate?

The underlying printed Greek text of our modern English New Testaments has its own story to tell. A landmark shift in the Bible's transmission arose with Johannes Gutenberg's invention of movable, cast-metal type (c. 1440–50). Before the introduction of the printing press and the fall of Constantinople (1453), European churches were dependent upon the Bible in hand-written Latin.[51] Whereas each MS copy was a unique edition of the biblical text all unto itself, copies of printed editions reproduced their imprints exactly and at a much cheaper cost. Still, general access to the Greek NT would have to wait for more than half a century after these momentous developments.

TEXTUS RECEPTUS

The famous Dutch scholar, Desiderius Erasmus, was the first to publish a printed Greek NT in AD 1516.[52] The following year, an Augustinian monk, named Martin Luther, posted his *Ninety-five Theses* on the chapel door in Wittenberg. Critical interest in the origins of Christian authority and demand for the earliest available form of Scripture swept European academies. There was enough demand that Erasmus printed a second edition just three years later.[53] This edition formed the basis of Martin Luther's German translation, the *September Testament* of 1522.[54] That same year, Erasmus released a third edition, the one which William Tyndale used for his pioneering translation work (1525/26).[55] (For more on Tyndale, turn to page 175.)

Erasmus's text was later reproduced in 1546 by the Parisian printer, Robert Stephanus.[56] In Stephanus's beautiful third edition (called "the royal edition" of 1550), he included a critical apparatus* (a concise system of references to his original MS sources) in

A sample of **Rom 1** from Erasmus' 1516 edition.

A sample of **Rom 1** from Robert Stephanus' 1550 ed.

The Best Bible?

its margins. It indicated seventeen Greek MSS, which he compared with his main text.[57]

Stephanus eventually fled Catholic-dominated Paris and found refuge and welcome in Protestant Geneva, where he printed a fourth edition (1551). In this edition, he introduced numbered verse divisions for reference.[58] William Whittingham, a Protestant refugee residing in Geneva during Queen Mary's reign in England, carried Stephanus's divisions over into his translation of the English NT (1557)—a decision that influences printed Bibles to this day.

Later, John Calvin's successor, Theodore Beza, reprinted Stephanus' Greek Testament in nine editions. His fourth or fifth edition (1588/9, 1598) formed the Greek basis for the King James Bible.

In 1633, the Elzevirs, a printing family from Leiden, Netherlands, printed their second edition based on Beza's first folio edition (1565).[59] This edition introduced an advertisement claiming that the reader had "the text now received by all (*textum . . . receptum*) in which we give nothing altered or corrupt."

These words form the collective label that scholars give all the editions from Erasmus to the Elzevirs—the *Textus Receptus*, which we consider our traditional "Received Text". So the *Textus Receptus* (TR) perpetuates a fairly consistent text with most variations due to edits intended to correct obvious typographical errors.[60]

TEXT-CRITICAL EDITIONS

For the next two centuries, the TR dominated biblical studies. Meanwhile, scholars busied themselves searching for the earliest available MSS and collecting lists of variations among the hand-written copies. This work culminated in several printed editions that launched and sustained an era of modern NT text-critical science.

In 1707, John Mill, an Oxford theologian,[61] published an edition of the *Textus Receptus* with one significant feature: His footnotes revealed an estimated 30,000 textual variants distribut-

A sample of **Rom 1** from John Mill's 1707 edition.

ed among a hundred Greek MSS, several printed editions, and a collection of NT passages quoted by early Christian writers.[62] (By comparison, Erasmus based his editions on just seven or eight late MSS.) Mill did not live long enough to hear his work criticized and condemned by those who felt it cast doubt on the apparent stability and reliability of the NT. After careful review, one scholar vindicated his work by concluding that none of the listed variants threatened any fundamental Christian doctrines.[63]

Mill's edition effectively launched the last three centuries of text-critical scholarship. Among his colleagues and successors were G. von Maastricht (1711),[64] R. Bentley (1720),[65] J. A. Bengel (1742),[66] J. J. Wettstein (1730, '51),[67] J. J. Griesbach (1796),[68] K. Lachmann (1842),[69] C. von Tischendorf (1849),[70] and S. P. Tregelles (1856),[71]

One of the significant English contributions to this discussion culminated in a publication by two British text critics, B. F. Westcott and F. J. A. Hort, titled *The New Testament in the Original Greek.*[72] Their proposed text formed the base of the English Revised Version (1881) and its transatlantic sister, the *American Standard Version* (1901).

Scholars and critics paired historic discoveries with critical analysis. In order to manage and organize a growing number of extant* (*i.e.,* surviving) MSS, they devised schemes for grouping them into families or text-types* based on similar features, like how closely their contents match each other, their proximity in age, or their provenance* (*i.e.,* their place of discovery or suspected origin). The general consensus recognized three or four families. The Byzantine text-type is the biggest family with the most MSS. It is named after its supposed place of origin—Byzantium, the old capital of the Eastern Roman empire. The family represented by the oldest extant MSS is the Alexandrian text-type named after Alexandria, Egypt, home to an early Christian scholarly community.[73] All editions of the TR predominantly reflect a later Byzantine family of Greek NT MSS, while Westcott and Hort's edition leans heavily on the Alexandrian family.[74]

Text critical studies has resulted in a sum of critical *principles* or *canons* ("guidelines") for determining the text of the original NT. These principles are better described as "arguments of probability," since the rules are by no means hard and fast and often require qualifications. The most fundamental argument is that *only one reading can represent the original wording among two or more variants*. The rest of the arguments are generally classified as either "external" or "internal" arguments. External arguments include:

Antiquity—the older a reading is, the more likely it serves as evidence for the original text. Physical characteristics are frequently factored in, including the *age* of its substrate* (*i.e.*, the material that the text is written on), the *kind* of substrate (*e.g.*, papyrus*, parchment*, or paper), or the *style* of its writing (majuscule* or minuscule*).

Numerical agreement—the majority of MSS, groups of MSS, or MS families whose readings agree with one another are more probably original.

Geographic distribution—readings which agree among MSS from a widespread number of locales are preferred as more likely genuine.

Internal arguments, on the other hand, deal strictly with the nature of the text as distinct from the its provenance or its substrate. These arguments examine textual variants for their probable origin. They try to answer "which variant reading gave rise to the others around it?" Internal arguments include:

Transcriptional probabalitities—these are tendencies of each scribe's writing habits. For example, harder readings are typically regarded as original, because scribes tended to smooth passages out and make them easier to read. Shorter readings were preferred, because it was assumed that scribes tended to add to the texts they copied: They would either add clarifications or combine variants when they were unsure which was original.

Intrinsic probabilities are arguments which lend more weight to readings that agree with the normal use of the source language, that fit the context, or that match the author's unique style.

Various text critics may prioritize their arguments differently and get different results. For instance, quotations of NT passages by early Christian writers also offer evidence for original NT readings. Those critics, who consider this argument as more important than the scribe's writing habits or the passage's NT context, make it a higher priority among the external arguments. Other critics may consider such evidence as an afterthought and class it as a lesser intrinsic probability among the internal arguments.

So, too, later discoveries can disrupt priorities and their assumptions. For example, some arguments preferred shorter readings and claimed that longer readings were recorded too late. These argument assumed that scribes tended to add words to their copies with each successive generation. But later discoveries of earlier papyrus MSS revealed that the opposite tendency is the case: Scribes tended to omit words and drop lines over time.[75] With such revelations, text critics are challenged to hold their arguments and priorities loosely and judge one variant at a time.

ECLECTIC EDITIONS

The standard editions of the Greek NT today are edited by text critics who balance the weight of internal and external evidences passage-by-passage and variant-by-variant. They reject a strictly consistent application of general principles for determining the most likely reading of a given passage. This is the approach promoted by editors of our modern "eclectic" editions.[76]

At the turn of the twentieth century, Eberhard Nestle edited a volume of the NT (with the Latin title, *Novum Testamen-*

The Best Bible?

tum Graece) which combined Westcott-Hort's critical text with editions by Tischendorf and R. F. Weymouth.[77] Wherever two or more of these critical texts agreed, Nestle set the result as his base text. Later, Eberhard's son, Erwin, expanded the work that his father began by developing the critical apparatus to make it more useful to scholars. For his 26th edition (Stuttgart: Deutsche Bibelgesellschaft, 1979), Erwin and his associate editor, Kurt Aland, sought to revise the base text and apparatus by building them directly from extant MSS instead of the majority agreement of existing printed editions.[78] Their stated ideal was a text that tried to balance internal and external arguments.[79]

The Nestle-Aland text was shared and developed with the United Bible Societies, who produced their own edition for translators.[80] Most modern English translations rely on these two editions as the base text for their New Testaments.

MAJORITY AND BYZANTINE PRIORITY TEXTS

One of the greatest criticisms against the critical editions of the 19th century is that they relied too heavily on one MS or on a single family of MSS. Some also argue that they relied too much on internal principles of textual criticism, which can result in a combined set of conjectural readings that, when taken together, have no precedent in existing MSS. In general, the early text-critics were biased against the *Textus Receptus* because of its relatively late date. Since they were primarily concerned with the earliest form of the NT, they tended to ignore the vast majority of MSS—the ones generally grouped in the Byzantine family.

Zane C. Hodges and Arthur L. Farstad were motivated by the idea that God had preserved his word faithfully amongst *all* the Greek MSS, not just in a late traditional text or among the earliest group of MSS. They produced *The Greek New Testament According to the Majority Text* (Nashville: Thomas Nelson Publishers, 1982, '85), which gave the total number of Greek MSS a vote.[81] Whichever reading had the greatest attestation* (*i.e.*, evidence) among the majority of MSS formed the base text of their edition. Wherever

ΠΡΟΣ

Paul Gree

ΑΥΛΟΣ, δοῦλος [¹] Ἰ
ἀφωρισμένος εἰς
γείλατο διὰ τῶν προφ
3 περὶ τοῦ Υἱοῦ αὐτοῦ, τ
κατὰ σάρκα, 4 τοῦ ὁρισ
Πνεῦμα ἁγιωσύνης ἐξ ἀν
τοῦ Κυρίου ἡμῶν, 5 δι᾽ (
εἰς ὑπακοὴν πίστεως
ὀνόματος αὐτοῦ, 6 ἐν
Χριστοῦ·
7 Πᾶσι τοῖς οὖσιν ἐν
ἁγίοις·
Χάρις ὑμῖν καὶ εἰρήνη
Ἰησοῦ Χριστοῦ.

Paul De

8 Πρῶτον μὲν εὐχαρις
[⁷]ὑπὲρ πάντων ὑμῶν ὅ
ὅλῳ τῷ κόσμῳ. 9 Μά
λατρεύω ἐν τῷ πνεύμα
αὐτοῦ, ὡς ἀδιαλείπτως
τῶν προσευχῶν μου
εὐοδωθήσομαι ἐν τῷ θε.
11 Ἐπιποθῶ γὰρ ἰδεῖν
πνευματικὸν εἰς τὸ στ

In Romans G = 𝔓⁴⁶ℵBAC

1 ʹB vs 𝔐 ℵA   8 ⸀περι

A sample of **Rom 1** from Hodges-Farstad's 2nd ed. (1985).

this external evidence tied for support or was too close to tell, their reconstruction of the MSS' family tree guided their decision.[82] One major English revision, the *New King James Version* (1982, '84), records their more significant findings in its footnotes.

Maurice A. Robinson and William G. Pierpont published *The New Testament in the Original Greek: Byzantine Textform* (Southborough, MA: Chilton Book Publishing, 2005) with which they intended to counter the perceived biases of earlier text-critics by giving more weight to the Byzantine MSS.[83] They argued that the relative consistency and stability of these MSS indicated that they were copied from much older exemplars. Those exemplars at the head of the Byzantine family tree would have been contemporary with the earliest extant MSS.[84] Since scribes tend to preserve their exemplars in their copies, and since the smaller number of early extant MSS vary more widely among themselves than do the many later Byzantine MSS, they argued that there is a greater probability that the Byzantine text better preserves the original wording of the NT.[85]

COHERENCE-BASED GENEALOGICAL METHOD

Within the last few decades, computers have grown to more ably process massive amounts of data efficiently. Today, a set of computer software tools facilitates the study of the NT variants in a process called the Coherence-Based Genealogical Method* (CBGM). This method analyzes sets of copyiest errors (variants) in each MS as if they were unique genetic markers. These sets uniquely identify the text of each MS and allow text-critics to relate the texts one to another in order to trace probable lines of descent from parent exemplars to children copies in a family tree. The CBGM allows scholars to analyze and compare the variant markers of very many NT MSS much more quickly than was previously possible.[86]

Despite new possibilities that computers afford, editorial decisions based on CBGM is still a massive undertaking. Some of the results of this method are published in the latest editions of Nestle-Aland (28th) and United Bible Societies (5th),[87] but only in the book of Acts and the general epistles so far. Detailed results with full apparati are being published in the *Editio Critica Maior*.[88]

IMPACT OF TEXTUAL CRITICISM ON THE NEW TESTAMENT

The Gospel and the major doctrines of Christianity are in no way obscured by the many variants distributed among the NT's many MSS. Nonetheless, some passages are re-evaluated in light of evidence. On occasion, translators and editors will mark passages where they differ between the more ancient MSS and the later traditional ones (*i.e.,* the *Textus Receptus*).

THE PERICOPE ADULTERÆ (or the 'Story of the Adulteress'). The ESV has printed a bracketed note in the main text that alerts readers, "The earliest manuscripts do not include [**John**] **7.53–8.11**". Its footnote elaborates,

> "Some manuscripts do not include **7.53–8.11**; others add the passage here or after **7.36** or after **21.25** or after **Luke 21.38**, with variations in the text."

The NRSV adds, "some mark the passage as doubtful." The NKJV footnote reads,

BIBLICAL SPELLING. When comparing early English versions of the Bible, one of the first things we notice is inconsistent spelling. Until the 18th century, English had no standard orthography* (standard spelling) against which to judge the "correct" spelling of words. Not until Samuel Johnson published his famous dictionary in 1755 did English society have anything respected enough to compare the standard use of words and their proper spellings.

The underlying Hebrew and Greek MSS had no explicit spelling standards either. For example, Some MSS record the names of Jesus' ancestors differently. In Matthew's Gospel, some MSS spell King David's name as *Dauid* (Δαυιδ), while others spell it *Dabid* (Δαβιδ).

Early Hebrew was spelled entirely with consonants, while later Hebrew made a few of the consonants perform double-duty as disambiguating vowels. Sometimes the same word is spelled with both the older and newer spellings, even in the same passage.[141]

Spelling differences of known words are not usually counted among estimates for the total number of textual variants. Those who hold to the doctrine of plenary-verbal inspiration* should not insist that inerrancy extends to the precise spelling of words, because there can be no perfect spelling without a perfect standard to spell by. ◄

"The words *But Jesus* through *sin no more* (**8.11**) are bracketed by [the Nestle-Aland and United Bible Society]Texts as not original. [But t]hey are present in over 900 manuscripts."[89]

THE LONGER ENDING OF MARK. The NIV introduces the longer ending of Mark with a caution,

> "The earliest manuscripts and some other ancient witnesses* do not have **Mark 16.9–20.**"

The NRSV goes into fuller detail by giving both the longer and a shorter ending. It further elaborates in its footnotes:

> "Some of the most ancient authorities* bring the book to a close at the end of verse **8**. One authority concludes the book with the shorter ending; others include the shorter ending and then continue with verses **9–20**. In most authorities verses **9–20** follow immediately after verse **8**, though in some of these authorities the passage is marked as being doubtful."

(Here "authorities" means significant MS witnesses.) The NKJV helpfully specifies,

> "Verses **9–20** are bracketed in [the N-A and UBS]Texts as not original. They are lacking in *Codex* Sinaiticus* and *Codex Vaticanus*, although nearly all other manuscripts of Mark contain them."

These notices alert text critics, scholars, and other serious Bible students, but sometimes they do little more than frighten or confuse casual readers. These notes exist as the editors' and translators' attempts at transparency. Their honest hope is to alert readers of the debate that surrounds these passages.[90, 91] Their notes should invite us to investigate the arguments more closely.

THE HEBREW-ARAMAIC OLD TESTAMENT

The Traditional Text & Masoretic Transmission

The Masoretic* transmission of the Hebrew OT forms the base text for all major modern Bible translations. The term "Masoretic" comes from the medieval Jewish scribes, called Masoretes,* who were responsible for copying both the ancient Hebrew letters and later written traditions surrounding the text. Originally, the Hebrew Scriptures were written with only consonants and word divisions. For an idea of what that's like, try to imagine what the following set of letters signify in English (bullets [•] represent word divisions):

HR•O•ISRL•Th•LRD•YOR•GD•Th•LRD•S•ON

שמע ישראל יהוה אלהינו יהוה אחד

(Note, Hebrew is written and read from right to left.)

Because the language was spoken by the community everyday, and because the Scripture was already familiar to them, Hebrew scribes could easily discern the consonants' meaning.

Much later, during the late medieval period (7th–10th centuries AD), the Masoretes added marks *in* and *around* the consonantal letters to indicate vowel sounds, accents, and punctuation. These marks guided generations of Jewish readers, who had been cut off from their linguistic heritage since the Jews' return from Babylonian exile.

Hear, O Israel: The LORD our God, the LORD is one.
(**Dt 6.4** ESV)

שְׁמַע יִשְׂרָאֵל יְהוָה אֱלֹהֵינוּ יְהוָה אֶחָד׃

(The same Hebrew verse with vowels and cantillation points.)

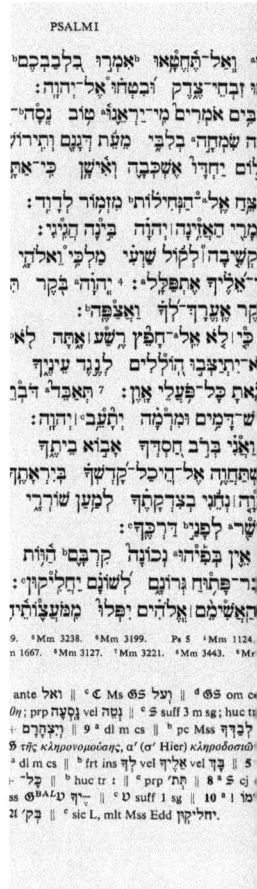

A sample of **Ps 5** in the *Biblia Hebraica Stuttgartensia* (BHS, 1997), a standard Hebrew text based on the Masoretic tradition.

To date, there are approximately 6,000 existing Masoretic MSS. About 2,700 of these are dated prior to the Reformation (before 1540), albeit only a few (thirty-eight) predate the twelfth century, with the earliest of them dated to the ninth.[92] Most printed editions of the Hebrew Bible are based on the Masoretic tradition as preserved in the *Aleppo* and *Leningrad Codices.**

Even though available MSS in the Masoretic tradition are relatively late (9th – 16th centuries), their reliable transmission is well attested by the Dead Sea Scrolls* (DSS) and other ancient versions (Greek, Latin, Aramaic, Coptic, Syriac, *et al.*).

The Dead Sea Scrolls (DSS) were discovered in the caves of Qumran by a young Bedouin goatherder in 1947.

The DSS include copied portions of the Hebrew Bible that were rediscovered somewhat recently (1947) in the ancient library of the old Qumran community. They were part of a collection that once perched inside the elevated caves along the western shore of the Dead Sea. They are roughly dated to the first century AD and are among the oldest extant witnesses to the OT.

The DSS demonstrate that the Hebrew scribes took meticulous care when they copied Scripture. One scholar, who compared the DSS version of **Isaiah** with modern, printed editions, observed that the texts "proved to be word for word identical . . . in more than 95 percent of the text. The five percent of variation consisted chiefly of obvious slips of the pen and variations in spelling."[93]

Conjectural Emendations

When evaluating the text of the Hebrew Bible, scholars can not always determine where the Masoretic tradition best reflects the original Hebrew-Aramaic sources. When in doubt, they check the text against other ancient versions, like the Greek Septuagint, Samaritan Pentateuch,* Aramaic Targums,* Syriac Peshitta,* or Jerome's Latin Vulgate, *etc.* If good evidence among the DSS, other ancient versions, and the Rabbinic sources differ from the Mas-

The Best Bible?

oretic Hebrew, then textual critics might alter the vowels and accents to match the consensus of the early versions and witnesses.

Because of the known antiquity of the consonants, modern text critics may only dare to venture and emend them when presented with an overwhelming amount of evidence. On occasion, where critics doubt the Masoretic tradition and where there is a lack of evidence to confirm those doubts, they may risk and "fix" the consonants or spaces between words, though with great hesitation.

For example, the Aramaic "square" script (in which the Hebrew Bible has been written since some time after the Jews' return from Babylonian exile) has several pairs of letters, which share similar shapes. The *dalet* (ד) and the *resh* (ר) are two such letters that are often confused. Before the discovery of the DSS, scholars suspected that the *dalet* in **Isaiah 33.8** which renders the phrase "he hath despised *the cities*" (ASV 1901, *emphasis added*) should, in fact, read *resh* in order to make "the cities" mean "witnesses". This guess used to be a conjectural emendation*, but it proved to be

ר

Hebrew letter
resh

ד

Hebrew letter
dalet

JOTS AND TITTLES. "Till heaven and earth pass, *one jot or one tittle shall in no wise pass from the law*, till all be fulfilled" (**Mt 5.18** KJV).

During Jesus Christ's first advent, the word "jot"—that is the Greek letter *iota* (ι) or its Hebrew-Aramaic counterpart, *yod* (י)—denoted the smallest or simplest letter that a scribe could write, consisting of a single short stroke. The word "tittle"—that is the Greek *keraia*—signified the horizontal stroke of the Aramaic letter *dalet* (ד) whose overlapping spur is the only thing distinguishing it from the letter *resh* (ר).

Jesus made it clear that he and his ministry by no means abandoned or discarded even the smallest letter of Moses' Law or the Old Testament prophets. Rather, where there was a Messiah-shaped hole in Scripture waiting to be filled, Jesus came and "fulfilled"—or completed—it. There are still promises in the Old Testament that have yet to be realized, but Jesus Christ assures us that not one "jot" or "tittle" will disappear until he completes them all. ◄

י

Hebrew letter
yod

ι

Greek letter
iota

a valid variant when the suspected *resh* was found in the earlier DSS, so that modern versions now read, "Covenants are broken, *witnesses* are despised, there is no regard for man." (RSV 1952, *emphasis added*). Happily, the evidence from this discovery clarifies the text and fits the context far better.

Reliability of the Hebrew Scribal Tradition

These "conjectural emendations," or scholarly guesses about how the original might have read, are discouraged because of the great likelihood that the originals are well preserved through the scribes' traditional practice. Hebrew copyists were known for the attention they gave to preserving the text of their exemplars; they had systems and policies for checking and correcting their copies. Whereas early Greek and Latin texts were written so that the words ran together (*scripta continua*), eastern scribes differentiated words from one another with dots or spaces, much like we do today, thus helping them copy more carefully. They would scrupulously count lines and words to ensure that both their copies and their exemplars reached the same numbers of both.[94] Depending on which standard was in use, columns of copied text were permitted to contain one to three corrected errors only.[95] Any more corrections per column and the copied scroll would be rolled up and removed from use.[96] Scribes took care since they aspired to faithfully reproduce their original sources and guard the stability of the text for future generations.[97]

TRANSMISSION PRIORITY IN ENGLISH TRADITION

The *Westminster Confession of Faith* (1647) reads that the "Old Testament in Hebrew ... and the New Testament in Greek ... , being immediately inspired by God and, by His singular care and providence, kept pure in all ages, are therefore authentical."[98] This doctrine of the providential preservation of Scripture is derived from Jesus's own words, "Till heaven and earth pass, one jot or one tittle

shall in no wise pass from the law, till all be fulfilled." (**Mt 5.18** KJV)
Some take this to mean that God has preserved the biblical canon
through one particular tradition of scribal transmission, namely
the Masoretic tradition for the Old Testament and the Greek *Textus Receptus* (TR) for the New.

The second part of the doctrine so reads, "[B]ecause these
original tongues are not known to all the people of God, who . . .
are commanded . . . to read and search them, therefore they are to
be translated into the vulgar language of every nation unto which
they come."[99] Some take this to mean that there is a single ideal
Bible translation that best reflects that scribal transmission. For
Germans, this could be Luther's last edition of 1545; for Spaniards, the Reina-Valera revision of 1602; and for English readers,
many consider it to be our landmark translation—the King James
Version of 1611.

To the credit of the King James Version, it does in fact reflect
the *Textus Receptus* better than most other modern translations.
In recent times, it has even been praised as the "noblest monument of English prose."[100] Despite scholars' tributes to the KJV's
success or the literary critics' accolades for its poetic cadence,
they both acknowledge that its Jacobean language serves to hinder most modern readers' ability to understand it. Since it was a
revision of almost a century's work of Bible translation starting
with William Tyndale, its antiquated language retained English
renderings that were out of date even when it was first published.
(See "Thy Fine English Tongue", page 215.)

As an example to modern readers, the KJV revisers rendered
the Apostle Paul's words:

"For they that have used the office of a deacon well purchase to
themselves a good degree" (**1Tm 3.13** KJV).

This does not mean that deacons ought to buy a graduate-level education (though it might help), but that they should "gain a good
standing" or "reputation".

Yet another example, **Psalm 119.147** reads,

"I prevented the dawning of the morning, and cried." (KJV)

Here, the psalmist is not claiming that he stopped the sun from shining with his tears. The word "prevented" stems from the Latin verb, *prævenio*, meaning "went before" or "preceded". This inspired poet is saying that "I rise before dawn and cry for help."

Or again, **Revelation 10.5–6** reads,

"[T]he angel which I saw stand upon the sea and upon the earth . . . sware . . . that there should be time no longer."

This does not mean that the angel swore an oath to stop time altogether. Rather, it means that the angel swore an oath, promising that "there should be no more delay" to the fulfillment of God's mystery that he announced to the prophets so long ago. (*Cf.* **vs. 7**. For more examples, see "Language Change" on page 212 and following.)

The apostle Paul instructed the church to make themselves clear and understandable, "So likewise ye, except ye utter by the tongue words easy to be understood, how shall it be known what is spoken? for ye shall speak into the air." (**1Co 14.9** KJV) Therefore, later renderings of the TR update the words so that Scripture can be readily understood by modern readers in the "vulgar", *i.e.*, common language, of our nation. Among these versions are the *New King James Bible* (NKJV, 1982), the *Modern English Version* (MEV, 2014), the *KJV II* (1971), the *21st Century KJV* (KJ21, 1994), the *Third Millennium Bible* (1998), and the *KJV 2000* (2011).

Though the King James Version reflects some of the best linguistic and biblical scholarship of its day, our collective knowledge of Scripture and language has since grown. Most contemporary Bible translations—the RSV, NIV, CSB, NRSV, NASB, *et al.*—are based on earlier MSS than those available to King James' scholars or on MSS that better reflect the Byzantine text transmis-

The Best Bible?

sion than does the TR. In fact, the King James Version follows the TR even where good MS evidence reveals that the TR is faulty or deficient. For example, Desiderius Erasmus did not possess the last few leaves of Revelation to complete his Greek edition, so he back-translated the last few chapters from the Latin Vulgate. Of the significant errors that both later, critical editions and the majority consensus of all MSS correct is **Revelation 22.19**, which reads in the King James Bible,

> if any man shall take away from the words of the book of this prophecy, God shall take away his part out of the *book of life* (KJV, *emphasis added*)

It should not read *"book* of life", but *"tree* of life" instead.[101]

COMMA JOHANNEUM.* Another famous example is the *Comma Johanneum*, which reads,

> For there are three that bear record in heaven, the Father, the Word, and the Holy Ghost: and these three are one. (**1 John 5.7** KJV).

This reading shows up in only eight Greek MSS, only one of which dates no earlier than the tenth century AD. It is not found in any of the early versions (Old Latin, Jerome's Vulgate, Syriac, Coptic, Armenian, *etc.*), nor do any of the early church fathers quote it. It seems to have been an old marginal gloss that a small number of scribes incorporated into the main text of their editions at a much later date.[102]

Critics may accuse modern translations for omitting portions of Scripture.[103] But caution is due when blaming them for dropping words, because the TR can just as well be condemned for adding words that were never there to begin with.[104] Though the *Comma Johanneum* seems like a strong proof-text for the doctrine of the Trinity, we should be wary when basing any doctrine on a single, weakly supported text. (After all, if the early church was able to arrive at trinitarian doctrine without the benefit of this passage, perhaps we can, too.)

In the words of one scholar-theologian, "No biblical doctrine would go unsupported if a favorite reading was abandoned in favor of a more valid variant. That does not mean, as is sometimes said, that no doctrine of Scripture is affected by textual variation. Rather, a doctrine that is affected by textual variation will always be adequately supported by other passages." [105]

Finally, the *Westminster Confession of Faith* clearly teaches that God preserves the purity of Scripture. Jesus Christ himself asserts as much. But we should note that Jesus never specified by *what means* (or by *what manuscript tradition*) or to *what extent* that Scripture should be preserved.[106] With the wealth of MSS available to us, we can be sure that there is no risk of losing God's written word. The originals—the *autographa*—may be lost to us, but they are only so beyond reach as is the object behind a mirror's reflection. The artifacts—the early MSS and versions—that we have today offer us a sufficiently clear reflection of the originals, even where the image is sometimes marred here and there by the scratches and dirt inflicted by historical happenstance.   ⌁

ENDNOTES FOR TEXTUAL DECISIONS

1 From Moses to John the Revelator; possibly longer, since the composition of **Job** (likely a contemporary with Abraham, *ca.* 1800 BC) cannot be exactly determined.

2 The Bible was written in Asia, Europe, and Africa. The bulk of the Bible's composition occurred in what is now the modern state of Israel and the Sinai peninsula. Portions of Jeremiah were written in Egypt (**Jer 43.7 ff**). Paul's missionary journeys took him to Europe from where he wrote several letters.

3 The Bible was written in Hebrew, Aramaic, and Greek. Passages written in classical Aramaic include **Jer 10.11; Dn 2.4b – 7.28; Ezr 4.8 – 6.18; 7.12–26**. We could count a fourth language, if we include the Latin loanwords in Mark's Gospel (*e.g., census,* **Mk 12.14;** *centurion,* **15.39, 44, 45;** *flagellum,* **15.15;** *legion,* **5.9, 15;** *modius,* **4.21;** *prætorium,* **15.16;** *quadrans,* **12.42;** *sextarius,* **7.4;** *speculator,* **6.27**).

4 The authority of some of these books were debated long after they were composed. For example, Jewish rabbis finally settled the dispute over **Song of Songs** and **Ecclesiastes** sometime in the third century AD.

5 *Tanakh* is the Hebrew acronym for the canon's three main sections (*Ta = Torah; Na = Nebi'im; Kh = Khetubim*). The existing Samaritan community holds only the first five books of Moses in Hebrew (the *Torah*) as canonical. Kairite Jews restrict their faith and practice to the *Tanakh,* but Orthodox Jews (Chasidim) adhere to an even broader canonical tradition, which includes the *Tanakh* and what's called the Oral Torah (*i.e.,* the *Mishnah*) and its commentary (the *Gemara*). (The *Mishnah* and *Gemara* together comprise the *Talmud,* of which there are two recensions: *Talmud Bavli* and *Talmud Yerushalmi*—the Babylonian and Jerusalem Talmuds).

6 The story of the **Macabees** is celebrated with the Jewish holiday, Hanukkah (*i.e.,* the Feast of Dedication, *cf.* **Jn 10.22**).

7 One early Christian author, Papias of Hierapolis (*ca.* 125–150 AD) *via* Eusebius (*Historia Ecclesiastica* 6.25.4), asserts that the Gospel of **Matthew** was originally composed in Hebrew or Aramaic and then translated or recomposed in Greek. Though a possibility, there is no extant manuscript to prove this one way or the other.

8 **Mark**, though not one of Jesus' earliest followers, was a disciple of the apostle Peter. He derived his gospel, so it is reasoned, from the apostle's experience.

Other gospels had been written (e.g, Gospel of Mathias, Gospel of Thomas) but were dismissed because they had either been written too late or their authorship could not be authenticated.

9   The author of **Hebrews** is anonymous, but from an early date the book was associated with the apostle Paul or someone through his ministry. Though its authorship is unknown, its inclusion in the NT canon was never disputed.

10 Eusebius, a church historian, tells us that the acceptance of **2 Peter, 2–3 John, James,** and **Jude** was disputed in his day (*ca.* 325 AD). The Syriac church's NT canon originally excluded **2 Peter, 2–3 John, Jude,** and **Revelation,** but since the Western Syriac church's ties with Europe and North Africa, it has adopted these works as authoritative *via* Thomas of Harqel's version (616 AD).

11 The early Christian apologists defended their faith from the LXX, to the consternation of Jewish leaders. By the 2nd c. AD, three new translations or revisions of the Greek OT were produced by Jews or Jewish converts. Aquila of Sinope (*ca.* 130 AD) was one who sought to concordantly* translate the Hebrew text. His version used different terms than those familiar to Christians, *e.g.,* at **Is 7.14,** he writes νεανίας ("young woman") instead of παρθένος ("virgin"); elsewhere he uses ἠλειμμένος ("anointed") instead of its more familiar synonym χριστός ("anointed" or *Christ*).

Symmachus (*ca.* 170) carefully retranslated the Pentateuch.

Theodotian's version (*ca.* 150), particularly his translation of **Daniel,** was frequently used by Christians.

Origen of Alexandria, a 3rd-century Christian theologian, transcribed (1) the LXX and the translations of (2) Aquila, (3) Symmachus, and (4) Theodotian, plus (5) the Hebrew Bible and (6) a transcription* of the Hebrew text into Greek letters, all into six parallel columns. This monumental work of scholarship, which we call the *Hexapla,* became the standard reference work for later translators, like Jerome in the early 5th c. AD. It is lost to us now, except for where it is cited by others or where it can be backtranslated from the versions that relied on it.

12 The Greek Orthodox Church's general consensus on the composition of Scripture is summed up in the results of the Council of Jerusalem as found in *The Confession of Dositheus* (AD 1672), Decree 18, Question 3, "[W]e call Sacred Scripture all those which Cyril [Lucaris] collected from the Synod of Laodicea, and enumerated, . . . [including the] Apocrypha; . . . For we judge these also to be

with the other genuine Books of Divine Scripture genuine parts of Scripture. . . . [A]ll of these we also judge to be Canonical Books, and confess them to be Sacred Scripture."

13 The Council of Florence (AD 1441) "accepts and venerates" those texts which were only later officially canonized by the Council of Trent (1546).

14 United States Catholic Conference, "The Canon of Scripture," *Catechism of the Catholic Church* (Libreria Editrice Vaticana, 1994), §120.

15 Michael Pomazansky, *Orthodox Dogmatic Theology: A Concise Exposition*, translated by Seraphim [Eugene Dennis] Rose (Platina, CA: St. Herman of Alaska Brotherhood, 1984), pp. 33–34.

16 Roman Catholics also consider those latter works (**1–2 Esdras, Prayer Man, Ps 151**, and **3Mc**) as apocryphal and not canonical. **2 Esdras** (**4 Esdras** according to the Catholic Douay Bible, which is known as the Latin Esdras because its most complete sources are only available in Latin) is rejected by Protestants, Catholics, and Greek Orthodoxy alike, yet it is accepted in Russian and other Eastern Slavic Orthodox churches. Eastern Orthodoxy considers **4 Maccabees** and **Prayer Man** of lesser authority, relegating them to an appendix.

17 Some of the apocryphal books included in the Tewahedo canon share the same names as those in the Eastern Orthodox canon yet differ in content.

18 Protestants of the Reformation era extended the application of the apostle Paul's words ("the Jews were entrusted with the oracles of God," **Ro 3.2** ESV) to the Rabbinic conclusions of a later century. This may seem like an anachronism, but the Jewish *Talmudim* do preserve traditions that were long-standing well before their publication.

19 *Cf.* Jerome, *Incipit prologus Sancti Hieronomi in libro regum*, i.e., the "helmeted" preface to **Samuel** and **Kings** (*ca.* 391 AD).

20 Flavius Josephus, the Babylonian Talmud (*b. Batra* 14b), and Melito of Sardis (*ca.* 160 AD) all omit mention of the apocryphal books in their enumerations of the Old Testament books. Origen of Alexandria (*ca.* 225), Eusebius of Cæsaria (*ca.* 325), and Athanasius of Alexandria (*ca.* 325) omit mention of apocryphal books or excplicitly set them aside from the "canonical" books. But this is not conclusive, since some books or collections could have been subsumed under larger works. For example, it is possible that a reference to **Daniel** might include **Sus, Bel & Drag**, and **Song of 3**; that **Jeremiah** could include **Bar** and **Ep of Jer**.

[21] With the exception of **Sir**, the apocryphal books have no clearly identifiable author, but neither do some books from the OT (*e.g.*, **Kings, Chronicles, Esther**) nor does **Hebrews** in the NT.

[22] For example, the author of **Jdt** incorrectly identifies Nebuchadnezzar as the king of the Assyrians instead of the Babylonians (**Jdt 1.1**); Judas Maccabees offers prayer for dead soldiers who wore pagan amulets to battle (a proof text for purgatory, **2Mac 12.38-46**).

[23] Though some Apocryphal books are alluded to in the NT, they are never explicitly quoted or given the same attention that quotations from the Hebrew canon receive. The NT authors cite or allude to works outside the Hebrew canon and the Greek Apocrypha, like 1 Enoch (**2Pt 2.4–5; Jd 14–15**) or the secular poet, Epimenides (**Tt 1.12**). But they never introduce any of these with any special formula as they do books from the Hebrew canon (*e.g.*, "it is written . . . ," ". . . in the Scriptures . . . ," "Moses said . . . ," or "the Lord said . . ."). Not all OT quotations are introduced this way, but all quotations that are thus introduced are limited to the books of the Hebrew canon.

[24] The author of **Sirach** asserts no divine origin for either his text or his calling, unlike the OT prophets or NT apostles. (Neither does **Esther**, for that matter, which was why it was debated in early Jewish tradition.) The author of **2 Maccabees** discloses his reliance on the human effort and research he needed to write his history (**2Mc 2.24–32**). Finally, the Reformers considered some apocryphal works as mere fables or legends whose inclusion in the canon would unneccessarily discredit the whole Bible. As the theologian, Edward Reuss, put it, "the scoffs thrown at the head of the little fish of Tobit will sooner or later destroy Jonah's whale" (*cf.* **Tb 6.17–18; 8.2–3;** *History of the Canon of the Holy Scriptures in the Christian Church* [Edinburgh: James Gemmel, 1887], pp. 361–2).

[25] Jewish tradition reports, "After the last prophets Haggai, Zechariah, and Malachi died, the Divine Spirit [of prophetic revelation] departed from the Jewish people" (*b. Yoma* 9b; *cf. b. Sotah* 48b; *b. Sanhedrin* 11a). Flavius Josephus agreed, "From Artaxerxes (5th century BC) to our own time (1st c. AD) the complete history [of the Jews] has been written, but has not been deemed worthy of equal credit with the earlier records, *because of the failure of the exact succession of the prophets*" (*Contra Apionem* 1.41, *emphasis mine*). The author of **1 Maccabees** (167–160 BC) tells us that the Jewish nation had to postpone

decisions regarding proper worship "until a trustworthy prophet should arise" (**1Mc 4.46; 14.41;** *cf.* **9.27**). So the consensus of Jewish tradition does not recognize as divinely inspired any work written after the last composition of the Hebrew canon.

26 John Calvin, *Institutes of the Christian Religion,* 1.7.5.

27 The general Protestant consensus is stated in the *Westminster Confession of Faith* (1647), chap. 1, sect. III, "The books commonly called Apocrypha, not being of divine inspiration, are no part of the canon of the Scripture; and therefore are of no authority in the Church of God, nor to be any otherwise approved, or made use of, than other human writings." The *Thirty-nine Articles* of the Church of England (1571) reads, "And the other Books (as Jerome says) the Church does read for example of life and instruction of manners; but yet it does not apply them to establish any doctrine" (Article 6). So Swiss Reformer, Œcolampadius (1530): "We do not despise [the Apocryphal books]; but we do not allow them divine authority with the other [Scriptures]."

28 This is the title page of Luther's Apocrypha (1534). In German it reads, "Apocrypha. Das find Bücher: fo nicht der heiligen Schrifft gleich gehalten: und doch nützlich und gut zu lefen find."

29 Today the British and Foreign Bible Society goes by the name of the Bible Society.

30 The Russian Synodal text does not follow the Septuagint (a.k.a. the "Alexandrian" canon), but rather the Masoretic Hebrew (the "Palestinian" canon) in accordance with the instructions of Metropolitan Philaret of Moscow.

31 For example, Catholicos Patriarch of the East, Mar Eshai Shimun XXI, wrote in 1957, the "originality of the *Peshitta* text, ... we wish to state, that the Church of the East received the scriptures from the hands of the blessed Apostles themselves in the Aramaic original, the language spoken by our Lord Jesus Christ Himself, and that the *Peshitta* is the text of the Church of the East which has come down from the Biblical times without any change or revision."
George M. Lamsa, ed., "Preface," *Holy Bible from the Ancient Eastern Text,* ed. (San Francisco, CA: Harper & Row, 1985).

32 The church historian, Eusebius (*fl. c.* AD 260–340), records in his *Historia Ecclesiastica* (book III, ch. 39, vs. 16) a report by Papias of Hierapolis (*c.* AD 125–50.): "Matthew collected the oracles (λογία, *i.e.,* the 'sayings' of or about Jesus) in the Hebrew language (Ἑβραΐδι διαλέκτῳ, or 'in the Hebrew style') and each interpreted (ἡρμήνευσεν, or 'translated') them as best he could."

[33] Published advocates of Aramaic primacy (*e.g.*, George M. Lamsa, Victor Alexander, and Andrew G. Roth) tend to equivocate later Syriac dialects with the older Aramaic langauge. Syriac is an eastern cognate language akin to the Galilean Aramaic that Jesus would have spoken. They share much of the same vocabulary and similar grammar. Yet, evidence for the NT's original composition in either Aramaic or Syriac falls woefully short: We have no early NT MSS in Aramaic. The text of the Old Syriac versions may date as early as 2nd century AD, but the twenty-two-book Syriac NT (called the *Peshitta* or "Simple" version) and its Philoxenian and Harklean emendations date much later (AD 5th – 7th centuries). The earlist existing copy of Matthew's Gospel in the Peshitta can be found in the British Library under the designation Add.MS 14470. It is dated to the 6th century.

All the earliest Syriac NT manuscripts (MSS) that we now possess post-date our Greek ones and show signs of their being translated from the Greek instead of from supposed Aramaic exemplars.* Rather, the *Peshitta* shows signs of its reliance on the Greek. For example, instead of translating the meaning of the Greek word *paraklētos* (παράκλητος) into a native Syriac equivalent, the Peshitta transliterates the term as *prqlta* (ܦܪܩܠܛܐ, *cf.* Jn 14.16; 15.26; 16.7; 1Jn 2.1). Instead of using Aramaic or Syriac forms of the names of Jesus and John (*Yeshua* and *Yochanan*), it renders Greek forms (*Yesous* and *Yohannes*).

[34] Whereas the Jewish Hebrew *Tanakh* is written in the Aramaic-derived square script (called *Ashuri* or "Assyrian" script), the Samaritan *Torah* is recorded in a script modelled closer to the ancient Phoenician or palæo-Hebrew script.

[35] The Samaritan Pentateuch is held as an authority in the Samaritan community. It supports their theological agenda against Jewish exclusivism.

Emanuel Tov, *Textual Criticism of the Hebrew Bible.* 2nd rev. ed. (Minneapolis, MN: Fortress Press, 1992), pp. 94–5.

[36] Greek Orthodoxy considers differences between the LXX and the Hebrew text to be changes made under divine inspiration. This view seems to rest on the legend of Aristeas as recalled by several early respected Christians: Justin Martyr in his *Hortatory Address to the Greeks*, Chapter 13; Irenæus, *Against Heresies*, 3.21.2ff; Cyril of Jerusalem, *Catechetical Lectures*, 4.34ff, *et al.* Yet, some members of the Eastern Orthodox communion (*e.g.*, the Russian Orthodox Church) place greater priority on the earlier Hebrew text (*cf.* Metropolitan Philaret of Moscow's *Larger Catechism* [approved 1830], Questions 28–43).

37 The Latin version, commonly called the Vulgate, was translated by Saint Jerome (Gk. Hieronymus) in the late fourth century AD from early Hebrew sources. It eventually surpassed the Old Latin version (*i.e.*, Vetus Latina, translated from the Greek NT and LXX) as authoritive in the Roman Catholic Church.

38 Council of Trent, "Decree Concerning the Edition and Use of the Sacred Books" (Trento: April 8, 1546), Session IV, Second decree.

39 Pope Pius XII, *Divino Afflante Spiritu* (Rome: September 30, 1943).

40 Second Vatican Council, *Dei Verbum*, by Pope Paul VI (Rome: November 18, 1965).

41 At times, fresh parchment was unavailable or too expensive, so scribes would sometimes scrape the ink off an already written parchment to proffer a place for their pen and record another text. This rewritten document is called a *palimpsest* (Greek for "scraped again").

42 Alan R. Millard, "In Praise of Ancient Scribes," *The Biblical Archaeologist*, vol. 45, no. 3 (Summer, 1982), pp. 143–53.

43 Papyri 52 ($\mathfrak{P}^{52}$), 66 ($\mathfrak{P}^{66}$), and 90 ($\mathfrak{P}^{90}$) all contain parts of John's gospel:

$\mathfrak{P}^{52}$ includes **John 18.31–33, 37–38**; it is currently housed in the John Rylands University Library (Gr. P. 457) in Manchester, UK.

$\mathfrak{P}^{66}$ includes **John 1.1–6.11; 6.35–14.26** and a fragment of **14.29–21.9**. It is located at the Fondation Bodmer (Papyrus Bodmer II) in Geneva.

$\mathfrak{P}^{90}$ includes **John 18.36–19.7**; it is currently located in the Sackler Library (Papyrology Rooms, P. Oxy. 3523) in Oxford.

The "Magdalen" papyrus 67 ($\mathfrak{P}^{67}$), includes **Matthew 3.9,15; 5.20–22, 25–28**. It can be found in the Fundacion San Lucas Evangelista (P. Barc.1) in Barcelona.

Papyrus 4 ($\mathfrak{P}^{4}$) includes **Luke 1.58–59; 1.62–2.1; 2.6–7; 3.8–4.2; 4.29–32, 34–35; 5.3–8; 5.30–6.16**. It can be found in Bibliothèque nationale de France (Suppl. Gr. 1120) in Paris. It is dated to the early part of the 1st century AD, approximately 30 years after the death of John the Elder, the author of Revelation.

Theses five ancient manuscript fragments were copied from even earlier exemplars.

44 By "traditional base text" I mean any edition of the *Textus Receptus* that many critical editions compare variants against.

45 Bruce M. Metzger, *A Textual Commentary on the Greek New Testament*. 2nd ed. (Stuttgart: Deutsche Bibelgesellschaft, 1994), p. 574.

46 For an example of external evidence, the traditional reading in **1Co 15.51**, "we will not a sleep, but we will all be changed" is supported by early majuscule

MSS, like the *Codex Vaticanus* (B/03) and the corrected hand of *Codex Claromontanus* (D/06), the majority of Greek MSS, as well as MSS in Syriac and Coptic.

47 Peter J. Gurry, "The Number of Variants in the Greek New Testament: A Proposed Estimate," *New Testament Studies*, vol. 62, no. 1 (2016): pp. 97–121, doi:10.1017 /S0028688515000314.

48 Differences of Greek word order within a sentence do not usually translate into English. Cases that do are insignificant (*e.g.*, "Jesus Christ" versus "Christ Jesus").

The Greek removable letter *nu* (ν) occurs occasionally at the end of certain verb forms (*e.g.*, ἐστιν) in order to make the transition to the next word sound better.

The addition or omission of a definite articles (ὁ, ἡ, τό) sometimes has no affect on the meaning of the words they modify.

49 As of 2011, Daniel Wallace estimated that there are between 300- to 400-thousand possible variants. Others indicate that number could be as high as 500,000 with the recovery of even more manuscripts, but we won't know for sure until scholars have finished collating* all extant manuscripts.

Daniel B. Wallace, "Lost in Transmision: How Badly Did the Scribe Corrupt the New Testament Text?" *Revisiting the Corruption of the New Testament* (Grand Rapids, MI: Kregel Publications, 2011), pp. 26–40;

Gurry, "The Number of Variants."

50 One percent of an estimated 500,000 textual variants equal 5,000 probable significant variants. If we divide 5,000 by the approximate total number of New Testament words (140,000), we get a little over 3 ½ percent of the total affected NT. This rough approximate ignores the fact that there are frequently more than one variant per textual unit, that is, several variant readings are counted on a single word or phrase, which reduces the percentage of the affected total of NT words. This percentage should suffice to give us at least a very rough estimate.

51 The fall of Constantinople (ancient Byzantium) to the Ottoman Turks marked the final destruction of the eastern half of the old Roman empire (the Byzantine empire). Scribes fled to the West bringing their Greek manuscripts with them. They were welcomed by interested philosophers and scholars in the early Italian printing houses.

52 Erasmus beat Spanish Cardinal Ximenes de Cisneros to publication, even though the latter had already printed the Greek New Testament two years earlier (in the Complutensian Polyglot, 1514) and was waiting for Papal approval, which he eventually received in 1520.

53 Erasmus' second edition corrected the first in 400 places, mostly typographical errors (perhaps due to Erasmus' haste to beat Ximenes' edition to market).

54 Luther translated his *September Testament* while hiding in Wartburg Castle disguised as a certain Junker Jörg (translated "Squire George").

55 Erasmus' third edition differed from the second in 118 places and introduced the *Johannine Comma* (**1 Jn 5.7**), which in turn found its way into the Tyndale-KJV tradition of English Bibles.

The *Johannine Comma* was not added to the German biblical tradition until much later.

Ezra Abbot, "I. John v. 7 and Luther's German Bible," *The Authorship of the Fourth Gospel and Other Critical Essays* (Boston: Geo. H. Ellis, 1888), pp. 458–63.

56 Robertus Stephanus is his Latin name, Robert Stephens is his English, and Robert Estienne, his French.

57 Two of the seventeen MSS (Stephanus' 11th and 16th sources) are unidentified; another two are uncertain (possibly minuscules 2298 and 237); another two are identified but not numbered (minuscules 42 and 111). An eighteenth source (which Stephanus numbers as his first) is the Complutensian Polyglot (printed in 1514).

58 Stephanus' fourth edition (1551) became the standard Greek edition in England.

59 The Elzevirs' reprint also included corrections from Beza's third octavo edition (1580).

60 F. H. A. Scrivener published the final edition of the *Textus Receptus* in 1881 to reflect the textual decisions made by the KJV revisers. In all there are approximately 28 different editions of the TR, from Erasmus to Scrivener.

61 John Mill, the theologian, is not to be confused with John Stuart Mill, the British philosopher, who espoused the doctrine of Utilitarianism in a later century.

62 Gerhard von Maastricht, "Prolegomena," Ἡ Καινὴ Διαθήκη. *Novum Testamentum.* (Amsterdam [*Amstelaedami*]: *Ex Officina Wetsteniana*, 1711), p. 25.

Adam Fox, *John Mill and Richard Bentley: A Study of the Textual Criticism of the New Testament 1675–1729* (Oxford: Basil Blackwell, 1954), p. 105.

Bruce M. Metzger and Bart D. Ehrman, *The Text of the New Testament: Its Transmission, Corruption, and Restoration*, 4th ed. (New York: Oxford U. Press, 2005), pp. 154–5.

63 Mill's contemporary, Johann Albrecht Bengel, while a student at Tübingen, "procured all the editions, manuscripts, and early translations available to him. After extended study he came to the conclusion that the variant readings were fewer in number than might have been expected, and that they did not shake any article of evangelic doctrine."

Metzger and Ehrman, *The Text of the New Testament*, p. 158.

64 von Maastricht, "Prolegomena," Ἡ Καινὴ Διαθήκη. *Novum Testamentum*, pp. 17–70.

65 Richard Bentley, Ἡ Καινὴ Διαθήκη *Graece. Novum Testamentum versionis Vulgatæ, per S^{tum} Hieronymum . . . Proposals for Printing.* (London: Knapton, 1720). *Dr. Bentley's Proposals for Printing a New Edition of the Greek New Testament . . .* (London: Knapton, 1721).

66 Johann Albrecht Bengel, "The Author's Preface," *Gnomon of the New Testament . . . with corrections and additions from the ed. secunda of 1759*, vol 1 (Edinburgh: T. & T. Clark, 1877), pp. 3–67. Bengel's *Gnomon* was originally published in 1742.

67 Johann Jakob Wettstein, *Prolegomena ad Novi Testamenti Graeci editionem accuratissimam . . .* (Amsterdam [Amstelaedami]: with R. & J. Wetsten & G. Smith, 1730); —, Ἡ Καινὴ Διαθήκη *Novum Testamentum Graecum Editionis Receptae cum Lectionibus Varaiantibus . . .*, 2 vols (Amsterdam [Amstelaedami]: [ex officina Dommeriana], 1751).

68 Johann Jacob Griesbach, *Novum Textum Græce . . .*, 2 vols (London and Halle: 1796/1806).

69 Karl Lachmann, "Praefatio . . . ," *Testamentum Novum Graece et Latine . . .*, vol 1 (Berlin [Berolini]: George Reimer [in Aedibus Georgii Reimeri], 1842), pp. v–li.

70 Constantine von Tischendorf, "Prolegomena," *Novum Testamentum Graece . . .*, 2nd ed (Leipzig [Lipsiae]: printed by Adolf [Adolphi] Winter, 1849), pp. vii–lvi.

71 Samuel P. Tregelles, *An Introduction to the Textual Criticism of the New Testament* (London: 1856).

72 B. F. Westcott and F. J. A. Hort, *Text*, vol. 1, and *Introduction, Appendix*, vol. 2 of *The New Testament in the Original Greek* (Cambridge and London: Macmillan and Co., 1881).

73 The two others families deserve mention, the Western text-type, named for unique texts generally found in the Western Roman empire, and the Caesarean text-type, often considered an offshoot of the Byzantine family.

74 Westcott and Hort's text was biased by their preference for a theoretical "Neutral" text, which largely reflected the Alexandrian family of mss as recorded in

the Codex Vaticanus (B/02). C. von Tischendorf's editions relied on his great discovery at St. Catherine's monastery in the Sinai wilderness, *viz.* the Codex Sinaiticus (ℵ/01). K. Lachmann's text leaned in favor of the Codex Ephraemi Rescriptus (C/04).

75 The tendencies of this accidental omission (haplography) or repetition (dittography) is likely caused by a confusion of words or of lines that begin with the same words (homeoarcton) or end with the same words (homeoteleuton).

Evidence of omission is given by Harry A. Sturz in his book, *The Byzantine Text-Type & New Testament Textual Criticism* (Nashville, TN: Thomas Nelson, Inc., 1984).

76 There are actually several "eclectic" schools of textual criticism. The one already described may be called "reasoned eclecticism" and may be more accurately called the "local genealogical" school. Critics who doubt the possibility of ever arriving at the original *autographa* and hope only to produce the *Ausgangstexten* (*i.e.,* the heads of the different traditions of textual transmission) are labled "radical eclectics."

77 Eberhard Nestle, *Novum Testamentum Graece cum apparatu critico ex editionibus et libris manu scriptis collecto* (Stuttgart: 1898). This edition included readings from R. F. Weymouth's *The Resultant Greek Testament* (London, 1892). Weymouth's text was eventually replaced with B. Weiss' edition, *Das Neue Testament: Berichtigter Text,* 3 vols. (Leipzig: 1896–1902) in Nestle's 3rd edition (1901).

78 According to Philip Comfort, the 25th and 26th editions of Nestle-Aland are virtually identical. The 26th edition makes a total of 176 changes based on the evidence of early Greek papyri. The 27th edition's text does not differ, except in some punctuation.

Philip W. Comfort, *The Quest for the Original Text of the New Testament,* (Grand Rapids, MI: Baker, 1992), p. 123.

79 "Being a critical edition of the Greek New Testament, the Nestle-Aland provides an eclectic text reconstructed from the tradition by means of a combination of external and internal criteria." Barbara & Kurt Aland, Johannes Karavidopoulos, Carlo M. Martini, Bruce M. Metzger, eds, "Introduction," *Novum Testamentum Graece . . . ,* 28th ed. (Stuttgart: Deutsche Bibelgesellschaft, 2012), p. 54*.

The text of the Nestle-Aland (N-A) Greek NT (28th ed.) does not stray far from its original Westcott-Hort (W-H) base, which tended to prefer the Alexandrian text-type (as represented by the Codex Vaticanus) over and above other MSS.

There are only about 700 differences between w-h and n-a. For context, each edition contains around 138,000 words. There is only about a half of a percent difference (0.54%) between them. For another "eclectic" NT edition, see: Michael W. Holmes, *The Greek New Testament: SBL Edition* (Atlanta, GA: Society of Biblical Literature, 2010).

80 Kurt Aland, Matthew Black, Bruce M. Metzger, Allen Wikgren, *The Greek New Testament* (New York: American Bible Society; London: British and Foreign Bible Society; Edinburgh: National Bible Society of Scotland; Amsterdam: Netherlands Bible Society; Stuttgart: Württemburg Bible Society, 1966).

81 Zane C. Hodges and Arthur L. Farstad, *The Greek New Testament According to the Majority Text*, 2nd ed. (Nashville, TN: Thomas Nelson Publishers, 1985).

82 Reliance on the family tree (genealogical stemmata) is prevalent among those portions that have the greatest number of collated and compared manuscripts, *viz.* the *Pericope Adulteræ* and the book of Revelation.

83 Maurice A. Robinson and William G. Pierpont, *The New Testament in the Original Greek: Byzantine Textform* (Southborough, MA: Chilton Book Publishing, 2005).

84 Evidence of readings unique to the Byzantine text family among the early papyri also argue for an early recension* on par with the other text families. See Harry A. Sturz's work, *The Byzantine Text-Type & New Testament Textual Criticism* (Nashville, TN: Thomas Nelson, 1984).

85 Maurice A. Robinson and William G. Pierpont, "Appendix: The Case for Byzantine Priority," *The New Testament in the Original Greek: Byzantine Textform* (Southborough, MA: Chilton Book Publishing, 2005), pp. 533–86.

86 James D. Price, "Ch. 1: Introduction," *A Genealogical History of the Greek Text of the Gospel of Matthew,* rev. ed. (2018) pp. 1–10.

87 Barbara and Kurt Aland, Iōan. D. Karavidopoulos, Carlo M. Martini, and Bruce M. Metzger, *Novum Testamentum Graece.* 28th ed. (Stuttgart: Deutsche Bibelgesellschaft, 2012).

Barbara and Kurt Aland, Iōan. D. Karavidopoulos, Carlo Maria Martini, Bruce M. Metzger, and Holger Strutwolf, *The Greek New Testament.* 5th rev. ed., 3rd corr. printing (Stuttgart: Deutsche Bibelgesellschaft, American Bible Society, United Bible Societies, 2016).

88 Union of German Academies of Sciences and Humanities (Union der deutschen Akademien der Wissenschaften), *Novum Testamentum Graece, Editio Critica Maior* edited by the Institut für Neutestamentliche Textforschung (Institute

for New Testament Textual Research) (Westphalia, Germany: University of Münster, 1997–2030[?]).

[89] Followup research reveals that the *Pericope Adulteræ* is found in 1,476 MSS.

James Snapp, Jr., *A Fresh Analysis of John 7:53 – 8:11: With a Tour of the External Evidence* (2016). Kindle edition.

[90] Regarding their acceptance: The *Pericope Adulteræ* may have been marked, not because its authority was doubted, but to indicate its exclusion from lectionary readings. Later scribes may have confused the marking as an instruction to omit it from their copies.

[91] Even the important manuscripts, Codices Sinaiticus and Vaticanus, show evidence that their scribes were aware of the longer ending of **Mark**. Early church writers were aware of these passages and of their use.

Snapp, *A Fresh Analysis of John 7:53 – 8:11.*

[92] Gleason Archer, *A Survey of Old Testament Introduction* (Chicago, IL: Moody Press, 1985), p. 25.

[93] Malachi Beit-Arié, "Some Technical Practices Employed in Hebrew Dated Medieval Manuscripts," *Litterae textualis*, vol. 2 in Codicologica: Eléments pour une codicoligie comparée (Leiden: E. J. Brill, 1978), p. 72.

[94] Millard, "In Praise of Ancient Scribes."

[95] Tov, *Textual Criticism of the Hebrew Bible*, p. 216.

[96] Discarded texts were not usually destroyed but were stored away from public use in spaces called *genizot* (singular *genizah*) of which the most famous is the Cairo Genizah in Egypt.

[97] The En-Gedi Scroll (discovered in 1970) is a charred parchment roll dated to the third or fourth c. AD. It contains portions of **Leviticus** discovered through micro-computed tomography scanning. The text deciphered so far is "completely identical" to that found in later Medieval manuscripts.

Michael Greshko. "Computers Decipher Burnt Scroll Found in Ancient Holy Ark," National Geographic Society website, last modified September 21, 2016, accessed September 7, 2019, https://www.nationalgeographic.com /news/2016/09/computers-decipher-ancient-hebrew-ein-gedi-scroll -bible-archaeology/.

[98] *Westminster Confession of Faith*, 1.18.

[99] "Search the scriptures; for in them ye think ye have eternal life: and they are they which testify of me." — Jesus Christ (**Jn 5.39** KJV)

[100] John Livingston Lowe, *Of Reading Books: Four Essays* (London: Constable & Co., LTD, 1930), pp. 47–77.

[101] This associates the passage with the *tree of life* in the garden of Eden (**Gn 2–3**).

[102] "The passage is absent from every known Greek manuscript except eight, and these contain the passage in what appears to be a translation from a late recension of the Latin Vulgate. Four of the eight manuscripts contain the passage as a variant reading written in the margin as a later addition to the manuscript."

Metzger, *A Textual Commentary on the Greek New Testament*, pp. 647–9.

The *Comma Johanneum* is not found in any Latin Gospel MS before the ninth c. AD. Medieval MSS do not clearly distinguish between marginal glosses and emendations to the text.

[103] "Statement of Faith," *Chick Publications* website, accessed March 29, 2019, http://chick.com/information/general/statementoffaith/.

Steven Anderson, *Faithful Word Baptist Church* (Tempe, AZ) website, accessed March 29, 2019, http://www.repentanceblacklist.com/081207p.mp3.

Gail A. Riplinger, *New Age Bible Versions* (Shelbyville, TN: Bible & Literature Missionary Foundation, 1993).

[104] As Scripture reads, "Add thou not unto [God's] words, lest he reprove thee, and thou be found a liar." (**Pr 30.6** KJV)

[105] David Alan Black, *New Testament Textual Criticism: A Concise Guide* (Grand Rapids, MI: Backer Academic, 1994), p. 25.

[106] The immediate context of **Matthew 5.17** indicates that Jesus was referring specifically to the Old Testament "law and the prophets". The Law, is generally understood as the Pentateuch (*i.e.*, *Torah* = The Five Books of Moses). The Prophets, according to the traditional Hebrew division of Scripture, includes the Former Prophets (from Joshua to 2 Kings) and the Latter Prophets (Isaiah to Malachi). But "prophets" could refer to any prophetic record in the Hebrew canon, including the Psalms.

[107] Martin Luther was the first to set the Apocrypha apart from the other books of the Old Testament canon.

Luther, *Biblia/das ist/die ganze Heilige Schrifft Deudsch. Mart. Luth. Wittemberg. Begnadet mit Kürfurstlicher zu Sachsen freiheit. Gedruckt durch Hans Lufft. M. D. XXXIIII.* 2 vols. (1534).

108   **Ezra** and **Nehemiah** are sometimes combined as **2 Esdras** in some editions of the LXX, while other editions separate **Nehemiah** into its own book. See page 15 for more about naming conventions in different faith traditions.

109   **4 Maccabees** is included as an appendix. It is not viewed as canonical within Orthodoxy.

110   Eastern and Coptic Orthodox, Armenian Apostolic, and Armenian Catholic Churches accept **Psalm 151** as canonical. Roman Catholics, Protestants, and Jews consider it apocryphal, though some Catholic Bibles include it as an appendix.

111   Josh D. McDowell and Clay Jones, "The Bibliographical Test," Josh McDowell's ministry website, last modified August 13, 2014, accessed March 28, 2019, https://www.josh.org/wp-content/uploads/Bibliographical-Test-Update -08.13.14.pdf. Emended by the author.

112   31 out of the 33 manuscripts of the *Annals* by Tacitus are late 15th century copies.

113   Numbers for Josephus' works are taken from Heinz Schreckenberg's *Die Flavius-Josephus-Tradition in Antike und Mittelalter* (Leiden, Netherlands: E. J. Brill, 1972), pp. 13–51.

114   Livy's *History of Rome* is preserved in 60 complete copies and 90 partial ones.

115   Graeme D. Bird, "Textual Criticism as Applied to Classical and Biblical Texts," *Multitextuality in the Homeric Iliad: The Witness of the Ptolemaic Papyri*, Hellenic Studies, vol. 43 (Cambridge, MA: Harvard University Press, 2010).

116   The Institute for New Testament Textual Research (Institut für Neutestamentliche Textforschung) updates their official catalogue of Greek New Testament manuscripts (MSS, singular MS) online with each new MS discovery (see the *New Testament Virtual Manuscript Room* at http://ntvmr.uni-muenster.de/liste). Though the database is mostly complete, it is unfortunately not altogether accurate, as it occasionally lists the same MS twice, or identifies two MSS which are really one, or recognizes Greek NT MSS that really are not, or excludes those that are. The total entries for Greek MSS listed in their database is 5,387 (or 5,838 according to the Gregory-Aland numbering system), but a good qualified number is somewhere between 5,100 to 5,400.

117   This number includes the many thousands of scrolls (roughly approx. 25,000) currently used in Jewish synagogues and seminaries. Most of these are relatively modern productions and have no text-critical value. Very few, if any,

publishers bother to transcribe the secular works when good printed editions are readily available.

Caspar René Gregory, *Die Griechischen Handschriften des Neuen Testaments* (Leipzig: J. C. Hinrichs'sche Buchhandlung, 1908).

[118] McDowell and Jones, "The Bibliographical Test."

[119] Desiderius Erasmus' Greek NT (published 1516) is based on seven or eight MSS. From Johannes Reuchlin, Erasmus borrowed Minuscules 1^{eap} (12th century; contains the entire NT except Revelation) and 1^{rk} (12th c.; unfinished Revelation). From the Dominican Library in Basel, he borrowed Minuscules 2^e (12th c.; Gospels), 2^{ap} (12th c.; Acts and Epistles), 4^{ap} (15th c.; Pauline epistles), 7^p (12th c.; Pauline epistles) and 817 (15th c.; Gospels).

[120] Robert Stephanus indicated sixteen MSS with Greek numerals in his apparatus. Identified sources include the Complutensian Polyglot, the codices *Bezæ*, *Regius*, *Victorinus*, and the minuscules 4, 5, 6, 2817, 8, 38, 9, and 398. Other possible sources are Miniscules 2298 and 237. Two of his unnumbered MSS are Miniscules 42 and 111. Two more sources remain unidentified.

[121] John Mill, Ἡ Καινὴ Διαθήκη. *Novum Testamentum....* (Oxford [Oxonii]: Sheldonian Theatre [e theatro sheldoniano], 1707).

[122] Gerard von Maestricht, "Prolegomena: De Collectionibus & Collectoribus variantium Lectionum," Ἡ Καινὴ Διαθήκη. *Novum Testamentum. . . .* (Amsterdam [Amstelaedami]: Johan Hendrik Wetstein [ex officina wetsteniana], 1711).

[123] Johann Jakob Wetstein, Ἡ Καινὴ Διαθήκη. *Novum Testamentum Graecum . . .* 2 vols. (Amsterdam: ex officina Dommeriana, 1751/52).

[124] F. H. A. Scrivener, *A Plain Introduction to the Criticism of the New Testament: For the Use of Biblical Students* (Cambridge: Deighton, Bell, and Co., 1861), p. 3.

[125] Constantin von Tischendorf and Caspar René Gregory, *Novum Testamentum Graece... Editio Octava Critica Maior,* vol. III, *Prolegomena,* parts 1–3 (Leipzig [Lipsiae]: J. C. Hinrichs, 1884–90)

[126] Benjamin B. Warfield, *An Introduction to the Textual Criticism of the New Testament* (London: Hodder and Stoughton, 1886), p. 13.

[127] Gregory, *Die griechischen Handschriften.*

[128] Eberhard Nestle and Ernst von Dobschütz, *Einführung in das Griechische Neue Testament,* 4th ed. (Göttingen: Vandenhœck & Ruprecht, 1923).

[129] H. J. Vogels and L. Pirot, "Critique textuelle du Nouveau Testament," in *Dictionnaire de la Bible: Supplément,* ed. Louis Pirot, 13 vols. (Paris: Librairie Letouzey et Ané, 1934), vol. 2, p. 226.

Léon Vaganay, *Initiation à la critique textuelle néotestamentaire,* in Bibliothèque catholique des sciences religieuses (Paris: Bloud & Gay, 1934), vol. 60, p. 9.

[130] Kurt and Barbara Aland, *The Text of the New Testament* (Grand Rapids, MI: Wm. B. Eerdmans, 1989), p. 74.

[131] Kenneth Clark, "The Textual Criticism of the New Testament," *Peake's Commentary on the Bible,* ed. Matthew Black and H. H. Rowley (London: Thomas Nelson, 1962), p. 669.

[132] Eldon Jay Epp, "Are Early New Testament Manuscripts Truly Abundant," *Israel's God and Rebecca's Children* (Waco, TX: Baylor University Press, 2007), p. 79.

[133] Bart D. Ehrman, *Misquoting Jesus: The Story Behind Who Changed the Bible and Why* (New York: HarperSanFrancisco, 2005), p. 89.

[134] Institut für Neutestamentliche Textforschung's online database *minus* duplicate entries.

[135] Peter J. Gurry, "The Number of Variants in the Greek New Testament."

[136] This sample comes from **1Co 15.51**. The base text is translated from the *Textus Receptus* (TR); MS 1 is translated from the Codex Alexandrinus (A 02, 5th century AD); MS 2, from Papyrus 46 ($\mathfrak{P}^{46}$, early 3rd c.); and MS 3, from Codex Sinaiticus (א 01, 4th c.).

[137] Constantin von Tischendorf, *Novum Testamentum Graece . . . Editio Octava Critica Maior,* vols. I–II, (Leipzig [Lipsiae]: J. C. Hinrichs, 1869–72).

[138] S. P. Tregelles, *The Greek New Testament,* (London: 1857–79).

[139] Scribal changes that make parallel passages agree with one another is called harmonization.*

[140] *NET Bible.* 2nd ed. (Biblical Studies Press, L.L.C., 2017). Read the **tc** (text critical) note at **Mt 5.22**.

[141] As an example of Hebrew spelling differences within the same passage, the plural word, "tablets", is spelled either as *lucht* (לוחת) or *lchot* (לחות) at **Dt 9.10, 11**.

Translation Decisions

Hitting the Targets

Friends frequently ask me, "Which Bible translation is the most accurate?" The short answer I give them is "It depends on the target."

The question is full of implications. No single answer is both simple and sufficient. To give a terse answer with so little explanation would treat my friends and those who labor in translation with so much contempt.

After determining which text to work from, translators must identify the *goals* of their translation. Most have one general target in mind—to faithfully render the text set before them. Their aim is to put the Bible into language that their intended audience can understand, to give those unfamiliar with Greek and Hebrew an idea of what the Bible is saying.

This goal is simple to state, but the actual aims are complex. That's because faithful and accurate translation looks different depending on the specific targets aimed for. We might ask, "Is the target to merely gloss the biblical words and grammatical forms?" Or, "Is it to clarify the biblical authors' intended meaning?" "Is it to reflect the emotional moods that the authors tried to evoke?" Or, "Is it to conform the text to the way we normally use English?" Each of these aims are fraught with their own problems, challenges, and technicalities that often compete with one another for adequate expression.

Since most translators aim to hit more than one target at the same time, they often miss the bullseye in any one of them. Instead, they usually land somewhere among the outer rings of overlapping targets. They all compromise to some extent, because they are all stuck in the tension between two extremes—two tensions constantly pulling in opposing directions. Translators are frequently forced to either (A) reflect the forms of the original languages or (B) interpret the implied meaning of the text.

Formal Precision — Contextual Precision

Modern English Idiom — Intended Meaning

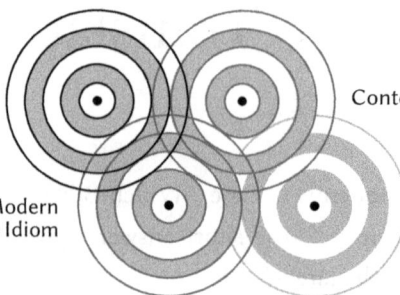

Translators always aim somewhere between competing translation goals. Also, the targets can vary in range and distance from one passage to the next.

We find evidence for this struggle in every Bible translation—from the Greek Septuagint to the Latin Vulgate, from Wycliffe to Tyndale, from the King James on up to our modern versions. Each translation is governed by those two competing priorities: (A) Formalism* and (B) functionalism.* (A) Formalism tries to convey *what is said* by prioritizing fidelity to the original word-forms and consistent representation of grammar and vocabulary. (B) Functionalism* tries to convey *what is meant* by expressing the ways in which the language is used.

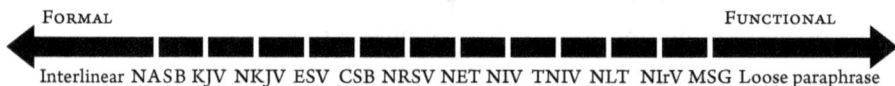

FORMAL ←——————————————————————→ FUNCTIONAL

Interlinear NASB KJV NKJV ESV CSB NRSV NET NIV TNIV NLT NIrV MSG Loose paraphrase

All Bible translations generally land somewhere on this formal-functional spectrum.

FORMAL TRANSLATION

Formal* translation goes by several designations, including "formal-" or "verbal-equivalence," "word-for-word," literal rendering,[1] or *ipsissima verba* (Latin for "the very words"). When translators refer to their work as "formal," they do not mean that it must sound archaic or dignified. That is, formalism does not imply the kind of high-register* expression we expect to hear at a formal inauguration or a ceremonial state dinner. Rather, translators who strive for a formal ideal work to let the original languages glimpse through their English renderings. They use several tools and techniques to do this:

The Best Bible?

Interlinear

The most formal way to show the correspondence between the English target and its base text is with an interlinear.* An interlinear Bible places English verbal* equivalents under the Greek or Hebrew text. This helps readers identify which English words represent their counterparts in the original languages. For example:

> ὡς   ἀρτιγέννητα βρέφη   τὸ   λογικὸν   ἄδολον γάλα   ἐπιποθήσατε,
> as   newborn   babes   [²the ⁵of the word ³pure   ⁴milk ¹desire]
>
> ἵνα   ἐν αὐτῷ   αὐξηθῆτε,   εἴπερ   ἐγεύσασθε   ὅτι   χρηστὸς
> that   [²thereby ¹you may grow] if indeed you have tasted that   [²gracious
>
> ὁ   κύριος.
> ¹the   Lord]   (*interlinear rendering*)
>
> as newborn babes, desire the pure milk of the word, that you may grow thereby, if indeed you have tasted that the Lord *is* gracious. (**1Pt 2.2–3**, NKJV)

The trouble with an interlinear is that it tends to obscure meaning by breaking up the natural English word order so as to conform it to the order of the original text. Also, this formal, one-to-one parallel makes it hard to identify English renderings that require more than one word to convey the meaning of a single Greek or Hebrew term. In fact, interlinears fail as true translations, because they merely gloss* the text. They do not arrange words into patterns that fit normal English syntax.

Transliteration

Another formal rendering is spelling Greek and Hebrew words with English letter-for-letter equivalents. This process, called transliteration,* is useful for identifying technical language unique in the original by giving it an equally unique referent in English. Familiar examples shared by most English versions include "angel" (from the Greek ἄγγελος, *angelos*), "apostle" (ἀπόστολος, *apostolos*), "baptize" (βαπτίζειν, *baptīzein*), "demon" (δαίμων, *daimōn*),

TRANSLATING THE NAME OF GOD. The word "God" is really a unique title like "Sir" or "Chief", but reserved solely for deity. When God revealed himself to Moses (**Ex 3.14,15**), the name he chose to give constituted four Hebrew consonants: *yod* (י), *hē* (ה), *waw* (ו), *hē* (ה)— read right to left—יהוה. These four letters in combination are called the Tetragrammaton*. Later scribes, out of respect for the name, feared to pronounce it aloud (*cf.* **Ex 20.7**). Instead, the Masoretes marked the four letters with the vowels of another word meaning "my Lord" or "my Master" (Heb. *adonai*).[29] The presence of these vowels remind readers to say "my Lord" whenever they read the divine name. This tradition was later transferred to the Septuagint (LXX), which uses the Greek equivalent for "Lord" (*kurios*) in every place where the Tetragrammaton occurs.

When later European scribes met the divine name, they attempted to transliterate it. The four Hebrew consonants were represented with the letters, I H V H or J H V H. (The and "Jehovah" (from the Hebrew Tetragrammaton—יהוה, YHWH).

One familiar transliteration is the Hebrew word for an "opponent," "adversary," or "enemy." The word "Satan" (*shatan*) is often used as a proper noun or a name for the enemy of God's people, as is fitting for the main antagonist in the book of **Job**, "So *Satan* went out from the presence of the LORD, and he afflicted Job" (**2.7** NET). But *shatan* can mean any "opponent" in general, as the distrustful Philistines regarded their ally, David, prior to their fight against the army of King Saul:

"Send that man back and let him return to the place you assigned him. He must not go down with us into battle only to become our adversary (*shatan*) during the battle." (**1Sa 29.4** CSB)

Essentially, transliteration is the same as borrowing loanwords* from foreign languages. This practice is not necessarily more "accurate" when the cultural associations tied to those words do not match how the words function in Scripture. Transliterations can actually hide the meaning or significance that a simple translation can reveal. For example, some confuse the familiar term "Christ" (Gk. *christos*) as Jesus's family name or surname. Rather, "Christ" functions as a unique title, which director Mel Gibson understood when he added the definite article ("the") to the title of his film *The Passion of* *the Christ* (Icon Productions, 2004). The Greek words, *ho christos,* is in fact a formal rendering of the term in Hebrew (*ha-mashiyach*), which simply translated means "the anointed [one]," that is, "someone smeared with an unguent."

This translation may seem pedestrian at first glance, because it loses the religious connotations we associate with "Christ." But, if we translate the Hebrew and Greek terms consistently, we may form new associations that we would otherwise miss. We discover that Jesus fits the pattern of several other "anointed" people in the Hebrew Old Testament: God "anointed" the Aaronic priests to show that they were his exclusive ministers in the Tabernacle; "the Anointed" was a title associated with God's choice of king (**1Sa 2.10**; *cf.* **Ps 2.2**); a unique "Anointed One" was predicted in Daniel's seventy-week prophecy (**Dn 9.25–26**); and the prophet Isaiah indicated that even a Gentile (a non-Jew) could be considered God's "Anointed" (*cf.* **Is 45.1**). The unifying theme of all these uses is the idea of God's election, or his choosing someone to serve or rule.[2]

Another example is a word often associated with Jesus's critical contempt towards the scribes and Pharisees, whom he described as "hypocrites". This transliteration from the Greek *hypokritai* (ὑπόκριται) misses the contemporary use of the word, which meant "actors", that is, "those who perform parts in a play." Though used metaphorically in the Septuagint (LXX) and New Testament, its contemporary use is illustrated in the *Letter*

Latin letters "ɪ" and "ɪ" were pronounced like "y" at the beginning of a word, and "v" was pronounced like an English "w.") When combined with the Masoretic vowels, they spelled "Jehovah," which became the standard spelling of the divine name in the *American Standard Version* (1901) and *New World Translation of the Holy Scriptures* (1984/2013).[30]

Some English translations approximate the original pronunciation as close as can be guessed. Recent renderings transcribe the divine name as "Yahweh" (HCSB, JB, NJB).[31] Most translations, though, set the traditional word in all capitals ("LORD") or in small caps with an initial capital letter ("LORD") in order to distinguish it from written occurrences of *adonai* ("Lord" or "lord" without caps). The familiar rendering, "Lord," has the convenience of translating the traditional spoken reading (*adonai*) while matching the same number of four letters as the written Tetragrammaton. ◄

of Aristeas, when the king of Alexandria asked one of his guests a question about living honorably. The guest answered,

> "For you must not appear to be worse than the actors (*tōn hypo-kritōn*), who study carefully the role, which it is necessary for them to play, and shape all their actions in accordance with it. You are not acting a part (*hypokrisei echeis*), but are really a king, since God has bestowed upon you a royal authority in keeping with your character." [3]

Concordance

Another formal method is to consistently render each original word or phrase with a single English equivalent. With this method, when the Greek word *baptīzein* is rendered "baptize" in the Gospels (*cf.* **Jn 1.33**), it is translated "baptize" wherever it appears in all other New Testament passages (*cf.* **1Co 1.17**). This creates a one-to-one correspondence and facilitates detailed word studies with the help of a concordance.*

This concordant* ideal, though valuable for consistent study, is frustrated when a Greek and Hebrew word expresses more than one meaning, since each word is affected by different contexts. For example, the Greek verb *katalambanein* can mean "to comprehend", "to overtake", or "to obtain" depending on how it is used in its context. As the apostle Peter realized, "Truly I *understand* (*katalambanomai*) that God shows no partiality" (**Ac 10.34** ESV), or as the apostle Paul says regarding the resurrection, "Not that I have already obtained all this, or have already arrived at my goal, but I press on *to take hold* (*katalabō*) of that for which Christ Jesus *took hold* (*katalēmphthēn*) of me" (**Php 3.12** NIV). There is no single English equivalent that functions the same way as this word does. This is why different translators find it tricky to translate **John 1.5**, which can be rendered in different ways, "The light shines in the darkness, and the darkness *has* not *overcome* it" (ESV), or "the darkness *did* not *comprehend* it" (NASB, KJV), or "the darkness *apprehended* it not." (RV/ASV)

Similar to English homographs*—words that are spelled the same but mean different things, like the English word "row" (as in "*row* your boat ashore" or "sit in the second *row*")—the different meanings of certain Greek and Hebrew words are missed entirely when they are not understood within their unique contextual settings.

Coinage

Yet another way to formally reflect the original text is to create new word called "coinages."* This method allows translators to represent an original concept while keeping to a formal priority with the creative use of a single descriptive word or compound word.

William Tyndale invented several new words in his pioneering translation work. We know how successful they are by how familiar they seem to us today: He coined words like "Passover" to replace the Latin transliteration *Pascha* (**Ex 12.26–27**), or "scapegoat" for the Hebrew *'azazel* (**Lv 16.10**), and words like "birthright," "longsuffering," "lovingkindness," "mercy seat," "shewbread," and "stiff-necked."

Formal Benefits & Challenges

Formal renderings prove useful for word study, because they alert us to thematic elements by using consistent turns of phrase. These uniform words and phrases make it easier for us to trace a concept or theme throughout Scripture. But formal renderings don't always convey a proper meaning, because Scripture sometimes uses high-context* language.

"High-context" situations require participants (*i.e.*, writers, speakers, and their audiences) to assume a prior understanding of their culture, environment, and situation in order to understand a story or conversation. So much meaning is implied or suggested by verbless cues (*e.g.* hand motions, facial expressions, gasps, *etc.*) that audiences must rely on their surrounding context to discern a speaker's intent. In contrast, low-context* cultures, like academic English and German engineering, value explicit, clear communication with ideas spelled out to the nth detail, with as few inferences as possible.

Because formal translations do not bother to clarify their higher context, they can tend to sound unnatural and foreign to English ears. This results in a kind of awkward biblical English that we sometimes call "biblish."* For example, the ESV tells us that

> the ants are a people not strong,
>> yet they provide their food in the summer;
> the rock badgers are a people not mighty,
>> yet they make their homes in the cliffs (Pr 30.25, 26 ESV)

Here we find that both ants and badgers (or hyraxes) are people, too! The word "people" in both verses is a formal translation of the Hebrew word, 'am. The NIV, on the other hand, interprets this passage's meaning,

> Ants are creatures of little strength . . .
> hyraxes are creatures of little power. (NIV 2011)

Here is another passage that can seem just as strange:

> He who planted the ear, shall He not hear?
>> He who formed the eye, shall He not see? (Ps 94.9 NKJV)

We're not sure which seeds God needs to plant in order to grow human ears, so, here, the GNB renders the general idea:

> God made our ears—can't he hear?
>> He made our eyes—can't he see? (GNB)

By breaking the literary "fourth wall", "biblish" reminds modern readers of our distance from that foreign, ancient world whose human authors wrote to us only indirectly. Such awareness is needed for objective study, but it can distract us from engrossing ourselves in the biblical message.

FUNCTIONAL TRANSLATION

On the other end of the translation spectrum is functional* translation, also known as "functional-" or "dynamic-equivalence," "thought-for-thought," idiomatic rendering, or *ipsissima vox* (Lat. "the very voice"). The need for functional translations arise when we recognize that words derive their meaning through their use or function in a given context. Translators working toward this ideal share two primary concerns:

First, when a Hebrew or Greek word can function different ways in different contexts (that is, where a word may have multiple meanings and the surrounding passage influences which is meant), translators choose an English rendering that best fits the immediate context. This is generally recognized as necessary for any good translation.

For example, in **Acts 2.2**, a sound like a violent "wind" (Gk. *pnoē*) blew from heaven. In **Acts 17.25**, God gives life and "breath" (also *pnoē*) to everyone. The same word is used in both verses, but the two settings affect its meaning in different ways. So, the same word was rendered differently according to its use in each context.

Second, at a higher level, functional translation smooths over rough passages. When a passage's meaning is not immediately apparent, functionalism mines the broader context of the biblical genre and its ancient cultural settings for clarity. Translators try to bridge that distance between the original text and the modern reader through paraphrase in order to make its meaning clear. Such renderings are criticized for reading into the text what ought to be left out for commentaries and exegetical* study. Yet a functional rendering is of great help for those unfamiliar with the Bible's ancient settings and unskilled in its technical language. Most translators apply this kind of interpretive paraphrase* in varying degrees.

For example, when Jesus's disciples rowed across the Sea of Galilee *en route* to Capernaum, they found themselves in a storm. Jesus appeared to them after they rowed about "twenty-five or thirty *stadia*" (**John 6.19** LEB, *cf.* KJV, RV/ASV). Roman *stadia* are unfamiliar to us who are accustomed to miles or kilometers. So, most current translations render the phrase with a modern equivalent—about "three or four miles" (or "five or six kilometers"; AMP, CSB, ESV, GNB, NASB, NET, NIV, RSV, NRSV).

Functional Precedent

Functional translation and paraphrase are staples of historic Bible translation. We even see functional methods at work within the New Testament itself:

> Taking her by the hand [Jesus] said to her, "Talitha cumi," which means, "Little girl, I say to you, arise" (**Mark 5.41** ESV).

Nowhere in the Aramaic phrase, *Talitha cumi*, does it indicate the words, "I say to you." The additional address is a Greek paraphrase.

For another example, Stephen, the proto-martyr, appears to be quoting the Greek Septuagint (LXX), which paraphrases Amos, the Hebrew prophet :

> "[I]t is written in the book of the prophets: 'Did you bring to me slain beasts and sacrifices, during the forty years in the wilderness, O house of Israel? *You took up the tent of Moloch and the star of your god Rephan,* the images that you made to worship; and *I will send you into exile beyond Babylon.*'" (**Acts 7:42b–43** ESV, *emphasis added*)

The LXX reads,

> You took up the tent of Moloch and the star of your god Rephan . . . And I will deport you beyond *Damascus* (**Amos 5.26, 27** NETS, *emphasis added*)

But the Hebrew reads,

> You shall take up *Sikkuth your king*, and *Kiyyun your star-god*...
> and I will send you into exile beyond *Damascus* (**Amos 5.26,
> 27** ESV, *emphasis added*)

Even though the Greek LXX already differs from the original Hebrew, Stephen paraphrased it further. Where Stephen says, "'I will
send you into exile beyond *Babylon*,'" the LXX and Hebrew read,
"I will deport you beyond *Damascus*." The purpose of these changes in the LXX and Stephen's quotation is to connect the implications of God's warning for an earlier generation (who would not
have anticipated a Babylonian exile) to a later one (for whom the
return from exile was a distant memory).

For generations, translators have shared this goal—to express
the *meaning* of Scripture, not just its mere words:

> "[M]y only object has been to prove that from my youth up,
> I at least have always aimed at rendering sense not words."
> — Jerome (AD 395), translator of the Latin Vulgate.[4]

> "First it is to know, that the best translating is ... to translate
> after the sentence (*i.e.*, the meaning), and not only after the
> words." — John Purvey, contributer to the second Wycliffe
> Bible (1388).[5]

> "[W]hat is the point of needlessly adhering so scrupulously
> and stubbornly to words which one cannot understand any-
> way? Whoever would speak German must not use Hebrew
> style. Rather he must see to it—once he understands the He-
> brew author—that he concentrates on the sense of the text,
> asking himself, 'Pray tell, what do the Germans say in such a
> situation?' Once he has the German words to serve the pur-
> pose, let him drop the Hebrew words and express the meaning
> freely in the best German he knows." — Martin Luther, who

translated his *September Testament* in 1522 and completed the German Bible in 1534.[6]

> "We have not tied ourselves to uniformity of phrasing, or to an identity of words, as some perhaps would wish that we had done . . . . For is the Kingdom of God become words or syllables? Why should we be in bondage to them if we may be free, use one precisely when we may use another, no less fit, as commodiously?" — Miles Smith, "The Translator to the Reader," preface to the King James Bible (1611)

Idiomatic Language and Functional Rendering

Idiomatic renderings rely on paraphrase to faithfully translate their meaning into English. Word order, word choice, diction, style, and even the required number of words may differ from the original text in order to reflect its intended meaning. In fact, without translating their sense, idioms* rendered word-for-word may obscure its meaning.

For example, French *hors d'œuvres* are typically served as an appetizer before the main meal, yet a formal translation of this dish fails to correspond to the food associated with it: *Hors d'œuvres* quite strictly means "outside [the] work"—something out of the ordinary course of other things. To convey the meaning of *hors d'œuvres* to someone who doesn't know what they are, I might paraphrase the meaning: "Oh! Those are *the little finger foods* they serve us before we all sit down to eat."

In the Gospels, when Jesus indicts the Pharisees for their hypocrisy, he provokes them by telling them to "fill up the measure" of their ancestors (**Mt 23.32**). Later translations add a word or two in order to clarify the phrase, "Fill up, then, the measure of your fathers' *guilt*" (NKJV, so NASB). The NLT paraphrases its implication, "Go ahead and finish what your ancestors started" (so NIV, *cf.* TNIV).

Another example: In the OT, Israel's ally, Gibeon, was under attack. Gibeon begged Israel to "slack not thy hand from thy servants"

(KJV, so RV/ASV, *cf.* ESV), which later translations interpret, "Do not abandon your servants" (NASB, so NKJV, NIV, NET, NRSV).

A paraphrased translation renders language familiar to modern readers and requires far less work to understand. Yet, it requires more work from translators to paraphrase well. Not only must they know the biblical languages and subjects, they must also be intimately knowledgeable of their own native English and its customary manners of speaking. For example: Read Paul's entreaty to the Corinthian church, first in a formal rendering,

> Our mouth is open to you, Corinthians, our heart is opened wide. You are not restrained in us, but you are restrained in your own bowels. Now in a like exchange—I speak as to children—open wide also. (*cf.* NASB 1995)

And now read its paraphrase,

> We have spoken freely to you, Corinthians, and opened wide our hearts to you. We are not withholding our affection from you, but you are withholding yours from us. As a fair exchange—I speak as to my children—open wide your hearts also. (**2Co 6.11–13** NIV)

Paraphrase is called for when passages seem vague or ambiguous. Sometimes ambiguity accompanies ignorance of the larger context or its historical setting. For example, the NASB formally translates God's rejection of Eli's priestly family,

> "Therefore the LORD God of Israel declares, 'I did indeed say that your house and the house of your father *should walk before Me* forever'; but now the LORD declares, 'Far be it from Me . . .'" (**1Sa 2.30** NASB, *emphasis added*)

The phrase, "should walk before Me," is a rather straightforward translation, but readers may miss the significance of its implication, which is more clearly rendered

> "Assuredly—declares the LORD, the God of Israel—I intended for you and your father's house *to remain in My service* forever. But now—declares the LORD—far be it from Me! For I honor those who honor Me, but those who spurn Me shall be dishonored." (**1Sa 2.30** NJPS, *emphasis added*)

Sometimes ambiguity results from insufficient data about a word that does not get enough use. Many words occur only once in the entire body of Scripture. These nonce* words we call *hapax legomena.** We infer their meaning from their context, from their etymology* (*i.e.*, the words' component parts), or from cognate* words (*i.e.*, related words that share similar characteristics and origins).

The most famous *hapax legomenon* in the New Testament is found in the Lord's prayer as recorded at **Matthew 6.11** and **Luke 11.3**, "Give us this day our *epiousion* bread." The Greek word, *epiousion*, occurs nowhere else in any body of Greek literature prior to its use in the Gospels. Formal Latin translations render the word according to its component parts, "Give us this day our *supersubstantial* bread" (Rheims; Lat. *super + substantialem* = Gk. *epi + ousion*). The Latin rendering does little more than reveal the inherent difficulty of the word. Most translations render the phrase based on the meaning suggested by its etymology. *Epiousion* evokes an idea of something needed for existence. This is why many translations retain the familiar English rendering, "Give us this day our daily bread" (KJV, NASB, CSB, NIV, ESV, NRSV), that is, the "bread for the coming day" (Ballantine, 1923). Or as the NLT reads, "Give us today the food we need."

At times ambiguity is deliberate. For example, authors may use intentionally obscure language, like euphemism,* in order to exclude some members of the audience from sharing a certain understanding. (For more on biblical euphemism, see page 93.)

What is *Said* and What is *Meant*: Problems with Paraphrase.

> "Translations are nothing less than extended interpretations, or controlled articulations of meaning. They are not equivalent to saying 'in other words,' but they are quite literally in *other* words." — Dr. Andrew Blaski [7]

In a real sense, all translation is a kind of paraphrase in that it puts obscure language into familiar words. Yet, paraphrase is tyically thought to be the interpretation of words without warrant or precedent. It is an attempt to smooth over textual difficulties or resolve ambiguities by adding words with no direct correspondance with or counterpart to the Hebrew or Greek sources.

Paraphrases may add clarifications and glosses that are foreign to the original text. This kind of functional translation is not exact enough to be used for precise and careful study, because it hides the very difficulties that scholars are looking for. Unless the translation reveals difficult passages in its footnotes, casual readers will blissfully read over any underlying issues without suspicion.

PARAPHRASE AND THE DOCTRINE OF INERRANCY

For those of us who uphold the doctrine of plenary-verbal* inspiration, excessive paraphrase poses a bigger problem. As one reviewer noted,

> "When a Hebrew sentence has been translated into an English sentence of equivalent meaning, the original words are of course lost. But they can never be left behind: each element of meaning in the English has to justify its existence by reference to the words of the original, and each element of the original

ought to be represented in some way in translation. This is because Holy Scripture is inspired at the level of its words." [8]

In other words, if translators are competent in both source and target languages, they should not expect to get more information out of their translation than can be found in their original source, and *vice versa.*

Paraphrase tends to rely on the translators' subjective judgments. These judgments should be constrained by diligent study in the original text and its settings. Without checks from careful research and contextual precedent, the more translators try to paraphrase the text into other words, the greater they risk delving into speculative interpretation and theological supposition. When translators choose the meaning of ambiguous or difficult passages, honest scholarship lets readers know in the marginal notes. Otherwise they risk obscuring difficulties in favor of their own biases or conjectures. (See "Theological Decisions" starting on page 103.) In this way, some translations block readers from the original intent instead of simply mediating between readers and the text. Too much paraphrase gives us a text without sufficient precedent or warrant and ventures into the error of adding to God's words.

Readability in Higher or Lower Registers

Competent translators consider the abilities of their reading audience; that is, they craft their translation to either fit or expand the range of their readers' vocabulary. A people's reading preference and ability is broadly measured by register. High-register* language freely uses technical or sophisticated words. We sometimes call this "formal" speech—not in the sense of formal translation, which tries to reflect the underlying forms of the Hebrew and Greek, but in the sense of sophisticated jargon, refined erudition, or even affected formality.

For example, Edward Harwood's rendering of the Lord's Prayer demonstrates highly affected paraphrase and artificial language in a high register:

Mt 6.7, 9 in Harwood's *A Liberal Translation of the New Testament* (1768)	Mt 6.7, 9 in the ESV (2016)
7 Think not the design of prayer is by the dint of importunity to teaze the Deity into compliance with our requests—Carefully avoid therefore the errour of the heathens who think that the supreme Being can be prevailed upon by enthusiastic clamours, and a constant unvaried repetition of noisy expressions. . . . 9 In order to guard you from mistakes in this important concern I will propose the following as a model for your devotions — O Thou great governour and parent of universal nature—who manifestest thy glory to the blessed inhabitants of heaven—may all thy rational creatures in all the parts of thy boundless dominion be happy in the knowledge of thy existence and providence, and celebrate thy perfections in a manner most worthy thy nature and perfective of their own!	7 "And when you pray, do not heap up empty phrases as the Gentiles do, for they think that they will be heard for their many words. . . . 9 "Pray then like this: 'Our Father in heaven, hallowed be your name.' "

Sometimes high-register language employs what we call inkhorn terms*—words chosen to give a text a sophisticated air or mystique. Writers may use these terms to either invite readers with similar interests and abilities or to exclude non-initiates. We hear language with this effect whenever mechanics and technicians use specialized jargon to efficiently share technical or insider knowledge. Some people even use inkhorn terms pretentiously in hope that they might find acceptance with an exclusive crowd.

Translations written at higher registers include the NEB, RSV, NRSV, NASB, and MEV. These versions are generally accessible to later high school or secondary school students. (The KJV is at a higher register due to changes in English language. It is accessible to those familiar with early modern English grammar and vocabulary.)[9]

Low-register* language, on the other hand, is written for general populations or for those with limited experience with the target language, like young children or beginning English students. Translations written for lower registers include works like the *EasyEnglish Bible, International Children's Bible, Bible in Basic English*, the *New International Reader's Version* (NIrv), the *God's Word* translation, and *The Living Bible*.

Mid-register translations, like the NLT, NKJV, GNT, NET, NIV, and CSB, are usually intelligible to later elementary (*i.e.*, primary) and junior-high school students.

The following are samples contrasting high- to low-register renderings of technical theological words and their more broadly familiar equivalents:

Higher Register	Middle Register	Lower Register
justification (**Ro 4.25; 5.16** KJV, NIV, ESV, CSB, NASB)	acquittal (NAB)	"to make us right with God" (NLT); "the undeserved gift of 'Not guilty!'" (GNB)
sanctification (**Ro 6.19** ESV, NASB, NRSV, CSB)	holiness (NKJV, NIV)	"so that you will become holy" (NLT); "which show that you belong to God" (*EasyEnglish Bible*)
Wadi Zered (**Dt 2.13** NRSV, NAB, NET, *et al.*)	**the watercourse of Zered** (CLV)	**Zered Valley** (CLV, NIV); **the brook Zered** (RSV, ESV)
My son, if you have **put up security** for your neighbor, have **given your pledge** for a stranger (**Pr 6.1** ESV)	My child, if you have **made a pledge** for your neighbor, if you have **become a guarantor** for a stranger (NET)	My child, suppose you **agree to pay the debt** of someone, who cannot repay a loan. (CEV); You may have **promised to pay the debts** of a friend or of a stranger. (*EasyEnglish Bible*)

Balancing Functional and Formal Priorities

No translation is ever purely formal or completely functional. Every translation finds itself somewhere on the spectrum between these two tensions. Some translations tend more towards the formal side (like the NASB, NKJV, ESV, MEV), while others swing the other way towards a functional approach (NLT, GNB, TNIV, NET, CEB). Others try to find a happy medium somewhere in between. To do this, they translate those passages that make clear English sense when rendered word-for-word in a formal manner, and passages that are less clear, they paraphrase (*e.g.* the NIV or CSB).

Even translations that tend one way or the other are not uniformly consistent. At times, the NLT, which pursues a functional approach, is more formal in those passages where the meaning of a formal translation is either apparent or familiar. For example, the NLT formally renders **Ac 13.22b** as,

> "'I have found David son of Jesse, *a man after my own heart.*'"
> (NLT, *emphasis added*)

This rendering has passed down into familiar use, though it is mostly found in religious contexts. A functional translation might paraphrase this passage for a broader audience,

> "'I have found *that* David son of Jesse *is the kind of man I like.*'"
> (GNB, *emphasis added*)

Translators often find themselves working under both tensions—formal and functional—at the same time. No single translation consistently hits only one priority. Either extreme would either confuse or mislead. If a translation were absolutely formal, it would fail to conform to regular English usage, or it would obscure meaning by failing to interpret ambiguities and idioms.* If it were completely functional, it might obscure meaning through over-interpretation and, thus, exclude other intended meanings, implications, or allusions.

LANGUAGE CHANGE

The fact that our language's forms, styles, and meanings change over time is well attested and undisputed. There are subtle changes to the accepted ways we talk even within the last fifty years. The *Oxford English Dictionary* has added over 3,800 new words to its collection over the last five years. That's more than two words a day, each day for the last half-decade—and that's not including the many thousands of new meanings and uses added to already existing words! [10]

The introduction of new technology affects our everyday choice of words: At one time, our grandparents turned the dial

Version	Age
Higher Register	
KJV	17+
RSV	
AMP	16
LEB	
MEV	
NRSV	
NASB	
ESV	15
Phillips	
NAB	14
CEB	12
GNT	
[H]CSB	
ISV	
NET	
NIV	
NKJV	
NLT	11
The Voice	
CEV	10
GW	
Message	9
TLB	
ICB	7
NCV	
NIrV	
Lower Register	

(Above) Translations listed in order of register (high to low) and suggested by reader's age.[32]

on a "wireless" to listen to news over the airwaves. Now we tune a "radio" or connect to a "WiFi" network. Even the word "telephone" has been clipped to just "phone," a term that now refers to a hand-held, interconnected computer.

Even our grammar changes. The "get" passive frequently re-places "to be" as a passive-forming helping word that expresses a non-continuous state. For example, "Our team *got* beat last night." (Instead of "Our team *was* beat last night.") Or, "Josh *got* promot-ed to a new position." (Instead of "Josh *was* promoted . . .")

Prescriptive English grammar teaches us that the word "shall" is required for expressing the first-person, future indicative (*e.g.,* "I *shall* win that," "I *shall* return," or "we *shall* read"). Nowadays, outside of historical drama, legal contexts, and parody, "shall" is often replaced with "will" (I *will* win that, *etc.*).

The problem for modern readers is that we, who are separated by centuries, have to work so much harder to understand what older generations meant. These changes may not seem all that drastic by themselves, but when we accumulate many similar cas-es over a period of four- or five-hundred years, they add up.

Writing and Wording Changes

English sounds and looks radically different than it did when it was first written. It has lost certain characters and symbols, like the letters "ꝑ" (spelled ᵽynn, pronounced *wynn*), " ð " (eð, *eth*), "þ" (þorn, *thorn*),[11] and "ȝ" (ȝogh, *yogh*); alternate forms, like "ſ" (long "s") and "ꝛ" ("r" rotunda); ligatures, like "æ" (æsc, *ash*); and symbols, like the "⁊" (tironian *et*).[12] Since English had no stan-dard orthography* (spelling) for centuries as it developed, words were spelled to fit how people talked in their local dialects.

However, the changes go deeper than the cosmetics of written language and regional variations. English grammar, with its de-clensions and conjugations, substantially changed. Its vocabulary grew and warped as a result of foreign invasions, missions, and colonization.

Among the earliest records in English is King Æthelberht's law code (written approximately AD 550 – 616).[13] The earliest English translations of Scripture include the West-Saxon gospels, dating to the 10th and 12th centuries. Here's an example from John's gospel, translated before the Norman Conquest could affect the insular language and infuse it with continental French.

Hwi ne cnawe ge mine spræce. for-þan þe ge ne magen ge-heren mine spræce.

Could you read that? Let's try a later version, this time from John Wycliffe's version (*ca.* 1382), translated during the Hundred Years' War and before the Great Vowel Shift,

Whi knowen ȝe not my ſpeche? for ȝe mown not heere my word.

If the meaning is not yet entirely clear, let's try a later version by William Tyndale (1526), translated at the dawn of the English Reformation,

Why do ye nott knowe my ſpeache: Be cauſe ye canot abyde the hearynge off my words.

Finally, let's read the KJV in its original spelling (1611),

Why doe yee not vnderstand my speech? euen because yee cannot heare my word.

Cosmetic improvements to the KJV were encouraged, no doubt, by London's literary respect for the first generally-accepted standard of English orthography—Samuel Johnson's famous dictionary (1755).[14] The Bible was lightly revised in 1769 by Dr. Benjamin Blaney of Oxford. His emendations corrected obvious printing errors, regularized the punctuation and typesetting, and standardized the spelling: "Jesus said unto them (the Pharisees), . . .

A glimpse of Tyndale's *New Testament* (1526). Note the use of black-letter print.

A glimpse of **Jn 8** in the King James Bible (1611).

Why do ye not understand my speech? even because ye cannot hear my word. (**John 8.42a, 43**)

Changes occur within words, too. For example, the Bishops' Bible gives us a strange rendering at **Ecc 11.1**,

Lay thy bread upon wet *faces*, and so shalt thou find it after many days. (*emphasis added*)

No, this is not some ancient beauty treatment. Though it could mean the front of a person's head, the word "face" generally meant "surface", like it does in **Genesis 2.6** ("[T]here went up a mist from the earth, and watered the whole *face* of the ground" KJV). Modern translations render the verse as, "Cast your bread on the *surface* of the waters" (NASB, *cf.* CSB), or they paraphrase it, like the KJV does, by omitting the word as it is not needed for clarity, "Cast your bread upon the waters" (NIV, so NKJV). And yet others, "Send your grain *overseas*" (NET, *cf.* NLT).

Older translations, like the KJV (so Wycliffe, Coverdale, Geneva, Bishops', Douay), render **Ps 26.2** as

Examine me, O LORD, and prove me; try *my reins* and *my heart* (*emphasis added*)

The apparent meaning of the word "reins" is deceptively misleading. In the 16th century, it did not refer to the leather straps that a driver used to steer his horse.[15] Rather, the word "reins" is an anglicized adaption of the Latin word, *rēnēs*, which formally translates the Hebrew word meaning "kidneys" (*cf.* **Ex 29.13**, Latin *duos renes*; KJV "two kidneys"; NIV "both kidneys"). In ancient Hebrew culture, the kidneys (Heb. *kilyôtay*) figuratively implied the seat of one's emotions and affections, the place modern English speakers typically associate with the "heart", whereas the heart (Heb. *libîy*) signified the seat of one's thinking and intention, which English associates with the "mind." Here is how most modern translations render *kilyôtay* and *libîy* in **Ps 26.2**:

> Test me, O LORD, and try me,
>> examine *my heart* and *my mind*
>> (NIV, so NASB, CSB, *emphasis added*).

The *NET Bible*, on the other hand, renders them more abstractly:

> Examine me, O LORD, and test me!
>> Evaluate *my inner thoughts* and *motives*!
>> (NET, *emphasis added*).

Gender Language

The controversy over gendered language in modern Bibles is more than a debate over the proper use of pronouns. It is an argument over the perceived accuracy of translation when the target language itself has changed and moved its position. There are both political and linguistic agenda pushing issues in this debate. But to understand the issues, we must learn what gender language entails and what is at stake.

GENDER LANGUAGE IN POLITICAL DEBATE

The current political debate over gender language began during the Anglo-American, anti-establishment, counter-cultural movements of the 1960s and '70s. With it came new expressions of feminism which questioned language that insisted on women's traditional roles. As British linguist, David Crystal, observed more than three decades ago, "[T]he issue is by no means silly, but is in danger of becoming worse than silly, now. What began as a healthy and constructive awareness of the limitations of language has degenerated into a shifty humourless self-consciousness about sexist expression."[16]

In turn, academia's low-context culture began to demand more inclusive references to people in general. Papers were graded, returned—and marked in red wherever students used "he" (*i.e.*, the generic masculine pronoun). It became increasingly accepted—and politically correct—to rush two pronouns together, to say "he/she," or to change the sentence altogether and use an ambiguous, third-person, plural pronoun ("they") instead. The realm of religion, including liturgical language, contemporary preaching, and corporate Bible study, was challenged to acknowledge participants of both sexes without using language that excluded one or the other. Each half of the English-speaking world paid careful attention to how they addressed the other half.

Against this cultural backdrop, the revision committee for the *New Revised Standard Version* (NRSV) carried out their work. They made one of their explicit goals to revise the Bible in accordance with the rising norm* of gender-inclusive language.[17] Understandably, their work was not universally appreciated: Several conservative churches rejected the NRSV as a liberal plot to undermine the traditional roles of men and women. Seven years after the NRSV's publication, and soon after the release of an anglicized* edition of the NIV with revised gender language, James Dobson (of Focus on the Family) and other conservative leaders responded by convening an evangelical council to agree on linguistic norms for upcoming translations. Their conclusions, which are recorded in the *Colorado Springs Guidelines* (revised September 1997), are embodied in both the *English Standard Version* (ESV) and the [*Holman*] *Christian Standard Bible* (HCSB/CSB).

Even if they are well-intended, gender-inclusive* or gender-neutral* agenda miss the mark when they *eisegete** (introduce foreign ideas into) a translation in the attempt to either include both sexes or remove specific references to gender. These agenda—feminist, ecumenical, or otherwise—can impose on the translators' role as careful interpreters. The goal of faithful Bible translation is to accurately render biblical meaning, so that whatever gendered language is found in most Bibles translations today is there to accurately render the meaning of Scripture without

The Best Bible?

hindering comprehension. (For more on this subject, see "Inclusive Language" starting on page 129.)

GENDER IN BIBLICAL LANGUAGES

Now, let's look at some of the unique characteristics of biblical gender language. All nouns in the Greek NT fit into a class system of three grammatical genders:* (1) masculine, (2) feminine, and (3) neuter. Nouns in the Hebrew OT fit into only two—masculine and feminine. Some of these nouns so happen to correspond with their natural gender.* For example, we'd naturally expect that "son" (*huios*) and "man" (*anēr*) are grammatically masculine, because they are physically male—and they are. Likewise, "woman" or "wife" (*gunē*) is grouped with the feminine nouns.

But Greek also places all sorts of "sexless" nouns (things without male or female attributes) into masculine or feminine grammatical categories. For example, the concrete noun, "book" (*biblos*), is grammatically masculine, while the abstract noun, "love" (*agapē*), is feminine. When English speakers refer to sexless nouns and abstract ideas in the third person (words like "faith", "error", "judgment", or "sword"), we use the neuter pronoun "it". For example, "Faith is required, because without *it*, we cannot please God." Greek considers these nouns (*pistis, planē, krisis, machaira*) as feminine, even though they have no particular feminine characteristics. And sometimes the reverse is true: Even when we know the biological (*i.e.*, the natural) gender of a person from the context of a passage, the Greek will refer to a "child" (*teknion* or *paidarion*) as a grammatically neuter "it" (*cf.* **Heb 11.23**).

A CASE FOR "PEOPLE"

Where English uses genderless, neuter words like "person(s)" or "people", Greek uses grammatically-gendered words to mean the same (*anthrōpos, anthrōpoi*). In fact, Greek uses the grammatically masculine plural whenever referring to any inclusive group—"people" (*anthrōpoi*), "nations" (*ethnoi*), "Hebrews" (*Hebraioi*, **Php 3.5**), "Greeks" (*Hellēnistes*, **Ac 11.20**), "saints" (*hagioi,*

Ro 1.7) "brothers and sisters" (*adelphoi*, **Ro 15.30**). This is true except for certain groups consisting of an all-female membership ("women" *gunaikes*, **Mt 28.5**; "sisters" *adelphai*, **Mt 13.56**).

Translators of yesteryear were comfortable rendering the grammatically masculine *anthrōpoi* as simply "men", which was understood to be shorthand for "mankind", "humanity", or "people" in general, as the 16th-century Bishop of London reported, "The Lord had but one pair of *men* in paradise [*i.e.*, in the Garden of Eden]."[18] General humanity is what William Tyndale undoubtedly meant, when he rendered Christ's words, "as ye would that *men* should to you, so do ye to them likewise." (**Luke 6.31**, Tyndale, so also KJV)

There is no small debate about the best and proper use of gender language in the Old Testament. **Ps 9.19–20** reads, "let the nations be judged before you! Put them in fear, O LORD! Let the nations know that they are but *men* (Heb. *'enôsh*)!" (ESV, *cf.* NASB) This passage does not exclude kingdoms that have never seen a queen sit on their thrones. Like the other examples, its meaning in this context involves all "people," particularly those who need a reminder of their vulnerability. This is why some modern translators render the passage, "Let the nations know that they are mere *mortals*" (NET, *cf.* Alter, NWT).

Yet, there is still value in rendering the Hebrew text with familiar masculine language: It reflects the cultural *milieu*, that is, the patriarchal society of the prophets and psalmists, which should remind most modern readers that, as they read, they might be peering through a perspective somewhat foreign to themselves.

A CASE FOR "BROTHERS AND SISTERS"

In Paul's letters, the apostle addresses both natural genders with the plural, grammatically masculine noun, *adelphoi*, which older English translations rendered simply and formally as "brothers". The contexts of Paul's letters reveal that he intends the inclusive meaning "brothers and sisters". For example, Paul requested of those, whom he addressed with the masculine *adelphoi*, to pray for him (**Ro 15.30**) and greet each other (**Ro 16.3ff**). Among those he addressed are several women (*e.g.*, Prisca, Mary, Tryphena, Typhosa, Nereus' sister, *et al. Cf.* **Col 4.15; 2Ti 4.21**). The broader context of Paul's letters affirms as the grammatical norm that the masculine plural form of *adelphoi* is inclusive of both sexes (*i.e.*, "brothers" and "sisters") when it is unaffected by any clarifying context.[19]

A CASE FOR "THEY"

There is yet another expression in English that needs a creative solution. How ought we to render a common-gender, third-person, singular pronoun? The plural, "they", is already ambiguous in gender, but it is plural in number. So, what should we use instead of "he" or "she" when we mean either? Finding appropriate alternatives was the explicit policy of some translations, like the NRSV, which adopts paraphrastic renderings "only sparingly, and then chiefly to compensate for a deficiency in the English language— the lack of a common gender third person singular pronoun."[20]

Like the plural collective nouns mentioned earlier, the biblical languages often use a (grammatically) masculine singular form to mean either a male or a female. For example, the Tyndale-KJV tradition uses the masculine-generic pronoun ("man") to render, "God cannot be tempted with evil, *neither* tempteth he *any man* (*oudena*)" (**Jas 1.13**, *emphasis added*). A strictly formal solution renders the verse, "he himself tempts *no one*" (RSV, cf. NRSV, ESV), but just as acceptable is the more traditional rendering, "*nor* does He Himself tempt *anyone*" (NKJV, cf. NASB, NIV, NLT). In fact, all three renderings translate the phrase accurately.

Another issue deals with how to elegantly render **Rv 3.20**, where Jesus Christ announces,

"Behold, I stand at the door, and knock: if *any man* (*tis*) hear my voice, and open the door, I will come in to *him* (*auton*), and will sup with *him* (*autou*), and he (*autos*) with me." (KJV)

Several translations hesitate to emend the masculine pronouns in this passage (*cf.* CSB, NET, ESV, NKJV, NIV '84). Yet others radically change the wording and bend its particular meaning:

> "if *you* (*tis*) hear my voice and open the door, I will come in to *you* (auton) and eat with *you* (*autou*), and *you* (*autos*) with me" (NRSV)

> "If *you* (*tis*) hear my voice and open the door, I will come in (*auton*?), and we will share a meal together as friends (*autou/ autos*?)" (NLT).

The following comes close, but loses something in its effect,

> "If *anyone* (*tis*) hears my voice and opens the door, I will come in (*auton*?) and eat with *that person* (*autou*), and *they* (*autos*) with me" (NIV '11).

The TNIV received criticism for using the third-person, plural, personal pronoun as a singular, gender-ambiguous pronoun (henceforth, the singular "they").

> "If *anyone* (*tis*) hears my voice and opens the door, I will come in (*auton*?) and eat with *them* (*autou*), and *they* (*autos*) with me." (TNIV)

Were the TNIV's Committee on Bible Translation justified in using a singular "them" and "they" in this passage?

Here are the facts. In 2010, the producers of the *Collins Dictionary* pulled data from over 4.4 billion words covering twenty years of published texts and sound recordings. In order to gather hard evidence for the contemporary use of gendered language, they analyzed the pool of all gendered and generic pronouns and determiners from their database. What they discovered confirmed what we suspected: In that twenty-year period, the use of masculine-generic pronouns ("he", "him", "himself", *etc.*) fell in use, from 22 percent to only eight percent. Instances of awkward alternative forms ("him or her", "his/her", "s/he", *etc.*) also fell, from twelve percent to eight. In contrast, the use of plural or gender-neutral pronouns and determiners ("they", "them", "one", "themselves", *etc.*) jumped from 65 percent in 1990 to 84 percent by 2009!

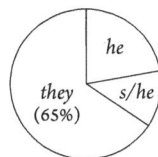

The preferred English generic pronoun as of 1990.

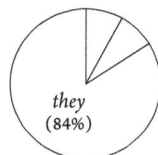

Nineteen years later, the preferred pronoun as of 2009.

Current style-guides (the arbiters of good sense in printed discourse) are still debating the sufficiency of "they" as a gender-ambiguous, single-person pronoun. *The Chicago Manual of Style* has wavered on its position from edition to edition. The 14th and 15th editions were both accepting, but the 16th rejected the use of the singular "they" and "their" claiming that, although in common use in casual settings, "neither is considered acceptable in formal writing."[21] The 17th edition appears to be cautiously supportive.[22] The *Publication Manual of the APA* encourages the use of gender-neutral language and the avoidance of "he" as a generic, third-person, singular pronoun. It recommends rewriting sentences in order to avoid the awkward "he/she" combination, but fails to mention anything about the use of the singular "they".[23] The *SBL Handbook of Style* also requires the disuse of the generic masculine, but also says nothing about singular "they".[24]

In contrast, The *Associated Press Stylebook* set a new precedent in 2017, "*They, them, their* . . . is acceptable in limited cases as a singular and-or gender-neutral pronoun, when alternative wording is overly awkward or clumsy. However, rewording usually is possible and always is preferable. Clarity is a top priority; gender-neutral use of a singular they is unfamiliar to many readers. We do not use other gender-neutral pronouns such as *xe* or *ze*."[25] (The *MLA Handbook* remains silent on the issue, relegating itself to merely solve documentation problems.)[26]

In fact, there is early precedent for the use of the singular "they" going as far back as John Wycliffe and throughout the Tyndale-King James tradition (1526–1611). We find its use in Wycliffe's Early Version (AD 1382), in the apocryphal* (*i.e.*, deutero-canonical*) book of **Sirach 38.34(35)**,

Alle þefe in þer hondis hopeden; and echon in þer ʼcraft is wys.

In modern English, the verse reads, "All these hoped in their hands; and *each one* is wise in *their* craft." Note how the antecedent "each one" is followed by the singular use of "their"? The following passages demonstrate other uses of singular "their":

"So likewise shall my heavenly father do unto you except ye forgive with your hearts each one to his brother their trespasses." (**Mt 18.35**, Tyndale, so also Geneva, Bishops', KJV; but not Coverdale, Rheims. "[H]is brother" is the antecedent to the singular "their".)

"Let nothing be done through strife or vainglory; but in lowliness of mind let each esteem other better than themselves" (**Php 2.3**, Douay, so KJV; but not Tyndale, Coverdale, Matthew, Bishops', Geneva. The antecedent "each" precedes "themselves".)

In the following examples, the antecedent "every one" is followed by singular "their".

"And the children of Israel did all as the LORD commanded Moses. And so they pitched under their banners, and took their journey, every one in his kindred, according to the house of their fathers." (**Nm 2.34**, Coverdale, so Geneva, Bishops', Douay, KJV; but not Tyndale, Matthew)

"According to the number that ye shall prepare to offer, so shall ye do to every one according to their number." (**Nm 15.12**, Geneva, so Bishops', KJV, RSV; but not Tyndale, Coverdale, Matthew, Douay)

"And Judah was put to the worse before Israel; and they fled every man to their tents" (**2Kg 14.12**, Geneva, so Bishops', Douay, KJV; but not Coverdale, Matthew. The singular possessive "their" takes "every man" as its antecedent.).

Despite resistance, singular "they" is gaining more momentum. Its popular rise—resurrection, rather—is precedented in early English literature and Bible translation. It is a contested solution to an awkward problem, where we've traded a gain in the ambiguity of *gender* for a loss of clarity in *number*. Nonetheless, it offers translators a valid option to consider.

EUPHEMISM

Community Concerns and Public Worship

Euphemism* is the linguistic practice of Mary Poppin's aphorism, "A spoonful of sugar helps the medicine go down." English societies tend to euphemize* anything dealing with uncomfortable circumstances, bodily fluids, intimate relations, or death. We say that we are "going to the bathroom" or "visiting the loo" while excusing ourselves from a prying public. Couples who "sleep together" imply far more than stationary rest. In the British Isles, expressions of "sanguine profusion" are deemed plain rude. In times of public worship—like a close-knit Bible study or a high-church liturgy—awkward renderings can result in sudden gasps, blushing faces, and nervous giggles which distract the assembly from venerable solemnity.

There are several ways of referring to those concepts that huddle under clouds of public shame. The foolhardy way is to expound the idea explicitly. This may be appropriate in the low-context cultures of academia, but it is sure to exclude some from polite society and deny them requests for public speaking. Another way is to omit the idea altogether, but this merely runs from discussion to avoid embarrassment. The socially acceptable way is to use euphemism*, a kind of speech that refers to sensitive ideas indirectly.

English speakers euphemize difficult ideas with a few different strategies or figures of speech. In other words, we use a variety of indirect linguistic associations. For example, we might use alliteration* and rhyme* instead of speaking an indiscreet word outright (*e.g.*, "darn," "balmy," or "ruddy"). We may employ a form of metonymy* or generalization, that is, we'll refer to the place where a sensitive activity may occur without mentioning the act itself ("bathroom," "bedroom," or "the grave"). Or we might use deliberate ambiguity or double *entendre* with the meaning understood only by those who share the same high context ("sick" for alcohol addiction, "pass away" for death). We apply these and other strategies to lighten somber circumstances and loosen tension.

Biblical Euphemism

Biblical languages have euphemized expressions like these long before any Bible translators have tried. For example:

Bodily functions	1 Samuel 24.3b	Saul went in (to the cave) *to cover his feet* (KJV, so RV/ASV, *emphasis added*)

The phrase "to cover his feet" meant that "Saul went in to *relieve himself*" (RSV, so NRSV, NASB, ESV, et al.) The phrase "to relieve himself" is itself a contemporary euphemism. Other translators felt the need to use acceptable idioms for their day and culture: "Saul went in to *do his easement*" (Geneva, Bishops'), or "Saul went in to *attend to his needs*" (NKJV).

Sexual relations	Genesis 4.1	Now Adam *knew* Eve his wife, and she conceived and bore Cain (NKJV, *emphasis added*)

The Hebrew word, "to know" (*yada*), is no mere mental exercise. It indicates experiential knowledge or specialized skill. In the higher context of this verse, we realize what kind of knowledge is meant, as the *NET Bible* (2006) spells out, "Now the man had marital relations with his wife Eve." The revisers of the *NET Bible*'s second edition (2017) felt that even this euphemism was too explicit for a public setting, and rendered it formally (and quite appropriately), "Now the man was intimate with his wife Eve."

Death	1 Kings 2.1–2	As David's time to die drew near, he charged Solomon his son, saying, "I am *about to go the way of all the earth*. Be strong, therefore, and show yourself a man." (NASB, *emphasis added*)

In this formal, yet figurative, rendition, David seemed to normalize the circumstance of his decline in order to ease the burden of its personal significance for his son Solomon's sake. Other translations force David to "cut to the chase"—"I am about to die" (NET, *cf.* NIrV).

Death	1Th 4.4	[I]f we believe that Jesus died and rose again, even so God will bring with Him those who have fallen asleep in Jesus (NASB, *emphasis added*)

Paul used a rather helpful euphemism, because it not only sweetens the bitterness of the situation, it also offers a hopeful metaphor: Just as a sleeper will rise and wake, so also will those, who have died in Christ, rise to resurrection life (*cf.* **1Co 15.6, 18–20;** **Jn 11.11**).

Monthly period	Gn 31.35	[Rachel] said to her father, "Let not my lord be angry that I cannot rise before you, for *the way of women is upon me*." (ESV, NRSV, *cf.* NASB, NKJV, *emphasis added*)

This word-for-word rendering states elegantly what other low-context translations make so clear, "Don't be angry, my lord, that I cannot stand up in your presence; I'm having my period" (NIV, NLT, NET).

Crass Language and Formal Renderings

Some Biblical expressions are inherently crude.[27] For example, the biblical writers can be vividly explicit when referring to human males. The KJV and its predecessors (Geneva, Bishops', Douay) faithfully and formally rendered the Hebrew of **1 Samuel 25.22**, where David derisively swore to destroy every last man in Nabal's service and household on account of Nabal's reluctance to repay David's mercenary band for their protection,

> "So and more also do God unto the enemies of David, if I leave of all that pertain to [Nabal] by the morning light any that pisseth against the wall."

This expression is deemed too close to course slang today, which is why most all modern versions temper its language and of others like it, "God do so to David and more also, if by morning I leave so much as one male of all who belong to him" (RSV, *cf.* RV/ASV, NRSV, NASB, ESV, NKJV, NLT).

Too Much Euphemism

Sometimes translators get overzealous when euphemizing potentially offensive language. One example is where the RSV and NASB render the Greek word, *porneia*, with an overly general term. This word means "prostitution" or "fornication" (KJV), though it can mean adultery ("unchastity") or allude to incest in certain contexts. In several passages, the RSV renders the word with the blanket term "immorality", which is so broad as to be devoid of significance, even when the context makes its meaning clear enough. For example, "[B]ecause of the temptation to *immorality, each man should have his own wife*" (**1Co 7.2b** RSV, *emphasis added; cf.* **1Co 5.1; 6.13, 18**). Since any act done outside God's moral code should be construed as "immoral", I ask then, is coveting my neighbor's paperweight, then, sufficient justification for finding a wife? The NRSV helpfully amends the word, "[B]ecause of cases of *sexual immorality*, each man should have his own wife" (*cf.* NLT, NKJV, *emphasis added*).

Too Little Euphemism

At other times, translators may go too far in clarifying the Bible's explicit meaning. The revisers of the *NET Bible's* second edition, recognized their need to lighten the tone so that their text could find wider acceptance in public worship: "References to explicit sexual body parts or sexual acts have been made more euphemistic like it is in the Hebrew and Greek. Sometimes a more transparent translation isn't always better, such as reading the Christmas story with young children."[28] For example:

NET Bible 1st ed.	Luke 1.34	Mary said to the angel, "How will this be, since I have not *had sexual relations* with a man?" (*cf.* CSB)
NET Bible 2nd ed.		Mary said to the angel, "How will this be, since I have not *been intimate* with a man?" (*emphasis added*)

The NKJV renders the passage more formally, "How can this be, since I do not know a man?" Other translations interpret the sense: "How can this be, since I am a virgin?" (NASB, *cf.* NIV, NLT, NRSV, ESV), and others render it euphemistically, but not with the same elegance or accuracy as the revised *NET Bible*: "But how? I've never slept with a man" (MSG), or "How shall this be, since I have no husband?" (RSV)

Initially, the translators felt the need to clarify the following passage with an explicit interpretation. The revisers thought better of it and chose to replace it with a popular euphemism.

NET Bible 1st ed.	Gn 6.4	the sons of God *were having sexual relations* with the daughters of humankind
NET Bible 2nd ed.		the sons of God *would sleep* with the daughters of humankind (*emphasis added*)

The next revision corresponds more formally with the Hebrew, which itself uses a euphemism common throughout the OT:

"Bring them out to us, that we may *know them.*" (**Gn 19.5b** ESV, *emphasis added*)

NET Bible 1st ed.	**Gn 19.5**	They shouted to Lot, "Where are the men who came to you tonight? Bring them out to us so we can *have sex with* them!"
NET Bible 2nd ed.		They shouted to Lot, "Where are the men who came to you tonight? Bring them out to us so we can *take carnal knowledge of* them!" (*emphasis added*)

Some may criticize the use of euphemism for catering to a broader audience. They would be partly right, because that is what it does. But, euphemism largely determines the tone and not the essential meaning of a passage. Any good translation can just as easily comfort or offend by the implications of its message. It doesn't need to weigh readers down with the baggage of needlessly distasteful words. Why not allow translators to hitch their skills to the broader biblical context and the audience's sensibilities and let the listener fill in what's missing? For those wary of what they're hiding, that's what the footnotes, commentaries, and formal versions are for.

Translation is both a science and an art. Its medium is words. The wonderful thing about words is that the Bible's beauty (and even its seediness) can be expressed in any human language. It may just take a few more pages.   ◁

ENDNOTES FOR TRANSLATION DECISIONS

1   "Literal" is a misleading term that requires some qualification. It is commonly thought that a "literal" rendering constitutes word-for-word (formal) correspondence. But, in truth, a "literal" translation considers all the figures of speech in a text with literary understanding and appreciation. A literal interpretation is one which clarifies figurative language with a logical equivalent. Thus, a literal rendering is one which expresses a text without any confusing figures of speech.

2   One version (*The Voice*) does render "Christ" (Gk. *ho christos*) as "God's Anointed," or "the Anointed One," or in certain places "God's Anointed, *the Liberating King*" (*cf.* **Mk 8.30; Lk 9.20**).
    Ecclesia Bible Society, "Preface," *The Voice New Testament* (Nashville, TN: Thomas Nelson, Inc., 2011).

3   "Letter of Aristeas," *The Apocrypha and Pseudepigrapha of the Old Testament in English*, ed. by R. H. Charles (Oxford: Clarendon Press, 1913), § 219.

4   Saint Jerome's Letter (LXVI) to Pammachius.

5   Adapted from Chapter 15 of John Purvey's prologue to the Wycliffe Bible (*c.* 1395).

6   Martin Luther, "On Translating: An Open Letter" (1530), in *Luther's Works*, vol. 35, trans. Charles M. Jacobs, ed. E. Theodore Bachmann (Philadelphia, PA: Muhlenberg, 1960), p. 193.

7   Andrew Blaski, "Myths About Patristics: What the Church Fathers Thought About Textual Variation," *Myths and Mistakes in New Testament Textual Criticism*, eds. Elijah Hixson and Peter J. Gurry (Downers Grove, IL: InterVarsity Press, 2019), p. 247.

8   Andrew G. Shead, "Burning Scripture with Passion: A Review of The Psalms (*The Passion Translation*)," *Themelios* vol. 34, no. 1 (April 2018): p. 59.

9   Renaissance English, or early modern English, is the the development of the English language dating from the Tudor period (*c.* AD 1485) until the restoration of the English monarchy (*c.* 1688).

10   Such words include "earworm"—an overly catchy tune; "Blu-ray"—a high capacity medium used for recording and retrieving audio and video; "flash mob"—an seemingly random public gathering where people assemble, perform, then disperse; and "brûlée"—yet another word that the French have introduced to

English "cuisine" (which is yet another word that the French have introduced to English).

[11] We still see remnants of "þ" (þorn, *thorn*) in Old English signage and Reformation-era literature. Black-letter fonts used by English printers did not have a unique glyph for the Gothic "þ" (𝔥), so they used the similarly written "y" (𝔶) instead. Whence come our funny-written signs, like 𝔶𝔢 𝔬𝔩𝔡 𝔱𝔯𝔦𝔭 𝔱𝔬 𝔧𝔢𝔯𝔲𝔰𝔞𝔩𝔢𝔪 (ye olde trip to jerusalem), which should still be pronounced as "The Old Trip to Jerusalem".

[12] The "7" (tironian *et*) functions like an ampersand (&) and is still used in modern Gælic signage.

[13] The earliest copy of Æthelberht's law code is found in the *Textus Roffensis* (AD 1122–1124).

[14] Samuel Johnson, *A Dictionary of the English Language*, 2 vols. (London: W. Stahan, 1755).

[15] Ronald Bridges and Luther A. Weigle, *The King James Bible Word Book* (Nashville, TN: Thomas Nelson, 1960, 1994), p. 285.

[16] David Crystal, "Language in Church," *The Tablet* (June 16, 1984): pp. 570–2.

[17] "The mandates from the Division [of Education and Ministry of the National Council of Churches of Christ] specified that, in references to men and women, masculine-oriented language should be eliminated as far as this can be done without altering passages that reflect the historical situation of ancient patriarchal culture."

Standard Bible Committee, "To the Reader," preface by Bruce M. Metger for the *New Revised Standard Version Bible* (Division of Christian Education of the National Council of the Churches of Christ in the U.S.A., 1989).

[18] John King, *Lectures vpon Ionas*, 1st ed., vol. 1 (Oxford: 1597). This phrase could perhaps incite scorn by both parties of another charged political debate raging today.

[19] Clarifying context may affect gender language, as in the case in the Gospels where Jesus Christ makes explicit reference to "brothers" (*adelphoi*) as distinct from "sisters" (*adelphai*, cf. Mt 19.29; Mk 10.29, 30; Lk 14.26). In this context, Jesus specified these groups among others in order to build an accumulative list, which illustrates that no one is exempted from his teaching.

[20] "To the Reader," *New Revised Standard Version Bible* (1989).

21 *The Chicago Manual of Style*. 16th ed. (The University of Chicago Press, 2010), §5.227, p. 303.

22 "Chicago Style for the Singular They," *CMOS Shop Talk*, posted April 3, 2017, http://cmosshoptalk.com/2017/04/03/chicago-style-for-the-singular-they/.

23 American Psychological Association, *Publication Manual of the APA*, 6th ed. (Washington, DC: 2009), §3.12.

24 Society of Biblical Literature, *SBL Handbook of Style* (Peabody, MA: Hendrickson Publishers, 1999), §4.3, p. 17.

25 Lauren Easton, "Making a case for a singular 'they'," the blog of the Associated Press, last modified March 24, 2017, https://blog.ap.org/products-and-services/making-a-case-for-a-singular-they.

26 Modern Language Association of America, *MLA handbook*, 8th ed. (New York: 2016) Accessed April 1, 2019.

27 The Old Testament is replete with tales of violence, some which may surprise us by their visceral detail, though, I suppose I have grown insensitive to the anguish that the thought of circumcision used to cause me.

28 "Preface," *NET Bible: New English Translation*, 2nd ed. (Nashville, TN: Thomas Nelson, 2017).

29 In the Masoretic tradition, the Tetragrammaton* (יהוה) is given the vowels for *adonai* (Heb. אֲדֹנָי "my Lord", so יְהֹוָה); or, if the previous or following word is already *adonai*, the vowels match *elohim* instead (Heb. אֱלֹהִים "God", so יֱהֹוִה). The composite *schĕwa* under the first letter of *adonai* (א) differs from that beneath the first letter of the Tetragrammaton (י), because Hebrew orthographic rules do not permit a *schĕwa* without a *patach* (i.e., a *hateph patach*) when placed under a gutteral consonant (א).

30 The *New World Translation of the Holy Scriptures* (NWT) is produced by the Watchtower Bible and Tract Society (New York: 1960, '84, 2013) and is popular among Jehovah's Witnesses.

31 The NLT renders the Tetragrammaton as "Yahweh" in only eleven places: **Gn 22.14; Ex 3.15, 16; 6.2, 3; 15.3; 17.15; 33.19; 34.5, 6; Jg 6.24.**

32 Jonathan Petersen, "Bible Translation Reading Levels," *BibleGateway Blog*, last modified June 21, 2016, accessed April 4, 2019, https://www.biblegateway.com/blog/2016/06/bible-translation-reading-levels/

Theological Decisions

Overcoming Bias and Agenda

Often, there is no single way to best render any given passage, so translators must select from the many options that our English language affords them. Therefore, a Bible translation is the product of millions of interpretive and editorial decisions. Some of these decisions are obvious, or they follow a line of explicit, logical reasoning, but many are highly intuitive and their reasons are obscure. When translators neglect to demonstrate or justify their translation choices, then their assumptions—their biases—are left to influence their work. We can only guess what biases guide their intuitive choices through the hints they offer in the printed text of their translation or through the clues they leave in comments and interviews.[1]

NATURE OF BIAS

Biases are the filters that shade our experience and the lenses that frame our worldview. They are the assumptions on which we form opinions or make assertions. They are those underlying beliefs about reality—those presuppositions—that govern our behaviors and bend our judgments.

Biases are pervasive; everyone has them and no one is exempt. No human is perfectly impartial and unbiased, including those who swear to neutrality, such as arbiters, judges, and research scientists. Our society often associates bias with moral and social ills, like racism, sexism, and religious bigotry, but biases are not necessarily evil.

We are creatures hardwired for reconciling the daily flood of facts—sensory stimulation and data input—with our emotions. We draw inferences, make assumptions, generalize, and form beliefs to connect what we learn with what we feel. This is so we can efficiently make decisions, get cloture, and move on with our lives.

Biases are the mental shortcuts we take so that we don't exhaust ourselves when processing all that information.

We are primed for bias even from birth. In early childhood, we learn what to believe while interacting with the world around us. We make meaning out of our experiences in order to cope with the mysteries of our vast, new world. Most of our early beliefs are never expressed in words. Nonetheless, they exist, because they dictate what we do. Biases are beliefs so basic, so intrinsic, and so intimate that we act on them even when our behavior betrays our personal creeds and stated values.[2]

Certain biases are so fundamental to our worldview, so basic to how we perceive reality, that we heavily invest and deeply commit ourselves to the presumption that they are really true. This is why emotions rise to the surface when our biases are confronted or contradicted. We feel threatened when our basic assumptions (and personal justifications) are questioned and challenged.

KINDS OF BIAS

We form different biases from different assumptions. For example, *ignorant bias** results from the assumptions we make in the absence of information. It believes an assertion when we don't know enough to know that it is false. It blind-sides us with our lack of knowledge so that we assume the truth of an untested theory. Ignorant bias is why novices are the least qualified to assess their own competence in any given field.

*Anchoring bias** is a belief founded on first impressions. The initial set of information—an introductory book or lecture, for example—frames all the information that we gain later on in that subject. In other words, everything we know now interprets everything we don't know yet. This is why we say "a little knowledge is dangerous,"[3] because we need more information to challenge and correct any false "facts" that we currently hold.

Unchecked bias results in *prejudice*. Prejudices (*i.e.*, "pre-judgments") make our choices for us before we've seen the options.

They answer the questions not raised. They decide debates before they're confronted with evidence.

Prejudice predisposes us to pay more attention to facts that support our preexisting beliefs. This attention is what we call *confirmation bias,** and it is particularly insidious. It cherry-picks the information that supports an assumption and ignores or minimizes anything else that seemingly contradicts it. It sways us to dismiss or downplay data that doesn't fit our worldview.

Even highly intelligent people are susceptible to confirmation bias, because they use their intellectual skills to buttress their own arguments and eloquently defend their own views. Intelligence doesn't necessarily encourage us to explore every vantage point. We could call confirmation bias "willful ignorance," except that it can be so implicit and habitual that one could be unaware of it, as it both blinds and steers a person's reason.

Different biases lead to different conclusions, even when confronted with the same data. These differences don't always lead to different translation results, but sometimes they do, and, at times, significantly so.

CONSCIOUS BIAS AND AGENDA

We may envision translators as *mediums* between a speaker and his audience, but they are, in fact, *mediators*. That is, translators are not passive avenues of meaning. They are active editors.

Since the Bible is filled with theological data—assertions about God's nature, activity, and relationship with his creation—a burden of responsibility rests on translators to check whatever biases shape their theological views. How effectively translators allow a biblical author to speak to us depends on how closely they adhere to the author's context. Translators transgress context when they impose artificial lenses upon his text, that is, when they allow ideas foreign to an author's writing, time, and culture to interfere with his intended meaning.[4] Editors gag an author when they ignore his use of words or his historico-cultural settings.[5] They do him another injustice by forcing simple inferences out of linguistic puzzles that neither syntax nor history can resolve.

At times, it is hard to know when a rendering results from the translator's unconscious bias or from some hidden agenda. Translators may reveal their biases when they are interviewed. Many clarify their agenda in a preface or an introduction. We can even identify certain theological assumptions when unique renderings are held in contrast with other versions. The rest of this chapter illustrates those very impositions and offers suggestions for identifying and correcting them.

WHERE TRANSLATION AND TRADITIONAL BIAS COLLIDE

Church and "Congregation"

When William Tyndale released his New Testament in England (1526), it was immediately condemned by authorities in the English church. Thomas More, King Henry VIII's right-hand man and Tyndale's most vocal critic, took particular offense with how Tyndale translated the word "church" (Greek *ekklēsia*). At this time, the idea of "church" in Europe and England was generally recognized as a single, hegemonous, hierarchical institution that spanned all of civilized Christendom. At least, that is the idea it conjured up at the time. By insisting on the word "congregation" instead, Tyndale challenged prevailing dogma by using a word that seemed to imply an autonomous, local assembly. Though, at times, the biblical word refers to the universal, collective body of believers, the word "congregation" does indeed better reflect how the Greek word is frequently used throughout the New Testament.

As we will see, new and novel renderings—even when perfectly justified by historic precedent and use in context—tend to unsettle the comfortable ties between familiar terms and traditional usage.

The Best Bible?

Baptism and "Immersion"

Alexander Campbell's NT translation, titled the *Sacred Writings* (1826), rendered the Greek verb *baptizein* with a clear English equivalent—"to immerse."[6] Even though his translation was consistent with Baptist theology and practice, the Baptist-backed American and Foreign Bible Society (founded 1836) and several other prominent Baptist ministers rejected it. It is likely that the Bible Society was simply put off by the kinds of controversy surrounding the Campbellite movement.[7] Regardless, the word as Campbell rendered it in his Bible differed too radically from the familiar transliteration ("to baptize") for it to be accepted. It differed too much from their cherished KJV.[8]

To date, no popular modern translation is willing to part with this traditional rendering, despite good precedent for the word's use in NT contexts. Such cases include Jesus's own example, which shows him "coming up out of the water" (Gk. *anebē apo tou hudatos*, **Mt 3.16; Mk 1.9**); the Ethiopian, who went "down into the water" (*katebēsan . . . eis to hudōr*, **Ac 8.38, 39**); and John the Baptist, who required "much water" (implying John's need for a volume of water large enough to submerge his followers, **Jn 3.23**). If we broaden the scope of our search, we find one of its few uses in the Septuagint, where Elisha instructs the Syrian commander, Naaman, to "dip" (*ebaptisato*) seven times into the Jordan River (**2Kg 5.14**). Even the mixed metaphors of burial and baptism imply full immersion in **Romans 6.3, 4**. (After all, can any Christian convert imagine being merely "sprinkled" into Jesus' death?)

When the word, *baptizein*, is used in a concrete, non-figurative sense, the evidence overwhelmingly supports one practice over another, as even the standard lexicons* evince.[9] In fact, the earliest explicit precedent for sprinkling is found in *The Didachē*, a document that only emerged after the NT was written (2nd c. AD). It describes "sprinkling" as a kind of last resort,

"[I]f you have neither [running, cold, or even warm water],
then pour water (*ekcheon . . . hudōr*) on the head three times
in the name of the Father, Son, and Holy Spirit".[10]

Yet, in some traditions, even something so apparent can be
overturned by a broader *de facto* canon of traditional practice.

Traditional Texts

Traditional doctrinal biases even choose which edition of text to
translate. The Trinitarian Bible Society's (TBS) constitution dic-
tates that their "aim shall be to produce or select versions whose
textual basis is as close as possible to the Hebrew Masoretic and
the Greek Received texts underlying both the English Authorised
Version (*i.e.*, KJV) and translations of comparable standing made
from these texts into other European languages at the time of the
Protestant Reformation."[11] TBS has selected these texts because
they believe that "*the providentially preserved true and authentic
text is to be found in the Hebrew Masoretic (i.e., the Second Rabbinic Bible, 1524–25) and the Greek Received Texts (i.e., the Textus
Receptus, 1516–98).* In so doing, [they believe that they are fol-
lowing] the historic, orthodox Protestant position of acknowledg-
ing as Holy Scripture the Hebrew and Greek texts consistently accessible to and preserved among the people of God in all ages."[12]

In other words, TBS believes that God has preserved the Bible
for all people at all times, but they assume he did so through this
particular, traditional form of the biblical text—a printed form
that coincided with the creation of the *Westminster Confession of
Faith* in 1643.

The translators of the NKJV, on the other hand, were well aware
of this theologically-motivated textual bias. Though they intended to revise the KJV using the same texts endorsed by the TBS, they
did not wish to leave their readers unaware of textual differences
between important manuscripts. So, they placed concise textual
notes in the margins to show any significant differences between
translations of the traditional text and the later critical editions.

The Best Bible?

This way, the translators and editors of the NKJV remained open about their textual bases without trying to push a particular doctrinal point of view.

Traditional Language and the *Status Quo*

For those of us who have grown up in ecclesiastical settings, we find that church language is loaded with all sorts of pre-existing associations. Practices, policies, titles, and roles in the church tend to receive traditional biblical labels, whether or not they are justified by the Bible's regular use of those terms.

This tendency to preserve traditional norms and practices is a persistent one. We react to challenges to these norms when we do not trust the challenger's authority, or when we do not know what to believe and do instead. Mastery of the familiar makes us feel competent and safe. A Bible whose language is taken for granted does not risk upsetting the *status quo*.

The push for understandable English Bibles faced resistance long after their popular and legal acceptance. The first attempt to translate an official Anglican Bible appropriate for use in the English church fizzled and failed in 1535. Seven years later, Archbishop Thomas Cranmer tried again to encourage the English bishops to collaborate on a revision of Coverdale's Great Bible. But, a certain Bishop (Steven Gardiner of Winchester) garnered a long list of words from the Latin Vulgate, which he insisted that this new revision should retain:

> *ecclesia* (a transliteration from Greek instead of "church" or "congregation"), *episcopus* (translit. from Gk., "bishop" or "overseer"), *apocalypsis* (translit. from Gk, "revelation"), *presbyter* (another translit. from Gk., "elder" or "senior"), *poenitentia* (Latin for "repentance"), *pontifex* (Lat. "priest"), *sapientia* (Lat. "wisdom"), *opera* (Lat. "work"), *spiritus sanctus* (Lat. "Holy Spirit"), *gratia* (Lat. "grace" or "favor"), *charitas* (Lat. "love" or "compassion"), *scientia* (Lat. "knowledge"), and many more, *etc.*

At this point, production ground to a halt, since Gardiner refused to compromise, and the effort eventually died off for a lack of support. A full revision would have to wait until the end of three monarchs' reigns (those of Henry VIII, Edward VI, and Mary I). Three decades after the last attempt, a revision called the Bishops' Bible was finally published during the reign of Queen Elizabeth I in 1568.

After Elizabeth's death and the accession of James I in 1603, the Anglican church took up the task of revising the Bishops' Bible, but only according to the strict set of rules set out by Archbishop Richard Bancroft. His third rule demanded that

> the old ecclesiastical words [are] to be kept, namely, as the word *Church* [is] not to be translated *Congregation, etc.*[13]

To this day, the general consensus of most modern popular translations is to preserve certain familiar, theologically-loaded terms ("baptism", "church", "justification", "pastors", *etc.*). The benefit of keeping the traditional and technical language is that it offers a line to historic theological discussion. It gives an entry to those who wish to commune with historic confessions, creeds, catechisms, and commentaries.

On the other hand, these terms force a barrier between novices and the theologically conversant. For those inexperienced in the Bible and historic Christianity, traditional renderings can hide passages of Scripture that functional translations make clear.

WHERE AMBIGUITY HAS THEOLOGICAL IMPLICATIONS

When the Standard Bible Committee released the *Revised Standard Bible* in 1952, they were greeted with general popular acclaim. But some also branded them as heretics! Certain conservative Christians condemned them for their rendering of a particular

Hebrew word in Isaiah's prophecy. In the KJV, the word 'almah is translated "virgin":

> "Therefore the Lord himself shall give you a sign; Behold, a virgin ('almah) shall conceive, and bear a son, and shall call his name Immanuel" (Isaiah 7.14 KJV).

But the revisers rendered the word as "young woman", instead. As a result, they were accused of abandoning Isaiah's messianic prophecy regarding Jesus' virgin birth. The way that the RSV revisers rendered the passage seemed to limit its reference only to King Hezekiah's immediate situation.

This controversy is, in fact, very old, going all the way back to the early Christian apologist, Justin Martyr (c. AD 130), who debated this point with a certain Jew named Trypho. Justin Martyr's understanding of Scripture was dependent on the Septuagint, which translates the Hebrew word 'almah (which generally means "young woman") with the Greek, parthenos (exclusively "virgin").

Trypho argued that the Hebrew word did not mean "virgin" but "young woman." In fact, in Hebrew Scripture, the word can refer to any marriageable young woman without regard to her sexual experience. Though the term may include young virgins, it does not do so exclusively.

Nonetheless, Justin Martyr argued that the Septuagint reflected a pre-Christian understanding of the passage. He insisted that if the child was born in the natural way, how could the event really be considered a "sign"? So he reasoned for the translation of "virgin" and its significance as predictive prophecy.

In another passage, the NRSV (one of the RSV's successors) renders Psalm 8.4 as

> "what are *human beings* that you are mindful of *them, mortals* that you care for *them*?"   (*emphasis* added)

This idiomatically renders what the RSV more formally reads,

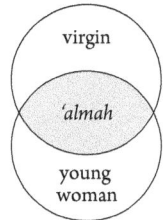

"what is *man* that thou art mindful of *him*, and *the son of man* that thou dost care for *him*?" (*emphasis* added)

Note the distinctions between the two renderings:

RSV	NRSV
man . . . him	human beings . . . them
the son of man . . . him	mortals . . . them

There is good precedent for the NRSV (on the right) to render the Psalm this way. Most Old Testament (OT) cases use the phrase "son of man" to recognize the distinction between humanity and divinity. For example, in the NRSV, **Gn 11.5** reads, "The LORD came down to see the city and the tower, which *mortals* (*the sons of men*, RSV) had built." **Nm 23.19**, "God is not a *human being*, that he should lie, or a *mortal* (a *son of man*, RSV), that he should change his mind." **Ps 144.3**, "O LORD, what are *human beings* that you regard them, or *mortals* (*the son of man* [singular], RSV) that you think of *them*?" **Ezk 3.4**, "He said to me: *Mortal* (*Son of man*, RSV), go to the house of Israel and speak my very words to them."

Where the author of the letter to the Hebrews quotes **Ps 8.4**, a problem occurs in the NRSV, because it renders this Psalm in the NT just like it does in the OT,

"What are human beings that you are mindful of them, or mortals, that you care for them?" (**Heb 2.6** NRSV, so CEB, GNB)

Here the NRSV pluralizes the predicates and pronouns, which strictly narrows the verse's referents to an inclusive group of people. Yet, the grammar and the context of Hebrews can only refer to a single person in this passage, namely, Jesus Christ. The NET and other translations render the NT occurrence of this verse more appropriately:

"What is man that you think of him or the son of man that you care for him?" (**Heb 2.6** NET, so KJV, RSV, NIV, NASB, NLT, ESV, NAB, CSB)

When confronting the difficulty of rendering OT passages quoted in the NT, it may help to address an underlying interpretive assumption: Not all OT prophecy is predictive in nature. Some of it is *typological.** That is, Jesus Christ's fulfillment of OT passages (as the NT frequently indicates) does not require that this Psalm refers to the Christ in a *predictive* prophetic sense.[14] Rather, Jesus fulfills OT Scripture here in the sense that he fits and completes OT patterns and paradigms.

Ambiguity and Bias

On occasion, a passage's meaning seems clear, but theological biases restrict other possible renderings. For example, **Acts 8.19** records the story of Simon the Magician, who was so impressed with the apostles' impartation of the Holy Spirit that he wanted to purchase the same skill,

"Give this authority to me as well, so that everyone on whom I lay my hands may receive the Holy Spirit." (NASB, so KJV, NIV, NAB, CSB, *et al.*)

The problem with this rendering is how it makes Simon seem to assume the significance of that Spirit's nature. There is no definite article ("the") in the original to distinguish this Holy Spirit from any other possible "holy spirit" that Simon might have imagined. There are no syntactical clues in the Greek. Nothing in the surrounding context (**Ac 8.15–19**) explicitly demands that translators narrow the reference to *the* Holy Spirit of God.[15] Translators are left with two options when rendering Simon's request—that he might receive "a holy spirit" or "the Holy Spirit". The deciding factor in most versions is the translators' orthodox Christian bias.

The *New World Translation of the Holy Scriptures* (NWT—a version distributed by the Jehovah's Witnesses) offers a third option that makes it seem like Simon is asking for some force, substance, or experience,

> "Give me also this authority, that anyone upon whom I lay my hands may receive holy spirit." (NWT, so Knox)

Notice the lack of article, definite or otherwise? The NWT's translation is not so bad in this context, and it could reflect Simon's own ignorance about the nature of the Holy Spirit. Nonetheless, the Watchtower Bible and Tract Society's own theological bias (which assumes the non-personal nature of the Holy Spirit) likely influences this rendering,[16] just as Christian orthodoxy does in evangelical and Catholic sponsored versions.[17]

Eisegesis—Reading Into the Passage

Bible translation is much more than a mechanical exercise—it is more than finding a single English word to match each corresponding word in the Greek or Hebrew dictionary. (See "Translation Decisions" starting on page 63 regarding the two tensions of translation.) Sometimes, clear translation requires translators to supply words that can't be found among the original words but are needed, because English norms require them, or because the grammatical tenses of Greek and Hebrew verbs imply them.

Sometimes translators must supply whole concepts missing in the original text in order to make sense of a passage. Those who aim for the most probable meaning of the original will pull these ideas from the original context (*i.e.*, from the history and culture contemporary to the Bible). But sometimes translators read concepts into a passage without sufficient precedent or justification to put them there. This is called *eisegesis,** a Greek word defined as the "interpretation of a word or passage by reading into it one's own ideas."[18]

Martin Luther was accused of improperly reading his own idea into the text of **Romans 3.28** in his 1522 edition of the New Testament. Eight years later, he defended his inclusion of the word *allein* (German for "alone", as in "justified by faith *alone*") in an open letter,

> "I knew very well that the word *solum* (Latin, 'alone' or 'only') is not in the Greek or Latin text . . . At the same time . . . it belongs there if the translation is to be clear and vigorous. I wanted to speak German, not Latin or Greek, since it was German I had undertaken to speak in the translation. But it is the nature of our German language that in speaking of two things, one of which is affirmed and the other denied, we use the word *solum* (*allein*) along with the word *nicht* ('not') or *kein* ('no'). For example, we say, 'The farmer brings *allein* ("only") grain and *kein* ("no") money . . . .'

> "This is the German usage, even though it is not the Latin or Greek usage. It is the nature of the German language to add the word *allein* in order that the word *nicht* or *kein* may be clearer or more complete." [19]

German does not absolutely need this addition for clarity, as other German translators did not require it in their Bibles.[20] Luther's paraphrase, by his own admission, takes a liberty where there is no immediate correspondence between the German words and the Greek text. Yet, a perusal of Paul's other writings validates Luther's implication, if not his translation. Righteousness (hence salvation) through faith alone is well-attested throughout the Pauline corpus* (*cf.* **Gal 3.11; Tt 3.5–6**).

When some word or phrase is unclear, theological intrusion (*i.e.,* eisegesis) tempts translators to jump to conclusions and make assumptions about what it means. The translators' first strategy for discerning its meaning is to refer to the normal rules of the source's language—its grammatical forms, regular syntax, and its general use of vocabulary. If the meaning is still hidden, translators throw their net wider and examine the context of the passage. If it is still obscure after examination, they extend their search to the rest of the biblical book, or to other books in the same genre, or by the same author, or in the same Testament. The search may continue through the entire biblical canon. If the passage is still obscure, translators may continue searching through the book's historical and cultural contexts (including archælogical finds and literature contemporary with the book's composition) or through early commentaries on the book or passage (e.g., Aramaic Targums or early Christian writings). This process for discerning meaning is an example of *exegesis*.* It serves to a guard against speculative or purely conjectural interpretation.

Determining context is not without its difficulties. To demonstrate, let's revisit **Isaiah 7.14** in the *NET Bible*,

> For this reason the Lord himself will give you a confirming sign. Look, this *young woman* (Heb. *'almah*) is about to conceive and will give birth to a son. You, young woman, will name him Immanuel." (NET, *emphasis added*)

Like the RSV, the NET renders the Hebrew word, *'almah*, as "young woman", even though this OT passage is quoted later in the NT as

> This all happened so that what was spoken by the Lord through the prophet would be fulfilled: "Look! *The virgin* (Gk. *parthenos*) will conceive and give birth to a son, and they will name him Emmanuel" (**Mt 1.22–23a** NET, *emphasis added*)

Notice that in **Isaiah 7.14** the translators used the word "this" to specify some woman in Hezekiah's presence? This rendering was intended to fix the context to Isaiah's historical situation. This also brings up a couple questions:

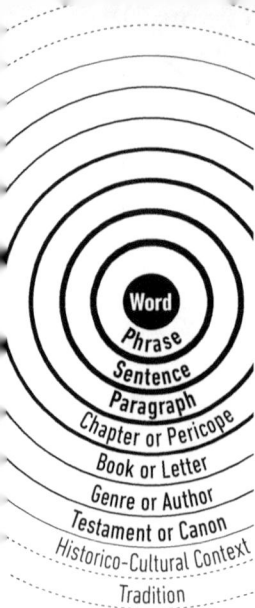

The further out from the passage that translators go in order to clarify its meaning, the more speculative (or narrow) their interpretation of the context tends to get.

The Best Bible?

(1) Does the translator translate the older passage (**Is 7.14**) with a view to the clarification that the later passage (**Mt 1.23**) brings, or (2) does the translator concentrate solely on the native context of the older passage?[21]

The NET translators decided to follow the second option based on a theological assumption they call "progressive revelation." Since the Bible is a collection of historic books, and since it was composed piecemeal over a long duration, they assume that God made himself known to humanity in portions at a time. He progressively revealed his character and intentions to people with each successive addition to Scripture. The Bible, then, binds together an accumulated series of God's acts and words into a single volume. Therefore, those who arrive later in history have access to more of the biblical canon so that they necessarily have access to more of God's revelation than those who lived before those biblical books were composed and completed.

The implication is that the prophet Isaiah's imagination was limited to what God had revealed in the *Torah* or in Israel's history up to his point in time. Nowhere in his mind could he have imagined a child born from a virgin. Only later generations could reflect on Isaiah's prophecy in light of Jesus's miraculous birth. Thus, the NET translators, with this view of historical context, tried to avoid reading a later NT context into this OT passage, as it was not likely intended by the OT author.

This view of progressive revelation finds some theological support in the NT. The introduction of the letter to the Hebrews reads, "*Long ago, at many times and in many ways,* God spoke to our fathers by the prophets, *but in these last days* he has spoken to us by his Son . . ." (**Heb 1.1–2b** ESV, *emphasis added*). This letter demonstrates how the later revelation of Jesus Christ is superior to the prophecies of those who had gone before him. Prior revelation merely outlined a shadow of the Christ, but Jesus filled in the details (*cf.* **Col 2.17; Gal 3.15–19**). Since we have access to later additions to the biblical canon, we necessarily have more revelation and, thus, a better conception of who God is.

But there are other possibilities to consider. For instance, it is probable that former generations did not record all the revelation they saw and heard. Moses probably did not transcribe all that God spoke to him (*cf.* **Ex 30.11**). John the evangelist claimed that "Jesus performed many other miraculous signs in the presence of the disciples, which are not recorded in this book," and that if "every one of them were written down, I suppose the whole world would not have room for the books that would be written." (**Jn 20.30; 21.25** NET) If such revelation was never recorded, it could only instruct those individuals or generations that witnessed it. Without a record, it could never be added to the canon, and, therefore, we miss out on what only they could have known.[22]

Also consider that some historic, documented revelation may be lost to us today. For example, the ancient Book of Jasher (literally "Scroll of the Upright One", *cf.* **Jos 10.13; 2Sa 1.18**) and the apostle Paul's letter to the Laodiceans (*cf.* **Col 4.16**) may have vanished due to persecutions, wars, wear and tear, natural deterioration, or something else that removed it from circulation. Mention of these lost works is evidence that the ancients had possible access to some amount of revelation that we can no longer witness.[23]

Here's a final counter to the NET's interpretation: The translators of the NET acknowledge the Bible's divine inspiration, which means that Scripture is effectively composed by two authors—one human and the other divine. What progressive revelation fails to address is the intentions of dual-authorship. Isaiah may have had no clue as to the meaning or implication of his prophetic utterance, but God certainly did. As Scripture itself teaches,

> Above all, you do well if you recognize this: No prophecy of scripture ever comes about by the prophet's own imagination, for no prophecy was ever borne of human impulse; rather, men carried along by the Holy Spirit spoke from God. (**2Pt 1.20–21** NET)

In other words, the ambiguity and future implication of the Hebrew 'almah was probably intended from the start, though, perhaps, not by Isaiah. This dual-intent, or fuller sense (Latin *sensus plenior*), may add to the implications of this passage, though it could never change or reduce the words in actual use there.[24]

EISEGETING THE TRANSLATOR'S IMAGINATION

Some paraphrases are intended to reimagine the historic biblical authors as if they were speaking to modern audiences. When acknowledged as a paraphrase, they can offer helpful analogies or commentary. For example, Clarence Jordan's *Cotton Patch Gospel* reimagines the NT as if it were set in the American Deep South. He introduces chapter two of Matthew's Gospel,

> When Jesus was born in Gainesville, Georgia during the time that Herod was governor, some scholars from the Orient came to Atlanta and inquired, "Where is the one who was born to be governor of Georgia? We saw his star in the Orient, and we came to honor him."

In Jordan's version, Joseph, the descendant of King David and Jesus' adopted father, is rechristened "Joe Davidson"; The Jewish sects, Pharisees and Sadducees, are labeled "Protestants" and "Catholics."

Eugene Peterson's *The Message* is another rendition that sometimes introduces ideas foreign to both the text and its setting in order to make a point. Peterson extensively paraphrases **Romans 8.3,**

> God went for the jugular when he sent his own Son. He didn't deal with the problem as something remote and unimportant. In his Son, Jesus, he personally took on the human condition, entered the disordered mess of struggling humanity in order to set it right once and for all. The law code, weakened as it always was by fractured human nature, could never have done

that. The law always ended up being used as a Band-Aid on sin instead of a deep healing of it. (MSG)

The Message's reference to a Band-Aid, a registered trademark for a modern medical product, would have been a radically foreign notion to the original audience. The translator was well aware of this and merely took the opportunity with this passage to illustrate and preach to his modern reader. Such extreme contextualization was never intended as a translation of words, but an approximation of ideas. For contrast, read the NASB's formal (and far more succinct) rendering of the same passage,

> For what the Law could not do, weak as it was through the flesh, God *did:* sending His own Son in the likeness of sinful flesh and *as an offering* for sin, He condemned sin in the flesh (**Ro 8.3** NASB)

Sometimes translators are guilty of reading concepts into a passage that are foreign even to its broader context. For example, the 2013 edition of the *Letters from Heaven by the Apostle Paul* (*The Passion Translation,* or TPT) has added words to **Galatians 6.6** with no correspondence between the English and the Greek text or from the rest of Paul's letter:

> *And those* who are taught the Word *will receive an impartation from their teacher; a transference of anointing takes place between them.* (TPT 2013, *emphasis added*)

This interpretation entirely misses the original idea of material provision for the teacher. For comparison, the RSV formally reads,

> "*Let him* who is taught the word *share all good things with him who teaches*" (RSV, cf. NRSV, KJV, NKJV, RSV, ESV, NASB, *emphasis added*)

and the NLT reads,

> *Those* who are taught the word of God *should provide for their teachers, sharing all good things with them.* (NLT, *emphasis added*)

In a later revision, the translator adjusted his text to read,

> *And those* who are taught the Word *will receive an impartation from their teacher; a sharing of wealth takes place between them.* (TPT 2016, *emphasis added*)

Though somewhat closer to the idea of the other translations, it still misses the Greek imperative. So he revised it again,

> *And those* who are taught the Word *must share all good things with their teacher; a sharing of wealth takes place between them.* (TPT 2018, *emphasis added*)

and again,

> *And those* who are taught the Word *must share all good things with their teacher.* (TPT 2020, *emphasis added*)

For another example of theologically motivated eisegesis, let us look again at the *New World Translation* (NWT). One of the NWT's unique features is how it renders the Greek work *kyrios* ("lord" or "Lord") as "Jehovah" 237 times out of the approximately 721 times it occurs in the New Testament. In an appendix at the end the NWT, the translators claim that the NT *autographa** (the original MSS) actually recorded the name of God in Hebrew, which they transcribe as "Jehovah" (or "Yahweh"). They admit that "many [Bible scholars] feel that [God's personal name, as represented by the Tetragrammaton (יהוה)] did not appear in the original text of the Christian Greek Scriptures."[25]

Only it's not a mere feeling. None of the nine arguments defending the editorial stance of the Watchtower Bible and Tract Society confront the hard physical evidence: Not one of the Greek NT MSS records the Hebrew Tetragrammaton in place of the word "Lord" (*kyrios*). The point is that all the 237 places in the NT that the Society chooses to translate "Jehovah" are there in accordance with a theological bias that will not allow them to conflate the identity of Jesus Christ with the eternal God.[26]

EISEGETING THE READER'S IMAGINATION

Translators aren't the only ones who get caught reading into Scripture. Some translations are more susceptible to the intrusion of their readers' illegitimate ideas.

The Amplified Bible (AMP) is unique in that it accompanies each significant word with a set of glosses and clarifying meanings within parenthesis ( ) and supplied senses or commentary in square brackets [ ]. For example, read **Col 2.13**,

> When you were dead in your sins and in the uncircumcision of your flesh (worldliness, manner of life), God made you alive together with Christ, having [freely] forgiven us all our sins. (AMP 2015)

The use of the word "flesh" is clarified by the parenthesized words "(worldliness, manner of life)." The bracketed word "[freely]" is supplied to comment on the manner of God's forgiveness.

Though not technically a translation as much as a cautious paraphrase, *The Amplified Bible*'s system allows careful readers to discern between the biblical text and the expanded paraphrase. Incautious readers mistreat the AMP when they assume that the parenthetic glosses offer alternate renderings instead of convenient clarifications. The difference is subtle: As clarification, the AMP intends the meaning as conveyed by the main, non-parenthetic text. The glosses in parentheses are meant to disambiguate or focus the meaning of the main text.

The Best Bible?

When readers see the parenthetical glosses as optional renderings, they tend to act as umpires of the text's meaning by selecting suitable options from the ones offered inside the parentheses. Or, they might try to imagine how *all* the parenthetic words somehow fit into the context. By reading into the context all the meanings associated with the glossed words in parentheses, the reader commits the crime of "illegitimate totality transfer," which is an attempt to force the entire range of a word's possible meaning onto the text, including unaffected meanings (general definitions or denotations) and affected meanings (connotations and nuances), without regard for its context.[27]

Conflicting Christology

IN THE BEGINNING . . .

> In the beginning was the Word, & the Word was with God, and the Word was God. (**Jn 1.1** KJV)

These are the familiar first words of John's Gospel when read in the Tyndale-KJV tradition. Later revisions (including the RSV, NASB, NKJV, NRSV, ESV) and newer translations (NLT, NIV, NAB) state it pretty much the same. But there are a handful of translations that render the verse rather differently.

For example, Coverdale's translation (1535) changes the English word order to match the order in the Greek,

> and God was the word (Gk., *kai theos ēn ho logos*)

Though Coverdale is faithful to form, because the Greek definite article (*ho*, "the") precedes the word "word" (*logos*), it marks "word" as the subject of the sentence and not "God." So, the familiar order of words, "the Word was God," better fits Greek syntax.

In a different rendering, James Moffatt's translation (1913) interprets the word "God" (Gk. *theos*) in a qualitative sense:

> the Logos was *divine* (Moffatt, so NEB, REB)

Some argue that a syntactical principle called "Colwell's Rule" demands that "God" should be rendered as a definite noun and not as an adjective.[28] Colwell's Rule does not require this, but Moffatt's use of "divine" could suggest references that are not exclusive to God, which is a notion not implied by the Greek source. Rather, a more acceptable translation should read something to the effect of "God was what the Word was."[29]

In contrast, the NWT interprets "God" as an indefinite noun:

and the Word was a god (NWT 2013)

The Watchtower Bible and Tract Society insisted that the word "God" (*theos*) has no definite article (*ho*, "the") in Greek, so it should be rendered as an indefinite noun in English ("a god"). Yet their grammatical argument is inconsistent, which becomes apparent in just the first eighteen verses of John's Gospel.[30]

v 6	There came a man who was sent as a representative of **God**	*egeneto anthrōpos apestalmenos para **theou***	No article, but the NWT makes God definite by capitalizing it.
v 12	as many as did receive him, to them he gave authority to become **God's** children	*hosoi de elabon auton, edōken autois exousian tekna **theou** genesthai*	No article, same as above.
v 13	they were born . . . from **God**	*ek **theou** egennēthēsan*	No article, same as above.
v 18	No man has seen **God** at any time; **the** only begotten **god** . . .	***theon** oudeis heōraken pōpote **ho** monogenēs **theos***	The first occurrence ("God") in this verse follows the same pattern as those listed above. The second occurrence ("god") is set in lowercase, yet it follows the definite article (*ho*, "the").

In sum, the Watchtower Bible and Tract Society shaped their translation of this passage to fit their theological agenda, which tries to avoid possible trinitarian interpretations and the essential divinity of Jesus Christ.[31]

ONLY BEGOTTEN OR ONE OF A KIND

Some translations are so familiar that we cannot imagine them being rendered any differently. **John 3.16** is a prime example:

> For God so loved the world, that he gave his *only begotten* Son, that whosoever believeth in him should not perish, but have everlasting life. (KJV, *cf.* Geneva, Bishops', Rheims, NASB, NWT, MEV; *emphasis added*.)

The words "only begotten" have so much theological weight tied to them that some institutions refuse to have the words translated any other way.[32]

"Only begotten" (which correctly translates a Latin mistranslation of the original Greek word) came down to us through the influence of the Geneva New Testament (1557). These words are a formal translation from Latin (*unigenitum*), which is itself a formal rendering of the Greek word, *monogenē*. Though the forms seem to match (*uni-* = *mono-*; *genitum* = *genē*), the Latin misses the Greek etymology: Latin *genitum* regards "birth" and "begetting", but Greek *genē* deals with the "kind" or "sort" of something.[33] William Tyndale's translation twenty years earlier (1526) was nearer the mark:

> For God so loveth the world that he hath given his *only* son that none that believe in him should perish: but should have everlasting life. (Tyndale, so Coverdale, Matthew, RSV, NAB, NRSV, ESV; *emphasis added*)

Tyndale's support for this rendering comes from the word's use in other contexts (see **Lk 7.12; 8.42; 9.38**). Other modern translations tend towards a compromise:

> For God so loved the world that he gave his *one and only* Son, that whoever believes in him shall not perish but have eternal life. (NIV, so NET, NLT, CSB; *emphasis added*)

Only a couple translations, including the *International Standard Version* (2010), seem to get it quite right.

> For this is how God loved the world: He gave his *unique* Son so that everyone who believes in him might not be lost but have eternal life. (ISV, *cf*. AMP; *emphasis added*)

Further justification for this last rendering is found at **Hebrews 11.17**, which describes the faith of Abraham, who was willing to sacrifice his *monogenē*—his son Isaac. He was Abraham's only child through Sarah, but he was certainly not Abraham's only son, for Abraham also had Ishmael through Hagar, his concubine, and other children through Keturah, whom he married after Sarah's death. God's covenantal promises, though, were made exclusively through Isaac, the specially, unique, "one-of-a-kind" son (*cf*. **Gal 4.23**).[34]

GRANVILLE SHARP'S RULE

William Tyndale rendered **Titus 2.13** according to the forms and the word positions of the Greek:

> looking for that blessed hope and glorious appearing of the mighty God and of our Saviour Jesus Christ (so Coverdale, Matthew, Bishops', Geneva, Rheims, KJV, ASV, NWT, NAB).

By repeating the genitive construction in English, readers could construe the passage as referring to two different persons ("of the mighty God" *and* "of our Saviour").

Our understanding of how the Greek language of the New Testament works has progressed since Tyndale and King James. Granville Sharp (1735–1813), a Christian abolitionist, musician, classicist, and biblical scholar discovered a syntactical pattern in the Greek NT relevant to the rendering of this passage,

> When the copulative *kai* ("and") connects two nouns of the same case, . . . if the article *ho* ("the"), or any of its cases, precedes the first of the said nouns or participles, and is not repeated before the second noun or participle, the latter always relates to the same person that is expressed or described by the first noun or participle. . . .[35]

Evangelical grammarian, Daniel Wallace, explains:

> In native Greek constructions, when a single article modifies two substantives (nouns) connected by *kai* (thus, article + substantive + *kai* + substantive), *when* both substantives are (1) singular (both grammatically and semantically), (2) personal, (3) and common nouns (not proper names or ordinals), *they have the same referent.* [36]

This construct (article "the" + *common noun* + "and" + *common noun*) functions similarly in English: When we read "Here comes the gentleman and scholar," we assume that "gentleman" and "scholar" are both referring to the same person. But if we add an *article*—"Here come the gentleman and *the* scholar"—we expect it means two separate individuals.

The two nouns in this passage meet the criteria: They share only one article ("the"); they are joined with a copulative conjunction ("and"); they are singular, personal, common nouns

("God", "savior")—Therefore, they must refer to the same person, the appositive,* proper noun "Jesus Christ." (*cf.* **2Pt 1.1**)

So, the text should read as most modern translations do,

> waiting for our blessed hope, the appearing of the glory of our great God and Saviour Jesus Christ (RV, RSV, NASB, NKJV, NIV, NRSV, ESV, NET, NLT, CSB, MEV).

Sacramental Prejudice

James Moffatt's translation poses a theological challenge in some circles. His paraphrase of **Matthew 26.26** reflects a rationalistic take on Jesus' words:

> "As they were eating [Jesus] took a loaf and after the blessing he broke it; then he gave it to the disciples saying, 'Take and eat this, it *means* my body.' "

The heart of the controversy surrounds the unwarranted use of the word "means" found in the phrase "it means my body." This debate goes back a long time.

Centuries earlier, in 1529, Martin Luther and the Swiss Reformer, Huldreich Zwingli, met at the castle of Marburg, Germany, to discuss the possibility of uniting two Protestant factions against the Roman Church. Of the fifteen points set forth, the Lutheran party could agree with the Zwinglian on fourteen, but they failed to form a consensus on the last point regarding the Eucharist. Zwingli and his followers interpreted Jesus' words as a figure of speech, that Jesus did not mean the bread to be understood in any real sense, but only to be taken symbolically. Luther, on the other hand, sought another way to combat the Roman understanding of the elements.[37] Luther feared that the words of Scripture would be forced to mean something other than what they said. He insisted that Jesus' words could not be understood any other way except that Christ's body was somehow mystically present "in, with, or under" the Eucharistic bread. Most modern translations solve the problem by rendering the Greek formally and simply, "Take, eat; this is my body" (Bishops', KJV, RSV, NASB, NKJV, NIV, *et al.*). This uncontroversial rendering allows the different opinions to stand as they do.

Inclusive Language

The rise of political feminism in the 1960s led to a re-evaluation of women's roles in English society. (See "Gender Language" starting on page 85.) This led to a reassessment of gender language in the public arena. Sensitivity towards the explicit inclusion of women led English speakers to seek out alternatives to the spoken norm. They looked for something other than male pronouns when intending a generic sense. That is, they preferred some word other than "he" when meaning anyone of either sex.

Biblical scholars sought to conform translations to modern usage while ensuring that the Bible's use of gender was rendered accurately. That is, translators gave more attention to how pronouns and gender were actually used in Scripture instead of mechanically translating gender in a strictly formal sense. This demanded more attention to linguistics and vocabulary. Their work resulted in translations which tend towards accuracy, because their interpretation was guided more by contextual precedent than subjective judgment. Translations and revisions begun with the explicit intention of rendering inclusive language include the NRSV, the *Good News Bible* (GNB, 1992), the *Contemporary English Version* (CEV, 1995), the 2011 update of the NIV, and the *Common English Bible* (CEB, 2011). Translations and revisions influenced by modern usage, despite their conservative backing, include the ESV, [H]CSB, and NLT (2004).

As political debate arose over traditionally male-dominated functions of pastor and elder in light of women's ordination, critics of the Church's founding Documents disparaged the biblical authors for their apparent patriarchialism. They viewed Scripture as culturally biased against women. Many simply wanted a translation of the Bible that could be read from a lectern or pulpit, which did not constantly require them to interject and explain that such and such a passage was meant to apply to both "men and women."

Others demanded that the Bible *itself* needed correcting. These were not content with the gains made through existing gender-accurate translations. They insisted that the Bible be conformed to the language of a modern egalitarian agenda. Revised translations, in turn, became tools of feminist activism and clerical reform.

At this point, it is helpful to grip the slippery terms thrown around the gender debate: Generally speaking, the phrase "gender inclusive" may refer to language that is either "gender neutral" or "gender accurate." "Gender neutral" refers to language that tries to eliminate any and all gender distinctions. "Gender accurate" refers to language that fits the linguistic norms (*i.e.*, natural gender) of people and things in the source text, even if it doesn't correspond to the exact grammatical forms of the words (grammatical gender). "Gender specific" language, on the other hand, refers to words referring exclusively to men, or to women, but not to both at the same time.

"Gender accuracy" is an attempt to render with contemporary words those distinctions that are either explicit or implied in the text. It requires more linguistic data than either "gender neutral" or "formal-equivalent" renderings do. "Gender accurate" translations entail both "gender inclusive" and "gender specific" renderings, but only as the context determines.

The editors of *The New Testament and Psalms: An Inclusive Version* (1995)—an adaptation of the NRSV—claim that their

New Testament and Psalms is a new version of the Bible that speaks more directly than ever before to today's social concerns, especially the move towards universal inclusivity. This revolutionary new version pushes the English language to new levels of inclusive expression. The noted scholars who produced this work address issues of gender, race and ethnicity more directly than ever before. [38]

The preface of *The Inclusive Bible: The First Egalitarian Edition* (2001) reveals that a group called the Priests for Equality took nineteen years to produce a complete Bible for Roman Catholics. The translators began their work by examining existing translations for sexist language. Before rendering their version, they judged whether the biblical text itself was expressing unconscious chauvinistic *bias* or whether it was sexist in *intent*.[39]

These two versions tend to neutralize (ambiguate and generalize) gender language to make it more inclusive. For example, **Genesis 2.7a, 22a, 24** in *The Inclusive Bible* reads,

> So YHWH fashioned an *earth creature* out of the clay of the earth, and blew into *its* nostrils the breath of life. . . . YHWH then fashioned the two halves into male and female, and presented them to *one another*. . . . This is why *people* leave their *parents* and become bonded to *one another*, and the two become one flesh. (*emphasis added*)

They also neutralized the gender in Christ's relationship with God the Father in **Mk 1.10–11**:

NT and Pss: An Inclusive Version	The Inclusive Bible
Just as Jesus was coming up out of the water, he saw the heavens torn apart and the Spirit descending to him like a dove. And a voice came from heaven, "You are my *Child*, the Beloved; [a] with you I am well pleased."	Immediately upon coming out of the water, Jesus saw the heavens opening and the Spirit descending on him like a dove. Then a voice came from the heavens: "You are my Beloved, my *Own*. On you my favor rests."

([a] Or my beloved Child)

One critic complained that *The Inclusive Bible* failed to go far enough,

> For God-language, they attempt to be gender-neutral. They consistently avoid "Lord" and "Son," and all masculine pronouns. For Father, they use "Abba God" or "Loving God." For

Son of Man, they use "Chosen One" or "Promised One" which seems to introduce later Christian theology. They use the initials YHWH for God in the Hebrew Bible. Since we still live in a largely androcentric culture, (and since YHWH and Abba are male in my vocabulary) most hearers are likely to continue to imagine a masculine referent. To broaden our image of God, we need expansive feminine images, not just in the few places they exist in scripture but much more broadly. An earlier version of the New Testament did use "Father-Mother God" to begin the Lord's Prayer, but they have retreated.[40]

Another observed, "[T]his translation typically just repeats 'God' rather than using a pronoun, when one occurs in the text, and substitutes 'Parent' for 'Father.'"[41]

These versions tend to ambiguate male and female relationships and roles. For example, *The Inclusive Bible* renders **Ephesians 5.21–24** so ambiguously that readers can read into the passage any kind of relationship that is not exclusive to male husbands and female wives:

> Defer to one another out of reverence for Christ. Those of you who are in *committed relationships* should yield to each other as if to Christ, because you are inseparable from each other, just as Christ is inseparable from the body—the church—as well as being its Savior. And the church yields to Christ, so you should yield to your *partner* in everything.

Another passage at **1 Timothy 3.11** regards women in ministry. It can be rendered four different ways, and each rendering can support one of four possible positions: (1) *Inclusionary* and (2) *neutralized renderings* both lend support to egalitarian positions; (3) *exclusionary rendering* can support complementarian or hierarchical positions; and (4) *formal rendering* can support a non-position. Often, these renderings are softened or offset by footnotes that demonstrate cultural or political difficulties.

(1) Inclusionary Rendering	(2) Neutralized Rendering

Deaconesses, in the same way, must be sober-minded women, not slanderers, but in every way temperate and trustworthy. (Weymouth, *cf.* Montgomery)
GNB **footnote** (**fn**): *Their wives*, or *Woman helpers*; NASB **fn**: I.e. either *deacons' wives* or **deaconesses**; NIV **fn**: Possibly *deacons' wives* or *women who are deacons*; NRSV **fn**: Or *Their wives*, or *Women deacons*

Their spouses, similarly, should be serious, mature, temperate and entirely trustworthy. (*The Inclusive Bible*)

(4) Formal Rendering

Women[a] likewise must be serious, not slanderers, but temperate, faithful in all things. (*NT and Pss: An Inclusive Version*, NRSV)

In the same way, **the women** are to be worthy of respect, not malicious talkers but temperate and trustworthy in everything. (TNIV, *cf.* RSV, NASB, NKJV, NIV, NAB)
CSB **fn**: Or *The women*

(3) Exclusionary Rendering

Likewise also **their wives** must be dignified, not slanderous, temperate, faithful in every respect. (NET, *cf.* Moffatt, ESV, CSB, GNB)
NIV **fn**: Or *Wives likewise*, or *Women likewise*; NRSV **fn**: Or *Their wives*, or *Women deacons*

The Inclusive Bible utterly disregards gender distinctions in the election of church elders (**Titus 1.6**):

> As I instructed you, presbyters must be irreproachable, *married only once*, and the parents of children who are believers and are known not to be wild and insubordinate. (*Inclusive Bible*)

Though, it is interesting how it renders **1Ti 2.12, 15** with gender-specific language:

> I don't permit a woman to teach or to have authority over a man. She must remain silent. . . . But women will be saved through childbearing—provided they continue in faith, love and holiness, with propriety. (*Inclusive Bible*)

This is because the editors considered the text "sexist in meaning" and rendered it formally.

In the attempt to reshape the liturgical language of the church by forcing the Bible into their agenda, these translators have failed to uphold the clarity and distinctions of the biblical sources. Ambiguous, gender-neutral renderings, particularly those in *The Inclusive Bible*, can leave readers thinking that the Bible's original authors used gender language ambiguously where, in fact, they did not.

Theological Translation?

Since much of the biblical data is inherently theological, should we strive to produce a "theological translation"? That is, shouldn't we ensure that our Bibles are shaped and conformed to a particular creed, catechism, or system of theology?[42]

If our doctrines depend on the Bible, a "theological translation" would be a classic case of setting the cart before the horse. Much of systematic theology rests upon the inductive study of Scripture. A "theological translation," on the other hand, would permit some doctrinal system to clip, expand, or change the meaning of the biblical text. Rather, an unbiased, neutral translation is ideal for the systemic formation of theological opinions. In other words, we should let the Bible influence doctrine, not the other way around.

NEUTRALITY IN BIBLE TRANSLATION

Neutrality in translation is ideal, if we want the Bible to speak on its own terms with as little intrusion or interruption as possible. But is impartial translation even achievable when we are so ingrained with bias?

Absolute neutrality is impossible to attain, since no translator is omniscient and, therefore, none are perfectly objective. In addition, most Bible translators and editors have deep commitments to biblical doctrines for personal (devotional) or professional reasons (*e.g.*, pastoral counseling, preaching, education). A translator's commitments to external agenda (theological or political positions, professorships, church functions) are possible blocks to objective translation work.

If none are free from their own biases, values, and preferences, then isn't impartial Bible translation a hopeless cause?

How Translators Mitigate Against Bias

It may be impossible to remove biases from translators, but translators can remove their biases from their work through careful preparation and through the process of translation itself.

HISTORICAL AND CULTURAL CONTEXTS

An effective way to mitigate against blind assumption is to pursue data relevant to the passage under examination. Translators can build a cultural backdrop for their text through the study of ancient history and archæology. Archæological finds unveil ancient material cultures with discoveries that illustrate every-day life in biblical times. Work tools, clay lamps, jars, winepresses, mill stones, scrolls, even threshing sledges (cf. **Is 28.27; 41.15**) give us a clearer picture of what the biblical authors meant when they mentioned these things in their writings. Social ideals, personalities, and historic events are often depicted in art through objects, like coins, signet rings and bullæ,* mosaics, sculptures, and monuments. Ancient documents illustrate the politics that frame the biblical events or the pagan beliefs that competed for devotion. Literature recorded during the time of the Bible's composition reveal the written norms for genres and literary devices used in the Bible.[43] All these pieces, together, form a kind of mosaic that depicts the Bible's ancient setting with greater clarity than if translators relied on their imaginations alone.[44]

LINGUISTIC CONTEXT

To ensure that translators don't impose their own values on a biblical author's choice of words or phrasing, they pursue a linguistic, or descriptive, approach to the text. That is, they seek to describe the language of the Bible as it is, not as it should be. They look for patterns in the text, like repeated syntactical constructions and vocabulary use. Modern grammars offer translators statistical measures for these patterns, which gives them valuable tools for approximating the most probable meaning of any passage.

As demonstrated elsewhere, "normal" English changes over time. (See "Language Change" starting on page 81.) So, good translators are students of the time they live in. They are attuned to how modern assumptions and political debates frame the use of our target language. They don't merely find English words that fit the biblical source. They also avoid those which conjure up misleading (and, sometimes, embarrassing) associations.[45]

COLLABORATION

Many Bible translators work together to share their knowledge and experiences with one another. Collaboration helps them see blind spots and holds them accountable to the quality of their work. Most of the versions reviewed and assessed in this book result from the collaboration of scholars, who hold varying—sometimes even opposing—theological positions.[46] Collaboration within diverse translation committees not only distributes theological representation, it also allows different sets of assumptions to check individual or in-group (clique) biases.

Peer-review within translation subcommittees has been the standard for popular versions since the KJV. Some translation committees even open participation to the public. *The Twentieth Century New Testament,* one of the early "modern" English versions, was produced entirely by volunteers.[47] Its open membership drew from all classes of society, including teachers, homemakers, and businessmen. Even its scholarly editorship was entirely voluntary.

More recently, the *NET Bible* (NET) opened the translation process to whoever was able and willing to offer insight and skill. The editors of the NET accumulated a database of knowledge by eliciting recommendations online.

Bible publishers are typically open to suggestions and recommendations even after their versions are finally published. Outside comments are welcomed, and if they can be supported, suggested edits frequently find their way into later editions.

BUILDING ON THE WORK OF PREDECESSORS

Wise translators listen to the insights of those who have gone before them. They engage in a multigenerational conversation when they turn the pages of past journals, commentaries, and monographs.[48] The commentaries of veteran translators are full of precious bits of wisdom. In them, modern translators find approaches to the text that they might have missed. The trails blazed by former generations help later translators avoid their pitfalls and mistakes.

Today, translators and editors can sift through volumes upon volumes of relevant data spanning centuries and covering every conceivable topic of Scripture—all of which are available to them at an instant. Thanks to the wealth of information readily available on the internet and high-capacity storage, access to these materials is no longer prohibited to those who live near a seminary library or who hold academic credentials. It is now a matter of mining the data and finding the best material in a convenient amount of time.

TRANSPARENCY

A single Bible translation has its limits. Translators are often forced to choose one among several possible renderings per passage due to the physical limits imposed by necessary convenience: They can only record so much information in a single volume without a book growing unwieldy and awkward to handle.

To accommodate these limits, editors give readers the translators' options in abbreviated form: Footnotes record alternative renderings of various possibilities where a text is ambiguous. Or, they clarify in the margins where the original source is clear, but where the translation is less so. In sum, the main text gives us the translators' decisions; the footnotes in the margins give us their options.

For example, the translators of the KJV debated the significance of the Greek word *typoi* in **1Co 10.11**. One of the revisers wished to translate this word as "types" or "archtypes," which implied that the Israelites in this context were paradigmatic models of what was wicked in the world. The rest of the committee resisted this interpretation and insisted that the word be translated "[en]samples" instead. This implied that the Israelites were not necessarily sinners but merely a fallible folk whose example was worth avoiding. The translation reads

> Now all thefe things happened vnto them for ᵃ enfamples : and they are written for our admonition, vpon whom the ends of the world are come. (KJV 1611)

The marginal note for this verse reads "ᵃ Or, Types." The note allows for the possibility of both interpretations and hints at the debate behind the scenes.[49]

Ideally, translators publish the justifications for their decisions in their own commentaries for the benefit of peers, colleagues, experts, or general readers. Usually, they are unable to record every translation decision they make due to lack of time, space, and memory. Those that they do offer are invaluable for understanding the reasons behind some of the more significant renderings—those which clarify the passage's context or underlie significant theological opinions. These justifications are too many to record in a single book, and, therefore, they must span several volumes. A single translation cannot convey all the discourse, grammatical, syntactical, and lexical information for every word, phrase, passage, and *pericope*.* Neither can a single translation demonstrate the cultural context within a convenient number of pages. Even the NET with its 60,000-plus notes offers only a curated selection of the most relevant decisions and clarifications. Therefore a series of commentaries are necessary to fill out all the details and clarify the entire biblical text.

The Best Bible?

Finally, honest translators admit when they do not (or cannot) know something. They acknowledge the limits of our collective human knowledge. Formal translations do this best when the obscurities of the original shows through in their translation.

For example, the age of King Saul and the duration of his reign (**1Sa 13.1**) was somehow lost in transmission when the Hebrew MSS were copied. Some translators refuse to risk any guesses and so leave gaps in strict formal correspondence with their source:

> Saul was . . . years old when he began to reign; and he reigned . . . and two years over Israel. (RSV, NRSV, SO NWT)

Other editors dredge the early versions and conjecture what would have likely been the original:

> Saul was *forty* years old when he began to reign, and he reigned *thirty*-two years over Israel. (NASB 1977)

But many versions cannot agree over the exact date:

> Saul was *thirty* years old when he began to reign, and he reigned *forty* two years over Israel. (NASB 2020, SO NLT, NIV);

> Saul reigned one year . . . reigned two years (KJV, NKJV, SO ESV);

> Saul was [thirty] years old . . . he ruled over Israel for [forty] years. (NET);

> Saul was forty years old . . . he had reigned two years over Israel (ASV).

All said, it may well be impossible to certify the duration of Saul's reign in this context. Apparently, in passages like this one, God was content to give humanity sufficient revelation instead of exhaustive knowledge. Still, we may hope to further clarify whatever confusing or obscure passages remain in light of new discoveries or fresh evidence.

The Readers' Responsibility

Translators are not the only ones responsible for checking their biases. Readers—you and I—both have a role to play. The first line of defense that translators offer us against our own encroaching assumptions is found in the margins of most Bibles: Footnotes offer us an opportunity to glimpse into their editorial process and answer the questions we would not have known to ask.

But reader, beware! Some translators use their footnotes to give us one-sided arguments in favor of their preferred reading. This risk is higher among versions edited by a lone translator, whose only consultant and editor is himself. Hence the value in comparing multiple translations.

Here are a few things to look for when comparing a number of versions:

(A) *Similar renderings between multiple versions show a consensus among translators.* This is especially valuable when the translations we are comparing are produced by those with divergent theological positions (*e.g.*, when comparing the NIV produced by evangelicals to the NJB produced by mainline Roman Catholics; or the NASB by orthodox Protestants, with the NWT by Jehovah's Witnesses). Passages that are the same or similar reveal no known controversy surrounding that portion of the text. Or, if translators borrowed renderings from other versions, they deemed that such renderings require no emendation or repair.

(B) *Meaningful differences between versions produced by translators who share similar theological positions* usually indicate different methodological approaches (*e.g.*, formal* versus functional,* see "Translation Decisions" starting on page 63). If the differences are not immediately reconcilable, check the

The Best Bible?

footnotes: They may have struggled with textual problems (*e.g.,* single-use words called *hapax legomena,* differences in the manuscript sources, *etc.*). These account for the majority of meaningful differences between versions like the NKJV and MEV in places where they are compared to the NASB, NIV, and CSB, all of which were produced by conservative evangelicals and orthodox Protestants.

(c) *Meaningful differences between versions produced by translators who hold radically different theological positions* usually indicate methodological differences and textual variants, but they can also highlight the passages on which hinge significant differences of theological opinion. These differences may reveal the intrusion of doctrinal bias and hermeneutical agenda.[50]

☜

ENDNOTES FOR THEOLOGICAL DECISIONS

1 A translator's denominational or academic association may suggest a particular bias, but that is inconclusive by itself.

2 *Cf.* **Jas 2.22**, "You see that faith was active along with his works, and faith was completed by his works" (ESV).

3 Even Scripture warns us that the "one who states his case first seems right, until the other comes and examines him" (**Pr 18.17**, ESV).

4 Authorial intent is hard to gauge with absolute certainty, since the apostles and prophets who composed Scripture are no longer available to consult with. Sometimes the purpose of a text is explicit (*cf.* **Jn 20.31; 1 Co 5.11; 2Pt 3.1**), or it can be inferred from its context. This discussion is important and complex and best belongs in its own volume on *hermeneutics**—the science and application of interpretive principles for clarifying meaning.

5 By no means ought translators to ignore figures of speech. Figures of speech follow patterns of use that identify them as figures.

6 Christian émigré from Scotland and minister of church reform, Alexander Campbell, founded Bethany College (now Bethany, West Virginia). The Stone-Campbell Movement (led by Thomas Cambell, Alexander Campbel [Thomas' father], and Barton W. Stone) eventually gave rise to the various congregational Christian Churches or Churches of Christ that sprung out of America's Second Great Awakening (c. 1790 – 1840).

7 Baptist clergy were annoyed with Campbell's rejection of all formal creeds and denominational distinctions.

8 Roland H. Worth, Jr., *Bible Translations: A History Through Source Documents* (Jefferson, NC: McFarland & Company, Inc., 1992), pp. 154–5.

9 Frederick W. Danker, ed., Walter Bauer, William F. Arndt, and F. Wilbur Gingrich, *A Greek English Lexicon of the New Testament and Other Early Christian Literature*, 3rd ed. (Chicago, IL: The University of Chicago Press, 2000), pp. 164–5.

   H. G. Liddell, R. Scott, Sir H. S. Jones, R. McKenzie, eds., *A Greek-English Lexicon with a Revised Supplement* (Oxford: Clarendon Press, 1940, '96), pp. 305–6; Supplement, p. 66.

   Johannes P. Louw and Eugene A. Nida, *Greek-English Lexicon of the New Testament Based on Semantic Domains*, 2nd ed., 2 vols. (New York: United Bible Societies, 1989), pp. 536, 537–8, 539.

Johan Lust, Erik Eynikel, and Katrin Hauspie, *Greek-English Lexicon of the Septuagint*, rev. ed. (Stuttgart: Deutsche Bibelgesellschaft, 2003), p. 102.

J. H. Moulton and G. Milligan, *Vocabulary of the Greek New Testament* (London: Hodder & Stoughton, 1930), p. 102.

10 *The Didachē*, 7.3 (*ca.* 2nd c. AD) in *The Apostolic Fathers: Greek Texts and English Translations*, ed. by Michael W. Holmes, 3rd ed. (Grand Rapids, MI: Baker Academic, 2007), p. 355.

11 Trinitarian Bible Society (TBS), "The Constitution of the Society" (1992), accessed December 12, 2019, https://www.tbsbibles.org/page/SocietyConstitution.

12 More specifically, the TBS identifies the Second Rabbinic Bible published by Daniel Bomberg (Venice, 1524–25) and F. H. A. Scrivener's *Textus Receptus* (1894) as ideal texts. Scrivener reconstructed his edition based on the editorial decisions of the KJV.

D. P. Rowland, "Statement of Doctrine of Holy Scripture," on the TBS's website, accessed April 24, 2015, https://www.tbsbibles.org/page/DoctrineofScripture (*emphasis added*).

13 Alfred W. Pollard, *Records of the English Bible* (London: Oxford University Press, 1911), p. 53.

14 More examples of the NT's use of the OT in *typological* fulfilment: **Mt 2.15; 2.17; 4.14; 5.17; Jn 13.18; 15.25; 18.19; 19.24; Col 2.17; Heb 10.1**, *etc.*

15 Similar passages include **Lk 2.25; 11.13; Jn 20.22; Ac 8.15, 17–19; 10.38; 19.2**.

16 The *New World Translation's* footnote at **Mt 1.18** exposes the Watchtower Bible and Tract Society's doctrinal bias. The verse reads, "[Mary] was found to be pregnant by holy spirit* before they were united," which the footnote identifies "* Or 'active force.'"

17 Comfort demonstrates how early Christian scribes identified each occurrence of the [Holy] Spirit in **Ac 8.15–19** as referring to divinity by how they recorded them as *nomena sacra**—abbreviations of theologically significant proper nouns, like God (Gk. $\overline{\Theta\Sigma}$, $\overline{\Theta Y}$, *etc.*), Father ($\overline{\Pi\Sigma}$, $\overline{\Pi HP}$, *etc.*), Son ($\overline{Y\Sigma}$, $\overline{YY}$, *etc.*), Jesus ($\overline{I\Sigma}$, $\overline{IY}$, *etc.*), Christ ($\overline{X\Sigma}$, $\overline{XY}$, *etc.*), Spirit ($\overline{\Pi NA}$, $\overline{\Pi NI}$, *etc.*), Lord ($\overline{K\Sigma}$, $\overline{KY}$, *etc.*), and others. Each occurrence of Spirit is abbreviated as a *nomen sacrum** in Papyri 46 (*ca.* AD 200) and 74 (7th century AD) and Codices Sinaiticus (4th cent. AD) and Bezæ (5th cent. AD).

Philip W. Comfort, *A Commentary on the Manuscripts and Text of the New Testament.* (Grand Rapids, MI: Kregel Publications, 2015).

[18] Quote taken and modified from the *Oxford English Dictionary*.

[19] Martin Luther, "On Translating: An Open Letter" (1530), *The Interpretation of Scripture*, vol. 6 in *The Annotated Luther*, ed. Euen K. Cameron (Minneapolis, MN: Fortress Press, 2017), pp. 29–30.

[20] Luther's 1545 Bible reads, "So halten wir es nu / Das der Menſch gerecht werde / on des Geſetzes werck / *alleine durch den Glauben*." (**Ro 3.28**, so also the Zurich Bible, *emphasis added*.) By contrast, Johannes Piscator's version (1602–4) reads, "So ſchlieſſen wir nun, daß der menſch gerechtgeſprochen werde *durch den glauben*, ohne deß geſätzes werck." (From Hortinus' edition of 1736, so also the later Schlachter version of 1951.) It's possible that Piscator omitted Luther's *allein* for theological reasons. In his public discourse, Luther adamantly taught the bondage of man's will, while Piscator had converted to a Arminian view of free-will and obligation. Piscator, therefore, may not have wished to exclude obedience as a necessary component for righteousness.

[21] W. Hall Harris, III, "Introduction to the First Edition," *The NET Bible: New English Translation*, 1st ed. (Richardson, TX: Biblical Studies Press, LLC, 2005), pp. 21*–22*.

[22] Certain traditions claim that some of God's judgments and decisions were passed down orally and weren't written down until generations later. The *Mishna* (or "Oral Torah") is an example of text, that tradition claims, records original revelation given alongside the books, which Moses wrote. It was supposedly preserved and transmitted by word of mouth until it was finally written down sometime in the 2nd or 3rd c. AD. It is considered canonical in Hasidic Judaism.

[23] Some folks take the opportunity offered by a title without a body to invent a missing text. For example, Jacob Ilive, a maker of type-faces, forged a purported translation of the Book of Jasher, which he published in 1751.

The letter to the Laodiceans is no longer extant in Greek, though a Latin text going by that name (*Epistola ad Laodicenses*) exists. This text was rejected by Jerome, and no such letter can be found among the lists of Scripture of the early church fathers. It's probably a short compilation of familiar Pauline sayings gathered from his other canonical letters.

[24] *Sensus plenior* and *polysemy* (having multiple meanings or senses) are distinct things. The first deals with a passage's authorial intent. The second with a word's usage.

25 Watch Tower Bible and Tract Society of Pennsylvania, "A5: The Divine Name in the Christian Greek Scriptures," in *New World Translation of the Holy Scriptures* (Wallkill, NY: Watchtower Bible Tract Society of N.Y., Inc., 2013), pp. 1736–41.

26 For example, the NWT translates κύριος (*kyrios*) at **Ro 14.11** with "Jehovah," while it translates the same word in that passage's verbal parallel (**Php 2.10–11**) with the familiar word "Lord." Without MS evidence, translations of supposed original Tetragrammata are speculative editorial decisions without any basis in fact.

27 James Barr, *The Semantics of Biblical Language* (London: Oxford University Press, 1961), pp. 218, 222.

28 Daniel B. Wallace, *Greek Grammar Beyond the Basics* (Grand Rapids, MI: Zondervan, 1996), pp. 267–70.

29 *NET Bible*. First Edition. footnote 3 (**tn** = translator's note).

30 Out of the 282 places in the New Testament where "God" has no article, in only sixteen places the NWT renders either "a god", "god", "gods", or "godly". The translators neglected their stated principle 94 percent of the time!
Wallace, *Greek Grammar, Ibid.*

31 The Watchtower Bible and Tract Society further argued that "Someone who is 'with' another person cannot be the same as that other person." (*Should You Believe in the Trinity?* New York: 1989. p. 27) Unfortunately, the Society failed to consider that not all predicate nominative constructions deal with convertible identity. That is, linking verbs ("is" or "was") do not always functions like equal signs (=). As in this case, it can function in a subordinate sense. For another example, **1Jn 4.8, 16**, reads, "God is love," which excludes the idea that "love is God." So also, "the Word" can be "God" (in essence), but "God" cannot be "the Word" (in total), as indicated by **John 1.14**.

32 For example, "The Gideons will not distribute a Bible that doesn't have 'only begotten Son.' Most Gideon Bibles are either KJV or NKJV. Zondervan did allow an edition of their Bible to be altered to appease the Gideon's objections. So there's actually a **John 3:16** Gideon Bible in NIV."
Will Lee, "Interview with Dr. Ed Blum, General Editor for the HCSB," *Anwoth*, last modified December 7, 2007, accessed September 4, 2011, http://www

.anwoth.org/2007/12/19/interview-with-dr-ed-blum-general-editor -for-the-hcsb/.

33 A more appropriate Latin word would be *unicum* instead of *unigenitum*. It's possible that the Latin translation was either based on a scribal error in some Greek exemplar, which slipped in an extra letter "ν" *nu* (μονογεννή *monogennē* instead of μονογενή *monogenē*), or it was made to conform to St. Augustine's African form of the Apostles' Creed: *Credo . . . in Iesum Christum, Filium eius* **unigenitum**, *Dominum nostrum* "I believe . . . in Jesus Christ, his **only-begotten** Son, our Lord."

34 Further support for rendering *monogenē* as "unique" stems from the theological idea at **Hebrews 2.10** (and **Gal 4.6**), that God has many sons (redeemed and "adopted" humans through Christ), but that Jesus Christ remains his unique, one-of-a-kind Son.

35 Granville Sharp, *Remarks on the Uses of the Uses of the Definitive Article in the Greek New Testament . . .* 3rd ed. (London: Vernor and Hood, et al., 1803), p. 3.

36 Daniel B. Wallace, *The Article with Multiple Substantives Connected by* kai *in the New Testament: Semantics and Significance* (Ph.D. diss., Dallas Theological Seminary, 1995), pp. 134–5.

37 Martin Luther rejected the notion of transubstantiation with its obscure filter of Greek philosophic thought necessary to understand the bread and wine as material forms to express a corporeal ideal of Christ's body and blood.

38 Victor R. Gold, et al., eds., *The New Testament and Psalms: An Inclusive Version* (Oxford: Oxford University Press, 1995). Dust-jacket cover.

39 Priests for Equality, *The Inclusive Bible: The First Egalitarian Edition* (Plymouth, United Kingdom: Rowman & Littlefield Publishers, Inc., 2007).

40 Joanna Dewey, "The Inclusive Bible: The First Egalitarian Translation. A Sheed and Ward Book," *Anglican and Episcopal History*, vol. 80, no. 4 (December 2011), pp. 436–8.

41 Craig Blomberg and Jennifer Foutz Markley, *A Handbook of New Testament Exegesis* (Grand Rapids, MI: Baker, 2010).

42 In a way, we've already started to shape Bibles into theological molds when we affirm which texts belong in our biblical canon.*

43 Among works that are contemporary with events in the Bible are the Gilgamesh epic (*c.* 22nd – 20th centuries BC), the Ugarit library (*c.* 13th and 12th centuries BC), Hammurabi's law code, classical Greek and Latin authors, and

even monumental propaganda inscribed by the Old World's ancient empires (Egypt, Babylon, Persia, Greece, Rome, *et al.*), among other ancient sources.

[44] Several published collections of translated primary sources are available which shed light on the Bible's historical and cultural context:

William W. Hallo and K. Lawson Younger, eds., *The Context of Scripture*, 3 vols (Leiden, The Netherlands: Koninklijke Brill NV, 2003);

James B. Pritchard, ed., *Ancient Near Eastern Texts Relating to the Old Testament*, 3rd ed. with supplement (Princeton, NJ: Princeton University Press, 1969).

[45] For example, we cannot read **James 2.3** in the KJV aloud without issuing some cautious clarification: "[Y]e have respect for him that weareth *the gay clothing* . . ." (KJV, so Wycliffe, Tyndale, Coverdale, Bishops', *etc.; emphasis added.*)

[46] J. J. M. Roberts knows the rewards of working with five other scholars on the NRSV. The insights that his subcommittee shared about the meaning of Isaiah were invaluable. But he also knows the frustration of prejudiced people in heated debate.

In one meeting, Roberts, who was responsibile for that day's agenda, recommended an emendation to the traditional Hebrew text at **Isaiah 9.3**. His suggestions fit the context better and had the support of a few Hebrew MSS, the Targums, and the Syriac version. He was able to demonstrate how the traditional text was likely corrupted in this verse during its transmission. Roberts expected that his recommendation would be welcomed as an obvious improvement, so he was surprised when another member in the group objected to the change "as an unwarranted emendation of the Masoretic Text." Debate ensued, which lasted for quite some time. During the arguments (some of which turned nasty), this member admitted to Roberts that his suggestion was probably what Isaiah wrote, but he could not allow for any change to the traditional text if any tolerable sense could be wrenched from it. As the debate burned hotter, another member threatened to resign from the NRSV committee if the group caved to "Masoretic fundamentalism," as he called it. Finally, the chair suggested a coffee break to let arguments simmer down. The grouped rejoined later with cooler heads. Not wishing to provoke further conflict, a vote was called, and a small majority rejected Roberts' proposal.

After a disappointing round, Roberts introduced the next proposal on his agenda, one that he thought should undergo serious debate. But, by this time, the group had lost all will to fight. Roberts remembers, "As a consolation for accepting defeat on the previous proposal, the group simply gave me the follow-ing proposal without discussion." Roberts' story is a reminder that even Bible translation committees can succumb to all the human passions and problems of any political arena.

J. J. M. Roberts, "An Evaluation of the NRSV: Demystifying Bible Translation," *Insights: A Journal of the Faculty of Austin Seminary*, vol. 108, no. 2 (Spring 1993): pp. 25–36.

[47] *The Twentieth Century New Testament: A Translation into Modern English*, rev. ed. (London: Horace Marshall & Son, 1904).

[48] For example, when Martin Luther produced his Old Testament (1534 AD), he relied on the earlier French commentator, Nicholas de Lyra (1270 – 1349), who, in turn, depended on the Jewish Rabbi Solomon ben Isaac (a.k.a. Rashi, *fl.* late 11th c. AD). Even older volumes of the *International Critical Commentary* hold valuable technical information that will only go out of date when English itself does.

[49] Adam Nicolson, *God's Secretaries: The Making of the King James Bible* (New York: HarperCollins, 2003), pp. 212–3.

[50] For example, compare the RSV (1952) with its Roman Catholic variant (the RSV-CE, or Catholic edition, published 1966). In the RSV, **Mt 12.46** reads, "While [Jesus] was still speaking to the people, behold, his mother and *his brothers* stood outside, asking to speak to him" (*emphasis added*). The RSV-CE reads, "his mother and *his brethren* stood outside," instead. The change from "brothers" to "brethren" likely reflects the Catholic belief that Jesus was Mary's only son, since Catholic dogma professes that Mary is a perpetual virgin, having never conceived children after Jesus' birth.

Typesetting Decisions

Punctuation and white space are easy to overlook in Bible translations, but they, too, play an important role when reading Scripture. Most of our earliest manuscripts do not demarcate words, sentences, and paragraphs. They have no periods, commas, parentheses, or quotation marks. Indentation was limited; letters were the same height; no distinction was made between upper- and lower-case. They had no chapter or verse numbers. Yet, ancient readers were familiar enough with their own languages to make sense of what they read without these additional helps. Punctuation was added later for the benefit those unfamiliar with the original languages and texts.

In the Geneva Bible, supplied words are set in *italics*. Note "for" and "me" in **Ps 5.3**.

To him that excelleth vpon "Nehiloth. A Pſalme of Dauid.

1 HEare my wordes, ô Lord: vnderſtand my ᵃ meditation.
2 Hearken vnto the voice of my crye, my King & my God: for vnto thee do I praie.
3 Heare my voice in the morning, ô Lord: for in the morning will I direct me vnto thee, and I wil ᵇ wait.
4 For thou art not a God that loueth ᶜ wickednes: nether ſhal euil dwel with thee.

SUPPLIED WORDS

Greek and Hebrew do not require all the same words that English does in order to make sense of a passage. Translators need to supply these words in order to clarify the sense or make the passage read smoothly in English. Often, they are the little words, like the linking verbs ("is", "be", or "are"), or the definite and indefinite articles ("the", "a", or "an"), and other helping words.

The Geneva NT (1557) was the first English version to distinguish words not found in the original text by setting them in a different type.[1] In the King James version (1611 edition), the words that correspond to the Greek and Hebrew are set in black letter,* while the supplied words are differentiated

In the KJV, supplied words are in Roman font. Note "*my prayer*" and "*up*" in **Ps 5.3**.

2 Hearken vnto the voice of my crie, my King, and my God: for vnto thee will I pray.
3 * My voyce ſhalt thou heare in the morning, O LORD; in the morning will I direct my prayer vnto thee, and will looke vp.

* Pſal 1 30 6.

1 Give ear to my words, O LORD,
Consider my meditation.
2 Give heed to the voice of my cry,
My King and my God,
For to You I will pray.
3 My voice You shall hear in the morning,
O LORD;
In the morning I will direct *it* to You,
And I will look up.
4 For You *are* not a God who takes pleasure
in wickedness,
Nor shall evil dwell with You.
5 The boastful shall not stand in Your sight;

In the NKJV,
supplied words
are *italicized*.
Note "*it*" in **Ps
5.3** and "*are*"
in verse **4**.

with Roman type. In later editions, the main text is set in Roman, while the supplied words are set in *Italic*. Still other translations place them inside square brackets [ ].

For example, in **1 Jn 3.17**, the KJV revisers clearly reveal what words they added to clarify a Greek idiom,

But whoso hath this world's good, and seeth his brother have need, and shutteth up his bowels *of compassion* from him, how dwelleth the love of God in him? (KJV)

The KJV added the words "of compassion" to make sense of a Greek expression, "shutting up his bowels," which here describes one person's disregard for another.

A special case in the KJV deserves attention: The entire second half of **1 Jn 2.23** was supplied by the Kings's revisers,

Whosoever denieth the Son, the same hath not the Father: (*but*) *he that acknowledgeth the Son hath the Father also*."

The conjunction in parentheses (*but*) was added to indicate the contrast between the first and second halves, but the rest of the supplied words indicate where there was a difference between the manuscripts that the revisers used: Some manuscripts had the second half of the verse and the others did not.[2]

Sometimes readers place undue attention on the supplied words thinking that the change in type indicates emphasis or that it requires some other mysterious interpretation. Modern Bibles (except the NKJV and the NASB) have largely done away with the practice of setting supplied words in a different type. Their uniform font does not reveal translation methods as clearly, but it improves the reading experience by removing distractions.

The Best Bible?

PUNCTUATION

We depend on certain typographical marks to identify the natural pauses that group words into unique and coherent thoughts. Periods, commas, quotation, exclamation, and question marks are all foreign to the Bible's earliest texts. They have been added to help modern readers. For the most part they really help, but now and again, they hide certain editorial choices that impose on the meaning of the text.

Periods

Even a mark as small as a period or a comma can spark real controversy. At **Romans 9.4, 5**, the RSV places a period between one significant proper noun ("Christ") and what many consider its appositive* ("God"). Many believe that the two words are paired to reveal their shared identity, but the editors of the RSV decided to split them into two separate sentences. The NIV uses a comma instead and reorders the words to make the apposition clear. The NRSV uses awkward punctuation, which reflects a compromise position:

RSV (cf. NWT)	NIV (cf. NKJV)	NRSV
They are Israelites . . . to them belong the patriarchs, and of their race, according to the flesh, is the Christ. God who is over all be blessed for ever. Amen.	[T]he people of Israel . . . [t]heirs are the patriarchs, and from them is traced the human ancestry of Christ, who is God over all, forever praised! Amen.	They are Israelites . . . to them belong the patriarchs, and from them, according to the flesh, comes the Messiah, who is over all, God blessed forever. Amen.

Sometimes editors make a decision where there is no one best option or where there is no explicit precedent. For example, it takes two translations to reflect an ambiguity at **John 1.3b–4**. Carefully note where each version has placed its period:

RSV	NRSV
without [the Word] was not anything made that was made. In him was life, and the life was the light of men.	without [the Word] not one thing came in to being. What has come into being in him was life, and the life was the light of all people.

The textual basis for each rendering is exactly the same. The only difference is where the editors decided to place a natural break. To demonstrate, here is the transliterated Greek source of each version, with a vertical line (|) indicating each editorial decision:

RSV's Greek source	NRSV's Greek source
*chōris [tou logou] egeneto oude hen ho gegonen	en autō zōē ēn kai hē zōē ēn to phōs tōn anthrōpōn*	*chōris [tou logou] egeneto oude hen	ho gegonen en autō zōē ēn kai hē zōē ēn to phōs tōn anthrōpōn*

In this case, both renderings are good ones. Both are accurate. Both nuance the meaning in subtly different ways. And both reflect a tolerable difference between two possible opinions.

Commas

Commas group related words together into smaller, bite-sized phrases. They also work well for delineating items into lists. Try reading the genealogies of **1 Chronicles 1 – 9** without commas and see how clear it is to identify each person:

> The sons of Ezrah: Jether Mered Epher and Jalon. These are the sons of Bithiah daughter of Pharaoh whom Mered married; and she conceived and bore Miriam Shammai and Ishbah father of Eshtemoa. (**1Ch 4.17** NRSV, *punctuation removed*)

Commas should remove ambiguity and confusion:

> The sons of Ezrah: Jether, Mered, Epher, and Jalon. These are the sons of Bithiah, daughter of Pharaoh, whom Mered married; and she conceived and bore Miriam, Shammai, and Ishbah father of Eshtemoa. (**1Ch 4.17** NRSV, *punctuation restored*)

The Best Bible?

Though they are immensely helpful in organizing biblical thoughts, even the subtle placement of a single comma can alter the Bible's meaning in a significant way. An early translation renders **Hebrews 10.12,**

> this man after he had offered *one sacrifice for sins*, *sits for ever* at the right hand of God. (Geneva, *emphasis added, cf.* Bishops', Douay)

This comma placement puts the duration's focus on Christ's current session (". . . , sits forever").[3] The KJV renders the same verse with a shifted comma and focuses the duration on the effect of Christ's sacrifice ("sacrifice . . . forever, . . ."):

> But this man, after he had offered *one sacrifice for sins for ever*, *sat down* on the right hand of God. (KJV)[4]

One misplaced comma has even influenced the way we sing Scripture: Handel based his famous oratorio, *Messiah*, on **Isaiah 9.6** as recorded in the KJV,

> For unto us a child is born, unto us a son is given: and the government shall be upon his shoulder: and his name shall be called Wonderful, Counsellor, The mighty God, The everlasting Father, The Prince of Peace. (KJV)

The KJV lists five titles, but in Hebrew there are only four pairs. Since the adjective "Wonderful" modifies the noun "Counsellor," the comma between them should be omitted, as most modern translations do (*cf.* NKJV, RSV, NASB, NET, NIV, *et al.*).[5]

Quotation marks

Thanks to the use of quotation marks, editors help us demarcate dialogue at a glance. They are particularly helpful when marking complex dialogue, as where the NIV renders **Isaiah 7.3–9,**

Then the Lord said to Isaiah, "Go out, you and your son Shear-Jashub, to meet Ahaz at the end of the aqueduct of the Upper Pool, on the road to the Washerman's Field. Say to him, 'Be careful, keep calm and don't be afraid. Do not lose heart because of these two smoldering stubs of firewood—because of the fierce anger of Rezin and Aram and of the son of Remaliah. Aram, Ephraim and Remaliah's son have plotted your ruin, saying, "Let us invade Judah; let us tear it apart and divide it among ourselves, and make the son of Tabeel king over it." Yet this is what the Sovereign Lord says:

"'It will not take place,
    it will not happen,
for the head of Aram is Damascus,
    and the head of Damascus is only Rezin.
Within sixty-five years
    Ephraim will be too shattered to be a people.
The head of Ephraim is Samaria,
    and the head of Samaria is only Remaliah's son.
If you do not stand firm in your faith,
    you will not stand at all.'" (**Isaiah 7.3–9**, NIV)

The NASB embeds these quotes somewhat differently. A summary of the two patterns of quotations looks something like this:

Is 7.3–9 *New International Version*	Is 7.3–9 *New American Standard Bible*	
Then the Lord said to Isaiah,	Then the Lord said to Isaiah	*verse* **3**
"Go out, you and your son . . .	"Go out now to meet Ahaz . . .	
'Be careful, keep calm . . .	'Take care and be calm . . .	**4**
"Let us invade Judah . . ."	"Let us go up against Judah . . ."	**6**
"Yet this is what . . .	'thus says the Lord GOD . . .	**7**
'It will not take place . . .'"	"It shall not stand. . ."'"	

The two schemes differ slightly so as to suggest different addressees. In the NIV, God addresses verses **7–9** to the prophet Isaiah as an aside (so RSV). But the editors of the NASB seem to think that the verses are addressed to King Ahaz as an addendum (so NET, NKJV).

On occasion, translations disagree where to delineate between the narration and the dialogue. One good example surrounds John 3.16: A few translations conclude Jesus's answer to Nicodemus with closing quotation marks after verse 15,

> " . . . whoever believes in him may have eternal life." (RSV, so NIV, NAB, TNIV, NET)

But several others continue Jesus' speech until the end of verse 21,

> " . . . he who does the truth comes to the light, that his deeds may be clearly seen, that they have been done in God" (NKJV, so NRSV, JB, NJB, NASB, NIrV, ESV, NLT, CSB, *et al.*).[6]

This reveals that modern scholars are still not sure to what extent Jesus spoke with Nicodemus that night. Most translations prior to the *American Standard Version* (1901), including the KJV, ignored this issue since they all forgo the use of quotation marks (which were never part of their Greek sources anyway).

Exclamation marks

Exclamation marks indicate emphasis and the expressiveness in a person's tone. Their presence affirms the excitement in someone's voice or the grave urgency in another's plea. Since we are separated from the original audience by a distance of millennia, we can only imagine the authors' faces when they spoke or wrote. Just as it is hard to decipher genuineness or sarcasm in plain text messages, so it can be difficult to know the intended emotional impact of ancient biblical expressions. Translators require detailed knowledge of idioms, figures of speech, contexts, writing genres, and styles before they can presume to know the emotional intent of a text.

Early English translations used exclamation marks only sparingly. The Geneva Bible has printed only 84 marks. The 1611 KJV has even fewer—53. The Blaney revision of the KJV (1769) added 297 more. As time progressed, translators and editors grew more accustomed to using these marks. The number of exclamation marks used in the Protestant edition of the RSV (1971) jumped to 1,669. Modern Bibles based on functional principles use many more—the NLT uses 4,248 and the NET, 5,343.[7]

PARAGRAPHS AND INDENTS

Paragraph indents group together those thoughts which share the same theme. They also mark breaks within larger arguments. They help reader's eyes from getting lost in a sea of text. Special indentation also alerts readers to the genre* they're reading. For example, the indented passages at **Genesis 2.23** and **1 Chronicles 16.7–36** show us at a glance the poetry surrounded by narrative—something we might have missed without special formatting:

> "This is now bone of my bones
>> and flesh of my flesh;
> she shall be called 'woman,'
>> for she was taken out of man." (**Gn 2.23** NIV)

Then on that day David first appointed the singing of praises to the LORD by Asaph and his kindred.

> O give thanks to the LORD, call on his name,
>> make known his deeds among the peoples.
>> . . .
> Blessed be the LORD, the God of Israel,
>> from everlasting to everlasting."

Then all the people said "Amen!" and praised the LORD. (**1Ch 16.7, 36** NRSV)

The Best Bible?

The KJV (1611) placed each verse on a new line, but this makes it difficult to identify paragraphs. To accommodate, the typesetters set pilcrows* (¶) to mark each paragraph break.[8] The NASB (1977 edition) and the original NKJV marked paragraphs by setting their first verse reference in bold type. For example, the embolded verse numbers (**23, 25,** and **26**) start new paragraphs:

19 Do not quench the Spirit;

20 do not despise prophetic utterances.

21 But examine everything *carefully*; hold fast to that which is good;

22 abstain from every form of evil.

23 Now may the God of peace Himself sanctify you entirely; and may your spirit and soul and body be preserved complete, without blame at the coming of our Lord Jesus Christ.

24 Faithful is He who calls you, and He also will bring it to pass.

25 Brethren, pray for us.

26 Greet all the brethren with a holy kiss.

27 I adjure you by the Lord to have this letter read to all the brethren.

28 The grace of our Lord Jesus Christ be with you.

(**1Th 5** NASB 1977)

Paragraph breaks are editorial decisions nowhere found in the earliest manuscripts. Paragraph indents can and do differ from one translation to the next. For example, some translations include **Galatians 5.1** with the previous paragraph. This makes an encouraging summary to resist spiritual coercion in light of the believers' position in Christ and identity in God's promise:

[4.31] . . . So then, friends, we are children, not of the slave but of the free woman. [5.1] For freedom Christ has set us free. Stand firm, therefore, and do not submit again to a yoke of slavery. (NRSV, so CEB)

Other translations place the verse at the start the following paragraph, at the beginning of Paul's urging to reject circumcision:

> ⁵·¹ For freedom, Christ set us free. Stand firm then and don't submit again to a yoke of slavery. ⁵·² Take note! I, Paul, am telling you that if you get yourselves circumcised, Christ will not benefit you at all. . . . (CSB, so ISV, NET)

Most versions make it stand alone as it's own paragraph (NIV, NLT, ESV, CEV, GNB, MEV, MSG, NAB, NASB, *et al.*):

> It was for freedom that Christ set us free; therefore keep standing firm and do not be subject again to a yoke of slavery. (**Gal 5.1** NASB)

CHAPTERS AND VERSES

The Bible contains a lot of text. So much so that it is rather like a library of books bound into a single volume. Many passages in these books allude to other sections throughout Scripture. New Testament writers and speakers often quote from earlier passages found in the Old Testament. Some of the Bible's history and stories are repeated in different books with nuanced variations. That's why students, scribes, and editors have overlaid the text of the Bible with reference systems to help them quickly locate passages and correlate portions of Scripture with each other.

One of the earliest reference systems, from the fourth century, was adapted to find similar passages in each of the four Gospels. This system, called the Eusebian Canons,* was the standard reference for many Greek manuscripts up until the 16th century.

In the 13th century, Scripture was arranged into numbered chapters* by Archbishop Stephen Langton while he taught in Paris. 300 years later, the Parisian printer, Robert Stephanus, segmented these chapters into shorter verses* for an edition of his Greek New Testament (1550).⁹ This chapter-and-verse system

The Best Bible?

made study so efficient and useful for biblical references (like concordances and topical indices) that it has remained virtually unchanged to this day. It is printed in the vast majority of modern Bibles as the primary reference system.

As useful as they are, chapter and verse numbers don't always correspond with the content they reference. Sometimes they break the logic of a paragraph or a sentence. For example, Paul, in instructs the church at Philippi in his letter,

> Therefore, my beloved, as you have always obeyed, so now, not only as in my presence but much more in my absence, work out your own salvation with fear and trembling, (**Php 2.12** esv)

This isolated sentence may leave readers in despair when they realize their own natural limits. Fortunately, it is not complete—the following verse concludes the thought:

> for it is God who works in you, both to will and to work for his good pleasure. (**Php 3.13** esv)

Another unfortunate break occurs in Paul's letter to the **Colossians** between chapters **2** and **3**. Chapter **3**, verse **1**, starts,

> If then you have been raised with Christ, seek the things that are above, where Christ is, seated at the right hand of God. (rsv)

It's not a bad way to start a passage, but the actual section begins earlier, in Chapter **2**, verse **20**, which reveals the contrast in related subject material,

> If you have died with Christ to the elementary principles of the world, why, as if you were living in the world, do you submit

yourself to decrees, such as, "Do not handle, do not taste, do not touch! . . . " (**2.20–21ff**, NASB)

Anyone who wishes to study a passage with any care must consider its surrounding context. There is nothing particularly sacred about a chapter reference or a verse number. They remain helpful so long as we use them in the way they were intended—as convenient references for finding our place in Scripture.

CITING THE BIBLE: CHAPTER AND VERSE. The system for citing specific portions (or passages) of the Bible is a fairly simple one to learn and use. The name of the biblical **book** is always written first (*e.g.* **John**, **1 Samuel**, or **2 Peter**), followed by the number for the **chapter**, and then a number for a **verse** within that chapter.

In the standard American system, a **colon** (:) is placed between the chapter and verse numbers. (The British system uses a period [.] instead.) **Commas** (,) are written between verse numbers in the same chapter, or just between chapter numbers when verses are unlisted. A **semicolon** (;) is placed between verses from different chapters. A **dash** (–) is placed between verses to specify a range within a single chapter, or between chapter numbers for a range of chapters where verses are not specified. (For examples, see the table on the following page.)

To save space, most book names are shortened to some standard abbreviation (*e.g.* **John** = **Jn**; **1 Samuel** = **1Sa**; **2 Peter** = **2Pe**). Bibles and biblical references usually include a table of book names and their abbreviations in the prefatory matter near the beginning of the volume. Abbreviations are frequently used in footnotes and marginal cross-references.

Chapter and verse numbers in the English OT do not always correspond to those in the Latin Bible, the Greek Septuagint (LXX), or the Hebrew *Tanakh*. For example, **Psalm 68** in English begins with a prefatory **title** ("To the Chief Musician. A Psalm of David. A Song.") before starting verse **1** ("Let God arise, Let His enemies be scattered . . ."). In the LXX, **Ps 68.1** *is* the title and the actual psalm starts at verse **2**. Elsewhere, **Daniel 4.1–3** in the English Bible corresponds to **Dn 3.31–38** in the Hebrew; English **Jeremiah 9.1** to Hebrew **Jer 8.23**. *&c.* ◄

The Best Bible?

Description of citation	Reference	Biblical passage
Citing a single chapter	John 3	The Gospel according to John, chapter 3
two chapters (chs.) only	Jn 3, 18	John, chapters 3 *and* 18
a range of sixteen chs.	Jn 3 – 18	John, chs. 3 *through* 18
a single verse (vs.)	Jn 3:18	John, ch. 3, verse 18
the second part of vs. 18	Jn 3:18b	John, ch. 3, only the second part of vs. 18
two separate vss. in the same ch.	Jn 3:1, 18	John, ch. 3, vss. 1 *and* 18 only
a range of vss. within a ch.	Jn 3:1–18	John, ch. 3, the passage *from* vs. 1 *thru to* vs. 18
a range of vss. and a separate vs. within a ch.	Jn 3:1–18, 36	John, ch. 3, *from* vs. 1 *to* vs. 18, *and* vs. 36
two vss. in two separate chs.	Jn 3:1; 18:36	John, only the two vss. 3:1 *and* 18:36
a range from one vs. in one ch. to another vs. in another ch.	Jn 3:1 – 18:36	John, the entire section *from* 3:1 *to* 18:36
two ranges of vss. in two separate chs.	Jn 3:1–18; 18:3–6	John, the two *passages* 3:1-18 *and* 18:3-6
three ranges of vss. in two chs.	Jn 3:1–2, 6–18; 18:3–6	John, 3:1-2; and 3:6-18; and John 18:3-6
one vs. followed by another vs.	Jn 3:18f	John, ch. 3, vss. 18 and 19 (or 18 and the *following* vs.)
one vs. followed by an unspecified number of vss.	Jn 3:18ff	John, ch. 3, vs. 18 and the *following* vss.

Formatting references for citing biblical passages.[14]

OLD TESTAMENT QUOTATIONS

Several modern translations mark where the New Testament quotes the Old with a change in font weight, letter case, or some kind of indentation. Look at Jesus' quote from Isaiah 54.13 in various translations (John 4.45). The NASB sets off the quotation with small-caps,

"It is written in the prophets, 'AND THEY SHALL ALL BE TAUGHT OF GOD.'"

The NKJV uses italics, as do the JB and NJB,

"It is written in the prophets, *'And they shall all be taught by God.'*"

The NET uses a bold-italic face,

"It is written in the prophets, **'And they will all be taught by God.'**"

The NAB carries and indents the quote,

"It is written in the prophets:
    'They shall all be taught by God.'"

Other translations follow the RSV (so NRSV, NIV, NLT, ESV) by neglecting to give any special typographic attention to these quotes besides enclosing them in quotations:

"It is written in the prophets, 'And they shall all be taught by God.'"

The RSV and NRSV give no indication outside the context that a passage quotes from the Old Testament. Other translations, like the NIV, NLT, ESV, and even the original KJV, place Old Testament references in the footnotes or margins.

Even though some editors do not give these quotes special formatting, complex quotes are often formatted according to their source's unique genre. Here is the poetry of **Psalm 2.1–2** as set in the narrative of **Acts 4.25–26**:

"You spoke by the Holy Spirit through the mouth of your servant,
  our father David:
  " 'Why do the nations rage
    and the peoples plot in vain?
  The kings of the earth take their stand
    and the rulers gather together
  against the Lord
    and his against his Anointed One.' " (NIV)

CAPITALIZATION AND
DIVINE PRONOUNS

The Bible was not originally written with capital letters. The ancient scribes employed scripts that used a single set of letters each. They did not have modern typesets in upper or lower cases.

Nonetheless, some versions, like the AMP, NASB, NKJV, MEV, and HCSB, use what some call "reverential capitalization," *i.e.*, they capitalize the pronouns ("He," "Him," "His," *etc.*) that refer to God (or any member of the Trinity: the Father; Jesus Christ, the Son; or the Holy Spirit). This is particularly valuable for those editions that start each verse on a new line. Line breaks tend to disrupt readers' attention to the larger context so that it is easier to miss the pronoun's antecedent* (*i.e.*, the word it refers back to).

Most translations (KJV, RSV, NRSV, ESV, CSB, NLT, *et al.*), however, do not capitalize divine pronouns. That's because capitalization sometimes requires interpretive decisions where the context is unclear or ambiguous.

For example, the NKJV renders Naomi's praise with a divine pronoun ("His"),

Blessed be he of the Lord, who has not forsaken *His* kindness to the living and the dead. (**Ruth 2.20** NKJV, *emphasis added*)

The NASB and the HCSB do not link the "kindness" with God (uppercase "His"), but with Boaz (lowercase "his"), who generously provided for Naomi's daughter-in-law,

> May he be blessed of the Lord who has not withdrawn *his* kindness to the living and to the dead. (**Ruth 2.20** NASB, *emphasis added*)

Capitalizing a single divine pronoun ("You") in the Gospel of Matthew makes the Pharisees seem like they recognize Jesus' divinity (which, at first, they clearly did not):

> "Teacher, we want to see a sign from You" (**Mt 12.38** NKJV, so NASB, *et al.*).

In OT messianic proclamations, the NKJV narrows the application to Jesus Christ,

> "My God, My God, why have You forsaken Me?" (**Ps 22.1**).

Capitalizing this final pronoun ("Me") eliminates other possible applications. Yet, even the NKJV is inconsistent with similar passages, like **Ps 16.10** (notice the lowercase "my"),

> "For You will not leave my soul in Sheol," (NKJV)

or in **Ps 41.9**,

> "Even my own familiar friend in whom I trusted, Who ate my bread, Has lifted up his heel against me." (NKJV)

Most modern translations have abandoned the practice of capitalizing divine pronouns for the reasons demonstrated above or for the lack of historic precedent, as the editors of the ESV make clear:

> "There is nothing in the original Hebrew and Greek manuscripts that corresponds to such capitalization." [10]

RED LETTERS

Rubricated, or red-letter, editions have been with us for centuries, but the method of using red print to distinguish the words of Jesus Christ from the rest of Scripture is a rather recent innovation.

The tradition of red-letter Bibles began when the editor and publisher of the *Christian Herald* magazine, Louis Klopsch, took note of Jesus' words in **Luke 22.20**, "This cup is the new testament in my blood, which I shed for you." (KJV) While pondering the symbolic significance of the blood, it occurred to him to print a Bible with Jesus' words in red type. He colored them, not just in the Gospels, but throughout the whole NT. His red-letter KJV Testament (1899) and Bible (1901) were immediately popular.[11]

Other publishers caught on to Klopsch's success, and the practice spread throughout the Bible printing industry. Red-letter editions remain popular to this day.[12] Several major translations are available in red-letter editions, including the KJV, NIV, NKJV, NASB, NLT, and ESV.

Red letters are most helpful in the KJV, which doesn't use quotation marks to distinguish Jesus' speech from the surrounding text. They also help readers to quickly spot Jesus' words found outside of the Gospels, like at **Ac 18.9** ("Do not be afraid, but speak, and do not keep silent") and **2Co 12.9** ("My grace is sufficient for you, for My strength is made perfect in weakness" [NKJV]).[13]

But red letters are not always so rosy: They can have the same effect on readers as verse references. They can encourage readers to take Jesus' words out of context. Sometimes, they impose editorial interpretations in the same way that quotation marks do at **John 3.10–21** (See "Quotation marks" on page 153). More critically, they have been used to form a "canon within a canon", where some exalt Jesus' words as being more "scriptural" than the rest of Scripture. Despite these difficulties, rubrication can be an effective help for readers in an increasingly distracted world.   ⌬

ENDNOTES FOR TYPESETTING DECISIONS

1. Technically, the first English Bible to set off words not considered original was Myles Coverdale's *Great Bible* (1539), which had bracketed renderings based on the Latin Vulgate. Sebastian Münster's Latin translation of the Hebrew Bible (1534–35) was the base text for Coverdale's version. It was the first to set supplied words in roman font inline with the rest of Münster's translation, which he set in black letter.
   Walter F. Specht, "The Use of Italics in English Versions of the New Testament," *Andrews University Seminary Studies*, vol. VI, no. 1 (January, 1968): pp. 88–109.

2. Robert Stephanus' third Greek edition (1550) places an asterisk (*) here in **1 Jn 2.23** and records the fuller reading of the second half on the inside margin (ὁ ὁμολογῶν τὸν υἱὸν, καὶ τὸν πατέρα ἔχει. *ho homologōn ton huion, kai ton patera echei.*).

3. Eschatologically (theologically), this is contested, since Christ is expected to break his session at the Father's right hand for the *Parousia*—his return. If he breaks the session, then it cannot be considered eternally constant.

4. The NKJV better renders the last phrase ". . . sat down at the right hand of God" (**Heb 10.12b**).

5. Jack P. Lewis, *The English Bible from KJV to NIV: A History and Evaluation* (Grand Rapids, MI: Baker Book House, 1982), pp. 95, 253, 299.

6. The *Good News Bible* concludes the conversation early with verse **13**. Other passages whose interpretation is influenced by quotation marks include **Jb 32.15–17; Jn 3.31; Lk 14.10; Ac 19.5**.

7. The NIV uses 34 exclamation marks in the book of Proverbs; *NET Bible*, 47; NLT, 66. One translation promotes itself as being more "passionate" than others, a claim substantiated by its frequent use of exclamation marks: *The Passion Translation* (TPT) uses 130 in Proverbs!

8. Unfortunately, the typesetters of the orginal KJV apparently ran out of pilcrow characters, because none are set after **Acts 20.36**.

9. The story goes that Stephanus, a Parisian printer, had just converted to Protestantism and fled for sanctuary in Geneva. He is supposed to have added the verse references during his flight on horseback, which, some explain, is why his verse numbers seem to land arbitrarily in some places.

10 "Preface to the English Standard Version," *The Holy Bible, English Standard Version*, text ed. 2016 (Wheaton, IL: Crossway, 2001, '16).

11 "The Origins of the Red-Letter Bible," *Crossway.org*, last modified March 23, 2006, accessed August 22, 2018, https://www.crossway.org/blog/2006/03/red-letter-origin/.

12 In fact, there was even a popular Christian song written in celebration of Jesus' words as portrayed in the "red letters" — DC Talk's "Red Letter" from their album, *Supernatural* (Fore front records, 1998).

13 Other places outside the Gospels where Jesus speaks or is quoted by others can be found at Acts 1.4–5, 7–8; 9.4, 5, 6, 11–12, 15–16; 18.9–10; 22.7, 8, 10, 18, 21; 23.11; 26.14, 15–18; 1 Corinthians 11.24–25; Rv 1–4; 16.15; 22.7, 12, 16, 20.

14 Felix Just, "Biblical References: Format, Examples, History," *Catholic Resources for Bible, Liturgy, Art, and Theology*, last modifed May 5, 2012, accessed September 5, 2018, http://catholic-resources.org/Bible/Biblical_References.htm.

Part Two

History of English Bibles

Timeline of Historic English Bibles

		1378–1415 Great Papal Schism.
Wycliffe's Bibles	1380s	1381 Peasant's Revolt in England.
		1401 English victory against the French at the Battle of Agincourt.
		1415 Jan Hus burned at the stake.
		1455 Johann Gutenberg prints his 42-line Latin Bible.
		1476 William Caxton introduces printing to England.
		1485 Henry VII Tudor crowned King of England after winning the Battle of Bosworth.
		1497 John Cabot claims Newfoundland for England.
		1509 Henry VII dies, succeeded by his son, Henry VIII Tudor.
		1513 English victory against the Scots at the Battle of Flodden Field.
Tyndale's *New Testament*	1526	
Coverdale's Bible	1535	
"Thomas Matthew's" Bible	1537	1536 William Tyndale strangled and burned at the stake.
Great Bible	1539	
Cranmer Bible	1540	1540 Society of Jesus (Jesuits) founded by Ignatius of Loyola.
		1547 Henry VIII dies, succeeded by his son, Edward VI Tudor.
		1553 Edward VI dies, succeeded by his sister, Mary I Tudor.
		1555 John Rogers burned at the stake.
		1556 Archbishop Thomas Cranmer burned at the stake.
		1558 Mary I dies, succeeded by her sister, Elizabeth I Tudor.
Geneva Bible	1560	
Bishops' Bible	1568	
Rheims New Testament	1582	
		1588 England's victory against the Spanish Armada.
		1603 Elizabeth I dies, succeeded by her cousin, James I Stuart of England (VI of Scotland).
		1605 Gunpowder Treason and Plot.
Douay Old Testament	1610	1607 Jamestown founded.
King James Version	1611	
		1620 Plymouth founded.
		1625 James I dies, succeeded by his son, Charles I Stuart.
		1649 Charles I beheaded by English Parliament.
		1657 Oliver Cromwell refuses the crown.

Wycliffe, Lollardy, & Suppression

The First Fully English Bible

ENGLISH MONARCHY AND THE ROMAN CHURCH

I n medieval England, what wasn't ruled by the king and his nobles was ruled by the church and her bishops through Canon Law, which dealt with domestic and economic matters as well as religious ones. An early dispute between King Henry II and Archbishop Thomas à Becket resulted in the English *Magna Carta,* which demonstrated that church and crown could not always agree over who ruled what.

Two centuries later, the debate persisted in Oxford's halls among students, readers, and professors.* One such professor sought to challenge the whole body of Canon Law by regulating it with Scripture. John Wycliffe taught that the Bible was foundational to the church. He believed that the church's teaching and judgments should find precedent and warrant in Scripture alone. To support his case, Wycliffe required that an accurate translation of the Bible be made in the common language so that the English people could know what God demanded of them.

Wycliffe and his followers translated their Bible from available Latin manuscripts and published their English copies by hand. With an English Bible for all to read and hear, Wycliffe could persuade laity and clergy alike from its authority. With the Bible in words they understood, common people could bypass the hierarchy of priests and bishops and appeal directly to God's revelation about matters of faith and practice.

Wycliffe's disciples, who became known as Lollards, preached the Bible throughout England. Their teaching contradicted offi-

---

* This is during the reign of Richard II (AD 1367–1400; reigned 1377–99).

cial church policies. For example, they rejected celibacy for priests, prayers for the dead, and pilgrimages—all of which lacked scriptural support and precedent. They went so far as to reject the Pope's authority from Rome, arguing from Scripture that the bishops are to be subject to civil courts.†

Following Wycliffe's death, King Henry IV of England issued a decree, judging that any person who was caught promoting Wycliffe's teaching and distributing the Bible in English should be burned at the stake, in order "that such punishment may strike fear in the minds of others."‡ Seven years later, Thomas Arundel, the Archbishop of Canterbury, wrote in the constitutions of the English church, "The translation of the text of Holy Scripture out of one tongue into another is a dangerous thing." Those who did and persisted after being warned to stop would "incur the sentence of the greater excommunication."§

Wycliffe died from a stroke in 1384. After was he was long buried, the Council of Constance declared Wycliffe a heretic and excommunicated him (1415). Later, his corpse was dug up and burned as the church's final act of defiance. The official indictment against Wycliffe's English Bible was in effect for more than a century. As late as 1512–22, nine Lollards from Coventry were burned to death at the stake. One was a widow who was caught hiding the Lord's Prayer, the Ten Commandments, and the Apostle's Creed up her sleeve—all written in English.

John Wycliffe's teaching was not contained in England. It spread throughout European academia and found followers as far as Bohemia (now the Czech Republic or Czechia). Jan Hus, an admirer of Wycliffe, was himself burned at the stake at the Council of Constance for promoting Wycliffe's teachings. These two, Wycliffe and Hus, were the forerunners of a great Reformation that would change the course of world history.

---

† Cf. Rom 13.1–7; 1Pet 2.13–17.
‡ *De Hæretico Comburendo* (AD 1401)
§ *Constitutions of Oxford* (AD 1408)

Jn 3.18 "he þat bileueþ ī hī is not demed; but he þat bileueþ not, is now demed, fo2 he bileueþ not ī þe name of þe oon bigetū fone of god." (Wycliffe, 1394)

Tyndale &
Black-Market Bibles

The First New Testament Translated From Greek

RENAISSANCE & REFORMATION

The seeds planted by John Wycliffe and his Lollards, though buried and hidden for over a hundred years, were fertilized by the prevailing thoughts and new technologies of the 15th century. Around 1440, an enterprising German perfected a method of copying texts using cast metal type and a modified wine press. Johannes Gutenberg invented a system of movable type that reshaped the way information was copied and distributed. The process eliminated the need for copying texts by hand and made books for less money in less time. As printing technology spread, so did access to significant religious and legal texts. Learning was on the rise.

Throughout Europe, interest in the classical origins of law and culture stirred scholars to search out their sources in ancient literature. Those refugees, who fled the collapsed remains of the Roman empire in the East (that is, the Fall of Constantinople to the Ottoman Turks in 1453), brought ancient Greek manuscripts with them as they sought shelter in the West. Among their parchments was the New Testament text in words that predated the Roman church's official Latin Bible.

In 1516, Desiderius Erasmus published a diglot* New Testament—Greek in one column and his fresh Latin translation in the other. His edition demonstrated the lack and limitations of the Latin Bible then employed by the church. In the preface to his first edition, Erasmus encouraged the translation of the Greek New Testament into the languages of the world. He wrote,

"I disagree very much with those who are unwilling that Holy Scripture, translated into the vulgar (*i.e.*, common) tongue, be read by the uneducated, as if Christ taught such intricate doctrines that they could scarcely be understood by very few theologians, or as if the strength of the Christian religion consisted in men's ignorance of it. The mysteries of kings, perhaps, are better concealed, but Christ wishes his mysteries published as openly as possible. I would that even the lowliest women read the Gospels and the Pauline Epistles. And I would that they were translated into all languages so that they could be read and understood not only by Scots and Irish but also by Turks and Saracens."

In England, young King Henry VIII wished to maintain good relations with the Catholic Church and proved his loyalty by defending the Roman Mass and Sacraments against the Lutheran teaching then sweeping Europe.* For this, the Roman Pope granted him the title, *Fidei defensor*—Defender of the Faith. Despite Erasmus' influence, Henry had no intention of upsetting Rome and changing a century's worth of legislation against the English Bible.

WILLIAM TYNDALE

At this time, a young Oxford theologian and polyglot proved himself capable in translating Greek. William Tyndale, a scholar of virtuous reputation, sought permission to translate the Bible in England, but the Bishop of London denied him authorization. Tyndale, convinced of the necessity of the work, crossed the English Channel and traveled to Germany where he quickly took to translating the New Testament. While Tyndale was publishing his translation of Matthew's Gospel, his work was discovered by the local authorities, and he was forced to flee to the Low Countries

---

* Tudor, Henry VIII. *Assertio Septem Sacramentorum.* (England: 1521)

(today's Belgium and the Netherlands). There he found refuge among the English merchants and continued his work.

In 1526, Tyndale published the entire New Testament in a convenient, pocket-sized octavo edition. His little books were immediately popular and in high demand. The story goes that once the Bishop of London saw the multiplication of Tyndale's Testaments in England, he sought to destroy as many as he could get his hands on. He struck a deal with a merchant, whom he paid to buy up as many Bibles as he could so that he could burn them all at Paul's Cross in London. The merchant, in turn, told Tyndale, who saw this as an opportunity to pay off his debts and finance a new, improved edition. "So forward went the bargain—the bishop had the books, [the merchant] had the thanks, and Tyndale had the money."† (Only three copies of this edition survive today from an estimated three to six thousand total.)

Tyndale eventually learned Hebrew and began translating the Old Testament. He published the first five books of Moses and the prophet **Jonah** and got as far as **2 Chronicles** before he was betrayed and imprisoned. In 1536, Tyndale was condemned as a heretic and set ablaze. Because of his status as a scholar and theologian, his executioners devised a way to choke him to death before the fire completely consumed him. His last words formed a prayer, petitioning God with his dying breath—"Lord, open the King of England's eyes!"

Three years after his death, Tyndale's prayer was answered. The influence of his pioneering work would be seen in every successive English Bible. Seventy-five years later, an estimated eighty percent of his Bible would be retained in the classic King James Version.‡

---

† *Hall's Chronicle containing the History of England* (London: Johnson, Rivington, *et al.*, 1809) pp. 762–3.

‡ Crystal, David. *Begat.* (Oxford, New York: Oxford University Press, 2010) More precisely, 83.7% of Tyndale's New Testament and about 76% of his work on the Old Testament is preserved in the KJV. (Nielson, Jon, Royal Skousen. "How Much of the King James Bible Is William Tyndale's? An Estimation Based on Sampling." *Reformation* (Vol 3. 1998. Issue 1) pp. 49–74.

worlde through hi / mynght be saved. He that beleveth on hym shall not be condempned. But he that beleveth nott / is condempned all redy / be cause he beleveth nott in the name off the only sonne off God. And this is the condempnaci

Jn 3.18 "He that beleveth on hym ſhall not be condempned. But he that beleveth not is condempned all redy be cauſe he beleveth nott in the name off the only ſonne off God." (Tyndale, 1526) ⊲

The newe Teſtamēt
as it was written / and
cauſed to be writtē /
by them which her
de yt. To whom
alſo oure ſa
veoure
Chriſt Jeſus
commaunded that
they ſhulde pre
ache it vnto al
creatures.

Title page to
Tyndale's 1526
New Testament.

The King, Coverdale, & Anonymity

The First Legal English Bibles

B y the early 1530s, England's ruler, King Henry VIII, had a change of heart. He had failed to get a dispensation from the Pope to annul his marriage with Queen Catherine,* so he decided to split with the Roman Church and set himself as the head of the Church of England. Thus he divorced his wife in order to marry Anne Boleyn. In the same stroke, King Henry effectively annulled the jurisdiction of Rome's Canon Law over England.†

While William Tyndale was laboring over the original languages in Europe, an Augustinian friar named Myles Coverdale, a sympathizer with the European reformers, fled to Germany and labored there to complete the entire Bible in English. Coverdale was not a well-trained a linguist like Tyndale was, but he made do with what he had. He used Tyndale's existing New Testament, Pentateuch, and prophet Jonah, and translated the rest from German and Latin sources (including Martin Luther's Bible, the Zurich Bible, the Vulgate, and Pagninus' Latin Bible). He published his work in 1535, but he had to wait before it could be printed in England. On its title page, he recorded the Apostle Paul's words, "Pray for us, that the word of God may have free passage and be glorified."‡

After Tyndale was killed in 1536, his friend, John Rogers, took Tyndale's surviving text and manuscripts and proceeded to edit them for a new edition of the entire Bible. It included portions of Tyndale's Hebrew Old Testament that couldn't be published before Tyndale's martyrdom. Rogers supplemented the

---

* Henry VIII married his elder brother's widow, Catherine of Aragon, in 1509.

† Henry declared Tyndale a heretic and condemned his works, especially his English translation, in a decree published in June 1530. Yet, his decree offered hope that the King might himself use his right to authorize a future translation.

‡ From the title page of the Coverdale Bible, quote taken from **2Th 3.1**.

missing pieces of his edition with Coverdale's Bible and translated a portion of the Apocrypha himself. When the book was published in 1537, Rogers could not credit Tyndale with any of the work, because Tyndale was still considered a heretic by the Church of England. So Rogers attributed the Bible to "Thomas Matthew," a fictitious name he gave to make the Bible acceptable to all English readers.

In 1537, the prayers of Tyndale and Coverdale were finally answered. King Henry was now inclined to license the publication and distribution of the English Bible, thanks in no small part to the influence of his principal secretary, Thomas Cromwell, and Archbishop Thomas Cranmer. Cranmer endorsed Coverdale's version, recommending that it be sold and read by every person "without danger of any act, proclamation, or ordinance heretofore granted to the contrary, until such time that we, the Bishops shall set forth a better translation, which I think will not be till a day after Doomsday."[§] Upon the reception of their endorsement for Coverdale's second edition, King Henry resolved, "If there be no heresies [in it], then in God's name let it go abroad among our people." He granted that Coverdale's edition and the "Matthew" Bible be printed with the words, "Set forth with the king's most gracious license."

Coverdale revised the "Matthew" Bible, and in 1539, his new version appeared with the following: "This is the bible appointed to the use of the churches." This Bible—called the Great Bible due to its immense size[¶]—was set as the official Bible of the Anglican Church. Its second edition, named after Archbishop Thomas Cranmer, who wrote the preface for it, served the churches until it was replaced by the Bishops' Bible twenty-eight years later.

---

§ Pollard. Letter from Th. Cranmer to Th. Cromwell, 4 Aug 1537. *Records of the English Bible*. p. 215.

¶ Its pages measure 11 inches × 16 ½ in!

The Best Bible?

the worlde might be faued by him. He that
l eleueth on him, fhal not be cõdemned. But
he that beleueth not, is cõdemned allready:
becaufe he beleueth not on the name of the
onely fonne of God. But this is ỹ cõdemp

Jn 3.18 "He that beleueth on him, fhal not be cõdemned. But he that beleueth not, is cõdemned allready: becaufe he beleueth not on the name of the onely fonne of God." (Coverdale, 1535)

ỹ pm myghc be He that beleueth on hym/ wall not be con=
faued ꝛc . The dempned. But he that beleueth not / is con=
worldheredoth dempned all redy/ becaufe he beleueth not in
only fygnifye ỹ the name of the only fonne of God. And thys
the chofen   is the condemnacion /that lyght is come in
and thofe

Jn 3.18 "He that beleueeth on hym, fhal not be condempned. But he that beleueth not is condempned all redy, becaufe he beleueth not in the name of the only fonne of God." (Matthew's, 1537)

BIBLIA

The Bible, that

is, the holy Scripture of the
Olde and New Testament, faithfully and truly translated out
of Douche and Latyn
in to Englishe.

M. D. XXXV.

S. paul. II. Tessa. III.
Praie for vs, that the worde of God maie
haue fre passage, and be glorified. zc.

S. paul Col. III.
Let the worde of Christ dwell in you plen
teously in all wyßdome zc.

Josue I.
Let not the boke of this lawe departe
out of thy mouth, but exercyse thyselfe
therin daye and nighte zc.

Title page to Coverdale's 1535 Bible.

The Best Bible?

The Genevan Study Bible
The First Bible to Completely Translate the Original Languages

Protestant King Edward VI died young at only fifteen. He survived his father, Henry VIII, by just six years. The Protestants in court hastened to secure their influence by crowning the successor whom Edward named—his first cousin once-removed, Lady Jane Grey. But the Privy Council swayed their support for her in favor of Edward's elder half-sister—Mary Tudor.*

Mary deposed her cousin, Lady Jane, and locked her away. When Mary learned that Jane's father participated in a failed revolt intended to resist Mary's marriage-alliance to the Catholic king, Philip of Spain, she had Lady Jane beheaded.

Staunchly Catholic, Mary Tudor sought to reverse whatever gains the Protestants made by reconnecting with Rome. She reinstated the old heresy acts, including old King Henry IV's† prohibitions against the Bible.‡ To prove she was sincere, her first victim was John Rogers, the editor of the "Matthew" Bible, whom she had burned at the stake in 1555. Her persecutions killed around three hundred heretics and sent several hundred more English Protestants into exile.

William Whittingham was one such exile who found welcome and refuge in Protestant Geneva, a center for Reformed doctrine and biblical scholarship. He worked diligently with several other English refugees, including Myles Coverdale (who published the Great Bible during the reign of Henry VIII) in order to produce a new version of the New Testament by 1557. They ensured that it was "conferred diligently with the Greek, and best approved translations." Only three years later, in 1560, the entire Bible was ready

---

* This Mary Tudor is also known as Mary I of England, or sometimes, "Bloody" Mary.
† Henry IV, a.k.a. Henry of Bolingbroke (born 1367, reigned 1399–1413)
‡ Revival of the Heresy Acts (1 & 2 Ph. & M. c.6) November 1554

and dedicated to a new Protestant English queen, Elizabeth I, who succeeded Mary Tudor, her half-sister, the year before.

The Geneva Bible, named after the place of its production, made several improvements over its predecessors. First, a couple members of the translation team were competent Hebrew scholars who revised and completed the translation of the Old Testament from the Hebrew-Aramaic sources. Second, the Bible was filled with explanatory notes, maps, illustrations, introductions to books, summaries of chapters, and other useful helps. Third, it was the first English Bible to sub-divide chapters into verses: Each verse started on a separate line for ease of reference. Other English Bibles had annotations, but the Geneva Bible's many marginal notes made it an exceptional study Bible—a kind of Protestant seminary in a book.

Due to its helpful features and its academic and linguistic qualities, the Geneva Bible quickly overtook all other English versions in popularity. This Bible went through no less than 120 editions since its publication in 1560 until the release of the King James version in 1611; for several decades it appeared in at least one new edition every year. It was this version that the Puritan Pilgrims brought with them to the Plymouth shores in 1620. It remained popular with the English and Scots nations right up to the English Civil War (1642–52).

Jn 3.18 "He that beleueth in him, fhal not be cōdemned: but he that beleueth not, is condēmned already, becaufe he hath not beleeued in ỹ Name of that onely begottē Sōne of God." (Geneva, 1560)

The Best Bible?

LEVI. SIMEON. RVBEN. PETER. ANDREWE. IAMES.

MATHEW. MARC.

IVDAH. IOHN.

DAN. PHILIP.

THE
BIBLE,
THAT IS,
THE HOLY SCRIPTVRES
conteined in the Old and New
TESTAMENT.
Translated according to the Ebrew and Greeke, and
conferred with the best Translations in
divers Languages.
With most profitable Annotations upon all hard places
and other things of great importance.

IMPRINTED AT LONDON
by the Deputies of Christopher Barker,
Printer to the Queenes most
Excellent Maiestie.
1599.

NEPHTHALI. BARTHOLO.

GAD. MATHEWE.

LVKE. IOHN.

ASHER. THOMAS.

ISACAR. IAMES.

IOSEPH. BENIAMIN. MATTHIAS. IVDE.

ZABVLON. SIMON.

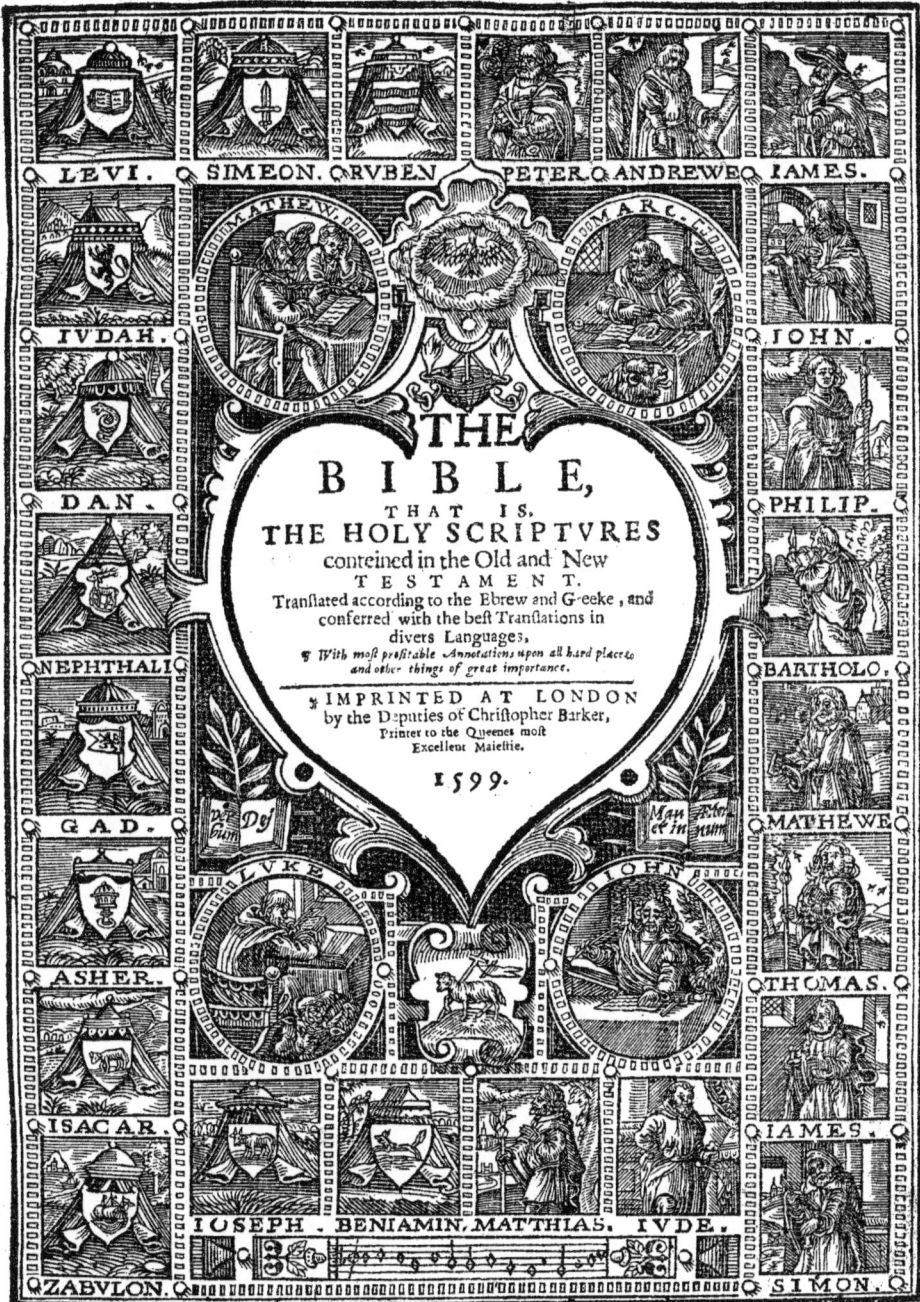

Title page to the 1599 Geneva Bible.

The Bishops' Bible
The First Bible by Committee

1 Paul sheweth by
18 The vengeaun
ingratitude and p

At the start of her reign in 1559, Queen Elizabeth I restored her father's (King Henry VIII) official injunction requiring each parish church to display the "whole Bible of the largest volume in English." But, due to her half-sister's persecutions, no new Bible had been printed since their brother, Edward VI, had died. What Bibles did survive official suppression, destruction, or constant use also contained variations from one another.

The bishops, abbots, and other Anglican clergy felt no strong compulsion to produce a new, uniform edition. They had dragged their feet ever since two previous attempts failed to make an official revision. During the reign of King Henry VIII, as early as 1534, Archbishop Thomas Cranmer tried to coordinate the clergy and assign them sections of the New Testament for revision. Not all those who were given assignments were willing to participate, so their revisions were never completed.

Cranmer tried again in 1542. This time, he divided the New Testament into fifteen parts for the clergy to review—some of whom were eminently qualified in the original languages. However, one bishop insisted that the language of the revision retain some one hundred Latin words and Greek transliterations, including *confessio, contritus, ecclesia, episcopus, olocausta, pontifex, presbyter, sacramentum, et al.* (See "Traditional Language and the Status Quo" on page 109.) His insistence, plus the lack of cooperation with Cambridge and Oxford Universities, blocked all progress until well after Cranmer's martyrdom and Mary I's eventual demise.

The arrival of the Geneva Bible in 1560 spurred the bishops to a new sense of urgency. This Bible—which was a product of French and Swiss Reformers and English Puritans—included many explanatory notes in its margins. The Anglican bishops considered these notes partisan and potentially disruptive to Queen

The Bishops' Bible

Elizabeth's "middle way" if not countered by an official Bible of their own. So work began anew under the supervision of Archbishop Matthew Parker and William Cecil, Elizabeth's secretary of state. Portions were parceled out to competent bishops and clerics for their recommendations. The work progressed for about seven years until William Cecil finally presented a completed Bible to Queen Elizabeth in 1568.

Though it was officially endorsed by the Anglican clergy and "authorized to be read in the churches," it was never authorized by royal decree like the Great Bible (1539) was. The popular Geneva Bible and Coverdale's familiar Great Bible overshadowed the influence of the Bishops' Bible, and its significance is limited to the Elizabethan age. It was begun during her reign in support of her ecclesiastical agenda, and no edition of it was printed after she died. Its greatest influence is that it formed the base for the most popular Bible revision to date—the King James version.

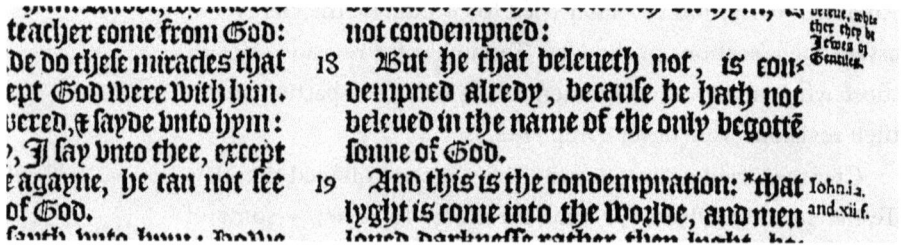

Jn 3.18 "But he that beleueth not, is condempned alredy, because he hath not beleued in the name of the only begottē sonne of God." (Bishops', 1568)

Rheims' New and Douay's Old Testaments

The First English Bible for Roman Catholics.

After Mary Tudor died, her sister, Elizabeth I ascended the throne.* In order to stabilize English society after Mary's persecutions, Elizabeth, herself a Protestant, insisted on a policy of compromise between Catholics and Protestants in what is known as the "middle way." After her accession as queen, she reinstated the *Book of Common Prayer* for liturgical use in the churches. All else she required from her subjects was their loyalty.

Things were peaceful enough until Elizabeth's cousin, Mary Stuart (Queen of Scots)† fled a Protestant rebellion in Scotland and sought refuge in England. Elizabeth wasn't sure she could trust her, because, at one time, she claimed the English throne as her own.‡ It was about this time that William Allen, a Catholic theologian who lost influence in the universities of Oxford and Cambridge, settled across the Channel in Flanders. There, he established a seminary at Douay to harbor disaffected English Catholics.

Then things took a turn for the worse between Elizabeth and Rome: Pope Pius V issued a papal bull condemning Elizabeth as a heretic, officially excommunicating her, and licensing those Catholics who remained on the British Isles to depose her. A year later, the Ridolfi plot was exposed: It failed to replace Elizabeth with her Catholic cousin, Mary. Elizabeth then issued the Treasons Act

---

* Mary Tudor was the daughter of Henry VIII's first wife, Catherine of Aragon. Elizabeth Tudor was the daughter of his second wife, Anne Boleyn.

† Mary Stuart was the grand-daughter of Henry VIII's older sister, Margaret Tudor, so she was Elizabeth's first cousin once-removed.

‡ Some English subjects considered Elizabeth illegitimate, because she came from Henry VIII's second wife, Anne Boleyn; they preferred the eldest child of Henry's older sister.

ENGLAND
Oxford
London
Douay
Rheims
Paris
FRANCE

of 1571, condemning any thought or intent against her right to rule.

Soon, Elizabeth heard reports from across the channel about the horrible slaughter of so many Huguenots (French Protestants) in Paris during .St. Bartholomew's Day (1572).[§] General English opinion hardened against Catholicism, and devoted Catholics were immediately suspected as traitors if they failed to comply with the liturgy of the Anglican Church.

At this time, Gregory Martin, a Jesuit scholar working at the Catholic seminary in Rheims with William Allen,[¶] Edmund Campion, and others, started work on a version of the Bible for Roman Catholics based on the Latin Vulgate.[**] At this point, it was too late to turn back the clock and wait for a fresh English Bible supervised and specially annotated by Rome. The flood of existing Bibles with Protestant marginal notes pushed the Jesuits at Rheims to respond by producing a New Testament which met the requirements set forth by the Council of Trent (1545–63). They conformed its language to the Latin Mass and prepared its use for clandestine missions work intended to encourage devout Catholics in England.

Gregory Martin finished his translation only a few months after his collaborator, Edmund Campion, was caught during a mission to England and executed. Soon after its completion, Martin succumbed to illness and also died. He never saw the completion

---

§ Estimates of the number of deaths from the St. Bartholomew's Day massacre vary widely, starting upwards from about 2,000 in Paris and an additional 3,000 to over 30,000 possible deaths in rural France. Whatever the toll, the deaths during this tragic event radically soured English opinions towards Roman Catholicism.

¶ The English seminary founded at Douai moved to Rheims in 1578.

** The translators revealed their prejudice, that they consider that the old Latin Vulgate "is not only better than all other Latin translations (i.e., Beza's or Erasmus'), but than the Greek text itself, in those places where they disagree." (New Testament, Preface, 1582)

The Best Bible?

of the Old Testament, which was finished in 1610 after the English seminary returned to Douay. Though the Douay-Rheims Bible had limited influence on the language of future English Bibles, its New Testament was one of the many references consulted by the translators of the King James version.

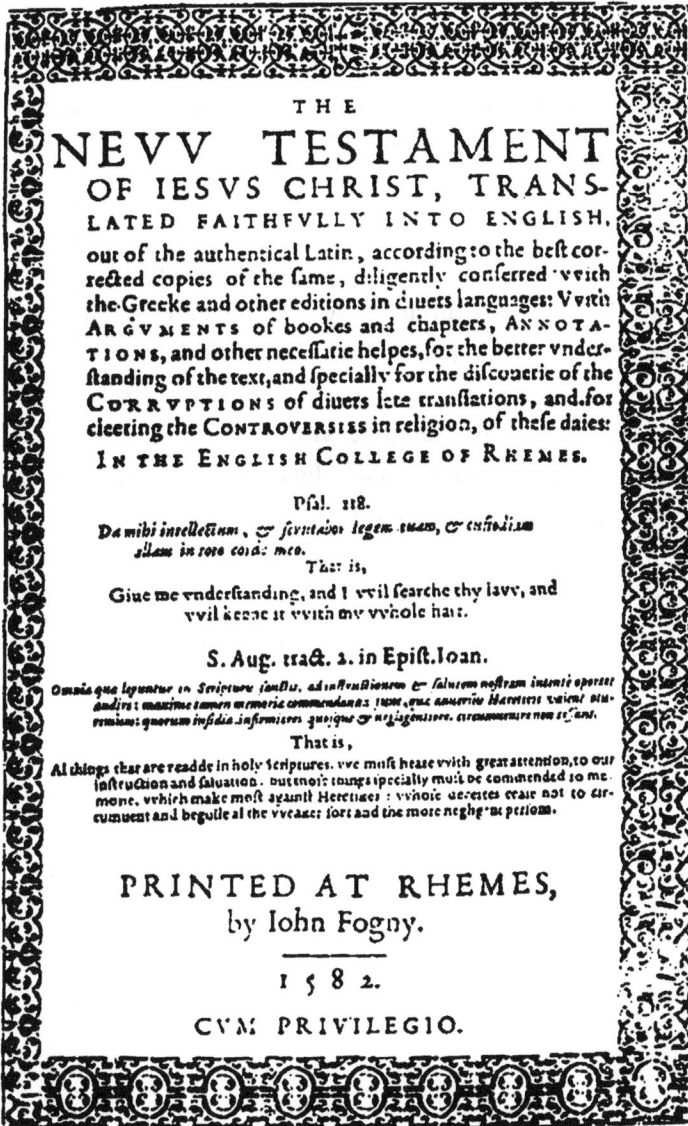

THE

NEVV TESTAMENT

OF IESVS CHRIST, TRANS-
LATED FAITHFVLLY INTO ENGLISH,

out of the authentical Latin, according to the best corrected copies of the same, diligently conferred with
the Greeke and other editions in diuers languages: Vvith
ARGVMENTS of bookes and chapters, ANNOTA-
TIONS, and other necessarie helpes, for the better vnderstanding of the text, and specially for the discouerie of the
CORRVPTIONS of diuers late translations, and for
cleering the CONTROVERSIES in religion, of these daies:

IN THE ENGLISH COLLEGE OF RHEMES.

Psal. 118.

*Da mihi intellectum, & scrutabor legem tuam, & custodiam
illam in toto corde meo.*

That is,

Giue me vnderstanding, and I vvil searche thy lavv, and
vvil keepe it vvith my vvhole hart.

S. Aug. tract. 2. in Epist. Ioan.

*Omnia quae leguntur in Scriptura sanctis, ad instructionem & salutem nostram intente oportet
audire: maxime tamen memoriae commendanda sunt, quae aduersus Haereticos valent plu-
rimum: quorum insidiae infirmiores quosque & negligentiores circumuenire non cessant.*

That is,

Al things that are readde in holy Scriptures, vve must heare vvith great attention, to our
instruction and saluation. but most things specially must be commended to me-
morie, vvhich make most against Heretikes: vvhose deceites cease not to cir-
cumuent and beguile al the vveaker sort and the more negligent persons.

PRINTED AT RHEMES,
by Iohn Fogny.

1582.

CVM PRIVILEGIO.

Title page to the 1582 Rheims New Testament.

16. For fo God loued the world, that he gaue his only-begotten Sonne; The (
that euery one that beleeueth in him, perifh not, but may haue life euer- vpon
lafting. ¶ 17. For God fent not his Sonne into the world, to iudge the in the
world, but that the world may be faued by him. 18. He that beleeueth weake
in him, is not iudged. But he that doth not beleeue," is already iudged:
becaufe he hath not beleeued in the name of the only-begotten Sóne of.
God.

Jn 3.18 "He that beleeueth in him, is not iudged. But he that doth
not beleeue is already iudged: becaufe he hath not beleeued in the
name of the only begotten Sóne of God." (Rheims, 1572)

The next part—Part Three: Contemporary English Bibles—
actually begins where this part ought to conclude—with the culmination of the King James Version (KJV). The KJV is included
with the next section so as not to repeat the same subject matter.

In fact, much more could be written (and has been written)
about significant historic Bibles following the 16th-century's
"golden era" of Bible translation. This overview should suffice to
demonstrate the challenges that these pioneering translators faced
and the courage they possessed to overcome and realize their vision of setting God's word before the eyes of their countrymen in
words that they could speak, hear, and understand.   ◁

Part Three

Contemporary English Bibles

Introduction

to the Contemporary English Bibles

TRANSLATION REVIEW SECTIONS

Each of the review chapters includes the following sections:

At a Glance *Overview • Historical Introduction • Stated Translation Ideals • Method • Text Bases • Contributors • Theological Assumptions • Features • Reception • Representative Samples • Revisions • Assessment • Endorsements • Copyright • Endnotes*

The *At a Glance* Overview

Each review chapter is prefaced with a page of summary information called the "At a Glance" overview. This overview includes a diagram titled *Formal/ Functional Tendencies*. On this diagram, each translation is listed horizontally by their initialism and set in relation to one another according to their general translation tendencies. For example, the NET tends to be rendered more formally than the NLT, though it could not be considered a formal translation.

The words "interlinear" and "free paraphrase" on opposing ends of the diagram indicate extreme renderings that cannot be considered translations. For example, even though the NASB is closer to the "Formal" end of the spectrum, it is

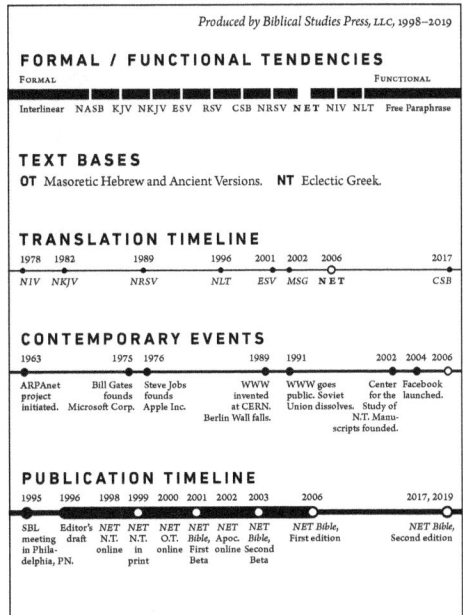

Produced by Biblical Studies Press, LLC, 1998–2019

FORMAL / FUNCTIONAL TENDENCIES

FORMAL   FUNCTIONAL

Interlinear NASB KJV NKJV ESV RSV CSB NRSV **N E T** NIV NLT Free Paraphrase

TEXT BASES

OT Masoretic Hebrew and Ancient Versions.   NT Eclectic Greek.

TRANSLATION TIMELINE

1978	1982	1989	1996	2001	2002	2006	2017
NIV	NKJV	NRSV	NLT	ESV	MSG	NET	CSB

CONTEMPORARY EVENTS

1963	1975	1976	1989	1991	2002	2004	2006
ARPAnet project initiated.	Bill Gates founds Microsoft Corp.	Steve Jobs founds Apple Inc.	WWW invented at CERN. Berlin Wall falls.	WWW goes public. Soviet Union dissolves.	Center for the Study of N.T. Manuscripts founded.	Facebook launched.	

PUBLICATION TIMELINE

1995	1996	1998	1999	2000	2001	2002	2003	2006	2017, 2019
SBL meeting in Philadelphia, PN.	Editor's draft N.T.	NET N.T. online in print	NET O.T. online	NET Bible, Apoc. First Beta	NET Bible, online Second Beta	NET	NET	NET Bible, First edition	NET Bible, Second edition

The *At a Glance* overview

a translation and not a gloss, so it could never be considered an "interlinear."

This book does not usually consider footnotes when characterizing the formal or functional tendencies of a translation's main text.

Translation Review Sections

The "Historical Introduction" begins each review and gives readers context for the circumstances by which the translation arose.

"Stated Translation Ideals," which may be read from a Bible's preface, jacket cover, marketing copy, or interviews with the translators and editors themselves, give readers an idea of the editors' general hope for the outcome of their work. In the following review chapters, I judge whether or not they met their goals by offering my conclusions under the "Assessments" heading.

The "Method" section describes how each translation or revision was organized and executed.

"Text Bases" gives a short bibliography of the original language sources used by each translation. Regarding such, translators and translation committees usually view their text bases with a critical eye. Standard texts (*e.g.* the Nestle-Aland/United Bible Societies or *Editio Critico Maior* Greek NTs) or traditional texts (the *Textus Receptus*) may be set as a base for reference, but final editorial decisions lay with the editors and translators themselves. Few, if any, follow their base texts blindly.

"Contributors" identifies some of the people who have worked on each translation either as editors, translators, or specialists in some related field. Some of these individuals are recognized for their work on other translations, which are indicated by their initialisms in parentheses following the contributor's name.

"Theological Assumptions" summarizes any explicit faith-claims held by the translators and editors.

"Features" lists the typical translation or typesetting features shared by a translation's printed editions.

"Representative Samples": I benefit from reading several translations all the way through. In preparing for this book, however, I could not read exhaustively all of the Bibles that are evaluated here in time for publication. Therefore, I approach the review of each translation as a modern archaeologist approaches a previously inhabited hill. Earlier generations of archaeologists would strip the entire surface of the hill layer-by-layer, one after the other. They would record their discoveries for one layer before continuing down to the next layer, and so on, until they reached the bottom. In contrast, later generations learned to plan ahead by cutting a length of trench straight through the entire hill. Thus they are able to quickly characterize the nature of the hill, distinguish and identify the site's habitation layers, examine a sampling of artifacts, give approximations of each layer's relative age, and determine where to look next—all without having to sift and record every potsherd and rock before proceeding to the next underlying layer.

So too, I do not need to read every page of each Bible translation in its entirety in order to get a good sense of that Bible's general character. All I require are "Representative Samples" to discern a translation's functional or formalistic tendencies and test the translators' theological assumptions. Some of these samples are listed in each review so that you may follow the method and know what kinds of passages to look for.

Many of the samples that are listed for comparison have Hebrew or Greek transcriptions to the left of their references. All of the references are included for specific reasons:

Familiar Passages (**Gn 1.1–2; Ps 23.1–2; 27.4; Jn 3.16**) offer a very quick glimpse into a translation's style and give a rapid comparison for those who already know these verses by heart.

Divine Name and Titles (**Gn 1.27a; Ex 6.3a; 1Sa 17.45b; Ps 24.1; 73.28b; 90.1b, Dn 9.3a; Mt 16.16b; Lk 20.42b**) summarizes the ways that references to God have been rendered throughout a translation.

New Testament Text Base (**Mt 17.21; 18.11; Ac 8.37; 1 Jn 5.7b–8a**) indicates significant text-critical passages which reveal the Greek textual basis for the translation's NT. For example, all of the passages in this section are generally found in the late Byzantine MSS used for the production of the *Textus Receptus* in the 16th century. They are not found in any of the standard critical Greek editions in use today (except as footnotes in the critical apparatus).

Gender Language (**Gn 9.6; Lv 24.17; Pr 15.5a; Mt 4.19; 5.9; Ro 2.6; Gal 5.13; 1Ti 3.11; Ti 1.6**) reveals the manner in which the translators and editors handled language related to gender. Some generic masculine nouns include both males and females when their meaning is unaffected by context (*e.g.* ʾ*ādām, nephesh, anthrōpoi*). Some exclusively masculine nouns, when influenced by context, may also extend to females (*huioi, adelphoi*). Some translations (*e.g.* NRSV) render specific male or female nouns in an inclusive manner for liturgical reasons without regard for their context (ʾ*āvîw, gynaikos, anēr*).

Two passages for *Difficult Renderings* were chosen, not because of any difficulty in rendering the words of their primary text base, but because of how difficult it is to judge what their original text-basis ought to be (**1Sa 13.1**) or how hard it is to render the intent of the words written there (**Is 28.13**).

Significant Renderings were picked for their traditional familiarity (**Pr 15.11; Mt 1.2; Jn 1.14**) or for the theological controversies surrounding those passages (**Is 7.14; Jn 18.36; Ro 3.22a; Tt 2.13**). For example, *she'ol ... ʾabaddon* in **Pr 15.11** are traditionally rendered as "Hell and Destruction" (KJV), but they are typically transcribed as "Sheol and Abaddon" in modern translations. Some fear that modern renderings mask a valuable doctrine by using terms that are unfamiliar to modern readers. On the other hand, there is a need to distinguish between notions of Hell, which have been conditioned by later societies influenced by Dante's *Inferno*, and the habitation of the dead as understood by ancient Israel and her contemporaries.

The words *tois ioudaiois* in **Jn 1.14** is controversial because of how its referent has been confused: If rendered formally ("to the Jews," so KJV, NASB) it can be construed to apply to Jews universally for their collective culpability in sending Christ to the cross, despite the handful of loyal Jewish followers who were powerless to do anything on his behalf at his trial. But when rendered in its context as "by the Jewish leaders" (NIV), the referent is narrowed to just those Jews who were directly involved with condemning Jesus to death.

Plenty has already been written about the rendering of *'almah* in **Is 7.14** regarding its historic translation and theological controversy. (See page 110 and following.)

The "Revisions" section: While preparing for this book, I have either collated and compared different text editions of the various translations under review or sifted through collations produced by the editors or publishers themselves. These collations demonstrate the improvements that translators and editors have made to their translations over time. A sampling of their revisions are included in each review chapter.

Some review chapters may include additional sections. For example the KJV chapter includes a section on "Language Changes."

WHY THESE TRANSLATIONS?

The twelve contemporary translations reviewed in the following chapters are here because of their popularity based on sales or readership or their significant influence on other translations.

An argument can be made that the King James Version (KJV) is not really a contemporary translation. It is included in this section, because it is still a text that is widely available. Its copyright status makes it profitable and popular among publishers (particularly in the United States). Though it is four hundred years old, it is still

26.22 Open Spaces] Ro
26.22 room] space
26.24 My] my
26.25 Yahweh,] the LOR
26.25 slaves] servants
26.29 ^done
26.29 done~
26.31 Then~
26.32 slaves] servants
26.33 ^still
26.33 to this day.] today
26.34 40] forty
26.34 Hittite,] Hethite,
26.34 Hittite.] Hethite.
27.2 /Take] /So now tak
27.7 the~
27.7 /Now obey every or
27.8 son.] son, listen to
27.20 worked] made
27.20 out] happen
27.25 "Serve] "Bring it c
27.25 ^closer
27.29 down] in worship
27.29 brothers;] relative
27.29 down] in worship
27.30 the hunt.] his hun
27.31 Then he] He
27.37 Esau:] Esau,
27.38 ^have
27.38 have~
27.38 /Then his] /His
27.39 him:] him,
27.46 Hittite women.] H
27.46 a Hittite woman] :
27.46 one of them,] thes
27.46 /Isaac] /So Isaac
28.1 him: "Don't take] hi
28.1 wife from the~
28.1 women.] girl.
28.6 woman."] girl."
28.12 heaven,] the sky,
28.12 /Yahweh] /The LO
28.13 Yahweh,] the LOR
28.13 that] on which
28.13 now sleeping on.]
28.20 on] during
28.20 journey,] journey
28.20 He] he
28.21 house,] family,
28.22 You] you
28.22 You] you

A sample collation of changes made between the HCSB (2009) and the CSB (2017) in **Gn 26–28**.

second in sales following the *New International Version* (NIV).[1] As of just five years ago, it was still held as the most popularly read and listened to translation, far surpassing the better-selling NIV.[2]

The *Revised Standard Version* (RSV) is included because it is still in print and found in the pews of many mainline liturgical churches today. It is also influential as the English base text for later translations and revisions, like the *New Revised Standard Version* (NRSV), the *English Standard Version* (ESV), and the *Revised Standard Version, Second Catholic Edition* (RSV2CE).

The NRSV is a familiar presence in mainline denominations, and can be found in many pews, seminary bookstores, and as a text of choice for religious courses in state colleges. It is currently undergoing revision.

The ESV has earned its reputation as a trusted evangelical translation and is now gaining ground in certain conservative Roman Catholic circles.

The *New American Standard Bible* (NASB) is a significant evangelical translation touted for its formalistic "literalism." It has recently been revised in two different versions: The NASB 2020 edition has moved in a more functional direction, while the *Legacy Standard Bible* has moved in a more formal one.

The *New King James Version* (NKJV) is a static translation that is still in print and supported with many study resources. It is an ideal version to set alongside the classic King James Bible.

The *New International Version* (NIV) has been a trusted evangelical translation for the last four decades and is today's best-selling version. Its revision history could use some explanation.

The *Christian Standard Bible* (CSB) is the successor to the *Holman Christian Standard Bible* (HCSB). It is a modern version that cleverly frames its balance between formal and functional translation methods. The CSB has a unique heritage extending to the success of the NKJV.

The *New Living Translation* (NLT) is here as a modern functional translation. It follows in the commercial success of *The Living Bible* paraphrase.

The *NET Bible: New English Translation* (NET) is a functional translation whose many thorough footnotes have influenced other familiar Bibles, including the ESV and the revised NIV.

The Message is a popular paraphrase which has received endorsements from those outside typical ecclesiastic circles.

The Passion Translation (TPT) is a work in progress, yet its future sales seems promising due to its popularity within Charismatic groups.

GENEALOGY AND TIMELINE

The following two charts illustrate the relationships of some of the more common and familiar English translations by their derivation and by their publishing history. The "Genealogy of Familiar Bible Translations" starts with the earliest, complete English biblical text (Wycliffe's Bible). Lines terminating with arrows show a direct relationship between translations (as between an ancestor and a descendant), whereas dotted lines indicate a lesser or a less strict influence.

The "Timeline of Modern English Bibles" sorts some of the more familiar and common modern English Bible translations by their initial publication dates, even though some of the more popular editions have been revised more recently. For example, the NIV is posted in 1969 (since the publication of its *Gospel of John*), yet it has been revised as late as 2011.

Genealogy of Familiar English Bible Translations

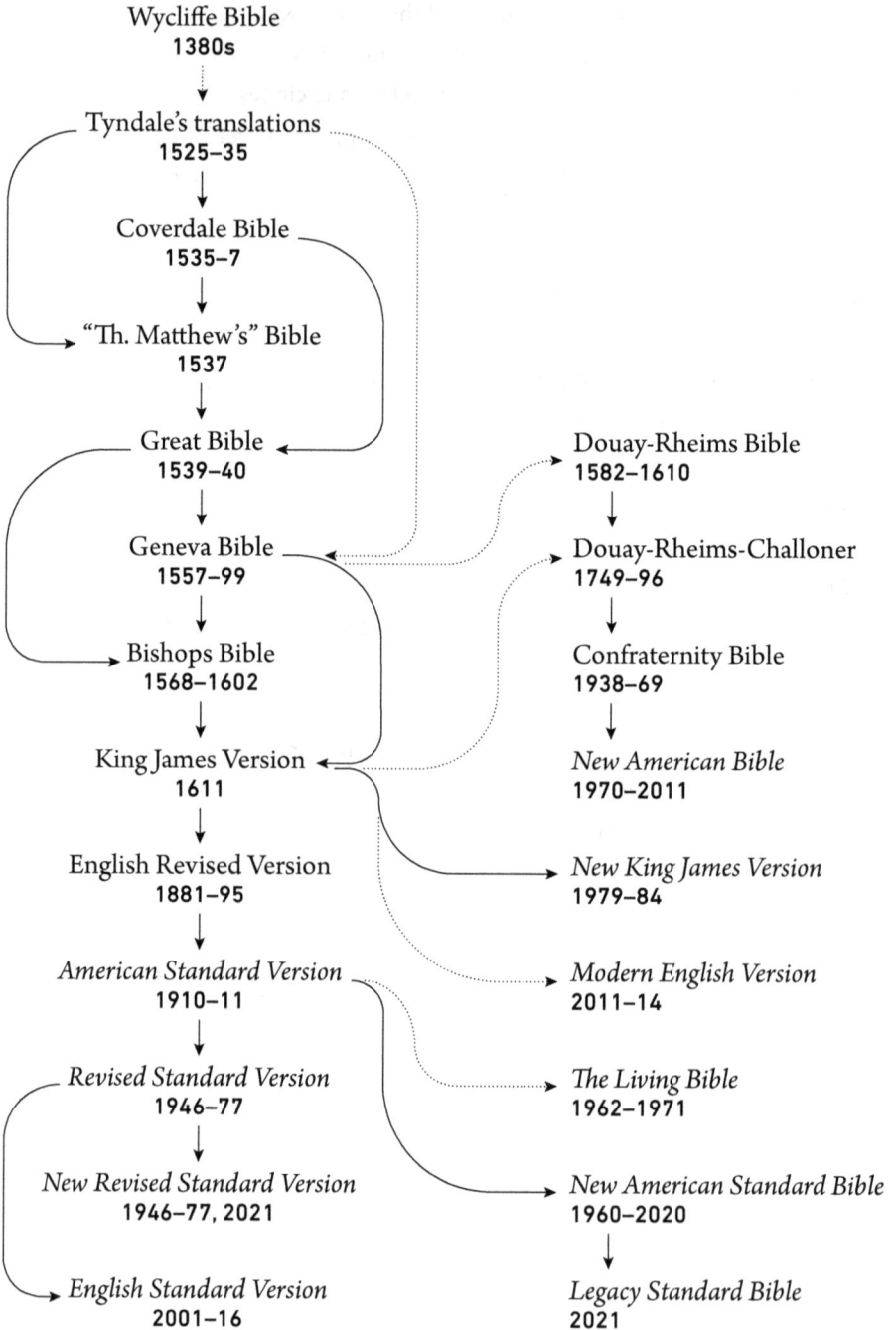

Wycliffe Bible
1380s

Tyndale's translations
1525–35

Coverdale Bible
1535–7

"Th. Matthew's" Bible
1537

Great Bible
1539–40

Geneva Bible
1557–99

Bishops Bible
1568–1602

King James Version
1611

English Revised Version
1881–95

American Standard Version
1910–11

Revised Standard Version
1946–77

New Revised Standard Version
1946–77, 2021

English Standard Version
2001–16

Douay-Rheims Bible
1582–1610

Douay-Rheims-Challoner
1749–96

Confraternity Bible
1938–69

New American Bible
1970–2011

New King James Version
1979–84

Modern English Version
2011–14

The Living Bible
1962–1971

New American Standard Bible
1960–2020

Legacy Standard Bible
2021

The Best Bible?

Timeline of Modern English Bibles

American Standard Version
1910–11

Confraternity Bible
1938–69

Jewish Publication Society *Tanakh*
1917

Revised Standard Version
1946–77

New World Translation
1950–2013

New English Bible
1961–70

Good News Bible
1964–92

New Jewish Publication
Society *Tanakh*
1958–1999

The Living Bible
1962–1971

Jerusalem Bible
1966

New American Standard Bible
1960–2020

The Living Bible
1962–1971

New International Version
1969–2011

New American Bible
1970–2011

New Jerusalem Bible
1985

New King James Version
1979–84

Revised English Bible
1989

New Revised Standard Version
1989–2021

Contemporary English Version
1991–99

NET Bible, New English Translation
1995–2017

The Message
1993–2018

New Living Translation
1996–2015

New International Reader's Version
1995–96

Holman Christian Standard Bible
1999–2009

Today's New
International Version
2001–05

Modern English Version
2011–14

Revised New
Jerusalem Bible
2018

English Standard Version
2001–16

Evangelical Heritage Version
2017–19

Common English Bible
2010–11

Christian Standard Bible
2017–20

Legacy Standard Bible
2021

ENDNOTES FOR THE INTRODUCTION

1 E.C.P.A., "Bible Translation . . . Best of 2020," *Christian Book Expo,* accessed January 26, 2021, https://christianbookexpo.com/bestseller/translations.php?id=BO20.

2 American Bible Society, "Prefered Bible Version," *State of the Bible 2015,* research by Barna Group (New York, NY: American Bible Society, February 2015), p. 16.

King James Version

The Holy Bible Containing the Old Testament and the New

Produced by various representatives from Oxford and Cambridge Universities and the Church of England, 1611

FORMAL / FUNCTIONAL TENDENCIES

FORMAL   FUNCTIONAL

Interlinear   NASB   **KJV**   NKJV   ESV   RSV   CSB   NRSV   NET   NIV   NLT   Free Paraphrase

TEXT BASES

English Base   Bishops' Bible, 2nd edition (1572, 1602).

OT Masoretic Hebrew and Ancient Versions.   **NT** *Textus Receptus.*

TRANSLATION TIMELINE

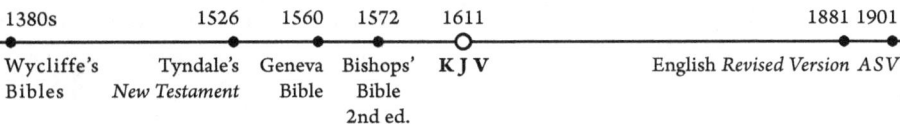

1380s	1526	1560	1572	1611	1881	1901
Wycliffe's Bibles	Tyndale's *New Testament*	Geneva Bible	Bishops' Bible 2nd ed.	**KJV**	English *Revised Version*	*ASV*

CONTEMPORARY EVENTS

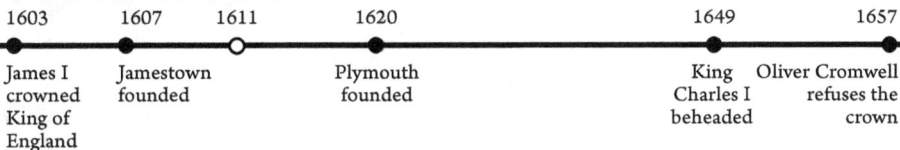

1603	1607	1611	1620	1649	1657
James I crowned King of England	Jamestown founded		Plymouth founded	King Charles I beheaded	Oliver Cromwell refuses the crown

PUBLICATION TIMELINE

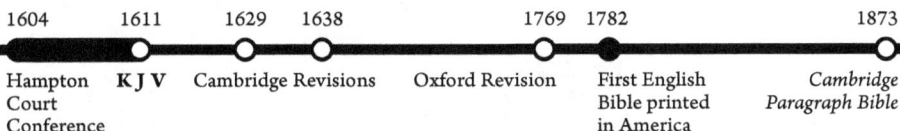

1604	1611	1629	1638	1769	1782	1873
Hampton Court Conference	**KJV**	Cambridge Revisions		Oxford Revision	First English Bible printed in America	*Cambridge Paragraph Bible*

At a Glance

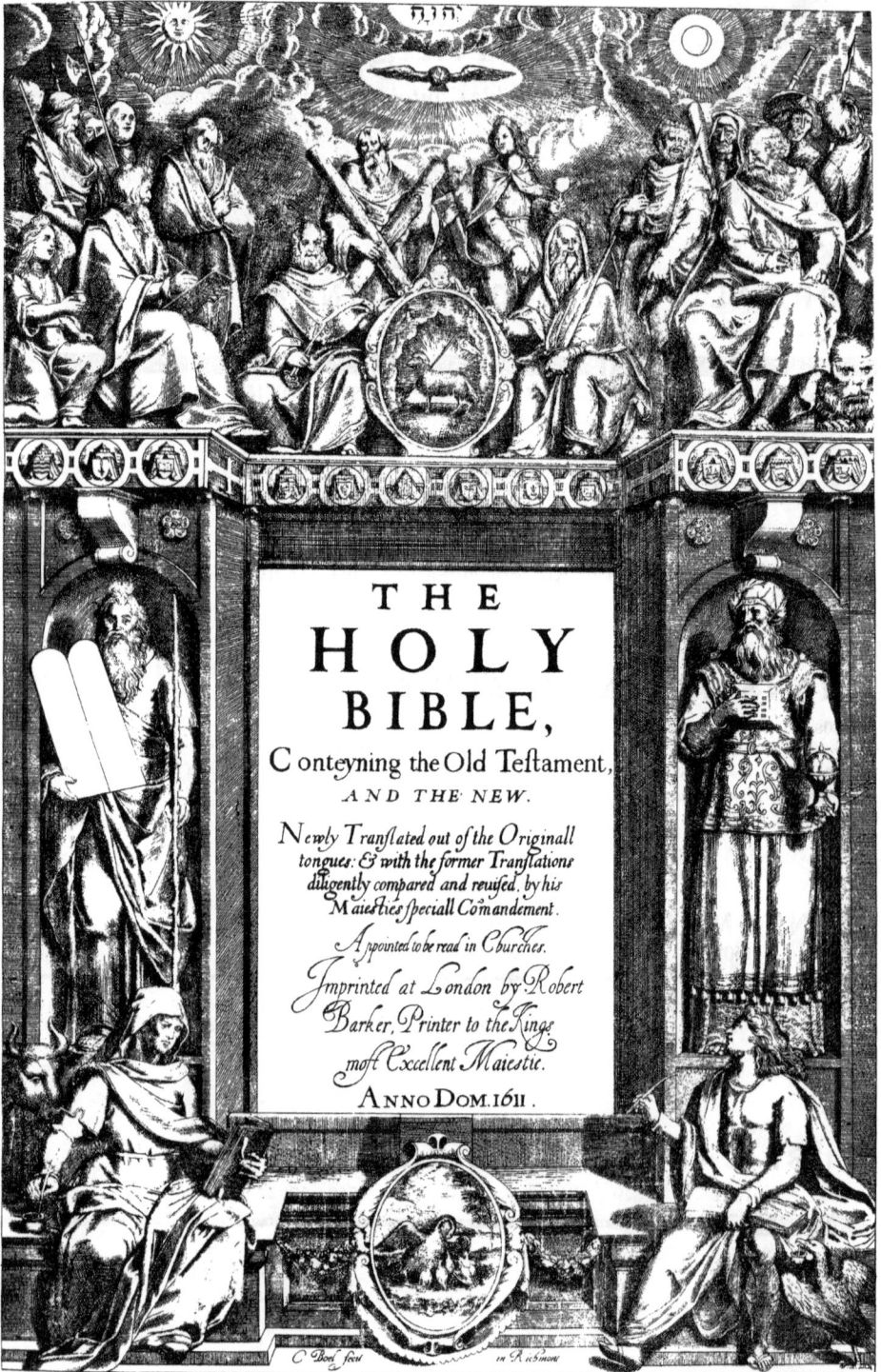

THE HOLY BIBLE,

Conteyning the Old Testament,

AND THE NEW.

Newly Translated out of the Originall
tongues: & with the former Translations
diligently compared and reuised, by his
Maiesties speciall Commandement.

Appointed to be read in Churches.

Imprinted at London by Robert
Barker, Printer to the Kings
most Excellent Maiestie.

ANNO DOM. 1611.

I n 1603, Queen Elizabeth I rested on her deathbed without a natural heir. Before dying, she implied that her second-cousin, James Stuart (*i.e.*, James VI, king of Scotland), should succeed to the English throne. She would leave him a kingdom rife with religious division and civil discord. Her own glorious reign preserved the island nation from Spanish invasion and Catholic plots, but the cost emptied England's coffers. The English Exchequer was left with outstanding debts and deficit spending.[1]

The English church, too, faced threats to its internal unity and its external peace: Elizabeth expelled English Catholics during her reign, yet Protestants were not all content with her Acts of Uniformity (1559), which governed church doctrine, practice, and polity, and vested authority over the church in the crown.

When Elizabeth died, James Stuart traveled to London with his retinue, *en route* to unify the two crowns of England and Scotland as the new English King James I. As he rode south surveying his new country, members of the English church intercepted him and offered him a petition signed by a thousand Puritan ministers.[2] Their petition humbly bade the king to cleanse the official Anglican liturgy from what they saw as remnants of Popism. The king promised to hold court the following year to discuss the matter.

James now had a kingdom held together by compromise and coercion. He did not need party divisions within his church, too. In 1604, the king met with Anglican bishops, clerics, and Puritan leaders at Hampton Court Palace in order to unite the church. However, the debates and decisions did not bode well for the Puritan sectarians. James refused all their requests—save one.

A certain Puritan leader, John Reinolds hoped to gain wider support for the popular Geneva Bible against the Anglican Bishops' Bible and other early translations. Reinolds may have doubted that his preferred version would gain the king's support. So he proposed the creation of a *new translation* in their stead. Reinolds defended his request with examples where the earlier renderings had mistreated the text.[3] One bishop there complained, "If every man's humour should be followed, there would be no end of translating!"

King James Version

ls zeale

EPISTLI
Apo

CHAP.
1 Paul commendeth his calling
9 and his defire to come to t
his Gofpel is , and the righte
fheweth. 18 God is angry
fin. 21 What were the finne

fed afoze by his Prophet
Scriptures,)
3 Concerning his S
Chzift our Lozd , which
the feed of Dauid accozdi
4 And declared to be
God, with power, accozdi
rit of holineffe, by the refu
the dead.
5 By whom we haue
and Apoftlefhip || foz obe
faith among all nations fc
6 Among whom are
led of Jefus Chzift.
7 To all that be in R
of God, called to be Saints
and peace from God our
the Lozd Jefus Chzift.
8 Firft J thanke my
Jefus Chzift foz you all, t
is fpoken of throughou
wozld.
9 Foz God is my wit
J feruell with my fpirit in
his Sonne, that witho
make mention of you, in
prayers,
10 Making requeft, (if b

King James had no love for the Geneva Bible, chiefly because he suspected its marginal notes. For the most part, the notes were politically innocuous and simply clarified the meaning of Scripture (though, later revisions made the notes more partisan and hostile towards Rome). The king took issue with certain notes that appeared to denigrate the monarch's divine right and authority—particularly those affixed to **Ex 3.19**, which permitted some people to disobey kings, and **2Ch 15.16**, which criticized another person for only deposing a regent instead of executing her.[4] James would not tolerate any reading of the Bible that questioned his right to rule.

Instead of dismissing Reinolds, James heartily assented to the Puritan's request and asked Cambridge and Oxford Universities to produce a new version with the support of church authorities. He "wished, that some special pains should be taken in that behalf for one uniform translation (professing that he could never, yet, see a Bible well translated in English, but the worst of all his Majesty thought the Geneva to be)."[5] King James hoped to unite his divided church and country around his new Bible—on condition that it contained no marginal notes.

STATED TRANSLATION IDEALS

The King James Version (KJV) is not a strictly word-for-word translation, as its preface indicates: "We (the translators) have not tied ourselves to uniformity of phrasing, or to an identity of words, as some perhaps would wish we had done."

"The old ecclesiastical words [were] to be kept, namely, as the word church [was] not to be translated congregation, etc." (in accordance with Archbishop Bancroft's Rule No. 3). This was to guard the church from controversies that Tyndale stirred up eighty-five years earlier in his debates with Sir Thomas More over which terms the Bible ought to employ. As the KJV's preface continues:

We have avoided the scrupulosity of the Puritans, who leave the old ecclesiastical words, and betake them to other, as when they put "washing" for "Baptism," and "Congregation" instead of "Church." [A]lso, on the other side, we have shunned the obscurity of the Papists, in the *Azimes, Tunike, Rational, Holocausts, Præpuce, Pasche,* and a number of such like, whereof their late Translation (*i.e.,* the Douay-Rheims Bible, 1582, 1609–10) is full, and that of purpose to darken sense. . . . But we desire that Scripture may speak like itself.

The translators made their goal clear: "Truly . . . we never thought from the beginning, that we should need to make a new translation, nor yet to make of a bad one a good one, . . . but to make a good one better, or out of many good ones, one principal good one, not justly to be excepted against; that has been our endeavour, that our mark."[6]

Read the original KJV preface at *booklink.id/ kjv-preface*

METHOD

King James wanted his Bible "to be done by the best learned in both the Universities [of Oxford and Cambridge], after them to be reviewed by the Bishops, and the chief learned of the Church; from them to be presented to the [King's] Privy Council; and lastly, to be ratified by his Royal authority, and so this whole Church to be bound unto it and none other."[7] Thus he intended, but James needed a way to pay for his translation. With a bare treasury, James had no money to offer his translators. Though, as the head of the Anglican Church, it was his right to fill the church's vacant positions whenever they opened with whomever he wished.[8]

Fifty-four scholars and theologians skilled in various languages were chosen to revise the Bible.[9] They were divided into six companies, two each for Oxford and Cambridge Universities and two for Westminster Abbey in London. Each company of seven or eight men was tasked with revising a portion of Scripture, including the Apocrypha.

The men in each company were expected to revise their portion, section by section. Each would translate the same section by himself. Then he would regroup and examine the others' work in that section. Whatever rendering they agreed upon would stand as the company's decision. They would then submit their revision to the other companies for their consideration (Bancroft's Rules 8 and 9).

Wherever words and phrases had several possible meanings, they were to be rendered consistently with writings of earlier Christian theologians, so long as they fit the immediate context and precedent found throughout Scripture. If there were still debates about the meaning of passages, they could be decided in a general conference. Two men from each of the six companies would settle the text when the companies' revisions were complete. If the revisers were still in doubt about the meaning of any passage, they could ask any available scholar in England for his judgment (Rules 4, 10–13).

From these twelve editors, three were responsible for further refining the work. The whole effort was finished by a general editor and assistant who made final edits and decisions before sending the text to print.

At last, after seven years, the KJV's text was published by the King's printer, Robert Barker, in 1611.[10] Eventually, this Bible would surpass its predecessors as a principal, standard version against which all modern English translations are still compared today.

For a complete list of translators, visit booklink.id/kjv-translator

> 18 ¶He that beleeueth on him, is not condemned: but hee that beleeueth not, is condemned already, because hee hath not beleeued in the Name of the onely begotten Sonne of God.

Jn 3.18 "¶He that beleeueth on him, is not condemned: but hee that beleeueth not, is condemned already, because hee hath not beleeued in the Name of the onely begotten Sonne of God." (KJV 1611)

The Best Bible?

TEXT BASES

English Text

The King James Bible is a revision of a 1602 edition of yet another revision—the Bishops' Bible (1568, '72).[11]

New Testament

Textus Receptus. The 4th (1588/9) or 5th (1598) major folio edition of Theodore Beza's Greek New Testament,[12] or the 3rd (1550) or 4th (1551) edition of Robert Stephanus. In 1881, F. H. A. Scrivener published an edition which conforms the Greek text to the editorial decisions of the KJV.[13]

Old Testament

Masoretic Hebrew-Aramaic text. Bomberg's second Rabbinic Bible (Venice, 1524–25), Complutensian Polyglot (1517), Pagninus (1528), Münster (1539), Antwerp Polyglot (1572).
  Ancient versions. Tremellius and Junius (Latin, 1590).

Apocrypha

Basel Bible (1545/50), Complutensian Polyglot (1517), Aldine Bible (1518). When the apocryphal books of Tobit and Judith differed between their Latin and Greek sources, the translators followed the Greek.[14]

CONTRIBUTORS

Fifty-four Anglican bishops and scholars worked on the KJV. Archbishop of Canterbury, Richard Bancroft (✝1610), oversaw the direction of the work. Lancelot Andrews (bishop of Ely, 1601; bishop of Winchester, 1618), John Harding (✝1610), and Edward

Lively (✝ 1605) were chosen to further review and edit the project. Miles Smith (who became the bishop of Gloucester in 1612) was the ultimate overseer and guided final production. He and Thomas Bilson (bishop of Winchester until 1616) put the final touches on the work before sending it through the printer.

THEOLOGICAL ASSUMPTIONS

Each of the translators of the KJV was a member of the official Church of England, but their loyalties were divided on church practice and polity. All upheld the *Thirty-nine Articles of Religion*, a Reformed Protestant and moderately Calvinist document imposed under Elizabeth I. All worked under Archbishop Bancroft's rules, which favored a conservative view of religious offices and practice.[15]

LANGUAGE CHANGE

Since the translators intended to revise the earlier Bishops' Bible (1568, '72), the language of the KJV reaches back to a previous century. In fact, the KJV held on to certain grammatical features and vocabulary that were starting to go out of style in its own day. The contrast with language we use today is so great that if someone exclusively reads the KJV without helps, they might question their faith in the perspicuity (*i.e.*, clarity) of Scripture.[16]

Sometimes the KJV uses words so old that they have altogether dropped from modern English use. These are what we call "dead words", such as:

"amerce" (which means to "punish with a fine," **Dt 22.19**),
"bolled" (to "swell," that is to "bud," **Ex 9.31**),
"beeves" (*i.e.*, "oxen," plural of "beef," **Lv 22.19**),
"bewray" (to "expose," "reveal," or "disclose," **Pr 29.24; Is 16.3; Mt 26.73**),
"crisping pin" (a tool for "crisping" or curling the hair, **Is 3.22**),

"trow" (to "trust" or "believe," **Luke 17:9**).

Several significant words have changed their meanings over time. Many of these words occur frequently. We call these words "false friends," because they sound or look familiar, but their earlier use radically differs from how they're used today.[17] They can trick modern readers, because their familiar spelling does not alert readers to check their definitions in a dictionary. For example:

Mk 1.30	Simon's wife's mother lay sick of a fever, and **anon** they tell him of her.	*"Anon" meant "immediately," not "after a time".*
Ro 5.8	God **commendeth** his love toward us, in that, while we were yet sinners, Christ died for us.	*"Commend" meant "display" or "show".*
Ps 50.23	[T]o him that ordereth his **conversation** aright will I shew the salvation of God.	*"Conversation" meant "manner of life" or "citizenship".*
1Kg 18.21	How long **halt** ye between two opinions?	*"Halt" meant "lame" or "to limp".*
Mt 18.8	[I]t is better for thee to enter into life **halt** or maimed, rather than having two hands or two feet to be cast into everlasting fire.	
Ro 1.13	But was **let** hitherto	*"Let" meant "prevent" in some cases.*
2Th 2.7	[H]e who now **letteth** will **let**	
Jn 14.2	In my Father's house are many **mansions**: if it were not so, I would have told you. I go to prepare a place for you.	*"Mansions" meant "rooms".*
Mk 8.8	So they did eat, and were filled: and they took up of the broken **meat** that was left seven baskets.	*"Meat" generally meant "food" or a "meal".*
Ps 119.147	I **prevented** the dawning of the morning, and cried: I hoped in thy word.	*"Prevent" meant "precede" or "go before".*
1Pt 4.5	Who shall give account to him that is ready to judge the **quick** and the dead.	*"Quick" meant "alive"; "quickened" meant "made alive"*

Pr 22.28	**Remove** not the ancient landmark, which thy fathers have set.	*"Remove" meant much more than "take from a place." It also meant "change", "replace", or "destroy".*
Ac 14.18	[W]ith these sayings **scarce** restrained they the people, that they had not done sacrifice unto them.	*"Scarce" was an adverb that meant "barely".*
1Ti 6.20	O Timothy, keep that which is committed to thy trust, avoiding profane and vain babblings, and oppositions of **science** falsely so called	*"Science" is an anglicized Latin word that meant "knowledge".*
Eph 2.13	[N]ow in Christ Jesus ye who **sometimes** were far off are made nigh by the blood of Christ.	*"Sometimes" meant "formerly", not "occasionally".*
2Ti 2.15	**Study** to shew thyself approved unto God, a workman that needeth not to be ashamed, rightly dividing the word of truth."	*"Study" meant "strive".*
1Co 10.24; cf. Ezr 9.12; Est 10.3	Let no man seek his own, but every man another's **wealth**	*"Wealth" meant "welfare".*
Ps 66.12	We went through fire and through water: but thou broughtest us out into a **wealthy** place.	*"Wealthy" meant "happy".*
2Co 8.1	We do you to **wit** of the grace of God	*"Wit" meant "know".*

The KJV revisers did not have as broad of a zoological understanding that we have today. Sometimes the identifications of certain animals were unknown. They interpreted some biblical animals as the medieval heraldic beasts that they were familiar with, or they borrowed from older translations in other languages:

Nm 24.8 is rendered, "God brought him (*i.e.* Israel) forth out of Egypt; he hath as it were the strength of an *unicorn*" (KJV, *emphasis added*, so Wycliffe, Tyndale, *et al.*). The word "unicorn" may conjure up an image of some fantastic heraldic beast, but it formally renders the Greek (LXX) *monokerōtos*—a creature with a single horn. The Douay Bible renders it "rhinoceros" from the Latin Vulgate *rinocerotis*, which itself is half-transcribed from its Greek source (*monokerōtos*). With further study, linguists learned that the underlying Hebrew word (*re'em*) actually meant a "wild ox" (RV/ASV, CSB, ESV, NASB, NIV, NLT, *et al.*; "wild bull" NET)—a much more fitting and familiar analogy in this passage and a better lexical fit for the number of times it occurs throughout the OT (*cf.* Dt 33.17; Jb 39.9, 10; Ps 22.21; 29.6; 92.10; Is 34.7).

Dt 32.33, "dragon" (instead of "serpent")

Is 11.8, "cockatrice" (also known as a *basilisk*. This fantastic, fire-breathing *chimera* is a cross between a rooster and a dragon. In all likelihood, the Hebrew word refers to the familiar venomous snake that we know today as an "adder"),

Is 13.21, "satyrs" (now known as "wild goats", *cf.* ESV, NET, NLT, CSB, NIV, GNB; but "goat-demons" NRSV, or "shaggy goats" NASB),

And there are some words and phrases that no preacher should say aloud without due caution:

THY FINE ENGLISH TONGUE. In late Middle English the plural, second-person pronoun (*ye, you, your*[*s*]) started to replace the singular forms (*thou, thee, thy, thine*). Shakespeare's English no longer held a regular distinction between the forms "ye" and "you." "Ye" eventually found itself consigned to poetry, while "you" became the norm for both subject *and* object. The singular, second-person pronouns (*thou, thee, thy, thine*) used to function as familiar address, but, thanks to the Bible's influence, they became the exclusive address to God.

Part of speech	2nd Person Singular	2nd Person Plural
Subject	Thou	Ye
Object	Thee	You
Possessive determiner	Thy, Thine	Your
Reflexive pronoun	Thyself	Yourself

The benefit of these older English forms is they better map the underlying grammars of Greek and Hebrew, which also use both singular and plural, second-person pronouns. For example:

Lk 5.24, "But that **ye** may know … I say unto **thee** … take up **thy** couch, and go into **thine** house." — Here, Jesus addresses the crowd before speaking to the individual.

(continued next page)

Jn 3.7, "Marvel not that I said unto **thee, ye** must be born again." — Though spoken to Nicodemus, Jesus' words apply to a broader audience.

2Sa 7.23, "And what one nation in the earth is like **thy** people, even like Israel, whom God went to redeem for a people to himself, and to make him a name, and to do for **you** great things and terrible, for **thy** land, before **thy** people, which **thou** redeemest to **thee** from Egypt, from the nations and their gods?" — In the midst of his public prayer to God, David addresses the people of Israel.

With the loss of the second-person, singular forms in modern English, we've also lost their corresponding verbal endings (*-est, -st, -t; -edst, -dst*). Also, the third-personal singular endings (*-eth, -th*) have yielded to other forms (*-es, -s*).

Verb ending	Present tense	Past tense
1st Person Singular	I walk, I am walking	I walked
2nd Per. Sg.	thou walkest	thou walkedst
3rd Per. Sg.	he walketh	he walked

Awareness of these kinds of language features help us read the KJV and earlier English Bibles accurately. It even gives us advantages where modern editions lack these specific language distinctions. ◄

"He purgeth it, that it may bring forth more fruit" (Jn 15.2)

"Solomon loved many strange women" (1Kg 11.1)

"Nevertheless even [Solomon] did outlandish women cause to sin" (Ne 13.26)

"Mt. Sinai was altogether on a smoke" (Ex 19.18)

"I will cut off from Ahab him that pisseth against the wall" (2Kg 9.8)

"And Jacob sod pottage" (Gn 25.29)

FEATURES

The KJV was not intended as a strictly concordant or formal translation. For example, the Greek word *splangchna*, whose unaffected meaning is "bowels", is rendered figuratively twice out of the eleven times it occurs in the New Testament (as "mercy" in Lk 1.78 and "inward affection" in 2Co 7.15).

Proper names were meant to follow traditional English use. They were not to follow the Catholic Vulgate's spelling or transliterate the Hebrew and Greek anew (Bancroft's Rule No. 2).

No marginal notes about controversial doctrines were allowed, as King James intended. There were marginal notes, however, that gave explanations or alternate renderings where the original language fought easy translation. And, if a Greek or Hebrew word allowed for multiple meanings, or if a formal rendering was too hard to understand, then an alternate or literal meaning would be printed in the margins. The revisers printed notes with references to parallel passages (Rules 6, 7).[18] And there were even notes indicating text-critical issues.[19]

The KJV was originally set in a thick, black letter font. Words that were inserted into the text to complete its meaning were distinguished by small, roman type. Modern editions set supplied words with *italic* or *oblique* fonts.

Chapters followed familiar, traditional divisions. (Bancroft's Rule No. 5) Originally, each verse started at the beginning of a new line. Paragraphs were indicated with pilcrows (¶).[20] Later editions, like the [*New*] *Cambridge Paragraph Bible* (1873, 2011), formatted the text into indented paragraphs.

The original KJV had headings and summaries at the beginning of each chapter. It also had a genealogy and a map of the Holy Land among other prefatory matter. Modern printed KJV Bibles usually omit these features.

RECEPTION

At the time of the KJV's publication, the Geneva Bible was still the most popular version available. In fact, the preface of the KJV, titled "The Translator to the Reader" (written by Miles Smith), quotes the Geneva Bible wherever it cites Scripture.

King James banned the continued production of the Geneva translation in 1616 in order to suppress competition in favor of his Bible. But European printers continued to publish and export it to England until 1644. Even Robert Barker, the King's printer, continued to print the Geneva Bible in England after its prohibition. He simply left the date, 1599, unaltered on its title page.

The KJV only started to gain influence after the death of King James and after the Bishops conspired to suppress the publication

THE NEWE

Testament of
our Lord and Sauiour
IESVS CHRIST.

¶ *Newly Translated out of*
the Originall Greeke : and with
the former Translations diligently
compared and reuised, by his
Maiesties speciall Com-
mandement.

¶ IMPRINTED
at London by *Robert*
Barker , Printer to the
Kings most Excellent
Maiestie.

ANNO DOM. 1611.

of the Geneva Bible. Also, Robert Barker invested much to obtain the rights to print the King James Bible. He was eager to promote the KJV since he had a significant financial investment that he hoped to recoup.

REPRESENTATIVE SAMPLES

Familiar Passages

Gn 1.1–2	In* the beginning God created the heaven and the earth. And the earth was without form, and void; and darkness was upon the face of the deep. And the Spirit of God moved upon the face of the waters.
	1611 marginal note *with original spelling* (mn): *Pfal.33.6. and 136.5. acts.14.15. and 17.24. hebr.11.3
Ps 23.1–2	The LORD *is* * my shepherd; I shall not want. He maketh me to lie down in † green pastures: he leadeth me beside the † still waters.
	mn: * Efa.40.11 Iere.23.5. Ezech. 34. Ioh.10.11.23. I.Pet.2.25. † *Heb. paftures of tender graffe.* † *Heb. waters of quietneffe.*
Ps 27.4	One *thing* have I desired of the LORD, that will I seek after; that I may dwell in the house of the LORD all the days of my life, to behold ‖ the beauty of the LORD, and to enquire in his temple.
	mn: ‖ *Or, the delight.*
Jn 3.16	¶* For God so loved the world, that he gave his only begotten Son, that whosoever believeth in him should not perish, but have everlasting life.
	mn: * I. Iohn 4.9.

KJV

Divine Name and Titles

Yhwh	Ps 24.1a	The earth *is* the LORD's, and the fulness thereof
adonai	Ps 90.1b	Lord, thou hast been our dwelling place † in all generations.
		mn: † *Heb.in generation and generation.*
elohim	Gn 1.27a	So **God** created man in his *own* image
adonai Yhwh	Ps 73.28b	I have put my trust in the **Lord God**
adonai elohim	Dn 9.3a	¶ And I set my face unto the **Lord God**
Yhwh saba'oth	1Sa 17.45b	I come to you in the name of the **LORD of hosts**
el shaddai	Ex 6.3a	And I appeared unto Abraham, unto Isaac, and unto Jacob, by the name of **God Almighty**
kyrios	Lk 20.42b	The **LORD** said unto my **Lord**, Sit thou on my right hand [21]
christos	Mt 16.16b	* Thou art the **Christ**, the Son of the living God
		mn: * Ioh.6.69.

New Testament Text Base

Mt 17.21	Howbeit this kind goeth not out but by prayer and fasting.
Mt 18.11	* For the Son of man is come to save that which was lost.
	mn: * Luke 19.10.
Ac 8.37	And Philip said, If thou believest with all thine heart, thou mayest. And he answered and said, I believe that Jesus Christ is the Son of God.
1Jn 5.7b–8a	. . . in heaven, the Father, the Word, and the Holy Ghost: and these three are one. And there are three that bear witness in earth, the spirit . . .

The Best Bible?

Gender Language

ʾādām	Gn 9.6	Whoso sheddeth **man's** blood, by **man** shall his blood be shed: for in the image of God made he **man**.
ʾîsh . . . nephesh	Lv 24.17	¶ * And **he** that †killeth **any man** shall surely be put to death. mn: * Exod 21.12.deu.19.21. † *Hebr. ſmiteth the life of* *a man.*
ʾāvîw	Pr 15.5a	* A fool despiseth **his father's** instruction mn: * Chap.10.1.
huioi	Mt 5.9	Blessed *are* the peacemakers: for they shall be called the **children** of God.
anthrōpōn	Mt 4.19	Follow me, and I will make you fishers **of men**.
hekastō . . . autou	Ro 2.6	Who will render **to every man** according to **his** deeds
adelphoi	Gal 5.13	For, **brethren**, ye have been called unto liberty; only *use* not liberty for an occasion to the flesh, but by love serve one another.
gynaikos anēr	Ti 1.6a	If any be blameless, **the husband of** one **wife**, having faithful children
gynaikas	1Ti 3.11	**The women** likewise must be serious, no slanderers, but temperate, faithful in all things.

Difficult Renderings

1Sa 13.1	Saul † reigned **one year**; and when he had reigned **two years** over Israel mn: † *Hebr.the ſonne of one yeere in his reigning.*
Is 28.13	But the word of the LORD was unto them **precept upon precept, precept upon precept; line upon line, line upon line; here a little, *and* there a little**; that they might go, and fall backward, and be broken, and snared, and taken.

Significant Renderings

'almah	Is 7.14	Therefore the Lord himself shall give you a sign; * Behold, **a virgin** shall conceive, and bear a son, and shall call his name Immanuel.
		mn: * Math.1.23.luc.1.31.
she'ol, 'abaddon	Pr 15.11	* **Hell** and **destruction** *are* before the LORD: how much more then the hearts of the children of men?
		mn: * Iob 26.6.
egennēsen	Mt 1.2	* Abraham **begat** Isaac; and * Isaac **begat** Jacob; and * Jacob **begat** Judas and his brethren;
		mn: * Gen.21.3. * Gene.25.26. * Gen.29.35. * Gen.38.27.
eskēnōsen	Jn 1.14	* And the Word was made flesh, and **dwelt** among us, (and we beheld his glory, the glory as of the only begotten of the Father,) full of grace and truth.
		mn: * Mat.1.16.
tois ioudaiois	Jn 18.36	Jesus answered, My kingdom is not of this world: if my kingdom were of this world, then would my servants fight, that I should not be delivered **to the Jews**: but now is my kingdom not from hence.
dikaiosunē theou, pisteōs Iēsou Christou	Ro 3.22a	Even **the righteousness of God** *which is* by **faith of Jesus Christ** unto all and upon all them that believe
Granville Sharp's rule not applied	Tt 2.13	Looking for that blessed hope, and the glorious appearing of **the great God** and **our Saviour Jesus Christ**

VARIANTS, MISHAPS, & REVISIONS

Even the first printed edition of the KJV had variations. The first edition's initial printing is called the "'He' Bible" (1611), while its second issue is the "'She' Bible" (1611–3), because of a debate over the interpretation of **Ruth 3.15** ("he [Boaz] / she [Ruth] went into the city"). Further corrections were made in 1616.

In 1629, two members of the original translation team (Samuel Ward and John Bois) revised the entire KJV, but omitted the Apocrypha. Supplied words were more thoroughly and consistently revised in the 1638 edition. After these revisions, the text was left alone for more than a century.[22]

During that time, certain editions were printed with curious errors. For example, in 1631, Robert Barker omitted a single word from a single sentence in what today is called the "Wicked" Bible. The word "not" was left out of the sixth commandment, so that it reads "Thou shalt commit adultery." Upon discovering the error, King James fined Barker, and he was forced to enter debtors' prison.[23] Here are few more errata from a handful of editions:

Year	Misprinted Edition	Error
1611	The "Judas" Bible	Mistook **"Jesus"** so that **Mt 26.36** reads, "Then commeth **Judas** with them unto a place called Gethsemane"
1631	The "Wicked" Bible	Omitted **"not"** so that **Ex 20.14** reads, "Thou shalt commit adultery."
1653	The "Unrighteous" Bible	Added a prefix **"un-"** so that **1Co 6.9** reads, "the **un**righteous shall inherit the kingdom of God."
1717	The "Vinegar" Bible	A heading at **Luke 20** reads "The Parable of the **Vinegar**" instead of the **"Vineyard"**
1795		Misprinted **"filled"** in **Mk 7.27** to read "Let the children be **killed**"
1801	The "Murderer's" Bibles	Mistook **"murmurers"** in **Jude 16** to read "These are **murderers**"
1804		Changed **"to death"** in **Nm 35.18** to read "the murderer shall surely be put **together**"
1823	The "Rebecca" Bible	Misspelled **"damsels"** in **Gn 24.61** so that Rebecca arose with her **"camels"**.

Drs. Francis S. Paris from Cambridge (1762) and Benjamin Blaney from Oxford (1769) corrected a number of errors, regularized spelling and punctuation, and added over 30,000 marginal references. Their text differs from the 1611 editions in almost 24,000 places. Blaney's text forms the basis of most modern editions. Most changes were insignificant, but a few are meaningful and important, such as:

Verse.	1611 original edition	1769 and later editions
Gn 6.5	God (*i.e.*, Elohim)	GOD (YHWH)
Gn 39.16	her lord	his lord
Nm 6.14	lambe	ram
Jos 3.15	at	All
Jg 11.2	his wives sons	his wife's sons
Ru 3.15	he	she
1Kg 8.61	your	our
2Ch 13.6	his LORD	his lord
2Ch 28.11	God	the LORD
2Ch 32.5	prepared	repaired
Jb 39.30	he	she
Dn 10.16, 17, 19	Lord	lord
Jn 15.20	his Lord	his lord
1Co 15.6	And	after [24]

ASSESSMENT

Besides recording divine revelation, Bible translations also function like balance sheets or snapshots of a language's development. Just as John Wycliffe preserved for us a picture of middle English from the late fourteenth century with his translations, so the KJV enshrines for us a portrait of early modern English idiom at the height of the Tudor era. Its style is simple, yet dignified. It is rightly praised for its cadence and rhythm, features intended by its revisers to make it more suitable for preaching.

The KJV's use of second-person, singular pronouns ("thee", "thou", *etc.*) give readers a greater degree of formal precision that modern translations altogether lack. Its number remains clear when context is silent so the pronoun is disambiguated. (For examples, see "Thy Fine English Tongue" on page 215).

The King James Bible has no copyright restrictions outside the British Commonwealth. With no demand for royalties, the KJV has the largest number of references and resources supporting it—though these vary in quality. The most popular and helpful of these tools is Strong's *Concordance*, ideal for thorough word studies and for finding passages when all one can remember is a single word.

What the KJV gains in linguistic precision, though, cannot compensate for its lack in accuracy. The KJV revisers were the greatest biblical scholars that England had produced—up to that time. However, scholarship does not stand still, and just as King James's men relied on the studies of those who had gone before them, so do modern translators. They could not anticipate the many significant discoveries made in the last 400 years since the KJV's publication. (See "New Discoveries of Old Sources" starting on page 21.) Those who originally labored over the KJV could not have imagined the increase of knowledge or the access to resources that are now at the fingertips of modern translators.

The language of the KJV can give readers a false sense of authority simply because of how strange it sounds. It sounds like how one might expect an ancient religious document ought to sound. But just as scholarship has moved on, so, too, has language. In particular, readers ought to beware of words in this version that look familiar, yet have changed their meaning over time. (See page 213 for examples of "false friends.")

Those who persist in the exclusive study of the KJV ought to become better acquainted with early modern English, so as not to read into its passages what its translators never meant to say. There are a number of useful references to this end, including *The King James Bible Word Book* (1994) from Thomas Nelson Publishers.

Read the original KJV preface at *booklink.id/kjv-preface*

Readers who study the language of the KJV benefit from a closer connection to earlier generations of English writers, a gift which modern translations cannot give. Familiarity with Elizabethan and Jacobine English offers readers access to historical treatments of Christian doctrine. It opens a door to old communities of faith and insight into the development of the English language.

Finally, readers will benefit from studying Miles Smith's original preface to the 1611 KJV, titled "To the Reader."

ENDORSEMENTS

King James I originally intended his Bible to be the sole official translation for the Anglican Church, but we have no evidence that he ever gave it any official authorization. Even though its title page reads "Appointed to be read in Churches," it was never officially acknowledged as the exclusive—the one and only—Bible for the Church of England. Nonetheless, some believe that its royal patronage and the ad copy on its title page give it official status, hence the KJV's British nickname—the "Authorised" Version (AV).

Members of the Anglican Communion—the Church of England, the Episcopal Church, and the Anglican Church of Canada, *et al.*—and the Christian Reformed Church in North America all authorize or approve the KJV/AV for use in public worship.[25] (The Reformed Episcopal Church considers the KJV their historic "standard Bible.") [26]

The Holy Synod of Bishops of the Orthodox Church in America has encouraged the use of the KJV in liturgical service and Bible study until such a time when a better alternative to the RSV and NRSV becomes available.[27]

There are some who persist in arguing for the superiority and sole authority of the KJV over and against all other English translations. The more sophisticated of such opinions are based on the conviction that the KJV is the culmination of a single, pure line of transmission extending from the original autographs.

The Best Bible?

COPYRIGHT

The King James Version has been in the public domain in the United States of America since 1776.[28]

For those in the United Kingdom, you may quote up to 500 verses from the King James Version in any form without prior written permission; the verses may not constitute a complete book of the Bible; they must comprise less than 25% of your work's content; they may not be quoted in a commentary or other biblical reference work; and your work must include the following copyright acknowledgment.

> Scripture quotations from The Authorized (King James) Version. Rights in the Authorized Version in the United Kingdom are vested in the Crown. Reproduced by permission of the Crown's patentee, Cambridge University Press.

Unless used exclusively, follow citations with the designation (KJV). For example:

Jn 1.4, "In him was life; and the life was the light of men." (KJV)

For permissions not covered here, write to the Permissions Department, Cambridge University Press, University Printing House, Shaftesbury Road, Cambridge CB2 8BS, U.K. (http://www.cambridge.org/about-us/rights-permissions /permissions/permissions-requests/).

ENDNOTES FOR THE KING JAMES VERSION

1   Elizabeth I not only inherited the debts of her spendthrift father, Henry VIII, she also spent deficits on foreign policy and national survival (*ala* the Spanish Armada). She left James I with a national debt of £365,254 in 1603, which is roughly £112.3 million ($140.5 million USD) as of late 2019.

   Graham E. Seel and David L. Smith, *The Early Stuart Kings, 1603–1642*, (London and New York: Routledge, 2001), p. 5.

   The current inflated value of the Tudor debts were determined by the Bank of England's inflation calculator, accessed June 1, 2020, https://www.bankofengland.co.uk/monetary-policy/inflation/inflation-calculator.

2   This petition, which was signed by the thousand Puritan leaders, is also known as the Millenary Petition.

3   John Reinolds (alternately Reynolds or Rainolds) gave **Gal 4.25; Ps 105.28; 106.30** as examples where earlier translations missed the meaning. The Geneva Bible, on the other hand, had rendered them all to Reinolds' satisfaction.

4   The marginal note at **Ex 1.19** reads, "Their disobedience in this was lawful, but their dissembling (deception) evil."; and the one at **2Ch 15.16**, "Or grandmother: & herein he showed that he lacked zeal, for she should have died both by the covenant (**2Ch 15.13**) and by the law of God, but he gave place to foolish pity & would also seem after a sort to satisfy the law."

5   William Barlow, *Summe and Substance of the Conference* (Clerkenwell, England: Bye and Law, Printers, 1804), p. 35.

6   Miles Smith, "The Translator to the Reader," preface to the KJV (London: the King's Printer [Robert Barker], 1611).

7   Barlow, *Summe and Substance*, p. 35.

8   The practicing of buying and selling church offices is a form of simony.

9   *The English Hexapla exhibiting the Six Important English Translations of the New Testament Scriptures.* . . . (London: Samuel Bagster and Sons, 1841).

10   Robert Barker (✝1643) inherited the royal patent (official monopoly) for printing Bibles from his father, Christopher Barker (✝1599).

11   One copy of the 1602 Bishops' Bible that the King James revisers worked from now sits in the Bodleian Library with this catalogue number: Bib. Eng. 1602 b. I.

12   There is some confusion as to how to number Beza's ten or eleven Greek NT editions. This is according to the best of my reckoning.

Donald L. Brake, *A Visual History of the King James Bible* (Grand Rapids, MI: Baker Books, 2011), pp. 141–2;

Bruce M. Metzger and Bart D. Ehrman, *The Text of the New Testament: Its Transmission, Corruption, and Restoration*, 4th ed. (Oxford: Oxford U. Press, 2005), pp. 151–2.

Daniel B. Wallace, "3. From the KJV to the RV (from Elegance to Accuracy)," *Bible.org*, last modified March 21, 2001, accessed July 3, 2020, https://bible.org/seriespage/3-kjv-rv-elegance-accuracy.

[13] Scrivener's "Appendix" identifies 190 places where the KJV departs from its Greek base (Beza 1598).

F. H. A. Scrivener, *The New Testament in the Original Greek According to the Text Followed in the Authorised Version....* (Cambridge University Press, 1881), pp. vii–xi.

[14] "Report on the Making of the Version of 1611 Presented to the Synod of Dort" (November 1618) in *Records of the English Bible*, ed. Alfred W. Pollard (Oxford University Press, 1911), p. 339.

[15] The KJV has been charged with theologically biased translation in some passages (*cf.* **Ac 2.47**; **Heb 6.6**; **10.29**), yet these verses follow precedent from earlier versions.

[16] Two-hundred, seventy-three years after the publication of the KJV, William Aldis Wright published *The Bible Word-book*, 2nd rev. and enlarged ed. (London: Macmillan & Co., 1884). It is filled with articles explaining 2,316 archaic words and phrases used in the KJV and the *Book of Common Prayer*. Aldis' work could be expanded now, 134 years later, to further demonstrate how a popular, revered translation can lose its usefulness when its meaning fades into obscurity.

[17] Mark Ward, "Dead Words and False Friends," in *Authorized: The Use and Misuse of the King James Bible* (Bellingham, WA: Lexham Press, 2018).

[18] According to F. H. A. Scrivener, the Old Testament had "6,637 marginal notes, 4,111 of which expressed the more literal meaning of the original Hebrew; 2,156 gave alternate renderings (indicated by "Or" preceding it); 63 gave meanings of proper names; 240 relate to harmonization of parallel passages; and 67 refer to variant readings of the Hebrew text which he listed."

The Cambridge Paragraph Bible of the Authorized English Version, ed. F. H. A. Scrivener (Cambridge University Press, 1873), pp. xxiv–xxv, *via* James D. Price, "A Response to Pastor Robert J. Sargent's pamphlet....," accessed March 1, 2019, http://www.jamesdprice.com/images/Price_A_Response_to_Pastor_Robert_J.pdf.

[19] Samples of text critical notes found in the KJV's margins (1611 edition):

Mt 26.26 "blessed it: Many Greek copies have, gave thanks";

Lk 17.36 "Two men shall be in the field, the one shall be taken, and the other left: This 36. verse is wanting in most of the Greek copies";

Ac 13.18 "suffered: Gr. ἐτροποφόρσεν (*etropophórsen*), perhaps, for ἐτροποφόρησεν (*etropophórēsen*) as a nurse beareth or feedeth her child, **Dt 1.31; 2Mc 7.27** according to the Sept[uagint] and so Chrysost[om]"

[20] Pilcrows (¶) indicate paragraphs as far as **Acts 20.36**.

[21] The 1611 editions of **Lk 20.42** do not set the initial "Lord" in [small-]caps; though, the 1769 Blaney edition does.

[22] Parliament even moved to make an official revision during the reign of Oliver Cromwell, but nothing came of the proposal.

[23] Robert Barker's fine for his misprint was £ 200. As of late 2020, Barker's debt would be valued at about £ 41,970 ($ 57,908 USD).

[24] James D. Price, *King James Onlyism: A New Sect* (Chattanooga, TN, 2006), p. 104.

[25] General Synod of the Church of England, "Versions of Scripture," by David Michael Hope, Archbishop of York (Eboracensis), October 9, 2002, GS Misc 698.

"Bible Translations" from the website of the Christian Reformed Church in North America, accessed September 6, 2019, https://www.crcna.org/welcome/beliefs/bible-translations.

"What We Believe: The Bible" from the website of The Episcopal Church, accessed September 6, 2019, https://www.episcopalchurch.org/bible/.

[26] Fifty-fifth General Council of the Reformed Episcopal Church, "Of Translations of the Bible," in *Constitution & Canons* (Dallas, TX, 2017), Title III, Canon 36.

[27] Bishop Tikhon, "Bishop's Pastoral Letter on the *New Revised Standard Version*," from the website of the Holy Trinity Cathedral, accessed September 6, 2019, https://www.holy-trinity.org/liturgics/tikhon.nrsv.html.

[28] The date, July 4, 1776, marks the American colonies' break with the English crown. Whenceforth, the citizens of the United States of America have refused to pay any of the British sovereigns' perpetual royalties for the publication of the "Authorised Version," beginning with the edition printed by Robert Aitken in Philadelphia, PA, in 1782.

Revised Standard Version®

The Holy Bible containing the Old and New Testaments

Initially produced for the International Council of Christian Education, 1946;
Production completed under the National Council of the
Churches of Christ in the USA, 1952–77

FORMAL / FUNCTIONAL TENDENCIES

FORMAL   FUNCTIONAL

Interlinear   NASB KJV NKJV ESV **RSV** CSB NRSV NET NIV NLT   Free Paraphrase

TEXT BASES

English Base *American Standard Version* (1901).
OT Masoretic Hebrew and Ancient Versions.   **NT** Eclectic Greek.

TRANSLATION TIMELINE

1611	1885	1901	1927	1952	1989	2001
KJV	English *Revised Version*	*ASV*	Goodspeed-Smith's *An American Translation*	**RSV**	*NRSV*	*ESV*

CONTEMPORARY EVENTS

1929	1933	1945	1947	1952	1954	1955	1962–5
Wall Street Stock Market Crash	Discovery of Chester Beatty papyri	World War II ends	Discovery of the Dead Sea Scrolls		McCarthy US Senate hearings	Discovery of the Bodmer Papyri	Vatican II Council

PUBLICATION TIMELINE

1928	1937	1946	1952	1957	1962	1966	1971	1973	1977
NCCC acquires *ASV* copyright from Th. Nelson	Revision begins	NT	OT	Apocrypha	*Harper Study Bible*	RSV Catholic edition	NT 2nd ed.	RSV *Common Bible*	RSV Expanded Apocrypha

THE
Holy Bible

Revised Standard Version

CONTAINING THE

OLD AND NEW TESTAMENTS

TRANSLATED FROM THE ORIGINAL TONGUES
BEING THE VERSION SET FORTH A.D. 1611
REVISED A.D. 1881-1885 AND A.D. 1901
COMPARED WITH THE MOST ANCIENT AUTHORITIES
AND REVISED A.D. 1952

THOMAS NELSON & SONS

TORONTO   CAMDEN, N.J.   LONDON

The *Revised Standard Version* (RSV) is a modern yet somewhat older version that has found a home in the pews of many churches. It is the update of an update—a revision of the *American Standard Version* (ASV).

The ASV and its transatlantic sister, the English Revised Version (RV), were themselves revisions of the classic King James Version. The KJV was feeling its age by 1870—259 years after its initial publication—when the Convocation of Canterbury called for its renewal. By this time, the meanings of certain English words had changed, certain parts of grammar had subsided and dropped from regular use, and both archæological research and later discoveries of older manuscripts shed new light on the original sources. The British revisers sought to bring the Bible into the modern era with contemporary scholarship. After fifteen years of work, a joint team of American and British scholars published the entire Revised Version in 1885 (and the Apocrypha in 1895). The American team later published their version (the ASV) in 1901, which included all of their recommendations that their British colleagues rejected from the RV.

In 1928, the predecessor to the Division of Christian Education of the National Council of Churches[1] obtained the ASV's copyright from its publisher, Thomas Nelson & Sons.[2] By this time, there had already been significant new archaeological and manuscript discoveries since the ASV's publication. Resources that reflected the latest scholarship in vocabulary, grammar, and *Koinē* Greek idiom had only recently been made available.

Beginning in 1930, the American Standard Bible Committee convened to start revising the ASV. Sadly, the Wall Street stock market crash forced the Committee to halt their work by 1932 due to a lack of funds. It wasn't until 1937, when they had raised enough capital to begin work again. They anticipated a completed Bible within five years, starting that December, but they could not foresee that the Second World War (1936–45) would delay their overall production. Submarine warfare cut off transatlantic collaboration between the American translators and their British colleagues and deprived them of scholarly contributions from Europe. Nonetheless, the Americans pressed on and completed their New Testament after the war's conclusion. It was finally published with great fanfare in February 1946, followed by the Old Testament in 1952. (The Apocrypha was published in 1957.)

The RSV has undergone several revisions since its initial publication. The edition of 1959 saw revisions to both Old and New Testaments, and the *Harper Study Bible* (1962) included some minor updates. In 1965, a Catholic edition of the NT was released (followed by a Catholic OT the following year).[3] A second edition of the NT was published in 1971, followed by an ecumenical edition, called the *Common Bible* (1973), and an expanded Apocrypha (1977), which includes **3** and **4 Maccabees** and **Psalm 151.**[4]

STATED TRANSLATION IDEALS

In contrast with the earlier English Revised and *American Standard Versions* (RV/ASV), which retained the Elizabethan vocabulary and style of the classic KJV, the RSV Bible Committee believed that the Bible should "not be disguised in phrases that are no longer clear, or hidden under words that have changed or lost their meaning. It must stand forth in language that is direct and plain and meaningful to people today." Yet, the RSV "is not a new translation in the language of today. It is not a paraphrase which aims at striking idioms. It is a revision which seeks to preserve all that is best in the English Bible as it has been known and used through the years." The revisers worked so that the RSV would "embody the best results of modern scholarship as to the meaning of the Scriptures" and express that meaning in an English diction designed for use in public and private worship and not just for reading and instruction.[5] They hoped that the RSV would supplant its classic predecessor and replace the role that the KJV had held for nearly three and half centuries.[6]

METHOD

The Standard Bible Committee consisted of both a Revision Committee (with its New and Old Testament Sections) and an ecumenical Advisory Board.

The NT Section originally consisted of nine members. The OT Section started with six members and elected nine more by the time of publication. An Apocrypha Committee of thirteen members convened after the OT was completed.

The NT Section finished their work first. Each portion of the New Testament was revised by one or two members. Drafts of their revisions were then typed, copied, and shared with the other members of the Section to consider before each meeting. Members then met to discuss and debate these drafted revisions. Their decisions were concluded by a simple majority vote, and their results were recorded in a second draft, which was then submitted to the Advisory Board for discussion before it was passed on to the OT Section for their review.

The members of the OT Section initially drafted fifteen chapters of the Old Testament each. At first, they met in pairs to discuss their work before submitting their results to the NT Section's members for review and recommendations—thus the revisers would have drafted each of the OT portions three times before submitting them to the Advisory Board.

But this method proved too time consuming and impractical. It was abandoned in favor of the OT Section's discussing each member's revisions in meetings led by the Section chair. Changes to the drafts were decided by simple majority vote. The new revised drafts were then submitted to the Advisory Board and the NT Section for their recommendations. By this time, changes could only be made with a two-thirds majority vote.

After all drafts were discussed, a final review considered each Section's recommendations before submitting the work to the Editorial Subcommittee. This Subcommittee prepared the text by

proofing, punctuating, and checking the revisions for consistency
before delivering the work to the printers.

TEXT BASES

English Text

The RSV is a revision of the *American Standard Version* (1901).

New Testament

Eclectic Greek text. Nestle's *Novum Testamentum Graece* 17th
and *Nestle-Aland* 25th editions (Stuttgart: Privilegierte Württembergische Bibelanstalt, 1941, 1963); *Greek New Testament*
1st, 2nd, and 3rd editions (United Bible Societies, 1966, 1968,
1975).

Old Testament

Masoretic Hebrew-Aramaic text. Likely Kittel's *Biblia Hebraica* 3rd edition (Stuttgart: Privilegierte Württembergische
Bibelanstalt, 1929–37). The revisers "have been circumspect
in the matter of emending the Masoretic text of the Old Testament,"[7] whch means they did not rely on Kittel's footnotes
or his suggested conjectural emendations, yet they felt free to
emend the vowels and consonants wherever they seemed to
need correcting.

    Ancient versions. Septuagint (Greek LXX) and Aqui-
la (Greek), Targums (Aramaic), Vulgate (Latin), Peshitta
(Syriac).

Apocrypha

Rahlf's *Septuaginta* (Stuttgart: Württemburg Bible Society, 1935); Greek papyri. **Tobit:** Codices Sinaiticus and Alexandrinus. **Add. to Daniel:** Theodotian (Greek). **Sirach:** Rahlf's *Septuaginta* (1935); Hebrew fragments; other editions. **2 Esdras:** Bensly (1895), Violet (1910); Oxyrhynchus Papyrus 1010; Syriac, Ethiopic, Arabic (in two forms), Armenian, Georgian.

CONTRIBUTORS

The RSV was an ecumenical effort led by the National Council of the Churches of Christ in the U.S.A. (NCCC). The initial Revision Committee (from 1937 to 1957) involved thirty-two biblical scholars representing numerous denominations from the United States, Canada, and the United Kingdom. The Advisory Board consisted of fifty representatives from many of the denominations affiliated with the NCCC, including Adventist, Baptist, Church of God, Disciples of Christ, Episcopal, Brethren (Quaker), Lutheran, Mennonite, Methodist, Moravian, Nazarene, Presbyterian, and Reformed. One Jew (Harry Orlinsky), five Roman Catholics, and a Greek Orthodox priest (Constantelos) also contributed to the work. In all, around 105 individuals contributed to the evolution of the RSV from its inception in 1930 until its final expansion in 1977.

For a complete list of translators, visit *booklink.id/ rsv-translator*

THEOLOGICAL ASSUMPTIONS

The revisers and translators were not obligated to agree on any particular view of inspiration or inerrancy. None were required to subscribe to any particular confession of faith or sign any doctrinal statement, though most came from some confessional, evangelical background.

Advertisement in *Life Magazine*, October 6, 1952.

The Best Bible?

FEATURES

The RSV consistently renders the Tetragrammaton as "LORD", in place of the ASV's "Jehovah" (see "Translating the Name of God" on page 66). No italics are used to distinguish translator-supplied words or paraphrase. Divine pronouns are kept in lower case. The text is formatted into thought-paragraphs with smaller, superscripted verse numbers inline with the text.

Most archaic language has been changed; Elizabethan remnants leftover in the ASV have been updated. The specific second-person, plural pronoun ("ye") has been completely dropped, but the second-person, singular pronouns ("thee", "thou", "thy", "thine") have not been completely eliminated: They remain in use for prayers and poetry when addressing God (but not when addressing Jesus Christ).

In the Old Testament, wherever the Standard Bible Committee differed from the consonantal text, they supplied a footnote to specify the ancient version or versions from which they derived the correction. Conjectural emendations of the Hebrew text, where it appears to have suffered in transmission, were indicated in the footnotes by the abbreviation "Cn" (*i.e.*, Correction). The Committee gave their translations of the Masoretic Text in the footnotes in both cases. The notes do not, however, alert readers where the Committee chose different wording from their Hebrew source based on their supplying different vowels than those in the Masoretic tradition.

Where the choice between two meanings was difficult or doubtful, they gave an alternative rendering in the footnote. The note indicates whether the Committee judged the meaning of a passage too uncertain or obscure, either because of some corruption during the text's transmission or because of limits to their available knowledge of the language at the time.

Among the notes added or changed in the 1971 NT revision are the modern equivalents of ancient currencies with a worker's contemporary wage for the day or year:

	NT (1952)	NT, second edition (1971)
Mt 18.24	"When he began the reckoning, one was brought to him who owed him ten thousand talents" *f*	
	Footnote (fn): *f* This talent was probably worth about a thousand dollars	**fn:** *f* This talent was more than fifteen years' wages of a laborer

REPRESENTATIVE SAMPLES

Familiar Passages

Gn 1.1–2	In the beginning God created the heavens and the earth.*a* The earth was without form and void, and darkness was upon the face of the deep; and the Spirit *b* of God was moving over the face of the waters.
	Footnote (fn): *a* Or *When God began to create* *b* Or *wind*
Ps 23.1–2	The Lord is my shepherd, I shall not want; he makes me lie down in green pastures. He leads me beside still waters *s*
	fn: *s* Heb *the waters of rest*
Ps 27.4	One thing have I asked of the Lord, that will I seek after; that I may dwell in the house of the Lord all the days of my life, to behold the beauty of the Lord, and to inquire in his temple.
Jn 3.16	For God so loved the world that he gave his only Son, that whoever believes in him should not perish but have eternal life.

Divine Name and Titles

Yhwh	Ps 24.1a	The earth is the **Lord**'s and the fulness thereof.
adonai	Ps 90.1b	**Lord**, thou hast been our dwelling place*e* in all generations.
		fn: *e* Another reading is *refuge*
elohim	Gn 1.27a	So **God** created man in his own image
adonai Yhwh	Ps 73.28b	I have made the **Lord God** my refuge
adonai elohim	Dn 9.3a	I turned my face to the **Lord God**.
Yhwh *saba'oth*	1Sa 17.45b	"I come to you in the name of the **Lord of hosts**"

The Best Bible?

el shaddai	Ex 6.3a	"I appeared to Abraham, to Isaac, and to Jacob, as **God Almighty**"[h]
		fn: *h* Heb *El Shaddai*
kyrios	Lk 20.42b	" 'The **Lord** said to my **Lord**, Sit at my right hand' "
christos	Mt 16.16b	"You are the **Christ**, the Son of the living God."

New Testament Text Base

Mt 17.21	———	**fn:** Other ancient authorities insert verse 21, *"But this kind never comes out except by prayer and fasting"*
Mt 18.11	———	**fn:** Other ancient authorities add verse, *For the Son of man came to save the lost*
Ac 8.37	———	**fn:** Other ancient authorities add all or most of verse 37, *And Philip said, "If you believe with all your heart, you may." And he replied, "I believe that Jesus Christ is the Son of God."*
1 Jn 5.7b–8a	———	(Omitted without notice)

Gender Language

'ādām	Gn 9.6	"Whoever sheds the blood of **man**, by **man** shall his blood be shed; for God made **man** in his own image."
'îsh … nephesh	Lv 24.17	**He** who kills **a man** shall be put to death.
'āvîw	Pr 15.5a	A fool despises **his father's** instruction
huioi	Mt 5.9	"Blessed are the peacemakers, for they shall be called **sons** of God."
anthrōpōn	Mt 4.19	"Follow me, and I will make you fishers **of men**."
hekastō … autou	Ro 2.6	For he will render **to every man** according to **his** works
adelphoi	Gal 5.13	For you were called to freedom, **brethren**; only do not use your freedom as an opportunity for the flesh, but through love be servants of one another.
gynaikos anēr	Ti 1.6a	if any man is blameless, **the husband of** one **wife**, and his children are believers

gynaikas	1Ti 3.11	**The women** likewise must be serious, no slanderers, but temperate, faithful in all things.

Difficult Renderings

1Sa 13.1		Saul was ... *j* **years** old when he began to reign; and he reigned ... **and two *k* years** over Israel.
		fn: *j* The number is lacking in Heb *k* *Two* is not the entire number. Something has dropped out.
Is 28.13		Therefore the word of the LORD will be to them **precept upon precept, precept upon precept, line upon line, line upon line, here a little, there a little**; that they may go, and fall backward, and be broken, and snared, and taken.

Significant Renderings

ʻalmah	Is 7.14	Therefore the Lord himself will give you a sign. Behold, **a young woman** *i* shall conceive and bear *j* a son, and shall call his name Immanu-el. *k*
		fn: *i* Or *virgin* *j* Or *is with child and shall bear* *k* That is *God is with us*
she'ol ... 'abaddon	Pr 15.11	**Sheol** and **Abaddon** lie open before the LORD how much more the hearts of men!
egennēsen	Mt 1.2	Abraham **was the father of** Isaac, and Isaac **the father of** Jacob, and Jacob **the father of** Judah and his brothers
eskēnōsen	Jn 1.14	And the Word became flesh and **dwelt** among us, full of grace and truth; we have beheld his glory, glory as of the only Son from the Father.
tois ioudaiois	Jn 18.36	Jesus answered, "My kingship is not of this world; if my kingship were of this world, my servants would fight, that I might not be handed over **to the Jews**; but my kingship is not from the world."
dikaiosunē theou, pisteōs Iēsou Christou	Ro 3.22a	**the righteousness of God** through **faith in Jesus Christ** for all who believe

Granville Sharp's rule applied	Tt 2.13 (cf. 2Pt 1.1)	while we wait for the blessed hope, the appearing of the glory of **our great God and Savior, Jesus Christ**

SIGNIFICANT REVISIONS

Improvements over the *American Standard Version*

A better understanding of history informs a better rendering of words. For example, it was later discovered that Pharaoh Neco and the King of Assyria were allies. King Solomon purchased his horses from a place called Kue, rather than in "droves".

	ASV (1901)	RSV (1952)
2Kg 23.29	Pharaoh-necoh king of Egypt **went up against** the king of Assyria	Pharaoh Neco king of Egypt **went up to** the king of Assyria
1Kg 10.28 (2Ch 1.16)	the king's merchants received them in **droves**	the king's traders received them from **Kue**
Jb 19.26	after my skin, even this body, is destroyed, Then **without my flesh** shall I see God	after my skin has been thus destroyed, then **from my flesh** I shall see God

Revisions within the *RSV*

The principles that guided the Committee to revise the ASV were applied again to a few changes of the RSV published in 1959. Most of these corrected punctuation, capitalization, and footnotes, though some words and phrases in the text were changed to be more consistent, clear, or accurate.

	New Testament (1946)	New Testament (1952)
2Kg 23.29	In him we live and move and **are**	In him we live and move and **have our being**
1Th 4.3	For this is the will of God, your **consecration**: that you abstain from immorality	For this is the will of God, your **sanctification**: that you abstain from unchastity

	RSV (1952)	RSV (1959)
1Ti 3.2 (cf 1Ti 3.12; 5.9)	Now a bishop must be above reproach, **married only once**, temperate, sensible, dignified, hospitable, an apt teacher	Now a bishop must be above reproach, **the husband of one wife**, temperate, sensible, dignified, hospitable, an apt teacher
Mt 27.54 (cf Mk 15.39)	the centurion . . . said, "Truly this was **a son** of God!"	the centurion . . . said, "Truly this was **the Son** of God!"
1Co 15.19	If in this life **we who are in Christ have only hope**, we are of all men most to be pitied.	If for this life **only we have hoped in Christ**, we are of all men most to be pitied.
Jn 16.23	"On that day you will ask **me no questions**."	"In that day you will ask **nothing of me**."
Rv 20.4 (cf v5)	They came to life **again**, and reigned with Christ a thousand years.	They came to life, and reigned with Christ a thousand years.

In 1965–66, the Catholic Biblical Association of Great Britain released a special Roman Catholic edition, which made no changes to the OT, but made several to the NT for liturgical or theological reasons. This edition included the OT Deuterocanon (Apocrypha, published in 1957).[8]

Two of the more significant changes included a re-estimation of the longer ending of Mark (16.9–20) and the *Pericope Adulteræ*, (*i.e.*, the woman caught in adultery at Jn 7.53–8.11), both of which were returned to the main text for canonical reasons. (In later editions, they are set off with extra line breaks and accompanied with different text-critical footnotes). In Protestant editions, these two passages were relegated to the margins where they had

The Best Bible?

stayed since the NT's initial publication in 1946 until the release of
a revised NT in 1971:

	New Testament (1959)	Catholic Edition NT (1965)
	k _____	Now when he rose early on the first day of the week, he ap-
		. . . .
		And they went forth and preached everywhere, while the Lord worked with them and confirmed the message by the signs that attended it. Amen. *k*
	1959 fn: *k* Other texts and versions add as 16.19–20 the following passage: 9 *Now when he rose early on the first day of the week, he ap-*	
	. . . .	
Mk 16.9–20	20 *And they went forth and preached everywhere, while the Lord worked with them and confirmed the message by the signs that attended it. Amen.* Other ancient authorities add after verse 8 the following: *But they reported briefly to Peter and those with him all that they had been told. And after this, Jesus himself sent out by means of them, from east to west, the sacred and imperishable proclamation of eternal salvation.*	**1965-CE fn:** *k* Other ancient authorities omit verses 9–20. Some ancient authorities conclude Mark instead with the following: *But they reported briefly to Peter and those with* . . . . *sacred and imperishable proclamation of eternal salvation.*

1971 fn: *k* Some of the most ancient authorities bring the book to
a close at the end of verse 8. One authority concludes the book by
adding after verse 8 the following: *But they reported briefly to Peter
and those with him all that they had been told*

. . . .

sacred and imperishable proclamation of eternal salvation.
Other authorities include the preceding passage and continue
with verses 9–20. In most authorities verses 9–20 follow immediately after verse 8; a few authorities insert additional material after
verse 14.

	New Testament (1959)	Catholic Edition NT (1965)
r ———		They went each to his own house, but Jesus went to the Mount of Olives. Early in the morning he came again to the . . . . "Neither do I condemn you; go, and do not sin again." *r*

Jn 7.53 – 8.11

1959 fn: *r* Other ancient authorities add 7.53–8.11 either here or at the end of this gospel or after Lk 21.38, with variations in the text
⁵³ *They went each to his own house,* 8.1 *but Jesus went to the Mount of Olives.* ² *Early in the morning he came again to the*

. . . .

"Neither do I condemn you, go, and do not sin again."

1965-CE fn: *r* Some ancient authorities insert 7.53–8.11 either at the end of this gospel or after Luke 21.38, with variations of the text. Others omit it altogether.

1971 fn: *r* The most ancient authorities omit 7.53–8.11; other authorities add the passage here or after 7.36 or after 21.25 or after Luke 21.38, with variations of text.

Catholic Bible editions require notes to instruct readers. While most are helpful or, at least, non-controversial, Protestants may bristle at the notes affixed to **Mt 16.18, 19:**

vs 18 fn: "The name 'Peter' comes from the Greek word for 'rock.' Jesus makes him the foundation on which the church is to be built. . . . **vs 19 fn:** "*the kingdom of heaven:* Peter has the key to the gates of the city of God. This power is exercised through the church. 'Binding' and 'loosing' are rabbinic terms referring to excommunication, then later to forbidding or allowing something. Not only can Peter admit to the kingdom; he also has power to make authoritative decisions in matters of faith or morals."

The Best Bible?

	New Testament (1959)	Catholic Edition NT (1965)
Mt 1.19	her husband Joseph, being a just man and unwilling to put her to shame, resolved **to divorce** her quietly.	her husband Joseph, being a just man and unwilling to put her to shame, resolved **to send** her **away** quietly.
Mt 12.46 (cf Mt 12.48f; Mk 3.31ff, Lk 8.19ff, Jn 7.34)	While he was still speaking to the people, behold, his mother and his **brothers** stood outside, asking to speak to him.	While he was still speaking to the people, behold, his mother and his **brethren** stood outside, asking to speak to him.
Lk 1.28	And he came to her and said, "Hail, **O favored one**, the Lord is with you!"	And he came to her and said, "Hail, **full of grace**,[b] the Lord is with you!"
		fn: b Or O favored one

A second revised edition of the NT was released in 1971, twenty-five years after its initial introduction in 1946. This revision resulted from suggestions given to the Standard Bible Committee by individuals and two denominational committees.

	NT (1959)	Second Edition NT (1971)
2Co 3.5 (cf v6)	Not that we are **sufficient** of ourselves to claim anything as coming from us; our **sufficiency** is from God	Not that we are **competent** of ourselves to claim anything as coming from us; our **competence** is from God
Mt 17.20b	"I say to you, if you have faith as a grain of mustard seed, you will say to this mountain, '**Move hence to yonder place**,' and it will move"	"I say to you, if you have faith as a grain of mustard seed, you will say to this mountain, '**Move from here to there**,' and it will move"
Mk 5.42	And immediately the girl got up and walked; **for** she was twelve years **old. And immediately** they were overcome with amazement.	And immediately the girl got up and walked (she was twelve years **of age**), **and** they were **immediately** overcome with amazement.

RSV

	NT (1959)	Second Edition NT (1971)
Lk 22.19b–20 (cf Lk 24.47a)	"This is my body." r ——— fn: *j* Other ancient authorities *which is given for you. Do this in remembrance of me."* [20] *And likewise the cup after supper, saying, "This cup which is poured out for you is the new covenant in my blood.*	"This is my body which is given for you. Do this in remembrance of me." And likewise the cup after supper, saying, "This cup which is poured out for you is the new covenant in my blood." fn: *j* Other authorities omit, in whole or in part, verses 19b–20 (*which is given . . . in my blood.*
Lk 17.34	"I tell you, in that night there will be two **men** in one bed; one will be taken and the other left."	"I tell you, in that night there will be two in one bed; one will be taken and the other left."
Lk 22.29	as my Father **appointed** a kingdom for me, so do I **appoint** for you	I **assign** to you, as my Father **assigned** to me, a kingdom
Ro 10.16	But they have not all **heeded** the gospel; for Isaiah says, "Lord, who has believed what he has heard from us?"	But they have not all **obeyed** the gospel; for Isaiah says, "Lord, who has believed what he has heard from us?"
2Co 5.19	**God was in Christ** reconciling the world to himself	**in Christ God was** reconciling the world to himself

Unique Renderings

On a rare occasion, the revisers were inconsistent in using archaic language for solely addressing God:

Rv 18.10b	"Alas! alas! thou great city, thou mighty city, Babylon!"

In the following, the word "only" is added without precedent. It neither corresponds to the Greek, nor is it suggested by the context:

Ro 11.20b	They were broken off because of their unbelief, but you stand fast **only** through faith.

Here, "immorality" (*porneia*) is misleading because it is too general. Perhaps the revisers felt that something more specific was inappropriate for public worship:

1Co 5.1 (cf. 1Co 6.13, 18; 7.2; 2Co 12.21; Gal 5.19; Eph 5.3)	It is actually reported that there is **immorality** among you

Once in a while, a rendering ought to be reworded before it is read aloud:

Ps 50.9	I will accept no bull from your house

(For more samples of awkward renderings that have been retained in the *English Standard Version*, see page 298.)

In an attempt to defend the of rendering **Is 7.14** with "young woman" (see "Where Ambiguity has Theological Implications" on page 110), other passages make clear the virginity of Mary, the mother of Jesus (**Mt 1.23; Lk 1.27**).[9]

The RSV's rendering of **Jn 7.8** omits the word "yet" for text-critical reasons (as does the ASV, but not the RV). It was suspected that the word was added by later scribes in order to remove an apparent discrepancy between verses **8** and **10**.[10] Without it, Jesus appears to mislead his brothers:

	KJV	RSV (1971)
Jn 7.8	Go ye up unto this feast: I go not up **yet** unto this feast; for my time is not yet full come.	"Go to the festival yourselves. I am not going to this festival, for my time has not yet fully come."

RECEPTION

The RSV's translators had high hopes for its success—hopes that were justified by the RSV's initial sales. In the first two months following its official launch on September 30, 1952, Thomas Nelson & Sons sold 1.6 million copies of the RSV Bible.[11] 1953 saw the RSV top the non-fiction best-sellers list (followed by Norman Vincent Peale's *The Power of Positive Thinking*).[12] Within its first ten years, a whopping 12 million copies were sold.[13] Even the Kennedy's presidential administration recognized its popular status when, in 1963, a copy of the RSV with the Apocrypha was included in a specially curated library installed in the White House.[14]

Yet, the RSV has had one of the most polarized debuts of any modern translation. Counter to its generally congenial reception, the RSV entered a political climate that witnessed the rise of the Red Scare and McCarthyism. At the time, Americans were generally anxious over Communist infiltration in mass institution. Even the RSV's sponsor, the National Council of the Churches of Christ in the U.S.A (NCCC), was accused of hosting Communist activists. The American Air Force Reserve distributed an official condemnation of the RSV as a product of a Communist plot within the ecumenical NCCC.[15] In answer, Luther A. Weigle, dean emeritus at Yale Divinity School and general editor on the Standard Bible Committee, released a public statement affirming that he in no way had any ties to the Communist Party. (He was, by admission, a Lutheran, a Republican, and a congregationalist.) To settle the matter, the Federal Bureau of Investigation, who had scrutinized the Communist Party's attempts to influence popular institutions, concluded that they had no reason to suspect the NCCC of either infiltration or subversion.

Such was the early suspicion and hostility that "one of the pastors of a church in Rocky Mount, North Carolina, [Reverend Martin] Luther Hux [of Temple Baptist Church], advertised in a newspaper that on a certain Sunday evening, he would 'testify to the truth' by burning publicly with a blowtorch a copy of this heretical, communist-tainted RSV Bible." (Rather, he tore out the page with **Isaiah 7.14** on it and burned that instead.)[16]

Weigle even received a tin-can with a note: "Enclosed you will find the ashes of a book that was once called the *Revised Standard Version*."[17] (Now that malcontents only burn translations and not their translators, perhaps we should consider these cases as real improvements!) Only four months after its initial publication, Dean Weigle admitted that the RSV "has been attacked as the product of 'modernists,' 'communists,' and 'un-believers,' but these attacks wither under honest scrutiny, and are largely inspired by opposition to the NCCC and to the ecumenical movement."

He triumphantly added, "Meanwhile it is coming into increasing use in public and private worship, as well as in private reading and in teaching. And not only here in America, but in many countries and languages, revision of the old translations of the Bible have been made or are under way."[18] Though the RSV was initially suspected by conservative evangelical groups, those same groups have grown to accept the RSV on the basis of its own merits, so that it has gained widespread respect. Today it can no longer be found among the top ten best-selling Bible translations, but two popular modern translations (the NRSV and the ESV) have sprung from the laurels of its success.

ENDORSEMENTS

Even though it was initially condemned by conservatives of all stripes, the RSV is the one English Bible that has merited the widest ecumenical support, trusted by Protestants, Roman Catholics, and Orthodox alike. Members of the Anglican Communion— the Church of England, the Episcopal Church, and the Anglican Church of Canada, *et al.*—authorize or approve the RSV for use in public worship. Both the RSV (1952) and the RSV *Common Bible* (1973) are approved for use in the Episcopal Church (USA).[19]

The Christian Reformed Church of North America (CRC) and the National Association of Evangelicals (NEA)—the two bodies who were later responsible for the NIV—initially rejected the RSV in 1954.[20] Though, after much study, they concluded that is was theologically safe and gave it their approval for use in public worship in 1969.[21]

The Catholic Bishops' Conference of England and Wales approve the RSV for use in the Liturgy, and suggest it as one of the optional translations when reading Scripture for the Divine Office or when reading the Canticles.[22] The RSV *Catholic Edition* (1965/66) was endorsed by the Archbishop of Westminster (Cardinal Heenan).[23]

The Holy Synod of Bishops of the Orthodox Church in America lamented the declining availability of the RSV, which they have preferred to use in their liturgy and Bible study.[24]

Eugene H. Peterson (†2018), who was responsible for *The Message* (2001), preferred the RSV for his own personal devotions.[25]

COPYRIGHT

You may quote up to 500 verses from the RSV in any form without prior written permission; the verses may not constitute a complete book of the Bible; they must comprise less than 50% of your work's content; and your work must include the following copyright acknowledgment.

When quoting from the Apocrypha:

The Best Bible?

cil of the Churches of Christ in the United States of America. Used by permission. All rights reserved worldwide.

Unless used exclusively, follow citations with the designation (RSV). For example:

John 1.4, "In him was life, and the life was the light of men." (RSV)

The title *"Revised Standard Version®"* and its initialism (RSV®), are registered trademarks with the U.S. Patent and Trademark Office by the National Council of the Churches of Christ.

For permissions not covered here, write to Riggins Rights Management, 2500 East Beltline Avenue SE, Suite G, Box #352, Grand Rapids, MI 49546; or contact NRSVcopyright@rigginsrights.com; or call (941) 621-6085.*

ENDNOTES FOR THE
REVISED STANDARD VERSION

[1] The International Council of Religious Education (ICRE) was founded in 1922. It merged with others to form the National Council of Churches of Christ in the U.S.A. (NCCC in the USA) in 1950, where it formed the Division of Christian Education. The NCCC has since been abbreviated to NCC—the National Council of Churches—an ecumenical body consisting of 38 participating communions of faith.

[2] The ICRE renewed the copyright the following year, in 1929.

[3] A later Catholic edition was published in 2006 by Ignatius Press (San Francisco, CA), and abbreviated RSV2CE for *Revised Standard Version*, Second Catholic Edition.

[4] The Readers' Digest Association published a condensed version of the Bible in 1982 (edited by Bruce M. Metzger *et al.*), titled *The Readers' Digest Bible: Condensed from the Revised Standard Version Old and New Testaments* (Pleasantville, NY).

Ronald Bridges and Luther Weigle, *King James Bible Word Book: A Contemporary Dictionary of Curious and Archaic Words Found in the King James Version of the Bible* (Nashville, TN: Thomas Nelson, 1994).

[5] "Preface to the Revised Standard Version," *Revised Standard Version of the Bible*, 2nd ed. (1971) in *The Oxford Annotated Bible* (Oxford University Press, 1977).

[6] "Well, the RSV was intended, you see, to play a role similar to the role that the King James [Version] has played. And—the impression that we had in the first years was that, in fact, it had done this quite successfully. . . . [M]y own informal impression is that the sense that the RSV could last for generations as the standard version for ordinary use, particularly in church worship—broke down only because of the lack of inclusive language." — George Lindbeck (†2018), emeritus professor, Yale Divinity School, Lutheran theologian, medievalist, and church ecumenicist.

National Council of Churches, Odyssey Productions, Linda Hanick, David J. Lull, *et al.*, *The Bible Under Fire: The Story of the RSV Translations.* (New York: Filmakers Library, 1999), minute 29:00–42.

[7] Harry R. Orlinsky, "The Hebrew Text and the Ancient Versions of the Old Testament," *An Introduction to the Revised Standard Version of the Old Testament* by

members of the Revision Committee of the Division of Christian Education of the NCCC (New York: Thomas Nelson & Sons, 1952).

8   The text of the RSV-CE received its *Nihil obstat* from Thomas Hanlon, S.T.L., L.S.S., Ph.L., and its *Imprimatur* from Gordon Joseph Gray, Archbishop of St. Andrews and Edinburgh, on May 17 (Pentecost Sunday) 1964, in the U.K. and from Peter W. Bartholome, D.D., Bishop of St. Cloud, Minnesota, on May 1, 1965, in the U.S.

9   There is also precedent in **Is 8.3–4** for the prophecy of a named child whose birth occurs within the prophet's lifetime.

10 The word "yet" (Gk. *oupō*) in **Jn 7.8** occurs in both early papyri ($\mathfrak{P}^{66,75}$) and the majority of Greek MSS.

11 "Sales of New Bible Reported a Record," *New York Times*, November 30, 1952.

12 Russell Lynes, "What Are Best-Sellers Made Of?" *New York Times*, December 27, 1959.

13 *Cambridge History of the Bible*, ed. by S. L. Greenslade, vol. 3 (Cambridge University Press, 1963), p. 378.

14 Four other versions joined the 1957 edition of the RSV with several other titles in the White House's library. They included the KJV, the ASV, a *New Catholic Edition of the Douay-Confraternity* Bible based on the Latin Vulgate (New York: Catholic Book Publishing Co., 1949), and a forerunner to the modern NJPS titled *The Holy Scriptures According to the Masoretic Text* (Philadelphia: Jewish Publication Society, 1955).

"The List of 1,780 Titles Compiled by Experts for Inclusion in White House Library," *New York Times*, August 16, 1963.

15 As recorded in the *Air Reserve Center Training Manual, Student Text*, NR. 45-0050, Increment 5, vol. 7, "National Council of Churches of Christ in the U.S.A. officially sponsored the *Revised Standard Version* of the Bible. Of 95 persons who served on this project, 30 have been affiliated with pro-Communist fronts, projects, and publications." In February 1960, the U.S. Air Force Secretary, Dudley Sharp, officially apologized for these remarks to James Wine, the associate general secretary of the NCCC.

"Military Affairs," *Life*, vol. 48, no. 9 (March 7, 1960): p. 82.

16 Bruce M. Metzger, *Reminiscenses of an Octogenarian* (Grand Rapids, IL: Baker Academic, 1997), p. 102.

17 National Council of Churches, *et al.*, *The Bible Under Fire*, minutes 23:34–47.

18 Weigle, "The Revised Standard Version."

19 "What We Believe: The Bible," from the website of The Episcopal Church, accessed September 6, 2019, https://www.episcopalchurch.org/bible/.

20 Peter J. Thuesen, *In Discordance with the Scriptures: American Protestant Battles over Translating the Bible*, Religion in America Series (New York: Oxford University Press, 1999), pp. 11, 119, 123, 132–3.

21 William W. Combs, "The History of the NIV Translation Controversy," *Detroit Baptist Seminary Journal* vol. 17 (2012), p. 11.

22 "Sacred Scripture: Versions approved for use in the liturgy," from the website of the Liturgy Office of the Catholic Bishops' Conference of England and Wales, accessed January 31, 2020, https://www.liturgyoffice.org.uk/Resources /Scripture/Versions.shtml.

23 *The Holy Bible: Revised standard version, containing the Old and New Testaments. Catholic edition, Prepared by the Catholic Biblical Association of Great Britain; With a Foreword by His Eminence John Cardinal Heenan, Archbishop of Westminster* (London: Nelson, 1966).

24 Bishop Tikhon, "Bishop's Pastoral Letter on the New Revised Standard Version," website of the Holy Trinity Cathedral, accessed September 6, 2019, https://www .holy-trinity.org/liturgics/tikhon.nrsv.html.

25 NavPress, "Eugene Peterson: The Bible Translation He Reads at Home," YouTube video, 41 seconds, posted December 19, 2017, https://www.youtube.com /watch?v=PiHtZxjqYM8.

New Revised Standard Version®

The Holy Bible containing the Old and New Testaments

Produced by the National Council of the Churches of Christ in the USA, 1989

FORMAL / FUNCTIONAL TENDENCIES

FORMAL   FUNCTIONAL

| Interlinear | NASB | KJV | NKJV | ESV | RSV | CSB | **NRSV** | NET | NIV | NLT | Free Paraphrase |

TEXT BASES

English Base *Revised Standard Version* (1971, 1977).

OT Masoretic Hebrew and Ancient Versions.   **NT** Eclectic Greek.

TRANSLATION TIMELINE

1901	1952	1977	1989	2001
ASV	*RSV*	*RSV* Expanded Apocrypha ed.	**NRSV**	*ESV*

CONTEMPORARY EVENTS

1962–5	1963	1965	1975	1989	1991	1993
Vatican II Council	*The Feminine Mystique* published	Joint Catholic-Orthodox Declaration	U.S. withdraws from Vietnam		Soviet Union dissolves	Tel Dan Inscription uncovered

PUBLICATION TIMELINE

1971	1974	1976	1977	1989	2021
RSV revised	NCCC authorizes work on *NRSV*	*RSV* Commitee meets at Princeton	Bruce M. Metzger chairs the *NRSV*	**NRSV**	*NRSV* revised

THE
HOLY BIBLE

containing the
Old and New Testaments
with the
Apocryphal/Deuterocanonical
Books

New Revised Standard Version

Thomas Nelson Publishers
Nashville

Title Page

After publishing a second revised edition of the RSV's New Testament (1971), the Policies Committee of the *Revised Standard Version* was convinced that even more changes were needed to make the RSV a truly modern Bible. The Committee admitted, "The decision to produce a further revision of the RSV was basically due to the social changes that took place during the 1960s and early '70s."[1] Many of those changes resulted in greater sensitivity to the use of gendered language and the use of more casual English in traditional liturgies. The RSV had already started the move from the Elizabethan and Jacobean English of the KJV to contemporary language, and a revised revision would bring the text fully up to date by replacing those lingering antique words ("thee", "thy", "thine", etc.) and sex-biased (male-dominated) language. This revision would give the Committee an opportunity to include a number of revisions based on later research and discoveries made since the RSV's last major update. They would also put into the main text the scholarship that was previously relegated to the margins.[2]

STATED TRANSLATION IDEALS

The English style of the NRSV follows that of the Tyndale-KJV tradition as filtered through the RSV. Yet the revisers were free to change the text on the basis of accuracy, clarity, euphony,* and current English style. The intended result is an essentially literal translation, or what the revisers marketed "as literal as possible, as free as necessary." Paraphrase is infrequent and mostly applied to "compensate for the lack of a common gender, third-person singular [pronoun]"; that is, the revisers reordered or reworded formalistic English to be more gender-inclusive when they understood the meaning of the text in this way.[3]

PROCEDURE

In order to keep up with the New Testament (NT) Section's relatively faster progress, more members were added to the Old Testament (OT) Section so that three OT subsections (each consisting of about six members and a graduate assistant) could meet in different places at the same time. "At least one member in each group was assigned a particular book for study, and for as much research as necessary. When the member's study was finished, he or she then drew up a detailed list of all the changes he or she felt were either necessary or desirable."[4] They then provided to the rest of their group's members an agenda of proposed changes to the biblical book that they were assigned.

The Bible Committee met twice a year at Princeton (for one week in January and one week in June) to discuss the agenda of proposed changes to the text. They sat in discussion and debate for almost ten hours a day to arrive at a consensus agreement over the revisions. Bruce M. Metzger recalled, "In rare instances, discussion of a single item could go on for an hour or two. If, finally, no consensus seemed possible, the issue was decided by simple majority vote. At the end of the week all the changes voted by all of the subcommittees, after further discussion when it seemed necessary, were ratified by the general meeting." [5]

After the Old and New Testament Sections finished their assignments, the results were smoothed and standardized by two Editorial Committees. On May 16, 1990, after fifteen years in production, the National Council of Churches (NCC) held a service to bless and commemorate the completed NRSV.[6]

TEXT BASES

English Text

The NRSV is a revision of the *Revised Standard Version* (RSV), second edition (1971) and its expanded Apocrypha (1977).

The Best Bible?

New Testament

Eclectic Greek text. *Greek New Testament* 3rd corrected and 4th revised editions (United Bible Societies, 1983, 1993), *Nestle-Aland Novum Testamentum Graece* 26th revised and 27th editions (Stuttgart: Deutsche Bibelgesellschaft, 1983, 1993).

Old Testament

Masoretic Hebrew-Aramaic text. *Biblia Hebraica Stuttgartensia* 1st and 2nd emended editions (New York: American Bible Society, 1967–77, 1984).

Ancient versions. Septuagint (Greek LXX) and Aquila (Greek), Targums (Aramaic), Vulgate (Latin), Peshitta (Syriac).

Apocrypha

Rahlf's *Septuaginta* (Stuttgart: Württemburg Bible Society, 1935); *Göttingen Septuagint.* **Tobit:** Codex Sinaiticus (as supported by the Dead Sea Scrolls). **Add. to Daniel:** Theodotian (Greek). **Sirach:** *Göttingen Septuagint* (1965); Syriac, Latin. **2 Esdras:** Weber's *Biblia Sacra Vulgata* (1971); Bensly (1895), Violet (1910); Syriac, Ethiopic, Arabic (in two forms), Armenian, Georgian. **Greek Esther:** *Göttingen Septuagint* (1983).

CONTRIBUTORS

Membership and personnel changed over the fifteen years it took to complete the project. Some members resigned due to professional obligations. Some of the long-standing members died from age-related health issues, and others took their place in the Committee. Herbert May, the chair of the Standard Bible Committee, died tragically in a car crash in 1977. Bruce M. Metzger, the NT Section chair, replaced him as his successor.

The NT Section consisted of ten members. By publication, the OT Section had twenty. The three OT subsections were vice-chaired by Robert C. Denton, Walter Harrelson, and one other member.

Other noted contributors include Phyllis A. Bird and Allen Wikgren. The inclusion of Eugene C. Ulrich (University of Notre Dame) and four other Roman Catholics, and Demetrios J. Constantelos (Greek Orthodox) demonstrated the Committee's ecumenical commitment. The return of Harry M. Orlinsky (Jewish, RSV, NJPS) was "intended as both an expression of goodwill and an assurance that the NRSV translation of the Hebrew Scriptures (*i.e.* the Christian OT) would contain nothing offensive to our Jewish neighbors."[7]

Nigel Lynn (of Oxford University Press) and Roger Coleman (editor of the *Revised English Bible*) were responsible for anglicizing the NRSV (1995).

For a complete list of translators, visit booklink.id/ nrsv-translator

THEOLOGICAL ASSUMPTIONS

The revisers who produced the NRSV either had history with the earlier RSV or were recognized for their scholarship. Though many of the NRSV contributors had denominational affiliations, none were required to sign a statement of faith or hold to any particular view of inspiration or inerrancy.

FEATURES

"The vowel signs, which were added by the Masoretes, are accepted in the main, but where a more probable and convincing reading can be obtained by assuming different vowels, this has been done. Departures from the consonantal text of the best manuscripts have been made only where it seems clear that errors in copying had been made before the text was standardized. Most of the corrections adopted are based on the ancient versions (*i.e.*, translations into Greek, Aramaic, Syriac, and Latin)"[8]

NRSV

"Occasionally it is evident that the text has suffered in transmission and that none of the versions provides a satisfactory restoration. Here we can only follow the best judgment of competent scholars as to the most probable reconstruction of the original text."[9]

The Committee changed the policy of the RSV so that archaic, second-person, singular pronouns ("thee", "thou", "thine") and verb forms ("art", "hast", "hadst") are no longer used in the Psalms or any other prayers addressed to God.

The mandates from the NCC's Division of Education and Ministry specified that

> in reference to men and women, masculine-oriented language should be eliminated as far as this can be done without altering passages that reflect the historical situation of ancient patriarchal culture. . . . In the vast majority of cases . . . inclusiveness has been attained by simple rephrasing or by introducing plural forms when this does not distort the meaning of the passage.[10]

Walter Harrelson (OT) explained, "That policy was quite simple: the committee should remove all masculine language referring to human being apart from text that clearly referred to men."[11] "To achieve this, the committee adopted a number of agreed conventions (chief among them the use of the plural instead of the singular) even in some instances in which the committee believed that only males were involved ("My child" for "My son" in Proverbs, for example). It was agreed that [they] would not use [the words] 'persons' or 'people,' unless no alternative could be found. We would use 'one' or 'someone' as necessary, but sparingly. When a Psalmist was referring to an enemy, [they] sometimes would retain the 'he' or 'his' in order not to lose the vivid, personal force of the psalm." For example, **Ps 109.6–7** reads

They say, "Appoint a wicked man against him; let an accuser stand on his right. When he is tried, let him be found guilty; let his prayer be counted as sin."

Ps 8.4 is an example of using plurals to generalize gender:

what are human beings that you are mindful of **them**, mortals that you care for **them**?

Samples of rephrasing include **Ps 41.8**, which change the view from third-person to first:

RSV	NRSV
They say, "A deadly thing has fastened upon **him; he** will not rise again from where **he** lies."	They think that a deadly thing has fastened on **me**, that **I** will not rise again from where **I** lie.

The Committee chose not to make neuter those whose natural genders were known. Individuals recorded in narrative or in parables where not generalized to be inclusive. The Committee opted for the generic "he" or "him" in only a very few cases of formal, legal language (*e.g.,* **Dt 21.22, 23; Lv 13**).

Only rarely did the Committee's punctuation of the NT text differ from the Greek editions of the United Bible Societies.

The Committee left section headings, cross-references, and clues to the pronunciation of proper names, (*i.e.,* self-pronouncing guides with special punctuation and diacritics) to the discretion of the NRSV's licensed publishers.[12]

The decision to use red-letters for the words of Jesus Christ was left to the licensed publishers, but with this caveat:

Members of the Standard Bible Committee have grave reservations about the propriety of issuing the Bible in such a format. Besides the difficulty of ascertaining which are the words of Jesus . . . , such a procedure not only destroys the unity of the text of NT books but also implies a theological judgment that what Jesus said is more significant than what he did.[13]

The editors use double brackets to enclose a few passages that they regarded to be later additions to the text. They were kept in the main text because of their "evident antiquity and their importance in the textual tradition."[14]

The NRSV's footnotes follow the pattern set in the RSV. Wherever the Committee differed from the consonantal text of the Hebrew Bible, they supplied a footnote to specify from which ancient version or versions they derived the correction. Conjectural emendations of the Hebrew text, where it appears to have suffered in transmission, are indicated in the footnotes by the abbreviation "Cn" (i.e., "Correction"). In both cases, the Committee has given their translations of the Masoretic Text in the footnotes.

The Committee made no indication in the notes where they chose different vowels than those added by the Masoretic scribes. This is due to their recognizing that the vowel points are less ancient and reliable than the consonants.

Occasionally, the Committee noted Jewish traditions about other textual readings (i.e., the Tiqqune Sopherim, "emendations of the scribes"). These are footnoted as "Ancient Heb tradition."

Strewn throughout the NT, the phrase "Other ancient authorities read" introduces readings preserved by Greek manuscripts and early versions.

In both Testaments, alternative renderings of the text are indicated by the word "Or."

ASSESSMENT

The NRSV's modern idiom, gender-inclusive policy, and careful attention to euphony make this translation ideal for smooth public reading. The language is natural and often dignified, even though it was published three decades ago with no subsequent revisions.

It is still a favorite among professors of college religion courses and seminaries in mainline Christian traditions.

Yet, the same feature that makes the NRSV ideal for public reading also make it a poorer choice for careful Bible study: Its inclusive policy requires paraphrases in places that reduce its lexical precision and formal correspondence. For this reason, some denominations have attached caution to it.

Its style is ideal for early high-school to college- or university-aged readers. It is also supported by numerous resources, including study Bibles, commentaries, and various curricula.

Anticipate an upcoming 2021 revision, which is being produced by the NCC in cooperation with the Society of Biblical Literature (SBL). It should result in a Bible with improved footnotes and greater textual, philological, and linguistic accuracy all while retaining its natural and euphonic style.

REPRESENTATIVE SAMPLES

Familiar Passages

Gn 1.1–2	In the beginning when God created *a* the heavens and the earth, the earth was a formless void and darkness covered the face of the deep, while a wind from God *b* swept over the face of the waters.
	footnote (fn): *a* Or *when God began to create* or *In the beginning God created* *b* Or *while the spirit of God* or *while a mighty wind*
Ps 23.1–2	The LORD is my shepherd, I shall not want. He makes me lie down in green pastures; he leads me beside still waters
Ps 27.4	One thing I asked of the LORD, that will I seek after: to live in the house of the LORD all the days of my life, to behold the beauty of the LORD, and to inquire in his temple.
Jn 3.16	"For God so loved the world that he gave his only Son, so that everyone who believes in him may not perish but may have eternal life."

Divine Name and Titles

Yhwh	Ps 24.1a	The earth is the **Lord**'s and all that is in it
adonai	Ps 90.1b	**Lord**, you have been our dwelling place *e* in all generations.
		fn: *e* Another reading is *our refuge*
elohim	Gn 1.27a	So **God** created humankind *c* in his image
		fn: *c* Heb *adam*
adonai Yhwh	Ps 73.28b	I have made the **Lord God** my refuge
adonai elohim	Dn 9.3a	Then I turned to the **Lord God**
Yhwh *saba'oth*	1Sa 17.45b	"but I come to you in the name of the **Lord of hosts**"
el shaddai	Ex 6.3a	"I appeared to Abraham, Isaac, and Jacob as **God Almighty**" *l*
		fn: *l* Traditional rendering of Heb *El Shaddai*
kyrios	Lk 20.42b	" 'The **Lord** said to my **Lord**, "Sit at my right hand" ' "
christos	Mt 16.16b	"You are the **Messiah**, *p* the Son of the living God."
		fn: *p* Or *the Christ*

New Testament Text Base

Mt 17.21	——— **fn:** Other ancient authorities add verse 21, *But this kind does not come out except by prayer and fasting*
Mt 18.11	——— **fn:** Other ancient authorities add verse 11, *For the Son of Man came to save the lost*
Ac 8.37	——— **fn:** Other ancient authorities add all or most of verse 37, *And Philip said, "If you believe with all your heart, you may." And he replied, "I believe that Jesus Christ is the Son of God."*
1Jn 5.7b–8a	——— **fn:** A few other authorities read (with variations) *7 There are three that testify in heaven, the Father, the Word, and the Holy Spirit, and these three are one. 8 And there are three that testify on earth:*

NRSV

Gender Language

'ādām	Gn 9.6	Whoever sheds the blood of **a human**,
		    by **a human** shall that person's blood be shed;
		for in his own image
		    God made **humankind**.

'îsh . . . nephesh	Lv 24.17	**Anyone** who kills **a human being** shall be put to death.
'āvîw	Pr 15.5a	A fool despises **a parent's** instruction
huioi	Mt 5.9	"Blessed are the peacemakers, for they will be called **children** of God."
anthrōpōn	Mt 4.19	"Follow me, and I will make you fish for **people**."
hekastō . . . autou	Ro 2.6	For he will repay according **to each one's** deeds
adelphoi	Gal 5.13	For you were called to freedom, **brothers and sisters**;[a] only do not use your freedom as an opportunity for self-indulgence,[b] but through love become slaves to one another.
		fn: a Gk *brothers* b Gk *the flesh*
gynaikos anēr	Ti 1.6a	if any man is blameless, **the husband of** one **wife**, and his children are believers
gynaikas	1Ti 3.11	**Women**[a] likewise must be serious, not slanderers, but temperate, faithful in all things.
		fn: a Or *Their wives*, or *Women deacons*

Difficult Renderings

1Sa 13.1	Saul was . . .[c] **years** old when he began to reign; and he reigned . . . **and two**[d] **years** over Israel.
	fn: c The number is lacking in the Heb text (the verse is lacking in the Septuagint). d Two is not the entire number; something has dropped out.

Is 28.13	Therefore the word of the LORD will be to them,
	    "**Precept upon precept, precept upon precept,**
	    line upon line, line upon line,
	    here a little, there a little;"[y]
	in order that they may go, and fall backward,
	    and be broken, and snared, and taken.

	fn: y Meaning of Heb of ths verse uncertain

The Best Bible?

Significant Renderings

'almah	Is 7.14	Therefore the Lord himself will give you a sign. Look, **the young woman** *r* is with child and shall bear a son, and shall name him Immanuel.*s*
		fn: *r* Gk *the virgin* *s* That is *God is with us*
she'ol, 'abaddon	Pr 15.11	**Sheol** and **Abaddon** lie open before the Lᴏʀᴅ, how much more human hearts!
egennēsen	Mt 1.2	Abraham **was the father of** Isaac, and Isaac **the father of** Jacob, and Jacob **the father of** Judah and his brothers
eskēnōsen	Jn 1.14	And the Word became flesh and **lived** among us, and we have seen his glory, the glory as of a father's only son,*d* full of grace and truth.
		fn: *d* Or *the Father's only Son*
tois ioudaiois	Jn 18.36	Jesus answered, "My kingdom is not from this world. If my kingdom were from this world, my followers would be fighting to keep me from being handed over **to the Jews.** But as it is, my kingdom is not from here."
dikaiosunē theou, pisteōs Iēsou Christou	Ro 3.22a	**the righteousness of God** through **faith in Jesus Christ** *k* for all who believe
		fn: *k* Or *through the faith of Jesus Christ*
Granville Sharp's rule applied	Tt 2.13	while we wait for the blessed hope and the manifestation of **the glory of our great God and Savior,** *f* Jesus Christ.
		fn: *f* Or *of the great God and our Savior*

Unique Renderings

Gn 1.2	while a **wind** from God *b* swept over the face of the waters
	fn: *b* Or *while the spirit of God* or *while a mighty wind*

NRSV

SIGNIFICANT REVISIONS

Improvements over the *Revised Standard Version*.

In many instances, the NRSV improves on the RSV by using more contemporary vocabulary and syntax, better informed cultural details (e.g., "Wadi" insted of "brook"), or less awkward English.

	RSV	NRSV
Gn 1.25 (cf. 7.21)	And God made the **beasts** of the earth according to their kinds	God made the **wild animals** of the earth of every kind
Gn 12.3b (cf. 18.18; 28.14)	by you all the families of the earth **shall bless themselves** *q* fn: *q* Or *in you all the families of the earth shall be blessed*	in you all the families of the earth **shall be blessed** *e* fn: *e* Or *by you all the families of the earth shall bless themselves*
Gn 22.18 (cf. 26.4)	by your descendants **shall** all the nations of the earth **bless themselves**, because you have obeyed my voice	by your offspring **shall** all the nations of the earth **gain blessing for themselves**, because you have obeyed my voice
Ex 20.19b	"You speak to us, and we will hear; but **let not** God speak to us, **lest** we die."	"You speak to us, and we will listen; but **do not let** God speak to us, **or we will** die."
Dt 2.13a	'Now rise up, and go over the **brook** Zered.'	"Now then, proceed to cross over the **Wadi** Zered."
2Co 11.25a	Three times I have been beaten with rods; once I **was stoned**.	Three times I was beaten with rods. Once I **received a stoning**.

Here, the NRSV replaces the adversative conjunction ("but") with the copulative conjunction ("and") in order to avoid a *negative* racial implication. (Also, the choice of the word "black" reverts to the KJV.)

Sg 1.5a	I am **very dark, but comely**, O daughters of Jerusalem	I am **black and beautiful**, O daughters of Jerusalem

Inclusive Language

Many inclusive-gender renderings are sufficiently warranted by how the original languages function. In these cases, the inclusive rendering better fits the intended meaning.

	RSV	NRSV
Jn 14.23a	Jesus answered him, "If **a man** loves me, **he** will keep my word"	Jesus answered him, "**Those who** love me will keep my word"
1Co 4.5	Then **every man** will receive his commendation from God.	Then **each one** will receive commendation from God.

Often, though, the Committee pluralized the number of persons to uphold their agenda. They supported the general meaning, but they lost some precision as a result:

Ps 1.1a	Blessed is **the man** who walks not in the counsel of the wicked	Happy are **those** who do not follow the advice of the wicked

Sometimes they paraphrased by adding a word or two:

1Co 12.1	Now concerning spiritual gifts,[x] **brethren,** I do not want you to be uninformed.	Now concerning spiritual gifts,[b] **brothers and sisters,**[a] I do not want you to be uninformed.
	fn: *x* Or *spiritual persons*	fn: *a* Gk *brothers* *b* Or *spiritual persons*
2Pt 1.21	no prophecy ever came by the impulse of man, but men moved by the Holy Spirit spoke from God.[e]	no prophecy ever came by human will, but men **and women** moved by the Holy Spirit spoke from God.[j]
	fn: *e* Other authorities read *moved by the Holy Spirit holy men of God spoke*	fn: *j* Other ancient authorities read *but moved by the Holy Spirit saints of God spoke*

Sometimes they paraphrased through omission:

Mt 10.38	"he who does not take **his** cross and follow me is not worthy of me"	"whoever does not take up **the** cross and follow me is not worthy of me."
Ro 2.1a	Therefore you have no excuse, **O man,** whoever you are, when you judge another	Therefore you have no excuse, whoever you are, when you judge others
1Th 5.27	I adjure you by the Lord that this letter be read to **all the brethren**.	I solemnly command you by the Lord that this letter be read to **all of them**. *p*
		fn: *p* Gk *to all the brothers*

And at other times they paraphrased in other ways:

Ro 4.1	What then shall we say about *e* Abraham, our **forefather** (Gk. *patera*) according to the flesh?	What then are we to say was gained by *n* Abraham, our **ancestor** according to the flesh?
	fn: *e* Other ancient authorities read *was gained by*	**fn:** *n* Other ancient authorities read *say about*
Mk 8.34b	"If any **man would come after me**, let him deny himself and take up his cross and follow me."	"If any **want to become my followers**, let them deny themselves and take up their cross and follow me."
Lk 1.34	And Mary said to the angel, "How shall this be, since I **have no husband**?"	Mary said to the angel, "How can this be, since I **am a virgin**?" *c*
		fn: *c* Gk *I do not know a man*

The Best Bible?

"We are assured [by Professor Metzger], however, that the masculine designations for God, Jesus Christ, and the Holy Spirit will be retained."[15] Yet at least one paraphrase contradicts consistent application of this rule in order to make a broader theological point:

	RSV	NRSV
1Ti 2.5	For there is one God, and there is one mediator between God and men, **the man** Christ Jesus	For there is one God; there is also one mediator between God and humankind, Christ Jesus, **himself human**

In some passages, the Committee altered the meaning:

	RSV	NRSV
1Th 4.10b (cf 5.4)	we exhort you, **brethren**, to do so more and more	we urge you, **beloved,** *j* to do so more and more **fn:** *j* Gk *brothers*
Mt 23.8	But you are not to be called rabbi, for you have one teacher, and you are all **brethren.**	But you are not to be called rabbi, for you have one teacher, and you are all **students.** *l* **fn:** *l* Gk *brothers*
Mt 25.40	And the King will answer them, 'Truly, I say to you, as you did it to one of the least of these **my brethren**, you did it to me.'	And the king will answer them, 'Truly I tell you, just as you did it to one of the least of these **who are members of my family,** *g* you did it to me.' **fn:** *g* Gk *these are my brothers*
Jn 21.23	The saying spread abroad **among the brethren** that this disciple was not to die	So the rumor spread **in the community** *p* that this disciple would not die. **fn:** *p* Gk *among the brothers*
Ro 7.4a	Likewise, my **brethren**, you have died to the law through the body of Christ	In the same way, my **friends,** *x* you have died to the law through the body of Christ **fn:** *x* Gk *brothers*

	RSV	NRSV
1Co 6.5–6	I say this to your shame. Can it be that there is no **man** among you wise enough to decide between **members of the brotherhood**, but **brother** goes to law against **brother**, and that before unbelievers?	I say this to your shame. Can it be that there is no **one** among you wise enough to decide between **one believer** *u* **and another**, but **a believer** *u* goes to court against **a believer** *u*—and before unbelievers at that?
		fn: *u* Gk *brothers*
1Co 10.13a	No temptation has overtaken you that is not common to **man**.	No testing has overtaken you that is not common to **everyone**.
Rv 12.10c	the accuser of our **brethren** has been thrown down	the accuser of our **comrades** *h* has been thrown down
		fn: *h* Gk *brothers*
Col 3.25	For the wrongdoer will be paid back for **the** wrong **he** has done, and there is no partiality.	For the wrongdoer will be paid back for **whatever** wrong has **been** done, and there is no partiality.
Gal 4.4	But when the time had fully come, God sent forth his Son, born of woman, born under the law, to redeem those who were under the law, so that we might receive adoption as **sons**.	But when the fullness of time had come, God sent his Son, born of a woman, born under the law, in order to redeem those who were under the law, so that we might receive adoption as **children**.
1Ti 3.2	Now a bishop must be above reproach, **the husband of one wife**	Now a bishop *h* must be above reproach, **married only once** *i*
		fn: *h* Or *an overseer* *i* Gk *the husband of one wife*

Doctrinal Concern

At **Jn 7.39**, the NRSV reads "as yet there was no Spirit." This seems as if the Spirit did not *exist* until Jesus's glorification. The words "had . . . been given" (Gk. *dedomenon*) were supplied in a small

The Best Bible?

handful of Greek manuscripts possibly to avoid contradicting the passage at **Heb 9.14** ("the eternal Spirit"). The problem goes away if we understand that this passage was written to accommodate the perspective of human experience and not to comment on the preexistence of the Holy Spirit.

	RSV	NRSV
Jn 7.39	for as yet the Spirit **had not been given**, because Jesus was not yet glorified.	for as yet there was **no** Spirit,ƒ because Jesus was not yet glorified.
		fn: ƒ Other ancient authorities read *for as yet the Spirit* (others, *Holy Spirit*) *had not been given*

Upcoming Revision

In 2017, the NCC announced an update to the NRSV, which is being managed by their partner, the Society of Biblical Literature (SBL) and will be released November 2021. The update will improve the text in four areas: (1) *text-criticism*, with regards to later discoveries and a fuller understanding of more original versions; (2) *philology*, the scholarly understanding of the meaning of ancient words and expressions; (3) *textual notes*, in order to make them more complete and consistent; and (4) *style and rendering*, to improve renderings that are awkward, inaccurate, or seemingly unclear.

nrsv
UPDATED EDITION

The SBL editorial board includes Sidnie White Crawford (CEB), Ronald Hendel, Michael W. Holmes (CEB), Robert S. Kawashima, Jennifer W. Knust, Judith H. Newman, and Eugene C. Ulrich (NRSV, NAB, NABRE).

The board's tools for updating the NT include Holmes' *The Greek New Testament: SBL Edition* (Atlanta, GA: SBL; Bellingham, WA: Logos Bible Software, 2010) and editions influenced by text-critical decisions using the Coherence-Based Genealogical Method (see page 34), including the *Greek New Testament, 5th Revised Edition* (New York: United Bible Societies, 2014), the 28th

edition (revised) of Nestle-Aland's *Novum Testamentum Graece* (Stuttgart: Deutsche Bibelgesellschaft, 2012), and the published volumes of the *Novum Testamentum Graecum, Editio Critica Maior* (Stuttgart: Deutsche Bibelgesellschaft, 1997–).

OT tools include Hendel's *The Hebrew Bible: A Critical Edition* (SBL Press, 2015–)[16] and the *Biblia Hebraica Quinta* (Stuttgart: Deutsche Bibelgesellschaft, 2004–).[17]

ENDORSEMENTS

The NRSV is endorsed by recognized authors and influencers, such as Marcus Borg, Frederick Buechner, Bart D. Ehrman, Richard J. Foster, Brian D. McLaren, John Ortberg, Anne Rice, William H. Willimon (bishop, United Methodist Church), John H. Thomas (president, United Church of Christ), Michael Leach (former president, Catholic Book Publishers Association), and professors including David A. deSilva (Ashland Theological Seminary), Scot McKnight (North Park University), and Kevin Mongrain (University of Notre Dame), among others.[18]

The Episcopal Church authorizes the NRSV for public worship.[19] The Church of England recognizes that the NRSV meets at least four of the necessary criteria for suitability of use during the course of public worship—though they advise an awareness of its tendency for gender inclusion and its departure from precision where it avoids masculine nouns and pronouns.[20] The Christian Reformed Church in North America has approved the NRSV for public worship since 1992.[21] The Catholic Bishops' Conference of England and Wales approves the NRSV for use in the Liturgy, but not in the production of a Lectionary without express permission from the Conference.[22] The United States Conference of Catholic Bishops approves the NRSV for private use and prayer or for personal Bible study.[23]

The Presbyterian Church (USA) does not officially endorse any one translation, but their publishing arm, the Presbyterian Publishing Corporation, and its imprints (Westminster John

Knox Press, Geneva Press, Witherspoon Press) frequently quote the NRSV in its publications.[24] Likewise, The United Methodist Church, through the The United Methodist Publishing House, its imprint, Abingdon Press, and its retailer, Cokesbury, prefer the NRSV in their curriculum and print resources.[25] (The NRSV is one of only two translations that the United Church of Christ sells on it online store.[26])

The 2014 *Style Guide* of the Evangelical Lutheran Church in America (ELCA) specifies the NRSV as their preferred text.[27] So the ELCA's publisher, Augsburg Fortress, uses the NRSV as the base text in their study references.[28] As such, the NRSV forms the base of the ELCA's *Lutheran Study Bible* (Minneapolis, MN: Augsburg Fortress, 2009).

The Holy Synod of Bishops of the Orthodox Church in America explicitly rejects the NRSV, which means they have "decided not to permit the use of the *New Revised Standard Version* in liturgical services and in Bible study."[29]

COPYRIGHT

You may quote up to 500 verses from the NRSV in any form without prior written permission; the verses may not constitute a complete book of the Bible; they must comprise less than 50% of your work's content; and your work must include the following copyright acknowledgment.

> Scripture is from the *New Revised Standard Version Bible,* copyright © 1989 by the Division of Christian Education of the National Council of the Churches of Christ in the United States of America. All rights reserved. Used with permission.

Unless used exclusively, follow citations with the designation (NRSV). For example:

Jn 1.4, "in him was life, and the life was the light of all people." (NRSV)

The title "*New Revised Standard Version*®" and its initialism (NRSV® and NRSV Updated Edition®) are registered trademarks with the U.S. Patent and Trademark Office by the National Council of the Churches of Christ, but the logomark is not.

For permissions not covered here, write to Riggins Rights Management, 2500 East Beltline Avenue SE, Suite G, Box #352, Grand Rapids, MI 49546, or contact <rights@rigginsrights.com>, or call 941-621-6085. <http://www.rigginsrights.com/>

N R Ṣ V

ENDNOTES FOR THE
NEW REVISED STANDARD VERSION

1. Bruce M. Metzger, Robert C. Dentan, and Walter Harrelson. *The Making of the New Revised Standard Version of the Bible* (Grand Rapids, MI: William B. Eerdmans Publishing Company, 1991), p. 5.

2. For example, the NRSV included the shorter ending of **Mk 16** between vss **8** and **9**, whereas the RSV left it in the footnotes.

3. The Standard Bible Committee, "To the Reader," preface by Bruce M. Metger for the *New Revised Standard Version Bible* (Division of Christian Education of the National Council of the Churches of Christ in the U.S.A., 1989).

4. Metzger *et al.*, *The Making of the NRSV*, p. 13.

5. *Ibid.*, p. 13.

6. Bruce M. Metzger, *The Bible in Translation: Ancient and English Versions* (Grand Rapids, MI: Baker Academic, 2001), p. 156.

7. *Ibid.*, p. 11.

8. "To the Reader," *New Revised Standard Version Bible*.

9. *Ibid.*

10. *Ibid.*

11. Metzger *et al.*, *The Making of the NRSV*, p. 76.

12. In 1991, the NRSV's seven licensed publishers included Cambridge University Press, Holman Bible Publishers, Thomas Nelson Publishers, Oxford University Press, World Bible Publishers, the Zondervan Corporation (later HarperCollins), William Collins Sons and Co. (in Glasgow, Scotland).
    Ibid., p. 62.

13. *Ibid.*, p. 62, footnote 8.

14. "To the Reader," *New Revised Standard Version Bible*.

15. Sakae Kubo and Walter F. Specht, *So Many Versions? Twentieth-century English Versions of the Bible* (Grand Rapids, MI: The Zondervan Corporation, 1983), p. 59.

16. *The Hebrew Bible: A Critical Edition*, accessed June 7, 2019, http://hbceonline.org/.

17. "NRSV Review and Update," *Society Report: Society of Biblical Literature* (2017) p. 7, accessed June 7, 2019, https://www.sbl-site.org/assets/pdfs/SocietyReport2017.pdf.

18. "Endorsements," website for the NRSV, accessed June 9, 2017, https://www.nrsv.net/about/endorsements/.

19 "What We Believe: The Bible" from the website of The Episcopal Church, accessed September 6, 2019, https://www.episcopalchurch.org/bible.

20 General Synod of the Church of England, "Versions of Scripture," by David Michael Hope, Archbishop of York (Eboracensis), October 9, 2002, GS Misc 698.

21 Christian Reformed Church in North America, "Bible Translations," accessed September 6, 2019, https://www.crcna.org/welcome/beliefs/bible-translations.

22 Liturgy Office of the Catholic Bishops' Conference of England and Wales, "Sacred Scripture: Versions approved for use in the liturgy," accessed January 31, 2020, https://www.liturgyoffice.org.uk/Resources/Scripture/Versions.shtml.

23 United States Conference of Catholic Bishops, "USCCB Approved Translations of the Sacred Scriptures for Private Use and Study by Catholics," accessed January 31, 2020, http://www.usccb.org/bible/approved-translations/index.cfm.

24 Presbyterian Publishing Corporation's website, http://www.ppcbooks.com.

25 Abingdon Press' website, https://www.abingdonpress.com.

26 United Church of Christ, "Bibles," *UCC Resources*, accessed June 7, 2019, https://www.uccresources.com/collections/bibles.

27 Evangelical Lutheran Church in America (ELCA), "Appendix 1: Credit Lines/Copyright Information for Key Resources: Versions of the Bible," ELCA *Style Guide*, Version 3 (Fall 2014), p. 73.

28 Augsburg Fortress' website, https://www.augsburgfortress.org.

29 Bishop Tikhon, "Bishop's Pastoral Letter on the *New Revised Standard Version*," from the website of the Holy Trinity Cathedral, accessed September 6, 2019, https://www.holy-trinity.org/liturgics/tikhon.nrsv.html.

English Standard Version®

The Holy Bible: English Standard Version, Containing the Old and New Testaments

Produced by Crossway Publishers, 2001

FORMAL / FUNCTIONAL TENDENCIES

FORMAL   FUNCTIONAL

Interlinear   NASB   KJV   NKJV   **E S V**   RSV   CSB   NRSV   NET   NIV   NLT   Free Paraphrase

TEXT BASES

English Base *Revised Standard Version* (1971).

OT Masoretic Hebrew and Ancient Versions.   **NT** Eclectic Greek.

TRANSLATION TIMELINE

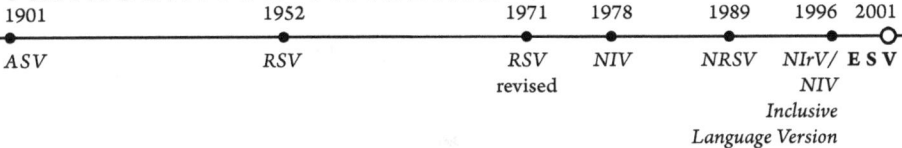

1901	1952	1971	1978	1989	1996	2001
ASV	*RSV*	*RSV* revised	*NIV*	*NRSV*	*NIrV/ NIV Inclusive Language Version*	**E S V**

CONTEMPORARY EVENTS

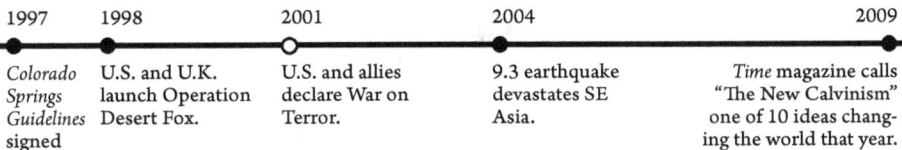

1997	1998	2001	2004	2009
Colorado Springs Guidelines signed	U.S. and U.K. launch Operation Desert Fox.	U.S. and allies declare War on Terror.	9.3 earthquake devastates SE Asia.	*Time* magazine calls "The New Calvinism" one of 10 ideas changing the world that year.

PUBLICATION TIMELINE

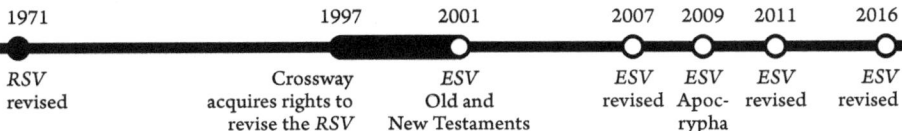

1971	1997	2001	2007	2009	2011	2016
RSV revised	Crossway acquires rights to revise the *RSV*	*ESV* Old and New Testaments	*ESV* revised	*ESV* Apocrypha	*ESV* revised	*ESV* revised

The

HOLY

BIBLE

ENGLISH
STANDARD
VERSION

CONTAINING THE

OLD AND NEW TESTAMENTS

CROSSWAY BIBLES

A DIVISION OF
GOOD NEWS PUBLISHERS
WHEATON, ILLINOIS

In the early 1990s, the president of Crossway Publishers, Lane T. Dennis, discussed with scholars and pastors the need for a new formal Bible translation.[1] At the time, there were several good functional translations available (*e.g.*, NIV, GNB, *etc.*). The NRSV, an update to the RSV, which many churches had come to trust and adopt, sadly disappointed the expectations of many conservatives churches. Critical reaction against the use of gender language in the *Today's New International Version* (TNIV, 1996) spurred urgency among these churches to find a suitable alternative.

One of the more vocal critics of the TNIV, who contended against its apparently unprecedented use of gender-inclusive language, was a professor at Trinity Evangelical Divinity School, named Wayne Grudem. In 1997, Grudem and Dennis began negotiating with the National Council of Churches (NCC) for the use of the 1971 edition of the RSV as a base text for a new revision. The following year, the NCC agreed to give Crossway the right to modify the RSV.[2] Three years later, Crossway published the *English Standard Version* (ESV®, 2001).

STATED TRANSLATION IDEALS

The ESV's Translation Oversight Committee intended the Bible to be "an 'essentially literal' translation that seeks . . . to capture the precise wording of the original text and the personal style of each Bible writer."[3] As such, it emphasizes " 'word-for-word' correspondence, at the same time taking into account differences of grammar, syntax, and idiom between current English and the original languages. Thus it seeks to be transparent to the original text, letting . . . reader[s] see as directly as possible the structure and meaning of the original" and allowing them "to understand the original on its own terms rather than on the terms of our present-day culture. . . . [It] lets the stylistic variety of the biblical writers fully express itself." The Committee has "sought to be 'as literal as possible' while maintaining clarity of expression and literary excellence."[4] In other words, they tried to be as clear as possible without glossing over ambiguities inherent in the original expressions.[5]

METHOD

The Translation Oversight Committee started with twelve members (later fourteen), who incorporated revisions into the 1971 edition of the RSV based on recommendations submitted by over fifty specialist scholars (designated the Translation Review Scholars). An Advisory Council of sixty additional pastors and Christian leaders submitted their recommendations for consideration.

TEXT BASES

English Text

The ESV is a revision of the *Revised Standard Version* (RSV), second edition (1971). The ESV Apocrypha (2009) is a revision of the RSV expanded Apocrypha (1977).

New Testament

Eclectic Greek text. *Greek New Testament* 4th revised edition (United Bible Societies, 1993); *Nestle-Aland Novum Testamentum Graece* 27th edition (Stuttgart: Deutsche Bibelgesellschaft, 1993).

Old Testament

Masoretic Hebrew-Aramaic text. *Biblia Hebraica Stuttgartensia* 2nd emended edition (1984).

Ancient versions. Dead Sea Scrolls (DSS), Septuagint (LXX, Greek), Samaritan Pentateuch (Hebrew), Peshitta (Syriac), Vulgate (Latin), *et al.*

The Best Bible?

Apocrypha

Göttingen Septuagint; ?4 **Maccabees:** Rahlf's *Septuaginta* (Stuttgart: 1935) "The *Göttingen Septuagint* served as the textual base for all of the books except 4 Maccabees (which was translated from the 1983 Vulgate published by the German Bible Society)."[6] **2 Esdras:** Weber-Gryson *Biblia Sacra Vulgata* 3rd edition (Stuttgart: Deutsche Bibelgesellschaft, 1984).

CONTRIBUTORS

116 people from around the English-speaking world and from various conservative evangelical denominations contributed to the production of the ESV's text. 52 served as Translation Review Scholars, and 54 were members on the Advisory Council.[7]

The Translation Oversight Committee consists of fourteen members, including Wayne A. Grudem, Vern S. Poythress, Leland Ryken, and Peter J. Williams (current warden of Tyndale House, Cambridge). The Committee also included classical scholars, J. I. Packer and Bruce Winter (former warden of Tyndale House), who were the more competent Greek scholars among those who worked on the New Testament.[8] Members who worked on the OT include C. John "Jack" Collins (OT committee chair; HCSB), Gordon Wenham (NLT), and Paul R. House (NLT, HCSB).

Among the over 52 Translation Review Scholars are Craig L. Blomberg (NIV, HCSB, ISV), Darrell L. Bock (Dallas Theological Seminary [D.T.S.], NLT, NET), George H. Guthrie (Union University, NLT, HCSB), Leon Morris (NIV), John Piper (author; Bethlehem College & Seminary), Thomas R. Schreiner (NLT, HCSB, CSB), Moisés Silva (NASB, NLT), James W. Voelz, Daniel B. Wallace (NET), and R. Albert Mohler (Southern Baptist Theological Seminary). Among the members of the Advisory Council are R. C. Sproul († 2017) and John F. Walvoord (D.T.S.).

For a complete list of translators, visit *booklink.id/esv-translator*

Members of the Translation Committee for the Oxford University Press' *Apocrypha* (2009) included David A. deSilva (CEB, NRSV 2021), Dan McCartney (CEB) and Bernard A. Taylor (CEB).[9]

An ESV Catholic Edition (ESV-CE) was prepared under the supervision of the Catholic Bishops of India.[10]

THEOLOGICAL ASSUMPTIONS

"This hundred-plus-member team shares a common commitment to the truth of God's Word and to historic Christian orthodoxy and is international in scope, including leaders in many denominations."[11]

FEATURES

According to Wayne Grudem, the ESV retains ninety-two percent of the RSV's text. That means, the ESV changes almost 60,000 words, about an eight-percent difference from the RSV.[12]

Since the ESV is a modest revision of the RSV (1971), it retains many of the RSV's features. Like the RSV, the word "'behold,' has usually been retained as the most common translation for the Hebrew word *hinnêh* and the Greek word *idou*. . . . Other than the word 'behold,' there is no single word in English that fits well in most contexts. Although 'Look!' and 'See!' and 'Listen!' would be workable in some contexts, in many other these words lack sufficient weight and dignity. Given the principles of 'essentially literal' translation . . . [t]he older and more formal word 'behold' has usually been retained . . . as the best available option."

The ESV consistently translates the Greek word *christos* as "Christ" throughout the NT. In fact, the ESV concordantly renders repeated "theological terminology—words such as 'grace,' 'faith,' 'justification,' 'sanctification,' 'redemption,' 'regeneration,' 'reconciliation,' 'propitiation'" because of their perceived importance in communicating Christian doctrine, and because "the underlying Greek words were already becoming key words and technical terms in NT times."[13]

Divine pronouns are not capitalized.

Paragraphs are formatted with indentation, and verse reference numbers are superscripted and inline. The ESV's grammar is structured to reflect the genres of its source; *e.g.*, it preserves the poetic structures of Psalms and Proverbs instead of rendering them in, perhaps, more readable prose.[14] So poetry is indented by stanzas and cola.

The word " 'anyone' replaces 'any man' where there is no word corresponding to 'man' in the original languages, and 'people' rather than 'men' is regularly used where the original languages refer to both men and women. But the words 'man' and 'men' are retained where a male meaning component (*i.e.*, where natural gender) is part of the original Greek or Hebrew. Similarly, the English word 'brothers' (translating the Greek word *adelphoi*) is retained as an important familial form of address between fellow-Jews and fellow-Christians in the first century. . . . In addition, the English word 'sons' (translating the Greek word *huioi*) is retained in specific instances because of its meaning as a legal term in the adoption and inheritance laws of first-century Rome. As used the apostle Paul's letters, this term refers to the status of all Christians, both men and women, who, having been adopted into God's family, who now enjoy all the privileges, obligations, and inheritance rights of God's children.

"The inclusive use of the generic 'he' has also regularly been retained . . . Similarly, where God and man are compared or contrasted in the original, the ESV retains the generic use of 'man' as the clearest way to express the contrast within the framework of essentially literal translation."[15]

Textual footnotes inform readers of textual variants and their difficulties and how the ESV's team of translators resolved them.

Some footnotes indicate the meaning of names in the original languages. For example,

Gn 17.19	God said, "No but Sarah your wife shall bear a son, and you shall call his name Isaac.[1] I will establish my covenant with him as an everlasting covenant for his offspring after him.
	footnote (fn): [1] *Isaac* means *he laughs*

Other notes give significant alternative translations for specific words or phrases when there is a strong likelihood that such words or phrases could be translated other ways. They sometimes offer explanations of technical terms or hard readings. Alternative rendering with the strongest support are placed in the text while other possibilities are given in the notes. For example,

Mt 26.38	Then he said to them, "My soul is very sorrowful, even to death; remain here, and watch[2] with me."
	fn: [2] Or *keep awake*; also verses 40, 41

Yet others give formal renderings of Hebrew or Greek words or phrases where they would be too awkward for use in the main text. For example,

1Pt 1.13	Therefore, preparing your minds for action,[1] and being sober-minded, set your hope fully on the grace that will be brought to you at the revelation of Jesus Christ.
	fn: [1] Greek *girding up the loins of your mind*

The ESV includes a number of explanatory notes. These clarify additional meanings that might not be obvious in the main text (*e.g.*, **Lv 13.2**, "*Leprosy* was a term for several skin diseases"). In some places, they clarify grammar that English readers are prone to miss (*e.g.*, **Gn 3.1**, In Hebrew *you* is plural in vss 1–5). Or they indicate where translators supply a referent for a pronoun in the English text (*e.g.*, **Mk 1.43**, "Greek *he*"). Or they give modern English equivalents for weights, measures, and monetary values.

"A recurring note is included to indicate that the term 'brothers' (*adelphoi*) was often used in Greek to refer to both men and women, and to indicate the specific instances in the text where this is the case."[16]

The Best Bible?

The ESV's cross-reference system is adapted from that used in the ASV and the English RV before it, which itself is based on the one developed for the original 1611 KJV. It is ideal for demonstrating *intertextuality* (*i.e.*, showing the internal relationships of the text) throughout the biblical canon.

This system uses different kinds of cross-references: References to specific words or phrases within the same chapter, book, or other books; comparative references, which tie passages with the same theme together; less direct references, which offer more detail about a specific theme; and quoted references, which reveal sources for passages or phrases quoted from elsewhere in Scripture.[17] Not every edition of the ESV is published with this system.

ASSESSMENT

The ESV is a conservative revision of the RSV that retains the best of the Tyndale-KJV tradition. Its revisers gave special attention to euphony* and strove to retain the rhythm and cadence that has made its predecessor, the KJV, so well loved. This makes it ideal for churches seeking continuity from one generation to the next. It is a good choice for those who want language more contemporary than that found in the RSV yet do not wish to alienate older readers. The language is modern, yet dignified. On occasion it retains some straggling awkwardness from the RSV.

The ESV's Translation Oversight Committee has proven their commitment to the longevity and support of the translation. Crossway Publishers ensures that it remains available and accessible in many different bindings and formats.

A few options are available for those who want an ESV version of the Apocrypha:[18]

- *ESV with Apocrypha* from Anglican Liturgy Press (2019),[19]
- *The Augustine Bible* (ESV-CE) from Augustine Institute (2019),[20]
- *The Apocrypha: The Lutheran Edition with Notes* (Concordia Publishing House, 2012),[21]

• *ESV Apocrypha Text Edition* (Cambridge University Press, 2021).[22]

REPRESENTATIVE SAMPLES

Familiar Passages

Gn 1.1–2	In the beginning, God created the heavens and the earth. The earth was without form and void, and darkness was over the face of the deep. And the Spirit of God was hovering over the face of the waters.
Ps 23.1–2	The LORD is my shepherd; I shall not want. He makes me lie down in green pastures. He leads me beside still waters.[1]
	footnote (fn): [1] Hebrew *beside waters of rest*
Ps 27.4	One thing have I asked of the LORD, that will I seek after: that I may dwell in the house of the LORD all the days of my life, to gaze upon the beauty of the LORD and to inquire[2] in his temple.
	fn: [2] Or *meditate*
Jn 3.16	"For God so loved the world,[3] that he gave his only Son, that whoever believes in him should not perish but have eternal life."
	fn: [3] Or *For this is how God loved the world*

Divine Name and Titles

YHWH	Ps 24.1a	The earth is the **LORD**'s and the fullness thereof[4]
		fn: [4] Or *and all that fills it*
adonai	Ps 90.1	**Lord**, you have been our dwelling place[5] in all generations.
		fn: [5] Some Hebrew manuscripts (compare Septuagint) *our refuge*
elohim	Gn 1.27a	So **God** created man in his own image

The Best Bible?

adonai Yhwh	Ps 73.28b	I have made the **Lord God** my refuge
adonai elohim	Dn 9.3a	Then I turned my face to the **Lord God**
Yhwh *saba'oth*	1Sa 17.45b	"I come to you in the name of the **Lord of hosts**"
el shaddai	Ex 6.3a	"I appeared to Abraham, to Isaac, and to Jacob, as **God Almighty**"[1]
		fn: [1] Hebrew *El Shaddai*
kyrios	Lk 20.42b	"'The **Lord** said to my **Lord**, Sit at my right hand'"
christos	Mt 16.16b	"You are the **Christ**, the Son of the living God."

New Testament Text Base

Mt 17.21	—— **fn:** Some manuscripts insert verse 21: *But this kind never comes out except by prayer and fasting*
Mt 18.11	—— **fn:** Some manuscripts add verse 11: *But the Son of Man came to save the lost*
Ac 8.37	—— **fn:** Some manuscripts add all or most of verse 37: *And Phillip said, "If you believe with all your heart, you may." And he replied, "I believe that Jesus Christ is the Son of God."*
1Jn 5.7b–8a	—— (Omitted without notice)

Gender Language

'ādām	Gn 9.6	"Whoever sheds the blood of **man**, by **man** shall his blood be shed, for God made **man** in his own image."
'îsh ... nephesh	Lv 24.17	"**Whoever** takes **a human life** shall surely be put to death."
'āvîw	Pr 15.5a	A fool despises **his father's** instruction
huioi	Mt 5.9	"Blessed are the peacemakers, for they shall be called **sons**[2] of God."
		footnote (fn): [2] Greek *huioi*; see preface
anthrōpōn	Mt 4.19	"Follow me, and I will make you fishers **of men**."
hekastō ... autou	Ro 2.6	He will render **to each one** according to **his** works:

adelphoi	Gal 5.13	For you were called to freedom, **brothers**. Only do not use your freedom as an opportunity for the flesh, but through love serve one another.
gynaikos anēr	Ti 1.6a	if anyone is above reproach, **the husband** of one **wife**,[1] and his children are believers [2]
		fn: [1] Or *a man of one woman* [2] Or *are faithful*
gynaikas	1Ti 3.11	Their **wives** likewise[1] must be dignified, not slanderers, but sober-minded, faithful in all things.
		fn: [1] Or *Wives likewise*, or *Women likewise*

Difficult Renderings

1Sa 13.1	Saul lived for **one year** and then became king, and when he had reigned for **two years** over Israel [2]
	fn: [2] Hebrew *Saul was one year old when he became king, and he reigned two years over Israel;* some Greek manuscripts give Saul's age when he began to reign as thirty years
Is 28.13	And the word of the LORD will be to them **precept upon precept, precept upon precept,** **line upon line, line upon line,** **here a little, there a little,** that they may go, and fall backward, and be broken, and snared, and taken.

Significant Renderings

'almah	Is 7.14	Therefore the Lord himself will give you a sign. Behold, **the virgin** shall conceive and bear a son, and shall call his name Immanuel.[3]
		fn: [3] *Immanuel* means *God is with us*
she'ol, 'abaddon	Pr 15.11	**Sheol** and **Abaddon** lie open before the LORD; how much more the hearts of the children of man!
egennēsen	Mt 1.2	Abraham **was the father of** Isaac, and Isaac **the father of** Jacob, and Jacob **the father of** Judah and his brothers

eskēnōsen	Jn 1.14	And the Word became flesh and **dwelt** among us, full of grace and truth; we have beheld his glory, glory as of the only Son[4] from the Father.
		fn: [4] Or *only One*, or *unique One*
tois ioudaiois	Jn 18.36	Jesus answered, "My kingdom is not of this world. If my kingdom were of this world, my servants would have been fighting, that I might not be delivered over **to the Jews**. But my kingdom is not from the world."
dikaiosunē theou, pisteōs Iēsou Christou	Ro 3.22a	**the righteousness of God** through **faith in Jesus Christ** for all who believe. For there is no distinction
Granville Sharp's rule applied	Tt 2.13	awaiting our blessed hope, the appearing of the glory of **our great God and Savior Jesus Christ**

SIGNIFICANT REVISIONS

Changes from the *Revised Standard Version*

The ESV simplified the RSV's punctuation by replacing semicolons with periods or commas:

	RSV (1971)	ESV (2001–16)
Gn 1.2–3	. . . and darkness was upon the face of the deep; **and** the Spirit[b] of God was moving over the face of the waters. And God said, "Let there be light"; and there was light.	. . . and darkness was over the face of the deep. **And** the Spirit of God was hovering over the face of the waters. And God said, "Let there be light," and there was light.
	fn: *b* Or *wind*	

The ESV also updated grammar, idioms and vocabulary:

Gn 1.11a	And God said, "Let the earth **put forth** vegetation"	And God said, "Let the earth **sprout** vegetation"

ESV

	RSV	ESV
Gn 1.29	And God said, "Behold, I have given you every plant yielding seed which is **upon** the face of all the earth"	And God said, "Behold, I have given you every plant yielding seed that is **on** the face of all the earth"
Gn 6.2a	the sons of God saw that the daughters of men were **fair**	the sons of God saw that the daughters of man were **attractive**
Gn 14.11	So the enemy took all the **goods** of Sodom and Gomorrah	So the enemy took all the **possessions** of Sodom and Gomorrah
Gn 15.9a	He said to him, "Bring me a heifer three years old, a **she-goat** three years old"	He said to him, "Bring me a heifer three years old, a **female goat** three years old"
Gn 16.12a	He shall be a wild **ass** of a man	He shall be a wild **donkey** of a man
Gn 20.16	To Sarah he said, "Behold, I have given your brother a thousand pieces of silver; it is **your vindication** in the eyes of all who are with you; and before every one you are **righted**."	To Sarah he said, "Behold, I have given your brother a thousand pieces of silver. It is **a sign of your innocence** in the eyes of all [1] who are with you, and before everyone you are **vindicated**." fn: [1] Hebrew *It is a covering of eyes for all*
Gn 26.14	He had possessions of flocks and herds, and **a great household**, so that the Philistines envied him.	He had possessions of flocks and herds and **many servants**, so that the Philistines envied him.
Gn 26.31a	In the morning they rose early and **took oath with one another**;	In the morning they rose early and **exchanged oaths**.
Gn 27.35	But he said, "Your brother came **with guile**, and he has taken away your blessing."	But he said, "Your brother came **deceitfully**, and he has taken away your blessing."

	RSV	ESV
Gn 25.29	Once when Jacob was **boiling pottage**, Esau came in from the field, and he was **famished**.	Once when Jacob was **cooking stew**, Esau came in from the field, and he was **exhausted**.
2Sa 11.5	And the woman conceived; and she sent and told David, "I am **with child**."	And the woman conceived, and she sent and told David, "I am **pregnant**."
Mk 1.7	And he preached, saying, "After me comes he who is mightier than I, the **thong** of whose sandals I am not worthy to stoop down and untie."	And he preached, saying, "After me comes he who is mightier than I, the **strap** of whose sandals I am not worthy to stoop down and untie."

Spelled-out numbers were converted to their Arabic equivalents, though not always.

	RSV	ESV
Nm 7.25a	his offering was one silver plate, whose weight was a **hundred and thirty** shekels, one silver basin of **seventy** shekels, according to the shekel of the sanctuary	his offering was one silver plate whose weight was 130 shekels, one silver basin of 70 shekels, according to the shekel of the sanctuary
Gn 46.27b	all the persons of the house of Jacob, that came into Egypt, were **seventy**.	All the persons of the house of Jacob who came into Egypt were **seventy**.

Sometimes, words are changed for their literary effect.

	RSV	ESV
Gn 1.26b	"and let them have dominion over the fish of the sea, and over the birds of the **air**"	"And let them have dominion over the fish of the sea and over the birds of the **heavens**"
Gn 10.24	Arpachshad **became the father** of Shelah; and Shelah **became the father** of Eber.	Arpachshad **fathered** Shelah; and Shelah **fathered** Eber.

Some changes were based on a broader understanding of the ancient cultures or geography surrounding the Bible:

	RSV	ESV
Gn 1.6	And God said, "Let there be a **firmament** in the midst of the waters, and let it separate the waters from the waters."	And God said, "Let there be an **expanse** in the midst of the waters, and let it separate the waters from the waters."
Gn 14.19	And he blessed him and said, "Blessed be Abram by God Most High, **maker** of heaven and earth"	And he blessed him and said, "Blessed be Abram by God Most High, **Possessor**[1] of heaven and earth"
		fn: [1] Or *Creator*; also verse 22

Since the discovery of the Dead Sea Scrolls (DSS) and their subsequent study, the scholars behind the ESV felt that the traditional OT text deserved greater weight against the RSV's conjectural emendations. Each translation committee recorded their stance in relation to the Hebrew Masoretic text:

The RSV's preface reads, "Departures from the consonantal text of the best manuscripts have been made only where it seems clear that errors in copying had been made before the text was standardized. Most of the corrections adopted are based on the ancient versions (translations into Greek, Aramaic, Syriac, and Latin), which were made before the time of the Masoretic revision and therefore reflect earlier forms of the text."[23]

And the ESV's stance: "The ESV is based on the Masoretic text of the Hebrew Bible as found in *Biblia Hebraica Stuttgartensia*... . The currently renewed respect among Old Testament scholars for the Masoretic text is reflected in the ESV's attempt, wherever possible, to translate difficult Hebrew passages as they stand in the Masoretic text rather than resorting to emendations or to finding an alternative reading in the ancient versions."[24]

	RSV	ESV
Gn 21.16b	And as she sat over against him, **the child** lifted up **his** voice and wept.	And as she sat opposite him, **she** lifted up **her** voice and wept.
Gn 22.18 (cf. 12.3)	"and by your descendants shall all the nations of the earth **bless themselves**, because you have obeyed my voice"	"and in your offspring shall all the nations of the earth **be blessed**, because you have obeyed my voice"
Ps 16.10	For thou dost not give me up to Sheol, or let thy godly one see **the Pit**.	For you will not abandon my soul to Sheol, or let your holy one see **corruption**.[1] fn: [1] Or *see the pit*
Ps 2.11–12	Serve the LORD with fear, with trembling kiss **his feet**,*a* lest he be angry, and you perish in the way; for his wrath is quickly kindled. Blessed are all who take refuge in him. fn: *a* Cn: The Hebrew of 11b and 12a is uncertain	Serve the LORD with fear, and **rejoice** with trembling. Kiss **the Son**, lest he be angry, and you perish in the way, for his wrath is quickly kindled. Blessed are all who take refuge in him.

The ESV has reverted to rendering some passages historically interpreted as referring to Christ (*cf.* Is 7.14).

	RSV	ESV
Ro 9.5	to them belong the patriarchs, and of their race, according to the flesh, is the Christ. God who is over all be blessed for ever. Amen.	To them belong the patriarchs, and from their race, according to the flesh, is the Christ, **who is** God over all, blessed forever. Amen.
Ps 45.6 (cf. Heb 1.8)	Your **divine throne** *h* **endures** for ever and ever. **Your royal scepter** is a scepter of equity fn: *h* Or *Your throne is a throne of God,* or *Thy throne, O God*	Your **throne, O God, is** forever and ever. **The scepter of your kingdom** is a scepter of uprightness

The ESV Committee felt that the word "expiation" held connotations that did not fit the broader NT context. So they opted to revert back to the word "propitiation" instead (so ASV, KJV).[25]

Ro 3.24–25a	they are justified by his grace as a gift, through the redemption which is in Christ Jesus, whom God put forward as an **expiation** by his blood, to be received by faith.	and are justified by his grace as a gift, through the redemption that is in Christ Jesus, whom God put forward as a **propitiation** by his blood, to be received by faith.

	RSV	ESV
Heb 2.17	Therefore he had to be made like his brethren in every respect, so that he might become a merciful and faithful high priest in the service of God, to make **expiation** for the sins of the people.	Therefore he had to be made like his brothers in every respect, so that he might become a merciful and faithful high priest in the service of God, to make **propitiation** for the sins of the people.

The ESV carries some awkward renderings that it has inherited from the RSV:

RSV and ESV

Pr 30.26	the rock badgers are a people not mighty, yet they make their homes in the cliffs
Ps 69.23b	make their loins tremble continually
Ps 94.9	He who planted the ear, does he not hear?
Ps 147.10	His delight is not in the strength of the horse, nor his pleasure in the legs of a man
Am 4.6	"I gave you cleanness of teeth in all your cities"
Lk 17.35	"There will be two women grinding together. One will be taken and the other left." [1] fn: [1] Other ancient authorities (RSV) / Some manuscripts add (ESV) verse 36: *Two men will be in the field; one will be taken and the other left*
Ac 1.26a	And they cast lots for them, and the lot fell on Matthias

RSV and ESV

Ro 14.22	The faith that you have, keep between yourself and God.
Gal 6.12	It is those who want to make a good showing in the flesh who would force you to be circumcised
1Ti 3.8	Deacons likewise must be dignified, not double-tongued (Gk. *dilogos*) **fn:** [2] Or *devious in speech*

On rare occasion the ESV has its own akward renderings.

Ac 20.12	And they took the youth away alive, and were not a little comforted.
Ac 21.39a	Paul replied, "I am a Jew, from Tarsus in Cilicia, a citizen of no obscure city."

Revisions within the *English Standard Version*.

As far as revisions within translations go, the ESV has faced comparatively few. The total number of revisions in the 2007 edition was only 86; in 2011, they totaled 269; and in 2016, only 29 verses were affected (for a total of 52 words). The following samples indicate how the revisions made the language more contemporary and international, improved grammar, or clarified meaning.

	ESV (2001)	ESV (2007)
Ro 12.16b	Never be **conceited.**	Never be **wise in your own sight.**
1Ti 5.1–2	Do not rebuke an older man but encourage him as you would a father. Treat younger men **like** brothers, older women **like** mothers, younger women **like** sisters, in all purity.	Do not rebuke an older man but encourage him as you would a father, younger men **as** brothers, older women **as** mothers, younger women **as** sisters, in all purity.
Jer 23.23	"Am I a God at hand, declares the LORD, and not a God **afar off**?"	"Am I a God at hand, declares the LORD, and not a God **far away**?"

ESV

	ESV (2001)	ESV (2007)
2Co 12.7a	So to keep me from **being too elated** by the surpassing greatness of the revelations,[1] a thorn was given me in the flesh	So to keep me from **becoming conceited** because of the surpassing greatness of the revelations,[1] a thorn was given me in the flesh
	fn: [1] Or . . . *hears from me, even because of the surpassing greatness of the revelations. So to keep me from being too elated*	fn: [1] Or *hears from me, even because of the surpassing greatness of the revelations. So to keep me from becoming conceited*
Jg 8.1b (cf. 11.6, 8, 9)	"What is this that you have done to us, not to call us when you went to fight **with** Midian?"	"What is this that you have done to us, not to call us when you went to fight **against** Midian?"

	ESV (2007)	ESV (2011)
Ex 12.45 (cf. Lv 19.13; 22.10; 25.6, etc.)	No foreigner or hired **servant** may eat of it.	No foreigner or hired **worker** may eat of it.

These changes made the text more formal, which improved its concordance:

	ESV (2001)	ESV (2007)
Gal 2.21	I do not nullify the grace of God, for if **justification**[1] were through the law, then Christ died for no purpose.	I do not nullify the grace of God, for if **righteousness**[1] were through the law, then Christ died for no purpose.
	fn: [1] Or *righteousness*	fn: [1] Or *justification*
Col 4.5	**Conduct yourselves wisely** toward outsiders, making the best use of the time.	**Walk in wisdom** toward outsiders, making the best use of the time.
Heb 6.4–6a	For it is impossible **to restore again to repentance those who have once been enlightened,** who have tasted the heavenly gift, and have shared in the Holy Spirit . . . **if they then** fall away	For it is impossible, **in the case of those who have once been enlightened,** who have tasted the heavenly gift, and have shared in the Holy Spirit . . . , **and then** have fallen away, **to restore them again to repentance**

The Best Bible?

	ESV (2007)	ESV (2011)
2Co 11.17	What I am saying with this boastful confidence, I say not **with the Lord's authority** but as a fool.	What I am saying with this boastful confidence, I say not **as the Lord would** [2] but as a fool.
		fn: [2] Greek *not according to the Lord*
Heb 10.29a	How much worse punishment, do you think, will be deserved by the one who has **spurned** the Son of God	How much worse punishment, do you think, will be deserved by the one who has **trampled underfoot** the Son of God
2Pt 1.10a	Therefore, brothers,[1] be all the more diligent to **make** your calling and election **sure**	Therefore, brothers,[1] be all the more diligent to **confirm** your calling and election
	fn: [1] Or *brothers and sisters*. The plural Greek word *adelphoi* (translated "brothers") refers to siblings in a family. In New Testament usage, depending on the context, *adelphoi* may refer either to men or to both men and women who are siblings (brothers and sisters) in God's family, the church	**fn:** [1] Or *brothers and sisters*. In New Testament usage, depending on the context, the plural Greek word *adelphoi* (translated "brothers") may refer either to *brothers* or to *brothers and sisters*
1Jn 2.16	For all that is in the world—the desires of the flesh and the desires of the eyes and pride **in possessions**—is not from the Father but is from the world.	For all that is in the world—the desires of the flesh and the desires of the eyes and pride **of life** [2]—is not from the Father but is from the world.
		fn: [2] Or *pride in possessions*
Ne 1.1 (cf. Ezr 6.2)	I was in Susa the **capital** [3]	I was in Susa the **citadel**
	fn: [3] Or *the fortified city*	

	ESV (2011)	ESV (2016)
2Ch 6.38a	if they repent with all their **mind** and with all their **heart**	if they repent with all their **heart** and with all their **soul**

English Standard Version   **301**

ESV

	ESV (2007)	ESV (2011)
Php 2.5–7	Christ Jesus [1] . . . did not count equality with God a thing to be grasped, but **made himself nothing**, by taking the form of a servant [2]	Christ Jesus [1] . . . did not count equality with God a thing to be grasped,[2] but **emptied himself**, by taking the form of a servant [3] . . . .
		fn: [1] Or *which was also in Christ Jesus* [2] Or *a thing to be held on to for advantage* [3] Or *slave* (for the contextual rendering of the Greek word *doulos*, see Preface)
	fn: [1] Or *which was also in Christ Jesus* [2] Gk *bondservant*	

Here, the revisers replaced a familiar, Latin cognate (which is tied to preexisting, religious connotations) with a clear English equivalent:

	ESV (2001)	ESV (2007)
Eph 4.11	And he gave the apostles, the prophets, the evangelists, the **pastors** and teachers [4]	And he gave the apostles, the prophets, the evangelists, the **shepherds** [4] and teachers [5]
	fn: [4] Or *the pastor-teachers*	fn: [4] Or *pastors* [5] Or *the shepherd-teachers*

The ESV even has some gender-inclusive revisions:

Rv 6.4b	Its rider was permitted to take peace from the earth, so that **men** should slay one another	Its rider was permitted to take peace from the earth, so that **people** should slay one another
	ESV (2007)	ESV (2011)
1Co 16.18 (cf. Mk 8.24; 1Ti 5.24)	Give recognition to such **men**.	Give recognition to such **people**.

Here is a theologically or thematically significant word choice:

1Sa 11.9	" 'Tomorrow, by the time the sun is hot, you shall have **deliverance**.' "	" 'Tomorrow, by the time the sun is hot, you shall have **salvation**.' "

The Best Bible?

The choice of "bondservant" instead of "slave" (for the Gk. word *doulos*) was argued in light of the United States' historic, cultural heritage. Slaves in ancient Roman society did not receive the same racial denigration as did slaves in antebellum America. Despite class disadvantage, Roman slaves could live well and gain fame and fortune. The ESV Committee's choice of word parallels that of the *Christian Standard Bible* (CSB).

	ESV (2007)	ESV (2011)
1Co 7.21a ff (cf Eph 6.5–8; Col 3.22; 4.1; 1Ti 6.1; Phm 1.16)	Were you a **slave**[1] when called? Do not be concerned about it.	Were you a **bondservant**[1] when called? Do not be concerned about it.
	fn: [1] Greek *bondservant*; also twice in verse 22 and once in verse 23 (plural)	fn: [1] For the contextual rendering of the Greek word *doulos*, see Preface; also verses 22 (twice), 23

A subtle difference in word choice indicates habitual action instead of incidental action, in order to better reflect the continuous aspect of the Greek participle (*ho poiōn*).

Jn 8.34	Jesus answered them, "Truly, truly, I say to you, everyone who **commits** sin is a slave[2] to sin."	Jesus answered them, "Truly, truly, I say to you, everyone who **practices** sin is a slave[2] to sin."
	fn: [2] Greek *bondservant*; also verse 35	fn: [2] For the contextual rendering of the Greek word *doulos*, see Preface; also verse 35

These examples are lexical or text-critical emendations for what the editors thought better reflected the Greek original:

	ESV (2007)	ESV (2011)
Mt 10.4	Simon the **Canaanean**	Simon the **Zealot**[3]
		fn: [3] Greek *kananaios*, meaning *zealot*

ESV

	ESV (2007)	ESV (2011)
Mt 18.22	Jesus said to him, "I do not say to you seven times, but **seventy times seven.**" [1]	Jesus said to him, "I do not say to you seven times, but **seventy-seven times.**"
	fn: [1] Or *seventy-seven times*	

	ESV (2011)	ESV (2016)
Lk 24.47	repentance **and forgiveness** of sins should be proclaimed in his name to all nations, beginning from Jerusalem.	repentance **for** [2] **the forgiveness** of sins should be proclaimed in his name to all nations, beginning from Jerusalem.
		fn: [2] Some manuscripts *and*

Finally, two recent and significant changes clearly link two passages that share the same unique Hebrew construction:

Gn 3.16b	To the woman he said, ". . . Your desire shall be **for** [3] your husband, **and** he shall rule over you."	To the woman he said, ". . . Your desire shall be **contrary to** [3] your husband, **but** he shall rule over you."
		fn: [3] Or *shall be toward* (see 4:7)
	fn: [3] Or *against*	
Gn 4.7	"If you do well, will you not be accepted? And if you do not do well, sin is crouching at the door. Its desire is **for** [4] you, but you must rule over it."	"If you do well, will you not be accepted? [4] And if you do not do well, sin is crouching at the door. Its desire is **contrary to** [5] you, but you must rule over it."
		fn: [4] Hebrew *will there not be a lifting up* [of your face]? [5] Or *is toward*
	fn: [4] Or *against*	

The Best Bible?

ENDORSEMENTS

The esv is endorsed by a number of evangelical influencers, including Darrell L. Bock (NLT, *The Message*, *NET Bible*), Francis Chan (author), Matt Chandler (pastor, The Village Church), Bryan Chapell (Covenant Theological Seminary), Kevin DeYoung (pastor), Joni Eareckson Tada, Steve Green (musician), David Platt (pastor, author, former president of the International Missions Board), Thomas R. Schreiner (NLT, HCSB, CSB), R. C. Sproul († 2017), and Daniel B. Wallace (*NET Bible*), among others.

The Church of England recognizes the esv as meeting at least four of the necessary criteria for suitability to use during the course of public worship, but noted (as of 2002) that it omitted the Apocrypha, which is needed for Anglican lectionaries.[26] (Perhaps the publication of the esv Apocrypha in 2009 and the recent edition from India, which combines the Bible and Apocrypha in a single volume, will encourage its popular acceptance and use in the Anglican Communion.) The Christian Reformed Church in North America has approved the esv for public worship since 2007.[27]

The Orthodox Presbyterian Church (O.P.C.) does not endorse any one translation, but the Committee on Christian Education of the OPC most frequently quotes from the esv in its publications.[28] Likewise, The Lutheran Church—Missouri Synod (LCMS) uses the esv as the base for the LCMS's *The Lutheran Study Bible* (St. Louis, MO: Concordia Publishing House, 2009).

The Translation Evaluation Committee of the Wisconsin Evangelical Lutheran Synod (WELS) is ambivalent about the esv, which they consider "a doctrinally acceptable, somewhat unidiomatic and inconsistent evangelical revision of the RSV. Nothing more and nothing less."[29] Nonetheless, WELS makes the esv available as one of six translations offered through their distributor, Northwestern Publishing House.[30]

ESV

The ESV *Catholic Edition* (ESV-CE) was approved by the Conference of Catholic Bishops of India on February 4, 2018 and granted the Imprimatur by Cardinal Oswald Gracias, a member of the Council of Cardinals. (The Vatican approved the ESV-CE *Lectionary* on December 9, 2019.)[31] Also, the Bishops' Conference of Scotland voted to use the ESV-CE as the basis for their new lectionary in July 2020.[32]

COPYRIGHT

You may quote up to 500 verses from the ESV in any form without prior written permission; the verses may not constitute a complete book of the Bible; they must comprise less than 25% of your work's content; and your work must include the following copyright acknowledgment.

> Scripture quotations are from the ESV® Bible (*The Holy Bible, English Standard Version®*), copyright © 2001 by Crossway, a publishing ministry of Good News Publishers. Used by permission. All rights reserved.

Unless used exclusively, follow citations with the designation (ESV). For example:

Jn 1.4, "In him was life, and the life was the light of men." (ESV)

The title *"English Standard Version®"*, its initialism (ESV®), and its logomark are registered trademarks with the U.S. Patent and Trademark Office by Good News Publishers.

For permissions not covered here, visit <https://www.crossway.org/permissions/print/>, or write to Crossway, 1300 Crescent Street, Wheaton, IL, 60187 USA.

ENDNOTES FOR THE
ENGLISH STANDARD VERSION

1   Crossway (Good News Publishers), "History—Celebrating God's Faithfulness and Glory: The ESV Bible," accessed February 5, 2020, https://www.crossway.org/history/.

2   David Bayly, "Decline of the NIV?" *World Magazine* (Asheville, NC: World News Group, June 5, 1999).

3   "Preface," *Holy Bible, English Standard Version* (Wheaton, IL: Crossway, 2001).

4   "Preface," *Holy Bible* . . . (2001).

5   C. John Collins, "What the Reader Wants and the Translator Can Give: First John as a Test Case," *Translating Truth: The Case for Essentially Literal Translation* (Wheaton, IL: Crossway, 2005), pp. 77–111.

6   "Preface," *The English Standard Version Bible with Apocrypha* (Oxford: Oxford University Press, 2009).

7   "Translation Team," website for the *English Standard Bible,* accessed January 16, 2006, http://www.esv.org/translation/team.

8   Suzanne McCarthy, "J I Packer and the ESV Team," *Better Bibles Blog*, last modified February 20, 2006, accessed February 5, 2020, http://englishbibles.blogspot.com/2006/02/j-i-packer-and-esv-team.html.

9   "Preface," *ESV with Apocrypha* (2009).

10 "The team of scholars which the Catholic Bishops of India entrusted with the task of revising the ESV for Catholic use included: Rev. Dr. Lucien Legrand, M.E.P., Rev. Dr. Assisi Saldanha, C.SS.R., Rev. Dr. Govindu Rayanna, Rev. Dr. A. Alfred Joseph, Rev. Dr. David Stanly Kumar, Sr. Dr. Prema Vakayil, C.S.S.T., Rev. Dr. Shabu Joseph Thottumkal, S.D.B., Rev. Dr. Stanislas Savarimuthu." "Frequently Asked Questions," accessed November 7, 2020, https://www.catholicbible.org/.

11 "Preface," *Holy Bible, English Standard Version.*

12 Wayne Grudem. *The Advantages of the English Standard Version* (ESV) *Translation,* uploaded February 2015, accessed January 31, 2017, http://www.waynegrudem.com/wp-content/uploads/2015/02/The-advantages-of-the-ESV.pdf.

13 *Ibid.*

14 Collins, "What the Reader Wants and the Translator Can Give," p. 88.

15 "Preface," *Holy Bible, English Standard Version.*

[16] *Ibid.*

[17] *Ibid.*

[18] These editions of the Apocrypha/Deuterocanon are based on the *English Standard Version Bible with Apocrypha* published by the Oxford University Press (January 2009).

[19] "[This] translation is an adaptation of the ESV *with Apocrypha* published in cooperation with Oxford University Press in 2009."

Anglican Liturgy Press, "ESV with Apocrypha," accessed February 4, 2020, https://anglicanliturgypress.com/shop/the-esv-bible-with-apocrypha/.

[20] Though based on the Oxford Apocrypha (2009), "the Book of Tobit . . . had to be retranslated from scratch. The translation was reviewed in accord with the norms of *Liturgiam authenticam.*"

Mark Giszczak, "ESV Catholic Edition Bible Now Available in the United States!" *Catholic Bible Student,* last modified December 13, 2019, accessed July 8, 2020, https://catholicbiblestudent.com/2019/12/esv-catholic-edition-bible-now-available-in-the-united-states.html.

Augustine Institute, "The Augustine Bible (ESV-CE)," accessed November 7, 2020, https://catholic.market/the-augustine-bible-esv-ce/.

[21] Concordia Publishing House, "The Apocrypha: The Lutheran Edition with Notes," accessed July 23, 2019, https://www.cph.org/p-21079-the-apocrypha-the-lutheran-edition-with-notes-ebook-edition.aspx.

[22] Cambridge University Press, "ESV Apocrypha Text Edition," accessed February 1, 2021, https://www.cambridge.org/us/bibles/all-titles/esv-apocrypha-text-edition-es530?format=HB.

[23] Division of Christian Education of the National Council of Churches in the U.S.A., "Preface," *The Holy Bible, Containing the Old and New Testaments . . . Revised Standard Version* (Holman Bible Publishers, 1982).

[24] Nonetheless, the ESV retains some of the emendations introduced by the RSV, such as "sons of God" in place of "children of Israel" in **Dt 32.8**.

"Preface," *Holy Bible, English Standard Version.*

[25] "Expiation" refers to *the removal of sin,* while "propitiation" refers to the broader aspect of Christ's act, which *appeases* God's anger and *puts him in a favorable relationship.*

Cp. "Expiation. *n.*" and "Propitiation, *n.*" in the *Oxford English Dictionary,* 3rd ed. (Oxford University Press, 2007).

26 General Synod of the Church of England, "Versions of Scripture," by David Michael Hope, Archbishop of York (Eboracensis), October 9, 2002, GS Misc 698.

27 Christian Reformed Church in North America, "Bible Translations," accessed September 6, 2019, https://www.crcna.org/welcome/beliefs/bible-translations.

28 Orthodox Presbyterian Church's publications website, accessed February 3, 2020 https://store.opc.org/.

29 Thomas P. Nass, "Some Thoughts on the ESV and Bible Translation," a paper presented at the St. Croix Pastors' Conference (Eden Prairie, MN, February 8, 2011) and at the New Ulm/Redwood Falls Pastors' Conference (Fairmont, MN, March 1, 2011).

30 Northwestern Publishing House, "English Standard Version ESV," accessed February 3, 2020, https://online.nph.net/bibles/bibles-by-translation/english-standard-version-esv.html.

31 "Frequently Asked Questions," accessed November 7, 2020, https://www.catholicbible.org/.

32 "A New Lectionary for Scotland," the website of the Archdiocese of St. Andrews and Edinburgh, last modified July 24, 2020; accessed November 24, 2020, https://archedinburgh.org/a-new-lectionary-for-scotland/.

New American Standard Bible®

The Holy Bible containing the Old and New Testaments

Produced by The Lockman Foundation, 1963–2020

FORMAL / FUNCTIONAL TENDENCIES

FORMAL   FUNCTIONAL

Interlinear **N A S B** KJV NKJV ESV RSV CSB NRSV NET NIV NLT   Free Paraphrase

TEXT BASES

English Base *American Standard Version* (1901).

OT Masoretic Hebrew and Ancient Versions.   **NT** Eclectic Greek.

TRANSLATION TIMELINE

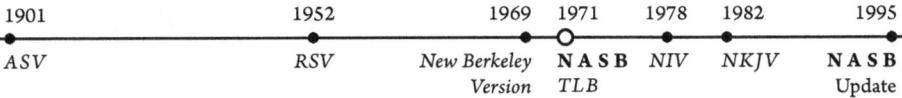

1901	1952	1969	1971	1978	1982	1995
ASV	*RSV*	*New Berkeley Version*	**N A S B** *TLB*	*NIV*	*NKJV*	**N A S B** Update

CONTEMPORARY EVENTS

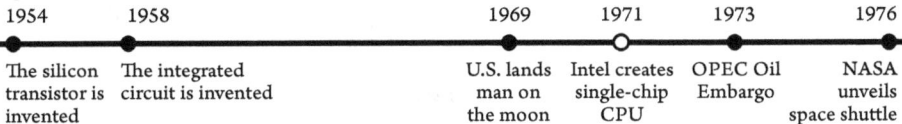

1954	1958	1969	1971	1973	1976
The silicon transistor is invented	The integrated circuit is invented	U.S. lands man on the moon	Intel creates single-chip CPU	OPEC Oil Embargo	NASA unveils space shuttle

PUBLICATION TIMELINE

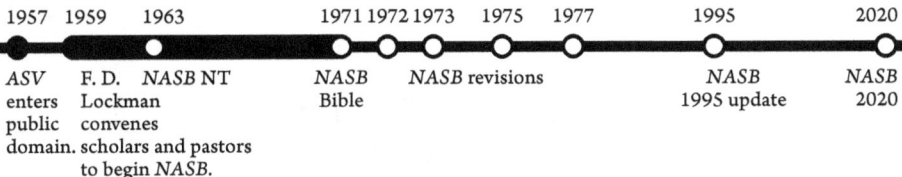

1957	1959	1963	1971	1972	1973	1975	1977	1995	2020
ASV enters public domain.	F. D. Lockman convenes scholars and pastors to begin *NASB*.	*NASB* NT	*NASB* Bible		*NASB* revisions			*NASB* 1995 update	*NASB* 2020

New

American Standard

Bible

⊰❧⊱

Text Edition

⊰❧⊱

MOODY PRESS
CHICAGO

In 1942, F. Dewey Lockman and his wife Minna sold three-quarters of their Imperial Ranch, a large citrus grove in La Habra, California.[1] They used their money to fund The Lockman Foundation, a non-profit organization with a mission of promoting Christian education and ministry.

By 1959, Lockman had funded Bible study programs for both adults and children. He had already financed a portion of one successful venture into Bible translation with the publication of the *Amplified New Testament* (1958). He now aimed to publish a new translation designed especially for Christian ministry. That year Lockman organized a group of scholars and pastors to produce such a translation, which would come to be known as the *New American Standard Bible* (NASB).

STATED TRANSLATION IDEALS

The *American Standard Version* (ASV) was considered to be a "rock of Biblical honesty," though it was rapidly falling into disuse. When the copyright of the ASV lapsed in 1957, "[it was felt that it was t]ime to restore its heritage before it was neglected and forgotten altogether."[2] "The producers of [NASB] were imbued with the conviction that interest in the *American Standard Version* should be renewed and increased."[3]

With the ASV as their model, the Editorial Board intended to make the NASB "adhere as closely as possible to the original languages of the Holy Scriptures, and to make the translation in a fluent and readable style according to current English usage."[4] They attempted "to render the grammar and terminology of the ASV in contemporary English." When they felt modern readers would not accept the word-for-word literalness of the ASV, they rendered the text with a more current English idiom. The Board then placed the formal renderings in the footnotes.

As stated in the "Fourfold Aim of the Lockman Foundation", the NASB (1) should be "true to the original Hebrew, Aramaic, and Greek," (2) it should be "grammatically correct," (3) it should be "understandable," and—in line with the Board's evangelical Christian faith—(4) it should "give the Lord Jesus Christ His proper place, the place which the Word gives Him."[5]

METHOD

Lockman formed a committee of four men to begin work in 1960. They settled on the ASV as the English text-base and model, though the NASB resulted as more of a new translation than a revision. Two of the men were scholars, who examined the translation work for accuracy, and two were pastors, who checked it for clarity and communicativeness.

They completed the *Gospel of John* that year. The committee then invited three more members the following year (1961) and finished the *Four Gospels* the next (1962). The *New Testament* was published in 1963. The number of those involved in the Bible's production grew to over forty-five by the time that the Bible was published. Finally on August 28, 1971, the NASB was commended to God during a service held at the First Baptist Church of Anaheim (Lockman's home church) and released to the world.[6]

TEXT BASES

English Text

The NASB is based on the *American Standard Version* (1901).

New Testament

Eclectic Greek text. Nestle-Aland *Novum Testamentum Graece* 23rd, 26th revised, and 28th editions (Stuttgart: Privilegierte Württembergische Bibelanstalt, 1957, 1983; Deutsche Bibelgesellschaft, 2012). *Novum Testamentum Graece, Editio Critica Maior* (Deutsche Bibelgesellschaft, 2013–) is used for **Acts** and the General Epistles (**Jas, 1–2Pt, 1–3Jn, Jd**).

Old Testament

Masoretic Hebrew-Aramaic text. Kittel's *Biblia Hebraica*, 3rd edition (Stuttgart: Privilegierte Württembergische Bibelanstalt, 1929–37); *Biblia Hebraica Stuttgartensia*, 2nd emended edition (Stuttgart: Deutsche Bibelgesellschaft, 1984); *Biblia Hebraica Quinta Editione* (Stuttgart: Deutsche Bibelgesellschaft, 2004–)

Ancient versions including the Septuagint (LXX) and the Dead Sea Scrolls (DSS).

CONTRIBUTORS

The members of the translation team were originally anonymous. Forty-two translators representing more than a dozen different evangelical denominations contributed to the Bible's publication in 1971.[7]

Reuben A. Olson served as the chairman of the editorial board. Other notables include Gleason Archer (NIV), Kenneth Lee Barker (NIV), Merrill C. Tenney (NIV), Bruce K. Waltke (NIV, TNIV), Kenneth S. Wuest (*The New Testament: An Expanded Translation*, 1961), and Moisés Silva (ESV, consultant for *The Message*).

Twenty more revisers and critical consultants took part in the NASB 1995 edition. Among them are George Blankenbaker, Frank G. Carver, Buist M. Fanning III (NET), Harold Walter Hoehner (ESV, NET), David K. Lowery (NET), Robert Saucy, Daniel B. Wallace (NET), and James White.[8]

Some of the revisers and consultants involved in the NASB 2020 edition include David Allen (CSB), Paul Enns, Robert "Bob" G. Lambeth (former president of The Lockman Foundation), H. Bruce Stokes, Ryan Stokes (NRSV 2021), and W. Don Wilkins, among others.

NASB

For a complete list of translators, visit *booklink.id/nasb-translator*

THEOLOGICAL ASSUMPTIONS

"The Fourfold Aim of the Lockman Foundation Publications . . . shall give the Lord Jesus Christ His proper place, the place which the Word gives Him."[9]

FEATURES

"The attempt has been made to render the grammar and terminology of the ASV in contemporary English. When it was felt that the word-for-word literalness of the ASV was unacceptable to the modern reader, a change was made in the direction of a more current English idiom."[10] The actual result is tends to be in understandable yet stilted English, as one should expect from a formal translation.

In the narrative and parables of the Gospels and Acts, the original authors often slipped into using the "historic present", *i.e.*, they used a Greek present continuous form while writing about past events. Story tellers do this, often without thinking, as they lead the imagination of their audiences into the events of the story. Most translations convert these Greek present verb forms into English past tense, and the NASB is no different, except the NASB indicates these forms with an asterisk ("*") to alert readers to the underlying "historic present" verbs.

Jesus *said to them, "Do you believe that I am able to do this?" They *said to Him, "Yes, Lord." (**Mt 9.28b** NASB)

In early editions of the NASB NT, a number of second person pronouns (singular or plural) were distinguished with superscripts when the context failed to clarify which was meant in English. Plurals were marked with "pl" and singulars with "s".

"You[pl] have heard that the ancients were told, 'You[s] shall not commit murder'" (**Mt 5.21a** NASB 1963)

The Best Bible?

This practice was discontinued with the publication of the full Bible in 1971.

In the 1995 update, "And" is not translated at the beginning of sentences in order to conform to modern English usage. The biblical idiom "answered and said" is sometimes reduced to "answered" or "said" depending on context.

Mt 9.26–27	**And** this news went out into all that land. **And** as Jesus passed on from there, two blind men followed Him, crying out, **and saying,** "Have mercy on us, Son of David!" (NASB 1977)	This news spread throughout all that land. As Jesus went on from there, two blind men followed Him, crying out, "Have mercy on us, Son of David!" (NASB 1995)

Likewise, the idiom "it came about [that]" has been dropped except when a major transition is needed in the OT.

Mt 4.4	**and it came about that** as he was sowing, some seed fell beside the road, and the birds came and ate it up.	as he was sowing, some seed fell beside the road, and the birds came and ate it up.
Jg 7.9	Now the same night **it came about that** the LORD said to him, "Arise, go down against the camp, for I have given it into your hands." (NASB 1977)	Now the same night **it came about that** the LORD said to him, "Arise, go down against the camp, for I have given it into your hands." (NASB 1995)

The most touted feature of the NASB editions from 1977 and earlier is how the editors consistently and transparently rendered Greek verb tenses. (This allows for fairly precise back-translation from English into Greek.) Greek imperfects are rendered as English past continuous ("He was doing"), as ingressive past (*i.e.,* inceptive past, "He began to do", "He started to do"), or customary past (*i.e.,* habitual past, "He used to do"). Greek aorists are translated as English simple past ("He did"), though not always: The translators determined from the context that some aorists are better represented by the English perfect tense ("He has done") or past perfect tense ("He had done").

The 1995 edition follows regular English usage more closely, and thus loses some of the grammatical transparency and precision shown by earlier editions.

Mk 6.7b	and He **was giving** them authority over the unclean spirits	and **gave** them authority over the unclean spirits
Lk 11.5	And He said to them, "Suppose one of you **shall have** a friend, and **shall go** to him at midnight, and say to him, 'Friend, lend me three loaves.'"	Then He said to them, "Suppose one of you **has** a friend, and **goes** to him at midnight and says to him, 'Friend, lend me three loaves.'"
Mt 9.29	"**Be it done** to you according to your faith." (NASB 1977)	"**It shall be done** to you according to your faith." (NASB 1995)

The NASB retains certain theological words, like "propitiation" (**Heb 2.17**), "justification" (**Ro 4.25**), "reconciliation" (**2Co 5.19**), and "saints" (**Eph 1.1; Php 1.1**).

Like the RSV, editions of the NASB from 1977 and earlier changed the second person pronouns, "thou", "thee", "thy", and "thine", to "you" and "your", *etc.*, except when addressing God in the language of prayer. In the 1995 update, these Divine pronouns have been changed to capitalized "You", "Your", and "Yours".

In the editions published from 1963–1995, each verse starts its own line. Sense paragraphs are indicated with **bold face** reference numbers or **bold** initial letters. Later print editions are available, which break paragraphs by sense with reference numbers placed inline inside the text. The 2020 edition prints verse numbers inline and indents the first line of paragraphs according to the sense.

In the NT, SMALL CAPS are used to indicate OT quotations or obvious references to NT texts.

Punctuation, including quotation marks for dialogue, is set according to current English use.

"*Italics* are used in the text to indicate words which are not found in the original Hebrew, Aramaic, or Greek but implied by it. Italics are used in the marginal notes to signify alternate readings for the text. . . . 'Began' is italicized if it renders an imperfect tense, in order to distinguish it from the Greek verb for 'begin.'

"Personal pronouns are capitalized when pertaining to Deity.

"Only such notations have been used as have been felt justified in assisting the reader's comprehension of the terms used by the original author."[11] The footnotes include readings of variant manuscripts, explanatory equivalents of the text, more literal renderings, and alternate renderings. Alternative translations are indicated by *italics* in the footnotes. Footnotes are referred to in the text with superscript numerals ([1]).

Cross-references are either placed in a column on the outer edge(s) of the page or they adjoin the text on the page, listed under the verse numbers to which they refer. Superscript letters ([a]) refer to cross-references. Cross references in *italics* are parallel passages (*e.g.*, at **Lk 18.35, 38**, note **Mt 20.29–34** and **Mk 10.46–52** below).[12] Not all editions carry a cross-reference system.

> **35** [a][b]As Jesus was approaching Jericho, a blind man was sitting by the road begging. **36** Now hearing a crowd going by, he *began* to inquire what this was. **37** They told him that Jesus of Nazareth was passing by. **38** And he called out, saying, "Jesus, [a]Son of David, have mercy on me!"
>
> ★**18:35**
> [a] Luke 18:35-43; *Matt 20:29-34; Mark 10:46-52*
> [b] Matt 20:29; Mark 10:46; Luke 19:1
>
> **18:38**
> [a] Matt 9:27; Luke 18:39

ASSESSMENT

The NASB's tendency towards formalism and concordancy make it ideal for careful word and thematic studies. It is one of only a handful of late translations that sets translator-supplied words in a different font. This and the translators' footnotes give readers a better vantage to glimpse into the translation process.

The NASB has a number of references and resources to support it, including a Strong's *Concordance*. These features and resources make the NASB ideal as a study Bible and for word studies in particular.

Yet, the same features that make the NASB good for study are also what make it difficult for casual reading. The translation is littered with wooden or stilted English, and this is despite the revisions it has received over the years. Yet the 2020 revision makes a better preaching Bible due to revisions that steer the translation towards more natural English and less rigid (formalistic) gender policies. The following samples are from the 2020 edition.

REPRESENTATIVE SAMPLES

Familiar Passages

Gn 1.1–2	In the beginning God created the heavens and the earth. And the earth was a [1] formless and desolate emptiness, and darkness was over the [2] surface of the deep, and the Spirit of God was hovering over the [2] surface of the waters.
	footnote (fn): 1:2 [1] Or *waste* [2] Lit *face of*
Ps 23.1–2	The LORD is my shepherd, I will not be in need. He lets me lie down in green pastures; He leads me beside [4]quiet waters.
	fn: 23:2 [4] Lit *waters of rest*
Ps 27.4	One thing I have asked from the LORD, that I shall seek: That I may dwell in the house of the LORD all the days of my life, To behold the [5] beauty of the LORD And to [6] meditate in His temple.
	fn: 27:4 [5] Lit *delightfulness* [6] Lit *inquire*
Jn 3.16	"For God so loved the world, that He gave His only Son, so that everyone who believes in Him will not perish, but have eternal life."

Divine Name and Titles

YHWH	Ps 24.1a	The earth is the LORD's, and [7]all it contains
		fn: 24:1 [7] Lit *its fullness*
adonai	Ps 90.1b	Lord, You have been our [8]dwelling place in all generations.
		fn: 24:1 [8] Or *hiding place;* some ancient mss *place of refuge*

elohim	Gn 1.27a	So **God** created man in His own image
adonai YHWH	Ps 73.28b	I have made the **Lord** [1]**GOD** my refuge
		fn: **73:28** [1] Heb *YHWH*, usually rendered LORD
adonai elohim	Dn 9.3a	So I gave my [2]attention to the **Lord God**
		fn: **9:3** [2] Lit *face*
YHWH *saba'oth*	1Sa 17.45b	"I come to you in the name of the **LORD of armies**"
el shaddai	Ex 6.3a	"and I appeared to Abraham, Isaac, and Jacob, as [3] **God Almighty**"
		fn: **6:3** [3] Heb *El Shaddai*
kyrios	Lk 20.42b	"'THE **LORD** SAID TO MY **LORD**, "SIT AT MY RIGHT HAND"'"
christos	Mt 16.16b	"You are the [4] **Christ**, the Son of the living God."
		fn: **16:16** [4] I.e., Messiah

New Testament Text Base

Mt 17.21	——— **fn:** Late mss add (traditionally v 21): *But this kind does not go out except by prayer and fasting."*
Mt 18.11	——— **fn:** Late mss add (traditionally v 11): *For the Son of Man has come to save that which was lost.*
Ac 8.37	——— **fn:** Late mss add as v 37: *And Philip said, "If you believe with all your heart, you may." And he answered and said, "I believe that Jesus Christ is the Son of God."*
1Jn 5.7b–8a	——— **fn:** A few late mss add . . . *in heaven, the Father, the Word, and the Holy Spirit, and these three are one. And there are three that testify on earth, the Spirit*

Gender Language

'ādām	Gn 9.6	"Whoever sheds **human** blood, By **man** his blood shall be shed, For in the image of God He made **mankind**."
gynaikos anēr	Ti 1.6a	*namely,* if any man is above reproach, **the husband of** one **wife**, having children who believe

'îsh … nephesh	Lv 24.17	Now if **someone** [1]takes any human **life**, he must be put to death.
		fn: 24:17 [1] Lit *strikes*
'āvîw	Pr 15.5a	A fool [2] rejects **his father's** discipline
		fn: 15:5 [2] Or *despises*
huioi	Mt 5.9	"Blessed are the peacemakers, for they will be called **sons** of God."
anthrōpōn	Mt 4.19	"[3]Follow Me, and I will make you fishers **of people**."
		fn: 15:5 [3] Or *Come after Me*
hekastō … autou	Ro 2.6	who WILL REPAY **EACH PERSON** ACCORDING TO **HIS** DEEDS
adelphoi	Gal 5.13	For you were called to freedom, **brethers *and sisters***; only *do not turn* your freedom into an opportunity for the flesh, but serve one another through love.
gynaikas	1Ti 3.11	[4]**Women** *must* likewise *be* dignified, not malicious gossips, but [5] temperate, faithful in all things.
		fn: 3:11 [4] I.e., either deacons' wives or deaconesses [5] Or *level-headed*

Difficult Renderings

1Sa 13.1	Saul was [6] ***thirty* years old** when he began to reign, and he reigned [7] ***forty* two years** over Israel.
	fn: 13:1 [6] As in some LXX mss, but very uncertain; MT *one year old* [7] See Acts 13:21; Heb *two years*
Is 28.13	So the word of the LORD to them will be, "[8]**Order on order, order on order, Line on line, line on line, A little here, a little there,**" That they may go and stumble backward, be broken, snared and taken captive.
	fn: 28:13 [8] See note v 10. The LORD responds to their scoffing by imitating their mockery, to represent the unintelligible language of a conqueror

The Best Bible?

Significant Renderings

'almah	Is 7.14	Therefore the Lord Himself will give you a sign: Behold, the ¹**virgin** will conceive and give birth to a son, and she will name Him ²Immanuel.
		fn: **7:14** ¹ As in LXX; MT *young unmarried woman* ² I.e., God is with us
she'ol, 'abaddon	Pr 15.11	¹**Sheol** and ²**Abaddon** *lie open* before the Lᴏʀᴅ, How much more the hearts of ³mankind!
		fn: **15:11** ¹ I.e., The netherworld ² I.e., place of destruction ³ Lit *sons of mankind*
egennēsen	Mt 1.2	Abraham **fathered** Isaac, Isaac **fathered** Jacob, and Jacob **fathered** ⁴Judah and his brothers.
		fn: **1:2** ⁴ Gr *Judas*; a name of a person in the Old Testament are given in its Old Testament form
eskēnōsen	Jn 1.14	And the Word became flesh, and **dwelt** among us, and we saw His glory, glory as of the only *Son* from the Father, full of grace and truth.
tois ioudaiois	Jn 18.36	Jesus answered, "My kingdom is not of this world. If My kingdom were of this world, then My servants would be fighting so that I would not be handed over **to the Jews**; but as it is, My kingdom is not ⁵of this realm."
		fn: **18:36** ⁵ Lit *from here*
dikaiosunē theou, pisteōs Iēsou Christou	Ro 3.22a	but *it is the* **righteousness of God** through **faith in Jesus Christ** for all those ⁶who believe; for there is no distinction
		fn: **3:22** ⁶ Or *who believe. For there is*
Granville Sharp's rule applied	Tt 2.13	looking for the blessed hope and the appearing of the glory of ⁷**our great God and Savior, Christ Jesus**
		fn: **3:22** ⁷ Or *the great God and our Savior*

SIGNIFICANT REVISIONS

In keeping with the promise "to make the translation in a fluent and readable style according to current English usage,"[13] the NASB has been revised several times since its initial publication, particularly within the first six years (1972, '73, '75, and '77). In 1995 and 2020 the NASB received significant revisions which brought its English style even closer to current usage.

The NASB 1995 Update

The major update published in 1995 resulted in around 21,800 changes in the NASB (approximately seventy percent of the Bible). Most changes resulted from revisers changing or hiding Hebrew *waw* consecutives and Greek *kai* conjunctives when they introduced new sentences. These were usually translated simply and consistently as "And . . ." in the more formal 1977 edition and earlier. Often, they added nothing that a simple period could not supply at the end of the previous sentence.

The 1995 edition improved punctuation by removing many unnecessary commas. The revisers also updated and improved its vocabulary. They swept away the archaic second-person singular pronoun when referring to God ("Thee", "Thou", "Thy", "Thine"), and they frequently replaced "shall" with "will".

	NASB (1977)	NASB (1995)
Gn 1.3–7	Then God said, "Let there be light" . . . **And** God saw that the light was good . . . **And** God called the light day . . . Then God said, "Let there be an expanse . . ." **And** God made the ¹expanse . . .	Then God said, "Let there be light" . . . God saw that the light was good . . . God called the light day . . . Then God said, "Let there be an expanse . . ." God made the ¹expanse . . .
	fn: **1:7** ¹ Or *firmament*	fn: **1:7** ¹ Or *firmament*

	NASB (1977)	NASB (1995)
Ps 2.9	" 'Thou shalt [1] break them with a rod of iron, Thou shalt shatter them like earthenware.' "	" 'You shall [1] break them with a rod of iron, You shall shatter them like earthenware.' "
	fn: 2:9 [1] Another reading is *rule*	fn: 2:9 [1] Another reading is *rule*
Pr 8.6a	"Listen, for I **shall** speak noble things"	"Listen, for I **will** speak noble things"

British or antique English was replaced by international English equivalents. The changes are most noticeable in the book of Proverbs. For example, the word "surety" is replaced with "guarantor" (**Pr 11.15**); "vain" with "worthless" (**12.11**); "vexation" with "anger" (**2.16**); "want" with "need" (**13.25**); "increase" with "revenue" (**14.14**); "bosom" with "heart" (**14.33**); "begets" with "sires" (**17.21**); "environs" with "vicinity" (**Mt 2.16**); "great multitude" with "large crowd" (**14.14**); "reckoned" with "credited" (**Ro 4.3ff**); "Glad tidings" with "good news" (**10.15**).

Some happier changes include: "pacifies contention" with "calms a dispute" (**Pr 14.18**); "the peck-measure" with "a basket" (**Mt 5.15**); "abundant seemliness" with "presentable" (**1Co 12.23**). Occasionally, they replaced concrete words with figurative equivalents—"lips" to "speech" (**Pr 4.24**); "weaker vessel" with "someone weaker" (**1Pt 3.7**).

On rare occasion, the revisers made changes based on new scholarly support for textual variants. For example, the 1995 edition includes some words that were not in the 1977 edition or in earlier translations since the RSV. The rendering reverts to the wording of older versions (ASV, KJV) after the revisers assessed later textual evidence:

NASB

	NASB (1977)	NASB (1995)
Col 3.6	For it is **on account** of these things that the wrath of God will come[1]	For it is **because** of these things that the wrath of God will come [1]**upon the** [2]**sons of disobedience**
	fn: **3:6** [1] Some early mss. add, *upon the sons of disobedience*	fn: **3:6** [1] Two early mss do not contain *upon the sons of disobedience* [2] I.e., people opposed to God

The NASB 2020 Edition

The latest edition of the NASB was begun in 2014 with the expectation that only a light revision was necessary to bring a fresh edition up to date for the following year. By 2016, The Lockman Foundation realized that they needed more time to give the text a thorough revision in order to make the NASB acceptable to younger, modern readers.

The goals of each NASB revision sets the text in tension with the NASB's original aims, that these "publications shall be true to the original Hebrew, Aramaic, and Greek" and they "shall be understandable."[14] Like all translations, this NASB 2020 revision has had to find a balance (*i.e.*, compromise) between faithfulness to text forms and faithfulness to the perceived intent and function of the biblical languages.

The NASB 2020 edition was published October 2020. It is not intended to replace the 1995 edition, since both will remain in print. Rather, the 1995 edition will continue to serve the needs of our current generation of preachers, while the 2020 will be of use to fresh Bible students.

Updated word choices: The 2020 edition more consistently capitalizes divine titles, pronouns, and referents and introduces updated and improved vocabulary:

	NASB (1995)	NASB (2020)
Dt 31.6	"Be strong and courageous, do not be afraid or **tremble** at them, for the LORD your God is the **one** who goes with you. He will not **fail** you or **forsake** you."	"Be strong and courageous, do not be afraid or **in dread** of them, for the LORD your God is the **One** who is going with you. He will not **desert** you or **abandon** you."
Ps 34:8-9	**O** taste and see that the LORD is good; How blessed is the man who takes refuge in Him! **O** fear the LORD, you His saints; For to those who fear Him there is no **want**.	Taste and see that the LORD is good; How blessed is the man who takes refuge in Him! Fear the LORD, you His saints; For to those who fear Him there is no **lack** *of anything*.
Is 53.4-5	**Surely** our [1]**griefs** He Himself bore, And our **sorrows** He carried; Yet we ourselves **esteemed Him stricken**, **Smitten of** God, and **afflicted**. But He was [2]pierced **through** for our **transgressions**, He was crushed for our **iniquities**; The **chastening** for our well-being *fell* upon Him, And by His **scourging** we are healed.	**However,** *it was* our **sicknesses** *that* He Himself bore, And our **pains** *that* He carried; Yet we ourselves **assumed that He had been afflicted**, **Struck down** by God, and **humiliated**. But He was [1]pierced for our **offenses**, He was crushed for our **wrongdoings**; The **punishment** for our [3] well-being *was laid* upon Him, And by His **wounds** we are healed.
	fn: **53:4** [1] Or *sickness* **53:5** [2] Or *wounded*	fn: **53:5** [1] Or *wounded* [3] Or *peace*

The word "engaged" was changed to "betrothed" (**Lk 1.27**) which fits the biblical culture better; "salutation" to "greeting"; "barren" to "infertile"; "one accord you may with . . ." to "one purpose *and* . . ." (**Ro 15.6**).

	NASB (1995)	NASB (2020)
Ro 15.6	[May God grant you to be of the same mind] so that with **one accord you may with one voice** glorify the God and Father of our Lord Jesus Christ.	[May God grant you to be of the same mind] so that with **one purpose** *and* **one** [1] **voice you may** glorify the God and Father of our Lord Jesus Christ.
		fn: **15:6** [1] Lit *mouth*
Jb 31.33	"Have I covered my **transgressions** like **Adam,** By hiding my **iniquity** in my bosom . . . ?"	"Have I covered my **wrongdoings** like a **man,** By hiding my **guilt** in my **shirt pocket** . . . ?"

"It is common today for readers to understand 'let us' to mean 'allow us.' So in effect, 'let us' has become unintentionally misleading to most readers. Therefore, the simple contraction 'let's' has emerged as the clearest expression because this form reflects the [original nuance]—that is, a proposal to do something.

Gn 11.4a	They said, "Come, **let us** build **for** ourselves a city, and a tower whose top *will reach* into heaven"	And they said, "Come, **let's** build ourselves a city, and a tower whose top *will reach* into heaven"

"However, in some situations 'Let Us' is retained for intimate discourse within the Godhead, as in **Gn 1.26,**

> Then God said, "Let Us make man in Our image, according to Our likeness"   (NASB 1995 and 2020)

"'Let us' is also kept when there is a request for permission (*e.g.,* **Dt 1.22**), and in some other select cases."[15]

Gender inclusive language: According to the revised preface, in "this edition Greek and Hebrew words that are not actually exclusive in gender as they are used in a given context are rendered by inclusive terms, such as 'people.' Just as important, when the words in the original languages are in fact referring only to males or females, the distinction is maintained in English."[16] The revisers were careful to use *italics* to indicate supplied words where there is no exact word-for-word, Greek-to-English correspondence.

	NASB (1995)	NASB (2020)
1Th 5.12	But we request of you, **brethren**, that you appreciate those who diligently labor among you, and have charge over you in the Lord and give you instruction	But we ask you, **brothers** *and sisters*, to recognize those who diligently labor among you and [1]are in leadership over you in the Lord, and give you [2]instruction
		fn: 5:12 [1] Or *care for you* [2] Or *admonition*
Jas 5.16b	The effective prayer of a righteous **man** can accomplish much.	A [3]prayer of a righteous **person**, when it is [4]brought about, can accomplish much.
		fn: 5:12 [3] Or *supplication* [4] I.e., granted by God

There are places where the revision has fully emerged from it old formalistic skin, but there are some spots where it had yet to finish molting. Note the use of "loins" and "behold!" in the following.

Heb 7.9–10	And, so to speak, through Abraham even Levi, who received tithes, paid tithes, for he was still in the loins of his father when Melchizedek met him.	And, so to speak, through Abraham even Levi, who received tithes, **has** paid tithes, for he was still in the loins of his [5]**fore**father when Melchizedek met him
		fn: 7:10 [5] Lit *father*

"Now behold, I Myself do establish My covenant with you, and with your descendants after you" (**Gn 9.9** NASB 1995, '20)

The *Legacy Standard Bible*

Evangelical Bible expositor, John F. MacArthur (of Grace Community Church, Los Angeles, CA), announced that he had sought

NASB

a conservative, formal translation with the help of The Master's Seminary and Master's University faculty in April 2020.[17] This translation, named the *Legacy Standard Bible* (LSB), is based on the NASB 1995 edition. It is expected to be a formal refinement of what is already considered to be a formal translation. MacArthur claims that the LSB will meet the expositors' need for a precise, concordant translation. It should give students a clearer view to the original, underlying Hebrew and Greek forms.

For example, the LSB reverts to the NASB 1977 edition in its treatment of *kai* conjunctives and its more careful distinction of Greek verb tenses.

	NASB (1995)	LSB
Mk 3.11a	Whenever the unclean spirits **saw** Him, they would fall down before Him	**And** whenever the unclean spirits **were seeing** Him, they would fall down before Him
Mk 9.11	They **asked** Him, saying, "*Why is it* that the scribes say that Elijah must come first?"	**And** they **began asking** Him, saying, "*Why is it* that the scribes say that Elijah must come first?"
Mk 9.15	Immediately, when the entire crowd saw Him, they were amazed and **began running up to greet** Him.	**And** immediately, when the entire crowd saw Him, they were amazed. And **as they ran up, they were greeting** Him.
Mk 11.32b	everyone **considered** John to have been a real prophet.	everyone **was regarding** John to have been a real prophet.

Here the LSB is more concordant where rendering the Greek word *thaumazō* or the phrase *ta peri* [*hymōn/eme*].

Mk 5.20b	and everyone was **amazed**	and everyone was **marveling**
Mk 6.6a	And He **wondered** at their unbelief.	And He **was marveling** at their unbelief.
Php 1.27b	whether I come and see you or remain absent, I will hear **of you**	whether I come and see you or remain absent, I will hear **about your circumstances**

	NASB (1995)	LSB
Php 2.19–20	But I hope in the Lord Jesus to send Timothy to you shortly, so that I also may be encouraged when I learn **of your condition**. For I have no one *else* of kindred spirit who will genuinely be concerned **for your welfare**.	But I hope in the Lord Jesus to send Timothy to you shortly, so that I also may be in good spirits when I learn **of your circumstances**. For I have no one *else* of kindred spirit who will genuinely be concerned **about your circumstances**.
Php 2.23	Therefore I hope to send him immediately, as soon as I **see how things go with me**	Therefore I hope to send him immediately, as soon as I **evaluate my own circumstances**

And a few more renderings that mark the LSB's character in the NASB's tradition of revisions.

Ps 110.1	**The LORD** says to my Lord: "Sit at My right hand Until I make Your enemies a footstool for Your feet."	*Yahweh* says to my Lord: "Sit at My right hand Until I make Your enemies a footstool for Your feet."
Mk 12.42	A poor widow came and put in two **small copper coins**, which amount to a cent.	And a poor widow came and put in two [1] **lepta**, which amount to a [2] **quadrans** fn: [1] Gr copper coin, approx $\frac{1}{128}$ of a laborer's daily wage [2] A Roman copper coin, approx. $\frac{1}{64}$ of a laborer's daily wage
Php 2.7	but emptied Himself, taking the form of a **bond-servant**, and being made in the likeness of men.	but emptied Himself, **by** taking the form of a **slave**, by being made in the likeness of men.
2Ti 3.16a	All Scripture is **inspired by God**	All Scripture is **God-breathed**

The LSB's New Testament, Psalms and Proverbs was published by 316 Publishing in March 2021. The rest of the Protestant Canon is to follow by the end of the year. The Lockman Foundation holds the LSB's copyright and helps in its promotion.

RECEPTION

In the late 1960s or early '70s, Lockman founded Foundation Press (later Foundation Publications) in order to print ministry materials, like bulletins and flyers, for churches. He also printed tracts and editions of the Gospel of John for Christian evangelism. Lockman did not have the capacity to print Bibles in large quantities. So he contracted the printing of the NASB and used his existing contacts with Christian ministries to market and distribute the new Bible.[18] As word spread and the NASB gained traction, other publishers gained interest in the NASB. Lockman eventually licensed the Bible to Creation House, World Bible Publishers, AMG, Moody, and Holman (later LifeWay) publishers in the format that Foundation Press had typeset it.[19]

Currently, the NASB ranks eighth in sales behind the NIV, KJV, NLT, ESV, NKJV, CSB, and NIrv.[20]

ENDORSEMENTS

The NASB has been endorsed by such noted conservative evangelical leaders as Dr. Charles F. Stanley (Pastor, First Baptist Church, Atlanta; President, In Touch Ministries), Joseph M. Stowell III (former President, Moody Bible Institute [1987–2005]), Dr. L. Paige Patterson (former President, Southwestern Baptist Theological Seminary), Dr. John F. MacArthur (Grace Community Church), Dr. R. Albert Mohler, Jr. (current President, Southwestern Baptist Theological Seminary), and Dr. R. C. Sproul.

The Christian Reformed Church in North America has approved the NASB for Bible study only (in contrast to public worship) since 1982.[21]

COPYRIGHT

You may quote up to 1,000 verses from the NASB in any form without prior written permission; the verses may not constitute a complete book of the Bible; they must comprise less than 50% of your work's content; and your work must include the following copyright acknowledgment.

Unless used exclusively, follow citations with the designation (NASB). For example:

Jn 1.4, "In Him was life, and the life was the Light of men." (NASB)

The titles *"New American Standard®," "New American Standard Bible®,"* and *"Legacy Standard Bible®"* and their initialisms (NAS®, NASB®, LSB®,) are registered trademarks with the U.S. Patent and Trademark Office by The Lockman Foundation, but the logo-marks are not.

For permissions not covered here, email your request through https://www.lockman.org/permission-to-quote-request -form/.

ENDNOTES

1   The Lockman Foundation, "About The Lockman Foundation" (2015), accessed June 3, 2019, http://www.lockman.org/tlf/tlfhistory.php, (site discontinued).

2   "Preface to the New American Standard Bible," *New American Standard Bible, New Testament* (La Habra, CA: The Lockman Foundation, 1995).

3   *Ibid.*

4   "Preface to the New American Standard Bible," *New American Standard Bible* (La Habra, CA: The Lockman Foundation, 1995).

5   "Fourfold Aim of the Lockman Foundation," *New American Standard Bible* (2020).

6   The Lockman Foundation, "The Lockman Foundation History," accessed January 28, 2021, https://www.lockman.org/history/.

7   Denominations represented by the translators include Presbyterian, Methodist, Southern Baptist, Church of Christ, Nazarene, American Baptist, Fundamentalist, Conservative Baptist, Free Methodist, Congregational, Disciples of Christ, Evangelical Free, Independent Baptist, Independent Mennonite, Assembly of God, and North American Baptist.

8   The Lockman Foundation, "New American Standard Bible" (2015) accessed June 3, 2019, http://www.lockman.org/nasb/nasbprin.php.
    "Translators of the New American Standard Bible®," *Wholesome Words*, ed. Stephen Ross, accessed June 3, 2019, https://www.wholesomewords.org/nasbtran.html.

9   "Fourfold Aim. . . . ,"*New American Standard Bible* (1995).

10 "Preface," *New American Standard Bible* (La Habra, CA: The Lockman Foundation, 1973), p. v.

11 *Ibid.*

12 "Preface," *New American Standard Bible* (1995).

13 "Foreword," *New American Standard Bible* (1995).

14 "Fourfold Aim . . . ," *New American Standard Bible* (2020).

15 "Preface . . . ," *Ibid.*

16 *Ibid.*

17 John F. MacArthur, "A Mid-Week Message from Our Pastor," published on *Facebook.com*, accessed January 21, 2021, https://www.facebook.com/watch/?v

=152984592694778 (https://player.vimeo.com/video/402824903), starting at 7:45.

— and Abner Chou, "Legacy Standard Bible," The Master's University website, https://www.masters.edu/news/legacy-article-bible.html.

18 Pike Lambeth [president of The Lockman Foundation], in discussion with the author, January 21, 2021.

19 This is why each of the early publishers printed editions of the NASB with pages identical to those published by the others.

20 E.C.P.A., "Bible Translation . . . Best of 2020," *Christian Book Expo*, accessed January 26, 2021, https://christianbookexpo.com/bestseller/translations.php?id=BO20;

I've excluded the Spanish *Reina Valera* version from this ranking.

21 Christian Reformed Church in North America, "Bible Translations," accessed June 2, 2020, https://www.crcna.org/welcome/beliefs/bible-translations.

New King James Version®

Holy Bible, The New King James Version, Containing the Old and New Testaments

Produced by Thomas Nelson, Inc., 1979–1982

FORMAL / FUNCTIONAL TENDENCIES

FORMAL   FUNCTIONAL

Interlinear   NASB   KJV   **NKJV**   ESV   RSV   CSB   NRSV   NET   NIV   NLT   Free Paraphrase

TEXT BASES

English Base   King James Version (1611).

OT Masoretic Hebrew and Ancient Versions.   **NT** *Textus Receptus.*

TRANSLATION TIMELINE

1611	1629, 1638	1769	1885	1901	1971	1982	1991	2014
KJV	*KJV revised*	*KJV revised*	*English Revised Version*	*ASV*	*King James II Version*	**NKJV**	*21st C. KJV*	*MEV*

CONTEMPORARY EVENTS

1969	1971	1973	1979	1981	1982
Sam Moore buys Thomas Nelson, Inc.	Time Magazine depicts Jesus on its cover.	*Roe v. Wade*	Jerry Falwell founds Moral Majority PAC.	Ronald Reagan wins American presidencey.	

PUBLICATION TIMELINE

1975	1979	1980	1982	1984
Guidelines for revision produced. Th. Nelson commissions 130 scholars and pastors to make the *NKJV*.	*NKJV* New Testament	*NKJV* Psalms and Proverbs	*NKJV* Bible	*NKJV* lightly revised

Holy Bible

The New King James Version

CONTAINING
THE OLD AND NEW TESTAMENTS

THOMAS NELSON PUBLISHERS

I n the 1980s, the King James Bible was still the preferred version among American readers.[1] As of the year 2000, the KJV still held nearly twenty percent of the market share among available English versions. Today, it is ranked the second-best selling Bible amongst evangelicals, following the NIV.[2] The translation has remained popular, even in today's electronic environment, despite its archaic language and occasionally obscure meaning.

But in 1969, a Lebanese immigrant and former door-to-door Bible salesman named Sam Moore purchased Thomas Nelson Publishers in the United States.[3] As a successful businessman, he pushed the American publishing company to profitability after its failure to keep up with demand for the *Revised Standard Version* in the 1960s.

The story goes that, in the early '70s, Moore's ten-year old son asked him, "Dad, you make a lot of Bibles. Can't you make one I can understand?"[4] Moore considered the potential of an updated version of the traditional King James Bible. So he decided that his company should fund a revision. Seven years later and at the cost of 4.5 million dollars, the complete *New King James Version* (NKJV®) was released in the United States. (In the United Kingdom, it was published as the *Revised Authorised Version* by Samuel Bagster and Sons.)

STATED TRANSLATION IDEALS

"Since the Bible is the divinely inspired Word of God, it is of great importance that translations of the Bible are faithful. There is no room for subjectivity in handling divine truth. Complete equivalence must be the primary goal of the Bible translator."[5] "The principle of complete equivalence seeks to preserve all of the information in the text, while presenting it in good literary form."[6] "For a standard Bible, then, we believe that a basically literal translation method, assisted by the findings of modern linguistics, will yield the optimum version."[7]

Yet, a "special feature of the *New King James Bible* is its conformity to the thought-flow of the 1611 version. The reader discovers that the sequence and identity of words, phrases, and clauses of the new edition, while much clearer, are so close to the traditional that there is remarkable ease in listening to the public reading of either edition while following with the other."[8]

METHOD

In 1975, Thomas Nelson Publishers invited a group of 68 people to draw up a set of guidelines to direct the revision.[9] Books of the Bible were portioned out to scholars based on each one's area of competence.

The revisers strictly adhered to the traditional texts—the *Textus Receptus* for the NT and the second edition of Jacob ben Chayyim's Masoretic Text for the OT. After analyzing the Hebrew and Greek, the scholars proposed revisions, which were submitted to Executive Editors for the Old and New Testaments who correlated and unified the proposed changes. The Editors submitted their results to the British Oversight Committee and the North American Overview Committee (consisting of clerical and lay advisors). Then, a Scholar Committee checked the accuracy of the editors' work. Final decisions were approved by an Executive Review Committee consisting of prominent evangelical scholars.[10] The NT Executive Review Committee completed their work within a year. The OT Executive Review Committee required more time due to the lengthier and more complex Hebrew text.

The NT was published in 1979. An edition of the NT with the Psalms and Proverbs was published the following year. Both Testaments were published together in 1982. Editions currently in print and available in digital format reflect minor revisions made since 1984.

NKJV

TEXT BASES

English Text

The NKJV is a revision of the King James Bible (1611, 1769).[11]

New Testament

Textus Receptus. The Greek text of the NKJV is the same as that underlying the KJV—the 4th (1588/9) or 5th (1598) major folio edition of Theodore Beza's Greek New Testament, the 3rd (1550) or 4th (1551) edition of Robert Stephanus, and F. H. A. Scrivener's Greek edition (1881), which conforms to the editorial decisions of the KJV.

Versions: The NKJV records the significant variations between the *Textus Receptus* and other modern Greek editions in its footnotes: Nestle-Aland *Novum Testamentum Graece* 26th revised edition (Stuttgart: Deutsche Bibelgesellschaft, 1983), *Greek New Testament* 3rd corrected edition (United Bible Societies, 1983); Hodges-Farstad *Greek New Testament according to the Majority Text* (1982).

One scholar on the New Testament Executive Review Committee admitted that "the [*Textus Receptus*] is a somewhat corrupt form of the traditional type of text."[12] This means that the scholars who developed the NKJV recognized that the traditional printed text underlying the KJV did not always represent the majority of hand-copied manuscripts from which it was based.

Old Testament

Masoretic Hebrew-Aramaic text. The Hebrew text of the NKJV is practically the same as that underlying the KJV. In the eight places that the *Biblia Hebraica Stuttgartensia* (1967–77) differs from Jacob ben Chayyim's text (*i.e.*, the Second Rabbinic Bible. Venice: Daniel Bomberg, 1524–25), the NKJV follows the text of Chayyim's second edition.[13]

Ancient versions. Septuagint (Greek LXX), Vulgate (Latin), Peshitta (Syriac), Dead Sea Scrolls (DSS).

CONTRIBUTORS

Thomas Nelson commissioned an international team of almost 130 scholars, editors, and church leaders from a number of denominations to work on the revision.

Of particular note, Arthur L. Farstad (from Dallas Theological Seminary) "gave up his academic appointment to become the New Testament editor."[14] James D. Price (Temple Baptist Theological Seminary, Chattanooga, TN; HCSB) served as the Old Testament editor. Both Executive Review Committees benefited from William H. McDowell (*Logos21*),[15] a Canadian professor at Florida Southern College, Orlando, who served as the English stylist. Textual scholar Harry A. Sturz participated as a member in the New Testament Executive Review Committee.

A number of revisers and Executive Committee members took part in other translations. Among the Old Testament scholars: Allen P. Ross (NLT, ESV, NET), Barry J. Beitzel (NLT), Elmer A. Martens (NASB), Eugene H. Merrill (NLT, HCSB), Gary V. Smith (HCSB), Louis Goldberg (NIV), Meredith George Kline (NIV), Victor Paul Hamilton (NIV), Willem A. VanGemeren (NLT, ESV); New Testament scholars: Edward M. Blaiklock (NIV), Lewis A. Foster (NIV); Old Testament Executive Review Committee: G. Herbert Livingston (NIV), Roland K. Harrison (NIV, NLT), New Testament Executive Review Committee: William Curtis Vaughan (HCSB); the Revision Committee of 1984 added James A. Borland and Zane C. Hodges (HCSB).

For a complete list of translators, visit booklink.id/nkjv-translator

THEOLOGICAL ASSUMPTIONS

"All participants in this project agree to sign the Statement of Faith that 'The Bible (both Old and New Testaments) alone, and the Bible in its entirety (plenary), is the infallible Word of God, and it therefore the in-errant (free from error), inspired* (God-breathed) Scriptures, in the autographs.* ' "[16]

FEATURES

The KJV's familiar "doctrinal and theological terms . . . have been retained except where the original language indicates need for clarification."[17]

Originally, the NKJV was printed so that each verse starts at a new line. If the verse does not start the beginning of a new sentence, it begins with a lowercase letter. Verse numbers in **bold** type indicate the beginning of paragraphs.

Poetry is formatted as contemporary verse to indicate the poetic form of the passage.

Other editions are now available, which break paragraphs by sense with reference numbers placed inline inside the text.

Oblique typeface in the text indicates an OT quotation. Their corresponding references are given in the footnotes.

In the 1979 NT, foreign words were set in *oblique* type, including *Abaddon* (**Rv 9.11**) and *Armageddon* (**Rv 16.16**), but interestingly not "Apollyon". This practice was discontinued in later editions.

Like the original KJV and the NASB, "[w]ords or phrases in *italics* indicate expressions in the original language which require clarification by additional English words"[18]

Pronouns referring to the Father, Son, and Holy Spirit, as well as a number of nouns relating to deity, are all capitalized, for example, "The Angel who spoke to spoke to him on Mount Sinai" (**Acts 7.38**), "Child" (**Mt 2.8–9; Lk 2.17; Rv 12.4–5, 13**), "One," "Coming One," "Boy," "Teacher," "Shepherd," "Son," "Babe," "Word," "Seed," "Beloved," "Potentate," *etc.* But not "cornerstone" or "head."

Family members, disciples, and opponents all address Jesus with capitalized pronouns, even when no reverence is intended. (*Cf.* **Jn 10.33; 4.7, 19, 26; 7.12, 15, 27; Mt 12.6**)

The NKJV is the only translation that succinctly specifies the sources of textual variants in the NT. Other translations may indicate that such variants exist among extant manuscripts but rarely offer anything more. Only the *NET Bible* gives a fuller account.

Notes prefaced with "NU-Text" indicate variations from the *Textus Receptus* (TR). "NU-Text" notes generally represent the so-called Alexandrian text-type predominating in the Greek editions published by the United Bible Societies. The "N" in the "NU-Text" stands for Nestle-Aland's *Novum Testamentum*, 27th edition; the "U" stands for the United Bible Societies' *Greek New Testament*, 3rd edition.

Notes prefaced with "M-Text" indicate variations in the Majority Greek text that differ from the TR.[19]

For example, a footnote for the *Comma Johanneum* reads in the 1979 edition,

> "The words from in 'heaven' (v. 7) through on 'earth' (v. 8) are from the Latin Bible, although three Greek mss. from the 15th Century and later also contain them."

The 1982 edition clarifies,

> "NU-Text and M-Text omit the words from *in heaven* (v. 7) through on earth (v. 8). Only four or five very late Greek mss. contain these words."

Paragraph or subject headings help readers identify subject matter or topics and logical transitions.

ASSESSMENT

The NKJV more accurately translates its text base than does the KJV itself. Its formal rendering and modern vocabulary make it ideal for Bible study, though, at times, its language is wooden and stilted (*cf.,* **2Co 13.2, 3**).

Its footnotes are helpful and scholarly. It is the only version which succinctly summarizes the major textual differences between the *Textus Receptus* (TR) and modern eclectic and majority editions of the Greek NT. As a revision of the KJV, it suffers from all the problems of the late manuscript tradition enshrined in the TR (*e.g.,* the *Comma Johanneum*, **1Jn 5.7–8**, and the end of Revelation). Fortunately, the NKJV's footnotes offset these problems.

With the exception of a very light revision in 1984, the NKJV has not undergone any revision since, and none are anticipated any time in the future, which leaves us with a very "stable" text. Though this ensures consistency among printed and digital editions, it also reveals the publisher's abandonment of the text's future development. (This gives new-comers a competitive edge.)

Though it is not the only translation claiming to update the KJV in direct succession,[20] it is the one with the widest availability in the greatest number of formats. It also has many supporting references and resources, including several study Bibles.

The NKJV is ideal for reading side-by-side with the KJV. It gives readers a better sense of what the KJV's language means. Its stability makes it a good choice for memorization and corporate Bible study, since future editions won't disrupt reading with subsequent revisions. In sum, the work of the NKJV revisers is like one "who brings out of his treasure *things* new and old" (**Mt 13.52**).

RECEPTION

The NKJV was generally well received by conservative evangelicals and Pentecostal assemblies in the United States. Yet, some scholars argue that its "text [base] is inferior, and its translation substandard," because it relied solely on the traditional text and tried to keep its word order consistent with the KJV.[21] Also, a number of those loyal to the KJV have been quick to denounce it and condemn it, even though it is based on the same Hebrew and Greek texts as its English ancestor (unlike the ASV/RSV). In sales, the NKJV generally ranks fifth behind the NIV, NLT, ESV, and the KJV.[22]

REPRESENTATIVE SAMPLES

Familiar Passages

Gn 1.1–2	In the beginning God created the heavens and the earth. The earth was without form, and void; and darkness *was* [a] on the face of the deep. And the Spirit of God was hovering over the face of the waters.
	footnote (fn): [a] Words in italic type have been added for clarity. They are not found in the original Hebrew or Aramaic
Ps 23.1–2	The LORD *is* my shepherd; I shall not want. He makes me to lie down in green pastures; He leads me beside the still waters.
Ps 27.4	One *thing* I have desired of the LORD, That will I seek: That I may dwell in the house of the LORD All the days of my life, To behold the beauty of the LORD, And to inquire in His temple.
Jn 3.16	"For God so loved the world that He gave His only begotten Son, that whoever believes in Him should not perish but have everlasting life."

Divine Name and Titles

Yhwh	Ps 24.1a, cf. Ex 6.3b fn	The earth *is* the **Lord**'s, and all its fullness, The world and those who dwell therein.
adonai	Ps 90.1b	**Lord**, You have been our dwelling place *ᵃ* in all generations. fn: *ᵃ* Septuagint, Targum, and Vulgate read *refuge*.
elohim	Gn 1.27a	So **God** created man in His *own* image
adonai Yhwh	Ps 73.28b	I have put my trust in the **Lord God**
adonai elohim	Dn 9.3a	Then I set my face toward the **Lord God**
Yhwh *saba'oth*	1Sa 17.45b	"I come to you in the name of the **Lord of hosts**"
el shaddai	Ex 6.3a	"I appeared to Abraham, to Isaac, and to Jacob, as **God Almighty**"
kyrios	Lk 20.42b	"'The **Lord** said to my **Lord**, "sit at my right hand"'"
christos	Mt 16.16b	"You are the **Christ**, the Son of the living God."

New Testament Text Base

Mt 17.21	"However, this kind does not go out except by prayer and fasting."*ᵃ* fn: *ᵃ* NU-Text omits this verse.
Mt 18.11	"For the Son of Man has come to save that which was lost."*ᵃ* fn: *ᵃ* NU-Text omits this verse.
Ac 8.37	Then Philip said, "If you believe with all your heart, you may." And he answered and said, "I believe that Jesus Christ is the Son of God."*ᵃ* fn: *ᵃ* NU-Text and M-Text omit this verse. It is found in Western texts, including the Latin tradition.
1Jn 5.7b–8a	. . . in heaven: the Father, the Word, and the Holy Spirit; and these three are one. And there are three that bear witness on earth:*ᵃ* the Spirit . . . fn: *ᵃ* NU-Text and M-Text omit the words from *in heaven* (verse 7) through *on earth* (verse 8). Only four or five very late manuscripts contain these words in Greek.

Gender Language

ʾādām	Gn 9.6	"Whoever sheds **man's** blood, By **man** his blood shall be shed; For in the image of God He made **man**."
ʾîsh . . . nephesh	Lv 24.17	"'**Whoever** kills **any man** shall surely be put to death.'"
ʾāvîw	Pr 15.5a	A fool despises **his father's** instruction
huioi	Mt 5.9	"Blessed *are* the peacemakers, For they shall be called **sons** of God"
anthrōpōn	Mt 4.19	"Follow Me, and I will make you fishers **of men**."
hekastō . . . autou	Ro 2.6	who *"will render to each one according to his deeds"*
adelphoi	Gal 5.13	For you, **brethren**, have been called to liberty; only do not *use* liberty as an opportunity for the flesh, but through love serve one another.
gynaikos anēr	Ti 1.6a	if a man is blameless, **the husband of** one **wife**, having faithful children
gynaikas	1Ti 3.11	**The women** likewise must be serious, no [a] slanderers, but temperate, faithful in all things.
		fn: [a] malicious gossips

Difficult Renderings

1Sa 13.1	Saul reigned **one year**; and when he had reigned **two years** over Israel [a]
	fn: [a] The Hebrew is difficult (compare 2 Samuel 5:4; 2 Kings 14:2; see also 2 Samuel 2:10; Acts 13:21).
Is 28.13	But the word of the LORD was to them, **"Precept upon precept, precept upon precept, Line upon line, line upon line, Here a little, there a little,"** That they might go and fall backward, and be broken And snared and caught.

The Best Bible?

Significant Renderings

'almah	Is 7.14	Therefore the Lord Himself will give you a sign: Behold, **the virgin** shall conceive and bear a Son, and shall call His name Immanuel. *a*
		fn: *a* Literally *God-With-Us*
she'ol, 'abaddon	Pr 15.11	**Hell** *a* and **Destruction** *b* are before the LORD; So how much more the hearts of the sons of men.
		fn: *a* Or *Sheol* *b* Hebrew *Abaddon*
egennēsen	Mt 1.2	Abraham **begot** Isaac, Isaac **begot** Jacob, and Jacob **begot** Judah and his brothers.
eskēnōsen	Jn 1.14	And the Word became flesh and **dwelt** among us, and we beheld His glory, the glory as of the only begotten of the Father, full of grace and truth.
tois ioudaiois	Jn 18.36	Jesus answered, "My kingdom is not of this world. If My kingdom were of this world, My servants would fight, so that I should not be delivered **to the Jews**; but now My kingdom is not from here."
dikaiosunē theou, pisteōs Iēsou Christou	Ro 3.22a	even **the righteousness of God**, through **faith in Jesus Christ**, to all and on all *a* who believe.
		fn: *a* NU-Text omits *and on all.*
Granville Sharp's rule applied	Tt 2.13	looking for the blessed hope and glorious appearing of **our great God and Savior Jesus Christ**

SIGNIFICANT REVISIONS

Changes from the King James Version.

The NKJV has a great number of changes from the King James Bible, most of which update the grammar, spelling, and vocabulary of the traditional version. The following illustrate typical changes.

	KJV (1611, 1769)	NKJV (1982)
Mt 12.40a	For as Jonas was three days and three nights in the **whale's belly**	For as Jonah was three days and three nights in the **belly of the great fish**
Mt 28.1	**In the end of the sabbath**, as it began to dawn toward the first day of the week, came Mary Magdalene and the other Mary to see the **sepulchre**.	**Now after the Sabbath**, as the first *day* of the week began to dawn, Mary Magdalene and the other Mary came to see the **tomb**.
Lk 6.17a	He came down with them, and stood **in the plain**, and the company of his disciples, and a great multitude of people	He came down with them and stood **on a level place** with a crowd of His disciples and a great multitude of people
Ac 2.6a	Now when this **was noised abroad**, the multitude came together	And when this **sound occurred**, the multitude came together
Ac 19.2a	Have ye received the Holy Ghost **since** ye believed?	"Did you receive the Holy Spirit **when** you believed?"

The revision updates personal pronouns:

	KJV (1611, 1769)	NKJV (1982)
Lk 19.2a	*there was* a man named Zacchaeus, **which** was the chief among the publicans	*there was* a man named Zacchaeus **who** was a chief tax collector

It uses language familiar to American readers:

	KJV (1611, 1769)	NKJV (1982)
Mt 12.1; Lk 6.1; Mk 2.23	At that time Jesus went on the sabbath day through the **corn**; and his disciples were an hungred, and began to pluck **the ears of corn**, and to eat.	At that time Jesus went through the **grainfields** on the Sabbath. And His disciples were hungry, and began to pluck **heads of grain** and to eat.

The NKJV fixes the famous printer's error:

	KJV (1611, 1769)	NKJV (1982)
Mt 23.24	Ye blind guides, which strain **at** a gnat, and swallow a camel.	"Blind guides, who strain **out** a gnat and swallow a camel!"

Revisions within the *New King James Version.*

In 1984, the OT and NT Translation Committees published revisions to improve the accuracy, clarity, and consistency of the NKJV.[23] At first, the publisher wished to revise the NKJV through the rejection of its TR base in favor of the modern critical editions of the NT, but the NT Committee successfully argued against it.[24] The revisions were never acknowledged by the copyright, but current print and online editions include all of the 1984 revisions.[25]

One example of improved accuracy includes:

	NKJV (1982)	NKJV (1984)
Zc 13.6a	"And *one* will say to him, 'What are these wounds **in your hands**?'"	"And *one* will say to him, 'What are these wounds **between your arms**?'"[a]
		fn: [a] Or *hands*

The next sample of improved consistency and concordance also shows an improvement in contemporary English usage, since the use of "glory" as a verb is no longer so familiar as it once was:

	NKJV (1982)	NKJV (1984)
2Co 5.12	For we do not commend ourselves again to you, but give you opportunity to **glory** on our behalf, that you may have an answer for those who **glory** in appearance and not in heart.	For we do not commend ourselves again to you, but give you opportunity to **boast** on our behalf, that you may have an answer for those who **boast** in appearance and not in heart.

Borland and Hodges updated or improved the idioms in a few other places, too:

1Sa 17.6a	And he had bronze **greaves** on his legs	And he had bronze **armor** on his legs
Is 51.7b	Do not fear the reproach of men, Nor be afraid of their **revilings**.	Do not fear the reproach of men, Nor be afraid of their **insults**.

	NKJV (1982)	NKJV (1984)
Ac 17.26	And He has ... determined their preappointed times and the boundaries of their **habitation**	And He has ... determined their preappointed times and the boundaries of their **dwellings**
Col 1.13	He has delivered us from the power of darkness and **translated** *us* into the kingdom of the Son of His love	He has delivered us from the power of darkness and **conveyed** [a] *us* into the kingdom of the Son of His love
		fn: [a] *transferred*
Dn 4.37b	And those who walk in pride He is able to **abase**.	And those who walk in pride He is able to **put down**.
2Co 3.3a	*you are* **manifestly** an epistle of Christ	**clearly** *you are* an epistle of Christ
Ro 7.5	For when we were in the flesh, the **passions of sins** which were aroused by the law were at work in our members to bear fruit to death.	For when we were in the flesh, the **sinful passions** which were aroused by the law were at work in our members to bear fruit to death.
Jn 6.41	The Jews then **murmured** about Him, because He said, "I am the bread which came down from heaven."	The Jews then **complained** [a] about Him, because He said, "I am the bread which came down from heaven."
		fn: [a] *grumbled*
Est 8.6	"Or how can I endure to see the destruction of my **kindred**?"	"Or how can I endure to see the destruction of my **countrymen**?"
1Co 6.7	Why do you not rather *let yourselves* be **defrauded**?	Why do you not rather *let yourselves* be **cheated**?

The Committees replaced ambiguous words and expressions with clearer renderings:

	NKJV (1982)	NKJV (1984)
1Sa 17.25b	"the king will ... give his father's house exemption in Israel"	"the king will ... give his father's house exemption *from taxes* in Israel"

	NKJV (1982)	NKJV (1984)
Heb 3.9, cf. Ps 95.9	"WHERE YOUR FATHERS TEST-ED ME, **PROVED** ME, AND SAW MY WORKS FORTY YEARS."	"WHERE YOUR FATHERS TEST-ED ME, **TRIED** ME, AND SAW MY WORKS FORTY YEARS."
Is 40.28b	The Creator of the ends of the earth, Neither faints nor is weary. **There is no searching of His understanding.**	The Creator of the ends of the earth, Neither faints nor is weary. **His understanding is unsearchable.**
1Co 10.23	All things are lawful for me, *a* but **all things are not** helpful; all things are lawful for me, *a* but **all things do not** edify. _____ fn: *a* NU-Text omits *for me*.	All things are lawful for me,*a* but **not all things are** helpful; all things are lawful for me,*a* but **not all things** edify.*b* fn: *a* NU-Text omits *for me*. *b* build up
Eph 5.1	Therefore be **followers** of God as dear children.	Therefore be **imitators** of God as dear children.

On rare occasions, a revision's meaning differs from an earlier rendering:

Ac 19.13b	"We *a* **adjure** you by the Jesus whom Paul preaches." _____ fn: *a* NU-Text reads *I*.	"We *a* **exorcise** *b* you by the Jesus whom Paul preaches." fn: *a* NU-Text reads *I*. *b* ad-jure, solemnly command
Ac 16.15c	So she **constrained** us.	So she **persuaded** us.

A more significant change was to use "bondservant" in the NT epistles, since it diverges from the KJV, and it does not consistent-ly translate the Greek word, *doulos*, which is translated "servant" everywhere else:

Jas 1.1, cf. Ro 1.1; Gal 1.10, etc.	James, a **servant** of God and of the Lord Jesus Christ	James, a **bondservant** of God and of the Lord Jesus Christ
Php 2.7	but made Himself of no reputation, taking the form of a **servant**, *and* coming in the likeness of men.	but made Himself of no reputation, taking the form of a **bondservant**, *and* coming in the likeness of men.

Unique Renderings

The NKJV offers wooden and stilted readings at times:

2Co 13.2–3	I have told you before, and foretell as if I were present the second time, and now being absent I write *a* to those who have sinned before, and to all the rest, that if I come again I will not spare— since you seek a proof of Christ speaking in me, who is not weak toward you, but mighty in you.
fn:	*a* NU-Text omits *I write*.

ENDORSEMENTS

The NKJV was endorsed by noted evangelical leaders and teachers, including John MacArthur (former president of The Master's College and The Master's Seminary), Jack W. Hayford (Founder and President, The King's University), Cornelius Van Til (Westminster Seminary, Philadelphia, Pennsylvania), Bill and Gloria Gaither, Dennis and Barbara Rainey, *et al.*[26]

The New Testament portion of the NKJV is incorporated into the *Orthodox Study Bible* (by St. Athanasius Orthodox Academy, published by Thomas Nelson, 1993 and 2008), which is endorsed by Metropolitan Maximos (formerly Bishop of Pittsburgh of the Greek Orthodox Archdiocese of America), Metropolitan Phillip (Primate of the Antiochian Orthodox Archdiocese of North America), and Metropolitan Theodosius (retired Archbishop of Washington, Orthodox Church in America).[27] They chose the NKJV because its text base is closer to the official text used by the Greek Orthodox Church than most other modern translations.[28]

COPYRIGHT

You may quote up to 500 verses from the NKJV in any form without prior written permission; the verses may not constitute a complete book of the Bible; they must comprise less than 50% of your work's content; and your work must include the following copyright acknowledgment.

Unless used exclusively, follow citations with the designation (NKJV). For example:

Jn 1.4, "In Him was life, and the life was the light of men." (NKJV)

The title *"New King James Version®,"* its initialism (NKJV®), and its stylized wordmark are registered trademarks with the U.S. Patent and Trademark Office by Thomas Nelson, Inc.

For permissions not covered here, write to HarperCollins Christian Publishing, Attention: Permissions Department, P.O. Box 141000, Nashville, TN 37214, http://www.harpercollinschristian.com/permissions/[29]

ENDNOTES FOR THE
NEW KING JAMES VERSION

1. Sakae Kubo and Walter F. Specht, *So Many Versions? Twentieth-century English Versions of the Bible* (Grand Rapids, MI: The Zondervan Corp, 1983), p. 273.

2. Evangelical Christian Publishers Association (ECPA), "Bible Translation Bestsellers, Best of 2019," *Christian Book Expo*, accessed June 2, 2020, http://christianbookexpo.com/bestseller/translations.php?id=B019.

3. Sam Moore is his Americanized his name. It is originally Sam Ziadi.

4. Jack Lewis, *English Bible from KJV to NIV* (Grand Rapids, MI: Baker Book House Co., 1982), p. 330.

5. James D. Price, "The Importance of Complete Equivalence," *Complete Equivalence in Bible Translation* (Nashville, TN: Thomas Nelson Publishers, 1987), p. 40.

6. "Preface," *The Holy Bible, New King James Version* (Nashville, TN: Thomas Nelson Inc., 1982).

7. Arthur Farstad, *The New King James Version: In the Great Tradition.* 2nd ed. (Nashville, TN: Thomas Nelson, Inc., 1993), p. 127.

8. "Introduction," *The New King James Bible: New Testament* (Nashville, TN: Thomas Nelson Inc., 1979), pp. iii–iv.

9. These individuals met twice: One meeting was held in Nashville, the other in Chicago.

   Michael Marlowe. "New King James Version," *Bible Research,* last modified October 2009, accessed June 10, 2019, http://www.bible-researcher.com/nkjv.html.

   Donald L. Brake and Shelly Beach, *A Visual History of the King James Bible* (Grand Rapids, MI: Baker Books, 2011), p. 222.

10. Kubo and Specht. *So Many Versions?* p. 275.

    Thomas Nelson Bibles, "NKJV: Frequently Asked Questions," accessed June 2, 2020, https://www.thomasnelsonbibles.com/nkjv/faq/.

11. The NKJV markets itself as the fifth major revision (1979–82) of the original KJV (1611; Cambridge ed. of 1629; Th. Buck and Rog. Daniel's ed. of 1638; Dr. Th. Paris' Cambrige rev. of 1762; Dr. Ben. Blaney's Oxford rev. of 1769).

    Thomas Nelson Bibles, "About the NKJV: History of the NKJV Translation," accessed October 29, 2020, https://www.thomasnelsonbibles.com/nkjv/about/.

[12] Referring to Dr. Alfred Martin, formerly Moody Bible Institute. When interviewed, Dr. James A. Borland confirmed the Committee's belief that the text of the *Textus Receptus* is inferior when compared to later printed editions of the Greek NT.

William E. Paul, "Farstad, Arthur," *English Language Bible Translators* (Jefferson, NC: McFarland & Company, Inc. Publishers, 2009), p. 79.

[13] The NKJV follows Bomberg's second edition in the eight places where it differs from BHS: **Pr 8.16; Is 10.16; 27.2; 38.14; Jer 34.1; Ezk 30.18; Zp 3.15; Ml 1.12.**

James D. Price, "The False Witness of G. A. Riplinger's Death Certificate for the New King James Version" (October 6, 1997), pp. 18–19.

[14] Kubo and Specht. *So Many Versions?* p. 275.

[15] *Logos21* = Arthur L. Farstad, *Living Water: The Gospel of John—Logos 21 Version* (1996), 71.

[16] Farstad, *The New King James Version: In the Great Tradition,* p. 55–56.

[17] "Introduction," *The New King James Bible: New Testament.* (Nashville, TN: Thomas Nelson Publishers, 1979).

[18] "Preface," *Holy Bible: The New King James Version, containing the Old and New Testaments* (Nashville, TN: Thomas Nelson Publishers, 1982).

[19] "M-Text" is the Majority Greek text as recorded in Zane C. Hodges and Arthur L. Farstad's *The Greek New Testament According to the Majority Text* (Nashville, TN: Thomas Nelson, 1982, '85).

[20] For example: MEV (2014), 21st C. KJV (1994), KJV II (1971), KJV2000 (2011), *Third Millennium Bible* (1998).

[21] D. A. Carson, A review of the *Revised Authorised Version* (1983), p 7.

Lewis, *English Bible from KJV to NIV,* p. 330.

[22] E.C.P.A., "Bible Translation . . . Best of 2020," *Christian Book Expo,* accessed January 26, 2021, https://christianbookexpo.com/bestseller/translations.php?id=BO20;

C.B.A. (formerly Christian Booksellers Association), "July 2018 Best-sellers," accessed September 26, 2018, http://cbaonline.org/wp-content/uploads/2018/08/0718-Best-Sellers.xlsx.

[23] Michael Marlowe, "New King James Version," *Bible Research,* last modified October 2009, accessed June 2, 2020, http://www.bible-researcher.com/nkjv.html.

[24] James A. Borland [emeritus professor of NT at Liberty University, Lynchberg, VA], in discussion with the author, May 31, 2020.

25 [Verbose Philosopher], "NKJV 1982 vs 1984/85," *The Verbose Philosopher* (January 4, 2012), accessed June 10, 2019, http://verbosephilosopher.blogspot.com/2012/01/nkjv-1982-vs-198485.html.

26 Thomas Nelson Bibles, "NKJV: Endorsements," accessed June 2, 2020, https://www.thomasnelsonbibles.com/nkjv/endorsements/.

27 "What North American Hierarchs have said . . . ," *Orthodox Study Bible: Old Testament Project,* accessed June 4, 2008, http://www.lxx.org/heirarch_quotes.htm.

28 The official New Testament text of the Greek Orthodox Church is the "Patriarchal" edition (1904) of the Ecumenical Patriarchate of Constantinople.

29 HarperCollins acquired Thomas Nelson Publishers in 2012, and thus obtained the NKJV's copyright.

New International Version®

The Holy Bible, New International Version,
Containing The Old Testament and The New Testament

Produced by the New York Bible Society International (now Biblica), 1973–2011

FORMAL / FUNCTIONAL TENDENCIES

FORMAL   FUNCTIONAL

Interlinear   NASB KJV NKJV ESV CSB NET **N I V** NLT TNIV NIrV MSG   Free Paraphrase

TEXT BASES

OT Masoretic Hebrew and Ancient Versions.   **NT** Eclectic Greek.

TRANSLATION TIMELINE

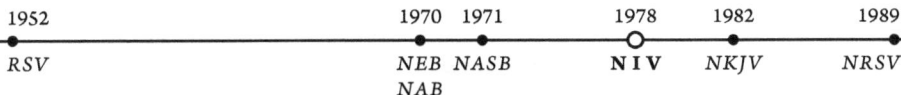

1952	1970	1971	1978	1982	1989
RSV	NEB	NASB	NIV	NKJV	NRSV
		NAB			

CONTEMPORARY EVENTS

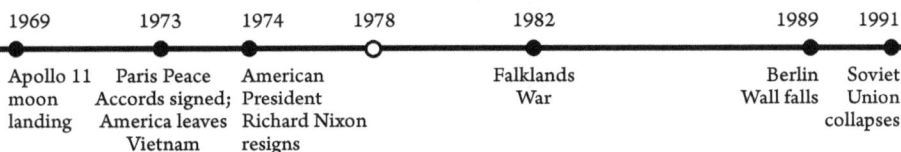

1969	1973	1974	1978	1982	1989	1991
Apollo 11 moon landing	Paris Peace Accords signed; America leaves Vietnam	American President Richard Nixon resigns		Falklands War	Berlin Wall falls	Soviet Union collapses

PUBLICATION TIMELINE

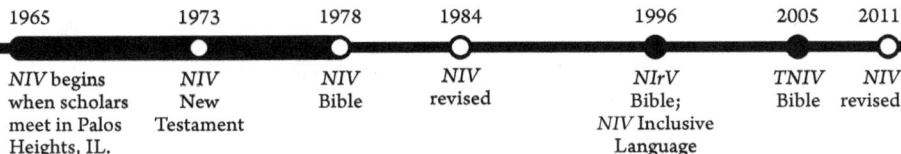

1965	1973	1978	1984	1996	2005	2011
NIV begins when scholars meet in Palos Heights, IL.	NIV New Testament	NIV Bible	NIV revised	NIrV Bible; NIV Inclusive Language	TNIV Bible	NIV revised

The

HOLY
BIBLE

NEW INTERNATIONAL VERSION

*Containing The Old Testament
and The New Testament*

ZONDERVAN BIBLE PUBLISHERS

GRAND RAPIDS, MICHIGAN

In 1955, Howard Long, an engineer with General Electric Company from Seattle, shared a dinner with a business associate while a guest at the Multnomah Hotel in Portland, OR.[1] During the course of their meal, Long had an opportunity to share about Jesus Christ. Intrigued, his friend took up Long's invitation to join him in the room where he was staying. There, Long opened an available Bible to passages that further demonstrated the Gospel. As he read a few verses, his friend's face turned red. Then his friend began to chuckle. Then he roared out laughing, claiming that it was the funniest thing he had heard of in years.

Long's spiritual discussion was interrupted by the absurd sounds of the antiquated Jacobean expressions in the King James Version. This experience drove Long and his pastor, Peter de Jong, to rally their church in pursuit of a new translation with the cooperation of their synod, the Christian Reformed Church.[2]

After expressing dissatisfaction with the results of the *Revised Standard Version* (RSV), separate committees from the Christian Reformed Church and the National Association of Evangelicals explored the possibility of making a new, modern translation.[3] They eventually combined their efforts, and in August 1965, they gathered a meeting of scholars from various denominations and theological backgrounds at Trinity Christian College in Palos Heights, IL. "The consensus was that, in spite of the fine features of many translations, there was a need for an up-to-date translation that was faithful to the original language."[4]

The meeting at Palos Heights agreed that a brand new, contemporary English translation should be undertaken as a cooperative effort by evangelical scholars and that a continuing committee of fifteen members (named the Committee on Bible Translation) should be established to move the work ahead.

STATED TRANSLATION IDEALS

"The *New International Version* tries to bring its readers as close as possible to the experience of the original audience: providing the best possible blend of transparency to the original documents and comprehension of the original meaning in every verse. The NIV® is founded on the belief that if hearing God's Word the way it was written and understanding it the way it was meant were the hallmarks of the original reading experience, then accuracy in translation demands that neither one of these two criteria be prioritized above the other."[5]

The Committee on Bible Translation (CBT) aimed for (1) a translation that would be exegetically accurate yet faithful to the thought of the biblical writers; (2) a translation that would be of such a clear and literary quality to be suitable for both public and private reading, teaching, preaching, memorizing and liturgical use; (3) some attempt at preserving continuity with the long tradition of translation of the scriptures into English; (4) and a translation that should be rendered idiomatically, but not idiosyncratically; with contemporary language, but not dated.

In sum, the "goals of the translation were fourfold: (1) Accuracy, (2) clarity, (3) contemporary idiom, and (4) dignity (that is, no slang, jargon, colloquialism, or over casualness).[6]

METHOD

According to the CBT's constitution, "The Committee, called into being by the Palos Heights Bible Translation Conference . . . , shall be a self-perpetuating body, independent of all ecclesiastical organizations, educational institutions, committees, and other associations."[7] It states: "The purpose of the Committee shall be to prepare a contemporary English translation of the Bible as a collegiate endeavor of evangelical scholars, and to pursue matters related thereto."[8]

Ultimate responsibility was placed in the hands of the CBT, a self-governing body of fifteen people. "This body made final decisions; it did not do all the work. Each translation went through several committees, the hands of literary experts complementing those of linguistic and biblical experts."[9]

The Best Bible?

Books of the Bible were distributed among twenty teams of five scholars each. For example, one scholar would draft a translation of a book and invite two others to work it over with him. Their result was submitted to the Intermediate Editorial Committee which sent comments back. The original translation team considered the comments: Some they accepted and others they rejected with explanations of their disagreement. The team turned their comments in to the CBT, which made the final decision with guidance from the English stylist.[10] "Their work then went to one of the General Editorial Committees, which checked it in detail and made another thorough revision.

"This revision in turn was carefully reviewed by the CBT," who "submitted the developing version to a number of stylistic consultants. Two of them read every book of both Old and New Testaments twice—once before and once after the last major revision—and made valuable suggestions. Samples of the translation were tested for clarity and ease of reading by various kinds of people—young and old, highly educated and less well educated, ministers and laymen." British anglicized editions were conformed to the spellings in the *Oxford English Dictionary*; American editions to *Webster's*.

"In this way the entire Bible underwent three revisions, during each of which the translation was examined for its faithfulness to the original languages and for its English style. All this involved many thousands of hours of research and discussion regarding the meaning of the texts and the precise way of putting them into English." "To the very end of the task, the senior committee encouraged open lines of communication, inviting criticism from those who thought they might have something to contribute."[11]

The New Testament portion was published in 1973. It was revised for publication with the entire Bible in 1978. (An anglicised edtion was published in the U.K. in 1979.)

Howard Long initially suggested that the cost of the NIV might total somewhere between 2 to 3 million dollars. According to the *New York Times*, his estimate was right: The translation's sponsors spent 2.25 million dollars and ten years to complete,[12] though actual editorial costs for the first edition reached roughly eight million dollars, including the translators' hourly rates, room and board, transportation, and other expenses, like secretarial labor, duplicating equipment, *etc.*[13] These costs were initially covered by the New York Bible Society until Zondervan Publishing House stepped in and advanced the costs in return for the sole right to publish the NIV.

The NIV was to never intended to stagnate, as Article VII of the CBT's constitution directed,

> "The Committee shall for a reasonable time provide for a periodic review and revision of the projected translation with a view to improving its renderings, embodying the fruits of future biblical scholarship, and keeping its idiom current.
> "This article shall be applicable also to any revision(s) of the projected version (NIV) under whatever name such revision(s) may be published."[14]

Through 1983–6, the NIV underwent a few light revisions (under a thousand changes),[15] which were embodied in an edition dated 1984. This became a standard evangelical edition that a generation of pastors and Bible students relied on thanks to the many biblical resources that its publisher, Zondervan, produced in its support.

In 1992, the CBT "made a decision . . . that the NIV should be made available in an inclusive-language edition."[16] The NT portion was first published in the U.K. in 1995 and the entire Bible followed in 1996. Sharp criticism from conservative news media and heated debate amongst evangelicals prevented the edition's reception in America.[17] Yet, revisions were still tested and marketed under different names: The *New International Reader's Version* (NIrV 1995, '96, '98) was published with young readers in mind; *Today's New International Version* (TNIV 2001, '05) was released a few years after the gender-language debates cooled following the publication of the *Colorado Springs Guidelines* (see "Gender Language in Political Debate" on page 85).

In January 2002, the International Bible Society, who owns the NIV copyright,[18] withdrew its endorsement of the *Colorado Springs Guidelines* (CSG), while affirming "the sanctity of the truth of sacred Scripture" and their obligation "to render the most accurate translation possible."[19] Among their reasons was that the NIV follows conflicting and less restrictive guidelines for rendering gender language, as shared by members of the International Forum of Bible Agencies.[20]

The NIVI, NIrV, and TNIV all preceded the current revision of the NIV published in 2011. Whereas the others were published under different titles as separate publications, the last is published as the familiar *New International Version* (NIV), only with a different year printed in the copyright page. Earlier editions of the NIV (1978, '84) have since been discontinued and are no longer in print.

TEXT BASES

New Testament

Eclectic Greek text. *Greek New Testament* 4th revised (United Bible Societies, 1993) and Nestle-Aland *Novum Testamentum Graece* 27th editions (Stuttgart: Deutsche Bibelgesellschaft, 1993); The editors' final decisions can be found in Goodrich and Lukaszewski's *A Reader's Greek New Testament* (2007).

Old Testament

Masoretic Hebrew-Aramaic text. Kittel's *Biblia Hebraïca* 3rd ed. (Stuttgart: Privilegierte Württembergische Bibelanstalt, 1929–37); *Biblia Hebraica Stuttgartensia* 1st and 2nd emended editions (New York: American Bible Society, 1967–77, 1984).

Ancient versions. Septuagint (Greek LXX) and Aquila, Theodotian, and Symmachus (Greek), Vulgate and Jerome's

Juxta Hebraica (Latin), Peshitta (Syriac), Targums (Aramaic), Samaritan Pentateuch (Hebrew), Dead Sea Scrolls.

CONTRIBUTORS

The Committee on Bible Translation (CBT) is a "group of biblical scholars charged with keeping abreast of advances in biblical scholarship and changes in English and issuing periodic updates to the NIV. The CBT . . . has sole responsibility for the NIV text."[21]

The original CBT team of fifteen members that assembled in 1966 included E. Leslie Carlson, Edmund P. Clowney (ESV), Ralph Earle, Burton L. Goddard, R. Laird Harris, Earl S. Kalland, Kenneth S. Kantzer (ESV), Stephen W. Paine, Charles F. Pfeiffer, Charles C. Ryrie, Francis R. Steele, John H. Stek, J. C. Wenger, and Marten H. Woudstra.[22] Edwin H. Palmer (from Westminster Theological Seminary) joined the CBT in 1968 as its full-time executive secretary and remained so until his death in 1980, after which Kenneth Lee Barker (NASB) took his place.

The initial translation team consisted of 97 people—87 Americans, three Canadians, three Britons, two New Zealanders, and two Australians.[23] "They were from many denominations and churches—including Anglican, Assemblies of God, Baptist, Brethren, Christian Reformed, Church of Christ, Evangelical Covenant, Evangelical Free, Lutheran, Mennonite, Methodist, Nazarene, Presbyterian, Wesleyan and others."[24]

Among the "translators whose services have been enlisted [were] a number of world-renowned scholars, including Gleason Archer, E. M. Blaiklock (NKJV), Ralph Earle, Roland K. Harrison (NKJV, NLT), William Hendriksen, William Lane (NASB), Leon Morris (ESV), Elmer B. Smick, and Donald J. Wiseman, to name but a few."[25]

For a complete list of translators, visit *booklink.id/ niv-translator*

The team of fifteen responsible for the 2011 update is "comprised of twelve American scholars, two British scholars and one Indian scholar. Of the fifteen committee members, thirteen are men and two are women. Most of the major theological traditions

The Best Bible?

of Protestant evangelicalism are represented."[26] They include Kenneth L. Barker, Craig Blomberg (HCSB, ESV), Jeannine K. Brown (*Common English Bible*), Gordon Fee, Richard T. France, David Instone-Brewer, Karen H. Jobes, Douglas Moo (CBT Chairman), William Mounce (ESV), Mark L. Strauss, Paul Swarup, Larry L. Walker, Bruce Waltke (NASB), Michael Williams, and Ronald Youngblood.

THEOLOGICAL ASSUMPTIONS

The *Constitution* of the NIV's standing Committee on Bible Translation reads:

> Only those shall be eligible for membership on the Committee who endorse the purpose for which the Committee exists, and who are willing to subscribe to the following affirmation of faith: "The Bible alone, and the Bible in its entirety, is the Word of God written, and is therefore inerrant in the autographs"; or to the statements on Scripture in the *Westminster Confession*, the *Belgic Confession*, the *New Hampshire Confession*, or the creedal basis of the National Association of Evangelicals; or to some other comparable statement.[27]

FEATURES

"Variation in the spelling of names in the original languages has usually not been indicated. Where a person or place has two or more different names in the Hebrew, Aramaic or Greek texts, the more familiar one has generally been used, with footnotes where needed."[28] For example, "Jehoash" in **2Kg 11.21** is rendered "Joash" to identify this Judahite king as the same person in **2Kg 11.2**.

The KJV's spellings of names are kept in the NIV, except where the traditional spelling uses the consonant cluster "ch". Since most English readers pronounce "ch" like "la*tch*" instead of "lo*ch*" or "Ba*ch*," the Committee replaced occurrences with either "k" or "c". For example: "Sabteka" (**Gn 10.7**), "Meshek" (**Gn 10.2**), and "Uruk" (**Gn 10.10**). (A few exceptions are the familiar traditional spelling of "Lamech," "Enoch," and "Zechariah.")

Approximate measurement equivalents for amounts and distance are also given in the footnotes.

Differences of versification between the NIV and other English translations of the Hebrew Bible, particularly in the Psalms, are noted in the footnotes.[29]

The Committee was responsible for the "[b]asic formatting of the text, such as lining the poetry, paragraphing (both prose and poetry), setting up of (administrative-like) lists, indenting letters and lengthy prayers within narratives."[30]

In the NT, verse numbers found in traditional Bibles (*i.e.*, KJV) for passages that are unsupported by "the best Greek manuscripts" are marked of with brackets ("[...]") and footnoted (*e.g.*, **Mt 17.[21]**).

The longer ending of Mark (**Mk 16.9–20**) and the story of the woman caught in adultery (**Jn 7.53–8.11**) are noted by bracketed annotations to indicate their debated stance in NT textual transmission. "A different typeface has been chosen for these passages to indicate their uncertain status."[31]

"[T]he issuing of 'red-letter' editions is a publisher's choice—one the Committee does not endorse."[32]

Cross references are found in the footnotes.

OT textual footnotes uses a system of notation where the words to the left the semicolon indicates the source of the words found in the main text. Words to the right of the semicolon indicate either the base text that the translators diverged from or some other early authoritative witness. For example, the footnote at **Jos 19.34** reads, "*a* 34 Septuagint; Hebrew *west, and Judah, the Jordan*."

NT footnotes indicate significant variants that cast doubt on what the actual original was. They are introduced by "Some manuscripts" or similar expressions.

Footnotes indicate variations of proper names and word-plays. Some footnotes indicate dynamic equivalents in the text.

In cases where the precise meaning of the original text couldn't be determined, footnotes introduced by "Or..." suggest an alternate rendering of the text.

Footnotes that call attention to places where there is uncertainty about what constitutes the original text have been introduced by the phrase "Some MSS add..." or "... omit..." or "... read....".

Approximate measurement equivalents for amounts and distance are also given in the footnotes.

The Committee inserted sectional headings hoping that they would prove more helpful than traditional chapter divisions. "They are not to be regarded as part of the NIV text, are not for oral reading, and are not intended to dictate the interpretation of the sections they head."[33]

RECEPTION

According to *The New York Times*, the NIV, which complemented "the booming evangelical Christian market... sold 1.2 million copies just four weeks after publication, most of them even before the ink was on the paper."[34] Since its initial publication, the NIV has outsold the ever-popular King James Version. It remains the number one, highest selling English translation of the Bible.

Revisions done between the 1984 and 2011 editions have not done as well. The NIV *Inclusive Language Edition* (1995, '96) was not published in the U.S. and was pulled from shelves not long after its release in the U.K. The TNIV has also been discontinued since it has been superceded by the 2011 update. The *New International Reader's Version* for youth and English-language learners remains popular, though, and typically ranks seventh in Bible sales behind the NIV, KJV, NLT, ESV, NKJV, and CSB.[35]

NIV

ASSESSMENT

The NIV's truly international English makes it useful from Brisbane to Bombay, from London to Los Angeles—wherever English is spoken.[36]

The Committee on Bible Translation's (CBT) permanence ensures an advocate for the NIV's future and development. The CBT's independence from publishers preserves the NIV's integrity from commercial influence, even though, their independence may put them at odds with the larger Christian community, who may not all agree with their decisions and for which the publishers could suffer.

The latest update (2011), though generally well-received, may not sit well with a generation who grew up reading and memorizing the NIV since 1984. This twenty-seven-year gap, though punctuated with significant editions like the NIVI, NIrV, and TNIV, seems like a long time to wait for an official, thorough revision of the NIV itself. Though only five percent of its text was emended, the changes are frequent enough (and sometimes significant enough) to disrupt public reading. Churches using both editions may startle members whenever a passage read aloud differs from what audiences read in front of them. (This problem is compounded in that churches can no longer stock their pews with new copies of the 1984 edition, which has been discontinued and replaced with the 2011 edition.)

Many good references and resources are available to support the NIV, including commentaries, dictionaries, and a concordance specially keyed to the NIV's wording.[37]

The NIV is a reliably accurate Bible translation ideal for intermediate English learners, middle school (sixth grade) and older.

REPRESENTATIVE SAMPLES

Familiar Passages

Gn 1.1–2	In the beginning God created the heavens and the earth. Now the earth was formless and empty, darkness was over the surface of the deep, and the Spirit of God was hovering over the waters.
Ps 23.1–2	The LORD is my shepherd, I lack nothing. He makes me lie down in green pastures, he leads me beside quiet waters
Ps 27.4	One thing I ask from the LORD, this only do I seek: that I may dwell in the house of the LORD all the days of my life, to gaze on the beauty of the LORD and to seek him in his temple.
Jn 3.16	For God so loved the world that he gave his one and only Son, that whoever believes in him shall not perish but have eternal life.

Divine Name and Titles

YHWH	Ps 24.1a	The earth is the **LORD**'s, and everything in it
adonai	Ps 90.1b	**Lord**, you have been our dwelling place throughout all generations.
elohim	Gn 1.27a	So **God** created mankind in his own image
adonai YHWH	Ps 73.28b	I have made the **Sovereign LORD** my refuge
adonai elohim	Dn 9.3a	So I turned to the **Lord God**
YHWH *saba'oth*	1Sa 17.45b	"I come against you in the name of the **LORD Almighty**"
el shaddai	Ex 6.3a	"I appeared to Abraham, to Isaac and to Jacob as **God Almighty**"*a*
		footnote (fn): *a* 3 Hebrew *El-Shaddai*
kyrios	Lk 20.42b	" 'The **Lord** said to my **Lord**, "Sit at my right hand" ' "

	Mt 16.16b	"You are the **Messiah**, the Son of the living God."
christos	Jn 17.3	"Now this is eternal life: that they know you, the only true God, and Jesus **Christ**, whom you have sent."

New Testament Text Base

Mt 17.21	——— **fn:** *20 Some manuscripts you.* [21] *But this kind does not go out except by prayer and fasting.*
Mt 18.11	——— **fn:** *10 Some manuscripts heaven* [11] *The Son of Man came to save what was lost*
Ac 8.37	——— **fn:** *36 Some late manuscripts baptized?"* [37] *Philip said, "If you believe with all your heart, you may." The eunuch answered, "I believe that Jesus Christ is the Son of God."*
1 Jn 5.7b–8a	——— **fn:** *7, 8 Late manuscripts of the Vulgate testify in heaven: the Father, the Word and the Holy Spirit, and these three are one.* [8] *And there are three that testify on earth: the* (not found in any Greek manuscript before the fourteenth century)

Gender Language

'ādām	Gn 9.6	"Whoever sheds **human** blood, by **humans** shall their blood be shed; for in the image of God has God made **mankind**."
'îsh ... nephesh	Lv 24.17	"'**Anyone** who takes the life of **a human being** is to be put to death.'"
'āvîw	Pr 15.5a	A fool spurns **a parent's** discipline
anthrōpōn	Mt 4.19	"Come, follow me, ... and I will send you out to fish for **people**."
huioi	Mt 5.9	"Blessed are the peacemakers, for they will be called **children** of God."
hekastō ... autou	Ro 2.6	God "will repay **each person** according to what **they** have done." [a] **fn:** *[a] 6 Psalm 62:12; Prov. 24:12*

NIV

adelphoi	Gal 5.13	You, my **brothers and sisters**, were called to be free. But do not use your freedom to indulge the flesh *a*; rather, serve one another humbly in love.
		fn: *a 13* In contexts like this, the Greek word for *flesh* (*sarx*) refers to the sinful state of human beings, often presented as a power in opposition to the Spirit; also in verses 16, 17, 19 and 24; and in 6:8.
gynaikos anēr	Ti 1.6a	An elder must be blameless, faithful to his **wife**, **a man** whose children believe *b*
		fn: *b 11* Or *children are trustworthy*
gynaikas	1Ti 3.11	In the same way, **the women** *c* are to be worthy of respect, not malicious talkers but temperate and trustworthy in everything.
		fn: *c 11* Possibly deacons' wives or women who are deacons

Difficult Renderings

1Sa 13.1	Saul was **thirty** *d* **years old** when he became king, and he reigned over Israel **forty-** *e* **two years**.
	fn: *d 1* A few late manuscripts of the Septuagint; Hebrew does not have *thirty*. *e 1* Probable reading of the original Hebrew text (see Acts 13:21); Masoretic Text does not have *forty-*.
Is 28.13	So then, the word of the LORD to them will become:
	Do this, do that,
	a rule for this, a rule for that;
	a little here, a little there—
	so that as they go they will fall backward;
	they will be injured and snared and captured.

New International Version   **373**

Significant Renderings

'almah	Is 7.14	Therefore the Lord himself will give you *a* a sign: **The virgin** *b* will conceive and give birth to a son, and *c* will call him Immanuel. *d*
		fn: *a 14* The Hebrew is plural. *b 14* Or *young woman.* *c 14* Masoretic Text; Dead Sea Scrolls *son, and he* or *son, and they* *d 14 Immanuel* means *God with us.*
she'ol, 'abaddon	Pr 15.11	**Death** and **Destruction***e* lie open before the LORD— how much more do human hearts!
		fn: *e 11* Hebrew *Abaddon*
egennēsen	Mt 1.2	Abraham **was the father of** Isaac, Isaac **the father of** Jacob, Jacob **the father of** Judah and his brothers
eskēnōsen	Jn 1.14	The Word became flesh and **made his dwelling** among us. We have seen his glory, the glory of the one and only Son, who came from the Father, full of grace and truth.
tois ioudaiois	Jn 18.36	Jesus said, "My kingdom is not of this world. If it were, my servants would fight to prevent my arrest **by the Jewish leaders**. But now my kingdom is from another place."
dikaiosunē theou, pisteōs Iēsou Christou	Ro 3.22a	**This righteousness** is given through **faith in** *f* **Jesus Christ** to all who believe.
		fn: *f 22* Or *through the faithfulness of*
Granville Sharp's rule applied	Tt 2.13	while we wait for the blessed hope—the appearing of the glory of **our great God and Savior, Jesus Christ**

SIGNIFICANT REVISIONS

The 2011 edition of the NIV is the culmination of all the editions that came before it, namely the *New International Version: Inclusive Language Edition* (NIVI 1995, '96), the *New International Reader's Version* (NIrV 1994, '96, '98), and *Today's New International Version* (TNIV 2001, '05). (On occasion the 2011 update even reverts to decisions made in the 1978 edition, *e.g.* **Ps 23.1.**) About 95 percent of the text of the 2011 edition is the same as its 1984 predecessor.[38]

The CBT gave three significant reasons for revising the NIV text. First, our English language changes over time. Old vocabulary can carry new associations. For example, the influence of film and television has so influenced the association of "aliens" with "extra-terrestrials" that the revisers sensed the need to replace the old word so as not to mislead modern readers.[39]

	NIV (1984)	NIrV (1998)	TNIV (2005), NIV ('11)
Gn 23.4	"I am an **alien** and stranger among you."	"I'm an **outsider. I'm** a stranger among you."	"I am a **foreigner** and stranger among you."

The following examples demonstrate improvements that reflect contemporary English idiom:

	NIV (1984), TNIV ('05)	NIrV (1998)	NIV (2011)
Ex 4.14b	"He is already on his way to meet you, and **his heart will be glad when he sees** you."	"He is already on his way to meet you. **He will be glad to see** you."	"He is already on his way to meet you, and **he will be glad to see** you."
Is 3.20	the headdresses and **ankle chains** and sashes, the perfume bottles and charms	their headdresses, **ankle chains** and belts. He'll take away their perfume bottles and charms.	the headdresses and **anklets** and sashes, the perfume bottles and charms

	NIV (1984), TNIV ('05)	NIV (2011)
Is 16.6 (cf. Jer 48.29)	"We have heard of Moab's pride— **her overweening pride and** conceit, her pride and her insolence— but her boasts are empty"	"We have heard of Moab's pride— **how great is her arrogance!**— **of her** conceit, her pride and her insolence; but her boasts are empty."
Jn 1.27	"He is the one who comes after me, the **thongs** of whose sandals I am not worthy to untie."	"He is the one who comes after me, the **straps** of whose sandals I am not worthy to untie."

Second, scholarship does not stagnate, but it progresses with new understanding. For example, the Greek word *harpagmon* is rare, only occuring once in the entire NT. Its meaning was uncertain until a later discovery clarified that it meant something that a person has in their possession yet does not use for their own personal gain.

	NIV (1984), NIVI ('95)	TNIV (2005), NIV (2011)
Php 2.6	[Christ Jesus], being in very nature *a* God, did not consider equality with God **something to be grasped**	[Christ Jesus], being in very nature *a* God, did not consider equality with God **something to be used to his own advantage**
	fn: *a*6 Or *in the form of*	fn: *a*6 Or *in the form of*

Further investigation led the translators to render some words more precisely or formally to improve accuracy (or shy away from over-interpreting):

	NIV (1984), TNIV (2005)	NIV (2011)
Gn 37.3	[Israel] made **a richly orna-mented* robe** for [Joseph]. fn: *a* 3 The meaning of the Hebrew for *richly ornamented* is uncertain; also in verses 23 and 32.	[Israel] made **an ornate** *a* robe for [Joseph]. fn: *a* 3 The meaning of the Hebrew for this word is uncertain; also in verses 23 and 32.

	NIV (1984), NIVI ('95)	TNIV (2005), NIV ('11)
Lk 2.7b	She wrapped him in cloths and placed him in a manger, because there was no **room** for them in **the inn.**	She wrapped him in cloths and placed him in a manger, because there was no **guest room available** for them.
Mk 15.27	They crucified two **robbers** with him, one on his right and one on his left	They crucified two **rebels** with him, one on his right and one on his left

	NIV (1984), TNIV ('05)	NIVI (1995)	NIV (2011)
Ro 8.3a (cf. Gal 5)	For what the law was powerless to do **in that** it was weakened by the **sinful nature,** *b* God did by sending his own Son in the likeness of sinful **man** to be a sin offering. fn: *b* 3 Or *the flesh;* also in verses 4, 5, 8, 9, 12 and 13	For what the law was powerless to do **in that** it was weak-ened by the **sinful nature,** *b* God did by sending his own Son in the likeness of sinful **humanity** to be a sin offering. *c* fn: *b* 3 Or *the flesh;* also in verses 4, 5, 8, 9, 12 and 13 *c* 3 Or *man, for sin*	For what the law was powerless to do **because** it was weak-ened by the **flesh,** *b* God did by sending his own Son in the likeness of sinful **flesh** to be a sin offering. *c* fn: *b* 3 In contexts like this, the Greek word for *flesh* (*sarx*) refers to the sinful state of human be-ings, often presented as a power in oppo-sition to the Spirit; also in verses 4–13. *c* 3 Or *flesh, for sin*

Third, the revisers of the 2011 edition were constantly aware of the need for clarity so that readers might have less justification to misinterpret or misapply a passage. For example:

	NIV (1984), NIVI ('95)	TNIV (2005), NIV ('11)
Php 4.13	I can do **everything** through him who gives me strength.	I can do **all this** through him who gives me strength.
Mt 1.16	Jacob the father of Joseph, the husband of Mary, **of whom was born** Jesus, who is called **Christ**.	Jacob the father of Joseph, the husband of Mary, **and Mary was the mother of** Jesus who is called the **Messiah**.

	NIV (1984), TNIV (2005)	NIV (2011)
Lv 4.19–20	[The priest] shall remove all the fat from it and burn it on the altar, and do with this bull just as he did with the bull for the sin offering. In this way the priest will make atonement for **them**, and they will be forgiven	[The priest] shall remove all the fat from it and burn it on the altar, and do with this bull just as he did with the bull for the sin offering. In this way the priest will make atonement for the **community**, and they will be forgiven.

	NIV (1984)	TNIV (2005)	NIV (2011)
Job 9.33	If only there were someone to **arbitrate** between us, **to lay his hand upon us both**	If only there were someone to **arbitrate** between us, **to lay a hand on us both**	If only there were someone to **mediate** between us, **someone to bring us together**

	NIV (1984), NIVI ('95)	TNIV (2005), NIV ('11)
1Co 7.1–2	Now for the matters you wrote about: It is good for a man not to **marry.**^a But since **there is so much immorality**, each man should have his own wife, and each woman her own husband. fn: ^a6 Or *"It is good for a man not to have sexual relations with a woman"*	Now for the matters you wrote about: "It is good for a man not to **have sexual relations with a woman**." But since **sexual immorality is occurring**, each man should have **sexual relations with** his own wife, and each woman **with** her own husband.

The revisers had over a decade and a half to test whether certain gender-inclusive renderings could stick. Some took hold, but not all survived scrutiny, for example:

	NIV (1984)	NIVI ('95), TNIV ('05), NIV ('11)
Nm 8.17a	"Every firstborn male in Israel, whether **man** or animal, is mine"	"Every firstborn male in Israel, whether **human** or animal, is mine"

	NIV (1984)	NIVI (1995), TNIV ('05)	NIV (2011)
Rv 3.20	"Here I am! I stand at the door and knock. If anyone hears my voice and opens the door, I will come in and eat with **him**, and **he** with me."	"Here I am! I stand at the door and knock. If anyone hears my voice and opens the door, I will come in and eat with **them**, and **they** with me."	"Here I am! I stand at the door and knock. If anyone hears my voice and opens the door, I will come in and eat with **that person**, and **they** with me."
1Co 15.21	For since death came through a **man**, the resurrection of the dead comes also through a **man**.	For since death came through a **human being**, the resurrection of the dead comes also through a **human being**.	For since death came through a **man**, the resurrection of the dead comes also through a **man**.

	NIV (1984)	NIVI (1995)	TNIV (2005), NIV ('11)
Jn 11.50	"You do not realize that it is better for you that one **man** die for the people than that the whole nation perish."	"You do not realize that it is better for you that one **person** die for the people than that the whole nation perish."	"You do not realize that it is better for you that one **man** die for the people than that the whole nation perish."

ENDORSEMENTS

The Church of England recognizes the NIV as suitable for use during the course of public worship, but they noted its lack of the Apocrypha, which is needed for Anglican lectionaries.[40] Both The Episcopal Church (USA) and the House of Bishops of the Anglican Church of Canada approve or authorize the NIV for use in public worship.[41] The Christian Reformed Church in North America has approved the NIV for public worship since 1980.[42]

The Orthodox Presbyterian Church (OPC) does not officially endorse any one translation, but the Committee on Christian Education of the OPC occasionally quotes from the NIV 1984 edition in its publications.[43] Likewise, The Lutheran Church—Missouri Synod formerly used the 1984 edition as the base for their *Concordia Self-Study Bible* (St. Louis, MO: Concordia Publishing House, 1986).

The Wisconsin Evangelical Lutheran Synod (WELS) has used the NIV in their publications since 1979 (*via* Northwestern Publishing House). The Translation Evaluation Committee of the WELS continues to endorse the NIV since its 2011 revision, not just because it improves the English idiom of the NIV 1984, but because they still do not have any clearly superior alternative, though that may change since the completion of their *Evangelical Heritage Version* (EHV).[44]

The Southern Baptist Convention (SBC) expressed profound disappointment with the gender-inclusive revisions in the NIV 2011 update. They formally requested that their publishing arm,

LifeWay Christian Resources, pull it from their inventory, as they could not commend the 2011 NIV to Southern Baptists or the larger Christian community.[45] Despite their formal request, LifeWay refused to remove the NIV 2011 from its stores, stating that the SBC was given invalid information about the revision when they made their decision.[46] It is still available in its latest editions in their online store.[47]

COPYRIGHT

According to the Constitution of the CBT, the "Committee shall see to the safeguarding of the integrity of the text of the projected translation by making adequate provision for its copyright."[48]

You may quote up to 500 verses from the NIV in any form without prior written permission; the verses may not constitute a complete book of the Bible; they must comprise less than 25% of your work's content; and your work must include the following copyright acknowledgment.

> Scripture is taken from *The Holy Bible, New International Version*®, NIV® Copyright © 1973, 1978, 1984, 2011 by Biblica, Inc.® Used by permission. All rights reserved worldwide.

Unless used exclusively, follow citations with the designation (NIV). For example:

> **Jn 1.4**, "In him was life, and that life was the light of all mankind." (NIV)

HarperCollins is the copyright administrator and one of the publishers of the NIV in the United States and Canada (Hodder & Stoughton, in Europe and the United Kingdom), but Biblica, Inc. holds the actual copyright and controls the text. The title *"New International Version*®*"* and its initialism (NIV®) are registered trademarks with the U.S. Patent and Trademark Office by Biblica, Inc., but its logomark is not.

For permissions not covered here, those working in the U.S. and Canada should write to HarperCollins Christian Publishing, Attention: Permissions Department, P.O. Box 141000, Nashville, TN 37214. For those working in Europe and the U.K., write to Hodder & Stoughton Ltd., a member of the Hodder Headline Plc. Group, 338 Euston Road, London NW1 3BH.

NIV✠

The Best Bible?

ENDNOTES FOR THE
NEW INTERNATIONAL VERSION

1 The historic Multnomah Hotel is now an Embassy Suites by Hilton Portland-Downtown.

2 Burton L. Goddard, "Clouds Small as a Man's Hand," *The NIV Story: The Inside Story of the New International Version* (New York: Vantage Press, 1989), pp. 5–8. "Made to Read," NIV Bible (blog), accessed November 24, 2020, https://www.thenivbible.com/50th-anniversary/made-to-read/. "Driven to Take Action," NIV Bible (blog), accessed November 24, 2020, https://www.thenivbible.com/driven-to-take-action/.

3 Christian Reformed Church of America. *1980 Agenda for Synod.* (Grand Rapids, MI: Board of Publications of the Christian Reformed Church, 1980).

4 Edwin H. Palmer, *"New International Version," What Bible Can You Trust?* (Nashville, TN: Broadman Press, 1974) *via* Roland Worth. *"New International Version," Bible Translations: A History through Source Documents* (Jefferson, NC: McFarland & Company, Inc., Publishers, 1992), p. 149.

5 Committee on Bible Translation (CBT), "Updating the *New International Version* of the Bible: Notes from the CBT" (August 2010), accessed February 3, 2020, https://www.thenivbible.com/wp-content/uploads/2014/11/2011-Translation-Notes.pdf.

6 *Ibid.*

7 *Committee on Bible Translation (CBT) Constitution,* Article I, Section 2, *via* John Stek, "The *New International Version*: How It Came to Be," *The Challenge of Bible Translation* (Grand Rapids: Zondervan, 2003).

8 CBT *Constitution*, Article II, Section 1.

9 D. A. Carson, review of the *New International Version of the Holy Bible.* (Deerfield, IL: 1979), p. 1.

10 Sakae Kubo and Walter F. Specht. *So Many Versions? Twentieth-century English Versions of the Bible.* (Grand Rapids, MI: The Zondervan Corp., 1983), p. 244. Thanks to Alan Millard for his insights into the drafting and editorial process.

11 Carson, review.

12 "New Bible for Evangelicals has Sold 1.2 Million Copies: 115 Worked on Project 'Biggest Selling Bible' Huge Religious Book Sales Paraphrase by One Man all United in Belief," *New York Times*, November 26, 1978.

[13] Goddard, "Counting the Costs", *The NIV Story*, p. 100.

[14] CBT *Constitution*, Article VII, Sections 4–5.

[15] Bruce M. Metzger, "English Translations of the Bible, Today and Tomorrow," *Bibliotheca Sacra* 150 (October–December 1993): 410–2.

[16] Committee on Bible Translation, "Preface to the Inclusive Language NIV," *Holy Bible, New International Version: Inclusive Language Edition, The New Testament, Psalms and Proverbs* (London: Hodder and Soughton, 1995), p. ix.

[17] Susan Olasky, "Femme Fatale," *World* magazine (March 29, 1997), pp. 12–5.

[18] Biblica is now the name (since 2009) of what was originally the New York Bible Society (1809–1971), then New York Bible Society International (1971–1973), then New York International Bible Society (1974–1988), then International Bible Society (1988–2009). These are the names of that institution which holds the NIV copyright, though it is now based in Colorado Springs, CO.

[19] Peter Bradley, a letter announcing International Bible Society's departure from the *Colorado Springs Guidelines* (January 18, 2002), accessed May 11, 2008, http://www.genderneutralbibles.com/ibs_letter_011802.php.

[20] Members of the International Forum of Bible Agencies (IFBA) include the American Bible Society, Biblica, Wycliffe Global Alliance, SIL International, New Tribe Missions, *et al.* United Bible Societies is a collaborating agency with IFBA.

[21] Biblica, Inc., "Preface," *The Holy Bible, New International Version* (Grand Rapids, MI: Zondervan, 2011).

[22] John H. Stek, "The *New International Version*: How It Came to Be," *The Challenge of Bible Translation,* edited by Glen G. Scorgie, Mark L. Strauss, and Steven M. Voth (Grand Rapids: Zondervan, 2003), p. 245.

The CBT was begun at the Palos Heights conference in 1965 and filled out its mandated membership of fifteen the following year.

[23] Metzger, "The New International Version (1978)," *The Bible in Translation: Ancient and English Versions* (Grand Rapids, MI: Baker Academic, 2001), p. 139.

[24] New York Bible Society International, "Preface," *The Holy Bible, New International Version* (Grand Rapids, MI: The Zondervan Corporation, 1978).

[25] Kubo and Specht, *So Many Versions?* p. 244.

[26] Biblica, Inc., "Updating the *New International Version* of the Bible. . . . ," *The Holy Bible, New International Version* (Grand Rapids, MI: Zondervan, 2011).

[27] CBT *Constitution*, Article II, Section 3.

28 International Bible Society, "Preface," *The Holy Bible, New International Version* (Grand Rapids, MI: Zondervan, 1984).

29 Biblica, "Preface," *The Holy Bible, New International Version.*

30 *Ibid.*

31 *Ibid.*

32 *Ibid.*

33 *Ibid.*

34 "New Bible for Evangelicals has Sold 1.2 Million Copies," *New York Times*, November 26, 1978.

35 E.C.P.A., "Bible Translation . . . Best of 2020," *Christian Book Expo*, accessed January 26, 2021, https://christianbookexpo.com/bestseller/translations.php?id=B020;

I've excluded the Spanish *Reina Valera* version from this ranking.

36 Admittedly, this international claim requires a variant edition, the NIVUK (2012), which is an anglicised version. This variant emends twelve percent of the NIV's verses for a total of 4,408 changes in order to match normal British punctuation, spelling, grammar, and idiom.

Robert Slowley, "Changes by book." *NIV comparison with the NIVUK*, accessed July 22, 2019, http://www.slowley.com/nivuk/books.html.

Thanks goes to Rev. Dr. David Instone-Brewer for pointing out that Slowley included punctuation. According to Instone-Brewer's count, only 2,369 total words were changed in the main text and footnotes.

37 John R. Kohlenberger, III, *The NIV Exhaustive Bible Concordance*, 3rd ed., (Grand Rapids, MI: Zondervan Academic, 2015), accessed July 24, 2019, https://www.zondervan.com/9780310262930/the-niv-exhaustive-bible-concordance-third-edition/. This Concordance is keyed with Goodrick-Kohlenberger (GK) numbers, which can be translated into the more familiar Strong's numbers with the numbering-system indices in the back.

38 "Frequently Asked Questions: About the Translation Process," NIV Bible website, accessed January 25, 2021, https://www.thenivbible.com/faqs/.

39 Science fiction and fantasy genres have profoundly influenced our collective imagination and language. Consider Steven Spielberg's blockbuster films, *Close Encounters of the Third Kind* (1977) and *E.T.* (1982); Gene Roddeberry's *Star Trek* (1966–69), George Lucas' *Star Wars* (1977–83), and Ridley Scott's *Alien* franchises (1979–97).

[40] General Synod of the Church of England, "Versions of Scripture," by David Michael Hope, Archbishop of York (Eboracensis), October 9, 2002, GS Misc 698.

[41] "What We Believe: The Bible" from the website of The Episcopal Church, accessed September 6, 2019, https://www.episcopalchurch.org/bible/.

General Synod of the Anglican Church of Canada, "List of Bible Versions Approved by the House of Bishops for use in Public Worship....," accessed February 3, 2020, http://www.anglican.ca/wp-content/uploads/2010/10/List -of-Bible-Versions-Approved-by-the-House-of-Bishops-for-use-in-Public -Worship-in-the-Anglican-Church-of-Canada.pdf.

[42] Christian Reformed Church in North America, "Bible Translations," accessed June 2, 2020, https://www.crcna.org/welcome/beliefs/bible-translations.

[43] Orthodox Presbyterian Church's publications website, accessed February 3, 2020 https://store.opc.org/.

[44] Translation Evaluation Committee, "Supplemental Report for the 2011 WELS Convention," accessed February 3, 2020, https://bibletranslation.welsrc.net /download-tlc/offical-reports/?wpdmdl=3251&ind=2.

[45] Southern Baptist Convention, "On The Gender-Neutral 2011 *New International Version*" (Phoenix, AZ: 2011), http://www.sbc.net/resolutions/1218/on-the -genderneutral-2011-new-international-version.

[46] Marty King, "LifeWay trustees vote to continue selling '11 NIV," *Baptist Press*, last modified February 15, 2012), accessed February 3, 2020, http://www .baptistpress.com/37181/lifeway-trustees-vote-to-continue-selling-11-niv.

[47] LifeWay Christian Resources, "*New International Version* (NIV) Bibles," accessed January 21, 2021, https://www.lifeway.com/en/shop/bibles/niv.

[48] CBT *Constitution*, Article VII, Section 2.

Christian Standard Bible®

The Holy Bible

*Produced by Holman Bible Publishers, an imprint of
LifeWay Christian Resources, 2017*

FORMAL / FUNCTIONAL TENDENCIES

FORMAL   FUNCTIONAL

Interlinear NASB KJV NKJV ESV RSV **CSB** NRSV NET NIV NLT Free Paraphrase

TEXT BASES

English Base *Holman Christian Standard Bible* (2004).

OT Masoretic Hebrew.   **NT** Eclectic Greek.

TRANSLATION TIMELINE

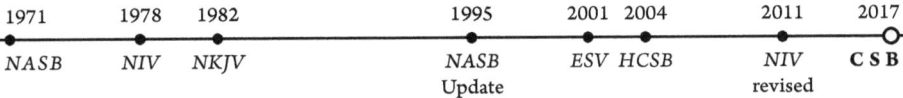

1971	1978	1982	1995	2001 2004	2011	2017
NASB	*NIV*	*NKJV*	*NASB* Update	*ESV HCSB*	*NIV* revised	**CSB**

CONTEMPORARY EVENTS

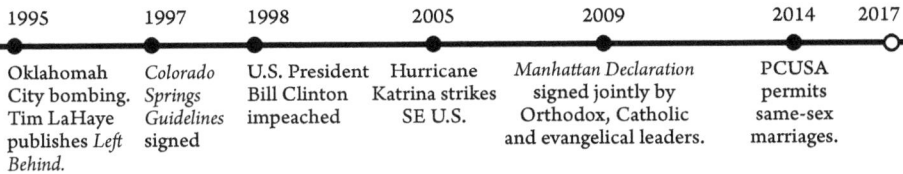

1995	1997	1998	2005	2009	2014	2017
Oklahomah City bombing. Tim LaHaye publishes *Left Behind*.	*Colorado Springs Guidelines* signed	U.S. President Bill Clinton impeached	Hurricane Katrina strikes SE U.S.	*Manhattan Declaration* signed jointly by Orthodox, Catholic and evangelical leaders.	PCUSA permits same-sex marriages.	

PUBLICATION TIMELINE

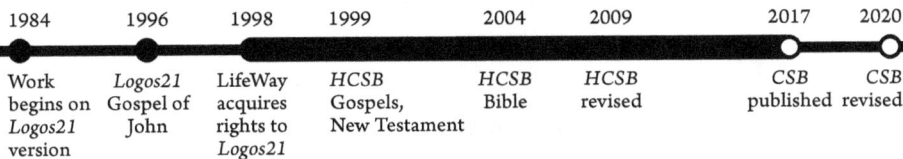

1984	1996	1998	1999	2004	2009	2017	2020
Work begins on *Logos21* version	*Logos21* Gospel of John	LifeWay acquires rights to *Logos21*	*HCSB* Gospels, New Testament	*HCSB* Bible	*HCSB* revised	*CSB* published	*CSB* revised

THE
HOLY BIBLE

CSB
CHRISTIAN
STANDARD
BIBLE®

HOLMAN®
BIBLES

HOLMAN BIBLE PUBLISHERS
NASHVILLE, TENNESSEE

Broadman & Holman Publishers (B&H), the trade publishing division of the Southern Baptist Convention's LifeWay Christian Resources, sought the rights to one of several existing Bible translations. First, B&H tried to negotiate with The Lockman Foundation on three different occasions in order to acquire the NASB, because they had hoped to avoid costly royalties altogether, but the negotiations fell through. Then, after trying and failing to obtain two other translations (the *NET Bible* and the *International Standard Version*), they approached Arthur L. Farstad and Edwin A. Blum, both of whom contributed significantly to the NKJV.[1]

Farstad and Blum had begun a modern translation (called the *Logos21* translation) immediately following their success with the NKJV. It was initially based on Farstad's and Zane C. Hodges' *The Greek New Testament According to the Majority Text* (1982, '85). They received financial backing for the project in 1996, but they lost funding when their backers decided not to finance an entirely new translation. By the time B&H approached them the following year, they had translated the four Gospels and started work on Acts and Romans.[2]

B&H acquired the project in April 1998 and set Farstad as its general editor. Sadly, Farstad died just five months later due to complications from a surgery. The editorship passed to his collaborator, Edwin Blum, who guided the project to completion.

The New Testament was published in 2001, and the Old in 2004. The entire Bible, titled the *Holman Christian Standard Bible* (HCSB), was revised for a second edition (2009), and several years later, it was overhauled again for its 2017 publication and renamed just the *Christian Standard Bible* (CSB).[3] The CSB underwent a handful of revisions in 2020 (less than one percent of the text).[4]

STATED TRANSLATION IDEALS

The HCSB and CSB Translation Committees' stated goal includes providing "English-speaking people worldwide with an accurate translation in contemporary English . . . for personal study, sermon preparation, private devotions, and memorization," with a "text that is clear and understandable, suitable for public reading, and shareable."[5] To these ends, "the CSB uses *optimal equivalence* as its translation philosophy," which means "in the many places throughout the Bible where a word-for-word rendering is understandable, a literal translation is used. When a word-for-word rendering might obscure the meaning for a modern audience, a more dynamic (that is, an idiomatic English) translation is used."[6] The intended result is a translation that "places equal value on fidelity to the original and readability for a modern audience."[7]

Another of the original Committee's stated goals was to conform the HCSB's gender language with the principles outlined by the *Colorado Springs Guidelines* (1997).[8] (Explicit mention of these principles was dropped in the 2017 CSB revision.)

METHOD

Arthur Farstad intended to produce a translation based on the Majority Greek Text (see page 33), but Broadman & Holman wanted it based on the eclectic text published by the United Bible Societies. So Farstad and B&H agreed to make two translations simultaneously: The HCSB would be based on the latest, standard, Greek critical edition, and Farstad's version on the Majority Text. His edition would have been published soon after the HCSB, but his vision was never realized.

Despite the death of their general editor, B&H did not take long to publish their New Testament, since the translation, which was begun by Farstad and Blum, was already mostly in draft form. After the first draft of the NT was complete, each book was submitted to a scholar who specialized in that particular book. Each sent their criticisms and proposals to a committee who pieced their recommendations into a second draft. This draft was then reviewed by an English stylist and others who marked up the draft and sent it to a committee in Dallas, Texas. This committee reviewed their notes and formed the final NT draft.

The NT had a head start when the project began, but no work had yet started on the Old Testament when B&H acquired the project. Editors were chosen for the four major OT sections (Pentateuch, History, Poetry, and Prophets), and an initial conference met in Nashville, Tennessee, to decide on significant translation issues. Next, a few English stylists were recruited to ensure the readability of the ensuing work.

For the first draft of the OT, the translators produced formal renderings of their books. They supplemented their text with five levels of footnotes:

(1) text-critical notes;

(2) either the formal "literal" rendering of what each translator put in natural English idiom, or an alternate rendering that, though less likely, was still noteworthy;

(3) vital historic or geographic information;

(4) cross-references;

(5) and OT texts cited in NT passages.

The books then moved from the translators to the section editor who recorded their criticisms and recommended changes.

Then an English stylist marked up the books to give the work a more natural, literary feel.

The books then moved on to their first committee, which included one or several Bible scholars and English stylists. This committee checked the books with recent commentaries and compared them with other translations before publishing a second draft.

The second OT draft underwent additional criticism by a new set of reviewers, including a scholar on staff with LifeWay, the executive director, and another English stylist. Their remarks went on to a second committee who produced yet another draft. This third and final draft was examined by a third and final committee of three to five people led by the general editor. The final committees and the general editor worked through every NT and OT book as least once. (Some books were reviewed many more times. The Gospel of **John**, for example, was reviewed twenty-one times, while **Isaiah** was reviewed only four times.)

Throughout the process, the translators and stylists were assisted by the latest available Bible software (Accordance®) to speedily compare existing translations and check for consistency.

The entire production of the first edition of the HCSB since LifeWay's involvement took about seven years and cost its backers approximately ten million dollars.[9]

TEXT BASES

English Text

The CSB is a revision of the *Holman Christian Standard Bible* (2009).

New Testament

Eclectic Greek text. *Greek New Testament,* 4th revised (5th printing) and 5th editions (United Bible Societies, 2001, 2014); Nestle-Aland *Novum Testamentum Graece,* 27th and 28th editions (1979, 2012).

Old Testament

Masoretic Hebrew-Aramaic text. *Biblia Hebraica Stuttgartensia,* 5th revised edition (1997).

CONTRIBUTORS

After Arthur Farstad's death, Edwin Blum served as the general editor of the HCSB. He worked with a team of over a hundred translators, lexicologists, stylists, and other scholars from around the world. The OT Section Editors included Mark Rooker (Pentateuch), James D. Price (historical books; NKJV), Duane Garrett (poetry; consultant on *The Message*), and Todd Beall (Prophets).

"Team members represent [seventeen][10] denominations, including Southern Baptists, Plymouth Brethren, Presbyterians (P.C.A.), Congregationalists, Church of England, Church of God, Evangelical Free Church, Methodists, Evangelical Mennonites, and Episcopalians."[11] The largest number of contributers (about one-third of the membership) were Baptist.

Participants included such noted evangelical scholars as David Alan Black (ISV), Craig L. Blomberg (ESV, NIV'11), George H. Guthrie (ESV, NLT), Zane C. Hodges (NKJV, *Logos21*), Walter C. Kaiser, Jr. (NIV), Andreas J. Köstenberger (ESV), Tremper Longman III (CEB, *The Message*, NLT, NCV), Eugene H. Merrill (NET, NKJV, NLT), and Robert H. Mounce (ESV, NIV, NLT). James D. Price (NKJV) wrote the translation philosophy (called "optimal equivalence") which guided the work.

The 2017 and 2020 CSB revisions were co-chaired by Thomas R. Schreiner (ESV, NLT) and David Allen, two of the ten-members on the Translation Oversight Committee responsible for ensuring the contemporary nature of any future revisions. They were joined by such scholars as David Alan Black (ISV), Constantine R. Campbell, Dorian G. Coover-Cox (NET), and Andrew E. Steinmann (GW). Michael Card (musician, song writer, author) participated as an English stylist for the CSB revision.

For a complete list of translators, visit *booklink.id/ csb-translator*

THEOLOGICAL ASSUMPTIONS

Even though the HCSB and CSB are products of LifeWay Christian Resources (which is the education arm of the Southern Baptist Convention) they are not an exclusively Southern Baptist Bibles. Arthur Farstad, who gave the HCSB its initial vision, was a member of the Plymouth Brethren. Ed Blum, who took over the editorship following Farstad's death, is Presbyterian.[12] The ten-member Translation Oversight Committee responsible for the major CSB revision (2017) consisted of three Southern Baptists, two non-denominational members, two Lutherans (E.L.S. and L.C.M.S.), two Presbyterians, and one Anglican.[13] All participants affirmed biblical inerrancy.[14]

FEATURES

Slavery and servitude in the ancient world differed from the kind of slavery formerly instituted in English territories and the Americas. In the ancient Middle East, Greece, and Rome, slavery was not tied to race or ethnicity, but to outstanding debts or military conquest. Slaves faced a range of circumstances: They might have been lowly galley slaves, pushing and pulling oars, or they might have administered wealthy households or gained fame and recognition.

The HCSB (2009) uses the word "slave" or "slaves" 316 times. It renders the NT Greek word *doulos* as "slave(s)" in all occurrences (*i.e.*, 128 times). After considering the cultural implications, both ancient and modern, the CSB revisers used the word "slave(s)" only 188 times for the entire Bible, opting to use "servant(s)" elsewhere. In the CSB NT, *doulos* is translated "slave(s)" only 36 times (*i.e.*, only 28 percent of occurrences). "The CSB retains use of 'slave' in contexts where slavery or a slave are clearly in view, but for references to Christian discipleship, 'servant' is used."[15]

	HCSB (2009)	CSB (2017)
Mt 18.32	" 'Shouldn't you also have had mercy on your fellow **slave**, as I had mercy on you?' "	" 'Shouldn't you also have had mercy on your fellow **servant**, as I had mercy on you?' "
Mt 24.45	"That **slave** whose master finds him working when he comes will be rewarded."	"Blessed is that **servant** whom the master finds doing his job when he comes."
Ro 1.1	Paul, a **slave** of Christ Jesus, called as an apostle and singled out for God's good news	Paul, a **servant** of Christ Jesus, called as an apostle and set apart for the gospel of God

The CSB reverts to rendering the Tetragrammaton as "Lord" in place of HCSB's "Yahweh" for a few good reasons: A consistent application of principles for rendering the divine name as "Yahweh" was not always clear in the HCSB.[16] The revisers concluded that consistently translating it as "Yahweh" confused or offended too many readers. Also both the Greek NT and the LXX use the title *kyrios* (Gk. "Lord") instead, as do most other translations.[17]

The HCSB (2004) translates the Greek word *christos* as either "Christ" or "Messiah" depending on its use in different NT contexts. For Gentile audiences, the word is rendered "Christ"; for Jewish, "Messiah." Bullets indicate that "•Messiah" receives fuller explanation in the back of the volume.[18]

The CSB continues this practice, but translates "Messiah" to a lesser extent. In contrast, the earlier NIV (1984) only renders the word "Messiah" twice, both times in John's Gospel where he transliterates the Hebrew term into Greek (*messian, messias*) and gives its interpretation (*christos*) for his readers (**Jn 1.41; 4.25**). In the CSB "Christ" is used "as the default translation wherever there is scholarly debate. When scholars are unanimous that Israel's messianic heritage is in view, the committee uses 'Messiah.'"[19]

The *Colorado Springs Guidelines* (a.k.a. "Guidelines for Translation of Gender-Related Language in Scripture") directed the policy for translating gender language in the [H]CSB (see page 85). The translators wished to avoid imposing any ideologically motivated inclusive agenda on the meaning of the text. While the HCSB avoids using "man" or "he" unnecessarily (*e.g.*, in contexts where grammatically masculine nouns included females), it does not restructure sentences in order to avoid gendered pronouns when they are in the text (as the NRSV does). They did not change "him" to "you" or to "them." They did not replace other masculine words, like "father" or "son" by rendering them with generic words, like "parent" or "child."

The 2017 CSB revision somewhat relaxed the gender language restrictions required by the original *Guidelines* without losing the traditional masculine referents to God ("Father," "Son," "King," "he," "him," "his"). The revisers knew that the Greek word *adelphoi* could demonstrably mean both "brothers and sisters," and that the Hebrew word *'ādām* and Greek *anthrōpos* both generally mean "people, mankind, human[ity]" in many contexts and, so, rendered them as such (though occasionally they still rendered "man" in the generic sense, *cf.*, **Heb 2.6**).[20]

Paragraphs are indented according to sense. Verse reference numbers are inline with the text. In dialogue, new paragraphs identify new speakers.

Many passages are formatted as dynamic prose, with separate block-indented lines, like poetry. The [H]CSB uses special block-indented formatting throughout the text for clarifying lists, series, genealogies, and more. The translators paid special attention to avoid breaking lines in poetry at awkward intervals.

All editions (2004, 2009, 2017, 2020) use bold type for OT quotations found in the NT.

The editors used modern forms of punctuation to clarify the text and make reading easier. They used *em* dashes (a long dash "—") to indicate sudden breaks in thought and to clarify long or difficult sentences. In a few places, they use parentheses to indicate words that are parenthetical in the original languages.

Italics are used for transliterations from the Greek or Hebrew. (E.g., **Jn 12.13b**, "*Hosanna!* Blessed is he who comes in the name of the Lord—the King of Israel!")

Where other versions use *italics* for the words supplied by their translators in order to complete the sense of a passage (as in the case of the KJV, NASB, and NKJV), the original HCSB (2004) demarcates supplied words with lower half brackets ("⌊ . . . ⌋") instead. After later consideration, the Translation Oversight Committee decided to remove the half brackets in the second revised edition (2009). They understood the practice of supplying words as normal for any translation, and, therefore, the questions these markers raised and distractions they caused for readers outweighed their supposed benefits.

Nouns and personal pronouns clearly referring to members of the Godhead are capitalized in the HCSB. The CSB discontinued this and revised divine pronouns to be in lower-case if they did not start a sentence (as does the RSV, ESV, NRSV, and NIV). They chose this because of difficulties regarding the referent in OT messianic prophecies (e.g., **Ps 22.1**) and in NT passages where readers could confuse what a character believed about the Jesus he was speaking to (**Mt 12.38**).

Red-letter editions of the CSB are available.

Arabic numerals are used for numbers 10 and greater and for fractions, except in a small number of cases, as when a number begins a sentence.

Unique to the first two editions (2004, 2009) is the use of bullets ("•") to indicate words and terms that are given further explanation in a glossary/dictionary in the back of the Bible. These are called the "HCSB Bullet Notes." (The Committee made the bullets in the second edition less distracting by superscripting them ["•"].)

Footnotes are frequent, averaging to around six per page. They give text-critical information or reveal alternate or difficult translations.

OT textual notes show important differences among Hebrew manuscripts and ancient OT versions, such as the Septuagint and the Vulgate.

NT textual notes indicate significant differences among Greek manuscripts (mss) and are normally indicated in one of three ways: (1) "Other mss read . . . ," (2) "Other mss add . . . ," or (3) "Other mss omit . . . "

Some textual-critical notes only give alternate textual readings, while others add the support for the reading chosen by the editors.

Other footnotes give alternate or less likely or more formal English translations of the same Hebrew, Aramaic, and Greek text.

Descriptive headings, printed above each section of Scripture, help readers quickly identify the contents of that section.

ASSESSMENT

The CSB is rendered in mostly contemporary language. It is readable and clear. Attention was given to how its words roll off the tongue. It may not feel as "dignified" or literary as those translations in the Tyndale-KJV tradition (e.g., the RSV, ESV and NRSV). Its many footnotes offer insights into the translators' decisions, though at times, they can busy the page or occasionally confuse readers with either too much or too little information.[21]

The CSB Translation Oversight Committee ensures the CSB's future development and continued relevance. LifeWay has made it available in many different bindings and formats, including a number of study Bibles. They have also incorporated it into various church curricula, for which this translation is particularly suited.

The CSB is a readable and accessible Bible for general English readers educated from grade school through college and university.

REPRESENTATIVE SAMPLES

Familiar Passages

Gn 1.1–2	In the beginning God created the heavens and the earth.[A] Now the earth was formless and empty, darkness covered the surface of the watery depths, and the Spirit of God was hovering over the surface of the waters.
	Footnote (fn): [A] Or *created the universe*
Ps 23.1–2	The LORD is my shepherd; I have what I need. He lets me lie down in green pastures; he leads me beside quiet waters.
Ps 27.4	I have asked one thing from the LORD; it is what I desire: to dwell in the house of the LORD all the days of my life, gazing on the beauty of the LORD and seeking him in his temple.

The Best Bible?

Jn 3.16		"For God loved the world in this way:^A He gave^B his one and only Son, so that everyone who believes in him will not perish but have eternal life."

fn: ^A Or *created the universe*   ^B Or *For in this way God loved the world, and so he gave,* or *For God so loved the world that he gave*

Divine Name and Titles

Yhwh	Ps 24.1a	The earth and everything in it . . . belong to the **Lord**
adonai	Ps 90.1	**Lord**, you have been our refuge ^C in every generation. fn: ^C Some Hb mss, LXX; other Hb mss read *dwelling place*
elohim	Gn 1.27a	So **God** created man in his own image
adonai Yhwh	Ps 73.28b	I have made the **Lord God** my refuge
adonai elohim	Dn 9.3a	So I turned my attention to the **Lord God**
Yhwh *saba'oth*	1Sa 17.45b	"I come against you in the name of the **Lord of Armies**"
el shaddai	Ex 6.3a	"I appeared to Abraham, Isaac, and Jacob as **God Almighty**"
kyrios	Lk 20.42b	"The **Lord** declared to my **Lord**, 'Sit at my right hand' "
christos	Mt 16.16b	"You are the **Messiah**, the Son of the living God."

New Testament Text Base

Mt 17.21	——— fn: Some mss include v. 21: *"However, this kind does not come out except by prayer and fasting."*
Mt 18.11	——— fn: Some mss include v. 11: *For the Son of Man has come to save the lost.*
Ac 8.37	——— fn: Some mss include v. 37: *Philip said, "If you believe with all your heart you may." And he replied, "I believe that Jesus Christ is the Son of God."*
1Jn 5.7b–8a	——— fn: A few late Gk mss and some late Vg mss add *testify in heaven: the Father, the Word, and the Holy Spirit, and these three are one. 8 And there are three who bear witness on earth:*

Gender Language

ʾādām	Gn 9.6	Whoever sheds **human** blood, by **humans** his blood will be shed, for God made **humans** in his image.
ʾîsh . . . nephesh	Lv 24.17	"If **a man** kills **anyone**, he must be put to death."
ʾāvîw	Pr 15.5a	A fool despises **his father's** discipline
huioi	Mt 5.9	"Blessed are the peacemakers, for they will be called **sons** of God."
anthrōpōn	Mt 4.19	"Follow me, . . . and I will make you fish for [A] **people**." fn: [A] Or *you fishers of*
hekastō . . . autou	Ro 2.6	He will repay **each one** according to **his** works [B] fn: [B] Ps 62:12; Pr 24:12
adelphoi	Gal 5.13	For you were called to be free, **brothers and sisters**; only don't use this freedom as an opportunity [C] for the flesh, but serve one another through love. fn: [C] Lit *a pretext*; a military term for abuse of position
gynaikos anēr	Ti 1.6a	An elder must be blameless, **the husband of** one **wife**, with faithful [D] children fn: [D] Or *believing*
gynaikas	1Ti 3.11	**Wives**,[E] likewise, should be worthy of respect, not slanderers, self-controlled, faithful in everything. fn: [E] Or *Women*

Difficult Renderings

1Sa 13.1	Saul was **thirty years old** [F] when he became king, and he reigned **forty-two years** [G] over Israel.[H] fn: [F] Some LXX mss; MT reads *was one year* [G] Text emended; MT reads *two years* [H] Some LXX mss omit v. 1
Is 28.13	The word of the LORD will come to them: "**Law after law, law after law, line after line, line after line, a little here, a little there**," so they go stumbling backward, to be broken, trapped, and captured.

The Best Bible?

Significant Renderings

ʿalmah	Is 7.14	Therefore, the Lord himself will give you [A] a sign: See, **the virgin** will conceive,[B] have a son, and name him Immanuel.[C]
		fn: [A] In Hb, the word *you* is pl [B] Or *virgin is pregnant, will* [C] = God With Us
sheʾol . . . ʾabaddon	Pr 15.11	**Sheol** and **Abaddon** lie open before the LORD— how much more, human hearts.
egennēsen	Mt 1.2	Abraham **fathered** [D] Isaac, Isaac **fathered** Jacob, Jacob **fathered** Judah and his brothers
		fn: [D] In vv. 2–16 either a son, as here, or a later descendant, as in v. 8
eskēnōsen	Jn 1.14	The Word became flesh and **dwelt** [E] among us. We observed his glory, the glory as the one and only Son [F] from the Father, full of grace and truth.
		fn: [E] Or *and dwelt in a tent*; lit and *tabernacled* [F] *Son* is implied from the reference to the Father and from Gk usage.
tois ioudaiois	Jn 18.36	"My kingdom is not of this world," said Jesus. "If my kingdom were of this world, my servants would fight, so that I wouldn't be handed over **to the Jews**. But as it is,[G] my kingdom is not from here."
		fn: [G] Or *But now*
dikaiosunē theou, pisteōs Iēsou Christou	Ro 3.22a	**The righteousness of God** is through **faith in Jesus Christ** [H] to all who believe
		fn: [H] Or *through the faithfulness of Jesus Christ*
Granville Sharp's rule applied	Ti 2.13	while we wait for the blessed hope, the appearing of the glory of **our great God and Savior, Jesus Christ**.

SIGNIFICANT REVISIONS

The *Holman Christian Standard Bible* (HCSB) has undergone four revisions. The first was published in 2009. The second was released in 2017 after the version was renamed by dropping *"Holman"* (CSB) from its title. A minor revision was published in 2020. Some of its more distinctive features (*e.g.*, brackets for supplied words and bullet references) were dropped in the later editions.

Some changes resulted from the Committee's preference for alternate ways of saying the same thing:

	HCSB (2004)	HCSB (2009)	CSB (2017, 2020)
Gal 3.17	**And I say this:** the law, which came 430 years later, does not **revoke** a covenant that was previously **ratified** by God, [A] **so as to** cancel the promise.	**And I say this:** The law, which came 430 years later, does not **revoke** a covenant that was previously **ratified** by God [A] **and** cancel the promise.	**My point is this:** The law, which came 430 years later, does not **invalidate** a covenant previously **established** by God [A] **and thus** cancel the promise.

fn: [A] Other mss add *in Christ*

Other changes clarify concepts, consider cultural differences, return to previously used or familiar language, make the text more formal and concordant in places, or reconsider the place for text critical decisions.

Changes for clarification

These following samples reveal how later revisions clarified the wording of earlier renderings. For example, the 2009 edition of **Gal 3.8** (see sample below) uses theological terms familiar to seasoned Bible students ("foresaw", "foretold"), but the later editions amended the text to read so that a broader audience can more readily understand it ("saw in advance", "proclaimed . . . ahead of time"). And at **1Pt 3.13**, the HCSB originally rendered the Greek word *zēlōtai* as "passionate," which connotes human lust and passions. Later revisers changed it to better fit both the immediate context and the general use of the word ("deeply committed to," or "devoted to").

The Best Bible?

	HCSB (2004)	HCSB (2009)	CSB (2017, 2020)
Gn 4.1a	**Adam knew** his wife Eve, and she conceived and gave birth to Cain.	**Adam was intimate with** his wife Eve, and she conceived and gave birth to Cain.	**The man was intimate with** his wife Eve, and she conceived and gave birth to Cain.
Php 1.10	so that you **can determine what really matters** and **can** be pure and blameless in[A] the day of Christ	so that you **can approve the things that are superior** and **can** be pure and blameless in[A] the day of Christ	so that you **may approve the things that are superior** and **may** be pure and blameless in the day of Christ

fn: [A] Or *until*

Gal 3.8	Now the Scriptures **foresaw** that God would justify the Gentiles by faith and **foretold** the good news to Abraham, saying, **All the nations will be blessed in you.**[C]	Now the Scripture **saw in advance** that God would justify the Gentiles by faith and **told** the good news **ahead of time** to Abraham, saying, **All the nations will be blessed through you.**[C]	Now the Scripture **saw in advance** that God would justify the Gentiles by faith and **proclaimed** the gospel **ahead of time** to Abraham, saying, **All the nations**[B] **will be blessed through you.**[C]

fn: [C] Gn 12:3; 18:18

fn: [B] Or *Gentiles*
[C] Gn 12:3; 18:18

Heb 5.11b	it's difficult to explain, since you have become **slow** to understand	it's difficult to explain, since you have become **too lazy** to understand	it **is** difficult to explain, since you have become **too lazy** to understand
1Pt 3.13	**And** who will harm[D] you if you are **passionate for** what is good?[E]	**And** who will harm[D] you if you are **deeply committed to** what is good?[E]	Who then will harm you if you are **devoted to** what is good?

fn: [D] Or *will mistreat, or will do evil to* [E] Lit *you are zealots, or you are partisans for the good, or you are eager to do good*

fn: [D] Or *mistreat, or do evil to* [E] Lit *you are partisans for the good; lit you are zealots*

Tt 1.7 contains a curious change in the CSB: The words "manager" and "administrator" are both slightly more concordant choices than "household" (for the Greek word, *oikonomon*),[22] though the later rendering may better convey the intended idea (so NLT). It also removes the notion that God somehow requires personal oversight and care. The second change, "an excessive drinker," broadens the concept to its more general implication—and lengthens the beverage list!

	HCSB (2004)	HCSB (2009)	CSB (2017, 2020)
Tt 1.7	**For** an •overseer, **as** God's **manager**, must be blameless, not arrogant, not quick tempered, not **addicted to wine**, not a bully, not greedy for money	**For** an ˙overseer, **as** God's **administrator**, must be blameless, not arrogant, not hot-tempered, not **addicted to wine**, not a bully, not greedy for money	**As** an overseer of God's **household**, **he** must be blameless, not arrogant, not hot-tempered, not **an excessive drinker**, not a bully, not greedy for money

The change from the semantically overlapping words, "rage" to "fury," in **Ps 59.13** was made so as not to imply that God is ever out of control:[23]

	CSB (2017)	CSB (2020)
Ps 59.13	consume them in **rage**; consume them until they are gone. Then people will know throughout[A] the earth that God rules over Jacob.	consume them in **fury**; consume them until they are gone. Then people will know throughout[A] the earth that God rules over Jacob.
	fn: [A] Lit *know to the ends of*	**fn:** [A] Lit *know to the ends of*

Cultural changes

The following changes were made for predominantly cultural reasons. **1Pt 2.11** was changed from "aliens" to "strangers" due to popular culture's cinematic influence. **Heb 7.8** changed from

The Best Bible?

"tithes" to "tenths" or "a tenth," because the earlier rendering has so many preexisting religious associations that undermine the word's basic meaning. **Tt 1.10** changed from "Judaism," which is the general implication of the underlying Greek words, *tēs peritomēs*, to "circumcision party"—"circumcision", which is an accurate lexical choice, and "party," a paraphrase that indicates the implication. The whole change tries to avoid the justification of anti-semitic attitudes.

	HCSB (2004)	HCSB (2009)	CSB (2017, 2020)
1Pt 2.11	Dear friends, I urge you as **aliens** and **temporary residents** to abstain from **fleshly** desires that war against you.ᴬ	Dear friends, I urge you as **strangers** and **temporary residents** to abstain from **fleshly** desires that war against you.ᴬ	Dear friends, I urge you as **strangers** and **exiles** to abstain from **sinful** desires that **wage** war against the soul.
fn:	ᴬ Lit *against the soul*		
Heb 7.8	In the one case, men who will die receive **tithes**; but in the other case, ⌊Scripture⌋ testifies that he lives.	In the one case, men who will die receive **tenths**, but in the other case, Scripture testifies that he lives.	In the one case, men who will die receive **a tenth**, but in the other case, Scripture testifies that he lives.
Tt 1.10	For there are also many rebellious people, **idle talkers** and **deceivers**, especially those from **Judaism**.ᴮ	For there are also many rebellious people, **full of empty talk** and **deception**, especially those from **Judaism**.ᴮ	For there are many rebellious people, **full of empty talk** and **deception**, especially those from the **circumcision party**.
fn:	ᴮ Lit *the circumcision*		
Jn 11.39	"Remove the stone," Jesus said. Martha, the dead man's sister, told Him, "Lord, **he already stinks. It's been** four days."	"Remove the stone," Jesus said. Martha, the dead man's sister, told Him, "Lord, **he's already decaying. It's been** four days."	"Remove the stone," Jesus said. Martha, the dead man's sister, told him, "Lord, **there is already a stench because he has been dead** four days."

	HCSB (2004)	HCSB (2009)	CSB (2017, 2020)
Tt 2.5	to be **sensible**, pure, **good homemakers**, and submissive to their husbands, so that God's **message** will not be slandered.	to be **self-controlled**, pure, **homemakers**, kind, and submissive to their husbands, so that God's **message** will not be slandered.	to be **self-controlled**, pure, **workers at home**, kind, and in submission to their husbands, so that God's **word** will not be slandered.

Formal changes

1Pt 2.2 was changed from "spiritual" to "of the word" to make it correspond more formally with its Greek source.

	HCSB (2004)	HCSB (2009)	CSB (2020)
1Pt 2.2	Life newborn infants, desire the **unadulterated spiritual** milk, so that you may grow **by it in** ⌐your⌐ salvation,[A] fn: [A] Other mss omit *in your salvation*	Like newborn infants, desire the **pure spiritual** milk, so that you may grow **by it for** your salvation,[A] fn: [A] Other mss omit *in your salvation*	Like newborn infants, desire the **pure** milk **of the word**, so that **by it** you may grow **up into** your salvation,
Heb 6.19	We have this ⌐hope⌐—**like a sure and firm** anchor of the soul—**that** enters the inner sanctuary behind the curtain.	We have this hope **as an** anchor **for our lives, safe and secure. It** enters the inner sanctuary behind the curtain.	We have this hope **as** an anchor **for the soul, firm and secure. It** enters the inner sanctuary behind the curtain.

Some formal changes improve the clarity of the passage:

	CSB (2017)	CSB (2020)
Mt 18.15	"If your brother sins against you,[A] go **and rebuke him in private**.[B] If he listens to you, you have won your brother.	"If your brother sins against you,[A] go **tell him his fault, between you and him alone**. If he listens to you, you have won your brother."
	fn: [A] Other mss omit *against you* [B] Lit *him between you and him alone*	**fn:** [A] Other mss omit *against you*

Functional changes

In **Eph 3.12** the first edition (2009) translated the Greek prepositional phrase, *en pepoithēsei*, as a noun ("and confidence"), but later editions translated it as a modifer ("confident") to another noun ("access").

Eph 3.12	in **whom** we have boldness, **access, and confidence** through faith in Him.[C]	In **Him** we have boldness **and confident access** through faith in Him.[C]	In **him** we have boldness **and confident access** through faith in him.[C]
	fn: [C] Or *through His faithfulness*		**fn:** [C] Or *through his faithfulness*

In **3Jn 5**, the CSB changes the noun from an accusative of direct object ("faith," "faithfulness") into an adverbial accusative ("faithfully").

	HCSB (2004)	HCSB (2009)	CSB (2017)
3Jn 5	Dear friends,[D] you are **showing your faith**[E] by whatever you do for the brothers, **and this ⌊you are doing⌋ for** strangers	Dear friend,[D] you are **showing faithfulness**[E] by whatever you do for the brothers, **especially when they are** strangers.	Dear friend, you are **acting faithfully** in whatever you do for the brothers **and sisters, especially when they are** strangers.
	fn: [D] Or *Beloved* [E] Lit *are doing faith*	**fn:** [D] Or *Beloved* [E] Lit *are doing a faithful thing*	

In **Eph 2.2**, we can see debate over the phrasing of the Greek clause, *tēs exousias tou aeros* ("of the power of the air"), unfold before our very eyes!

	HCSB (2004)	HCSB (2009)	CSB (2020)
Eph 2.2	in which you previously •**walked** according to **this worldly age**, according to the ruler **of the atmospheric domain**,[A] the spirit now working in the disobedient.[B]	in which you previously •**walked** according to **the ways of this world**, according to the ruler **who exercises authority over the lower heavens**,[A] the spirit now working in the disobedient.[B]	in which you previously **walked** according to **the ways of this world**, according to the ruler **of the power of the air**, the spirit now working in the disobedient.[B]
	fn: [A] Lit *ruler of the authority of the air* [B] Lit *sons of disobedience*	**fn:** [A] Lit *ruler of the domain of the air* [B] Lit *sons of disobedience*	**fn:** [B] Lit *sons of disobedience*

The following change in **Lv 1.9** is less formal, but it makes it clear what kind of offering it is. (*I.e.*, it's *not* some Zoroastrian fire offering.)

	CSB (2017)	CSB (2020)
Lv 1.9b	Then the priest will burn all of it on the altar as a burnt offering, a **fire offering**, a pleasing aroma to the LORD.	Then the priest will burn all of it on the altar as a burnt offering, a **food offering**, a pleasing aroma to the LORD.
Jn 2.4	"What **does that have** to do with **you and** me,[C] woman?" Jesus asked. "My hour has not yet come."	"What **has this concern of yours** to do with me,[C] woman?" Jesus asked. "My hour has not yet come."
	fn: [C] Or *"You and I see things differently;* lit *"What to me and to you;* Mt 8:29; Mk 1:24; 5:7; Lk 8:28	**fn:** [C] Or *"What does that have to do with you and me;* lit *"What to me and to you;* Mt 8:29; Mk 1:24; 5:7; Lk 8:28

Lexical Correspondence

The wording "self-made religion" in **Col 2.22–23** and "distort" in **Gal 1.7** was decided in the CSB to make the passage conform to the standard lexical reference.[24]

	HCSB (2004)	HCSB (2009)	CSB (2017, 2020)
Col 2.22–23	²²All these ⌊regulations⌋ refer to what is **destroyed** by being used up; they are **human** commands and doctrines. ²³Athough these have a reputation of wisdom by promoting **ascetic practices**, humility, and severe treatment of the body, they are not of any value **against fleshly** indulgence.	²²All these regulations refer to what is **destroyed** by being used up; they are commands and doctrines **of men**. ²³Although these have a reputation of wisdom by promoting **ascetic practices**, humility, and severe treatment of the body, they are not of any value **in curbing self**-indulgence.ᴬ	²²All these regulations refer to what is **destined to perish** by being used up; they are **human** commands and doctrines. ²³Although these have a reputation for wisdom by promoting **self-made religion**, **false** humility, and severe treatment of the body, they are not of any value **in curbing self**-indulgence.ᴬ
		fn: ᴬ Lit *value against indulgence of the flesh*	
Gal 1.7	not that there is another ⌊gospel⌋, but there are some who are troubling you and want to **change the gospel of Christ**.	not that there is another gospel, but there are some who are troubling you and want to **change the good news**ᴮ **about the ·Messiah**.	not that there is another gospel, but there are some who are troubling you and want to **distort the gospel of Christ**.
		fn: ᴮ Or *gospel*	

Paraphrase

In **1 Jn 3.17**, the Committee decided on "a fellow believer" against "his brother," perhaps to make the text more inclusive in its application.

	HCSB (2004)	HCSB (2009)	CSB (2017)
1 Jn 3.17	If anyone has this world's goods and sees **his brother** in need but **shuts off his compassion from him**— how can God's love reside in him?	If anyone has this world's goods and sees **his brother** in need but **closes his eyes to his need**— how can God's love reside in him?	If anyone has this world's goods and sees **a fellow believer**[A] in need but **withholds compassion from him**— how does God's love reside in him?
			fn: [A] Lit *sees his brother or sister*

Fine-tuning

These examples demonstrate where the CSB returns to the wording of an earlier edition of the HCSB or to an older translation of the Bible. For example, the CSB's rendering of **Is 53.10** ("guilt offering") is a reversion to language familiar to readers of the earlier NIV'84, NASB, and ESV, while **Gal 1.7** in the CSB reverts back to the first edition of the HCSB.

	HCSB (2004)	HCSB (2009)	CSB (2017, 2020)
Is 53.10	Yet the LORD was pleased to crush Him, **and He made Him sick.** When[C] You make Him a •**restitution** offering, He will see ⌊His⌋ •seed, He will prolong His days, and the **will of the LORD will succeed** by His hand.	Yet the LORD was pleased to crush Him **severely.**[B] When[C] You make Him a •**restitution** offering, He will see His •seed, He will prolong His days, and by His hand, the **LORD's pleasure will be accomplished.**	Yet the LORD was pleased to crush him **severely.**[B] When[C] you make him a **guilt** offering, he will see his seed, he will prolong his days, and by his hand, the **LORD's pleasure will be accomplished.**
	fn: [B] Or *If*	**fn:** [B] Or *Him; He made Him sick.* [C] Or *If*	**fn:** [B] Or *him; he made him sick.* [C] Or *If*

CSB

	HCSB (2004)	HCSB (2009)	CSB (2020)
Gal 1.15–16a	But when God, who from my **mother's womb** set me apart and called me by His grace, was pleased ¹⁶ to reveal His Son in me	But when God, who from my **birth** set me apart and called me by His grace, was pleased ¹⁶ to reveal His Son in me	But when God, who from my **mother's womb** set me apart and called me by his grace, was pleased ¹⁶ to reveal his Son in me
Gal 6.17	From now on, let no one cause me trouble, because I **carry** the **marks** of Jesus on my body.	From now on, let no one cause me trouble, because I **bear** on my body **scars for the cause** of Jesus.	From now on, let no one cause me trouble, because I **bear** on my body **the marks** of Jesus.

	HCSB (2004)	HCSB (2009)
	Then I said, "See, **I have come**—it is written about Me in **the volume of** the scroll—to do Your will, O God!" ᴬ	Then I said, "See— it is written about Me in **the volume of** the scroll—**I have come** to do Your will, God!" ᴬ

Heb 10.7	CSB (2017)	CSB (2020)
	Then I said, "See— it is written about me in the scroll—**I have come** to do your will, O God." ᴬ	Then I said, "See— it is written about me in the scroll—**I have come** to do your will, God." ᴬ

fn: ᴬ Ps 40:6–8

In **Col 2.20**, the supplied word "forces" was removed from "elements" (*tōn stoicheiōn*), which conforms to the standard lexical gloss,²⁵ and the title "Christ" was reverted back from "Messiah" as it is in the first edition.

In the case of **Mk 14.3**, the words *tou leprou* which describe the condition of Jesus' host, Simon, were initially paraphrased as "who had a serious skin disease" (HCSB). This is for two likely reasons: (1) to explain what his condition was, since a more formal rendering might obscure the likely nature of his disease,²⁶ and (2) to dissociate the person's identity from his disease, as the NLT does. The reversion to "the leper" is a formal change that appeals to those already familiar with word and its concept.

	HCSB (2004)	HCSB (2009)	CSB (2017, 2020)
Col 2.20	If you died with **Christ** to the elemental **forces** of this world, why do you live as if you still belonged to the world? Why do you submit to regulations:	If you died with the **Messiah** to the elemental **forces** of this world, why do you live as if you still belonged to the world? Why do you submit to regulations:	If you died with **Christ** to the elements of this world, why do you live as if you still belonged to the world? Why do you submit to regulations:
Ps 146.9	The LORD protects **foreigners** and helps the fatherless and the widow, but He frustrates the ways of the wicked.	The LORD protects **foreigners** and helps the fatherless and the widow, but He frustrates the ways of the wicked.	The LORD protects **resident aliens** and helps the fatherless and the widow, but he frustrates the ways of the wicked.

	HCSB (2004, 2009)	CSB (2020)
Mt 18.21	Then Peter **came to** Him and **said**, "Lord, how many times **could** my brother sin against me **and I forgive him**? As many as seven times?"	Then Peter **approached** him and **asked**, "Lord, how many times **must I forgive** my brother **or sister who** sins against me? As many as seven times?"

	HCSB (2004, 2009)	CSB (2017, 2020)
Mk 14.3 (cf. 1.40, 42; Mt 8.2–3; 10.8; 26.6; Lk 4.27; 7.22; 17.12)	While He was in Bethany at the house of Simon **who had a serious skin disease**, as He was reclining at the table, a woman came with an alabaster jar of pure **and** expensive **fragrant oil** of nard. She broke the jar and poured it on His head.	While he was in Bethany at the house of Simon **the leper**,[A] as he was reclining at the table, a woman came with an alabaster jar of **very** expensive **perfume** of pure nard. She broke the jar and poured it on his head.
		fn: [A] Gk *lepros*; a term for various skin diseases; see Lv 13–14

The Best Bible?

	HCSB (2009)	CSB (2017)	CSB (2020)
Ro 3.25	God presented Him as **a propitiation**[A] **through faith in** His blood, to demonstrate His righteousness, because in His restraint God passed over the sins previously committed.	God presented him as **an atoning sacrifice**[A] **in** his blood, **received through faith,** to demonstrate his righteousness, because in his restraint God passed over the sins previously committed.	God presented him as **the mercy seat**[A] **by** his blood, **through faith,** to demonstrate his righteousness, because in his restraint God passed over the sins previously committed.
	fn: [A] Or *as a propitiatory sacrifice,* or *as an offering of atonement,* or *as a mercy seat*; 2Co 5:21; Heb 9:5	**fn:** [A] Or *a propitiation,* or *a place of atonement*	**fn:** [A] Or *propitiation,* or *place of atonement*
Eph 2.2	in which you previously ˙**walked** according to the ways of this world, according to the ruler **who exercises authority over the lower heavens,**[B] the spirit now working in the disobedient.[C]	in which you previously **lived** according to the ways of this world, according to the ruler **of the power of the air,** the spirit now working in the disobedient.[C]	in which you previously **walked** according to the ways of this world, according to the ruler **of the power of the air,** the spirit now working in the disobedient.[C]
	fn: [B] Lit *ruler of the domain of the air* [C] Lit *sons of disobedience*	**fn:** [C] Lit *sons of disobedience*	

	CSB (2017)	CSB (2020)
Gn 37.3	Now Israel loved Joseph more than his other sons because Joseph was a son born to him in his old age, and he made a **robe of many colors**[D] for him.	Now Israel loved Joseph more than his other sons because Joseph was a son born to him in his old age, and he made a **long-sleeved robe**[D] for him.
	fn: [D] Or *robe with long sleeves;* see 2Sm 13:18,19	**fn:** [D] Or *an ornate robe;* see 2Sm 13:18,19

Christian Standard Bible 413

Text-critical changes

On occasion, the Committee made changes based on the later judgments of text critics. For example, **Jude 5** changed a word from "Lord" to "Jesus."

	HCSB (2004)	HCSB (2009)	CSB (2017)
Jude 5	Now I want to remind you, though you know all these things: **the Lord, having first of all**[B] saved a people out of Egypt, later destroyed those who did not believe	Now I want to remind you, though you know all these things: **The Lord**[A] **first**[B] saved a people out of Egypt and later destroyed those who did not believe	Now I want to remind you, **although** you **came to** know all these things **once and for all, that Jesus**[A] saved a people out of Egypt and later destroyed those who did not believe
	fn: [B] Other mss place *first of all* after *remind you*	**fn:** [A] Other mss read *Jesus/Joshua, God,* or *God Christ* [B] Other mss place *first* after *remind you*	**fn:** [A] Other mss read *the Lord,* or *God*

Where the HCSB bracketed **Ac 8.37**, the CSB moved the passage out of the main text and into the footnotes

	HCSB (2004, 2009)	CSB (2017)
Ac 8.36–37	The eunuch said, "Look, there's water! What would keep me from being baptized?" [[37] And Philip said, "If you believe with all your heart you may." And he replied, "I believe that Jesus Christ is the Son of God."][C]	The eunuch said, "Look, there's water! What would keep me from being baptized?"[C]
	fn: [C] Other mss omit bracketed text	**fn:** [C] Some mss include v. 37: *Philip said, "If you believe with all your heart you may." And he replied, "I believe that Jesus Christ is the Son of God."*

The Best Bible?

CSB

Regarding disputed passages or portions with textual bases deemed inadequate, the CSB gives more explanation than the HCSB.

	HCSB (2004, 2009)	CSB (2017)
Mk 16.9–20		[Some of the earliest ms conclude with 16:8]
	[⁹ Early on the first day of the week . . . ²⁰ . . . and confirmed the word by the accompanying signs.]^A	
	fn: ^A**16:9–20** Other mss omit bracketed text	fn: ^A**16:8** Other mss include vv. 9–20 as a longer ending. The following shorter ending is found in some mss between v. 8 and v. 9 and in one ms after v. 8 (each of which omits vv. 9–20): *And all that had been commanded to them they quickly reported to those around Peter. After these things, Jesus himself sent out through them from east to west, the holy and imperishable proclamation of eternal salvation. Amen.*

UNIQUE RENDERINGS

The [H]CSB is intended to communicate to a broad audience in a familiar register. Its greatest strength is its clarity of expression. Though, on rare occasion, its language may sound a bit too familiar.

	HCSB (2004, 2009)	CSB (2017, 2020)
1Kg 18.24	"Then you call on the name of your god, and I will call on the name of the Yahweh. The God who answers with fire, he is God." All the people answered, "That **sounds good**."	"Then you call on the name of your god, and I will call on the name of the LORD. The God who answers with fire, he is God." All the people answered, "That**'s fine**."

| 1Sa 10.27 | But some wicked men said, "How can this guy save us?" They |
| (cf. 1Kg 22.27; 2Ch 18.26) | despised him and did not bring him a gift, but Saul said nothing. |

ENDORSEMENTS

The CSB is endorsed by noted evangelical ministry leaders and professors, including Daniel Aiken (president, Southeastern Baptist Theological Seminary), Alistair Begg (author, speaker), David Dockery (president, Trinity International Univsersity), Tony Evans (pastor, author), David Platt (pastor, author, former president of the International Missions Board), and Robert L. Plummer (professor at Southern Baptist Theological Seminary), among many others.

The Southern Baptist Convention (SBC) publicly acknowledged the CSB's predecessor (the HCSB) in a 2004 press release in which they commend their publisher, LifeWay Christian Resources, for commissioning the translation.[27] Indeed, the curriculum that LifeWay publishes for the SBC is largely developed around the CSB.[28]

The CSB Review Committee under the Translation Evaluation Committee of the Wisconsin Evangelical Lutheran Synod found they could "recommend the CSB for reading, preaching, and teaching" in the church.[29]

COPYRIGHT

You may quote up to 1,000 verses from the CSB in any form without prior written permission; the verses may not constitute a complete book of the Bible; they must comprise less than 50% of your work's content; and your work must include the following copyright acknowledgment.

Unless otherwise noted, all Scripture quotations are taken from the *Christian Standard Bible*®, Copyright © 2017 by Holman Bible Publishers. Used by permission. *Christian Standard Bible®* and CSB® are federally registered trademarks of Holman Bible Publishers.

Unless used exclusively, follow citations with the designation (CSB). For example:

Jn 1.4, "In him was life, and that life was the light of men." (CSB)

The titles *"Holman Christian Standard Bible®"* and *"Christian Standard Bible®"* and their initialisms (HCSB®, *Holman* CSB®, CSB®) are registered trademarks with the U.S. Patent and Trademark Office by LifeWay Christian Resources of the Southern Baptist Convention, but their logomarks (the HCSB's "Sword and Shield" logo and the CSB's "True North" logo without their initialisms) are not.

For permissions not covered here, write to Holman Bible Publishers, One LifeWay Plaza, Nashville, TN 37234.

ENDNOTES FOR THE CHRISTIAN STANDARD BIBLE

1 E. Ray Clendenen and David K. Stabnow, *The* HCSB: *Navigating the Horizons in Bible Translation* (Nashville, TN: B&H Publishing Group, 2012), pp. 13–17.

2 Andy Cheung, "College Interview (Ed Blum)," *King's Evangelical Divinity School* (February 2008), accessed May 2, 2019, https://www.kingsdivinity.org /theological-articles/121-college-interview-ed-blum.

3 The CSB 2017 revision made around 34,000 changes to the text of the 2009 HCSB.

4 CSB Translation Oversight Committee, *Christian Standard Bible: Text Revisions* (January 2020), accessed October 30, 2020, https://csbible.com/wp-content /uploads/2020/05/CSBTextRevisions2020.pdf.

5 "Introduction to the *Christian Standard Bible*," *Holy Bible: Christian Standard Bible* (Nashville, TN: Holman Bible Publishers, 2017).

6 *Ibid.*

7 *Ibid.*

8 *Ibid.*

9 Ken Walker, "*Holman Christian Standard Bible* New Testament now available," *Baptist Press* (July 20, 2001), accessed June 3, 2019, http://www.bpnews.net/11363 /holman-christian-standard-bible-new-testament-now-available.

10 "HCSB Translation Team," the CSB's website, accessed October 2, 2014, http:// hcsb.org/pages/hcsbpages/aboutus.aspx.

11 "FAQ," the Christian Standard Bible website, accessed November 19, 2020, https://csbible.com/about-the-csb/faqs/#faq/what-denominations -were-involved-in-creating-the-christian-standard-bible

12 Will Lee, "Interview with Dr. Ed Blum, General Editor for the HCSB," *Anworth*, last modified December 19, 2007, accessed December 10, 2010, https://anwoth .wordpress.com/2007/12/19/interview-with-dr-ed-blum-general-editor -for-the-hcsb/.

13 "*Holman Christian Standard Bible*: Original Translation Team" and "*Christian Standard Bible*: Translation and Review Team," the CSB's website, accessed November 19, 2020, https://csbible.com/wp-content/uploads/2016/08 /TranslationTeam_HCSB-CSB-1.pdf.

14 Clendenen and Stabnow, *The* HCSB (2017), p. 19.

"History of the CSB," the CSB's website, accessed November 19, 2020, https://csbible .com/about-the-csb/history-of-the-csb/.

15 Q&A: Translation Decisions for the *Christian Standard Bible*," the CSB's website, accessed November 19, 2020, https://csbible.com/about-the-csb/history-of-the-csb/.

16 There were, in fact, principles in place:

"Although the HCSB usually follows the traditional 'the LORD,' whenever God's name is particularly relevant in the context it uses 'Yahweh.' About 200 times this involves explicit reference to His "name," as in the following verses": **Ex 15.3; Dt 28.58; Ps 83.18; Is 42.8; 54.5; Ho 12.5.**

"'Yahweh' is found where [he is] distinguished from any other god": **Gn 14.22; Ex 4.22; 12.12; 18.11; Jos 24.15; Jg 10.6.**

"Other passages using 'Yahweh' are those that contain the phrase 'I am Yahweh' and those that deal with God's covenant with Israel": **Dt 7.9; Ne 1.5.**

Clendenen and Stabnow, *The HCSB . . .* , pp. 97–99.

17 "Q&A," accessed November 19, 2020;

Mark L. Strauss, "A Review of the *Christian Standard Bible*," *Themelios*, vol. 44, no. 2, (August 2019), p. 263.

18 "Introduction to the *Holman Christian Standard Bible*," *Holy Bible: The Old and New Testaments. Holman Christian Standard Bible* (Nashville, TN: Holman Bible Publishers, 2019);

"HCSB Bullet Notes: Messiah," *Ibid.*

19 "FAQ," accessed November 19, 2020.

20 "Q&A," accessed November 19, 2020.

21 The two footnotes at **2Pt 3.10** in the 2009, '17, and '20 editions give more information than its target audience likely knows what to do with: "Other mss read *will be burned up*" and "Some Syriac and Coptic mss read *will not be found*"

The one at **Jn 1.18** reads with little explanation, "Other mss read *The one and only Son, who is at the Father's side.*"

22 Compare the CSB's use of the words "overseer of God's household" (*ton episkopon . . . oikonomos theou*) here in **Tt 1.7** with Paul's words in **1Co 4.1–2**, "A person should think of us in this way: as servants of Christ and managers (*oikonomous*) of the mysteries of God. In this regard, it is required that managers (*en tois oikonomois*) be found faithful" (CSB). Thanks to Dr. A. Andrew Das for pointing out the justification of rendering in Tt based on the commen-

tary of Luke Timothy Johnson's *Letters to Paul's Delegates: 1 Timothy, 2 Timothy, Titus,* in *The New Testament in Context* series (Valley Forge, PA: Trinity Press International, 1996), p. 224.

23 "Improvements to the *Christian Standard Bible,*" the CSB's website, accessed November 23, 2020, https://csbible.com/wp-content/uploads/2020/01/CSB-Improvements-2020-v3.pdf.

24 Walter Bauer, Frederick W. Danker, William F. Arndt, F. Wilber Gingrich, *A Greek-English Lexicon of the New Testament and Other Early Christian Literature,* rev. ed. (Chicago, IL: University of Chicago Press, 2000), s.vv. ἐθελοθρησκία, μεταστρέφω.

25 *Ibid.,* s.v. στοιχεῖον.

26 Clendenen and Stabnow, *The HCSB . . .* , pp. 102–105.

27 Southern Baptist Convention, "On the *Holman Christian Standard Bible*" (Indianapolis, IN: 2004), accessed February 3, 2020, http://www.sbc.net/resolutions/1140/on-the-holman-christian-standard-bible .

28 LifeWay Christian Resources, "Bible Studies," accessed February 3, 2020, https://www.lifeway.com/en/shop/bible-studies.

29 Wisconsin Evangelical Lutheran Synod, *Book of Reports and Memorials.* (Waukesha, WI: May 2019), pp. 7–8, accessed February 3, 2020, http://www.sew-wels.net/home/180019805/180019805/docs/BoRaM%202019.pdf.

New Living Translation®

Holy Bible, New Living Translation

Produced by Tyndale House Publishers, 1996–2015

FORMAL / FUNCTIONAL TENDENCIES

FORMAL   FUNCTIONAL

Interlinear NASB KJV NKJV ESV CSB NRSV NET NIV TNIV **N L T** NIrV MSG Free Paraphrase

TEXT BASES

English Base *The Living Bible* (1971).

OT Masoretic Hebrew and Ancient Versions.   **NT** Eclectic Greek.

TRANSLATION TIMELINE

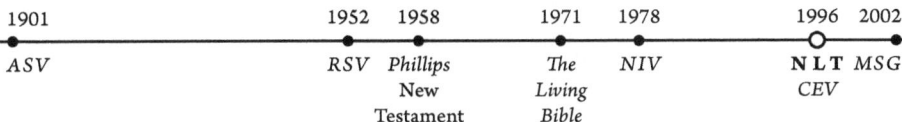

1901	1952	1958	1971	1978	1996	2002
ASV	*RSV*	*Phillips New Testament*	*The Living Bible*	*NIV*	*N L T CEV*	*MSG*

CONTEMPORARY EVENTS

1963	1971	1996	2001	2008
Billy Graham's 156th crusade in Los Angeles, CA	Billy Graham's 209th crusade in Oakland, CA		September 11 attack on New York	U.S. "Emergency Economic Stabilization" Act signed

PUBLICATION TIMELINE

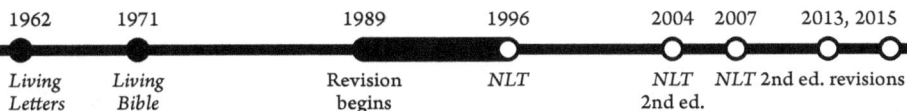

1962	1971	1989	1996	2004	2007	2013, 2015
Living Letters	*Living Bible*	*Revision begins*	*NLT*	*NLT 2nd ed.*	*NLT 2nd ed. revisions*	

Holy Bible

NEW LIVING
TRANSLATION
™

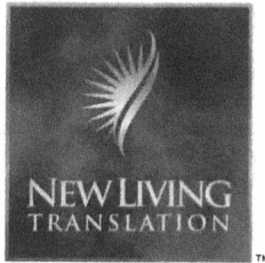

Tyndale House Publishers, Inc.
WHEATON, ILLINOIS

Kenneth N. Taylor produced a popular paraphrase called *The Living Bible* (1971) based on the *American Standard Version* (1901). It received glowing endorsements from eminent Christian ministers, like Billy Graham, and it went on to receive great popular and financial success. The profits from Taylor's work funded the expansion of his ministries and publishing company, Tyndale House. When Ken Taylor retired, he passed the responsibility of Tyndale over to his son, Mark.

In 1986, Mark D. Taylor and Ronald A. Beers (who would become Tyndale's Editor-in-Chief) discussed how they might make *The Living Bible* more acceptable to pastors. They agreed that an independent board of seminary professors and Bible scholars ought to revise *The Living Bible*. So in 1987, Tyndale House held a conference with several professors and formed a Bible Translation Committee consisting of six General Reviewers (later called Senior Translators).

Work began in earnest in 1989. At first, the translators set themselves to correct *The Living Bible* to make it more accurate. As work progressed, they realized that the revision demanded more translation work in order to make it correspond more closely to the original languages. So, they labored to translate the bulk of the Bible anew.

The result was the *New Living Translation* (NLT®), published in 1996. This edition was well received, but the translators felt that there was more they could do to improve it. A second revised edition (NLTse) was issued later in 2004. Minor revisions followed in 2007, 2013, and again in 2015.

STATED TRANSLATION IDEALS

"The translators of the *New Living Translation* set out to render the message of the original texts of Scripture into clear, contemporary English. As they did so, they kept the concerns of both formal-equivalence and dynamic-equivalence in mind. On the one hand, they translated as simply and literally as possible when that approach yielded an accurate, clear, and natural English text. . . .

"On the other hand, [they] rendered the message more dynamically when the literal rendering was hard to understand, was misleading, or yielded archaic or foreign wording. They clarified difficult metaphors and terms to aid in the reader's understanding. . . . Their goal was to be both faithful to the ancient texts and eminently readable. The [intended] result is a translation that is both exegetically accurate and idiomatically powerful."[1]

METHOD

Initially, the six General Reviewers intended to revise *The Living Bible* (TLB) while plans were laid for a new, state-of-the-art, functional translation. The plan was to sell the revised TLB alongside the new translation, but the revisions demanded more work than the Reviewers anticipated.

Each of the Reviewers (later known as the Senior Translators on the Bible Translation Committee) were responsible for one of six major portions of the Bible. Each Translator was tasked to recruit at least three other respected scholars for each book or sub-section of the Bible—scholars who had proven competence in those books. Every invitation the Translators sent out was accepted, and over nintey other scholars were added to the translation team.

The Senior Translators would revise or re-translate their portions of *The Living Bible*, and send initial drafts to the groups of scholars assigned to those books or sub-sections, and await their responses. The Translators would then evaluate the scholars' feedback. If two out of three in a group agreed to a change, the Translator was bound to accept it (though he could suggest a different wording).[2]

Then the Translator would work with members of a general review committee (which might include stylists, translators, and editors), who would rate the translation for its accuracy and clarity. He would then send his results back to the scholars for more feedback. This process of feedback and revision might happen a few more times until the Translator was content to move the work on from their little book committee to a final editorial committee. The members of the final editorial committee, who decided the final translation, included the Executive Director, Chief and Senior Stylists, the NT and OT Coordinating Editors, the six Senior Translators, and a Special Reviewer.

The translators generally followed the functional (dynamic-equivalent, thought-for-thought) approach to translation (though sometimes they rendered passages formally, if they did not require special work for the passage to make sense or if certain expressions were generally familiar to their target reader, *e.g.,* **Ac 13.22b**).

The revised (rather re-translated) *Living Bible* was completed in 1996 and sold as the *New Living Translation* (NLT). After eight more years of work, a revised *New Living Translation* second edition (NLTse) was released in 2004. The second edition embodied the Bible Translation Committee's original plan for a new functional translation, though with special attention paid to make the text more formally concordant where it did not hurt its readability.

TEXT BASES

English Text

The NLT is a complete and thorough revision of the *The Living Bible* (1971), which was itself a paraphrase of the *American Standard Version* (1901). The work is so extensive, that the majority of the NLT should be considered a fresh translation instead of a revision.

New Testament

Eclectic Greek text. *Greek New Testament* 4th revised edition (United Bible Societies, 1993), Nestle-Aland *Novum Tes-*

tamentum Graece 27th edition (Stuttgart: Deutsche Bibelge-sellschaft, 1993).

Old Testament

Masoretic Hebrew-Aramaic text. *Biblia Hebraica Stuttgarten-sia* 1st edition (New York: American Bible Society, 1967–77).

Ancient versions. Dead Sea Scrolls (DSS), Septuagint and other Greek manuscripts, Samaritan Pentateuch (Hebrew), Peshitta (Syriac), Vulgate (Latin), *et al.*

CONTRIBUTORS

Mark D. Taylor served as the chief stylist; Daniel W. Taylor, the senior stylist; Ronald A. Beers, the executive director and stylist. The general translators were Barry J. Beitzel (NKJV), Daniel I. Block (ESV), Norman R. Ericson, Tremper Longman III (NCV, HCSB, *The Message,* CEB), Douglas Moo (NIV), Grant R. Osborne, and John N. Oswalt (NIV, *The Message,* ESV). Mark R. Norton served as the managing editor and the coordinating editor for the Old Testament; Philip W. Comfort was the coordinating editor for the New Testament and Apocrypha/Deuterocanon.

Among the many prominent translators and revisers were Craig L. Blomberg (NIV, ESV, HCSB), Darrell L. Bock (*The Message,* ESV), Paul R. House (HCSB, *The Message,* ESV), Eugene H. Merrill (NASB, NKJV, NET), Allen P. Ross (ESV, NKJV, NET), and Thomas R. Schreiner ([H]CSB, ESV).

Special reviewers included Kenneth N. Taylor (*The Living Bible*) and F. F. Bruce.

In all, nearly 100 professors and scholars contributed to the *New Living Translation* and its subsequent revisions.

For a complete list of translators, visit *booklink.id/ nlt-translator*

THEOLOGICAL ASSUMPTIONS

All contributers to the *New Living Translation* were conservative evangelical theologians and scholars.

FEATURES

"For the sake of clarity, [the editors] have maintained lexical consistency in areas such as divine names, synoptic passages, rhetorical structures, and non-theological technical terms (*i.e.*, liturgical, cultic, zoological, botanical, cultural, and legal terms)." For theological terms, they allowed for a broader semantic range of acceptable English words or phrases for a single Hebrew or Greek word. "For example, [they] avoided using words such as 'justification' and 'sanctification'. In place of these words[, they gave] renderings such as 'we are made right with God' and 'we are made holy.'"[3]

The editors tried to use a single spelling for any one individual, even for those who go by different names. For example, to clearly distinguish the identity of Kings Joash or Jehoash of Israel or Judah, the Israelite king is consistently rendered Jehoash, while the king of Judah goes by Joash. When a biblical writer had an apparent theological reason for recording a variant name (e.g., Eshbaal/Ishbosheth), the different name is explained in the footnotes.[4]

"For the names of Jacob and Israel, which are used interchangeably for both the individual patriarch and the nation, [the editors] generally render it 'Israel' when it refers to the nation and 'Jacob' when it refers to the individual." Where they render a name that differs from the source text, they indicate the difference with a footnote.[5]

In some cases, the editors use the transliteration, "'Yahweh', when the personal character of the name is used to contrast another divine name or the name of some other god (e.g., **Ex 3.15; 6.2–3**)."

In NT narrative (*i.e.*, Gospels and Acts) "the Greek word *christos* has normally been translated as 'Messiah' when the context assumes a Jewish audience. When a Gentile audience [is] assumed (which is consistently the case in the Epistles and Revelation), *christos* has been translated as 'Christ'."

The editors expressed ancient weights and measures with recognizable contemporary equivalents. They converted them to modern English (*i.e.*, American) equivalents. They expressed ancient currency values generally, in terms of weights in precious metals. For example, the "two denarii" in **Lk 10.35** becomes

> "The next day he handed the innkeeper **two silver coins**, telling him, 'Take care of this man. If his bill runs higher than this, I'll pay you the next time I'm here.' "

The NLT rendered literal Hebrew or Greek measures, along with their metric equivalents or currency values in the footnotes.

Ancient Hebrew months are rendered with their closest modern equivalent. Specific times of day are rendered according to our "Standard Time" system. "On occasion, translations such as 'at dawn the next morning' or 'as the sun began to set' have been used when the biblical reference is general."

Words often translated "city" or "mountain" often don't match modern notions, so they are better translated as "towns" and "villages" or "hill".

The NLT often translates place names that are transliterated in other versions. In these cases, the editors give the traditional transliteration in a footnote. For example, the name usually transliterated "Havvoth-jair" in **Jg 10.4** has been translated "the Towns of Jair," with a footnote that gives the traditional transliteration: "Hebrew *Havvoth-jair*."

The Greek words *hoi Ioudaioi* are formally translated "the Jews" in many English translations. But in the Gospel of John this doesn't always refer to the Jewish people in general. In some contexts, it refers more particularly to the Jewish religious leaders. The NLT tries to reflect this by using terms such as "the people" or "the Jewish leaders" where the editors thought appropriate.[6] For example:

The Best Bible?

Jn 6.41	Then the people ᵃ began to murmur in disagreement because he had said, "I am the bread that came down from heaven." **Footnote:** *a* Greek *Jewish people*; also in 6:52.

The editors sought to preserve the ancient context while making the translation clear to modern readers, who tend "to read male-oriented language as applying only to males." So, they usually render the Greek word *adelphoi* as "brothers and sisters".

In many instances the editors used plural pronouns ("they", "them") in place of the generic masculine singular ("he", "him"), where the text applies to people or to the human condition in general. Sometimes, they even replace generic, third-person pronouns with second person pronouns ("you"). (*Cf.* **Pr 22.6; Pr 26.27**) Yet, "all masculine nouns and pronouns used to represent God (*e.g.*, 'Father') have been maintained without exception."[7]

The first edition of the NLT (1996) only formatted the Psalms and portions the text explicitly identified as poetry and song as poetic verse. Books, like Proverbs and Lamentations, were set in prose even though they fit the poetic genre. This changed with the second edition (2004) and later: Any content that the editors considered poetic is rendered in English poetic form (e.g. **Ecc 10** or the book of **Lamentations**). Wherever possible, they tried to represent Hebrew parallel phrases in natural poetic English.

Where OT passages are clearly quoted in the NT a footnote, a footnote indicates the OT reference.

Where the NT clearly quotes the Septuagint (LXX), and these quotes significantly differ from the Hebrew, the editors also place footnotes at the OT locations. These notes include renderings of the LXX with cross-references to the NT passages where they are cited. (*E.g.,* **Ps 8.2; 53.3; Pr 3.12**)

The editors indicated in footnotes where they chose variant readings that differ from their Hebrew or Greek text base. They also footnoted cases where their text omits entire verses that are included in the *Textus Receptus* (TR). In these cases, the editors offer translations of the traditional text in the footnotes.

When the meanings or wordplays of proper names help readers understand the text, they are clarified in the footnotes. For example, the note at **Gn 3.20** reads: "*Eve* sounds like a Hebrew term that means 'to give life.'"

Alternative translations are introduced with the word "Or . . ." Occasionally, the editors give notes on words or phrases that diverge from traditional translations. These notes are introduced with the words "Traditionally rendered . . ." For example, the first note at **Lv 13.2** reads: "Traditionally rendered *leprosy*. The Hebrew word used throughout this passage is used to describe various skin diseases." The second note reads: "Or *one of his descendants.*"

Some footnotes offer cultural and historical insights to clarify places, things, and people that are likely unfamiliar to most readers. *E.g.,* **Ac 12.1** "Greek *Herod the king.* He was the nephew of Herod Antipas and a grandson of Herod the Great."

ASSESSMENT

The NLT is one of the clearest and most understandable translations available. It is rendered in natural American English and its style is conversational and easy to follow. At times it is clear and comprehensible even where its original source is not clear or is ambiguous. The translators sometimes clarify the significance of metaphors and other figures of speech that general readers might miss.[8] The NLT also adds affective (*i.e.,* emotive) language where the translators imply it from context.[9]

The NLT is ideal for those new to the Bible and its genres, for those who want help reading the Bible in a year, or for anyone who wishes to read Scripture in a more casual setting. It is also a good choice for beginning to intermediate English readers (*e.g.* 4th grade through high-school).

An edition of the NLT with the Apocrypha is also available as the *Holy Bible, New Living Translation, Catholic Reader's Edition* (2015).[10] The only differences between it and the Protestant editions is the inclusion of the Deuterocanon.

REPRESENTATIVE SAMPLES

Familiar Passages

Gn 1.1–2	In the beginning God created the heavens and the earth.* The earth was formless and empty, and darkness covered the deep waters. And the Spirit of God was hovering over the surface of the waters. **Footnote (fn):** **1:1** Or *In the beginning when God created the heavens and the earth, . . .* Or *When God began to create the heavens and the earth, . . .*

Ps 23.1–2	The Lord is my shepherd;
	    I have all that I need.
	He lets me rest in green meadows;
	    he leads me beside peaceful streams.

Ps 27.4	The one thing I ask of the Lord—
	    the thing I seek most—
	is to live in the house of the Lord all the days of my life,
	    delighting in the Lord's perfections
	    and meditating in his Temple.

Jn 3.16	"For this is how God loved the world: He gave* his one and only Son, so that everyone who believes in him will not perish but have eternal life." fn: **3:16** Or *For God loved the world so much that he gave.*

Divine Name and Titles

Yhwh	Ps 24.1a	The earth is the **Lord**'s, and everything in it.
adonai	Ps 90.1b	**Lord**, through all the generations you have been our home!
elohim	Gn 1.27a	So **God** created human beings* in his own image. fn: **1:27** Or *the man*; Hebrew reads *ha-adam.*
adonai Yhwh	Ps 73.28b	I have made the **Sovereign Lord** my shelter
adonai elohim	Dn 9.3a	So I turned to the **Lord God**
Yhwh *saba'oth*	1Sa 17.45b	I come to you in the name of the **Lord of Heaven's Armies**

New Living Translation   431

el shaddai	Ex 6.3a	"I appeared to Abraham, to Isaac, and to Jacob as **El-Shaddai—'God Almighty'"*** **fn: 6:3** *El-Shaddai*, which means "God Almighty," is the name for God used in Gen 17:1; 28:3; 35:11; 43:14; 48:3.
kyrios	Lk 20.42b	"'The **LORD** said to my **Lord**, Sit in the place of honor at my right hand'"
christos	Mt 16.16b	"You are the **Messiah**,* the Son of the living God." **fn: 16:16** Or *the Christ. Messiah* (a Hebrew term) and *Christ* (a Greek term) both mean "anointed one."

New Testament Text Base

Mt 17.21	—— **fn:** Some manuscripts add verse 21, *But this kind of demon won't leave except by prayer and fasting.* Compare Mark 9.29.
Mt 18.11	—— **fn:** Some manuscripts add verse 11, *And the Son of Man came to save those who are lost.* Compare Luke 19:10.
Ac 8.37	—— **fn:** Some manuscripts add verse 37, *"You can," Philip answered, "if you believe with all your heart." And the eunuch replied, "I believe that Jesus Christ is the Son of God."*
1 Jn 5.7b–8a	—— **fn:** A very few late manuscripts add *in heaven—the Father, the Word, and the Holy Spirit, and these three are one. And we have three witnesses on earth.*

Gender Language

'ādām	Gn 9.6	"If anyone takes a **human life**, that person's life will also be taken by **human hands**. For God made **human beings*** in His own image." **fn: 9:6** Or *man*; Hebrew reads *ha-adam*.
'ish ... nephesh	Lv 24.17	"**Anyone who** takes **another person's life** must be put to death."
'āvîw	Pr 15.5a	A fool spurns **a parent's** discipline **fn: 15:5** Hebrew *father's.*

huioi	Mt 5.9	"God blesses those who work for peace, for they will be called the **children** of God."
anthrōpōn	Mt 4.19	"Come, follow me, and I will show you how to fish for **people**!"
hekastō ... autou	Ro 2.6	He will judge **everyone** according to what **they** have done.
gynaikos anēr	Tt 1.6a	An elder must live a blameless life. **He** must be faithful **to his wife,*** and his children must be believers fn: **1:6** Or *must have only one wife*, or *must be married only once*; Greek reads *must be the husband of one wife.*
gynaikas	1Ti 3.11	In the same way, their **wives*** must be respected and must not slander others. They must exercise self-control and be faithful in everything they do. fn: **3:11** Or *the women deacons.* The Greek word can be translated *women* or *wives.*

Difficult Renderings

1Sa 13.1	Saul was **thirty*** **years old** when he became king, and he reigned for **forty-two years.*** fn: **13:1a** As in a few Greek manuscripts; the number is missing in the Hebrew. **13:1b** Hebrew *reigned ... and two*; the number is incomplete in the Hebrew. Compare Acts 13:21.
Is 28.13	So the LORD will **spell out his message for them again,** **one line at a time,** **one line at a time,** **a little here,** **and a little there,** so that they will stumble and fall. They will be injured, trapped, and captured.

Significant Renderings

'almah Is 7.14	All right then, the Lord himself will give you the sign. Look! **The virgin*** will conceive a child! She will give birth to a son and will call him Immanuel (which means 'God is with us'). fn: **7:14** Or *young woman.*

she'ol . . . 'abaddon	Pr 15.11	Even **Death** and **Destruction** hold no secrets from the LORD. How much more does he know the human heart!
		fn: 15:11 Hebrew *Sheol and Abaddon*.
egennēsen	Mt 1.2	Abraham **was the father of** Isaac. Isaac **was the father of** Jacob. Jacob **was the father of** Judah and his brothers.
eskēnōsen	Jn 1.14	So the Word became human* and **made his home** among us. He was full of unfailing love and faithfulness.* And we have seen his glory, the glory of the Father's one and only Son.
		fn: 1:14a Greek *became flesh*. **1:14b** Or *grace and truth*; also in 1:17.
tois ioudaiois	Jn 18.36	Jesus answered, "My Kingdom is not an earthly kingdom. If it were, my followers would fight to keep me from being handed over **to the Jewish leaders**. But my Kingdom is not of this world."
dikaiosunē theou, pisteōs Iēsou Christou	Ro 3.22a	**We are made right with God** by placing **our faith in Jesus Christ**. And this is true for everyone who believes
Granville Sharp's rule applied	Tt 2.13	while we look forward with hope to that wonderful day when the glory of **our great God and Savior, Jesus Christ**, will be revealed.

SIGNIFICANT REVISIONS

The 2004 Second Edition

Shortly after the NLT's initial publication in 1996, the Bible Translation Committee began an eight-year process to improve the NLT's precision (*i.e.*, formal-equivalence), but without sacrificing its clarity. In 2004, Tyndale House published a thoroughgoing revision that affected approximately 25,000 verses. (or eighty percent of the verses in the Bible). A "Note to Readers" in the second edition claimed that the revised NLT was now a "general-purpose text especially good for study."[11]

Most of these changes are characterized by greater word-for-word correspondence to (*i.e.*, concordance with) the Hebrew and Greek sources. They are not enough to class the NLT as a formal translation. It is still very much a functional, or "dynamic" translation, but its paraphrase is less free than it was when the version first appeared in 1996. In all, the NLT is a combination of formal and functional renderings: It is formal where the word-for-word translation makes apparent English sense, and functional where the revisers sensed that a formal rendering would be too obscure.

	NLT (1996)	NLT (2004)
Isaiah 34.7	**The strongest will die — veterans and young men, too.** The land will be soaked with blood and the soil enriched with fat.	**Even men as strong as wild oxen will die — the young me alongside the veterans.** The land will be soaked with blood and the soil enriched with fat.
1 Corinthians 11.3	But there is one thing I want you to know: **A man is responsible to** Christ, **a woman is responsible to her husband**, and Christ **is responsible to** God.	But there is one thing I want you to know: **The head of every man is** Christ, **the head of** woman **is man**, and **the head of** Christ **is** God.
Romans 6.3	Or have you forgotten that when we **became Christians and were baptized to become one** with Christ Jesus, we **died with** him?	Or have you forgotten that when we **were joined** with Christ Jesus **in baptism**, we **joined** him **in his death**?

2007, 2013, and 2015 Revisions

Later revisions to the 2004 second edition continue in the same spirit. Only about a thousand relatively minor changes followed (in 2007, 2013, and 2015). These changes were made to include a broader English audience, to improve formal correspondence,

and to correct footnotes. The revisers tried to bring greater clarity
to some passages by rendering them in more idiomatic English.

More formal or concordant:

	NLT (2004–2013)	NLT (2007–2015)
Gn 46.4b	"**But** you will die in Egypt **with** Joseph **attending** to you."	"You will die in Egypt, **but** Joseph **will be with** you **to close your eyes.**"
1Co 13.10	But when **full understanding** comes, these partial things will become useless.	But when **the time of perfection** comes, these partial things will become useless.
Rv 13.6	[The beast] spoke terrible words of blasphemy against God, slandering his name and his **temple**—that is, those who **live** in heaven.	[The beast] spoke terrible words of blasphemy against God, slandering his name and his **dwelling**—that is, those who **dwell** in heaven.
Ac 16.15a	[Lydia] **was** baptized **along with other members of** her household	[Lydia] **and** her household **were** baptized
Ac 16.16b	we met a **demon-possessed** slave girl. **She was a fortune-teller**	we met a slave girl **who had a spirit that enabled her to tell the future**
1Co 7.12ff	If a **Christian man** has a wife who is not a believer and she is willing to continue living with him, he must not leave her.	If a **fellow believer** has a wife who is not a believer and she is willing to continue living with him, he must not leave her.
1Co 16.20	All the brothers and sisters here send greetings to you. Greet each other with **Christian love**.	All the brothers and sisters here send greetings to you. Greet each other with **a sacred kiss.**

	NLT (2004–2013)	NLT (2007–2015)
Mt 6.7	"When you pray, don't babble on and on as **people of other religions** do."	"When you pray, don't babble on and on as **the Gentiles** do."

The Best Bible?

Improved clarity or accuracy:

	NLT (2004–2013)	NLT (2007–2015)
Gn 46.4	this bread must be laid out before the LORD. **The bread is to be received from the people of Israel as a requirement** of the eternal covenant.	this bread must be laid out before the LORD **as a gift from the Israelites; it is an ongoing expression** of the eternal covenant.
2Sa 20.24	Adoniram was in charge of **the labor force**.	Adoniram was in charge of **forced labor**.
Jer 40.7a	he leaders of the Judean **guerrilla bands** in the countryside heard that the king of Babylon had appointed Gedaliah son of Ahikam as governor	The leaders of the Judean **military groups** in the countryside heard that the king of Babylon had appointed Gedaliah son of Ahikam as governor
1Pt 2.13	For the Lord's sake, **respect** all human authority—whether the king as head of state,	For the Lord's sake, **submit to** all human authority—whether the king as head of state
Mt 6.22b–23a	When your eye is **good**, your whole body is filled with light. But when your eye is **bad**, your whole body is filled with darkness.	When your eye is **healthy**, your whole body is filled with light. But when your eye is **unhealthy**, your whole body is filled with darkness.
Tt 3.7a	Because of his grace he **declared** us **righteous**	Because of his grace he **made us right in his sight**

General English usage:

Gn 1.26a	Then God said, "Let us make human beings in our image, to be like **ourselves**."	Then God said, "Let us make human beings in our image, to be like **us**."
Gn 31.26a	"What do you mean by **stealing away** like this?"	"What do you mean by **deceiving me** like this?"
Jos 24.32a	The bones of Joseph . . . were buried at Shechem, in the **parcel of ground** Jacob had bought	The bones of Joseph . . . were buried at Shechem, in the **plot of land** Jacob had bought

Idiomatic English:

	NLT (2004–2013)	NLT (2007–2015)
Pr 18.18	**Casting lots** can end arguments; it settles disputes between powerful opponents.	**Flipping a coin*** can end arguments; it settles disputes between powerful opponents.
		fn: **18:18** Hebrew *Casting lots*
1Pt 1.17b	So you must live in reverent fear of Him during your time as **"foreigners in the land."**	So you must live in reverent fear of him during your time here as **"temporary residents."**
1Jn 4.15	All who **confess** that Jesus is the Son of God have God living in them, and they live in God.	All who **declare** that Jesus is the Son of God have God living in them, and they live in God.
1Ti 3.1	This is a trustworthy saying: "If someone aspires to be **an elder,*** he desires an honorable position."	This is a trustworthy saying: "If someone aspires to be **a church leader,*** he desires an honorable position."
	fn: **3:1** Or *an overseer,* or *a bishop;* also in 3:2, 6.	fn: **3:1** Or *an overseer,* or *a bishop;* also in 3:2, 6.

Improved footnotes:

For example, a 2007 revision adds insights (in **bold** here) about Sarai's name change to Sarah in **Genesis 17.15**:

"Sarai and Sarah both mean 'princess'; **the change in spelling may reflect the difference in dialect between Ur and Canaan.**"

The following change in a footnote turned a text critical judgment into a simple observation:

	NLT (2004–2013)	NLT (2007–2015)
2Sa 13.37	**footnote:** the Hebrew text **omits** this sentence.	**footnote:** the Hebrew text **lacks** this sentence.

The Best Bible?

Swapped main text for footnote:

	NLT (2004–2007)	NLT (2013)	NLT (2015)
Jas 4.5	**What** do you think the Scriptures **mean when** they say that the spirit God has placed within us **is filled with envy*?**	Do you think the Scriptures mean **have no meaning when** they say that the spirit God has placed within us **is filled with envy?** *	Do you think the Scriptures **have no meaning**? They say that God **is passionate that** the spirit **he** has placed within us **should be faithful to him.** *
	fn: **4:5** Or *that God longs jealously for the human spirit he has placed within us?* or *that the Holy Spirit, whom God has placed within us, opposes our envy?*		fn: **4:5** Or *They say that the spirit God has placed within us is filled with envy;* or *They say that the Holy Spirit, whom God has placed within us, opposes our envy.*

And finally, some corrections:

1Kg 3.15b	He returned to Jerusalem and stood before the Ark of the **Lord's** Covenant	He returned to Jerusalem and stood before the Ark of the **Lord's** Covenant
Ac 2.38	"be baptized in the name of Jesus Christ **to show that you have received** forgiveness **for** your sins."	"be baptized in the name of Jesus Christ **for** the forgiveness **of** your sins."
Tt 1.7	For an elder must live a blameless life.	An elder **is a manager of God's household, so he** must live a blameless life.

ENDORSEMENTS

The NLT was endorsed by evangelist Billy Graham and other evangelical leaders, such as Greg Laurie (Harvest Crusades), Josh Mc-

Dowell (Christian apologist), Hyatt Moore (former U.S. Director of Wycliffe Bible Translators), John Ortberg (pastor, Menlo Park Presbyterian), Esteban Shedd (music artist), and Charles R. "Chuck" Swindoll (pastor, Stonebriar Community Church).

Though the NLT has received its *Nihil obstat* and *Imprimatur* from the Roman Catholic Church in 2015, it has not been approved for liturgical use.

COPYRIGHT

You may quote up to 500 verses from the NLT in any form without prior written permission; the verses may not constitute a complete book of the Bible; they must comprise less than 25% of your work's content; and your work must include the following copyright acknowledgment.

Unless used exclusively, follow citations with the designation (NLT). For example:

Jn 1.4, "The Word gave life to everything that was created, and his life brought light to everyone." (NLT)

The title *"New Living Translation®,"* its initialism (NLT®), and its logomark are registered trademarks with the US Patent and Trademark Office by Tyndale House Publishers, Inc.

For permissions not covered here, write to Tyndale House Publishers, Inc., 351 Executive Drive, Carol Stream, IL 60188 (https://www.tyndale.com/permissions/form)

The Best Bible?

ENDNOTES FOR THE
NEW LIVING TRANSLATION

1 "Translation Process." *New Living Translation, Tyndale House Publishers, Inc.,* accessed September 12, 2018, https://www.tyndale.com/nlt/translation-process/.

2 Tremper Longman III, in discussion with the author, May 27, 2020.

3 "Introduction to the *New Living Translation,*" *Holy Bible, New Living Translation* (Carol Stream, IL: Tyndale House Publishers, Inc., 2015).

4 "Introduction . . . ," *Holy Bible, New Living Translation* (1996).

5 *Ibid.*

6 "Introduction . . . ," *Holy Bible, New Living Translation* (2015).

7 "Introduction . . . ," *Holy Bible, New Living Translation* (1996).

8 For examples of clarified figures of speech, in **Sg 7.4** the NLT adds "as fine" in order to clarify the significance of the figure, "Your nose is **as fine** as the tower of Lebanon." And again in **Ecc 12.1–7**, the translators explain (in bold here) what the figures point to, "Remember [your Creator] before **your legs**—the guards of your house—start to tremble; and before **your shoulders**—the strong men—stoop. Remember him before **your teeth**—your few remaining servants—stop grinding; and before **your eyes**—the women looking through the windows—see dimly" (v **3**).

9 For examples of added emotive language, in **Ps 130.9** the NLT adds the possessive "my" in "Can **my** dust praise you?" with no justification from the Hebrew. **Jn 8.7** adds the first few words without precedent from Greek, "They kept demanding an answer, so he stood up again and said, '**All right, but** let the one who has never sinned throw the first stone!'" These additions are implied from the situation.

10 The text of the NLT's 2nd edition (NLTse) received its *Nihil obstat* from Gali Bali, Bishop of Guntur, and its *Imprimatur* from Oswald Cardinal Gracias, Archbishop of Bombay and President of the Conference of Catholic Bishops of India on April 29, 2015.

"Catholic Holy Bible Reader's Edition" at *Tyndale.com,* accessed February 4, 2021, https://www.tyndale.com/p/catholic-holy-bible-readers-edition /9781496414014.

An edition of the NLT's first text edition (titled the *Holy Bible: Catholic Reference Edition*) was marketed to Catholic readers with the Deuterocanon (in 2002) but it did not receive the Church's official stamp of approval.

[11] "Introduction . . . ," *Holy Bible, New Living Translation* (2015).

NET Bible®

NET Bible, New English Translation

Produced by Biblical Studies Press, LLC, 1998–2019

FORMAL / FUNCTIONAL TENDENCIES

FORMAL   FUNCTIONAL

Interlinear   NASB KJV NKJV ESV   RSV   CSB NRSV   **N E T** NIV NLT   Free Paraphrase

TEXT BASES

OT Masoretic Hebrew and Ancient Versions.   **NT** Eclectic Greek.

TRANSLATION TIMELINE

1978	1982	1989	1996	2001	2002	2006	2017
NIV	*NKJV*	*NRSV*	*NLT*	*ESV*	*MSG*	**N E T**	*CSB*

CONTEMPORARY EVENTS

1963	1975	1976	1989	1991	2002	2004	2006
ARPAnet project initiated.	Bill Gates founds Microsoft Corp.	Steve Jobs founds Apple Inc.	WWW invented at CERN. Berlin Wall falls.	WWW goes public. Soviet Union dissolves.	Center for the Study of N.T. Manuscripts founded.	Facebook launched.	

PUBLICATION TIMELINE

1995	1996	1998	1999	2000	2001	2002	2003	2006	2017, 2019
SBL meeting in Philadelphia, PN.	Editor's draft	*NET* N.T. online	*NET* N.T. in print	*NET* O.T. online	*NET Bible,* First Beta	*NET* Apoc. online	*NET Bible,* Second Beta	*NET Bible,* First edition	*NET Bible,* Second edition

NET

BIBLE®

FIRST EDITION

A NEW APPROACH TO TRANSLATION, THOROUGHLY DOCUMENTED WITH 60,932 NOTES BY THE TRANSLATORS AND EDITORS

www.bible.org

ccording to the preface of the *NET Bible* (NET), "The project began on a rainy night in November 1995 in Philadelphia, Pennsylvania at the annual meeting of the
Society of Biblical Literature. There a group of Old and New Testament scholars met over dinner at a fine Italian restaurant with
the sponsor of the project. Later that same night in a hotel lobby
they were joined by a larger group of scholars to discuss at greater
length a new translation of the Bible. The topic of conversation
was the possibility of an English translation for electronic distribution over the Internet. A revision and update of some existing
English translation was initially discussed, but in subsequent discussions the biblical scholars themselves insisted that a completely new translation was both possible and indeed preferable."[1]

The translators intended it to be the first Bible ever released to
be freely available for all at the time of its publication. They did
this by hosting the translation online, where it would be accessible to anyone with internet access.

Because its initial format was digital, the translators could write
fuller notes to explain their decisions in detail without worrying
about the limited space of a printed book. Their notes are what
make this translation so valuable to students, scholars, and other translators. The editors of the NET frequently make reference
to technical commentaries, periodicals, and standard reference
works. The second print edition, released in 2017 (through Biblical Studies Press) and 2019 (through Thomas Nelson), contains a
whopping 60,000+ notes.[2]

STATED TRANSLATION IDEALS

"The 19th century conservative Christian scholar Henry Alford
stated it best: 'a translator of Holy Scripture must be . . . ready to
sacrifice the choicest text, and the plainest proof of doctrine, if the
words are not those of what he is constrained in his conscience to
receive as God's testimony.'" "One of the primary goals of the NET
has been to stay abreast of current research." "As our understand-

ing of these languages improves, naturally it will affect the translation of particular passages."[3] The translators have placed scholarly findings in the Bible's extensive footnotes.

The translators of the NET sought to accurately translate passages "consistently and properly within their grammatical, historical, and theological context[s]." They prioritized an accurate rendering of Greek and Hebrew grammar, while historical and theological contexts set parameters to check and balance against idiosyncrasies. (Their used of "theological context" assumes that the Bible is a result of progressive and accumulating revelation.)[4]

Regarding the translators' target English style, "[t]he language of average adults had priority. The translation attempts to use good style but is not overly formal or embellished. [It] is intended to be understandable to non-Christians as well as Christians, so liturgical language or Christian 'jargon' (and archaism) has been avoided." They have sought to render a "gender-accurate translation", while avoiding "ideological gender inclusivity".[5]

METHOD

The effort was lead by a general editor, with senior editors appointed for each Testament. Translation teams consisting of anywhere between four to ten members were responsible for translating each of the seven major sections of the Bible. Very few members joined only one team; most worked on two or more.

Though the translation is largely functional (dynamic equivalent), the translators relied on the use of computerized concordance programs and electronic search engines in their production to ensure greater consistency. They compared and contrasted parallel passages in the Gospels for how closely they matched in the Greek. The translators wanted to render exact parallels in exactly the same way. Where the parallels differ, even slightly, the NET reflects that, even where other translations harmonize them.

The translators never wanted the work to remain a static publication. They fully intended it to undergo continuous revision, which is far easier to do in digital publishing than it is in traditional print.

The New Testament was released online in 1999, the Old Testament in 2000, and the Apocrypha in 2003. Printed Beta editions containing the Old and New Testaments were released in 2001 and 2003. The first edition was published in 2005, and twelve years later a revision was published as a second print edition (2017) with minor revisions following in 2019.

TEXT BASES

New Testament

Eclectic Greek text. Nestle-Aland *Novum Testamentum Graece* 27th and 28th editions (Stuttgart: Deutsche Bibelgesellschaft, 1993, 2012); "For the NT the Greek text to be used by individual translators was decided by the textual consultant."[6] "The Greek text of the NET NT differs from the Nestle-Aland 27 in about 500 places."[7]

Old Testament

Masoretic Hebrew-Aramaic text. *Biblia Hebraica Stuttgartensia* 2nd emended and 5th revised editions (1984, '97).
Ancient versions. Dead Sea Scrolls (DSS), *et al.*

CONTRIBUTORS

The NET is largely the product of the faculty of Dallas Theological Seminary (DTS). Its general editor, W. Hall Harris III, is a professor of New Testament at DTS, and has contributed to the *Lexham English Bible* (LEB) and the NASB. Robert B. Chisholm was the senior OT editor and Daniel B. Wallace (ESV), the senior NT editor. In total, twenty-seven people are recorded as responsible for the publication of the first edition (2006).[8]

NET

For a complete list of translators, visit *booklink.id/ net-translator*

Among the Old Testament specialists were Richard E. Averbeck (HCSB, *The Message*), William D. Barrick (ESV, LEB), Dorian Coover-Cox (CSB, LEB), Donald R. Glenn (NIV, *The Message*), Michael A. Grisanti (ESV, LEB), Gordon H. Johnston (LEB), Eugene H. Merrill (NKJV, NLT, HCSB), and Allen P. Ross (NKJV, NLT, ESV).

Among the New Testamant specialists: Darrell L. Bock (NLT, *The Message*, ESV), Buist M. Fanning III (NASB), John D. Grassmick, Harold W. Hoehner (ESV, NASB), and David K. Lowery (NASB).

THEOLOGICAL ASSUMPTIONS

The large majority of the NET's contributors are on staff with Dallas Theological Seminary. They uphold conservative evangelical tenets of faith.*

Like the RSV, the editors sought to render the Old Testament passages relating to New Testament fulfillment in a way that narrows their interpretation and application to their immediate OT contexts. This is likely due to the particular way that some of them viewed progressive revelation: Later revelation might add to the meaning of an earlier passage as a fulfillment of an OT type and pattern, but the human authors of the OT can not have anticipated any meaning other than what was obvious to them at the time. Hence, parallel OT and NT passages cannot be expected to match.

Is 7.14	Mt 1.26
"Look, this **young woman** is about to conceive and will give birth to a son."	"Look! The **virgin** will conceive and bear a son" (NET)

Ho 11.1	Mt 2.15
I summoned my **son** out of Egypt	"I called my **Son** out of Egypt." (NET)

---

* The doctrinal statements that the DTS faculty subscribe to are listed online (https://www.dts.edu/about/doctrinal-statement/).

The Best Bible?

FEATURES

The translators and editors of the NET worked to avoid "ideological gender inclusivity" and pursued an approach which they called "gender-accurate translation."

For example, there are a small number of instances where the Greek word *anēr* ("man", *i.e.*, an adult male, or "husband"), is rendered as "someone" or (very rarely) as a generic. For example, **Jas 1.23**,

> For if someone merely listens to the message and does not live it out, he is like **someone** who gazes at his own face in a mirror. (NET)

And **Ac 17.34**,

> But some **people** joined him and believed. Among them . . . a woman named Damaris, and others with them. (NET)

The Greek word *adelphoi* is rendered "brothers and sisters."
Greek participles translated "the one who" or "the person who" with the pronoun is kept masculine, due to a lack of a third-singular, gender-inclusive pronoun in English. For example, **Jn 7.18**,

> The person who speaks on **his** own authority desires to receive honor for **himself** (NET)

Verse numbers are included in **boldface** type. "In almost all cases the verse divisions follow standard English practice. In the few instances where there is a difference between the versification of the standard critical editions of the Greek NT and most English versions this is indicated by a translators' note (marked '**tn**')." [9]
The basic unit of translation is the paragraph. Paragraph indentations were determined by the translators and editors according to the sense. Poetry is indented as stanzas and cola.

NET Bible: New English Translation

NET

NT quotations from the OT are indicated by a combination of "***boldface and italic***" type. Less direct allusions to OT passages are indicated by "*italic*" type only. In both cases, a footnote (marked "**sn**") gives the OT reference.

The NET follows standard English conventions. "In cases where embedded quotations would require the use of more than three layers of quotation marks, a more streamlined approach has been followed to eliminate excess layers of quotation marks by the use of colons and commas."[10]

Divine pronouns are not capitalized (so RSV, NRSV, ESV, NIV, NLT, *et al.*).

The translators produced 60,932 notes for the first edition (2006) in which they recorded the issues and options confronting them as they worked. For the second edition (called 2.0, published in 2017), the editors deleted over three thousand footnotes that they deemed unnecessary and superfluous, such as "*de* has not been translated" or "*kai* has not been translated due to differences in Greek and English style." The latest edition (2.1), published through Thomas Nelson (2019), revised the notes to reflect updates to its NT text base.[11] It contains 60,000+ notes.

Cross-references and references to OT quotations or allusions in the NT are placed in footnotes marked "**sn**".

Text-critical notes (indicated by "**tc**") discuss variant readings found in the various Hebrew and Greek manuscripts (mss) and groups of mss. "They indicate historically important readings, exegetically significant readings, or readings accepted by the translation that are different from standard critical editions. Where the translation follows a different reading than that found in Nestle-Aland's *Novum Testamentum*, 27th edition, a '**tc**' note is preceded by a double dagger (‡)."[12]

"Translators notes (marked '**tn**') introduced by 'Or . . . ' give alternate translations that are regarded by the translators and editors as equally good to that which is given in the main text, with a choice made between them for reasons of style, euphony, other characteristics of contemporary English usage, or slight exegetical preference.

"Translators notes introduced by '*Heb* . . .', '*Aram* . . .', or '*Grk* . . .' give a gloss that approximates formal equivalence to the sources.

"Study notes (marked '**sn**') are explanatory notes that provide supplementary information: *E.g.*, historical details, cultural differences, explanation of obscure phrases or brief discussions of context, wordplays, technical terms, discussions of the theological point made by the biblical author, etc."[13]

Map notes (marked "**map**") indicate geographic information referenced to the satellite maps in the back of the volume.

The translators and editors added section headings to assist readers. They are not an integral part of the text.

A limited system of cross-referencing to principal parallel texts, cross-references, or significant allusions is found in the notes.

ASSESSMENT

The NET's most outstanding feature is its thorough set of footnotes, which explains everything from translation decisions to text-critical issues. The notes are scholarly and should appeal to serious Bible students. In fact, the editorial teams of both the ESV and the NIV *Study Bible* (2008) consulted the NET's notes for their editions.

Its language tends to be higher-register and lower-context, which results from the translators' striving for accuracy over general appeal. Even though this version tends towards concordancy, it remains faithful to context.

There are many good binding through Thomas Nelson publishers and a robust online reading environment besides (https://netbible.org).

The NET is ideal for Bible students and scholars who want to peer into the editorial process of an accurate, modern Bible translation.

REPRESENTATIVE SAMPLES

Familiar Passages

In the beginning [A] God [B] created [C] the heavens and the earth. [D]
Now [E] the earth [F] was without shape and empty, [G] and darkness [H] was over the surface of the watery deep, [I] but the Spirit of God [J] was moving [K] over the surface [L] of the water. [M]

Gn 1.1–2

Footnote (fn): [A] **tn** The translation assumes that the form translated "beginning" is in the absolute state rather than the construct... [B] **sn** *God.* The ending of the Hebrew term אֱלֹהִים (*'elohim*) is commonly used to indicate plural nouns... [M] **sn** *The water.* The text deliberately changes now from the term for the watery deep to the general word for water. The arena is now the life-giv-... *etc.*

The LORD is my shepherd, [N]
I lack nothing. [O]
He takes me to lush pastures, [P]
he leads me to refreshing water. [Q]

Ps 23.1–2

fn: [N] **sn** *Psalm 23.* In vv. 1–4 the psalmist pictures the Lord as a shepherd who provides for his needs and protects him from danger.... [Q] **tn** Both genitives in v. 2 indicate an attribute of the noun they modify: דֶּשֶׁא (*deshe'*) characterizes the pastures as... *etc.*

I have asked the LORD for one thing—
this is what I desire!
I want to live [R] in the LORD's house [S] all the days of my life,
so I can gaze at the splendor [T] of the LORD
and contemplate in his temple.

Ps 27.4

fn: [R] **tn** Heb "for me to live." [S] **sn** *The Lord's house.* This probably refers to the tabernacle (if one accepts Davidic authorship) or the temple (see Judg 19:18; 1 Sam 1:7, 24; 2 Sam 12:20; 1 Kgs 7:12, 40, 45, 51). [T] **tn** Or "beauty."

For this is the way [U] God loved the world: He gave his one and only [V] Son, so that everyone who believes in him will not perish [W] but have eternal life. [X]

Jn 3.16

fn: [U] **tn** Or "this is how much"; or "in this way." The Greek adverb οὕτως (*houtōs*) can... [X] **sn** The alternatives presented are... *etc.*

Divine Name and Titles

Yʜwʜ	Ps 24.1a	The **Lord** owns the earth and all it contains
adonai	Ps 90.1b	O **Lord**, you have been our protector [A] through all generations! fn: [A] **tn** Or "place of safety." See Ps 71:3.
elohim	Gn 1.27a	**God** created humankind [B] in his own image fn: [B] **tn** The Hebrew text has the article prefixed to the noun (הָאָדָם, *ha'adam*). The article does not dist-…*etc.*
adonai Yʜwʜ	Ps 73.28b	I have made the **Sovereign Lord** my shelter
adonai elohim	Dn 9.3a	So I turned my attention [C] to the **Lord God** [D] fn: [C] **tn** Heb "face." [D] **tn** The Hebrew phrase translated "Lord God" here is אֲדֹנָי הָאֱלֹהִים (*'adonay ha'elohim*).
Yʜwʜ *saba'oth*	1Sa 17.45b	"I am coming against you in the name of the **Lord of Heaven's Armies**"
el shaddai	Ex 6.3a	"I appeared to Abraham, to Isaac, and to Jacob [E] as **God Almighty**" [F] fn: [E] **tn** The preposition *bet* (בְּ) in this construction should be classified as a bet essentiae … [F] **tn** The traditional rendering of the title as "Almighty" is reflected in LXX and Jerome. But there is still little agree-… *etc.*
kyrios	Lk 20.42b	" 'The **Lord** said to my [G] **lord**, "Sit at my right hand" ' " fn: [G] **sn** *The Lord said to my lord.* With David being the speaker, this indicates his respect for his descendant (referred to as *my lord*). Jesus was arguing, as the ancient exposition assumed, that the passage … *etc.*
christos	Mt 16.16b	"You are the **Christ**, [H] the Son of the living God." fn: [H] **tn** Or "Messiah"; both "Christ" (Greek) and "Messiah" (Hebrew and Aramaic) mean "one who has been anointed." **sn** See the note on *Christ* in 1:16.

New Testament Text Base

Mt 17.21	——— **fn: tc** Many significant MSS (ℵ* B Θ 0281 33 579 892* e ff¹ sy s c sa) do not include 17:21 "But this kind does not go out except by prayer and fasting." The verse is included in ℵ² C D L W Γ Δ f¹.¹³ 565 579 700 1241 1424 𝔐 *al* lat sy(p) h . . . *etc.*
Mt 18.11	——— **fn: tc** The most important MSS (ℵ* B L* Θ* f¹.¹³ 33 892* *pc* e ff¹ sy s sa) do not include 18:11 "For the Son of Man came to save the lost." The verse is included in D Lmg W Θc 078vid ℵ lat sy c, p, h, but is almost certainly not original, being borrowed from the parallel in Luke 19:10. The present translation fol-. . . *etc.*
Ac 8.37	——— **fn: tc** A few later MSS (E 36 323 453 945 1739 1891) add, with minor variations, 8:37 "He said to him, 'If you believe with your whole heart, you may.' He replied, 'I believe that Jesus Christ is the Son of God.'" Verse 37 is lacking in 𝔓⁴⁵, ⁷⁴ ℵ A B C 33 614 vg sy p, h co. It is clearly not a part of the original . . . *etc.*
1Jn 5.7b–8a	——— **fn: tc** Before τὸ πνεῦμα καὶ τὸ ὕδωρ καὶ τὸ αἷμα, the *Textus Receptus* (TR) reads ἐν τῷ οὐρανῷ, ὁ πατήρ, ὁ λόγος καὶ τὸ ἅγιον πνεύμα, καὶ οὗτοι οι τρεῖς ἕν εἰσι. 5.8 καὶ τρεῖς εἰσιν οι μαρτυροῦντες ἐν τῇ γῇ ("in heaven, the Father, the Word, and the Holy Spirit, and these three are one. 5:8 And there are three that testify on earth."). This reading, the infamous *Comma Johanneum*, has been known in the English-speaking world through the King James translation. However, the evidence—both external . . . *etc.*

Gender Language

ʾādām	Gn 9.6	"Whoever sheds **human** blood,A by other **humans** B must his blood be shed; for in God's image C God D has made **humankind**."
		fn: A **tn** *Heb* "the blood of man." B **tn** *Heb* "by man," a generic term here for other human beings. C **sn** See the notes on the words "humankind" and "likeness" in in Gen 1:26, as well . . . *etc.* D **tn** Heb "he"; the referent (God) has been specified in the translation for clarity.

The Best Bible?

ʾîsh … nephesh	Lv 24.17	"'If **a man** beats **any person** to death,[A] he must be put to death.'"
		fn: [A] **tn** *Heb* "And if a man strikes any soul [נֶפֶשׁ, *nefesh*] of mankind." The idiom seems to derive … *etc.*
ʾāvîw	Pr 15.5a	A fool despises **his father's** instruction
huioi	Mt 5.9	"Blessed are the peacemakers, for they will be called the **children**[B] of God."
		fn: [B] **tn** *Grk* "sons," though traditionally English versions have taken this as a generic reference to both males and females, hence "children" (cf. KJV, NAB, NRSV, NLT).
anthrōpōn	Mt 4.19	"Follow me, and I will turn you into fishers **of people!**"[C]
		fn: [C] **tn** The Greek term ἄνθρωπος (*anthrōpos*) is used here in a generic sense, referring to both men and women, thus "people." **sn** The kind of fishing envis-… *etc.*
hekastō … autou	Ro 2.6	He[D] *will reward*[E] **each one** *according to* **his** works[F]
		fn: [D] **tn** *Grk* "who." The relative pronoun was converted to a personal pronoun … [E] **tn** Or "will render," "will recompense." In this context Paul … [F] **sn** A quotation from Ps 62:12; Prov 24:12; a close approxima-… *etc.*
adelphoi	Gal 5.13	For you were called to freedom, **brothers and sisters**; only do not use your freedom as an opportunity to indulge your flesh, but through love serve one another.
gynaikos anēr	Ti 1.6a	An elder must be blameless,[G] **the husband of** one **wife**,[H] with faithful children[I]
		fn: [G] **tn** *Grk* "if anyone is blameless…" as a continuation of … [H] **tn** Or "married only once," "devoted solely to his wife." See the note … [I] **tn** Or "believing children." The phrase could be translated "believing … *etc.*
gynaikas	1Ti 3.11	Likewise also their **wives**[J] must be dignified, not slanderous, temperate, faithful in every respect.
		fn: [J] **tn** Or "also deaconesses." The Greek word here is γυναῖκας (*gunaikas*) which literally means "women" or "wives." It is possible that this refers to women who serve as deacons, "deaconesses." The evidence is as follows: (1) The immediate context refers to deacons; (2) the author mentions nothing about wives in … *etc.*

NET Bible: New English Translation

Difficult Renderings

1Sa 13.1	Saul was [**thirty**] [A] **years old** when he began to reign; he ruled over Israel for [**forty**] [B] **years**. fn: [A] **tn** The MT does not have "thirty." A number appears to have dropped out of the Hebrew text here, since as it stands the MT (literally, "a son of a year") must mean that Saul was only . . . [B] **tc** The MT has "two years" here. If this number is to be accepted as correct, the meaning apparently would be that after a lapse of two years at the beginning of Saul's reign, he then went about the task of consolidating an army as described in what follows . . . *etc.*
Is 28.13	So the LORD's message to them will **sound like** **meaningless gibberish,** **senseless babbling,** **a syllable here, a syllable there.** [C] As a result, they will fall on their backsides when they try to walk, [D] and be injured, ensnared, and captured. [E] fn: [C] **tn** Heb "And the message of the Lord will be to them, '*tsav latsav*,' etc." See the note . . . [C] **tn** Heb "as a result they will go and stumble backward." Perhaps an . . . [D] **sn** When divine warn- . . . *etc.*

Significant Renderings

ʿalmah	Is 7.14	For this reason the Lord himself will give you a confirming sign. [E] Look, **this** [F] **young woman** [G] is about to conceive [H] and will give birth to a son. You, young woman, will name him [I] Immanuel. [J] fn: [E] **tn** The Hebrew term אוֹת (ʾot, "sign") can refer to a miraculous . . . [F] **tn** Heb "the young woman." The Hebrew article has been rendered as a de- . . . [G] **tn** Traditionally, "virgin." Because this verse . . . [H] **tn** Elsewhere the adjective הָרָה (harah), when . . . [I] **tn** Heb "and you will call his name." The words "young woman" . . . [J] **sn** The name Immanuel means "God [is] with us."

The Best Bible?

she'ol . . . 'abaddon	Pr 15.11	**Death** and **Destruction**[A] are before the LORD – how much more[B] the hearts of humans![C]

fn: [A] **tn** *Heb* "Sheol and Abaddon" (שְׁאוֹל וַאֲבַדּוֹן) (*she'ol va'avaddon*); so ASV, NASB, NRSV; cf. KJV "Hell and destruction"; NAB "the nether world and the abyss." . . . [B] **tn** The construction אַף כִּי (*'af ki*, "how much more!") introduces . . . [C] **tn** *Heb* "the hearts of the sons of man," although here "sons. . .*etc.*

egennēsen	Mt 1.2	Abraham **was the father**[D] of Isaac, Isaac **the father of** Jacob, Jacob **the father of** Judah and his brothers

fn: [D] **tn** *Grk* "fathered."

eskēnōsen	Jn 1.14	Now[E] the Word became flesh[F] and **took up residence**[G] among us. We[H] saw his glory—the glory of the one and only,[I] full of grace and truth, who came from the Father.

fn: [E] **tn** Here καί (*kai*) has been translated as "now" . . . [I] **tn** Or "of the unique one." Although this . . . *etc.*

tois ioudaiois	Jn 18.36	Jesus replied, "My kingdom[J] is not from this world. If my kingdom were from this world, my servants would be fighting to keep me from being[K] handed over[L] **to the Jewish authorities.**[M] But as it is,[N] my kingdom is not from here."

fn: [J] **sn** The kingdom (of God) is a major theme of Jesus' teaching. The nature of . . . [N] **tn** Grk "now."

dikaiosunē theou, pisteōs Iēsou Christou	Ro 3.22a	namely, **the righteousness of God** through **the faithfulness of Jesus Christ**[O] for all who believe

fn: [O] **tn** Or "faith in Christ." A decision is difficult difficult here. Though traditionally translated . . . *etc.*

Granville Sharp's rule applied	Ti 2.13	as we wait for the happy fulfillment of our hope in the glorious appearing[P] of **our great God and Savior, Jesus Christ.**[Q]

fn: [P] **tn** *Grk* "the blessed hope and glorious appearing." [Q] **tn** The terms "God and Savior" both . . . *etc.*

SIGNIFICANT REVISIONS

The editors of the NET intended to revise its text in five-year in-crements beginning in 2010, while the notes would undergo con-stant revision, improvement, and expression. The first of these revisions was actually released in 2017. Additional revisions were made after the publishing agreement with Thomas Nelson pub-lisher in the fall of 2019.

The revisers improved awkward language and consistent ren-dering. In particular, they changed how they rendered sexual language. Originally, the translators wrote these passages explic-itly for a low-context academic audience, but realized later that such language was not appropriate for their ideal audience—the general reader. To fix this, they most frequently rendered sexual references into the formal euphemistic language inherent in the original Hebrew and Greek.

Imagine reading the nativity story and Mary's reply to the an-gel aloud in public. Which will draw more unwanted attention?

	NET Bible (2006)	NET Bible (2017)
Lk 1.34	"How will this be, since I have not had **sexual relations** [A] with a man?"	"How will this be, since I have not had **been intimate** with [A] a man?"
	fn: [A] **sn** Grk "have not known." The expression in the Greek text is a euphemism for sexual relations. . . . *etc.*	
Gn 25.22a	But the children struggled [B] inside her, and she said, "**If it is going to be like** this, **I'm not so sure I want to be pregnant!**" [C]	But the children struggled [B] inside her, and she said, "**Why is** this **happening to me?**" [C]
	fn: [C] **sn** Heb "If [it is] so, why [am] I this [way]?" Rebekah wanted to know what was happening to her, but the question itself reflects a growing despair over the struggle of the unborn children. . . . *etc.*	
Gn 6.4	**were having sexual relations**	**would sleep**

Ex 20.16		goes to bed
Jg 21.12	sexual intercourse	marital relations
Lv 20.17		intimate . . . in bed
Gn 4.1	had marital relations	was intimate

Other revisions bring about greater concordance, formalism, or consistency:

	NET Bible (2006)	NET Bible (2017)
1Kg 8.7	The **cherubs'** wings extended over the place where the ark sat; the **cherubs** overshadowed the ark and its poles.	The **cherubim's** wings extended over the place where the ark sat; the **cherubim** overshadowed the ark and its poles.

The example above replaces the English plural ending with ("–s") the Hebrew ("–im"), thus removing its association with winged babies.

Heb 6.2	teaching about **baptisms**, laying on of hands, resurrection of the dead, and eternal judgment	teaching about **ritual washings**, laying on of hands, resurrection of the dead, and eternal judgment

	NET Bible (2006)	NET Bible (2017)	NET Bible (2019)
Jg 2.1	The LORD's **angelic messenger** went up from Gilgal to Bokim.	The LORD's **angel** went up from Gilgal to Bokim.	The **angel of the** LORD went up from Gilgal to Bokim.

Technical language, especially regarding the feasts, the tabernacle, and topography, is made more consistent:

	NET Bible (2006)	NET Bible (2017)
Gn 23.10b	Ephron the **Hethite** replied to Abraham in the hearing of the sons of Heth	Ephron the **Hittite** replied to Abraham in the hearing of the sons of Heth

	NET Bible (2006)	NET Bible (2017)
Lv 4.6	The priest must dip his finger in the blood and sprinkle some of it seven times before the LORD toward the front of the **veil-canopy** of the sanctuary	The priest must dip his finger in the blood and sprinkle some of it seven times before the LORD toward the front of the **special curtain** of the sanctuary.
Lv 8.15	Moses then took the blood and put it all around on the horns of the altar with his finger and **decontaminated** the altar	Moses then took the blood and put it all around on the horns of the altar with his finger and **purified** the altar
Lv 16.2c	"I will appear in the cloud over the **atonement plate**."	"I will appear in the cloud over the **atonement lid**."
Mt 13.25	"But while everyone was sleeping, an enemy came and sowed **weeds** among the wheat and went away."	"But while everyone was sleeping, an enemy came and sowed **darnel** among the wheat and went away."
Ex 5.1b	"**Thus says** the LORD, the God of Israel, 'Release my people so that they may hold a pilgrim feast to me in the **desert**.'"	"**This is what** the LORD, the God of Israel, **has said**, 'Release my people so that they may hold a pilgrim feast to me in the **wilderness**.'"

On the other hand:

Lv 16.10	but the goat which has been designated by lot for Azazel is to be stood alive before the LORD to make atonement on it by sending it away to Azazel into the **wilderness**.	but the goat which has been designated by lot for Azazel is to be stood alive before the LORD to make atonement on it by sending it away to Azazel into the **desert**.

Divine names and epithets are made more consistent:

Gn 6.3a	So the LORD said, "My **spirit** will not remain in humankind indefinitely, since they are mortal."	So the LORD said, "My **Spirit** will not remain in humankind indefinitely, since they are mortal."

The Best Bible?

	NET Bible (2006)	NET Bible (2017)
1Sa 1.3	Lord **of Hosts**	Lord **of Heaven's Armies**
1Kg 18.15	Lord **who rules over all**	

Most of the revisions for the 2019 Thomas Nelson edition were improvements made to punctuation and conversions of written numbers to arabic numerals, though some stylistic improvements and echoes to more familiar language were made:[14]

	NET Bible (2017)	NET Bible (2019)
Ps 27.1	The Lord **delivers and vindicates me!**[A] I fear no one![B] The Lord protects my life! I am afraid of no one![C]	The Lord **my light**[A] and **my salvation.** I fear no one.[B] The Lord protects my life. I am afraid of no one.[C]
	fn: [A] **sn** "Light" is often used as a metaphor for deliverance and the life/blessings it brings . . . Another option . . . "light" refers here to divine guidance . . . [B] **tn** Heb "Whom shall I fear?" . . . *etc.*	
Is 9.6b	He shoulders responsibility[D] and is called:[E] **Amazing** Adviser,[F] Mighty God,[G] Everlasting Father,[H] Prince of Peace.[I]	He shoulders responsibility[D] and is called[E] **Wonderful** Adviser,[F] Mighty God,[G] Everlasting Father,[H] Prince of Peace.[I]
Jer 17.15	Listen[J] to what they are saying to me. **They are saying, "Where are the things the Lord threatens us with? Come on! Let's see them happen!"**[K]	"Listen[J] to what they are saying to me, 'Where are the things the Lord threatens us with? **May it please** happen!'"[K]
	fn: [J] **tn** The Hebrew particle הִנֵּה (*hinneh*) calls particular attention to something. [K] **tn** Heb "Where is the word of the Lord? Let it come [or "come to pass"], please." The use of "please" is probably sarcastic.	

	NET Bible (2017)	NET Bible (2019)
Jon 2.10	Then the LORD commanded [A] the fish and it **disgorged** Jonah on dry land.	Then the LORD commanded [A] the fish and it **vomited** Jonah **out** onto dry land.
	fn: [A] **tn** Heb "spoke to." The fish functions as a literary foil to highlight Jonah's hesitancy to obey God up to this point. In contrast to Jonah who immediately fled when God commanded him, the fish immediately obeyed.	
Mk 1.41	Moved with **compassion**,[B] Jesus [C] stretched out his hand and touched [D] him, saying, "I am willing. Be clean!"	Moved with **indignation**,[B] Jesus [C] stretched out his hand and touched [D] him, saying, "I am willing. Be clean!"
	fn: [B] **tc** The reading found in almost the entire NT MS tradition is σπλαγχνισθείς (*splanchnisthei*, "moved with compassion"). Codex Bezae (D) and a few Latin MSS (a ff² r¹*) here read ὀργισθείς (*orgisthei*, "moved with anger").... *etc.*	
Ro 3:3	What then? If some **did not believe, does** their **unbelief** nullify the faithfulness **of** God?	What then? If some **were unfaithful**, their **unfaithfulness will not** nullify God's faithfulness, **will it?**

ENDORSEMENTS

The NET is endorsed by conservative evangelical leaders and scholars, several of whom hold strong ties with Dallas Theological Seminary, including Kenneth L. Barker (general editor of the NIV; NASB), Tony Evans (pastor, Oak Cliff Bible Fellowship), Wayne Grudem (ESV), Robert H. Gundry, Howard G. Hendricks († 2013), J. Ed Komoszewski (*Christian Research Journal*), Roger L. Omanson, Klyne Snodgrass (NLT), Chuck Swindoll (chancellor, Dallas Theological Seminary), and John F. Walvoord (former president, Dallas Theological Seminary).[15]

COPYRIGHT

Those who published the NET hold a radically different copyright position than most other Bible publishers. Biblical Studies Press is guided by the principle of "Ministry First" in order to make it easy for anyone to quote and use the NET.

For non-commercial (non-sales) purposes: You may quote any number of verses from the NET in any form without prior written permission, but your work must include the copyright acknowledgment below.

For commercial purposes: You may quote any number of verses from the NET in any form without prior written permission; the verses must comprise less than 50% of your work's content; they may not be quoted in a commentary or other biblical reference work; and your work must include the following copyright acknowledgment.

Audio presentations require an emailed notice to the Biblical Studies Press, which gives them permission to use your audio on their websites (like Bible.org), and the following acknowledgment as an audio insert.

Unless used exclusively, follow citations with the designation (*NET Bible*®) or (NET) if space is limited. For example:

Jn 1.4, "In him was life, and that life was the light of men." (NET)

NET

The title "*NET Bible®*" is a registered trademark with the U.S. Patent and Trademark Office by Biblical Studies Press, but its popular initialism (NET) is not.

For permissions not covered here, visit <https://bible.org/contact?category=Permissions>, or write to Biblical Studies Foundation, PO Box 831119, Richardson, TX 75083-1119.

ENDNOTES FOR THE
NET BIBLE: NEW ENGLISH TRANSLATION

1 "Preface to the First Edition," *NET Bible: New English Translation,* 1st ed. (Richardson, TX: Biblical Studies Press, LLC, 2005).

2 The *NET Bible* Second Edition (designated NET 2.0) claims to contain 58,506 translators' notes, yet the *NET Bible* published by Thomas Nelson (NET 2.1) is advertized as having more than 60,000. The difference is due to an initial miscount of footnote numbers. When the editors submitted the text with revised notes to Th. Nelson, they realized they had counted only the numbers without counting the actual notes under each number. Some numbers listed one, two, or even three notes each (a **sn**, a **tn**, and a **tc** note). This means that the *NET Bible* Second Edition (2.0) has always been published more than 60,000 notes, even when the number advertised was 58,506.

3 *Ibid.*

4 *Ibid.*

5 *Ibid.*

6 The textual consultant was most probably none other than Dan Wallace himself. *Ibid.*

7 Daniel B. Wallace, "Innovations in the Text and Translation of the *NET Bible, New Testament,*" paper presented to the Society of Biblical Literature's (SBL) Annual Meeting (Nashville, TN, November 18, 2000), accessed July 22, 2019, https://netbible.com/innovations-text-and-translation-net-bible-new-testament.

8 "The *NET Bible* Team," *NET Bible,* 1st ed.

9 "Introduction to the First Edition," *NET Bible,* 1st ed., p. 23*, 24*.

10 *Ibid.,* p. 24*.

11 The NT marginal notes of *NET Bible* (2.1) were revised to reflect Nestle-Aland's *Novum Testamentum Graece* 28th edition, which accounts for revisions in about 600 text critical notes.

12 *Ibid.*

13 *Ibid.,* p. 25.

14 "What changes were made in the Second Edition from version 2 to version 2.1?," *New English Translation*'s website, accessed November 16, 2020, https://netbible.com/faq/.

¹⁵ "Endorsements," *New English Translation*'s website, accessed February 3, 2020, https://netbible.com/endorsements/.

The Message®

The Bible in Contemporary Language

Produced by NavPress, 1993–2002

FORMAL / FUNCTIONAL TENDENCIES

FORMAL   FUNCTIONAL

Interlinear NASB KJV NKJV ESV CSB NRSV NET NIV NLT TNIV NIrV **MSG** TPT   Free
Paraphrase

TEXT BASES

OT Masoretic Hebrew and Ancient Versions.   **NT** Eclectic Greek.

TRANSLATION TIMELINE

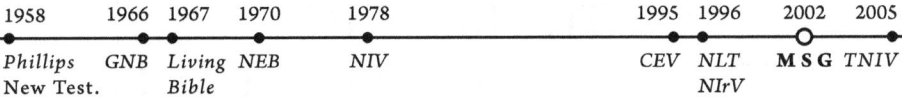

1958	1966	1967	1970	1978	1995	1996	2002	2005
Phillips New Test.	*GNB*	*Living Bible*	*NEB*	*NIV*	*CEV*	*NLT NIrV*	**MSG**	*TNIV*

CONTEMPORARY EVENTS

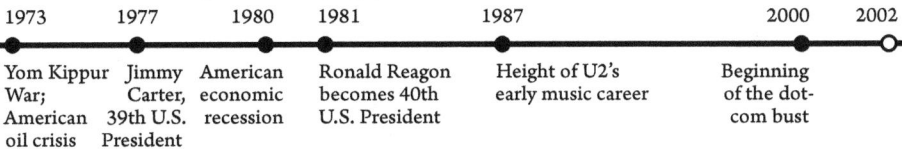

1973	1977	1980	1981	1987	2000	2002
Yom Kippur War; American oil crisis	Jimmy Carter, 39th U.S. President	American economic recession	Ronald Reagon becomes 40th U.S. President	Height of U2's early music career	Beginning of the dot-com bust	

PUBLICATION TIMELINE

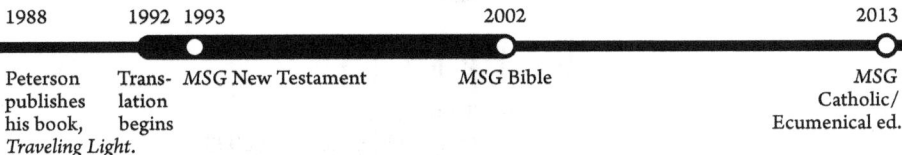

1988	1992	1993	2002	2013
Peterson publishes his book, *Traveling Light.*	Trans-lation begins	*MSG* New Testament	*MSG* Bible	*MSG* Catholic/ Ecumenical ed.

The

MESSAGE

THE BIBLE IN
CONTEMPORARY LANGUAGE

EUGENE H. PETERSON

NAVPRESS

Bringing Truth to Life
P.O. Box 35001, Colorado Springs, Colorado 80935
www.navpress.com

I t was during the economic downturn of the early 1980s when Eugene Hoiland Peterson, pastor of a Presbyterian church in Maryland, watched his congregation become unsettled by the turmoil surrounding them. Peterson was angered that they somehow failed to grasp the sufficiency of God's grace, which he had been teaching them for the past months. So, he intended to teach them all over again, even if he had to do it in Greek.

Instead of teaching biblical languages to his congregation (which he discovered had very little impact), Peterson began delivering messages that he had translated and paraphrased from the Greek New Testament. He rendered Paul's words from Galatians in contemporary "street" language that his congregation could relate to. He later published this in a small book titled *Traveling Light* (1982).[1]

Feedback on his messages and books was encouraging, but it would take another eight years (1990) before an editor from NavPress would read his initial translation and urge Peterson to continue translating the entire New Testament. By then, the time was ripe for such a project, since he was retiring the pastorate and seeking a full-time writing position.

Peterson took two years to complete his New Testament. He consulted with a number of scholars who reviewed his work before is publication. In 1993, NavPress published *The Message, The New Testament in Contemporary Language*. Peterson released portions of the Old Testament as he finished them and concluded his translation of the Bible and its review in 2002. (William Griffin completed the Apocrypha based on the *Nova Vulgata* for Roman Catholic readers in 2013.)[2]

STATED TRANSLATION IDEALS

Eugene Peterson intended to paraphrase *The Message* "in the rhythms and idiom of contemporary language."[3] "The goal is not to render a word-for-word conversion of Greek into English, but rather to convert the tone, the rhythm, the events, the ideas, into the way we actually think and speak."[4] "*The Message* is a reading Bible. It is not intended to replace the excellent study Bibles that are available. [Peterson's] intent here . . . is simply to get people reading it who don't know that the Bible is read-able at all . . . and to get people who long ago lost interest in the Bible to read again."[5]

Peterson intended "to recapture the tone, to bring out the subtleties and nuances of the Hebrew and Greek languages while keeping a sense of firsthand experience for contemporary readers. He often asked himself, 'If Paul were the pastor of my church, how would he say this?' or 'If Jesus were here teaching, what would it sound like?'"

The publishers initially considered *The Message* a "translation of tone" or a "paraphrase from the original languages."[6]

TEXT BASES

New Testament

Eclectic Greek text. The specific Greek text base was not specified, but when comparing his text to the *Textus Receptus* and Nestle-Aland/United Bible Society text, the MSG's renderings mostly conform to N-A/UBS.

Old Testament

Masoretic Hebrew-Aramaic text. Not specified.

CONTRIBUTORS

The Message started as a private translation by Eugene H. Peterson. Peterson acknowledged several scholars with whom he consulted to review his work. His NT consultants were Darrell L. Bock (ESV, NET, NLT), Donald A. Hagner (NLT), William W. Klein, Moisés Silva (ESV, NASB), and Rodney A. Whitacre.

OT consultants were Robert L. Alden (NIV), Richard E. Averbeck (HCSB, NET), Bryan E. Beyer (HCSB), Lamar E. Cooper, Sr., Peter E. Enns, Duane A. Garrett (HCSB), Donald R. Glenn (NET, NIV), Paul R. House (NLT, HCSB, ESV), Robert L. Hubbard (CEB), V. Philips Long (ESV, NLT), Tremper Longman III (HCSB, CEB, NCV, NLT), John N. Oswalt (ESV, NLT, NIV), Richard L. Pratt, Jr. (NLT), John H. Walton, Prescott H. Williams, Jr., and Marvin R. Wilson (NIV).

All consultants held faculty positions from a broad number of evangelical seminaries.

THEOLOGICAL ASSUMPTIONS

Eugene H. Peterson (1932–2018) was ordained in the Presbyterian Church (U.S.A.). He believed that Scripture was authoritative for Christian life and practice. Therefore, his official stance on marriage as between one man and one woman contradicted the doctrinal stance of his denomination.

FEATURES

When Peterson released his rendition of the Psalms in 1994, he used "Yahweh" for God's distinctive personal name (*i.e.*, the Tetragrammaton). In the 2001 release of his NT and Psalms and later editions, he translates the name as "GOD" in small-caps instead.

Peterson explains that he left out verse numbers to encourage unimpeded reading.[7] Later editions are available that place reference numbers in the outer margin.[8]

Peterson consistently rendered the author's self reference in Ecclesiastes as "the Quester," whereas other translations use "the Preacher" or "the Teacher." He translated place names instead of transliterating them, for example he translated "Havvoth-jair" in **Jg 10.4** as "Jair's Villages." He also used the generic, masculine-singular pronoun (*cf.* **1Co 8.10; Gal 6.1**), not because of any stated agenda, but because it was most natural to his speaking.

The *Message* was published with no footnotes or cross-references: Peterson did not wish to hamper the reading experience.

ASSESSMENT

The Message is an expanded paraphrase—the product of a capable English stylist, whose familiarity with Hebrew and Greek is filtered through his experience as a pastor. Its variety of expressions is refreshing. Sometimes Peterson renders passages with high-register, literary attainment. Sometimes he's plain-spoken and down-to-earth.

Often he writes colloquially, though perhaps too frequently. Peterson's intent was to convey the impact, and not merely the words, of the original, though we cannot be sure how successful he is at conveying the same connotations and emotional effects intended by Scripture's original authors or felt by its first audience.

The Message is a treasure trove for preachers looking for interesting figures of speech and sermon illustrations. It is not ideal for serious study, partly because its radical contemporization loosens it from its linguistic and historic moorings, but it is enjoyable for casual reading and useful for a fresh perspective.

THEMESSAGE®

REPRESENTATIVE SAMPLES

Familiar Passages

Gn 1.1–2	First this: God created the Heavens and Earth—all you see, all you don't see. Earth was a soup of nothingness, a bottomless emptiness, an inky blackness. God's Spirit brooded like a bird above the watery abyss.

Ps 23.1–2	God, my shepherd!
	  I don't need a thing.
	You have bedded me down in lush meadows,
	  you find me quiet pools to drink from.

Ps 27.4	I'm asking GOD for one thing,
	  only one thing:
	To live with him in his house
	  my whole life long.
	I'll contemplate his beauty;
	  I'll study at his feet.

Jn 3.16	"This is how much God loved the world: He gave his Son, his one and only Son. And this is why: so that no one need be destroyed; by believing in him, anyone can have a whole and lasting life."

Divine Name and Titles

YHWH	Ps 24.1a	**GOD** claims Earth and everything in it
adonai	Ps 90.1b	**God**, it seems you've been our home forever
elohim	Gn 1.27a	**God** created human beings; he created them god-like, Reflecting God's nature.
adonai YHWH	Ps 73.28b	I've made **Lord GOD** my home.
adonai elohim	Dn 9.3a	I turned to the **Master God**
YHWH *saba'oth*	1Sa 17.45b	I come at you in the name of **GOD-of-the-Angel-Armies**
el shaddai	Ex 6.3a	"I appeared to Abraham, Isaac, and Jacob as **The Strong God**"
kyrios	Lk 20.42b	"**God** said to my **Master**, "Sit here at my right hand""
christos	Mt 16.16b	"You're the **Christ**, the **Messiah**, the Son of the living God."

MSG

New Testament Text Base

Mt 17.21	——	(Absent without footnote)
Mt 18.11	——	(Absent without footnote)
Ac 8.37	——	(Absent without footnote)
1Jn 5.7b–8a	——	(Absent without footnote)

Gender Language

ʾādām	Gn 9.6	Whoever sheds **human blood**, by **humans** let his blood be shed, Because God made **humans** in his image reflecting God's very nature.
ʾîsh . . . nephesh	Lv 24.17	"**Anyone** who hits and kills **a fellow human** must be put to death."
ʾāvîw	Pr 15.5a	Moral dropouts won't listen to **their elders**
huioi	Mt 5.9	"You're blessed when you can show people how to co-operate instead of compete or fight. That's when you discover who you really are, and your place in God's **family**."
anthrōpōn	Mt 4.19	"Come with me. I'll make a new kind of fisherman out of you. I'll show you how to catch **men** and **women** instead of perch and bass."
hekastō . . . autou	Ro 2.6	Make no mistake: In the end **you** get what's coming **to you**
gynaikos anēr	Ti 1.6a	As you select them, ask, "Is **this man** well-thought-of? Is **he** committed to his **wife**? Are his children believers?"
gynaikas	1Ti 3.11	No exceptions are to be made for **women**—same qualifications: serious, dependable, not sharp-tongued, not overfond of wine.

The Best Bible?

Difficult Renderings

1Sa 13.1	Saul was **a young man** when he began as king. He was king over Israel for **many years.**
Is 28.13	So GOD will **start over with the simple basics and address them in baby talk, one syllable at a time**—"Da, da, da, da, blah, blah, blah, blah. That's a good little girl, that's a good little boy." And like toddlers, they will get up and fall down, get bruised and confused and lost.

Significant Renderings

ʻalmah	Is 7.14	So the Master is going to give you a sign anyway. Watch for this: **A girl who is presently a virgin** will get pregnant. She'll bear a son and name him Immanuel (God-With-Us).
she'ol . . . 'abaddon	Pr 15.11	Even **hell** holds no secrets from GOD— do you think he can't read human hearts?
egennēsen	Mt 1.2	Abraham **had** Isaac, Isaac **had** Jacob, Jacob **had** Judah and his brothers
eskēnōsen	Jn 1.14	The Word became flesh and blood, and **moved into the neighborhood.** We saw the glory with our own eyes, the one-of-a-kind glory, like Father, like Son, Generous inside and out, true from start to finish.
tois ioudaiois	Jn 18.36	"My kingdom," said Jesus, "doesn't consist of what you see around you. If it did, my followers would fight so that I wouldn't be handed over **to the Jews.** But I'm not that kind of king, not the world's kind of king."
dikaiosunē theou, pisteōs Iēsou Christou	Ro 3.22a	**The God-setting-things-right** that we read about has become **Jesus-setting-things-right for us.** And not only for us, but for everyone who believes in him.
Granville Sharp's rule applied	Tt 2.13	and is whetting our appetites for the glorious day when **our great God and Savior, Jesus Christ,** appears.

SIGNIFICANT REVISIONS

When comparing Peterson's earlier work, *Traveling Light* (1982),[9] with *The Message* (1993), we can see how Peterson strives to communicate the gist of Scripture to contemporary audiences by the kinds of changes he has made between the two editions. Some of his revisions included corrected spelling and improved punctuation (fewer semicolons, and more periods) to make reading simpler. Other revisions include paraphrastic clarifications:

	Traveling Light (1983)	The Message (2002)
Gal 1.16b; 3.14; cf. 3.28	Now he has intervened and revealed his son to me so that I might joyfully tell **Gentiles** about him.	Now he has intervened and revealed his Son to me so that I might joyfully tell **non-Jews** about him.
Gal 1.23	There was only this report: "That man who once persecuted us is now preaching the very **faith** he used to **lay waste.**"	There was only this report: "That man who once persecuted us is now preaching the very **message** he used to **try to destroy.**"
Gal 1.24	Their response was to **glorify** God because of me.	Their response was to **recognize and worship** God because of me!
Gal 2.17b	And are you ready to make the accusation that since people like me, who **seek to be justified by Christ**, aren't perfectly virtuous, Christ must therefore be an accessory to sin? The accusation is frivolous.	And are you ready to make the accusation that since people like me, who **go through Christ in order to get things right with God**, aren't perfectly virtuous, Christ must therefore be an accessory to sin? The accusation is frivolous.

Peterson had chaged his language to make it even more contemporary and relevant to modern audiences:

The Best Bible?

	Traveling Light (1983)	The Message (2002)
Gal 1.6	I can't believe your fickleness—how easily you have turned traitor to him who called you by the grace of Christ **to** a variant **gospel**!	I can't believe your fickleness—how easily you have turned traitor to him who called you by the grace of Christ **by embracing** a variant **message**!
Gal 1.11	Know this—I am most emphatic here, friends—this **good news that** I delivered to you is not mere human optimism.	Know this—I am most emphatic here, friends—this **great Message** I delivered to you is not mere human optimism.
Gal 2.20b	I am no longer driven to **please** God. Christ lives in me.	I am no longer driven to **impress** God. Christ lives in me.
Gal 2.21c	If a living relationship with God could come by rule-keeping, then Christ died **gratuitously**.	If a living relationship with God could come by rule-keeping, then Christ died **unnecessarily**.
Gal 3.17	A will, earlier ratified by God, is not annulled by an **a codicil that is** attached 430 years later, negating the promise of the will.	A will, earlier ratified by God, is not annulled by **an addendum** attached 430 years later, **thereby** negating the promise of the will.
Gal 3.19c	[The law] was arranged by angelic messengers through **the hand of the mediator**, Moses.	[The law] was arranged by angelic messengers through **a middleman**, Moses.
Gal 4.6	Thus we have been set free to experience our rightful sonship. Because you are now children, God sent the Spirit of his Son into our lives crying out, "**Abba**! Father!"	You can tell for sure that you are now fully adopted as his own children because God sent the Spirit of his Son into our lives crying out, "**Papa**! Father!"
Gal 6.18	May what our **Lord** Jesus Christ gives freely, be deeply and personally yours, my friends. **Amen.**	May what our **Master** Jesus Christ gives freely be deeply and personally yours, my friends. **Oh, yes!**

	Traveling Light (1983)	The Message (2002)
Gal 6.7b–8a	The person who plants self-ishness, ignoring the needs of others—ignoring God!—harvests a crop of **corruption**.	The person who plants selfishness, ignoring the needs of others—ignoring God!—harvests a crop of **weeds. All he'll have to show for his life is weeds!**

In some places, Peterson must have felt the need to reign in some of his paraphrase (Gal 2.14; 3.1; 5.22–23) or make it more consistent (*Cf.* Gal 1.1b).

	Traveling Light (1983)	The Message (2002)
Gal 1.1b	My authority . . . comes directly from Jesus **Christ** and God the Father who raised him from the dead: I'm God-commissioned.	My authority . . . comes directly from Jesus **the Messiah** and God the Father, who raised him from the dead. I'm God-commissioned.
Gal 2.14–15a	We, **who were born sinners in the Jewish way rather than the gentile, well know** that **a person** is not set right with God by rule keeping but only through personal faith in Jesus Christ.	We **Jews know that we have no advantage of birth over "non-Jewish sinners." We know very well** that **we** are not set right with God by rule-keeping but only through personal faith in Jesus Christ.
Gal 5.22a	What happens when we live God's way? **Quite without any effort on our part things begin to appear in** our lives, much the same way that fruit appears in an orchard	**But** what happens when we live God's way? **He brings gifts into** our lives, much the same way that fruit appears in an orchard
Gal 5.23b	No one can make us do these things; at the same time no one can prevent us from being such persons. These qualities of life develop as surely as fruit on a well-cultivated tree.	Legalism is helpless in bringing this about; it only gets in the way.

NavPress has partnered with Tyndale House Publishers since 2014 and released a limited number of revisions (only around 570 changes to the text) in 2018 to improve comprehension for contemporary readers (usually at a lower or more general register). These changes were intended as an "'aesthetic revision' of *The Message*, with spot-specific changes that would support ongoing readability over time. [They] were made with the oversight of biblical scholars and authorized by Eugene Peterson" before he died.[10] For example:

	Traveling Light (1983)	The Message (2002)	The Message (2018)
Gal 3.1a	You crazy Galatians! Did someone **give you a hallucinatory drug?**	You crazy Galatians! Did someone **put a hex on you? Have you taken leave of your senses?**	You crazy Galatians! Did someone **put a spell on you? Have you taken leave of your senses?**
Gn 4.1a	Even then God had **designs** on me. Why, when I was still in my mother's womb he chose and called me **by his grace!**	Even then God had **designs** on me. Why, when I was still in my mother's womb he chose and called me **out of sheer generosity!**	Even then God had **his eye** on me. Why, when I was still in my mother's womb he chose and called me **out of sheer generosity!**

	The Message (2002)	The Message (2018)
Mt 8.27	The men rubbed their eyes, astonished. "What's going on here? Wind and sea **come to heel** at his command!"	The men rubbed their eyes, astonished. "What's going on here? Wind and sea **stand up and take notice** at his command!"
Mt 9.34	The Pharisees were left sputtering, "**Hocus-pocus.** It's nothing but **hocus-pocus.** He's probably made a pact with the Devil."	The Pharisees were left sputtering, "**Smoke and mirrors.** It's nothing but **smoke and mirrors.** He's probably made a pact with the Devil."
Mt 22.29; cf. Mk 12.24	Jesus answered, "You're off base on two counts: You don't know **your Bibles,** and you don't know how God works.	Jesus answered, "You're off base on two counts: You don't know **what God said,** and you don't know how God works.

The Message

	The Message (2002)	The Message (2018)
Lk 4.33–34a	In the meeting place that day there was a man demonically disturbed. He screamed, "**Ho**! What business do you have here with us, Jesus?"	In the meeting place that day there was a man demonically disturbed. He screamed, "**Stop**! What business do you have here with us, Jesus?"

Any contemporary paraphrase, such as *The Message*, will necessarily feel dated and want an occasional brush up to stay relevant to modern readers.

DOCTRINAL CONCERNS

As a paraphrase, The Message will never fit an expositor's need for a careful translation to serve in Bible study. This was never Peterson's intent with his rendition, anyways. He preferred the RSV for public preaching and personal devotions.[11]

Sometimes Peterson's paraphrase resorts to generalization. This makes certain passages ambiguous which other translations make clear. For an example, a couple of the more controversial renderings are compared:

Ro 1.26–27	Worse followed. Refusing to know God, they soon didn't know how to be human either—women didn't know how to be women, men didn't know how to be men. Sexually confused, they abused and defiled one another, women with women, men with men— all lust, no love. And then they paid for it, oh, how they paid for it—emptied of God and love, godless and loveless wretches. (*The Message*)	For this reason God gave them over to dishonorable passions. For their women exchanged the natural sexual relations for unnatural ones, and likewise the men also abandoned natural relations with women and were inflamed in their passions for one another. Men committed shameless acts with men and received in themselves the due penalty for their error. (*NET Bible*)

	Don't you realize that this is not the way to live? Unjust people who don't care about God will not be joining in his kingdom. Those who use and abuse each other, use and abuse sex, use and abuse the earth and everything in it, don't qualify as citizens in God's kingdom.	Do you not know that the unrighteous will not inherit the kingdom of God? Do not be deceived! The sexually immoral, idolaters, adulterers, passive homosexual partners, practicing homosexuals, thieves, the greedy, drunkards, the verbally abusive, and swindlers will not inherit the kingdom of God.
1Co 6.9–10		
	(*The Message*)	(*NET Bible*)

Some readers have noted certain renderings that seem to smack of New Age influence.[12] For example, at **Mt 6.9b–10**, the Lord's prayer reads

> Our Father in heaven,
> Reveal who you are.
> Set the world right;
> Do what's best—as above, so below. (*The Message*)

The unique rendering "as above, so below" forms an identical aphorism attributed to the hermetistic *Emerald Tablet*.[13] It is not possible to measure Peterson's intentions when he used this language: Was he consciously trying to relate to English speakers familiar with Wiccan or New Age philosophy? More than likely, he just wished to poetically convey the more familiar (and, therefore, the more easily dismissed) renderings "on earth as it is in heaven" (RSV, NRSV, NASB, NKJV, NIV, GNB, NET, NLT, CSB, *etc.*) or "as in heaven, so on earth" (RV/ASV). (*Cf.* **Col 1.16**)[14]

Some accuse Peterson's rendering of **Eph 4.4–6** (*cf.* **1Co 15.22**) of supporting ecumenical universalism and panentheism because the capitalized word "Oneness" in his added summary (in **bold** here):

You were all called to travel on the same road and in the same direction, so stay together, both outwardly and inwardly. You have one Master, one faith, one baptism, one God and Father of all, who rules over all, works through all, and is present in all. **Everything you are and think and do is permeated with Oneness**. (Eph 4.4–6, *The Message*)

Like all passages, these ought to be read in their context before judging them as outright perversions or distortions of Christian doctrine. Remember that no paraphrase can give a satisfactory basis for careful exegesis, anyway.

ENDORSEMENTS

The Message and its various portions have been endorsed by a wide spectrum of society, most notably by Bono, the lead singer of the music group, U2. Other noted personalities include Stuart and Jill Briscoe (pastors), Frederick Buechner (author), Carnegie Samuel Calian (president emeritus, Pittsburgh Theological Seminary), Michael Card (CSB; recording artist), Gordon D. Fee (TNIV, NIV'11; professor, Regent), Harold Fickett (director The Milton Center, author), Vernon Grounds († former president and chancellor, Denver Seminary), Harry J. Harm (translator, Wycliffe), Walter C. Kaiser, Jr. (HCSB, NIV; OT professor, Gordon-Conwell Theological Seminary), Madeleine L'Engle (author), Tremper Longman III (CEB, HCSB, NCV, NLT), Mark Lowry (comedien), Max Lucado (pastor, author), Harold L. Myra (president, Christianity Today, Inc.), Tricia Rhodes (author, speaker), Rebecca St. James (recording artist), Virginia Stem Owens (author), J. I. Packer († ESV; former professor of theology, Regent College), Brock and Bodie Thoene (authors), and Walter Wangerin, Jr. (author).[15]

COPYRIGHT

You may quote up to 500 verses from the *The Message* in any form without prior written permission; the verses may not constitute a complete book of the Bible; they must comprise less than 25% of your work's content; and your work must include the following copyright acknowledgment.

Unless used exclusively, follow citations with the designation (MSG). For example:

Jn 1.4, "What came into existence was Life, and the Life was Light to live by." (MSG)

The title *"The Message®"* and its stylized wordmark are registered trademarks with the U.S. Patent and Trademark Office by The Navigators, but its popular initialism (MSG) is not.

For permissions not covered here, write to Tyndale House Publishers, Inc., 351 Executive Drive, Carol Stream, IL 60188 (https://www.navpress.com/permissions/form)

ENDNOTES FOR THE MESSAGE

1   Eugene H. Peterson, *Traveling Light* (Downers Grove, IL: Inter-Varsity Press, 1982, '88).

2   NavPress, "History and Frequently Asked Questions," last modified 2007, accessed August 19, 2008, http://navpress.com/Message/HistoryAndFaqs/.

3   Peterson, *The Message: The New Testament in Contemporary English* (Colorado Springs, CO: NavPress Publishing Group, 1993), dust jacket cover.

4   Peterson, "Introduction," *The Message: The New Testament in Contemporary English*.

5   Peterson, "Preface: To the Reader," *The Message: The Bible in Contemporary Language* (Colorado Springs, CO: NavPress Publishing Group, 2002).

6   NavPress, "History & Frequently Asked Questions," accessed August 19, 2008, http://navpress.com/Message/HistoryAndFaqs/.

7   Peterson, "Preface: To the Reader."

8   Peterson, *The Message: The Bible in Contemporary Language*, Numbered edition (Colorado Springs, CO: NavPress Publishing Group, 2005).

9   Peterson, *Traveling Light* (Downers Grove, IL: Inter-Varsity Press, 1982).

10   NavPress, "Frequently Asked Questions: Why were updates made to *The Message*?" accessed November 16, 2020, https://messagebible.com/faq/.

11   NavPress, "Eugene Peterson: The Bible Translation He Reads at Home," *YouTube.com* video, 41 seconds, last modified December 19, 2017, https://www.youtube.com/watch?v=PiHtZxjqYM8.

     Seth Nelson, "My Meeting with Eugene Peterson," Faith Lutheran Church's website, last modified January 5, 2015, accessed February 3, 2020, http://www.flcronan.org/blog/my-meeting-with-eugene-peterson.

12   "Why does 'The Message Bible' paraphrase 'on earth as it is in heaven' into the Hermetic 'as above, so below'?" *Quora* (March 3, 2017), accessed August 15, 2019, https://www.quora.com/Why-does-The-Message-Bible-paraphrase-on-earth-as-it-is-in-heaven-into-the-Hermetic-as-above-so-below.

13   The *Emerald Tablet* is a supposedly ancient, Egypto-Greek, hermetic text by Hermes Trismegistus from the early 4th century AD. It is likely written much later between the sixth and eighth centuries, and translated from Arabic into Latin in the 12th century.

14   If we consider one testimony about this, Peterson was supposedly warned about this rendering in 1993. Peterson responded to the reader who had contacted

him and said had he known that "as above, so below" was a phrase used in New Age circles, he would have never used it. Apparently, Peterson never considered the phrase's association a strong enough concern as it was never changed in any later edition.

Warren B. Smith, "NEW BOOKLET: Eugene Peterson's Mixed Message: A Subversive Bible for a New Age," Lighthouse Trails Research Project website, updated February 19, 2019, accessed November 17, 2020, https://www.lighthousetrailsresearch.com/blog/?p=29709.

[15] Endorsements are taken from the flaps of various editions and from the official website, accessed August 15, 2019, http://messagebible.com /endorsements/.

The Passion Translation®

The New Testament with Psalms, Proverbs, and Song of Songs

Produced by BroadStreet Publishing, 2013–

FORMAL / FUNCTIONAL TENDENCIES

FORMAL   FUNCTIONAL

Interlinear NASB KJV NKJV ESV CSB NRSV NET NIV TNIV NLT NIrV **T P T** MSG Free Paraphrase

TEXT BASES

English Base Translations from the Syriac *Peshitta* (2010, 2012).

OT Masoretic Hebrew and Ancient Versions.   **NT** Eclectic Greek.

TRANSLATION TIMELINE

1958	1966	1967	1996	2002	2018
Phillips *New Test.*	*GNB*	*Living* *Bible*	*NLT*	*MSG*	**T P T**

CONTEMPORARY EVENTS

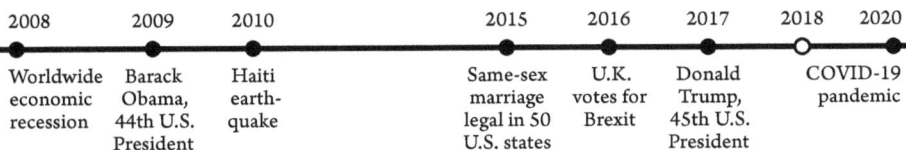

2008	2009	2010	2015	2016	2017	2018	2020
Worldwide economic recession	Barack Obama, 44th U.S. President	Haiti earth-quake	Same-sex marriage legal in 50 U.S. states	U.K. votes for Brexit	Donald Trump, 45th U.S. President		COVID-19 pandemic

PUBLICATION TIMELINE

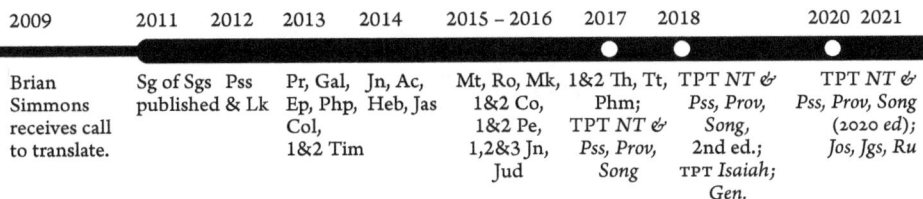

2009	2011	2012	2013	2014	2015 – 2016	2017	2018	2020 2021
Brian Simmons receives call to translate.	Sg of Sgs published	Pss & Lk	Pr, Gal, Ep, Php, Col, 1&2 Tim	Jn, Ac, Heb, Jas	Mt, Ro, Mk, 1&2 Co, 1&2 Pe, 1,2&3 Jn, Jud	1&2 Th, Tt, Phm; TPT NT & Pss, Prov, Song	TPT NT & Pss, Prov, Song, 2nd ed.; TPT Isaiah; Gen.	TPT NT & Pss, Prov, Song (2020 ed); Jos, Jgs, Ru

THE
PASSION
TRANSLATION

THE
NEW TESTAMENT
with PSALMS, PROVERBS, and SONG of SONGS

BroadStreet
PUBLISHING

B
rian Simmons, the sole translator of *The Passion Translation* (TPT®), was converted to Christ during the "Jesus
People" movement in 1971. He and his family later joined
a mission sending agency for eight years in the late 1970s and early
'80s. During their tenure on the mission field, Simmons acquired
some linguistic training to prepare for the translation of the New
Testament for the Paya-Kuna people, who live near the Central
American border between Panama and Colombia.[1]

After returning to and settling in the United States, Simmons
pastored a church in Connecticut for eighteen years (1990–2009).[2]
Near the end of his pastorship, Simmons relates that he received
a supernatural call from Jesus Christ to translate the Bible, which
he has since obediently followed.

Titled *The Passion Translation* since its inception, it has undergone many revisions over the past decade before the New Testament, Psalms, Proverbs, and the Song of Songs were published in
a single volume in 2017. A second revised edition was released in
2018 and a third, in late 2020. To date, Simmons has completed
the NT and portions of the OT, including Genesis, Isaiah, Joshua, Judges, and Ruth. The work is still ongoing, and Simmons ex-
pects to complete the Protestant canon by 2026.

STATED TRANSLATION IDEALS

Simmons writes that there "is no such thing as a truly literal translation of the Bible, for there is not an equivalent language that perfectly conveys the meaning of the biblical text. It must be understood in the original cultural and linguistic settings. This problem
is best addressed when we seek to transfer meaning, not merely
words, from the original text to the receptor language. . . .[3]

"The purpose of *The Passion Translation* is to reintroduce the
passion and fire of the Bible to the English reader. It doesn't merely
convey the literal meaning of words. It expresses God's passion for
people and his world by translating the original, life-changing message of God's Word for modern readers. . . . Our goal is to trigger

inside every English-speaking reader an overwhelming response to the truth of the Bible. This is a heart-level translation, from the passion of God's heart to the passion of [the reader's] heart." [4]

Simmons says, "[TPT] is an *emoticon* Bible, it's a *scratch-and-sniff*. It's something that takes you past the letters on the page into the heart of God. . . . When it comes to the emotions of God's heart, we want to amplify those. We want to come across clearly. Language can get tepid; language can get diluted. . . . Why can't we read a Bible that will really bring that passionate fire and love and strength into our hearts." [5]

METHOD

As the lone translator and primary editor of TPT, Brian Simmons has considerable freedom in how he chooses to render his text. This autonomy allows for consistency in direction, and indeed we see Simmons' unique style of rendering throughout his work.

TPT is typified by what Simmons sees as the homonymic (or homographic) character of Semitic languages. That is to say, in the Hebrew and Aramaic OT, Simmons swaps or adds the meanings of those different words which share similar sounds (or spellings) in order to enrich his text. [6] So that he can do the same in the Greek NT, Simmons relies on what he supposes are the NT's Aramaic originals. This results in many double-interpretations and amplifications in both Testaments with many footnotes asserting Semitic (specifically Aramaic) sources. Simmons justifies this approach based on his broad characterization of Semitic languages as primarily poetic in nature, in contrast with Greek, which he generalizes as tending towards literalism and analysis. [7]

Because Simmons equivocates all translation with paraphrase, he can justify adding exposition to his text, just as we might expect a paraphrase to do. Sometimes he marks those clarifications in italics. He also "amplifies" affective (*i.e.*, emotional) language with the use of additional adverbs, adjectives, or punctuation (like "very" or "passionately" or the frequent use of exclamation marks), which he derives from circumstances surrounding the passage.

The Best Bible?

TEXT BASES

English Text

Victor Alexander, *Aramaic Bible: Disciples New Testament* (CreateSpace, 2010); Glenn David Bauscher, *The 1st Century Aramaic New Testament in Plain English—with Psalms & Proverbs* (Lulu.com, 2010); Andrew Gabriel Roth, *Aramaic English New Testament* (Bellingham, WA: Netzari Press, 2012)[8]

New Testament

Eclectic Greek text. Nestle-Aland *Novum Testamentum Graece* 27th edition (United Bible Societies, 1993).
   Versions: *Peshitta* (Syriac)

Genesis, Psalms, Prov., Song, Isaiah

Masoretic Hebrew-Aramaic text. *Biblia Hebraica Stuttgartensia* (1977).
   Ancient versions. Septuagint (Greek LXX), *Peshitta* (Syriac)

CONTRIBUTORS

Brian Simmon's role is that of a lead translator. Besides his wife, Candace (an editorial reviewer) and David Sluka (an acquisitions and editorial director for BroadStreet Publishing Group) no one else is listed on his translation team. The publisher has identified a handful of reviewers, including Jeremy Bouma, Jacqueline Grey (dean of theology, Alphacrucis College), Gary S. Greig (vice president of Gospel Light Publications), and Rick Wadholm, Jr. (adjunct professor of Biblical and Theological Studies, SUM Bible College & Theological Seminary).[9]

THEOLOGICAL ASSUMPTIONS

Stated on the F.A.Q. page of the publisher's website: "TPT … is a fresh approach to translating the original Greek, Hebrew, and Aramaic manuscripts that intentionally transcends denominational barriers. It is not rooted in any one tradition or denomination, but desires to help the wider Body of Christ encounter the heart of God anew in the language of today." [10]

In fact, Simmons interprets his text according to a number of unique filters. First, he is an evangelical Christian who ministers within Charismatic circles. All the contributors to TPT (listed above) are associated with Pentecostal or conservative evangelical Christian institutions or assemblies.

In his rendering of the **Song of Songs**, Simmons refuses to let his rendering result in any kind of eroticism.[11] Instead, he gives a mystical, allegorical interpretation of the book based on preexisting suppositions about its nature. Simmons revealed his allegorical bias to the book when he asserted that

> "Solomon and the Shullamite woman share the same Hebrew root word; one feminine, one masculine—we are one Spirit with Jesus Christ. *It is a book of mystical, beautiful union with Jesus.*" [12]

But George Athas, professor of Hebrew (Semitics) and Old Testament at Moore Theological College assessed,

> "I can assure you that this translation does not reflect either the words or the meaning of *Song of Songs*, contrary to what it claims. It's not that the translation is careless—rather, it's eisegesis. It is imposing pre-conceived ideas onto the text and then claiming that the change is due to the translation strategy."[13]

FEATURES

Simmons has transcribed certain names to reflect their Hebrew or Greek forms in order "to better convey their cultural meaning and significance." For instance, TPT renders certain Greek names with their Hebrew equivalents, *e.g.*, Jacob instead of James, and Judah instead of Jude.[14]

Simmons rendered "male-oriented pronouns and terms in a gender-inclusive way when it was clear God's message applied not merely to men but to men and women collectively."[15] (*E.g.*, **Gal 4.12**, "**Beloved ones**, I plead with you, **brothers and sisters**, become like me, for I became like you. You did me no wrong.")

Divine referents (pronouns, titles, *etc.*) were capitalized in editions prior to TPT second edition (2018).

TPT *italicizes* certain words or phrases which are not in the Hebrew, Aramaic, and Greek manuscripts. Simmons "made these implications explicit for the sake of narrative clarity and to better convey the meaning of God's Word."[16] For example:

Ps 42.1	I long to drink of you, O God, *drinking deeply from the streams of pleasure* flowing from your presence.
Jn 4.21	"Believe me, dear woman, the time has come when you won't worship the Father on a mountain nor in Jerusalem, *but in your heart*."
Jn 5.34	"I have no need to be validated by men, but I'm saying these things so that you will *believe* and be rescued."
Jn 16.16	Soon you won't see me any longer, but then, after a little while, you will see me *in a new way*."
Jn 16.16	Actually, there are numerous advantages. Most important, God *distinguished the Jews from all other people* by entrusting them with the revelation of his prophetic promises.

Simmons nowhere explains any consistent system within TPT's more than 20,000 footnotes. He states simply that readers "will find ample footnotes throughout this translation to assist you in your study."[17] For example:

Jn 7.24	"Stop judging based on the superficial. First you must *embrace the standards of mercy* [b] and truth."
	fn: *b* 7:24 Jesus is teaching that the law of mercy (healing the lame man) overrides the laws of Moses (regulations of the Sabbath). Seeing situations and people with the lens of mercy gives us true discernment.
Jn 10.10	"A thief has only one thing in mind—he wants to steal, slaughter, [a] and destroy. But I have come to *give you everything in abundance,* [b] *more than you expect* [c]—life in its fullness until you overflow!"
	fn: *b* 10:10 Implied in the Aramaic text. *c* 10:10 Implied in the Greek text.

Like most translations aimed at general audiences, TPT tends to break up longer sentences into smaller ones in order to assist readers' concentration. For example, **Eph 1.3–14**, which is one, long, run-on sentence in Greek, is broken down into sixteen smaller sentences in TPT.[18]

RECEPTION

TPT is gaining popularity among Charismatic evangelical Christians thanks in large part to endorsements by pastors from influential churches and denominations like Bethel (Redding, CA) and Hillsong (Australia). As of February 2021, the TPT *New Testament with Psalms, Proverbs, and Song of Songs* has sold over 500,000 copies between its various editions.[19]

Despite its growing commercial success, several translators and scholars have denounced the TPT for lacking as a translation and regard it as a highly interpretive paraphrase or "targum."[20] Even Simmons' former mission sending agency (Ethnos360) has condemned the text for lacking as a translation.[21]

ASSESSMENT

This assessment is much longer than those in other review chapters due to the official claims made about TPT and its actual results. Note, this review does not discriminate against Simmons' role as a sole translator, otherwise it might as well reject out of hand other translations or paraphrases by Saint Jerome, Desiderius Erasmus, William Tyndale, Martin Luther, James Moffatt, Richard F. Weymouth, J. B. Phillips (*The New Testament in Modern English*), Kenneth N. Taylor (*The Living Bible*), or Eugene H. Peterson (*The Message*). Nor does it criticize Simmons' theological beliefs. It assesses TPT's merits, not Brian Simmons' qualifications as a linguist or theologian.

BroadStreet Publishing hails TPT as "an excellent translation you can use as your primary text to seriously study God's Word."[22] The marketing tries to set TPT apart from other paraphrases.[23] Now, all translations paraphrase to some degree, but this assessment demonstrates how TPT adds meanings that are foreign to their biblical contexts and goes beyond the kind of exposition that we should expect even in a paraphrase.

First, let me note that Brian Simmons renderings flow easily and TPT is very readable: Its language is mostly modern, vivid, and energetic. For example, in **Mk 7.6**, "Jesus replied, 'You are hypocrites! How accurately did Isaiah prophesy about you phonies . . .'" The use of "hypocrites" is a traditional Greek transcription going back to Wycliffe and Tyndale. TPT helpfully clarifies the word's use here with the addition of "phonies."

The leper's request to Jesus in **Mk 1.40** sounds contemporary, "You have the power to heal me right now if only you really want to!" And again, the disciples' answer to Jesus in **Mk 6.37b**, "It would cost a small fortune to feed all these thousands of hungry people." And again, Jesus' teaching in **Mk 7.19**, "For the food you swallow doesn't enter your heart, but goes into your stomach, only to pass out into the sewer" (so NLT, NET).

Yet again, the request of Herodias' daughter in **Mk 6.25**, "I want you to bring me the head of John the Baptizer on a platter—and I want it right now!" The last few words, which highlight the urgency or impetuousness of her request, are implied from the manner in which she approached the king earlier in the verse. Even John's title as the "Baptizer" (**Mk 3.1; Mk 6.25** above) is a clever choice, since it removes connotations as if John were somehow a member of a later Baptist convention, all while retaining a familiar "biblical" ring. And again, in **1Co 5.8**, "we can celebrate our continual feast, not with the old 'leaven,' the yeast of wickedness or bitterness, but we will feast on the freshly baked bread of innocence and holiness."

In line with modern practice, TPT rejects the traditional word "gentiles" for its clearer equivalent "non-Jews," as do other modern translations (so NLT, GNB).

TPT occasionally reverts to "biblish." For example, "flesh and blood" in **1Co 15.50**. And again, in **Mk 15.23**, "There they offered [Jesus] a mild painkiller, drink of wine mixed with gall, but he refused to drink it." "Gall" is a leftover from the Tyndale-KJV tradition (and repeated in the ESV, CSB). It meant "bile" specifically (so NASB 2020), but it could refer to anything bitter in general (including certain poisons). TPT already adds exposition in this verse taken from its parallel passage in **Mt 27.34**, so just a little more paraphrase here might help (like "*bitter* gall" as in the NLT).

No sophisticated system for italicizing supplied words is described, yet TPT's *italics* indicate ideas pulled either from a passage's *immediate (near) context* or from its *far context*. Many of these italics prove helpful. Good examples of *near context* include **Mk 1.32**, "Later in the day, *just after the Sabbath ended at sunset*" (see v. **21**), and **Mk 1.43**, "Don't say anything to anyone *about what just happened*" (verses **40–42**).

Some far-context additions are imported from parallel passages: **Mk 2.4**, "they lowered the paralyzed man on a stretcher *right down in front of him!*" (*Cf.* **Lk 5.19**.) And again in **Mk 4.14**, "Let me explain: The farmer sows the *message of the kingdom*." A more formal translation would read simply, "The farmer sows the word

(Greek *logon*)." TPT possibly narrows the application of this passage, but support for this rendering comes from its parallel in **Mt 13.19** ("the word of the kingdom," *cf.* **Lk 8.11**).

Sometimes TPT reaches for context that is not apparent: **Mk 16.6**, "I know that you're here looking for Jesus of Nazareth, who was crucified. He isn't here—he has risen *victoriously!*" Theologically, I agree with TPT's exposition in *italics*, but what context did it have to pull from in order to add the word "victoriously"? Perhaps **1Co 15.50**ff? Certainly nothing in the near context determines it.

Only some of TPT's additions are italicized, and it is among these non-italicized additions that I sense Simmons' linguistic training. For example, **Mk 7.26** offers a clear rendering with compact exposition: "born in the part of Syria known as Phoenicia." And again, **Mk 15.38**, "At that moment the veil in the Holy of Holies was torn in two from the top to the bottom." The veil's location is implied from an OT context and transported here (*cf.* **Heb 9.3**). The Greek source doesn't explicitly refer to this part of the Temple, although it is the only place from which the veil would have hung. New readers might appreciate an explanatory footnote for this verse.

Unfortunately, TPT frequently adds unwarranted or speculative words and phrases. The following passage taken from **Ro 3.24** may be theologically correct on its own, but there is simply no precedent from its surrounding context for the italicized words: "Yet through his powerful declaration of acquittal, God freely gives away his righteousness. His gift of love and favor now cascades over us, all because Jesus, the Anointed One, has liberated us from *the guilt, punishment, and power of* sin!" And again, **Eph 1.19**, "I pray that you will continually experience the immeasurable greatness of God's power made available to you through faith. *Then your lives will be an advertisement of this immense power as it works through you! This is the mighty power.*" Yet again, **Eph 2.6**, "He raised us up with Christ the exalted One, *and we ascended with him into the glorious perfection and authority of the heavenly realm, for we are now co-seated as one with Christ!*"

In the next few samples, there are no italics to show what TPT adds (which is in discordance with its stated features):

Eph 3.20, "*Never doubt* God's mighty power to work in you and accomplish all this. He will achieve infinitely more than your greatest request, your most unbelievable dream, and exceed your wildest imagination! He will outdo them all, for his miraculous power constantly energizes you."

A formal translation reveals the paraphrastic (or, rather, *periphrastic*) character of that rendering, "Now to the one who is able to do beyond all measure more than all that we ask or think, according to the power that is at work in us" (LEB)

TPT shares a tendency with most paraphrases in that its additions narrow the meaning of some passages and disallow other possible interpretations:

Mk 4.25, "Then [Jesus] said to them, 'Be diligent to understand the meaning behind everything you hear, for as you do, more understanding will be given to you. And according to your longing to understand, much more will be added to you.'"

Though this passage undoubtedly applies to wisdom and knowledge, it can also apply to other areas of life as well, an idea which a more formal rendering could have permitted ("For whoever has, more will be given to him, and whoever does not have, even what he has will be taken away from him." LEB).

Ro 8.14, "The mature children of God are those who are moved by the impulses of the Holy Spirit."

The addition of the word "mature" narrows what the original does not. The narrowed meaning introduces the notion of class distinctions between "mature" children and "immature" children, whereas only members of one class are so moved by the Spirit (an idea that is foreign to Paul's point).[24]

The following three verses in **1Co 11** shows that TPT is not always consistent with its interpretation:

> **1Co 11.4**, "Any *man who leads public worship,* and prays or prophesies with a shawl hanging down over his head, shows disrespect to his head, which is Christ."

The first set of italics shows what has been added, but there is nothing in the original that limits application of this verse only to those men *"who lead public worship."*

> **1Co 11.5a**, "And if any woman *in a place of leadership* within the church prays or prophesies in public with her long hair disheveled, she shows disrespect to her head, *which is her husband."*

Why don't words in italics (*"in a place of leadership"*) parallel the addition in the verse before (*"who leads public worship"*), since both are implied the same way? TPT give two separate meanings with two distinct applications for the same sort of *ellipses* (omissions).

> **1Co 11.6a**, "If a woman who wants to be in leadership will not conform to the customs of what is proper for women"

The phrase "who wants to be in leadership" ought to be italicized, just like its parallels in verses **4** and **5** above.

I agree with Brian Simmons when he says "the 'best' translation . . . is the one that makes the Word of God clear and accurate, no matter how many words it takes to express it."[25] Some may criticize TPT for using so many more words than other translations do, but additional words are necessary in most translations, and exposition is expected in paraphrase. Not all of TPT's additions are unwarranted, but unjustified emendations proliferate. Someone without another translation handy or experience in the original languages will not likely be able to discern which additions belong and which don't. In other words, TPT does not apply italics nearly enough to reflect all of its significant additions.

TPT renders and notes the etymology of many words, particularly proper nouns and names, but not in a consistently persuasive manner. For example TPT alternately renders Jesus' betrayer as "Judas Iscariot" in one Gospel (**Mk 3.19**) and "Judas the locksmith" in the others (**Mt 10.4; 26.14; Lk 6.16; 22.3; Jn 12.4**).

Mt 26.14

One of the twelve apostles, Judas the locksmith,*a* went to the leading priests

fn: *a* 26:14 Or "Judah Iscariot." Iscariot is not his last name or the name of a town. It means "locksmith." *Iscariot* comes from an Aramaic word for "brass lock." The one who held the key to the finances of the twelve disciples brazenly wanted to lock up Jesus.

This rendering lacks adequate justification. The etymological footnotes at **Mt 26.14** and **Mk 14.10** fail to connect the dots: I've found nothing in Hebrew or Aramaic (*i.e.*, Syriac) that points to any kind of "lock." In fact, several etymologies have been proposed for *Iscariot*, but none are so conclusive as this footnote asserts.[26]

And again, in TPT's introduction to the letter of **James (Jacob)**, Simmons writes, "By calling this book James instead of Jacob the church loses a vital component of our Jewish beginnings. There is no 'James' in Greek; it is Jacob. We would never say that God is the God of Abraham, Isaac, and James."[27] I'm not sure how necessary the name "Jacob" is to our Jewish understanding of the letter, since "James" originates from "Jacob" in the first place.[28] (The introduction ignores the benefit of using the different names to distinguish individuals.) The real issue here is a matter of consistency. Elsewhere, TPT uses the Hebrew/Aramaic equivalent of "Judah" (*i.e.* the "cultural name")[29] in place of the familiar Latin transcription "Jude" (Gk. *Ioudas*, *cf.* **Jd 1**), but this is not done in every place. For example, Jesus' ancestor is rendered "Judah" (also *Ioudas*, **Mt 1.2, 3**), but not Jesus' betrayer—"Judas" (also *Ioudas*,

The Best Bible?

Mk 14.43). Others in the text are not given their cultural names: There is no *Miriam* for "Mary," *Yochanan* for "John," or *Yeshua* (or "Joshua") for "Jesus."[30]

TPT is also selective in its cultural exposition. **Mk 9.42** reads, "it would be better for him to have a heavy boulder tied around his neck and be thrown into the sea than to face the punishment he deserves!" It's very probable that Mark intended to describe the size or weight of the "boulder" in his Gospel, but Mark used an adjective which specifies the rock as a "millstone" (Gk. *mylikos*). If TPT can narrow the meaning "bread" to "flatbread" (Gk. *artos*, **Mk 8.5**) in order to make it fit culturally, then why not render these words with something like a "*heavy* millstone" instead?

And again, **Mk 5.9**, "Jesus said to him, 'What is your name?' 'Mob,' he answered. 'They call me Mob because there are thousands of us in his body!'" There are perfectly good linguistic, cultural, and historical reasons for rendering the word as "Legion" or "Army" instead of "Mob." The word is a Greek transcription of a specific concept borrowed from Roman culture (as TPT's footnotes suggest). Roman legions were a part of the NT landscape and had been already for some time. "Mobs and "legions" are not the same things, since "mob" is undisciplined and chaotic, typically with no leader or orchestration, and a "legion" is a highly disciplined military unit. Elsewhere, TPT renders the word as "armies," as in **Mt 26.53**, where Jesus says, "And instantly he would answer me by sending twelve armies (**fn:** Or"twelve legions") of the angelic host to come and protect us." (Apparently, TPT considers spiritual beings as "mobs" only when they are evil.)

Neither is TPT consistent in rendering "brothers" (or "brothers *and sisters*") for the Greek word *adelphoi*. For example, in **Ro 8.12** it is rendered, "beloved ones" and in **12.1**, "beloved friends." Indeed siblings in God's family are expected to have affection for one another and ought to love each another, but such a variety of renderings reflect the imprecision of loose paraphrase and not of consistent translation.

And again, **Ro 1.1a**, "Paul, a loving and loyal servant (Gk *doulos*) of the Anointed One, Jesus." The footnote asserts that the "Greek word *doulos* signifies more than a servant; it is one who has chosen to serve a master out of love, bound with cords so strong that it could only be severed by death." Both text and footnote ignore the historical reality of coerced slavery common in the Græco-Roman world. The text and footnote sound pleasant, but TPT's assertion is without merit.

And again, **Gal 3.28**, "And we no longer see each other in *our former state*—Jew or non-Jew, rich or poor, male or female–because we are all one through our union with Jesus Christ." The words "rich or poor" seem to contemporize the passage, but it does miss the referent. TPT's footnote here offers readers a more accurate rendering ["enslaved or free"], but why was this rendering withheld from the text in the first place?

Yet again, **Sg 5.15**, the language is figurative here, as revealed by the NIV: "His legs are pillars of marble set on bases of pure gold." But TPT interprets all the figurative language away: "He's steadfast in all he does. His ways are the ways of righteousness, based on truth and holiness." Through this kind of interpretation, TPT transforms Hebrew poetry into English prose and effectively loses the very images that gives biblical poetry its force in the first place.

TPT frequently embellishes the text with adverbs and adjectives that are not italicized but should be. For example, in **Jas 5.16b**, "for tremendous power is released through the passionate, heartfelt prayer of a godly believer!" The words "passionate" and "heartfelt" seem to reflect the KJV ("effectual fervent"), but the intensity of emotion (*i.e., affect*) is not the point here; the result (*effect*) is. And again, **1Co 1.5**, "In him you have been made extravagantly rich" Nothing in the context specifies the degree of wealth implied. I get a sense that these additions express what Simmons believes his readers ought to feel about the text.

My reviews in this book do not usually look too deeply at footnotes, since its priority is each translation's main text, but the TPT

The Best Bible?

is an exception, because the footnotes give insight into the interpretive methods that Brian Simmons employed.

TPT's footnotes tend to be of several kinds: *Expositional, linguistic, devotional,* or *allegorical.* A good number of footnotes contain helpful insights or clarification, but it is hard for the uninitiated to discern and identify those that are helpful facts, those that are devotional insights, or those that are factually misleading.

Among linguistic notes, TPT offers etymological insights into many words. Now, the etymology (*i.e.,* historical formation) of a word has value when determining the meaning of a word's first occurrence, a coinage, a personal or place name, or a *hapax legomenon* (a word occurring only once). But the etymology of a common or familiar word gives no clear indication of its meaning and can mislead readers into confusing the origin of a word with its use in a particular context.

For example, the footnote at **Ro 1.4** reads, "

Or 'marked [appointed] as God's Son immersed in power.' The Greek word for 'set apart' comes from *horizo,* meaning 'the horizon.' It means 'to mark out the boundaries,' 'to decree,' or 'to define.' The horizon we move toward is Jesus!"

This etymological note follows the same bad reasoning that the later English word "dynamite" comes from the old Greek *dynamis* ("ability," "power"), therefore the Greek word means "*explosive force.*" This approach is simply anachronistic and misguided.

An etymological error occurs in the footnote at **Sg 2.1**. It asserts that the "word Sharon [in 'a rose of Sharon'] can be translated 'his song.' She now sees herself as the one he sings over. The root word for 'rose' (Hb. *habab*) can mean 'overshadowed.'" TPT's claim is simply unwarranted. *Sharon* is a geographic place-name, and the ending -*on* does *not* mean "his" (*i.e.,* it is not a third-person, singular, possessive pronominal suffix).

TPT makes frequent appeals to "the Aramaic" sources in its footnotes in order to justify certain renderings or offer interesting linguistic insights (frequently for devotional purposes).[31] Simmons buttresses his reliance on the Aramaic by appealing to scholars Craig S. Keener and Michael F. Bird,[32] but Keener himself denounces TPT's dependence on the Aramaic. He writes,

> "[T]here is a fatal flaw that pervades the entire translation (TPT): its dependence on Aramaic. Although Jesus spoke Aramaic, that was not the language of Jews in Asia Minor, Greece or Rome, areas to which most of the NT is addressed. It is not the language of our Greek NT (with a few snippets of Aramaic words or phrases here and there), which Christians take to be canonical. Scholars are virtually unanimous on these points because a massive quantity of inscriptions, graffiti and other sources from antiquity renders them beyond dispute."[33]

Observations from "the Aramaic" (*i.e.*, the Syriac *Peshitta*) sometimes help us better understand the original compositions in Hebrew and Greek, but they are unable to add to the meaning intended by the original authors. Translations are simply incapable of producing new revelation from their sources. They only convey the revelation that's already there (and they may do that adequately, but not completely.) The *Peshitta* is no exception, and reconstructions of supposed Aramaic originals are speculative at best. (See endnote 33 on page 50.)

To illustrate TPT's use of "the Aramaic," let us look at **Eph 6.9,**

> "And to the caretakers of the flock I say, do what is right with your people by forgiving them when they offend you, for you know there is a Master in heaven that shows no favoritism."

The footnote claims, "As translated literally from the Aramaic. The 'caretakers of the flock' can refer to both leadership in the church and in the workplace." This supposed "literal" translation from Aramaic is demonstrably false, since the word is not "caretaker of the flock" but "lord" or "master" with no exclusive reference to

The Best Bible?

sheep (Syr. *marayya'*, cf. **Col 4.1**, **1Ti 6.2**, but **1Pt 5.3**). Instead, TPT alters the entire referent, from [slave-]masters (Greek *kyrioi*) to church and business leaders. If this is an attempt to contemporize the language, then the passage is no longer an accurate translation, because it changes the author's point.

And again, at **Mt 3.7** the footnote reads, "The word viper in the Aramaic is *akidneh*, which is really a reference to a scorpion." TPT correctly identifies the Syriac word *dakidneh*, which is itself a transcription from Greek (*echidnōn*), but Syriac lexica identify it as a reference to a snake (an "asp" or "viper," like its Greek source) and not a scorpion.[34] As such, there is little benefit to the reader to refer to "the Aramaic" here.

At **Mk 1.9** the note reads,

> It is possible to translate the Aramaic as "Then one day Jesus came from victorious revelation" to be baptized by John. The word Nazareth can mean "victorious one," and the word Galilee can be translated "the place of revelation."

Both assertions demand a rather big leap of faith for suspecting readers.[35] Since TPT does not give anything more clear, we're left with speculative etymology *via* Simmons' homonymic principle of interpretation.[36]

TPT also contains devotional footnotes, like the one affixed to **Mk 3.17**, "Jesus chose twelve men who were all different in their personality types. It was no doubt humorous to Jesus to observe how different these twelve men were and how difficult it was to form them into a band of brothers" And again at **Mk 4.34**, "Jesus still delights to mystify those who follow him, but he waits until we are alone with him, and then he reveals the wonders of his grace and truth to our hearts." And at **Mk 1.3** ("clear a straight path inside your hearts for him!"), the footnote claims, "This 'way' is not a road, but preparing the heart, making room for the ways of the Lord." Here TPT excludes material expressions of preparation. This may have been what Mark intended John the Baptizer to mean, but it does narrow and confine other possible applications of meaning.

Footnotes at **Mt 13.3** and **Mk 4.2** record Simmons' view on the allegorical method of interpretation,

> "As a true prophet, one of Jesus' preferred methods of teaching was allegory. To deny the validity of allegorical *teaching* is to *ignore the teaching methods* of Jesus, the living Word." (emphasis added)

I am not sure what Simmons is getting at. There are good reasons why modern interpreters should reject modern attempts at allegorical *interpretation*: Namely, Jesus and his first generation of apostles have a unique *doctrinal authority* in the Church that later generations of believers cannot hope to imitate or repeat. Later teachers need to assure that their doctrine is "sound," unlike that which "is tossed with every wave of teaching" (**Eph 4.14; 2Ti 4.3**). Such teaching requires controls, like precedent and warrant, to keep it from spinning off into speculation and conjecture. (We call these controls *principles of interpretation* or *hermeneutics*.)

The footnote in **Mk 1.6** records one of Simmons' attempts at allegorical exposition:

> "[John's rough camel-hair garment] was considered to be the wardrobe of a prophet and was identical to what the prophet Elijah wore . . . . With a diet of locusts John points back to the four varieties of locusts mentioned in Joel 1:4. Locusts (grasshoppers) are an emblem of intimidation that will keep believers from taking their inheritance by faith. Israel thought themselves to be like grasshoppers in their own eyes because of the intimidation of the fierce inhabitants of the land. John the Baptizer arrives on the scene and makes locusts his food, eating up that symbol of intimidation (devouring the devour-

er). And he drank honey, which is a biblical metaphor of the revelation of God's Word that is sweeter than honey . . . . John's ministry was a prophetic statement from God that a new day had come, a day of leaving dead formalism and embracing new life in Jesus without intimidation."

This analogy breaks down very quickly: "Locusts represent intimidation; Israel viewed themselves as locusts." This should mean that Israel saw themselves as the ones doing the intimidating, but, *no!* they were the intimidated. (Should it not mean, too, that John *ate* the Israelites?) All of this allegorical exposition is reminiscent of some early Church writers, who would go from one loose association to the next. Simmons does not demonstrate any controls to govern or guard his interpretation. Therefore, this footnote cannot be weighed the same as other kinds of exposition based on hard facts or some consistent method of hermeneutics.

The **Song of Songs** is rendered as an allegorical interpretation (not a translation) throughout. By narrowing its interpretation to only one possibility—a romantic allegory between Christ and his church—TPT is leaving other legitimate interpretations on the cutting-room floor. Thus TPT has imported concepts into the book that are unsupported by its text. For example, **Sg 1.2**, "Let him smother me with kisses—his Spirit-kiss divine." The words "Spirit-kiss divine" have no warrant in the Hebrew. They are an invention based on Simmons' allegorical bias. And again, **Sg 1.14**, "He is like a bouquet of henna blossoms—henna plucked near the vines at the fountain of the Lamb." The footnote reads, "Or 'at En-gedi.' En-gedi means 'fountain of the Lamb.'" The problem is, *En-gedi* does not mean "fountain of the *lamb*", because, first, it is a geographical place-name for a sheltered oasis in the Judæan wilderness, and second, *En-gedi* derives from words that mean "fountain of the *goat*" (a different species with a distinct significance).

There is good warrant and precedent for a limited kind of allegorical interpretation that comes with guardrails called biblical "symbols" or "types." This is where an expositor will follow an image or idea throughout the whole of Scripture and link what is common to all (or most) occurrences. The interpreter can then draw out the unifying elements and themes and then read those back into the text. A good example is Paul's use of the word "sleep" in **1Co** and **2Ti**, which in Paul's writing, becomes a metaphor for "natural death" (**1Co 7.39; 11.30; 15.6; 1Ti 4.13–14**). TPT, however, does not seem to employ this method.

If translation is a controlled articulation of meaning (in order to differentiate it from loose paraphrase) and if TPT purports to be a Bible worthy of study, then the TPT needs more consistent controls:

First of all, by placing exposition within the main text, TPT limits or narrows its interpretation and excludes other possibilities. Any added exposition and clarifications in the main text should be italicized or they should be moved to the footnotes. This change will make good on TPT's stated claim regarding italics without misleading readers.

Second, TPT's dependence on homonymic, triliteral (three-letter), Semitic roots is its Achilles' heel. The entire reason these words are classified as homonyms (or homographs) is because their meanings are *not* interchangeable. Some Hebrew words truly are polysemous (*i.e.*, they carry more than one meaning), but only on rare occasions can multiple meanings be intended in the same context (*e.g.,* **Sg 2.12**). Homographs, polysemes, and etymologies simply do not offer translators legitimate options where the words are constrained by context and usage (*e.g.,* **Jn 19.30**).

Third, it is unnecessary to appeal to "the Aramaic" in those texts, which are, in all likelihood, composed in Greek (*i.e.,* the entire NT, with a possible exception of **Mt**) or Hebrew (**Pss, Pr, Sg**), unless it is with the purpose of identifying what is written in the original languages. If Simmons persists with "the Aramaic" (*i.e.,* Syriac) as a supposed source of revelation not expressed in the original sources, then he has a lot more work to do. He will require a translation of the Greek NT into Galilæan Aramaic, since the Syriac *Peshitta* is too late of a text to rely on. He will want to con-

The Best Bible?

sistently supply Galilæan Aramaic transcriptions in TPT's notes wherever he refers to "the Aramaic" so as to lend some semblance of credibility to his claims.

Fourth, readers would benefit from a clear distinction of its several kinds of footnotes. As they are, they are a mixed hodge-podge of facts (*i.e.,* etymologies, places, alternate meanings), devotional applications and allegories, cross-references, and associations (homonyms). Some notes offer a real aid to understanding the text, others are merely interesting, while others are unnecessary, unhelpful, or misleading (*e.g.,* observations from "the Aramaic" in the **Pss** and **Pr**). Readers would benefit from a consistent system that differentiates one kind of footnote from another (say, between personal applications or linguistic facts). In this way readers may better judge how such notes bear on the meaning of the text.

Fifth, TPT ought to cite its sources and "show its work." References to "some scholars" in the footnotes may sounds authoritative, but few works or names are given to support its many assertions. It ought to give supporting evidence when referring to such "scholars" (*e.g.,* **Mt 26.6–7; Mk 8.10; 16.18; Lk 1.1–4**).

Finally, TPT's marketing claims that the "text was interpreted from the original languages, carrying *its original meaning and giving you an accurate, reliable expression of God's original message*" (*emphasis* added).[37] It further states that "Dr. Simmons used *the same widely-used standards marked by mainstream Evangelical translations* to make TPT an accurate, faithful, clear, readable translation for twenty-first century English readers" (*emphasis* added).[38] This marketing claim is false, since TPT's methods are in fact condemned by recognized evangelical scholars precisely for failing to adhere to said standards and for adding meaning without good justification.[39] (They laud the intent, but condemn the practice.)

In sum, TPT suffers from what James Barr criticized in 1961 as the theological misuse of biblical language:

"[W]here linguistic evidence has been used in aid of a theological argument, and where I believe that evidence to have been misused, I do not necessarily believe the conclusion of the theological argument to be itself wrong in particular. Quite often I think that theological arguments . . . would have been better and more convincing without the linguistic evidence which has been used in their support. But while in some such cases I do not hold the particular point argued to have been disproved because of bad use of evidence, I commonly do think that such misuse of evidence argues a wrong understanding of biblical interpretation in general and almost certainly implies a seriously faulty theological method."[40]

Brian Simmons writes in his preface, "TPT is committed to bringing forth the potency of God's Word in relevant, contemporary vocabulary *that doesn't distract from its meaning or distort it in any way.*"[41] (emphasis added) Though I sympathize with his goal ("to communicate God's heart of passion for his people")[42] I sense that Simmon's zeal and personal "passion" has muddied the text in his attempt to elicit an artificial response from readers instead of allowing the Holy Spirit to speak to them through a clear and lucid translation. If TPT purports to carry the original meaning without distorting or detracting from the Word of God (*i.e.,* the original text), so that it may be used as advertised, then TPT ought to be revised on the basis of consistent and valid interpretive methods. In the mean-time, its marketing should be reworded so as not to mislead unsuspecting readers.

Despite its drawbacks, TPT has great hope for change and revision. On many occasions, Simmons has altered passages where his renderings have received criticism. (For example, see the "Significant Revisions" on page 517.) The question remains: Will TPT surpass its foundations and shine through its defects in order to become the translation that it is marketed to be?

REPRESENTATIVE SAMPLES

Familiar Passages

The Lord is my best friend and my shepherd.*a*
  I always have more than enough.*b*
He offers a resting place for me in his luxurious love.*c*
  His tracks take me to an oasis of peace near *the quiet brook of bliss.d*

Ps 23.1–2

fn: *a* 23:1 The word most commonly used for "shepherd" is taken from the root word *ra'ah*, which is also the Hebrew word for "best friend." This translation includes both meanings. The unique term for shepherd is *ro'eh tzon*—"lover of the flock." This teaches us that a shepherd was not just a responsible overseer, but a caring father figure, tending to his flock out of a deep sense of love. Shepherds were also fierce protectors of their flocks. Jesus is the Fierce Protector of his people.

b 23:1 Or "I lack nothing." What a wonderful declaration over your life! To never be in lack, always possessing more than enough. Our God meets our emotional, physical, and spiritual needs.

c 23:2 Or "in spring [green] meadows." A good shepherd knows where to pasture his flock. These green meadows would be a resting place, free from all fear. The Greek verb "to love" is *agapao*, which is a merging of two words and two concepts. *Ago* means "to lead like a shepherd," and *pao* is a verb that means "to rest." Love is our Shepherd leading us to the place of true rest in his heart.

d 23:2 The Hebrew word *menuhâ* means "the waters of a resting place." See Isa. 11:10.

Here's the one thing I crave from Yahweh,
   the one thing I seek above all else:
   I want to live with him every moment in his house,*e*
   beholding the marvelous beauty*f* of Yahweh
   filled with awe, delighting in his glory and grace.
   I want to contemplate*g* in his temple.

Ps 27.4

fn: *e* 27:4 A temple had not yet been built when David wrote this psalm. He was saying that he longs to be surrounded with God's presence, enclosed and encircled with holiness.

f 27:4 The meaning of the Hebrew word for "beauty" (*no'am*) is not easily conveyed by one English word. It can also be translated "sweetness," "pleasantness," "friendliness," "graciousness," "goodness," "loveliness," "splendor," or "delightfulness." Take each of these terms and read the verse again, inserting the possible alternatives. We must be captured by the awesomeness of God each time we come before him and rejoice in his friendship.

g 27:4 The Hebrew verb *baqar* can also mean "inquire," "meditate," "take pleasure in," and, in a general sense, "worship," "pray," or "seek [guidance]." However, *baqar* comes from a root word that means "to arise at dawn." Perhaps David was saying that he would arise every dawn to take pleasure in God.

For this is how much God loved the world—he gave his one and only, unique Son *as a gift.*e* So now everyone who believes in him*e* will never perish but experience everlasting life.

Jn 3.16

fn: *c* 3:16 Or "God proved he loved the world by giving his Son." *d* 3:16 Or "believe into him." Salvation and regeneration come only by faith. True faith (Gr. *pistis*) contains a number of components: acceptance, embracing something (someone) as truth, union with God and his Word, and an inner confidence that God alone is enough.

Divine Name and Titles

Yʜᴡʜ	Ps 24.1a	**Yahweh** claims the world as his.
adonai	Ps 90.1b	**Lord**, you have always been our eternal home
elohim	Gn 1.27a	So **God** created man *and woman* and shaped them with his image inside them.
adonai Yʜᴡʜ	Ps 73.28b	. . . **Lord Yahweh**, for your name is good to me.

The Best Bible?

adonai elohim	Dn 9.3a	———
YHWH *saba'oth*	1Sa 17.45b	———
el shaddai	Ex 6.3a	———

kyrios	Lk 20.42b	"The **Lord Yahweh** said to my **Lord**,*f* 'Sit near me in the place of authority'"
		fn: *e* 20:42 A Hebrew translation of this passage would read "Yahweh said to my Adonai." Paraphrased it would read "The Lord (God) said to my protecting Lord (Messiah)."
christos	Mt 16.16b	"You are the **Anointed One**,*g* the Son of the living God!"
		fn: *e* 16:16 Or "the Christ" (Messiah).

New Testament Text Base

Mt 17.21	"But this kind of demon is cast out only through prayer and fasting." *d*
	fn: *d* 17:21 As translated from the Hebrew Matthew, Aramaic, and some Greek manuscripts. Many reliable Greek manuscripts do not have this verse, and it is not included in many modern translations.
Mt 18.11	"The Son of Man has come to give life to anyone who is lost." *k*
	fn: *k* 18.11 As translated from the Hebrew Matthew, the Aramaic, and a few Greek texts. Many reliable Greek manuscripts do not have this verse, and it is missing in many modern translations. See Ezek. 34:16.
Ac 8.37	Philip replied, "If you believe with all your heart, I'll baptize you." The man answered, "I believe that Jesus is the Anointed One, the Son of God."
	fn: *k* 18.11 Although only a few later Greek manuscripts include v. 37, it is found in one of the oldest Aramaic texts (Harklean Syriac Version, AD 616) and one Greek uncial from the eighth century. There is widespread consensus among scholars of both Greek and Aramaic texts that v. 37 was added as an ancient Christian confession of faith.)

Gender Language

ʾāvîw	Pr 15.5a	You're stupid to mock the instruction of **a father**
huioi	Mt 5.9	"How blessed you are when you make peace! For then you will be recognized as a **true child** of God." *k*
		fn: *h* 5:9 See Pss. 72:3–7; 122:8–9; Isa. 26:12.
anthrōpōn	Mt 4.19	"Come and follow me, and I will transform you into men who catch **people** for God." *k*
		fn: *e* 4:19 Or "fishers of men." The Aramaic word can mean either "fishers" or "hunters." See Ezek. 47:1–10.
hekastō…autou	Ro 2.6	He will give to each one in return for what he has done. *k*
		fn: *e* See Ps. 62:12; Prov. 24:12; Matt. 16:27.
adelphoi	Gal 5.13	**Beloved ones**, God has called us to live a life of freedom. But don't view this wonderful freedom as an excuse to set up a base of operations in the natural realm. Constantly love each other and be committed to serve one another.
gynaikos anēr	Ti 1.6a	Each of them must be above reproach, devoted solely to his wife, *k* whose children are believers and not rebellious or out of control.
		fn: *e* 1:6 Or "the husband of one wife" or "married only once."
gynaikas	1Ti 3.11	And the women *k* also who serve the church should be dignified, *k* faithful in all things, *k* having their thoughts set on truth, and not known as those who gossip.
		fn: *b* 3:11 The word used here can mean "women" or "wives." This may refer to women deacons. Phoebe is called a deacon in Rom. 16:1. *c* 3:11 As translated from the Greek, the Aramaic can be translated "modest." *d* 3:11 Or "temperate."

The Best Bible?

Difficult Renderings

1Sa 13.1	—— (I **Samuel** has yet to be translated.)
Is 28.13	Therefore, the word of Yahweh will be to them **"Do, do this, and do, do that,** **a rule about this and a rule about that,** **here a little, there a little,"** in order that they will stumble backwards and be broken and captured.

Significant Renderings

ʿ*almah*	Is 7.14	The Lord himself will give you a sign. Behold—**the virgin** will conceive and give birth to a son and will name him God Among Us
sheʾol . . . ʾabaddon	Pr 15.11	Even **hell** itself holds no secrets from the Lord God, for before his eyes, all is exposed— and so much more the heart of every human being.
egennēsen	Mt 1.2	Abraham **had a son named** Isaac, **who had a son** **named** Jacob, **who had a son named** Judah (he and his brothers became the tribes of Israel)

eskēnōsen	Jn 1.14	And so the Living Expression
		  became a man and **lived** among us!
		  And we gazed upon the splendor of his glory,
		  the glory of the One and Only
		  who came from the Father overflowing
		  with tender mercy and truth!

tois ioudaiois	Jn 18.36	Jesus looked at Pilate and said, "The royal power of my kingdom realm doesn't come from this world. If it did, then my followers would be fighting to the end to defend me from **the Jewish leaders**. My kingdom realm authority is not *f* from this realm." *g*
		fn: *f* 18:36 The Aramaic is "not yet from here." *g* 18:36 The Greek text is not "world," but liter- ally "this side" or "this realm." The Aramaic word used here can be translated "not of this age."

dikaiosunē theou, pisteōs Iēsou Christou	Ro 3.22a	It is **God's righteousness** made visible through the **faithfulness of Jesus Christ**. And now all who believe in him receive that gift.
Granville Sharp's rule applied	Tt 2.13	For we continue to look forward to the joyful fulfillment of our hope in the dawning splendor of the glory of **our great God and Savior, Jesus, the Anointed One**.

Again, this application to the Trinity could prove useful as an illustration, but it is considered a faulty translation.

Simmons claims that his New Testament is based on the Greek NT and that he has "implemented" the Aramaic. In sum, where the footnotes indicate his reliance on the Aramaic, that's where he has relied on English renderings of the Syriac *Peshitta* or the medieval *Shem Tov* (though at times, not even this is apparent).

Matthew 5.4a	What delight comes to you when you wait upon the Lord!

Here, Simmon's footnote reads "As translated from the Hebrew Matthew," the medieval, which he identifies as the Shem Tov elsewhere.[43]

1 Timothy 2.12	I don't advocate that the newly converted women be the teachers in the church
1 Jn 5.7b–8a	——— **Footnote:** There is considerable historical and theological debate surrounding vv. 7–8. Some later, less reliable manuscripts have for vv. 7–8: "There are three that testify in heaven: the Father, the Word, and the Holy Spirit. And these three are one." This is known as the *Comma Johanneum*. But there has been a nearly complete agreement of scholars that this reading was added by copyists, with many theories of who it was. Although there is nothing heretical about this addition, it seems to have been inserted to reinforce the doctrine of the Trinity. It is not included in modern versions nor in the Aramaic.

SIGNIFICANT REVISIONS

TPT has undergone many hefty revisions throughout its publishing history. In Simmon's own words (spoken in 2018):

"I asked the Lord once, 'Why are there so many critics?' And he said, 'Because they will make me a better man and a better translator.' So I've done my best to listen to the critics. I've made hundreds of changes in the text over the last eight years. We plan on revising the work every two or three years and put out a new edition."[44]

	TPT (2014)	TPT (2015)	TPT (2017–20)
Ps 1.1	What delight comes to those [a] who follow God's ways! [a] **They** won't walk in step with the wicked, nor share the sinner's way, **nor sits in the circle of scoffers**	What delight comes to those [a] who follow God's ways! [a] **They** won't walk in step with the wicked, nor share the sinner's way, **or be found sitting in the scorner's seat.**	What delight comes to the one who follows God's ways![a] **He** won't walk in step with the wicked, nor share the sinner's way, **nor be found sitting in the scorner's seat.**

fn: *a* 1:1 The Hebrew text is actually "that One," and refers prophetically to the Lord Jesus Christ, our Tree of Life. Every one of us who belongs to "that One" can also walk in the light of this psalm. *b* Psalm 1 is the contrast of those who follow God's ways and those who choose their own path. Read through this psalm with the purpose of learning how to live with God in first place.

fn: 1:1 Psalm 1 is the contrast of those who follow God's ways with those who choose their own path. Read through this psalm with the purpose of learning how to live with God in the first place.

TPT

	TPT (2014, 2015)	TPT (2018 2nd ed)	TPT (2020)
Ps 23.1	**The Lord** is my **Fierce Protector** and my shepherd.[a] I always have more than enough.	**The Lord** is my **best friend** and my shepherd.[a] I always have more than enough.[b]	**Yahweh** is my **best friend** and my shepherd.[a] I always have more than enough.[b]

fn: *a* 23.1 The word most commonly used here is *shepherd*. In the days when David wrote this, a shepherd was as much a warrior as a gentle caregiver for sheep. Living in the wilderness with wild beasts, shepherds were both brave and strong.

fn: *a* 23:1 The word most commonly used for "shepherd" is taken from the root word *ra'ah*, which is also the Hebrew word for "best friend." This translation includes both meanings. The unique term for shepherd is *ro'eh tzon*—"lover of the flock." This teaches us that a shepherd was not just a responsible overseer, but a caring father figure, tending to his flock out of a deep sense of love. Shepherds were also fierce protectors of their flocks. Jesus is the Fierce Protector of his people.
b 23:1 Or "I lack nothing." What a wonderful declaration over your life! To never be in lack, always possessing more than enough. Our God meets our emotional, physical, and spiritual needs.

	TPT (2014, 2015)	TPT (2018 2nd ed)	TPT (2020)
Pr 1.7a	**How then does a man gain the essence of wisdom?** We cross the threshold of true knowledge when we live in **complete awe and adoration of** God.[c]	**How then does a man gain the essence of wisdom?** We cross the threshold of true knowledge when we live in **obedient devotion to** God.[c]	We cross the threshold of true knowledge when we live in **obedient devotion to** God.[c]

fn: *c* Many translations render this "the fear of the Lord." This is much more than the English concept of fear. It also implies submission, awe, worship, and reverence. The Hebrew word used here is found fourteen times in Proverbs. The number fourteen represents spiritual perfection. The number fourteen is mentioned three times in the genealogy of Jesus (Matthew 1:1-17). It is also the number for Passover. You will pass from darkness to wisdom's light by the *fear* of the Lord.

The Best Bible?

TPT (2014)	TPT (2018 2nd ed)	TPT (2020)
Lord, I passionately love you! **I want to embrace you,**[b] **for now you've become my Power!**	Lord, I passionately love you **and I'm bonded to you,**[a] **I want to embrace you,**[b] **for now you've become my power!**	**I love you, Yahweh, and** I'm bonded to you,[a] **my strength!**

fn: *b* 18:1 The Hebrew word used here for "love" is not the usual word to describe love. It is a fervent and passionate word that carries the thought of embrace and touch. It could actually be translated, "Lord, I want to hug you!" Haven't you ever felt like that?

Ps 18.1

fn: *a* 18:1 David doesn't employ the common Hebrew word for "love," *'ahav*, but instead uses the Hebrew word for "pity" or "mercy." How could David have mercy for God? The word he uses, *raham*, is the word used for a mother who loves and pities her child so much it manifests with a deep love and emotional bond. This concept, although difficult to convey in English, is brought forth as David is saying, "I love you passionately and my life is forever bonded to you!"

b 18:1 The Hebrew word used here for "love" is not the usual word to describe love. It is a fervent and passionate word that carries the thought of embrace and touch. It could actually be translated "Lord, I want to hug you!" Haven't you ever felt like that?

fn: *a* 18:1 David didn't employ the common Hebrew word for "love," *'ahav*, but instead used the Hebrew word for "pity" or "mercy." How could David have mercy for God? The word he used, *racham*, is the word for a mother who loves and pities her child so much it manifests with a deep love and emotional bond. This concept, although difficult to convey in English, carries the thought of embrace and touch. It could actually be translated "Lord, I want to hug you." Haven't you ever felt like that?

	TPT (2014, 2015)	TPT (2018 2nd ed, 2020)

Pr 2.4–5	For if you keep seeking it like
	  a man would seek for
	  sterling silver,
	  searching in hidden places for
	  cherished treasure,
	Then you will discover the fear
	  of **God**
	  and **truly worship him in
	  the awe and wonder that
	  he deserves.**
		For if you keep seeking it like
		  a man would seek for
		  sterling silver,
		  searching in hidden places for
		  cherished treasure,
		then you will discover the fear
		  of the **Lord**
		  and **find the true knowledge
		  of God.**

	TPT (2015)	TPT (2018 2nd ed, 2020)

Pr 3.7b	for wisdom comes when
	  you adore him with
	  awe and wonder
	and avoid everything that's
	  wrong.
		for wisdom comes when
		  you adore him with
		  undivided devotion
		and avoid everything that's
		  wrong.

	TPT (2013–15)	TPT (2018 2nd ed, 2020)
1Ti 1.7	They presume to be expert teachers of the Law,[a] but they don't have the slightest idea of what they're talking about. **They are dogmatic about peripheral issues** and they simply love to argue!	They presume to be expert teachers of the law,[a] but they don't have the slightest idea of what they're talking about and they simply love to argue!

fn: *a* 1:7 Or "Torah."

The Best Bible?

TPT (2014)	TPT (2015)
In the **very** beginning[a] **God** was already there. And **before his face**[b] **Was his Living Expression.** And **this** "Living Expression" Was with God, yet fully God.[c] They were together—face to face, In the very beginning.[e] And through his creative inspiration This "Living Expression" made all things,[f] For nothing has existence Apart from him!	In the **very** beginning[a] **the living expression** was already there.[b] And the "Living Expression" was with God, yet fully God.[c] They were together—face to face,[d] in the very beginning.[e] And through his creative inspiration this "Living Expression" made all things,[f] for nothing has existence apart from him!

TPT (2017 2nd ed)	TPT (2020)
In the **very** beginning[a] **the Living Expression**[b] was already there. And the Living Expression was with God, yet fully God.[c] They were together—*face-to-face*,[d] in the very beginning.[e] And through his creative inspiration this Living Expression made all things,[f] for nothing has existence apart from him!	In the beginning[a] **the Living Expression**[b] was already there. And the Living Expression was with God, yet fully God.[c] They were together—*face-to-face*,[d] in the very beginning.[e] And through his creative inspiration this Living Expression made all things,[f] for nothing has existence apart from him!

Jn 1.1–3

fn: *a* 1:1 Most scholars consider the first eighteen verses of John to be the words of an ancient hymn or poem that was cherished by first-century believers in Christ.

b 1:1 The Greek is *logos*, which has a rich and varied . . .

c 1:1 The Living Expression (Christ) had full participation . . .

d 1:2 The Greek word used here and the Hebraic concept . . .

e 1:2 Both Gen. 1:1 and John 1:1–2 speak of the beginning . . .

f 1:3 Or "all things happened because of him and nothing happened apart from him." The Aramaic is, "everything was in his hand" (of power). See Ps. 33:6; Isa. 44:24.

	TPT (2014)	TPT (2018 2nd ed)	TPT (2020)
2Ti 3.16	Every Scripture [a] has been **written by the Holy Spirit, the breath of God.** It will empower you by its instruction and correction, giving you the strength to take the right direction and lead you deeper into the path of godliness.	Every Scripture [a] has been **inspired by the Holy Spirit, the breath of God**. It will empower you by its instruction and correction, giving you the strength to take the right direction and lead you deeper into the path of godliness.	**God has transmitted his very substance into** every Scripture,[a] **for it is God-breathed.**[b] It will empower you by its instruction and correction, giving you the strength to take the right direction and lead you deeper into the path of godliness.

fn: *a* 3:16 Keep in mind that when Paul wrote this he was referring to the Torah and all the Old Testament writings. Today, "every Scripture" would include the New Testament as well.

b 3:16 The Word of God is inspired. Scripture is not simply a book that tells about God, it actually contains God. His breath is embedded in his Word.

	TPT (2013)	TPT (2017)
Gal 6.6	And those who are taught the Word **will receive an impartation** [a] **from** their teacher; **a transference of anointing** [b] **takes place between them.**	And those who are taught the Word **will receive an impartation** [a] **from** their teacher; **a sharing of wealth** [b] **takes place between them.**

a Or "blessings." *b* Literally "wealth."

	TPT (2018 2nd ed)	TPT (2020)
	And those who are taught the Word **must share all good things with** their teacher; **a sharing of wealth takes place between them.**	And those who are taught the Word **must share all good things with** their teacher.

	TPT (2013–17)	TPT (2018 2nd ed)	TPT (2020)
Gal 4.12	Beloved ones, I plead with you, **follow my example and become free from the bondage of religion.** I once became **as one of** you,[a] **a Gentile, when I lived among you**—**now** become free like me. **When I first came to minister to you,** you did me no wrong. **I can't believe you would do wrong to me now!**	Beloved ones, I plead with you, **follow my example and become free from the bondage of religion.** I once became **as one of** you,[a] **a gentile, when I lived among you**—**now** become free like me. **When I first came to minister to you,** you did me no wrong. **I can't believe you would do wrong to me now!**	Beloved ones, I plead with you, **brothers and sisters,** become like me, for I became **like** you. You did me no wrong.

fn: *a* 4:12 Or "imitated you." Paul is using sarcasm and saying, "I imitated you; now you should imitate me!"

Unique Renderings

Because TPT is supposed to be a dynamic (functional) translation, and because it results in so many periphrastic circumlocutions and paraphrastic interpretations, it has a large number of unique renderings. As discussed in the "Assessment," there are many renderings that have no correspondence or precedent in the original language or immediate context. In the examples below, words in **bold** type have no precedent in the Hebrew or in any of the ancient versions.

Sg 1.2a	Let him smother me with kisses—**his Spirit-kiss divine.**
Sg 1.12	As the king surrounded me at his table, the sweet fragrance of my **praise** perfume awakened the night

The allegory in **Sg 1.2** and the inclusion of "praise" in **Sg 1.12** may serve to illustrate a sermon, but they fail to convey the meaning in the text.

Not infrequently, TPT's footnotes reveal Brian's allegorical interpretation.

Sg 1.11	**Footnote:** "This is the Trinity ('we'), which will be involved in making every Shulamite holy and radiant."

Simmon's supposed back-translation from Greek into Hebrew gives him a strange rendering in John's Gospel:

Jn 19.30	When he had sipped the sour wine, he said, 'It is finished, my bride!'ᵃ Then he bowed his head and surrendered his spirit to God.
	fn: *a* This is from the Hebrew word *kalah*, which has a homonym that means "fulfilled [completed]" and "bride." Jesus finished the work of our salvation for his bride. This translation has combined both concepts. For a fascinating study of the Hebrew word used for "bride" and "finished," with its universe of meaning, see *Strong's Concordance*, Hb. 3615, 3616, 3617, 3618, and 3634. Although the completed work of salvation was finished on the cross, he continues to work through his church today to extend God's kingdom realm on the earth and glorify the Father through us. He continues to work in us to accomplish all that his cross and resurrection have purchased for us, his bride. His cross fulfilled and finished the prophecies of the Messiah's first coming to the earth. There was nothing written that was not fulfilled and now offered to his bride.

ENDORSEMENTS

Ché Ahn and James W. Goll (members with Simmons on the Apostolic team of Harvest International Ministry), John and Lisa Bevere (authors), Graham Cooke (author), Lou Engle (founder, The Call), Johnny Enlow (author), Brian and Bobbie Houston (pastors, Hillsong Church), Bill and Beni Johnson (pastors, Bethel Church, Redding, California), Patricia King (founder, Patricia

King Ministries), Banning Liebscher (pastor, Jesus Culture), and Dutch Sheets are among the ministers who endorse the TPT.

COPYRIGHT

ENDNOTES FOR
THE PASSION TRANSLATION

[1] Brian Simmons produced rough-draft translations of the first twenty or so chapters of Genesis for teaching purposes. He also helped some on a NT translation for the Kuna people. The translation was overseen and completed by Keith Forster, a translator who was with the Summer Institute of Linguistics (SIL). Simmons left the mission in 1988. The NT was published in 1995.

Jonathan Welton, interview with Brian Simmons, "Brian Simmons — An Interview With The Man Behind The Passion Translation," *The Jonathan Welton Show*, podcast audio, June 13, 2017, accessed May 5, 2019, https://podcasts.apple .com/us/podcast/brian-simmons-interview-man-behind-passion -translation/id716354571?i=1000420212509, starting at 14:53.

Bob Creson, "Part of the Team: The Whole Bible for the Kuna," Wycliffe Bible Translators website, October 14, 2014, accessed March 11, 2021, https://www .wycliffe.org/blog/posts/part-of-the-team-the-whole-bible-for-the-kuna.

[2] Brian and his wife, Candice, were established as senior leaders at Faith Christian Church (later Gateway Christian Fellowship) in the United States from about 1990 – 2009.

"Our Story," Gateway Christian Fellowship website, accessed March 11, 2021, https://www.yourgateway.com/our-story.

[3] Simmons, "About The Passion Translation," *The Passion Translation: The New Testament with Psalms, Proverbs, and Song of Songs,* 2nd ed. (Savage, MN: BroadStreet Publishing Group, LLC, 2018)

[4] Simmons, "About The Passion Translation."

[5] Interview with Simmons regarding his book of Genesis in *The Passion Translation* on the Shaun Tabatt Show (Episode #370), April 20, 2020, accessed February 24, 2021, https://www.youtube.com/watch?v=nq3ZDL1qMHc, starting at 9:26.

[6] Simmons asserts, "You're taking a big ax and chopping off all kinds of meaning when you insist on having a word-for-word translation.... I'm sure you've heard of the phrase 'lost in translation.'... We're going to the cutting-room floor and picking up all the nuances and treasures that have been cut off because of a 'strict, literal, word-for-word translation' mindset that eliminates great, great meanings to the text that maybe go outside the common translations."

Daniel Lovett, interview with Simmons, "The Passion Translation, Interview with Brian Simmons on Sozo Talk Radio EP[isode]020," December 1, 2018, accessed February 24, 2020, https://www.youtube.com/watch?v=Gu9zLxi4Y08, starting at 5:00.

7   This is of course an unfair assessment of both languages. It ignores the fact that both have literature in several different genres. The vast majority of ancient Hebrew literature is biblical, which includes both poetry and prose as well as other styles of writing. Ancient Greek includes an entire library of classical poetry. The facts that biblical poetry is found almost exclusively in the Hebrew OT and that the authors of the Greek NT rarely found opportunities to express themselves in meter and verse is not a good basis for assuming a language's character as a whole.

8   Andrew Chapman, "Brian Simmons' adaptation of Galatians 1.4a in the Passion [Anti-]Translation," *River of Life*, March 3, 2017, accessed June 18, 2020, http://theriveroflife.com/2017/03/03/brian-simmons-adaptation-of-galatians-1-4a-in-the-passion-anti-translation/.
Welton, interview with Simmons, *The Jonathan Welton Show*, 27:53.

9   Please note that the reviewers make recommendations, which Simmons and editors at BroadStreet Publishing either accept or reject.

10   "Does TPT represent any particular tradition or denomination," F.A.Q.s, TPT website, accessed February 24, 2021, https://www.thepassiontranslation.com/faqs/.

11   Simmons said, "[The Song of Songs] is my favorite book in the Bible. [It] speaks of divine romance, not erotica. . . . [If] the wisest man on earth would write a book, I don't think he would talk about his sex life. And if it really is just a book of erotica, then God is legitimizing one of Solomon's thousands of affairs with women and putting it in the Bible. I just—I can't see that."
Welton, interview with Simmons, *The Jonathan Welton Show*, 8:47.

12   Michael Lombardo, interview with Brian Simmons, "'The Passion Translation' with Dr. Brian Simmons," *YouTube.com*, November 17, 2017, accessed December 20, 2018, https://www.youtube.com/watch?v=1NYmwSBrWl8.

13   "George Athas reviews Song of Songs," *Reading the Passion Bible*, July 28, 2019, accessed June 3, 2020, http://readingthepassionbible.com/george-athas-reviews-tpt/.

14 Simmons, *John: Eternal Love*, in *The Passion Translation* (Racine, WI: BroadStreet Publishing Group, LLC, 2015), p. 10.

15 "FAQs: What is the approach to gender usage in *The Passion Translation?*" *The Passion Translation* website, accessed February 3, 2020, https://www .thepassiontranslation.com/faqs/.

16 Simmons, *John: Eternal Love*.

17 Simmons, *Matthew: Our Loving King*, in *The Passion Translation* (Racine, WI: BroadStreet Publishing Group, LLC, 2015), p. 5.

18 Even though sentences are smaller, readers will have to contend with more words. For example, **Eph 1.3–14** in TPT requires 429 words. By comparison, *The Message* uses 306 words for the same number of sentences (16); NLT, 309 words for 15 sentences; NIV, 262 words for seven sentences; ESV, 244 words for five sentences; LEB, 254 words for just the one. (Greek editions average around 180 – 200 words.)

19 Email from BroadStreet Publishing Group, February 24, 2021.

20 Nijay K. Gupta, "The Passion Translation: Galatians," p. 4.

21 Ethnos360's official statement regarding Simmon's and translation reads, "TPT obviously does deliver on its stated goal, to trigger an 'overwhelming response' using the 'love language of God.' However, the focus on creating an emotive impact has been made at the cost of accuracy to the original Scriptures." Email from an Ethnos360 representative on July 8, 2020.

22 "Is *The Passion Translation* considered a good translation for serious study?" F.A.Q.s, TPT website, accessed March 1, 2021.

23 Biblical paraphrases are not limited to rewrites of existing translations (like TLB); they can also be loose renderings from the original languages (like *The Message*). "Why is *The Passion Translation* described as a 'translation' rather than a 'paraphrase'?" F.A.Q.s, TPT website, accessed March 1, 2021.

24 Douglas Moo, "A Brief Evaluation of *The Passion Translation* of Romans," *Bible Thinker* website, accessed March 8, 2021, https://biblethinker.org/images/Notes/PassionProject/FINAL_Moo_TPT_ _-_Romans.pdf, p. 2.

25 Simmons, "A Note to Readers," *The Passion Translation* (Savage, MN: BroadStreet Publishing Group, 2020), p. viii.

26 *Iscariot* could derive from a Latin word for a group of assassins called the *Sicarii* (though the term may be too late for these events); or another Latin word for

"leather bag" (*scortea*); or it could be based on one of several possible Hebrew roots: *š K R, *Q R R, *Q R H, *Q R'; or the Hebrew for "small cities" (קריות). Syriac ("the Aramaic") does not offer any real help here, since the word seems to have entered its vocabulary after the NT was translated. In other words, Simmons' claim about *Iscariot*'s meaning is purely speculative.

27 *The Passion Translation* (2020), p. 638.

28 The NASB 2020 translation team acknowledges that "An accurate [*i.e.* formal] translation would render ['James' as] 'Jacob.' Unfortunately, many would find it confusing to suddenly change the name 'James' to 'Jacob.'" Simmons probably exaggerates this feature's importance, and I would not call this a "vital" or necessary fact to understand the book's message and its place in the NT. However, Rick Wadholm, Jr., one of TPT's reviewers, explained that "Jacob" suggests an author writing to the "twelve tribes of Israel" as if he were a father writing to his children (**Jas 1.1**). Necessary for understanding the book? *No.* Helpful as a footnote? *Sure!*

Oxford English Dictionary, 2nd ed. (Oxford: Oxford University Press, 2004), *s.v.* "James, *n.*"

"Preface," *New American Standard Bible* (La Habra, CA: The Lockman Foundation, 2020).

29 *The Passion Translation* (2020), p. ix.

30 Cultural names for these figures are relegated to TPT's footnotes, although earlier editions include some of them in the main text (*e.g., Miriam* for "Mary" in **Jn 2.2–3**).

31 TPT's marketing pushes a view of language that is uncharacteristic in linguistics. It asserts that "Aramaic and Hebrew . . . are considered to be emotional and poetic. Greek speaks to the mind while Aramaic and Hebrew speak powerfully to the heart." It does not seem appropriate to characterize Greek and Semitic languages by the genres they are written in, since the Greek literary library contains many volumes of poetry (with all their affective language), and the Hebrew Bible records facts in prose, precepts in law, and poetry in parallel.

"Why were Aramaic texts used as supplemental source material throughout *The Passion Translation*?" F.A.Q.s, TPT website.

32 *Ibid.*

³³ Craig S. Keener, "Brief Comments on the Passion Translation," *Bible Background*, August 28, 2018, accessed December 21, 2018, http://www.craigkeener.com/brief -comments-on-the-passion-translation/.

³⁴ Toma Audo, *Treasure of the Syriac Language: A Dictionary of Classical Syriac* (Mosul: Imprimerie des pères dominicains, 1897 – [1901]. Reprinted: Piscataway, NJ: Gorgias Press, 2008) vol. 1, p. 25 *via* sedra.bethmardutho.org, tagged by George A. Kiraz, accessed March 4, 2021; Sebastian P. Brock and George A. Kiraz, *Gorgias Concise Syriac-English, English-Syriac Dictionary* (Piscataway, NJ: Gorgias Press, 2015), *s.v.* ܐܪܥܐ *via* sedra.bethmardutho.org, accessed on March 4, 2021.

³⁵ "Galilee" cannot likely be translated as "the place of revelation." At least in Hebrew, the root is *G L L (גלל, "place" or "region"), not *G L H (גלה, "disclose" or "expose"), and there is no H (ה or ܗ) in the *Peshitta* here (*daglila'* ܓܠܝܠܐ).

³⁶ A place where Simmons' homonymic double-translation *does* makes sense is **Sg 2.12** (הַזָּמִיר for "singing" and "pruning"). Both renderings can fit the passage's context and poetic structure (as a "*janus* parallelism" according to the NET).

Examples of footnotes with speculative homonymic interpretations can be found at **Ps 22.2** (where תַעֲנֶה is supposed to mean "answer" *and* "affliction" in the same place); **37.25** (נַעַר for "immature" *and* "driven out"); **Pr 18.10** (מִגְדָּל for "tower of strength" *and* "bed of flowers"), **Sg 1.4** (נִשְׂמְחָה for "rejoice" *and* "spinning in a circle" or "dance"), or **Jn 19.30** (Gk. τετέλεσται [back-translated into Heb. כָּלָה, כָּלֶה, כְּלֵה, כַּלָּה or כָּלַל] for "fulfilled" or "completed" *and* "bride").

³⁷ "Is TPT considered a good translation for serious study?" F.A.Q., TPT website, accessed March 1, 2021, https://www.thepassiontranslation.com/faqs/.

³⁸ "What is the translation process and methodology for The Passion Translation?" F.A.Q., TPT website, accessed March 1, 2021, https://www .thepassiontranslation.com/faqs/.

³⁹ The following four reviews are published by Mike Winger, "The Passion Project: Scholars Review The Passion Translation," *BibleThinker.org*, accessed March 11, 2021, https://biblethinker.org/index.php/the-passion-translation.

Dr. Tremper Longman III (*Distinguished Scholar of Biblical Studies, Westmont College*), "*The Passion Translation* is a deeply flawed presentation of the *Song of Songs*. Its imposition of an allegorical interpretation represses the primary meaning. One can't hear God's intended message in this translation." ("Evaluation of The Passion Translation: Song of Songs," [Montecito, CA: Westmont College] accessed January 26, 2021);

530   *Endnotes*

Dr. Douglas Moo (*Kenneth T. Wessner Professor of NT, Wheaton College*), "However, I find [TPT] has several problems that, together, mean it is an unreliable guide to the meaning of Scripture." ("A Brief Evaluation of *The Passion Translation* of Romans," [Wheaton College] accessed January 27, 2021);

Dr. Craig L. Blomberg (*Distinguished Professor of the NT, Denver Seminary*), "Despite some of the wonderful passion and turns of phrase, there are also enough problems with it that it probably should have had a surgeon general's warning on it about its potential hazards." ("Review of 1 Corinthians in *The Passion Translation*" [Littleton, CO: Denver Seminary, April 2020] accessed January 18, 2021);

Dr. Darrell L. Bock (*Senior Research Professor of NT studies, Dallas Theological Seminary*), "I will treat [TPT] as a paraphrase and not a translation, because it is *not* a translation. This rendering is only a paraphrase, at best." ("Assessment of *The Passion Translation* of Ephesians" [Dallas Theological Seminary] accessed January 27, 2021);

[40] James Barr, *The Semantics of Biblical Language* (Oxford University Press, 1961), p. 6.

[41] Simmons, "A Note to Readers," *The Passion Translation* (2020), p. vii.

[42] *Ibid.*, p. viii.

[43] In his Gospel of Matthew, Simmons refers to the text of a "Hebrew Matthew" written by Shem Tov (alternately, Shem-Tob, **Mt 2.6; 24.41**). Simmons' comments omit any further identification. "Hebrew Matthew" is part of Shem Tov ben Isaac ben Shaprut's work titled *The Touchstone* (Heb. *Eben Boḥan*), which is a later medieval manuscript dating to the 14th century as part of Jewish polemic against Spanish Christianity.

In his footnote for **Mt 2.6**, Simmons claims that **Mi 5.2** in the LXX and Shem Tov's "Hebrew Matthew" reads differently than his translation. Shem Tov supposedly reads "out of you will come to me a Ruler who will be King of Israel." (Howard's translation of Shem Tov reads, "from you shall come forth to me one to be ruler in Israel.") This is close to the same as that found in the Latin Vulgate's version of **Mi 5.2**, *ex te mihi egredietur qui sit dominator in Israhel* ("out of you will come to me who is to be the ruler in Israel").

We cannot be sure that Shem Tov translated his "Hebrew Matthew" or copied it from an earlier composition. Considering the late date of Shem Tov's work and that no early manuscripts of any other Hebrew Gospels exist, it is likely that Shem Tov's "Hebrew Matthew" is based on a translation of a later Latin version of the NT, not on some ancient, original Hebrew source.

George Howard, *Hebrew Gospel of Matthew* (Macon, GA: Mercer University Press, 1995), p. 7.

[44] The future edition that Simmons referred to was published as the third, 2020 edition of TPT.

Sam Hailes, interview with Brian Simmons, "The Passion translation: Dr Brian Simmons responds to his critics," *Premier Christianity*, May 2018, accessed December 27, 2018, https://www.premierchristianity.com/Past-Issues/2018 /May-2018/The-Passion-translation-Dr-Brian-Simmons-responds -to-his-critics.

[45] "Why were Aramaic texts used . . . ?" F.A.Q.s, TPT website.

Glossary

A

alliteration *noun.* A figure of speech that repeats and plays on the same sound or letter. *E.g.: Peter Piper picked a peck of pickled peppers.*

anglicize, anglicise *verb.* to make English (rather, British) in spelling.

achoring bias *n.* A cognitive bias that weighs judgment towards the first piece of evidence, which frames all information that is learned later about a topic or case. *The professor's covenantal view was an anchoring bias which stilted his teaching on progressive revelation.*

antecedent *n.* A word or phrase to which another refers back.

Apocrypha *n.* Books added to the Septuagtint* that are not found in the Hebrew canon* and are regarded as non-canonical. *The Greek additions to Daniel and Esther are among the Apocrypha.*

apocryphal *adj.* (1) Regarding the Apocrypha.* *Protestants and Catholics alike consider 3 and 4 Esdras as apocryphal.* (*cf.* deuterocanonical*) (2) That which is considered fictional, spurious, false, fabulous, or mythical; inauthentic.

B

appositive *n.* An appositive is a noun or phrase that re-identifies another noun in close proximity to it.

Aramaic *n.* (a.k.a., Chaldæan) An ancient language in which certain later portions of the Old Testament were composed. (*cf.* Greek,* Hebrew*; Latin,* Syriac*)

Ausgangtext(en) *n.* (German "source-text[s]") The form of a text* at the start of a particular transmission,* *i.e.*, at at the beginning of a textual tradition.

attest(ed) *v.* To testify to the genuineness of something.

attestation *n.* A testimony or a witness.*

authority (-ies) (1) *n.* The power or right to influence the conduct and actions of others. (2) *n.* A significant manuscript witness* which gives evidence for a particular reading.*

autograph(a) *n.* A manuscript* or manuscripts written by an author's own hand.

B

base text (1) *n.* The text* that translators build their translation from. (2) *n.* A text used by text-critics* to compare manuscript* witnesses* (*i.e.*, copies) against.

Bible *n.* (1) Generally, a single bound collection of authoritative writings. (2) Specifically, Holy inspired* Scripture.*

biblical *adj.* Regarding the Bible.*

"biblish" *adj.* A manner of speaking or writing that reflects the idiosyncracies of the biblical* languages instead of familiar English forms and usage.

black letter *n.* A heavy, thick printing type based on handwriting, as contrasted to Roman type.

bulla(e) *n.* (Latin > "round seal[s]") an inscribed clay token used for authenticating legal documents.

C

canon *n.* (Greek > "reed", or a straight stick or rule used to measure length or alignment) A collection or list of biblical books accepted as authoritative, genuine, and/or divinely inspired.* *A sacred canon is the standard for establishing and evaluating a community's doctrine and practice.*

canon priority *n.* The translators' reliance on the text in a particular biblical canon* perceived to have greater precedent or priority over other canons. (*cf.* language primacy,* transmission priority*)

canonicity *n.* The status and facts of a work's inclusion in a canon.*

chapter(s) *n.* A main division or section of a biblical book.

codex (codices) *n.* An early manuscript* form of the modern book format. *The Aleppo Codex was the oldest extant* manuscript* of the Hebrew Bible until the discovery of the Dead Sea Scrolls.* *

cognate *n.* and *adjective.* A language or word that shares common ancestry with a family of related languages or words. *Syriac is a cognate with Palestinian Aramaic* since they both originate from Imperial Aramaic.* *

Coherence-Based Genealogical Method (CBGM) *n.* A method of textual criticsm* which uses computer software tools for efficiently making decisions about the relation of manuscripts.*

coinage(s) *n.* The formation of a new word or words. (*verb* "coin")

collate(d) *v.* To set side-by-side for comparison. *Text-critics* collate many manuscript* witnesses* against a standard base text.* *

comma *n.* (Greek > "a stamp, impression" or "short clause") A clause or short group of words.

Comma Johanneum *n.* A section in the epistle of **1 John** (**5.7–8**) found in the *Textus Receptus,* * but not in the earlier Greek manuscripts.*

concordance (1) *n.* A translation policy which renders each unique

The Best Bible?

vocabulary word in the base text* with a consistent equivalent in the target language. (2) *n.* A book which shows where and in how many passages of Scripture* any word occurs.

concordant   *adj.* (*see* concordance, sense (1)*)

confirmation bias   *n.* a cognitive bias which tends to find new information to support of one's preexisting theory or belief. *The presenter's confirmation bias reinforced his faith in Aramaic* primacy* despite only spurious evidence to support it and in contradiction to all the hard evidence against it.*

conjectural emendation   *n.* A correction to a text made without any manuscript* attestation* in the language in which it was composed, but whose authenticity is considered possible when compared to other early versions.*

corpus   *n.* A body or collection of texts.* *The Lukan corpus consists of both Luke's Gospel and its sequal, the Book of Acts.*

critical apparatus   *n.* A system of tools (usually written or printed) for the critical study of a document.

D

Dead Sea Scrolls (DSS)   *n.* The earliest extant* manuscript copies of the Old Testament. *The DSS were found in 1947 by a young Bedouin goatherd who discovered them by accident when he threw a rock into the caves near Qumran.*

Decalogue   *n.* (Greek > "the ten sayings") the Ten Commandments (**Ex 20.1–17; Dt 5.4–21**).

Deuterocanon   *n.* (Greek > "second canon") Books included in the Septuagint,* but not in the Hebrew canon,* that were formally canonized by the Roman Catholic Church at the Council of Trent in 1546. *Tobit, Judith, and the additions to Daniel and Esther are among the Catholic Deuterocanon.*

deuterocanonical   *adj.* Regarding the Deuterocanon.* *He read the deuterocanonical passage of Sir. 26.13–14 from the wedding liturgy during the couple's nuptial mass.* (*cf.* apocryphal*)

diglot   *n.* (Greek > "speaking two languages") A book or version written in two languages; bilingual.

E

eisegete *v.* (Greek > "one who proposes or introduces") To interpret a passage from the Scriptures* by reading into it one's own ideas. (*cf.* eisegesis,* exegesis*)

eisegesis *n.* The practice of reading one's own ideas into the interpretation of words or passages from Scripture.* (*cf.* eisegete,* exegesis*)

emendation *n.* A correction to a text* made through addition, omission, or change.

error *n.* In textual criticism, an error consitutes any mistake a scribe makes when copying from an exemplar.*

etymology *n.* The facts surrounding a word's origin; the historical development of a word's form and meaning.

euphemism *n.* (Greek > "something well said") A figure of speech that uses a less distasteful word or phrase in place of something harsher or more offensive.

euphemize *v.* (*see* euphemism*)

Eusebian Canons *n.* (a.k.a. Ammonian sections) An early system of dividing the four Gospels and correlating their parallel sections to one another.

exegesis *n.* (Greek > "interpretation")An explanation or interpretation of a text.* (*cf.* eisegete*)

exegetical *adj.* (see exegesis*)

exemplar(s) *n.* A manuscript* from which another is copied.

extant *adj.* Existing, or surviving. *An extant witness* is a MS* that has survived time and decay and is still accessible, as opposed to those lost, destroyed, or missing.*

external evidence *n.* Evidence in support of a reading* derived from circumstances or considerations outside of the text* itself. *Text-critics* count the age of a manuscript* as external evidence.* (*cf.* internal evidence*)

F

form(al, -alism) *n.* A translation priority that strictly adheres and corresponds to the grammatical forms, order, or spellings of the words in a text.* (*cf.* function(al, -alism)*)

function(al, -alism) *n.* A translation priority that emphasizes how the language of a text* communicates, processes thoughts, or performs socially, as distinguished from its formal or grammatical aspects. (*cf.* form[al, -alism]*)

G

gender(s) *n.* The classification of words or things into two or three classes: male, female, or neuter. (*see* grammatical gender,* natural gender*; gender-inclusive,* gender-neutral*)

gender-inclusive *adj.* Describes language (in general) or translation (in particular) that ambiguates gender so as to refer to either male or female. (*see* gender*; *cf.* gender-neutral*)

gender-neutral *adj.* Describes language (in general) or translation (in particular) that nullifies gender distinctions so as to refer to neither male nor female. (*see* gender*; *cf.* gender-inclusive*)

general epistles *n.* The general epistles, include the New Testament books of **James**; 1 and **2 Peter**; 1, 2, and **3 John**; and **Jude**. (a.k.a. Catholic Epistles)

genre(s) *n.* A kind or style of expression. *The psalms of David are grouped in the genre of biblical poetry.*

gloss *n.* and *v.* A word inserted between the lines or margins of a document as an explanatory equivalent of a foreign or obscure word in a text.*

grammatical gender *n.* A division within a classification system for noun inflections. *Grammatical gender is assigned to words based on linguistic factors.* (*see* gender*; *cf.* natural gender*)

Greek *n.* and *adj.* An ancient language in which the Old Testament was translated and the New Testament was composed. (see *Koinē*; *cf.* Hebrew,* Aramaic*; Latin,* Syriac*)

H

hapax legomenon *n.* (Greek > "a thing written once", pl. *hapax legomena*) a word that is recorded only once in a text* or corpus.*

harmonization *n.* The act or result of bringing one or more things into agreement with another. *Tatian produced a harmonization of the four Gospels.*

Hebrew *n.* An ancient language in which most of the Old Testament was composed. (*cf.* Aramaic,* Greek*; Latin,* Syriac*)

hermeneutics *n.* (Greek > "relating to interpretation") (1) A system of interpretive principles. (2) The application of such a system for discerning the meaning of Scripture.*

high-context *n.* and *adj.* Describes language that communicates through implication and depends on context, tone, and non-verbal cues to convey intended meaning. (*cf.* low-context*)

high-register *n.* and *adj.* A style of language typically used in formal occasions, or polite address, or to enter exclusive encounters, or to demonstrate the possession of prestige or sophistication. (*see* register*; *cf.* low-register*)

homograph(s) *n.* A word with the same spelling as another, but with a different meaning. *E.g.: A strong wind won't let us wind the sail.*

I

idiom(s) *n.* (1) An expression whose meaning cannot be understood by through it component parts. *My Brazilian colleague responded to my American idiom with a puzzled look when I told him that his presentation really "hit it out of the park."* (2) A regional speech or dialect. *Jesus and his disciples spoke in the Galilean idiom.*

ignorant bias *n.* A cognitive bias that forms a theory or belief in the absence of relevant information. *Ignorant bias prevented them from understanding the word "evil" as non-moral, so they were understadably confused when they read Ex 32.14 for the first time in the* KJV.

inkhorn terms *n.* Words used amongst a literary or bookish society. *Thanks to the abecardian nature of these appendices, it should not be so arduous a task to recall the situation of certain inkhorn terms as they are posited herein.*

inspired *adj.* (*see* inspiration*)

inspiration *n.* The influence of God's Spirit in the authorship and production of the biblical text*; implies the divine origin and authority of Scripture* (*cf.* **2Ti 3.16**). (*cf.* plenary-verbal inspiration*)

internal evidence *n.* evidence in support of a reading* derived from the nature or content of the text* itself, rather than from circumstances or considerations outside of the text.* (*cf.* external evidence*)

interlinear *n.* A document with the same text* written or printed with different languages in alternating lines.

The Best Bible?

K

Koinē *n.* and *adj.* A dialect of the Greek language . *The New Testament was composed in* Koinē *Greek, which was popularized in the Hellenistic period through the conquests of Alexander the Great.*

L

language primacy *n.* the translators' dependence on a biblical text* in a particular language, because they perceive it to have greater precedent or priority over other languages. *Hebrew holds the choice for language primacy in Protestant and Catholic translation due to the Old Testament's composition in that language.* (*see* canon priority,* transmission priority*)

Latin *n.* An ancient language in which the Bible was translated. *The Old Testament in the Old Latin texts* (a.k.a., Vetus Latina) were translated from the Greek* Septuagint*; but St. Jerome translated the* OT *from the Hebrew in his Latin Vulgate.* (*cf.* Syriac*; Greek,* Hebrew,* Aramaic*)

lexicon(s) *n.* A book of words and their glosses or definitions; a dictionary.

literal *adj.* (1) Free from metaphor,* exaggeration, allusion, or other figures of speech. (2) Verbally exact; formal.*

loanword(s) *n.* A word or words borrowed from another language.

low-context *n.* and *adj.* Describes language that communicates in a direct, explicit, and precise manner. (*cf.* high-context*)

low-register *n.* and *adj.* A style of language typically used for casual encounters, informal situations, or to address general audiences. (*see* register*; *cf.* high-register*)

M

manuscript(s) *n.* (alternatively "MSS") A document or documents written by hand and not printed.

Masorete *n.* (pl. "Masoretes") A Medieval Jewish scribe responsible for transmitting* the Masoretic text of the Hebrew Bible. The name comes from the *masorah*, or written traditions surrounding the Hebrew consonantal letters, including vowel points and critical marginal notes. *The Masoretes faithfully copied the Hebrew Bible for generations.*

Masoretic *adj.* (*see* Masorete*)

majuscule *n.* and *adj.* A style of hand-written script that uses large capital letters, called uncials. (*cf.* minuscule*)

metaphor   *n.* A figure of speech in which a name, a descriptive word, or a phrase expresses a likeness to something analagous, but without signs of comparison.

metonymy   *n.* (Greek > "a change of name") A figure of speech in which one word or phrase is substituted for another related word or phrase. *E.g., Jesus used metonymy when he referenced the writings of the Hebrew Bible, "They have Moses and the prophets; let them listen to them."* (**Lk 16.29**)

minuscule   *n.* and *adj.* A style of hand-written script that uses smaller, "lower-case" letters. *Minuscles are generally more efficient to write than majuscules,* and they almost look like cursive.* (*cf.* majuscule*)

MS (MSS)   (*see* manuscript(s)*)

N

natural gender   *n.* The biological sex of a person or an animal. *Natural gender is assigned to people according to a binary system of classification (either male or female) and is determined by physical or genetic traits.* (*see* gender*; *cf.* grammatical gender*)

nomen sacrum (**nomena sacra**)   *n.* A standard contracted form of a word with particular religious significance as written by early Christian scribes.

nonce word   *n.* and *adj.* A word that is used for one specific occurrence or in a single corpus.* (*see hapax legomenon**)

norm   *n.* A type, a standard, or a pattern.

O

orthography   *n.* The correct or appropriate spelling according to accepted norms.*

P

papyrus   *n.* (pl. "papyri") An early kind of paper made from flattened papyrus reeds. *Most early manuscripts* and manuscript fragments from the 1st–3rd centuries were written on papyri.* (*cf.* parchment*)

paraphrase   *n.* and *v.* An interpretation or explanation of a text* with more clarity and precision than the author(s) of the text expressed in their own words. (*see* function(alism)*)

parchment   *n.* and *adj.* A manuscript* made from the skin of a livestock. *Most later manuscripts from the 3rd–15th centuries were written on parchment.* (*cf.* papyri*)

Pentateuch *n.* The first five books of the Hebrew canon, also called the five books of Moses, or the Hebrew *Torah.*

pericope *n.* (Greek > "a cutting all-around", "a section", or "an outline") A short passage or a section of a text* marked for public reading.

Pericope Adulteræ *n.* The passage in John's Gospel (**Jn 7.53–8.11**) about the woman caught in adultery.

Peshitta *n.* An early version of the Bible translated into Syriac.* *The oldest extant* copies of the Peshitta are from the early 5th century* AD, but they probably preserve a text* that was translated in the 2nd century.*

pilcrow(s) *n.* A symbol (¶) that marks the beginning of a paragraph.

plenary-verbal inspiration *n.* The belief that God influenced the authorship of Scripture* completely (< plenary), even to the choice of individual words (< verbal). (*see* inspiration*)

Protocanon *n.* (Greek > "first canon") A Roman Catholic designation for books in the Hebrew* canon* and in the New Testament whose inclusion was never debated by the Christian Church.

provenance *n.* The origin or source of something, particulary the place a manuscript* was discovered.

R

reading(s) *n.* The particular form or order of a word or words in a passage as recorded in a copy or an edition of a text.*

recension *n.* A particular form or version of a text* resulting from a revision.

register *n.* The variety or level of the language used by a writer or speaker for a particular occasion. Register is determined by the social context and is marked by the range of vocabulary, pronunciation, and syntax. (*see* high-register,* low-register*)

rhyme *n.* and *v.* The repetition of identical or similar sounds at the ends of two or more words or metrical lines.

S

Scripture(s) *n.* (1) The sacred writings of the Christian Church (OT and NT); the Holy Bible.* (2) The sacred writings of the Jewish synogogue (*Torah,* Prophets, and Writings); Hebrew Scripture(s). (3) Any collection of sacred writings. (*cf.* Bible*)

Septuagint (LXX) *n.* An early translation of the Hebrew Old Testament into *Koinē** *Greek.* *The* LXX *was produced in Alexandria, Egypt sometime between* 275–130 BC.

substrate *n.* In textual studies, the material upon which something is written. *Ancient* NT MSS* *are typically written on two main substrates—papyrus* or parchment.**

Syriac *n.* An ancient language in which the Bible was translated. *Syriac is a cognate* language derived from Imperial Aramaic.** (*see* Peshitta*)

T

Tanakh *n.* (alternatively *Tanach*) The Hebrew canon* of Scripture, containing the same books as the Protestant Old Testament, though in a different order. *Tanakh is an acryonym for its three main divisions: Torah (Law), Nebi'im (Prophets), and Khethuvim (Writings)—**T**aNa-**Kh**.*

Targum(s) *n.* Early Aramaic* paraphrases of the Hebrew Pentateuch.*

Tetragrammaton *n.* (Greek > "the word of four letters") The spelling of the sacred Hebrew name for God—YHWH, or JHVH (Hebrew יהוה).

text *n.* A spelling and ordering of written words in a document.

text critic(s) *n.* A person or persons who specialize in the study of textual variants.*

text-type(s) *n.* A grouping of manuscripts* according to shared features, such as provenance* or similar textual variants.* *The Textus Receptus* is based on manuscripts* categorized within the Byzantine text-type.*

textual criticism *n.* The analysis and establishing of a text through the study and comparing of its extant* witnesses* (*i.e.*, its existing copies).

textual variant(s) *n.* A change in the text* of a witness* (*i.e.*, a manuscript* copy) that differs from a base text.*

Textus Receptus (TR) *n.* The text of the Greek New Testament based on an early printed tradition beginning with the Dutch humanist scholar, Desiderius Erasmus, in 1516 AD.

transliteration *n.* The conversion of a word or words made with letters in one alphabet into those of another.

transmission *n.* The passing of a message from one iteration or generation to the next. (*verb* "transmit")

The Best Bible?

transmission priority *n.* The translators' reliance on a text in a particular tradition or edition of the Bible*
perceived to have greater precedent
or priority over others. (*see* canon
priority,* language primacy*)

typological *adj.* Regarding typology.*

typology *n.* The study of *types*,
symbols that are emblematic or
representative of objects or persons
(called *antitypes*). Biblical typology
focuses on those prophetic prefig-
urings (types occuring in the OT)
for persons and things (antitypes)
in the NT.

V

variant(s) (*see* textual variant(s)*)

verbal *adj.* Regarding or affecting
words.

verse(s) *n.* A section into which
a biblical chapter is subdivided,
sometimes corresponding to a
couplet of Hebrew poetry.

versions *n.* A rendering of a text*
from one language into another; a
translation.

Vulgate *n.* Editions of the Latin
translation of the Bible produced
by St. Jerome (Hieronymus) and
later revised.

W

witness *n.* (pl. "witnesses") A manuscript* or an early version* which
offers evidence of authenticity for
a text.* *Instead of merely counting
the number of witnesses in support
of a particular reading,* a text-critic*
weighs the merits of each witness as
evidence.*

Scripture Index

Luke

Acts

Acts 314
Ac 1.4–5, 7–8 168
Ac 1.26a 298
Ac 2.2 71
Ac 2.6a 350
Ac 2.38 439
Ac 2.47 229
Ac 4.25–26 162–3
Ac 7.38 343
Ac 7:42b–43 72
Ac 8.15, 17–19 143
Ac 8.15–19 . . . . 113, 143
Ac 8.19 113
Ac 8.36–37 414
Ac 8.37 . . . . 198, 220,
 241, 267, 291, 321, 347,
 372, 399, 414, 432, 454,
 474, 513
Ac 8.38, 39 107
Ac 9.4, 5, 6, 11–12, 15–16
168
Ac 10.34 68
Ac 10.38 143
Ac 11.20 87
Ac 12.1 430
Ac 13.18 230
Ac 13.22b 81, 425
Ac 14.18 214
Ac 16.15a 436
Ac 16.15c 353
Ac 16.16b 436
Ac 17.25 71
Ac 17.26 352

Ac 17.34 449
Ac 18.9 165
Ac 18.9–10 168
Ac 19.2 . . . . 143, 350
Ac 19.5 167
Ac 19.13b 353
Ac 20.12 299
Ac 20.36 . . . . . 167, 230
Ac 21.39a 299
Ac 22.7, 8, 10, 18, 21 . . . .
168
Ac 23.11 168
Ac 26.14, 15–18 168

Romans

Ro 1.1 . . . . 353, 394, 502
Ro 1.4 503
Ro 1.7 87–88
Ro 1.13 213
Ro 1.26–27 480
Ro 2.1a 272
Ro 2.6 . . . . 198, 221, 241,
 268, 291, 322, 348, 372,
 400, 433, 455, 474, 514
Ro 3:3 462
Ro 3.22a . . 198, 222, 242,
 269, 293, 323, 349, 374,
 401, 434, 457, 475, 516
Ro 3.24 497
Ro 3.24–25a 298
Ro 3.25 413
Ro 3.28 . . . . 115, 144
Ro 4.1 272
Ro 4.3ff. 325

Ro 4.25 . . . . 80, 318
Ro 5.8 213
Ro 5.16 80
Ro 6.3 435
Ro 6.3, 4 107
Ro 6.19 80
Ro 7.4a 273
Ro 7.5 352
Ro 8.3 . . . . 119, 120, 377
Ro 8.12 501
Ro 8.14 498
Ro 9.4, 5 151
Ro 9.5 297
Ro 10.15 325
Ro 10.16 248
Ro 11.20b 249
Ro 12.1 501
Ro 12.16b 299
Ro 14.11 144
Ro 14.22 299
Ro 15.6 . . . . 327, 328
Ro 15.30 . . . . . 87–88, 89
Ro 16.3ff. 89

1 – 2 Corinthians

1Co 508
1Co 1.5 502
1Co 1.17 68
1Co 4.1–2 419
1Co 4.5 271
1Co 5.1 . . . . 96, 249
1Co 5.8 496
1 Co 5.11 142
1Co 6.5–6 274

Apocrypha /
Deuterocanon

Subject Index

The Best Bible?

Ad Fontes
P R E S S

Thank you for picking up this copy of my book. I sincerely hope that it serves you well. If you have any suggestions or concerns about this book or its contents, please feel free to reach me through my publisher, Ad Fontes Press, online at ww.adfontespress.com/connect or call 1 (503) 897-8118.   — MATTHEW J. BARRON

| Offer suggestions or corrections at booklink.id/ bestbible-recom | Report printing defects at booklink.id/ bestbible-defect | Report broken web links or QR codes at booklink.id/ bestbible-link |